ALL ■ IN ■ ONE

Oracle Cloud Infrastructure Architect Associate

EXAM GUIDE

(Exam 1Z0-1072)

ALL ■ IN ■ ONE

Oracle Cloud Infrastructure Architect Associate

EXAM GUIDE

(Exam 1Z0-1072)

Roopesh Ramklass

New York Chicago San Francisco
Athens London Madrid Mexico City
Milan New Delhi Singapore Sydney Toronto

McGraw-Hill Education books are available at special quantity discounts to use as premiums and sales promotions, or for use in corporate training programs. To contact a representative, please visit the Contact Us pages at www.mhprofessional.com.

Oracle Cloud Infrastructure Architect Associate All-in-One Exam Guide (Exam 1Z0-1072)

1 2 3 4 5 6 7 8 9 LCR 24 23 22 21 20

Library of Congress Control Number: 2019954401

ISBN 978-1-260-45259-4
MHID 1-260-45259-X

Sponsoring Editor
Lisa McClain

Editorial Supervisor
Patty Mon

Project Manager
Radhika Jolly, Cenveo® Publisher Services

Acquisitions Coordinator
Emily Walters

Technical Editor
Simon Pane

Copy Editor
Nancy Rapoport

Proofreader
Paul Tyler

Indexer
Ted Laux

Production Supervisor
James Kussow

Composition
Cenveo Publisher Services

Illustration
Cenveo Publisher Services

Art Director, Cover
Jeff Weeks

You are the one to walk the mountains with, Ameetha.
Your strength, wisdom, and tenacity inspire me
and your love gives meaning to my life.

ABOUT THE AUTHOR

Roopesh Ramklass is an Oracle Certified Master with expertise in Cloud, infrastructure, middleware, and database architecture. He has worked for Oracle Global Support, Advanced Customer Services, and Oracle University. He is actively involved in the Oracle community, speaking at Oracle conferences, serving as an executive of the Toronto Oracle Users Group, and participating in the Oracle ACE program. Roopesh is the author of several Oracle technology books and blogs and is passionate about serving others through education.

About the Technical Editor

Simon Pane is an Oracle Certified Professional, Oracle Certified Expert, Oracle ACE, and a member of several formal industry and community Advisory Boards. Working with the Oracle database since version 7, he enjoys various aspects of Oracle core technologies and, of course, the Oracle Cloud.

Simon loves sharing technical knowledge. He is a regular blogger and has presented at many user groups and at almost every major conference in North America and Europe, including at Oracle OpenWorld many times. Simon is also a UKOUG speaker and IOUG SELECT Journal award winner.

CONTENTS AT A GLANCE

Chapter 1 Oracle Cloud Infrastructure Concepts 1
Chapter 2 OCI Identity and Access Management.................................. 27
Chapter 3 OCI Networking 73
Chapter 4 Compute Instances.. 141
Chapter 5 Storage 187
Chapter 6 Databases 239
Chapter 7 Automation Tools.. 321
Chapter 8 OCI Best Practice Architectures 343
Appendix About the Online Content... 363
Glossary 367
Index... 379

CONTENTS

Acknowledgments xvii
Introduction xix
Exam 1Z0-1072 xxi

Chapter 1 Oracle Cloud Infrastructure Concepts 1

Introduction to OCI 1
    Exercise 1-1: Create a New OCI Account 4
Cloud Computing Models 9
OCI Features and Components 11
    Regions and Availability Domains 11
    Exercise 1-2: Explore Your Availability Domain and Region 14
    Off-Box Network Virtualization 15
OCI Concepts and Terms 16
    Identity and Access Management 16
    Networking 18
    Compute 20
    Storage 20
    Database Cloud Service 22
Chapter Review 24
    Questions 24
    Answers 26

Chapter 2 OCI Identity and Access Management 27

Explain IAM Concepts 27
    Resources 28
    Tenancy and Compartments 29
    Users 31
    Groups 33
    Policies 34
    Dynamic Groups 38
Describe Resource Locations and Identifiers 39
    Resource Locations 39
    Exercise 2-1: Subscribe to Another Region 41
    Exercise 2-2: Create a Compartment and a VCN 44
    Resource Identifiers 47
    Managing Tags and Tag Namespaces 49
    Advanced Policies 52
Create IAM Resources 56
    Create Compartments 57
    Exercise 2-3: Create Compartments for Organization 57

Create Groups, Users, Policies 60
Exercise 2-4: Create Groups, Users, and Policies 61
Federate OCI with Various Identity Providers 64
Set Up Dynamic Groups 66
Chapter Review 69
Questions 70
Answers 71

Chapter 3 OCI Networking 73
Networking Concepts and Terminology 73
CIDR 75
Exercise 3-1: Expand CIDR Notation 78
Virtual Cloud Networks 79
Subnets 81
Gateways 86
Use Virtual Cloud Networks 95
Exercise 3-2: Create VCNs and Subnets 96
Exercise 3-3: Deploy a NAT Gateway 100
Exercise 3-4: Deploy a Service Gateway 103
Exercise 3-5: Set Up Local VCN Peering 106
Exercise 3-6: Set Up Remote VCN Peering 111
DNS in OCI 115
DNS Concepts and Features 116
Creating and Managing DNS Records 121
Exercise 3-7: Set Up a DNS Zone and Resource Records ... 123
Load Balancers in OCI 126
Load Balancer Terminology and Concepts 126
Exercise 3-8: Set Up a Load Balancer 132
Design and Secure OCI Networks 135
VCN Design 135
Edge Security 137
Chapter Review 137
Questions 138
Answers 140

Chapter 4 Compute Instances 141
Compute Service Components 142
Compute Shapes 142
Compute Images 144
Instance Management 152
Create Compute Instances 152
Exercise 4-1: Create an SSH Key Pair 154
Exercise 4-2: Create a Compute Instance to
Use as a Web Server 156
Exercise 4-3: Create and Use a Custom Image 162

Exercise 4-4: Create a Load Balancer to Route Traffic to Web Servers 167
Exercise 4-5: Create and Connect to a Windows Compute Instance 170
Manage Compute Instances 174
Instance Configurations, Pools, and Autoscaling 175
Instance Console Connections 179
Chapter Review 182
Questions 183
Answers 185

Chapter 5 Storage 187

Block Storage 188
Create Block Volumes 189
Exercise 5-1: Create a Block Volume 190
Attaching Block Volumes 192
Exercise 5-2: Attach a Block Volume to a Linux Instance 194
Connecting Block Volumes 195
Exercise 5-3: Connect a Block Volume to Your Linux Volume Using iSCSI and CHAP 195
Exercise 5-4: Format a Block Volume, Create a File System, and Mount the Volume 198
Exercise 5-5: Present a Block Volume to a Windows Instance 200
Block Volume Backup Options 204
Exercise 5-6: Create a Full Backup of a Block Volume 207
Exercise 5-7: Create and Back Up a Volume Group 208
Delete and Recover Block Volumes 210
Exercise 5-8: Restore a Block Volume Backup to a New Block Volume 210
Exercise 5-9: Recover a Block Volume Backup in a Different Region 212
Object Storage 213
Buckets and Objects 213
Exercise 5-10: Upload, Restore, and Download Using an Archive Tier Bucket 216
Exercise 5-11: Upload, Restore, and Download Using a Standard Tier Bucket 218
Pre-Authenticated Requests 220
File Storage Service 222
FSS Concepts 222
Create, Configure, and Mount a File Storage Service 225
Exercise 5-12: Create a File System, Mount Target, and Mount with NFS Clients 225
FSS Snapshots 232

Chapter Review 234
Questions 235
Answers 236

Chapter 6 Databases 239

Database Cloud Service 240
DBCS on Bare Metal 242
DBCS on Exadata (Exadata Cloud Service) 247
DBCS on VM 250
Network Requirements for DBCS 250
Exercise 6-1: Configure a Public Subnet with Internet Gateway for Your DB System 252
Exercise 6-2: Create a DB System on a VM 257
Exercise 6-3: Connect to the Database System with SSH, SQL*Plus, and asmcmd 262
Exercise 6-4: Connect to the Database System with SQL Developer 264
dbcli 265
DBCS Backups 267
Exercise 6-5: Make a Disk-Based Database Backup Using dbcli 268
Exercise 6-6: Back Up Your TDE Wallet to Object Storage Using dbcli 270
Exercise 6-7: Back Up Your Database to Object Storage Using RMAN 275
Exercise 6-8: Create a Standalone Managed Backup Using the Console 278
Exercise 6-9: Enable Automatic Incremental Backups Using the Console 279
DBCS Patching 282
Advanced Database Features 283
Database Licensing 283
Data Encryption 287
High Availability 287
Autonomous Databases 293
Create an Autonomous Database 294
Exercise 6-10: Create an ATP Database Using the Console 294
Connecting to an Autonomous Database 297
Exercise 6-11: Connect to an ATP Database Using the SQL Developer 298
Back Up and Recover an Autonomous Database 300
Operating an Autonomous Database 301
Database Migration 303
Connectivity 304
Data Transfer Service 304

Approaches to Migration 306
SQL*Loader 310
Export and Import 311
Data Guard 312
RMAN 313
Data Pump 313
Multitenant Migration Approaches 314
SQL Developer 315
Chapter Review 316
Questions 317
Answers 319

Chapter 7 Automation Tools 321

OCI CLI 321
Install and Configure OCI CLI 322
Exercise 7-1: Install the OCI CLI Using the Quickstart Installation Script 323
Exercise 7-2: Configure OCI CLI 325
Use OCI CLI 328
Exercise 7-3: Use the OCI CLI to List Supported Oracle Databases 331
Terraform 333
Install and Configure Terraform and the Provider for OCI 334
Exercise 7-4: Install and Configure Terraform and the Provider for OCI on Linux 334
Use Terraform 336
Exercise 7-5: Use Terraform to Create and Remove an OCI VCN 337
Chapter Review 340
Questions 340
Answers 342

Chapter 8 OCI Best Practice Architectures 343

Design Highly Available Disaster Recovery (HADR) OCI Solutions 344
Regions and Availability Domains 345
VCNs, Load Balancers, and Compute Instances 346
VPN and FastConnect 348
Storage and Compute Instances 350
Performance-Based HADR 351
Database HADR 351
Leverage OCI Security Features to Protect Your Cloud Infrastructure 356
IAM 357

Networking 357
Compute Instances 358
Chapter Review 358
Questions 359
Answers 360

Appendix About the Online Content 363

System Requirements 363
Your Total Seminars Training Hub Account 363
Privacy Notice 363
Single User License Terms and Conditions 363
TotalTester Online 365
Technical Support 365

Glossary 367

Index 379

ACKNOWLEDGMENTS

This book was written during the Cloud Wars, the most aggressive and competitive software development period I have witnessed in the technology industry. The wars are not over. Cloud vendors vie for market share with new features being released on an ongoing basis as they attempt to gain an advantage over the competition.

Completing this book to a standard I am satisfied with during this time of massive change would not have been possible without the love, support, encouragement, and friendship of my wife, Dr. Ameetha Garbharran. I am also fortunate to receive positive energy and loads of support from my parents, Harriesagar and Sabita Devi Ramklass.

I am grateful, too, for the meticulous attention to detail of the technical editor, Simon Pane, who kept me focused on the quality of this endeavor. I appreciate the support from my friend and colleague Christine Kivi and the team at Eclipsys Solutions led by Michael Richardson.

Finally, thank you to the team at McGraw-Hill, specifically Lisa McClain, Claire Yee, Emily Walters, and Radhika Jolly, who kept me on track with my deadlines and showed patience and understanding while I realized that the more things changed in the Cloud space, the more they stayed the same.

INTRODUCTION

Very simply, Cloud represents the future of IT. It is folly to deny this as the inevitable wave of technology progress marches on. Your choice is to either be left behind administering silos of on-premises infrastructure or embrace this new world of opportunity.

I have been an IT professional for the last 25 years, acquiring generalist knowledge over my career as a problem solver as I endeavored to get to the bottom of issues that impacted one or another mission-critical system. My foray took me into too many data centers to remember, doing everything from setting up networks and servers, to architecting and deploying massive clustered database and middleware infrastructure, to setting up business intelligence, e-commerce applications, websites, and email systems. I am probably missing a few things, but the point is that Cloud lets me apply so much of what I know about technology in a simple, unbelievably powerful paradigm, without needing to leave the comfort of my design studio, or half-freeze to death in a cold, dead data center. I can barely express the liberation and exhilaration of architecting a fully operational infrastructure solution, codifying it for repeatability or mass deployment, and with a few commands sit back and watch as the design comes to life without me setting foot in a data center or fiddling with cables or disk drives.

This book is aimed at IT professionals who want to know more about Cloud in general and more specifically more about Oracle Cloud Infrastructure. The breadth of OCI spans the breadth of modern IT on-premises infrastructure. So, if you are looking to retool and are a storage engineer; network, systems, security, or database administrator; architect; developer; or designer, this book has you covered. If you are a sales or management professional with an interest in OCI and data governance, you will find the content explained in simple, clear terms, but you may have to skip over the more technical sections.

Writing this book has been quite challenging because of the constant evolution of OCI. During the initial writing of this book, Oracle changed the rules of the game a few times, and content had to be updated. This presented an opportunity to tell the Cloud story as an exciting evolving journey. There is massive competition in this market. And this is great for all of us. Oracle, AWS, Google, Microsoft, and other Cloud vendors innovate at an incredible rate, spurring one another to release equivalent or better technologies.

OCI was built on lessons learned from the Oracle Classic Cloud as well as the best-of-breed practices from other vendors. Oracle has constructed a solid, scalable foundation upon which to innovate, and it is fantastic. You are guaranteed to see updated screens in the OCI console compared to the point-in-time snapshots in the book as a result of the rapid rate of innovation. The foundation, however, remains stable and constant and that is the hallmark of this book. You will learn OCI from its roots and build upon this knowledge as new features are released.

When I started writing this book, there was a single exam for IaaS and PaaS–Data Management, which was the OCI Certified Architect Associate exam. As of this writing, there are three tiers of OCI IaaS certification exams and three tiers of OCI PaaS–Data Management exams, as well as a few specialist exams. The following table lists some of these certifications where there is overlap between the content covered in this book and the certification objectives provided for these exams.

Exam Number	Certification	Certification Path	Track
1Z0-1067	OCI Certified Cloud Operations Associate	Associate	IaaS–OCI
1Z0-932	OCI Certified Architect Associate	Associate	IaaS–OCI
1Z0-997	OCI Certified Architect Professional	Specialist	IaaS–OCI
1Z0-160 or 1Z0-998	Oracle Database Cloud Service Operations Certified Associate	Associate	PaaS–Data Management
1Z0-160	Oracle Database Cloud Administrator Certified Associate Prerequisite: 11g or 12c DBA Oracle Certified Associate	Associate	PaaS–Data Management
1Z0-160	Oracle Database Cloud Administrator Certified Professional Prerequisite: 11g or 12c DBA Oracle Certified Professional	Professional	PaaS–Data Management
1Z0-950 or 1Z0-1044	Oracle Cloud Platform Data Management Certified Associate	Associate	PaaS–Data Management
1Z0-931	Oracle Autonomous Database Cloud Certified Specialist	Specialist	PaaS–Data Management

This book is written as a reference book, not just a study guide for a specific exam. This book completely covers the content in the associate exams and mostly covers the content in the professional and specialist exams. An exam object list is available with each exam on the Oracle website, and this list represents the current set to be tested for each certification exam. The object map that follows lists the chapters in this book and maps these to the exam objectives tested in the OCI Certified Architect Associate exam at the time of this writing.

Exam 1Z0-1072

Official Exam Objective	Chapter	All-in-One Coverage
Identity and Access Management (IAM)		
Apply core identity and access management components	2	Explain IAM concepts
Explain resource locations	2	Describe resource locations and identifiers
Design federation with various identity providers	2	Federate OCI with various identity providers
Apply IAM, governance, and security best practices	8	Leverage OCI security features to protect your cloud infrastructure
Networking		
Apply design concepts related to VCN components	3	Networking concepts and terminology
Describe public and private IP addresses and virtual NICs	3	Networking concepts and terminology
Apply VCN connectivity options	3	Use virtual cloud networks
Understand remote network connectivity	3	Networking concepts and terminology
Apply OCI load balancer concepts	3	Load balancers in OCI
Understand OCI Edge services	3	DNS in OCI
Apply OCI networking best practices	3	Design and secure OCI networks
Compute		
Understand compute and sizing	4	Compute service components
Troubleshoot options using console connections and boot volume	4	Instance management
Architect High Availability and Disaster Recovery solutions	8	Design Highly Available Disaster Recovery (HADR) OCI solutions
Describe image options	4	Compute service components
Storage		
Understand OCI storage options	5	Block storage, object storage, File Storage Service
Design storage solutions for applications and database	5	Block storage, object storage, File Storage Service
Database		
Describe OCI database options	6	Database Cloud service
Explain OCI database operations	6	Advanced database features
Architect HA and DR solutions	8	Design Highly Available Disaster Recovery (HADR) OCI solutions
Manage Autonomous Database	6	Autonomous databases

Official Exam Objective	Chapter	All-in-One Coverage
Launching Bare Metal and Virtual Compute Instances		
Describe the components of Compute service, including shapes, images, and custom images	4	Compute service components
Create and manage a Compute Virtual Machine (VM) instance	4	Instance management
Advanced Database		
Use advanced database features, such as Dataguard, BYOL, Data encryption, RAC, and EXADATA	6	Advanced database features
Architecting Best Practices		
Architect High Availability (HA) using OCI	8	Design Highly Available Disaster Recovery (HADR) OCI solutions
Design for Security using OCI	8	Leverage OCI security features to protect your cloud infrastructure
Instantiating a Load Balancer		
Discuss Load Balancer terminology and concepts	3	Networking concepts and terminology
Set up a Load Balancer	3	Load balancers in OCI
Advanced Networking Concepts		
Manage your cloud network components, such as Virtual Private Network (VPN), Fast Connect, Multiple vNICs, and IP addresses	3	Networking concepts and terminology

Many of these topics are tested in other exams listed in the previous table and have been included to provide a complete set of foundational information. To derive the most value from this book, I recommend choosing an exam you wish to attempt and cross-referencing the exam objectives from the Oracle certification website with the objectives listed in the table of contents to identify overlap and any exceptions.

One of the first exercises in this book involves signing up for an Oracle Cloud account. Oracle has blazed the trail here again by providing a Free Tier account that never expires. Other Cloud vendors may follow suit in due course. Study the material and experiment with your cloud tenancy as you work through the exercises and sample questions and become more familiar with the Oracle environment. You will realize that there is one golden rule: When in doubt, try it out.

CHAPTER 1

Oracle Cloud Infrastructure Concepts

In this chapter, you will learn how to

- Discuss OCI and cloud computing models
- Describe the features and components of OCI
- Describe the OCI concepts and terms

Oracle has reinvented its infrastructure cloud as the best platform for hosting Oracle technology and one of the leading cloud vendors for non-Oracle workloads. The first-generation cloud offering, known as Oracle Cloud Infrastructure Classic, offers a limited set of compute, storage, and networking offerings. The second-generation cloud offering, and the focus of this book, is Oracle Cloud Infrastructure, or OCI. Learning from both its initial foray into the cloud space and its competitors, Oracle has designed a unique infrastructure cloud offering that is open and extensible with some great features.

This chapter introduces the underlying concepts supporting OCI and provides a broad overview of the various components and features while highlighting how the puzzle pieces fit together. We discuss core concepts and terms to provide the foundation required to master the topics related to Oracle Cloud Infrastructure.

Whether you are an experienced Oracle professional or you are just entering the game, have no illusions—cloud computing is here to stay and it is the future. With the advent of OCI, there has never been a more exciting time to embrace Oracle technology. Coupling your understanding of Oracle Cloud Infrastructure with your experience with Oracle software can be both invigorating and exciting to your career.

Introduction to OCI

OCI has been engineered to be simple yet powerful. Modern computer systems, whether hosted on your desktop or in a data center, consist of four primary elements:

- Non-volatile storage components that retain data after power is recycled and are usually some form of persistent disk storage.

- Volatile storage components that are typically memory modules or RAM. These modules tend to be faster or offer higher IOs per second (IOPS) than persistent storage and are generally more expensive. Volatile storage also does not survive a power cycle event.
- Networks that support communications between systems that rely on interfaces to connect to network routing infrastructure.
- CPUs, or compute processing components, are the brains of the outfit, performing logical processing operations.

Infrastructure as a Service or IaaS (frequently pronounced *i-as*) is an abstraction of infrastructure components, including the four mentioned earlier. It is available in an online marketplace, enabling you to choose the most appropriate combination of these elements to meet your computing requirements. OCI and other IaaS vendors provide this basic service. Figure 1-1 shows a subset of the infrastructure components that may be provisioned.

Virtualization of resources is the underlying philosophy behind IaaS. On premises, virtualization technologies like Oracle Virtual Machine (OVM) paved the way for consolidation and pooling of resources and sharing these between VMs to optimize hardware and infrastructure efficiency. This approach is very prevalent but presents several challenges. On premises, virtualization requires an initial capital outlay for hosting servers and setting up the VM environments. Provisioning a new VM system is generally faster than traditional methods, but ongoing maintenance is expensive and ecosystem growth is limited by the size of the physical virtual servers. OCI solves these problems by making a practically inexhaustible supply of resources accessible to you on demand, absolving you of the responsibility of maintaining storage, network, and servers, while refreshing the hardware transparently to ensure your systems are running on a modern supported kit.

An important feature provided by OCI relates to disaster recovery and high availability. On-premises solutions include hosting servers in multiple data centers and ensuring high-speed network connectivity between them. Backups are usually also taken and are sometimes moved to offsite storage locations.

OCI represents a collection of resources, both virtualized and bare-metal systems grouped in data centers known as *availability domains* (ADs). One or more ADs are

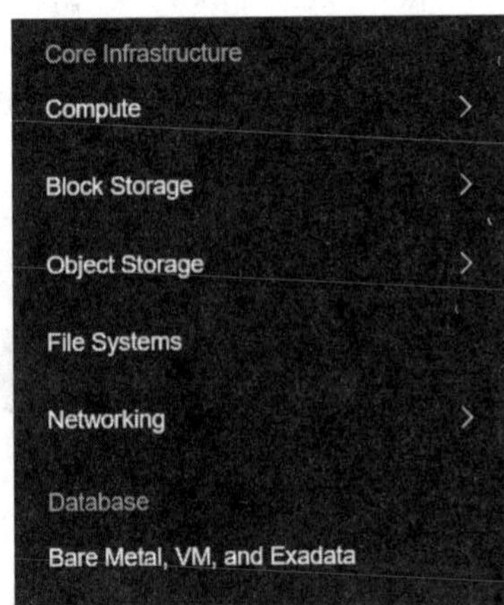

Figure 1-1 IaaS options from OCI

grouped into a region. You get access to multiple Disaster Recovery (DR) locations and access to archival storage for offsite backups with just a few clicks. The value proposition is staggering.

With OCI, you choose the processing or compute power for a system you want to spin up. Oracle was the first cloud vendor among other IaaS providers to offer both virtual and bare-metal machines. Virtual machine instances may be provisioned based on available compute shapes, which are preset bundles of RAM, and compute power called OCPU (Oracle CPUs). Figure 1-2 shows several VM shapes, highlighting the VM.Standard2.1 shape with one OCPU and 15GB RAM. Other instance provisioning items allow you to specify network configuration and to allocate storage. The infrastructure options available allow rapid provisioning of a wide range of systems from Windows desktops to Exadata Engineered systems.

Various infrastructure options exist for most components and more options are added as new technology is bolted onto OCI. For example, the first set of bare-metal x86 servers available with OCI was the X5 generation. These were replaced with the X7 generation of servers. OCI infrastructure follows a classical hardware refresh cycle and is periodically updated with modern replacements. At the storage layer, there are options for block storage, usually used for server file systems or database storage. These vary from slower devices to high-speed Non-Volatile Memory (NVMe) storage.

Traditionally, a new project implementation lifecycle would reach a stage where computing power resources are estimated and suitable server hardware is identified and ordered. After delivery and installation in one or more data centers, the system is ready for software implementation. Delivery and installation times vary widely and are inconsistent and unpredictable. This approach is inefficient and time-consuming, and these systems are usually over-provisioned.

Historically, the trend has been to design and architect systems for the worst-case scenario. It is common for enterprise software to be licensed based on the number of processors active on a server. A common trend is that many more CPU cores are licensed than actually required to cater to increased load on a few days of the year (for example, Black Friday and Boxing Day for retailers or Admissions week at colleges). During these peak times, there is a spike in processing power demand, while the system usually needs only a fraction of these resources for the vast majority of the year. OCI resolves this inefficiency

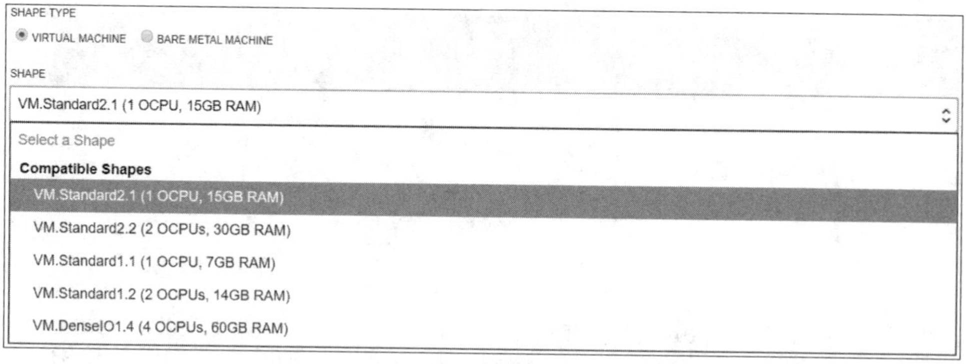

SHAPE TYPE
VIRTUAL MACHINE
BARE METAL MACHINE
SHAPE
VM.Standard2.1 (1 OCPU, 15GB RAM)
Select a Shape
Compatible Shapes
VM.Standard2.1 (1 OCPU, 15GB RAM)
VM.Standard2.2 (2 OCPUs, 30GB RAM)
VM.Standard1.1 (1 OCPU, 7GB RAM)
VM.Standard1.2 (2 OCPUs, 14GB RAM)
VM.DenseIO1.4 (4 OCPUs, 60GB RAM)

Figure 1-2 VM shape types

by offering bursting-on-demand or the dynamic provisioning of processing power during peak loads, which is another very compelling reason you should consider OCI.

NOTE OCI-Classic, launched in 2014, was known as Oracle Public Cloud (OPC). The first-generation IaaS offering supports only virtual machines (VMs) and was based on cloud infrastructure management software called Nimbula Director (acquired in 2013 by Oracle), which was a Xen-based hypervisor. OPC was renamed OCI-Classic in 2017. Cloud at Customer currently utilizes a similar hypervisor to OCI-Classic.

Oracle provides free credits to get you started with OCI. As you work your way through this book, we strongly recommend that you do so with access to your own OCI account.

Exercise 1-1: Create a New OCI Account

In this exercise, you will create a new OCI account. If you already have access to an OCI account, you can skip this exercise. To register for the free credits, you need an email address that, preferably, has not been used previously to register for OCI. You will also need a credit card. Note that unless you upgrade to the paid option, you will not be charged. It is still safest to use a credit card with a low credit limit. As of this writing, the workflow to create a new OCI account is as follows. These steps may vary as OCI interfaces are updated.

1. Navigate to http://cloud.oracle.com and choose Try For Free.

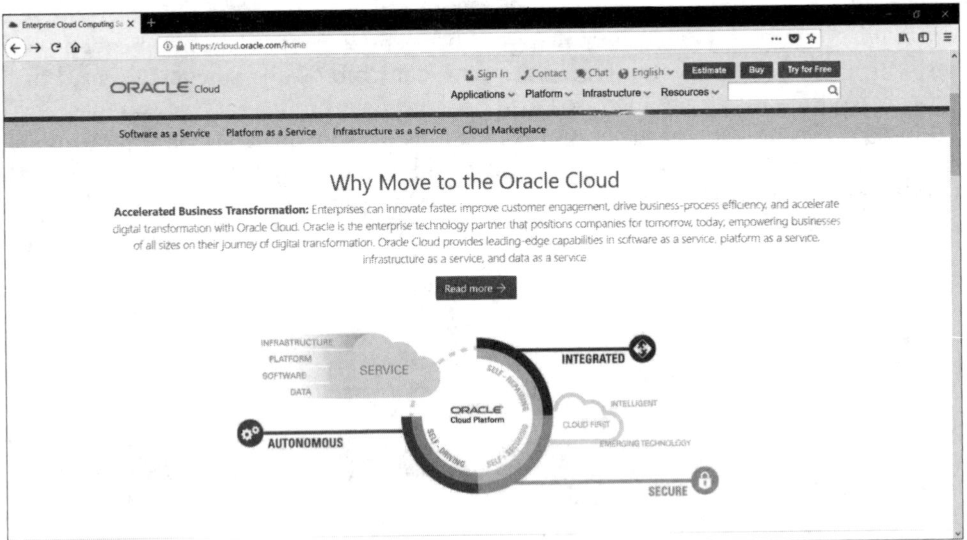

2. Complete the required fields to sign up. Pay attention to the cloud account name. This must be unique, and because this will appear in some URLs related to this account, you may wish to choose a recognizable name. The email address you

provide will also be your username. After providing name and address information, the second section verifies that you have a mobile phone from a supported country. You are required to enter a verification code texted to your mobile device and click the Verify button. The third section validates your credit card information. If you accept the terms and conditions, check the box and click Complete. You should land at the getting-started portal where Oracle thanks you for signing up and begins provisioning your account. There are some interesting videos on this page, well worth a watch while you wait for the provisioning email to show up in your Inbox.

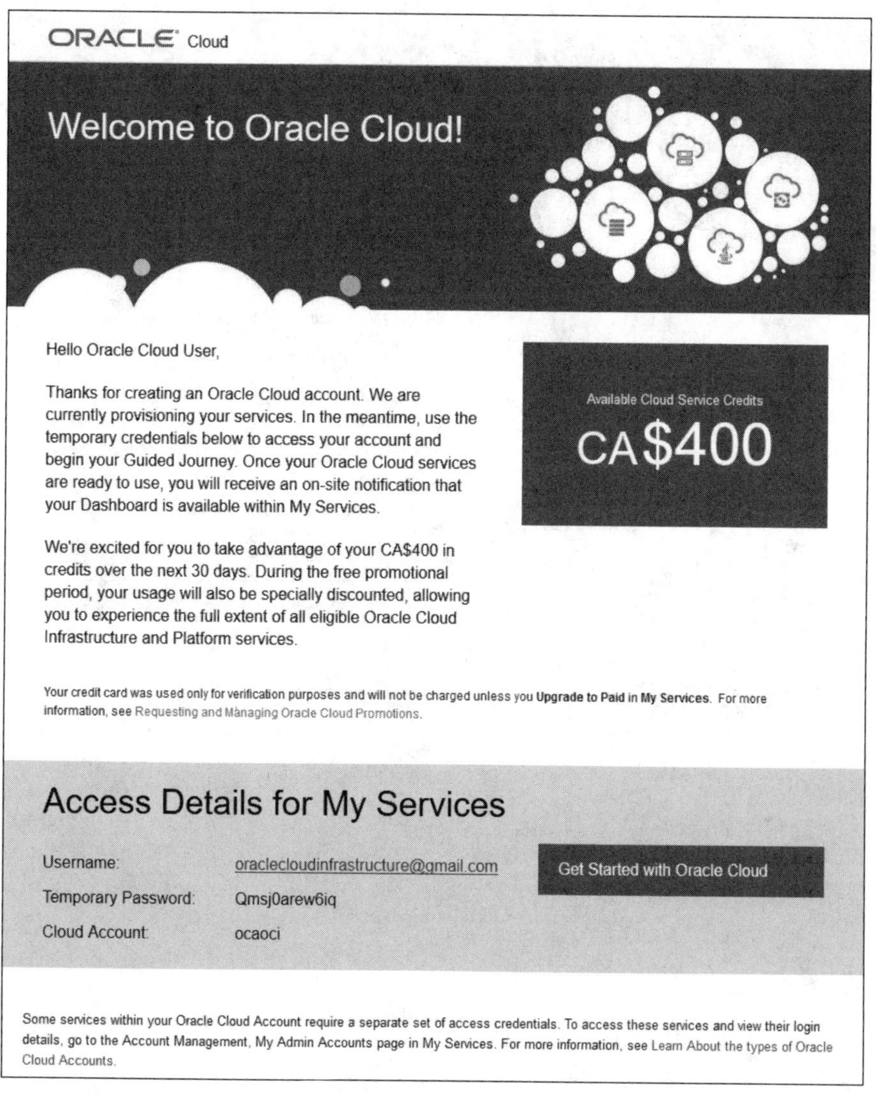

3. After signing up, you should receive several emails initially. One provides credentials, including a temporary password for My Services. Take note of the cloud account name that you provided when registering. In this example, the

cloud account is called ocaoci. Clicking the Get Started With Oracle Cloud button takes you to a login screen labeled Identity Cloud Service. Sign in with the credentials in the email, and you will be prompted to set a new password, language, and time zone preferences.

4. You have just signed into your cloud account, authenticated with Oracle Identity Cloud Service (IDCS).

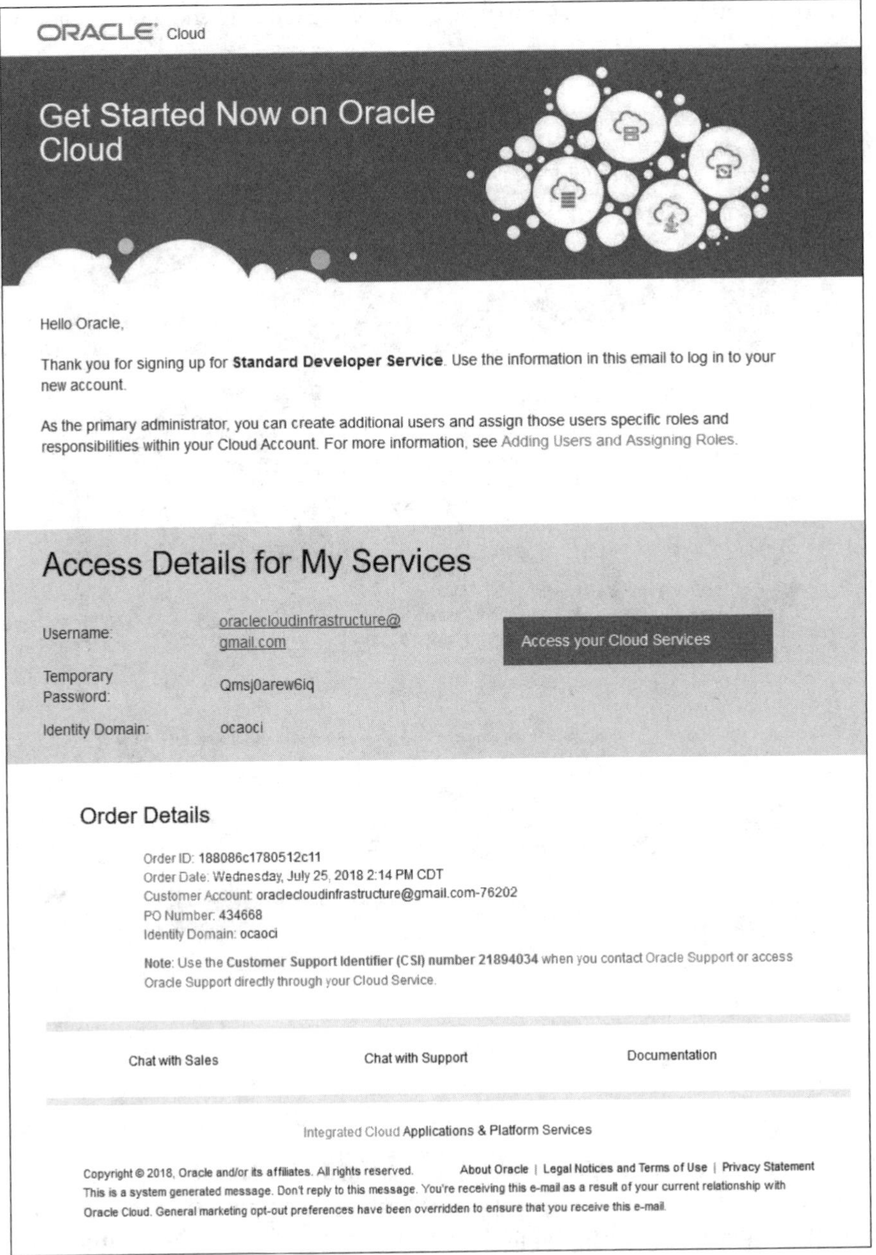

5. You will receive another email to confirm that you signed up for the Standard Developer Service. It also provides additional account information, such as your order details and even a Customer Support Identifier (CSI) number you may use when accessing Oracle Support on http://support.oracle.com. Notice that an Identity Domain has been created with the same name as the cloud account name. Choosing to Access Your Cloud Services strangely takes you to a different login screen, labeled Traditional Cloud Account.

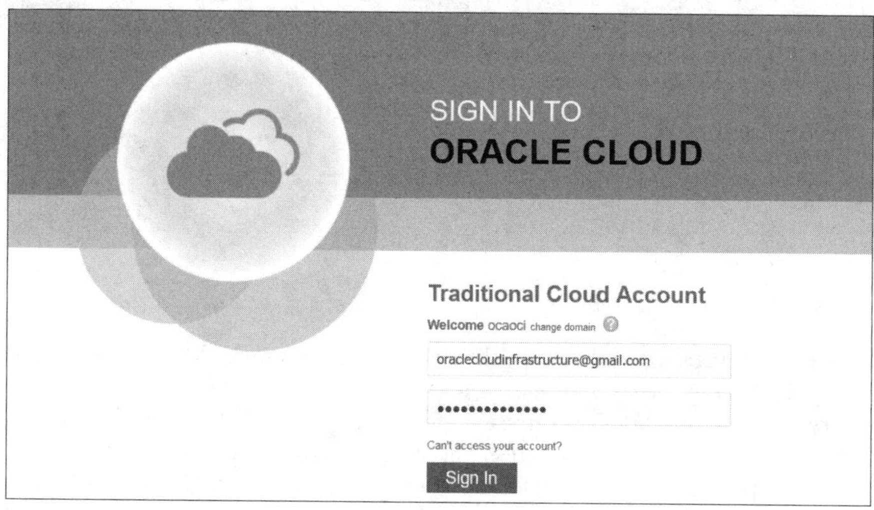

6. It gets tricky at this point. If you have been following along, you would have chosen a new password that is different from the temporary password emailed to you in an earlier step. However, when signing in to the Traditional Cloud Account, you have to use the temporary password from the email. Once authenticated, you are prompted by Oracle Identity Self Service to set a new password and to register challenge questions for your account. You now have two different types of cloud account: the traditional account and the Identity Cloud Service account. These different account types will be explored in the next chapter. For most of the exercises in this book, you will use your IDCS authenticated account.

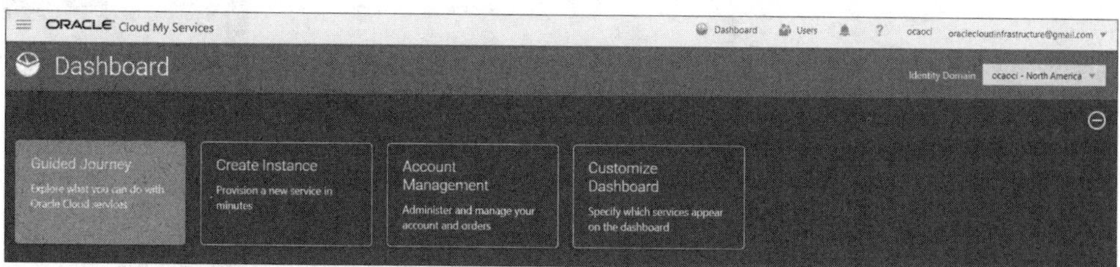

7. Explore the Dashboard interface. It may appear quite simple, but you have access to many powerful services. Note the Identity Domain drop-down list related to the two types of cloud accounts. The traditional and standard identity domains let you access the OCI-Classic and OCI features respectively. Choose Guided Journey to access various guided services.

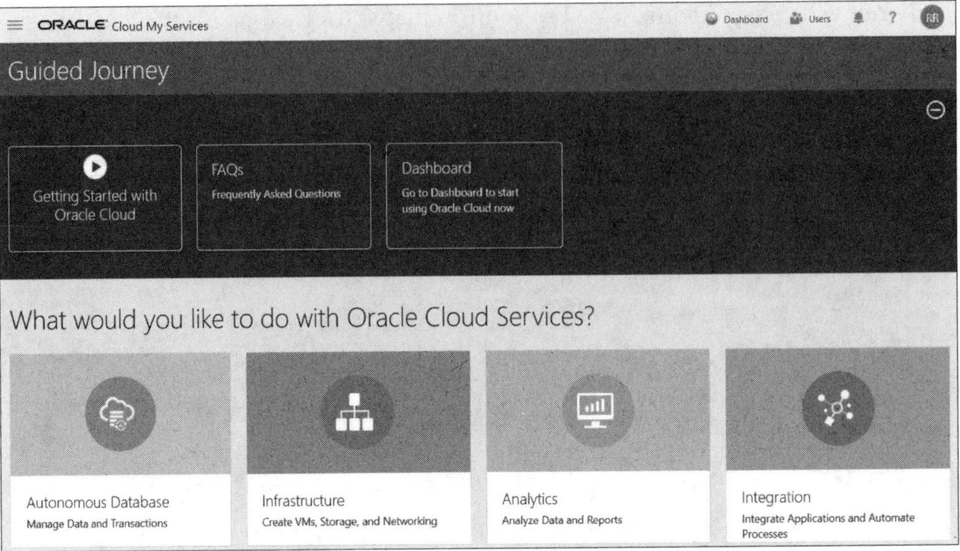

8. There are several ways to launch the OCI console from the My Services interface, including using the hamburger menu and choosing the Compute option in the Services menu or choosing Infrastructure from the Guided Journey screen and selecting Create Compute Instance. Various OCI console options are explored in this book, so prepare to become very familiar with this interface. You primarily navigate the OCI console using the burger menu. Choose Menu | Administration | My Services Dashboard to return to the dashboard or choose Oracle Cloud Infrastructure next to the burger menu to access the OCI console Quick Launch page.

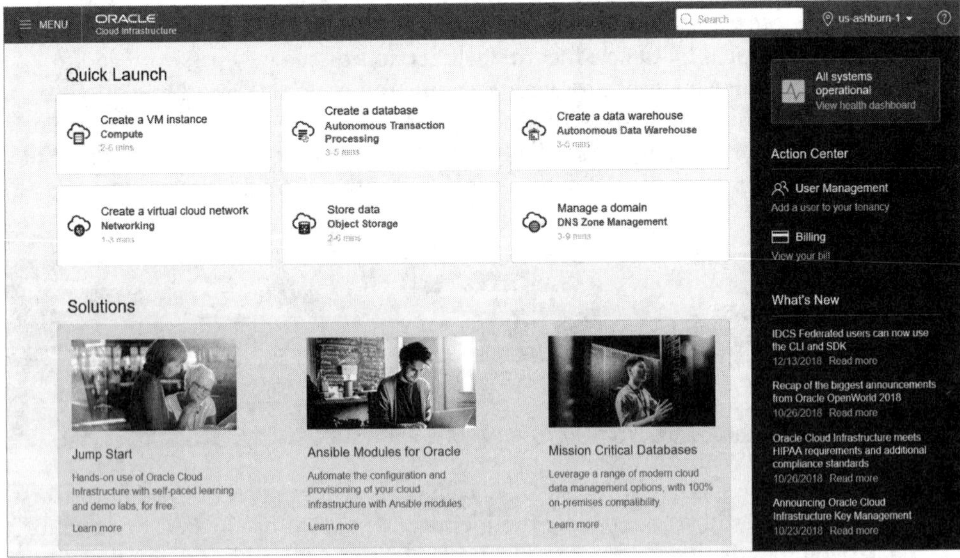

Cloud Computing Models

Modern cloud computing refers to a collection of applications, the platform, servers, storage, and network infrastructure resident in a data center, exposed as services. Three primary models of cloud computing typically implemented as services are Infrastructure, Platform, and Software as a Service—or IaaS, PaaS and SaaS.

- **IaaS** A collection of servers, storage, and network infrastructure onto which you deploy your platform and software. This is most akin to provisioning your own hardware in an on-premises data center. Teams of hardware engineers, storage specialists, network specialists, system administrators, and database administrators are usually involved in installing and configuring on-premises infrastructure. With IaaS, no hardware engineers or storage specialists are required. A good cloud architect (like you) is all that is required to design and provision this infrastructure. The cloud vendor provides the hardware engineers and storage specialists.
- **PaaS** A collection of one or more preconfigured infrastructure instances usually provided with an operating system, database, or development platform onto which you can deploy your software. The primary benefit of PaaS is convenience as the cloud vendor provides and supports the underlying infrastructure and platform. A subset of PaaS is Database as a Service (DBaaS). Figure 1-3 shows how you could provision an Oracle database instance with the required compute, memory shape, version, and block storage with a few clicks. Behind the scenes, OCI creates a machine, deploys an OS, installs the requested database version, and provides a functional platform in minutes. You may then connect to the machine where an Oracle database is ready and waiting. There is no need for explicit hosting and maintaining hardware infrastructure, operating systems, and databases.
- **SaaS** Applications are deployed on a cloud and all you do is access them through your browser. These could range from webmail to complex ERP and BI Analytic systems.

Oracle Cloud encompasses the Oracle Public Cloud, which represents a collection of infrastructure, platforms, and applications exposed as services on cloud.oracle.com. Figure 1-4 highlights two important factors on the same spectrum when considering cloud computing models: control and convenience. The convenience offered by SaaS and PaaS comes at the cost of less control. IaaS offers the most control but requires the most effort. With IaaS, you have complete access to the infrastructure you provision. For example, when you provision a compute instance, you have the option to choose the operating system image. With PaaS, if you provision a database, you will have administrator privileges, but you have fewer options. For example, when you provision a database, you cannot choose the operating system on the compute instance created. SaaS offers maximum convenience, but you are dependent on the cloud vendor for maintenance and support.

The placement of the OS (operating system) in the IaaS tier is sometimes debated. Some argue that IaaS refers to just the virtualized or physical infrastructure and therefore the OS forms a part of the PaaS layer. However, the NIST definition (https://nvlpubs.nist.gov/nistpubs/Legacy/SP/nistspecialpublication800-145.pdf) specifies IaaS as "The capability

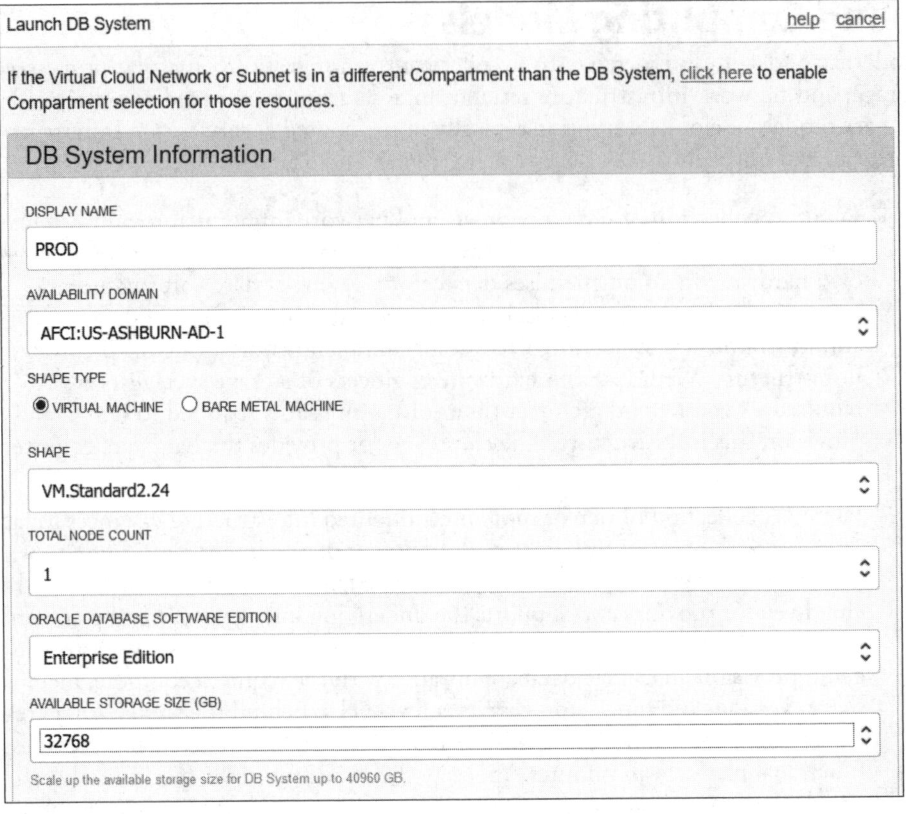

Figure 1-3 Database as a Service

provided to the consumer is to provision processing, storage, networks, and other fundamental computing resources where the consumer is able to deploy and run arbitrary software, which can include operating systems and applications." OCI appears to be congruent with this definition.

Some highly regulated and sensitive environments cannot consume public cloud services because of data residency (data must reside in a particular locale) and data sovereignty (data may only be managed by resources located in a particular region). For organizations in countries without local OCI data centers, Oracle offers IaaS, PaaS, and SaaS through an on-premises solution such as the Cloud at Customer products discussed in Chapter 8. Oracle Cloud comprises SaaS, PaaS, OCI-Classic (OCI-C), and OCI. OCI is all about IaaS and the focus of this book and exam.

EXAM TIP The three primary cloud-computing models are Infrastructure, Platform, and Software as a Service, better known as IaaS, PaaS, and SaaS. Compute, Storage, and Network resources fall under IaaS. Java and Database Cloud Services are examples of PaaS while ERP, SCM, and Analytics Cloud applications are examples of SaaS.

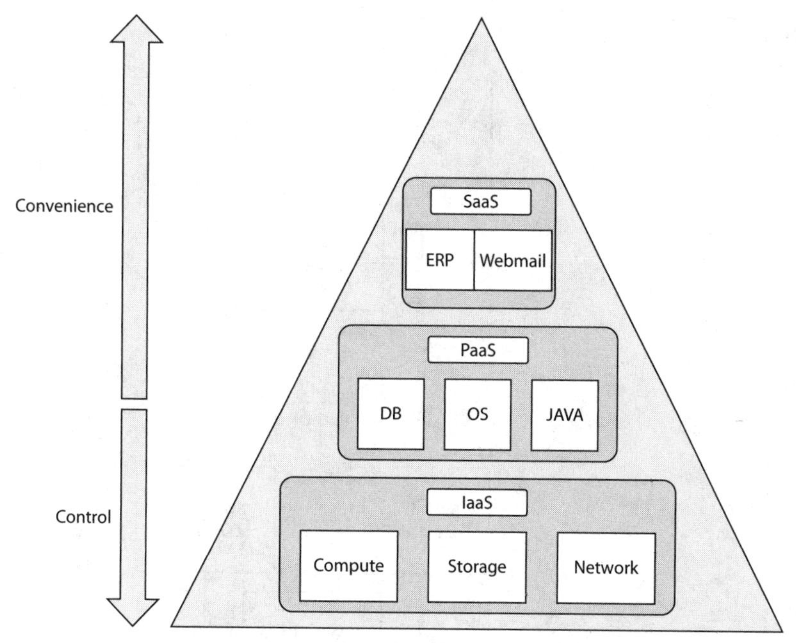

Figure 1-4 IaaS, PaaS, and SaaS

OCI Features and Components

OCI was engineered from the ground up using expertise and learning derived from OCI-Classic as well as other mainstream cloud vendors. OCI shares many features common to most mainstream cloud vendors. However, several features that are unique to OCI are key differentiators. Amazon Web Services (AWS) offers a plethora of services targeting the entire spectrum of cloud consumers. OCI focuses on enterprise consumers and has specifically catered to hosting Oracle workloads while still providing a general-purpose IaaS framework. For example, OCI regions and availability domains have AWS parallels called regions and availability zones, while OCI has off-box networking that is not provided by most other cloud vendors. This constantly evolving feature set is explored in the next section.

Regions and Availability Domains

Cloud infrastructure consists of servers, storage, and networking equipment. These reside in data centers. Data centers with resilient and redundant components that do not have a single-point of failure are referred to as fault-tolerant data centers. In OCI *cloud-speak*, a fault-tolerant data center is an availability domain (AD). One or more availability domains located in a metropolitan area connected with high-speed networks are grouped into a region. Figure 1-5 describes two regions, each comprising three availability domains.

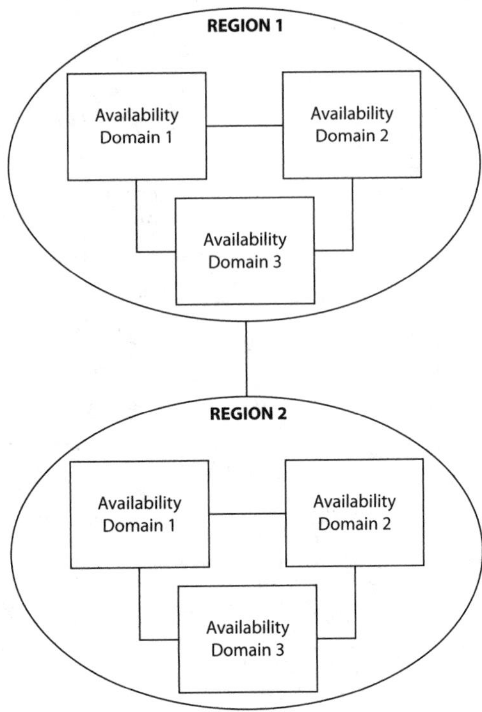

Figure 1-5 Regions and availability domains

Each AD contains three fault domains. A fault domain is an infrastructure grouping that allows your instances to be distributed so they do not reside on the same physical hardware within an AD. When creating instances you may optionally specify the fault domain to control instance placement. Fault domains offer additional protection at a physical server level against unexpected hardware failures and improves availability during planned outages.

The predictable consistent network performance available in OCI is a key differentiator due to the off-box network architecture that will be discussed in the next section. Table 1-1 lists the initial five OCI regions generally available, in various countries across several continents.

Region Location	Region Name	Region Key
Phoenix, Arizona, US	us-phoenix-1	PHX
Ashburn, Virginia, US	us-ashburn-1	IAD
Frankfurt, Germany	eu-frankfurt-1	FRA
London, UK	uk-london-1	LHR
Toronto, Canada	ca-toronto-1	YYZ
Seoul, South Korea	ap-seoul-1	ICN
Tokyo, Japan	ap-tokyo-1	NRT

Table 1-1 OCI Regions

Regions including Brazil and India as well as several government regions in the United States form the second wave of provisioned OCI regions. You have access to all regions, or you can subscribe to specific regions for data residency compliance or performance requirements. Placing your primary infrastructure in a geographical region nearest to your users reduces network latency.

Network performance is typically measured by the metrics *bandwidth* and *latency*. Bandwidth refers to the throughput or volume of data that can be transferred over time. For example, 5Gb/s means that five gigabits of data will be transferred over the network from one endpoint to another per second. Latency refers to the delay or time taken for a data packet to traverse a network. It is usually measured as the Round Trip Time (RTT).

Oracle claims the network bandwidth between servers in each AD is 10 Gbps with a latency of less than 100 microseconds. This network is a flat high-speed non-oversubscribed *Clos* network that provides around one million network ports per AD. Oracle promises a maximum of two network hops between Compute and Storage resources regardless of the size and scale of the estate. The bandwidth between ADs in each region is 1 Tbps with a latency of less than 5,000 microseconds. Finally, the bandwidth between regions, which are geographically vast distances apart, is 100 Gbps with a latency of less than 100 milliseconds. These network performance metrics are listed in Table 1-2.

The high-performance AD and region network architecture provides two key benefits:

- **Isolation** Each AD is self-contained, contains highly fault-tolerant computing resources, and is isolated from the other ADs in the region. ADs in a region do not share power, cooling, or the internal AD network. Failure of one AD is very unlikely to impact the availability of other ADs in the region. High availability and DR zero data loss architectures such as Oracle Maximum Availability Architecture (MAA) may be built within a single region utilizing the low-latency, high-bandwidth network, supporting near real-time data replication between availability domains.
- **Disaster recovery** It is unlikely that multiple ADs within a region will fail simultaneously. However, natural disasters and other compliance requirements may necessitate an architecture (usually DR strategy) spanning multiple regions. This is supported by a cloud backbone and direct peering that enables private connections between regions.

Object	Context	Bandwidth	Latency
Server A to Server B	AD	10 Gbps	<100µs
Availability Domain 1 to Availability Domain 2	Region	1 Tbps	<5000µs
Region 1 to Region 2	OCI Network Backbone	100 Gbps	<100ms

Table 1-2 Network Performance Between Servers, ADs, and Regions

Exercise 1-2: Explore Your Availability Domain and Region

1. Navigate to http://cloud.oracle.com and choose Sign In. Provide the cloud account name you specified when registering, and choose My Services.

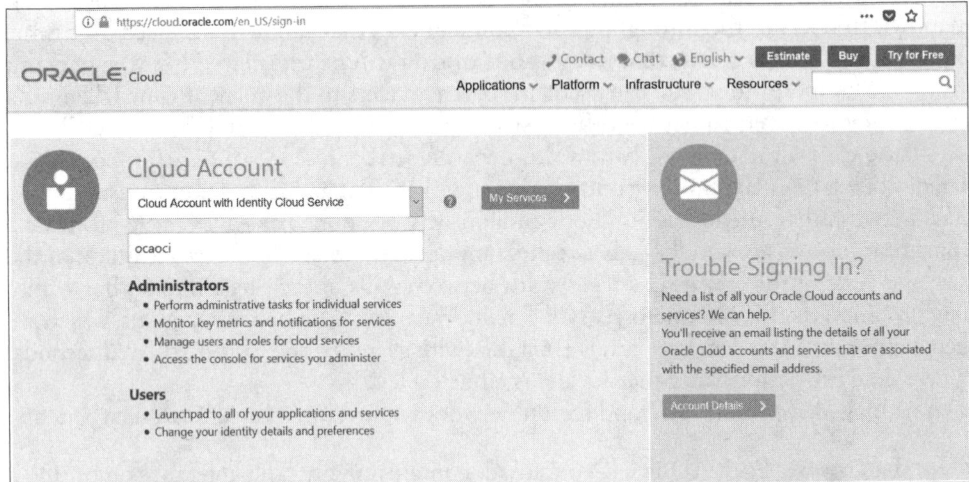

2. Upon login, find your way to the OCI interface. One route is to choose the Create Instance from the My Services dashboard. At the OCI interface, note your home region to the right of the search box.

3. When registering your cloud account in the previous exercise, you specified a cloud account name as well as a Default Data Region.
4. When registering the *ocaoci* cloud account, North America was selected as the Default Data Region. In the OCI console, navigate to Administration| Tenancy Details. The cloud account name is the OCI tenant name and is listed under Tenancy Information. OCI randomly allocates a home region close to the Default Data Region specified. OCI allocated the us-ashburn-1 region as the home region for this tenancy. Note the OCI console URL. In this tenancy, the URL is https://console.us-ashburn-1.oraclecloud.com. Your OCI console URL should begin with your home region.

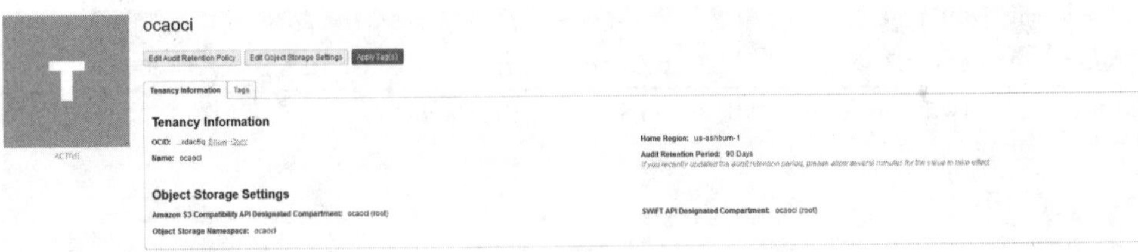

5. Note the Home Region, tenant name, and OCID (sometime pronounced *o-sid*). Your OCID uniquely identifies your OCI environment. Copy your OCID and keep this safe. Choose another available region, such as uk-london-1, and select Subscribe To This Region.

Regions
Displaying 1 Regions
R Name: eu-frankfurt-1 Subscribe To This Region
R Name: us-ashburn-1(Home Region)
R Name: uk-london-1 Subscribe To This Region
R Name: us-phoenix-1 Subscribe To This Region

6. The encircled R icon adjacent to the newly selected region turns from gray to orange, indicating work-in-progress, and a short time later turns green. You have just added your tenancy to another OCI region across the world. Choose the new region and examine your Tenancy OCID. This value has not changed and uniquely identifies your tenancy across regions. Each Oracle Cloud Infrastructure resource has a unique, Oracle-assigned identifier called an Oracle Cloud ID (OCID).

Off-Box Network Virtualization

One of the key design decisions taken by the OCI development architects was to implement off-box network virtualization. Traditional cloud vendors use hypervisors on servers to run multiple workloads through virtualized operating system and network functions, including I/O calls. In OCI, I/O virtualization has been relocated from the hypervisor layer to the network.

This separation has several important implications. A common cloud performance issue occurs when I/O from multiple VM workloads overwhelms the hypervisor, which leads to server performance degradation. This *noisy neighbor* situation cannot occur when I/O virtualization is off-box (off the server). Relocating the network and I/O virtualizations out of the software stack and into the network layer allows dedicated physical servers with a full software-defined layer 3 network topology to be defined. Figure 1-6 shows this layer as the Virtual Network. Off-box network virtualization enables OCI to support VMs and bare-metal compute instances, RAC (clustered) databases, and engineered systems.

EXAM TIP The noisy neighbor phenomenon occurs when VMs sharing a physical server are impacted by one or more VM workloads overwhelming the hypervisor. This situation is avoided in OCI through off-box network virtualization.

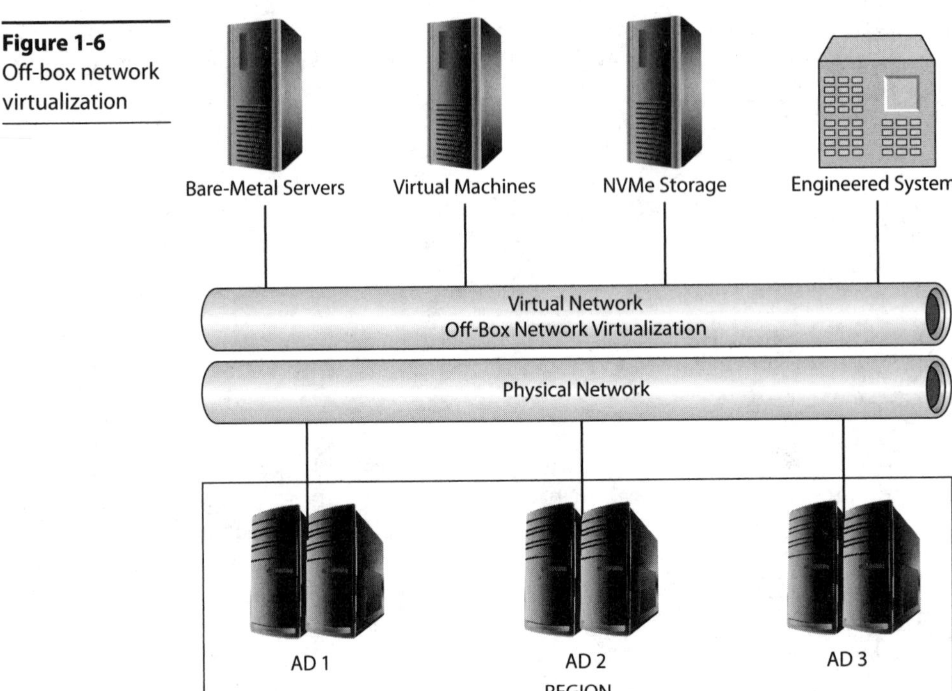

Figure 1-6 Off-box network virtualization

OCI Concepts and Terms

The sheer volume of offerings from cloud vendors can be overwhelming. Figure 1-7 offers a framework that may be useful for classifying some of the popular OCI offerings. This is not an exhaustive list but provides a context for readers new to OCI to frame the plethora of cloud services. The concepts are described in a typical order of provisioning. Identity and access management is addressed first, then networking because resources associated with these concepts are usually provisioned first in cloud architectures. You could then create compute instances, allocate storage, or take advantage of the Database Cloud Service, a popular platform service. Strictly speaking, compute, storage, and networking services are pure IaaS offerings. In the Oracle world, PaaS offerings such as Database Cloud Service and Java Cloud Service are so prevalent that these, along with Container services and other popular offerings, are available on OCI.

Identity and Access Management

When starting with OCI, some of the first decisions you usually make relate to Identity and Access Management (IAM) entities. If you have registered an OCI account, you already have defined your tenancy, which is your cloud account. One of the next IAM constructs you create is called a compartment, which is a logical collection of related cloud resources. Compartments are used to isolate resources.

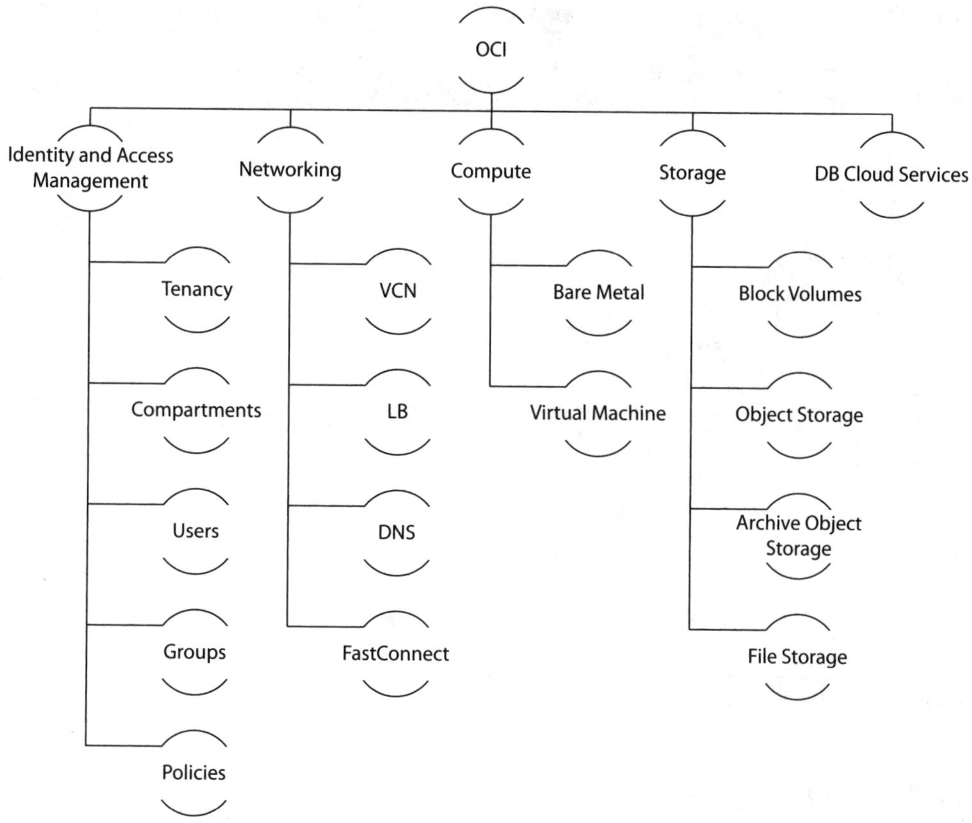

- OCI
  - Identity and Access Management
    - Tenancy
    - Compartments
    - Users
    - Groups
    - Policies
  - Networking
    - VCN
    - LB
    - DNS
    - FastConnect
  - Compute
    - Bare Metal
    - Virtual Machine
  - Storage
    - Block Volumes
    - Object Storage
    - Archive Object Storage
    - File Storage
  - DB Cloud Services

Figure 1-7 OCI taxonomy

Users may be created, deleted, and have their accounts managed. Figure 1-8 shows a user named Jason who belongs to the ESC_NetworkAdmins group. Groups may be created with collections of Users. One of the really neat things that IAM on OCI offers is the natural, descriptive language used by IAM policies to grant access:

```
Allow group Developers to manage all-resources in compartment Lab
```

IAM resources have global scope and are available in each Compartment, AD, and Region. IAM Compartments, Groups, Users, and Policies are discussed in detail in the next chapter.

EXAM TIP As new users are signed up for OCI, the cloud administrator should make use of IAM policies to grant appropriate access to Groups and then create Users.

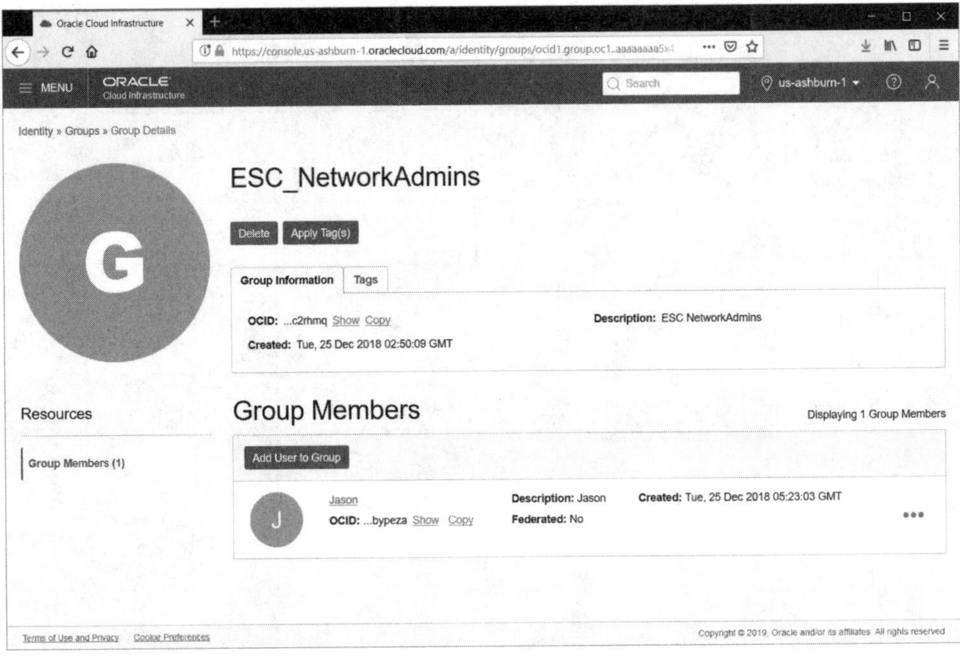

Figure 1-8 IAM resources

Networking

OCI networking is elegantly simple yet powerful and has direct parallels to networking in an on-premises data center.

Virtual Cloud Network

The first networking element you set up is your virtual cloud network (VCN), which works much like a traditional private on-premises network. The VCN is defined at a Compartment level so you could have multiple VCNs. At least one VCN must be set up before instances may be provisioned. There are simplified options to choose while creating a VCN that provisions related resources including subnets, a gateway, and a set of route rules to start you off with a working VCN. If you create your VCN manually, you have to provide a Classless Inter-Domain Routing (CIDR often pronounced *cider*) block, which specifies a range of IP addresses that may be allocated in that VCN.

When the VCN named ocaoci was provisioned, three subnets were automatically created, one for each availability domain. The VCN spans all ADs in a region. Notice in Figure 1-9 that the CIDR blocks allocated to each subnet do not overlap. A default route table is created along with an Internet Gateway, allowing your compute instances to connect to the Internet if desired. A default security list is also created with several default ingress rules, one of which permits SSH access on port 22 to provide remote login and access to your compute instances. An ingress rule permits incoming traffic, while an egress rule permits outgoing traffic. The Internet Gateway provides a network path for traffic between the VCN and the public Internet.

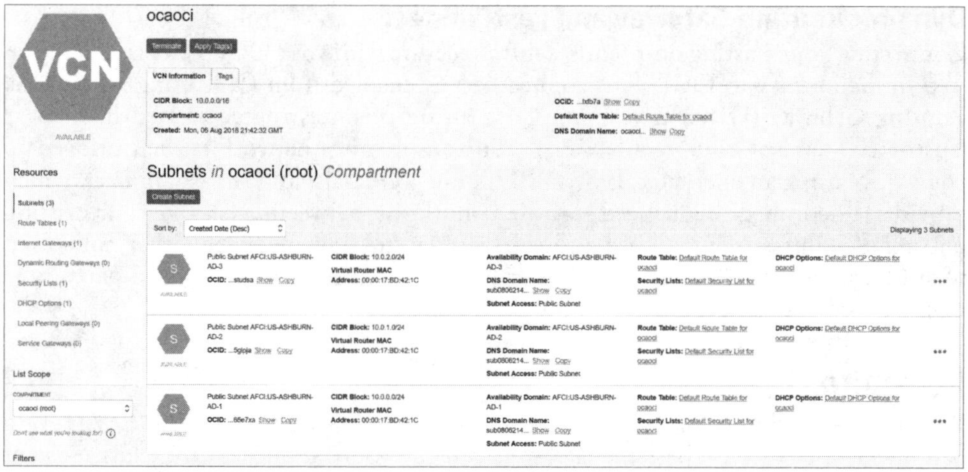

Figure 1-9 Virtual cloud network

Load Balancers

A Load Balancer (LB) is a network device you may provision that receives incoming traffic on an IP address and routes the traffic to one or more underlying instances. The OCI LB service is a regional service that distributes traffic to instances either within the same availability domain or across multiple availability domains.

The protocol and ports being serviced by an LB are specified in an entity called the Listener. When creating an LB, you specify the VCN in which incoming traffic is accepted as well as whether it will be a private or public LB. You also choose the shape of the LB, which limits the speed at which network traffic is routed. LBs are commonly used to support high availability and scaling out of web servers.

LBs distribute traffic to backend servers based on a set of policies known as a *backend set*. Routing algorithms, including Weighted Round-Robin, IP Hash, and Least Connections, are specified when creating the backend set. Path Route Sets specify a set of rules to route requests to different backend sets but this is optional and is only used if this level of sophistication is necessary. Finally, backend sets reference one or more hostnames, which are the target compute instances, which may be running a web server.

EXAM TIP OCI load balancers support three protocols: TCP, HTTP, and WebSockets.

Domain Name Service

OCI also provides a Domain Name Service (DNS) that lets you create and manage DNS zones, add records to zones, and allow the VCN to resolve DNS queries from your on-premises domain and vice versa. One of the primary services DNS provides is hostname resolution. For example, it is DNS that allows you to connect to http://cloud.oracle.com instead of http://23.9.97.203. This abstraction provides network resiliency to underlying network changes.

Dynamic Routing Gateway and FastConnect

Connecting your existing on-premises infrastructure with your OCI VCN is a common step in the journey to OCI. This connectivity is enabled from OCI using a Dynamic Routing Gateway (DRG) that connects to an on-premises router created in OCI as Customer Premises Equipment (CPE). Your on-premises network is then bridged to your VCN using an encrypted IPSec VPN tunnel. OCI also offers FastConnect, which provides a dedicated, high-speed, private connection between OCI and your existing on-premises infrastructure. FastConnect requires that you must be either collocated with Oracle in a FastConnect location or that you connect through a third-party FastConnect provider that is already connected to Oracle.

Compute

When you provision a compute instance, you can choose a virtual machine (VM) or a bare-metal (BM) server. Bare-metal servers provide your instance with exclusive use of the hardware. Not sharing hardware with other instances comes at a cost and bare-metal instances are more expensive that similarly sized virtual machines. BM servers are only available with a much higher CPU and memory footprint than entry-level VMs.

When you provision a new compute instance, you specify a name; the AD it resides in; a boot volume, which may be an Oracle-provided image such as Oracle Linux 7.5; and the shape type, which is either BM or VM. Depending on the operating system image and the shape type chosen, you can select compatible shapes. For example, you could provision a VM with the shape labeled VM.DenseIO2.16 (16 OCPUs, 240GB RAM, 12.8TB NVMe SSD) or a bare-metal instance with the BM.Standard1.36 (36 OCPUs, 256GB RAM) shape. The shape names contain several useful identifiers. Standard means that only block storage is available while DenseIO refers to local NVMe drivers being present. The last digits in the shape name refer to the number of OCPUs, or Oracle Compute Units. An OCPU provides CPU capacity equivalent to one physical core of an Intel Xeon processor with hyperthreading enabled. Each OCPU corresponds to two hardware execution threads, known as vCPUs.

You are also required to provide a secure shell (SSH) public key. SSH keys are created in pairs. The matching private key, which must be stored safely, will allow you to connect to the instance using the SSH protocol once it is provisioned.

Storage

Once your compute instance is provisioned, it will have a boot volume and usually no other storage. Four storage types are available on OCI:

- Block volumes
- Object storage
- Archive storage
- File storage

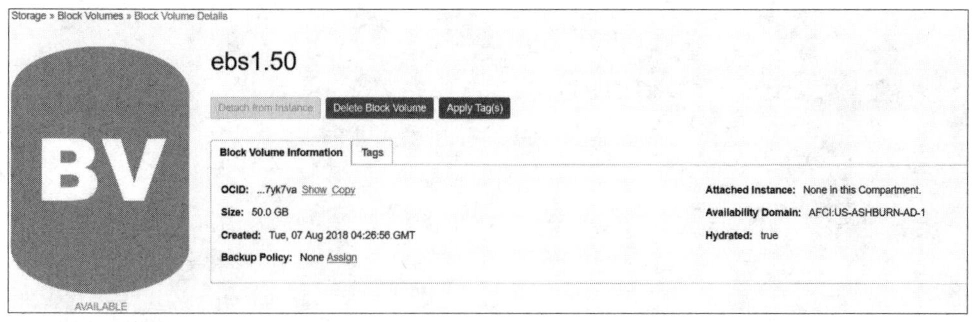

Figure 1-10 Block storage volume

Block Storage Volume

Block volumes are often used for user-created file systems as well as database storage and reside in a specific AD.

Figure 1-10 shows a 50GB block volume that resides in AD1 in the US-ASHBURN region. This block volume is not initially attached to any compute instance. After attaching the block volume to a compute instance using an iSCSI interface, OCI provides a handy list of commands to attach and detach the volume to your operating system, if required. I/O performance of block volume storage using iSCSI over Ethernet is comparable with modern SAN disks. Block volumes may be dismounted from one instance and mounted to another instance in the same AD without data loss.

Object and Archive Storage

Standard object storage (referred to as object storage hereafter) and archive storage are different tiers of the same storage solution. Using HTTP-based protocols, you can access these virtually unlimited durable and secure storage services. This storage is based on buckets, which may be private or public. Objects are uploaded to or downloaded from these buckets. There are developer tools available for interfacing with the object storage service.

Object and archive storage have parallels with AWS S3 and Glacier storage services. Object storage provides a scalable, readily available, and accessible storage service. Archive storage is durable but much slower. It is designed for extremely low-cost long-term data retention. It can take a long time to retrieve data from archive storage as the data must first be restored before it can be downloaded. You pay a slightly higher price for object storage where your objects are immediately ready for download. Figure 1-11 describes a bucket named Backups created in the standard storage tier (as opposed to the archive storage tier). One object, a file called EXACM.pdf, has been uploaded to this bucket. Examining the details of the object reveals several unusual properties, such as the URL path (URI), https://objectstorage.us-ashburn-1.oraclecloud.com/n/ocaoci/b/Backups/o/EXACM.pdf, and the visibility property, which is set to private. Object and file system storage systems differ in several aspects, the primary difference being that there are no

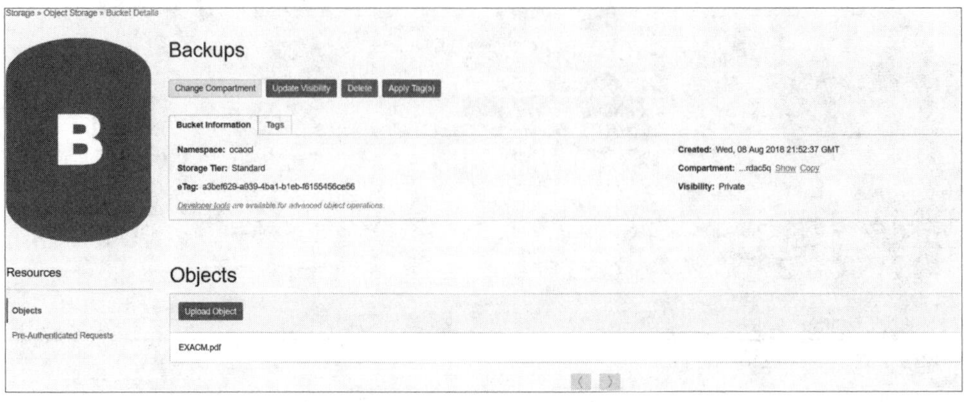

Figure 1-11 Object storage bucket

directories and subdirectories in object storage systems. Common use cases include storing daily and weekly backups using object storage while historical data that must be retained for compliance purposes is placed in archive storage.

File Storage Service

Most enterprise architectures contain one or more Network File Systems (NFS), which allow users access to remote shared storage that is mounted on their computers as if they are local file systems. NFS storage is typically mounted by multiple clients and is commonly used for backups, file sharing, and sometimes even for database storage.

The OCI File Storage Service provides durable NFS storage that you can connect to from any bare metal, virtual machine, or container instance in your virtual cloud network. The nfs-filer file system in Figure 1-12 is created in the ASHBURN-AD-1 availability domain and may be mounted by instances using the IP address and path name associated with the NFS mount target.

Database Cloud Service

Oracle Database Cloud Service (DBCS) is easily the most utilized PaaS offering on OCI. It is enthralling to contemplate that, with a few mouse clicks, you can provision a fully operational Oracle Database in minutes.

When provisioning a DBCS instance, you choose the shape of the compute instance, the database software version, edition, and license type. The compute instances may be virtual machines, bare metal, or Exadata, which is Oracle's leading-edge engineered system with converged infrastructure. The available database software versions vary and, as of this writing, versions 11.2.0.4, 12c, and 18c are available. DBCS software editions include the on-premises Standard and Enterprise Editions and additionally offer two new editions: Enterprise Edition High Performance and Enterprise Edition Extreme Performance (available only on Exadata).

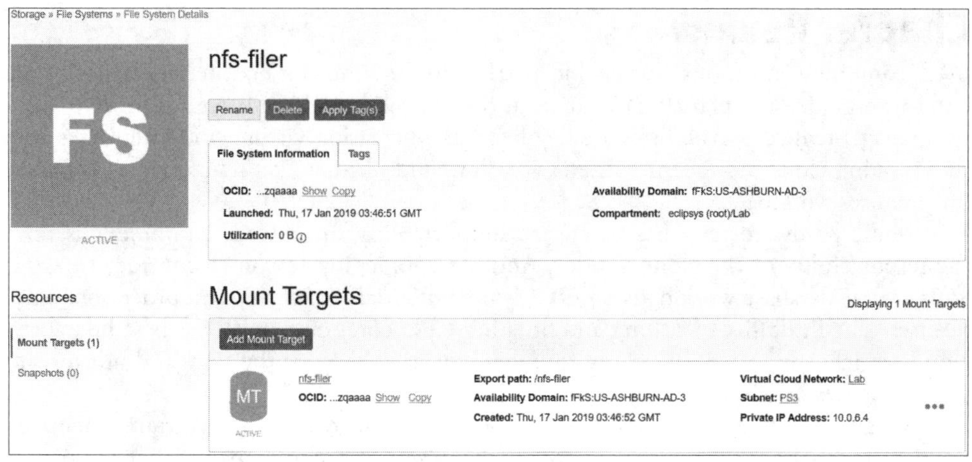

Figure 1-12 File storage service

Figure 1-13 shows an 18.2 Standard Edition database being provisioned on an instance with compute shape VM.Standard2.1 (1 OCPU, 15GB memory) and 256GB storage.

You can choose to provision a database with the license included or bring your own license (BYOL). The BYOL model is often used when migrating on-premises database workloads to OCI, allowing existing licenses to be reused. Massive license optimizations are often seen due to innovative features such as capacity on-demand bursting that allows you to license just what you need most of the time and not what you might need at peak load. Unsurprisingly, Oracle makes running its database most cost-effective on its own cloud compared to other cloud vendors.

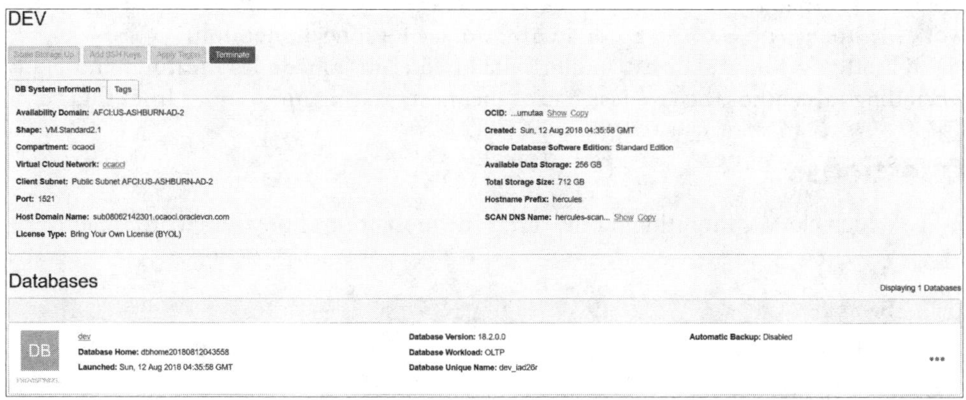

Figure 1-13 Oracle database provisioned by DBCS

Chapter Review

OCI combines enormous power and a deceptively simple user interface to offer an enterprise-grade IaaS platform. Virtualization, consolidation, and removal of data center management responsibilities are key benefits to creating virtual cloud networks and provisioning cloud architecture as an extension, and ultimately a replacement, for your on-premises workloads.

Periodic hardware refreshes to ensure supportability on current equipment is now the responsibility of the cloud vendor. Another compelling reason to consider running your Oracle database workloads on OCI is the potential cost savings on processor-based licenses. The flexibility of scaling and bursting CPU cores on some OCI-based database cloud services supports CPU sizing for what you need most of the time and not for the worst-case scenario.

High availability and disaster recovery options are provided for by arrangements of fault-tolerant data centers known as *availability domains* clustered together to form a region. Regions are geographically dispersed, some on different continents, and may be linked together to accommodate Maximum Availability Architectures.

Off-box networking is a key differentiator of OCI from most other cloud vendors and promotes predictable performance and uniquely enables OCI to support both VMs and bare-metal compute instances, RAC databases, and Engineered Systems.

An Identity and Access Management framework isolates environments using compartments and uses simple language policy statements to enforce the IAM framework on users and groups.

A full suite of virtualized network entities may be provisioned, including the virtual cloud network, internet and dynamic routing gateways, load balancers, route tables, and security lists.

Compute instances may be provisioned as virtual or bare-metal machines based on a selection of available compute shapes comprising various combinations of OCPUs and memory, operating systems, and even some PaaS options such as DBaaS. Block volume storage may be added to your compute instances and systems may be backed up to network file storage, object storage, or archive storage for longer retention.

OCI offers a continually expanding suite of enterprise-grade IaaS features and many (including this author) believe it is one of the most exciting innovations from Oracle.

Questions

1. Which cloud computing model offers the most control of your environment?

   A. PaaS

   B. SaaS

   C. IaaS

   D. DBaaS

2. What infrastructure resource cannot be provisioned in OCI?
   - **A.** NVMe storage
   - **B.** Networks
   - **C.** CPU and RAM
   - **D.** KVM switches
3. Which of the following statements is false?
   - **A.** VM instances may be created based on available compute shapes.
   - **B.** Block storage volumes can be added only to bare-metal machines.
   - **C.** VM instances may share resources on physical servers with other tenants.
   - **D.** Block storage volumes can be added to both virtual and bare-metal machines.
4. What is the OCI term for a fault-tolerant data center?
   - **A.** Availability zone
   - **B.** Region
   - **C.** Virtual cloud network
   - **D.** Availability domain
5. Which of the following statements is true?
   - **A.** An availability domain is a collection of regions.
   - **B.** A region is a collection of availability domains.
   - **C.** An availability zone is a collection of regions.
   - **D.** Two or more regions in a metro area are grouped into an AD.
6. Network performance is typically measured by which two metrics? (Choose two.)
   - **A.** Bandwidth and latency
   - **B.** Round Trip Time and latency
   - **C.** Throughput and bandwidth
   - **D.** Isolation and disaster recovery
7. Which of the following statements is false?
   - **A.** Instances in one region can connect to instances in another region.
   - **B.** Availability domains in a region share power and cooling.
   - **C.** Each AD is self-contained and highly fault tolerant.
   - **D.** Failure of one AD is very unlikely to impact the availability of other ADs in the region.

8. Choose four storage types available on OCI.
   A. Block volumes, object storage, archive storage, SSD
   B. Block volumes, file storage, archive storage, SSD
   C. Block volumes, object storage, archive storage, file storage
   D. Block volumes, buckets, file storage, SSD
9. A Load Balancing Router routes traffic to backend servers based on which backend set routing algorithms?
   A. IP Hash, Weighted Round-Robin
   B. IP Hash, Weighted Round-Robin, Least Connections
   C. Weighted Round-Robin, Least Connections
   D. IP Hash, Weighted Round-Robin, Least Connections, Shortest Path
10. What is the unique, Oracle-assigned identifier for Oracle Cloud Infrastructure resources known as?
   A. OCID
   B. Tenant ID
   C. ACID
   D. Cloud account name

Answers

1. **C.** IaaS provides you access to a collection of servers, storage, and network infrastructure onto which you deploy your platform and software. You have complete control of your environment.
2. **D.** KVM switches are not available or relevant in OCI. OCI allows NVMe storage, networks, CPU, and RAM to be provisioned.
3. **B.** Block storage volumes can be added to both virtual and bare-metal machines.
4. **D.** An AD is a fault-tolerant data center.
5. **B.** A region is a collection of availability domains.
6. **A.** Bandwidth and latency are key metrics used to measure network performance.
7. **B.** Availability domains in a region do not share power and cooling.
8. **C.** Block volumes, object storage, archive storage, and file storage are four storage options available on OCI.
9. **B.** IP Hash, Weighted Round-Robin, and Least Connections are valid backend set routing algorithms that a Load Balancing Router can use to route traffic to backend servers.
10. **A.** Each Oracle Cloud Infrastructure resource has a unique, Oracle-assigned identifier called an Oracle Cloud ID (OCID).

CHAPTER 2

OCI Identity and Access Management

In this chapter, you learn how to

- Explain IAM concepts
- Describe resource locations and identifiers
- Create IAM resources
- Federate OCI with various identity providers
- Set up dynamic groups

Management of on-premises IT equipment increases in complexity as the infrastructure scale increases. It is not uncommon to encounter huge server farms in data centers dedicated to single organizations. These servers are connected by countless networking interfaces, devices, and cables to banks of disk and tape storage devices in a seemingly endless, often overwhelming, infrastructure sprawl. Frequently, teams of engineers and administrators supporting systems, networks, storage, the database, and security roam these halls in an effort to meet ever-increasing and demanding service-level agreements (SLAs) with the respective lines of business that depend on the harmonious operation of both human and machine infrastructure resources.

The Identity and Access Management (IAM) service enabled by default in OCI encompasses the three A's of security: authentication, authorization, and access. Through a simple, yet powerful, set of entities comprising groups, users, and dynamic groups of principal instances, IAM constructs allow for secure access and governance of OCI resources, including compute instances, block volumes, and VCNs.

This chapter explains the IAM concepts supporting OCI and provides a detailed overview of the policy language, passwords, and keys, and a discussion on identity federation with various identity providers.

Explain IAM Concepts

IAM in OCI revolves around several novel concepts such as tenancy and compartments, while utilizing relatively familiar constructs such as users, groups, and policies. Figure 2-1 depicts policies as the mediating construct between groups of users interacting with OCI

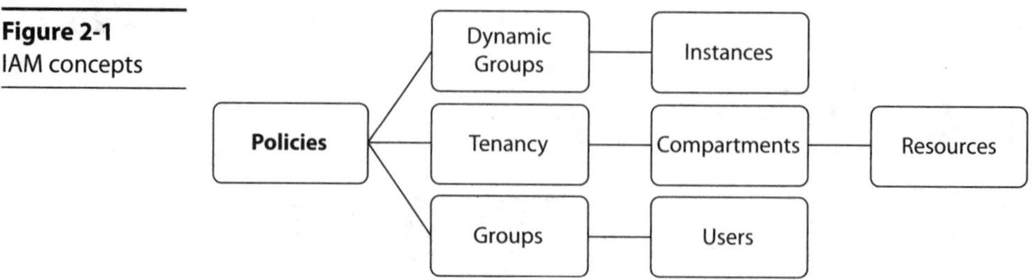

Figure 2-1 IAM concepts

resources that are logically separated into one or more potentially nested levels of compartments residing within your tenancy.

Resources

Typical on-premises IT infrastructure resources include servers, SANs, and network infrastructure. OCI infrastructure resources have a parallel definition and refer to artifacts, including compute instances, block storage volumes, object storage buckets, file system storage, virtual cloud networks (VCNs), load balancers, and Dynamic Routing Gateways. The previous list is not exhaustive and is constantly expanding as new computing resources and technologies are activated on OCI.

Your OCI resources may also fall victim to infrastructure sprawl unless a well-planned, standards-based architecture and nomenclature for resource management is established at an early stage in your OCI adoption. If such a system is already in place with your on-premises resources and is working well, it will provide a great baseline onto which the new concepts can be bolted.

Bear in mind that cloud infrastructure adoption should be transparent to your end-users. At the end of the day, your HR executive probably cares more that the people management applications are available, performant, and meeting SLAs, and less about the underlying infrastructure.

Some organizations have data residency regulations that restrict the geographical location of data. These requirements may be accommodated if there are geographically local OCI regions. For example, the initial OCI regions came online in the United States. Many public sector organizations in Canada have a regulatory restriction on data leaving Canadian soil. Oracle has provisioned a Canadian region with an availability domain in Toronto, which has opened the door for widespread OCI adoption in that region. Another design consideration to bear in mind relates to data sovereignty. Some organizations have regulatory limitations on the location of the staff who work on their data. For example, a large Canadian insurance corporation has a legal obligation to its policy holders guaranteeing that their data is never worked on by non–Canadian-based staff. This poses a challenge to infrastructure management which is met by a simple, guaranteed mechanism to logically segregate OCI resources discussed in the next section.

OCI resources are categorized by resource-types. An individual resource-type is the most granular and includes `vcn`, `subnet`, `instance`, and `volume` resources. Individual resource-types are grouped into family resource-types such as `virtual-network-`

`family`, `instance-family`, and `volume-family`. Resource-types may also be referenced as an aggregation of all resources at both compartment and tenancy levels as `all-resources`. These resource-types are important for defining resource management policies.

Tenancy and Compartments

OCI resources are collectively grouped into compartments. When an OCI account is provisioned, several compartments are automatically created, including the root compartment of the tenancy. An OCI resource can only belong to one compartment. Because compartments are logical structures, resources that make up or reside on the same VCN can belong to different compartments.

Figure 2-2 shows a VCN called msvcn created in the Managed_Services compartment, with a subnet called db_support_subnet created in the DB_Support compartment. Although this subnet resides in the msvcn VCN in the DB_Support compartment, compute instances that use the db_support_subnet do not have to reside in the DB_Support compartment. You could create an instance in any other compartment using the db_support_subnet. It is useful to think of compartments as responsibility areas. You may want the Networks team to create and maintain the network resources such as the VCN, subnets, route tables, and security lists grouped in the Networks compartment. You may want the Systems team to manage the compute instances in the Systems compartment that use a VCN from the Networks compartment. In this regime, each team manages and maintains resources appropriately using compartments to segregate duties and responsibilities.

A tenancy is synonymous with your cloud account and comprises a hierarchy of compartments with the root compartment at the top. There can be many compartments, and as of this writing, compartments may have child compartments nested six levels deep.

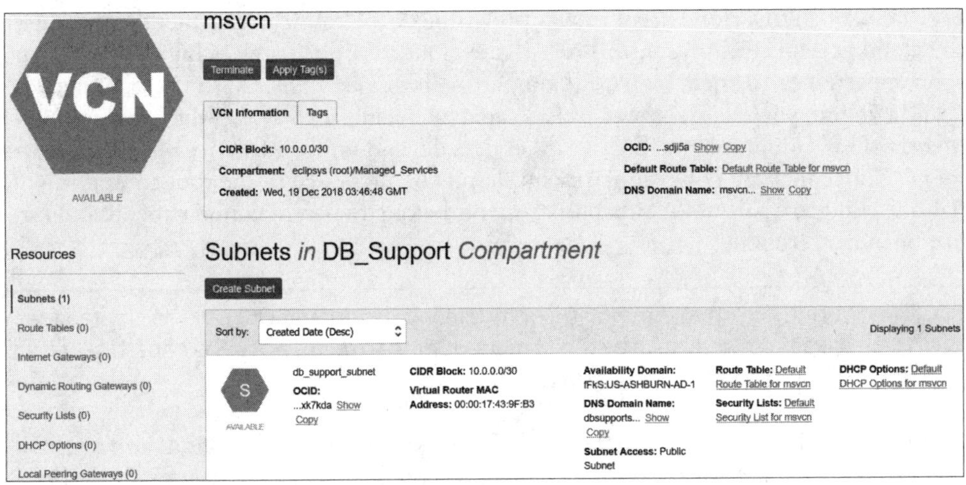

Figure 2-2 Resources in multiple compartments

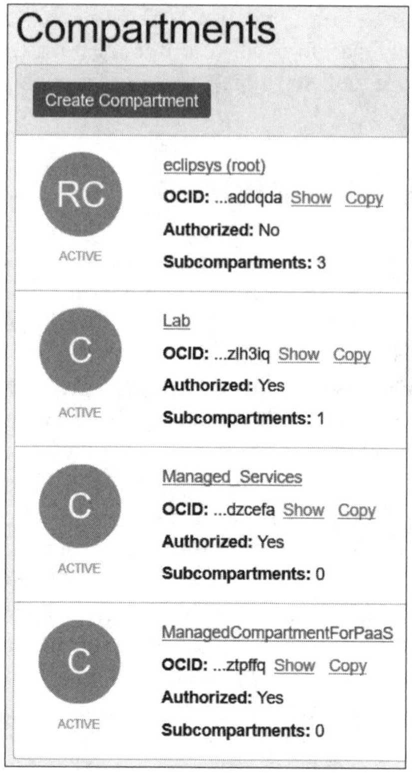

Figure 2-3 Compartment list

Figure 2-3 lists the root compartment (RC) along with three nested or child compartments (subcompartments) named Lab, Managed Services, and ManagedCompartmentForPaaS. When this cloud account was provisioned, the root compartment named after the cloud account (eclipsys in this case is the cloud account name being used) and one subcompartment (named ManagedCompartmentForPaaS) were automatically created. Avoid renaming or deleting the objects created by default such as the ManagedCompartmentForPaaS compartment. OCI PaaS services depend on the existence of this compartment. Notice that the Lab compartment, despite being nested in the root compartment, has one child compartment. Subcompartments belong to parent compartments and cannot be moved around.

CAUTION Avoid removing or modifying the default OCI objects created for PaaS services such as the ManagedCompartmentForPaaS compartment and any seeded policies.

Tenancy and compartments are global resources and span across regions and availability domains. In other words, this mechanism supports resource segregation or grouping regardless of the physical location of the resource.

Business units within organizations are typically clients of the IT department. It may be convenient to group all infrastructure resources consumed by a specific department into their own compartment. A trend in infrastructure support is to track infrastructure usage for cost management. There are many compelling reasons for this trend. This model supports accurate financial budgeting, improves capacity planning, and reduces infrastructure sprawl. Compartments support this model. A typical organization usually has HR and Sales departments. Infrastructure that hosts HR applications is often different from the infrastructure used by Sales applications. It is a simple matter to create HR and Sales compartments and provision their respective infrastructure resources by logical compartment groupings. You then have an accurate understanding of resource consumption. This approach supports the implementation of an internal chargeback mechanism. Compartments also allow resources to be secured and managed as a single entity. Once a compartment is created, it is typical to create a policy to allow appropriate access to the resources in the compartment.

EXAM TIP Compartments, users, groups, and policies are global resources and span regions. When you create these IAM entities, they exist in all regions to which your tenancy or cloud account has subscribed.

Users

An OCI user is an individual or system that requires access to OCI resources. There are three types of users:

- Local users
- Federated users
- Provisioned (or synchronized) users

Local users are created and managed in OCI's IAM service. Local users can only access OCI services. For example, user Jason is created using OCI's IAM service by navigating to Identity | Users and selecting Create User. After providing a name and description and choosing Create, a new local user is created. This user has a local password and, by default, is capable of logging in to the OCI console. When the tenancy is provisioned, the administrator receives a customized URL for your cloud account and a base URL, as in these examples:

```
https://console.us-ashburn-1.oraclecloud.com/?tenant=<your cloud tenancy name>
https://console.us-ashburn-1.oraclecloud.com
```

When you connect to the console using either of these URLs (explicitly specifying the tenancy when using the latter URL), you will be challenged for an OCI username and password. Once these credentials are provided, you sign in to the console with your local user.

Federated users are created and managed in an identity provider outside of OCI's IAM service such as Microsoft Active Directory or Oracle Identity Cloud Service (IDCS).

The identity provider discussed from here on will be IDCS, but the principles discussed next apply to other identity providers as well.

Provisioned users are automatically created in OCI's IAM service based on federated users in an identity provider. A provisioned user does not exist without a corresponding federated user. If your tenancy has been federated to another identity provider and you attempt to access the OCI console using the preceding URLs, you will be prompted to either use a single sign-on (SSO) credential or to specify your local username and password. Provisioned users allow federated users to sign in to the OCI console using a password managed by their identity provider—for example, IDCS.

Users have one or more user credentials.

User Credentials

Users connect to OCI using several types of credentials. Your username and password are authenticated when you sign in to the OCI console. When you access a Linux compute instance, you need an SSH key (see Chapter 4) to make a connection to the operating system. Figure 2-4 shows a federated user named neo with a list of user resources on the bottom left, including API keys, Auth tokens, SMTP credentials, customer secret keys, and the number of groups to which the user belongs. Usernames may also be simple names or based on email addresses.

An Oracle-generated Auth token is required when authenticating users with third-party APIs that do not support OCI signature-based authentication. Customer secret keys may be used to connect to your object storage bucket with Amazon S3–compatible APIs. This allows you to utilize existing scripts that already work with S3 buckets to interface with your OCI object storage buckets. SMTP credentials are used with the Email delivery service.

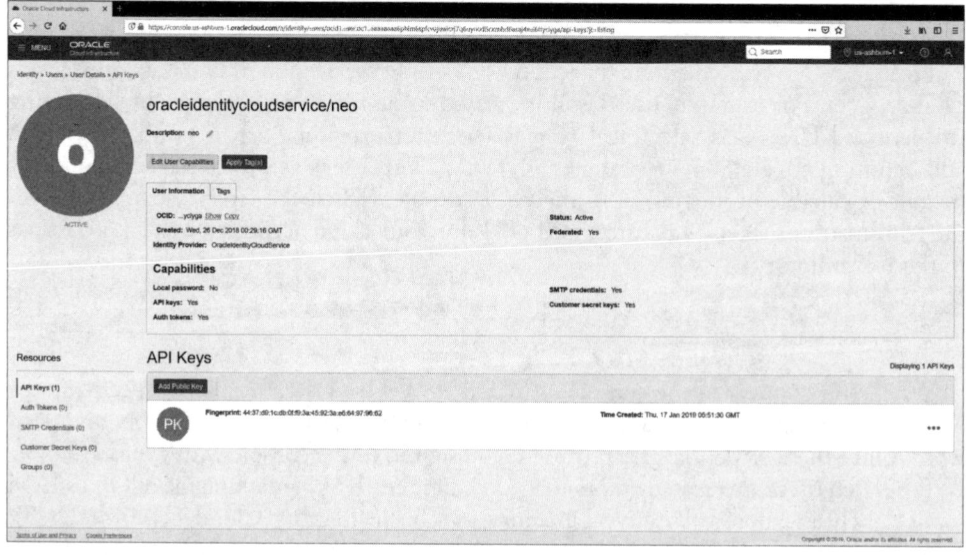

Figure 2-4 OCI user management

Your API signing keys are used for authenticating your user when accessing protected OCI service APIs. You generate a private and public key pair in PEM format and associate the public key with your user. You can then use the private key to access OCI service APIs programmatically through the command-line interface or one of the SDKs (discussed later in this chapter).

User management tasks such as creating or resetting passwords, and restricting or enabling user capabilities, may also be performed by administrators through this console interface.

Groups

OCI users are organized into groups. A user may belong to many groups. When your OCI account is created, a default Administrators group is created. The Administrators group initially has a single member—the user that was created when the tenancy was provisioned. As an administrator, you may create additional administrator users and add them to this group or create other groups for duty separation. The administrator users have complete control over all resources in the tenancy so access to this group should be tightly regulated. It is good practice to set up groups for teams of users who perform similar work.

For example, you may have a team of network administrators in your organization that is placed in a NetworkAdmins group. For applications or systems that have data sovereignty requirements, you could create a group of users who reside in a specific locale—for example, Canadian Network Admins. This group could be given permission to manage the network resources in the Canadian HR compartment to meet the data sovereignty requirement. Groups cannot be nested. Figure 2-5 shows the default Administrators group along with two custom groups: Managed_Services and NetworkAdmins.

Your nomenclature and group management strategy may already be in place with on-premises resource management, and OCI user and group management may be a natural extension of this system. If a well-defined strategy is not in place, this is an important design decision. The current segregation of your infrastructure and, more importantly,

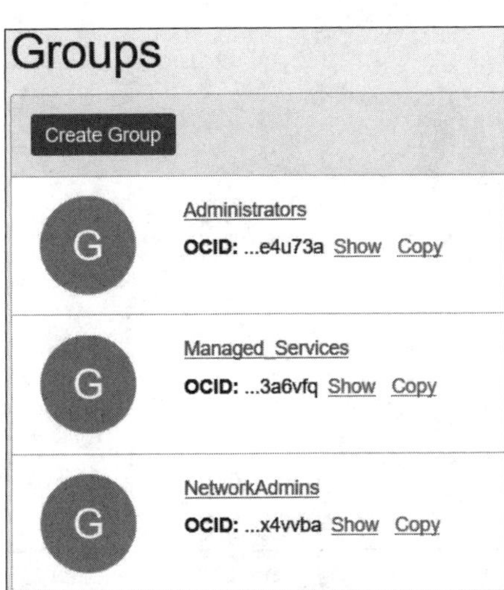

Figure 2-5 OCI groups

the current partitioning of your human resources into technical teams are often good models on which to base OCI groups. These teams may support specific applications or technologies or different infrastructure layers such as OS, storage, network, Oracle or other databases, or Oracle or other middleware. They may also support specific departments or business units. Aligning OCI group design with your existing human team divisions often simplifies the IAM nomenclature and group management strategy. As the volume of users and infrastructure grows, management of OCI resources inevitably grows in complexity. Groups are that piece of the IAM solution essential for practical, auditable user and infrastructure governance.

Policies

Policies are the glue that determines how groups of users interact with OCI resources that are grouped into compartments. You may want the HR application administrators to manage all resources in a compartment dedicated to the HR department:

```
Allow group HRAdmins to manage all-resources in compartment HR
```

This policy statement expressed in simple language is all that is required to authorize the users that belong to the HRAdmins group to manage all resources in the HR compartment. The manage verb is the most powerful and includes all permissions for the resource. The policy statements are submitted as free-form text. As of this writing, there is no tool provided to assist with constructing these policy statements.

Figure 2-6 zooms into the NetPol1 policy that is created on the VCN resources in the Lab compartment. This policy comprises a single statement but at the time of this writing can contain up to 50 statements. These limits may be modified by requesting a service limit change.

CAUTION A single policy by default can accommodate up to 50 statements. There are similar default limits on other IAM resources, like 100 policies, 100 users, 50 groups, and 50 compartments permitted per tenancy.

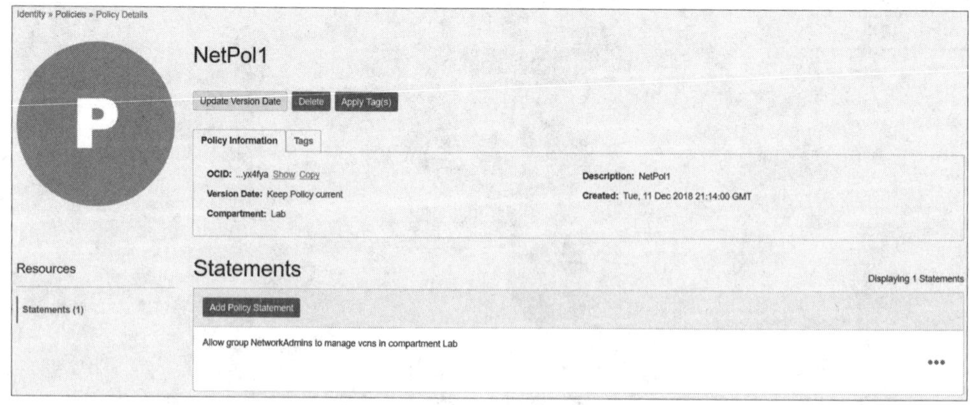

Figure 2-6 Policy to manage VCNs in the Lab compartment

The policy statement follows this syntax:

```
Allow <subject> to <verb> <resource-type> in <location> where <condition>
```

The policy statement in Figure 2-6 references the `NetworkAdmins` group as the subject, `manage` as the verb, `vcns` as the resource-type, and the `Lab` compartment as the location. There are no where conditions specified but the ability to specify conditions in policy statements supports more sophisticated policy features. For example, you could create a policy on the root compartment with this statement:

```
Allow group NetworkAdmins to manage vcns in tenancy
where target.compartment.name != 'Lab'
```

This statement grants all permissions required to manage all VCNs in all compartments in the tenancy except the Lab compartment to the users that belong to the NetworkAdmins group.

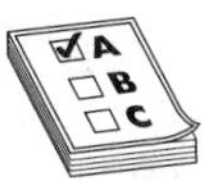

EXAM TIP Policies are inherited by their child compartments. If a policy is created in the root compartment, it applies to all compartments. A policy created in a child compartment with no subcompartments applies only to the relevant resources within that child compartment.

Subjects in the policy syntax specify one or more comma-separated groups by name or OCID. Chapter 1 introduced the unique identifier that each OCI resource is assigned, called an Oracle Cloud ID (OCID). In addition to the group name and group OCID, other valid subjects are dynamic groups (discussed later in this chapter), and a reserved collective noun called `any-user`, which refers to all users in your tenancy. Figure 2-7 shows the policy syntax expansion for the subject component. The Allow keyword grants permission to one or more subjects to interact with OCI resources. These subjects are currently limited to either all users in the tenancy, one or more groups of users or instances (dynamic groups), or any combination of these subjects.

The candidates for subjects, verbs, resource-types, and locations are an evolving list, but the essential terms are articulated in various policy syntax diagrams in this chapter. Figure 2-8 expands the policy verbs: inspect, read, use, and manage, which has been used in examples provided so far. These verbs have a generic meaning that determines your level of access to a resource. The exact meaning of each verb depends on the resource-type it acts upon.

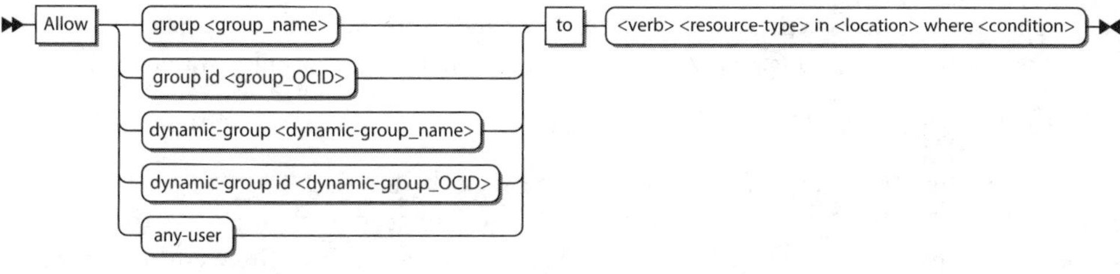

Figure 2-7 Policy syntax expansion for the subject component

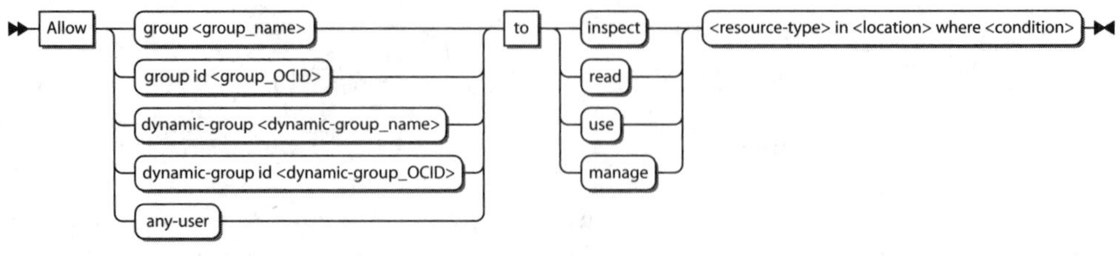

Figure 2-8 Policy syntax expansion for the verb component

EXAM TIP The verbs to authorize groups to interact with resources in order of lowest to highest levels of permission are inspect, read, use, and manage.

The inspect verb offers the least access to a resource. It provides the ability to list and get resources. This level of authorization is typically reserved for external or third-party limited access to the resource. All resources have a set of APIs (application programmer interfaces) that provide a programmatic interface for dealing with the resource. One or more related APIs are collectively grouped into permissions, which represent an atomic unit of authorization that determines the interactions between users and specific resources.

EXAM TIP Focus on understanding the policy syntax. APIs and permissions covered by policy verbs have a practical utility but are not measured in the exam.

For example, the object storage buckets resource has two APIs, `HeadBucket` and `ListBucket`, covered by the permission `BUCKET_INSPECT`. The `HeadBucket` API checks if a bucket exists, while the `ListBucket` API lists all the buckets in a compartment. When the Financial_Auditors group is allowed to inspect the object storage resources in the Finance compartment, the `BUCKET_INSPECT` permission in granted internally, which permits users in the group to interface with the resource using the associated APIs. The corresponding policy statement may be

```
Allow group Financial_Auditors to inspect buckets in compartment Finance
```

The read verb includes the permissions of the inspect verb and additionally provides access to user-specified metadata about the resource and access to the actual resource. This level of authorization is typically reserved for internal oversight and monitoring. Let's stay with the example of the buckets resource; consider the following policy statement:

```
Allow group Financial_Analysts to read buckets in compartment Finance
```

Users in the Financial_Analysts group receive both the `BUCKET_INSPECT` permission and the `BUCKET_READ` permission because the read verb includes the permissions of the inspect verb. The `BUCKET_READ` permission exposes three additional APIs: `GetBucket`, `ListMultipartUploads`, and `GetObjectLifecyclePolicy`.

Users in the Financial_Analysts group can access these five bucket-related APIs: `HeadBucket`, `ListBuckets`, `GetBucket`, `ListMultipartUploads`, and `GetObjectLifecyclePolicy`.

The use verb cumulates the permissions from the read verb with the ability to actually work with the resource. Let's continue with the example of the buckets resource; consider the following policy statement:

```
Allow group Financial_Controllers to use buckets in compartment Finance
```

Users in the Financial_Controllers group will be granted the permissions that the inspect and read verbs granted, which were `BUCKET_INSPECT` and `BUCKET_READ`, as well as the `BUCKET_UPDATE` permission, which fully covers two additional APIs—`UpdateBucket` and `DeleteObjectLifecyclePolicy`—and partially covers `PutObjectLifecyclePolicy`, which additionally requires other permissions such as `OBJECT_CREATE` and `OBJECT_DELETE`. Partially covered APIs are excluded from this discussion. Users in the Financial_Controllers group can access these seven bucket-related APIs: `HeadBucket`, `ListBuckets`, `GetBucket`, `ListMultipartUploads`, `GetObjectLifecyclePolicy`, `UpdateBucket`, and `DeleteObjectLifecyclePolicy`.

Generally, the use verb permits you to use and update a resource but not to create or delete that type of resource. This level of authorization is typically reserved for end-users of the resource. Bear in mind that these are general guidelines for these verbs and actual permissions vary depending on the resource-types involved. For some resource-types, the update operation is equivalent to the create operation, which is covered by the manage verb, so for these resources, the use verb precludes the update permission. Table 2-1 lists the verbs, permissions and APIs associated with the policies resource-type. Note that the inspect, read, and use levels of permission for this resource-type are identical.

NOTE The permissions granted by various policy verbs are entirely dependent on the OCI resource-type. Generally, the inspect verb lets you list available resources, the read verb lets you uncover user-specified metadata about that resource, the use verb lets you use and change the actual resource as long as that change is not effectively dropping and recreating it. Finally, the manage verb lets you create and delete the resource-type. Some resource-types have limited APIs so, for example, the inspect, use, and read levels of authorization for policies provide identical permissions. The important take-away is that each resource-type must be understood carefully while assigning permissions because each level exposes unique resource-specific APIs and you need to have a clear understanding of exactly what permissions are being granted.

Verb	Permissions	APIs
inspect, read, use, manage	POLICY_READ	ListPolicies, GetPolicy
manage	POLICY_CREATE	CreatePolicy
manage	POLICY_DELETE	DeletePolicy

Table 2-1 Permissions, APIs, and Verbs for the Policies Resource-Type

Verb	Permissions	APIs
inspect, read, use, manage	BUCKET_INSPECT	ListBuckets, HeadBucket
read, use, manage	BUCKET_READ	GetBucket, ListMultipartUploads, GetObjectLifecyclePolicy
use, manage	BUCKET_UPDATE	UpdateBucket, DeleteObjectLifecyclePolicy
manage	BUCKET_CREATE	CreateBucket
manage	BUCKET_DELETE	DeleteBucket
manage	PAR_MANAGE	GetPar, ListPars, DeletePar

Table 2-2 Permissions, APIs, and Verbs for the Bucket Resource-Type

The manage verb includes all permissions for the resource. It effectively combines the read permissions with the abilities to create and destroy the resource-type. It is the highest level of permission that can be granted on a resource-type and is generally reserved for administrator groups. To complete the example of the buckets resource, consider the following policy statement:

```
Allow group Financial_Admins to manage buckets in compartment Finance
```

Users in the Financial_Admins group will be granted all permissions on this resource, including `BUCKET_INSPECT`, `BUCKET_READ`, and `BUCKET_UPDATE` granted through the use verb, as well as the `BUCKET_CREATE`, `BUCKET_DELETE`, and `PAR_MANAGE` permissions, which cover six additional APIs: `CreateBucket`, `DeleteBucket`, `CreatePar`, `GetPar`, `ListPars`, and `DeletePar`. The latter four APIs relate to pre-authenticated requests discussed in Chapter 5. Users in the Financial_Admins group can access the bucket-related APIs shown in Table 2-2.

The exploration of the verbs in the policy syntax introduced several new concepts, such as APIs and permissions. These are key building blocks for advanced policy design, which is discussed later in this chapter.

When you create a policy, you are prompted for the policy versioning scheme you would like to use. The options are to Keep Policy Current, which adapts the policy dynamically to stay current with any future changes to the IAM services definition of verbs and resources, or to Use Version Date, which is to limit access to resources based on the definitions that were current on a specific date. It is likely to be a safer bet to use the version date approach on production policies.

Dynamic Groups

A powerful feature closely related to the notion of self-driving, self-tuning, automated systems involves granting groups of compute instances permission to access OCI service APIs. If you require aggregations of compute instances to interface with OCI resources, you create a dynamic group and add compute instances as members. Instances in dynamic groups act as IAM users to provision compute, networking, and storage resources based on IAM policies.

EXAM TIP Dynamic groups authorize member instances to interact with OCI resources at a tenancy level by using IAM policies.

The next section describes resource locations and resource identifiers as well as how they pertain to policy formation.

Describe Resource Locations and Identifiers

Resources are the building blocks of your infrastructure. In data centers all over the world, there are thousands of racks of servers, storage, and networking equipment tethered together with miles of cabling. The OCI software layer abstracts this massive collection of hardware into infrastructure resources in many digestible shapes and sizes. Through interfaces like the OCI console, you can carve out an infrastructure architecture with just the resources you need and with just a few commands. The OCI console, however, is not the only interface you can use to work with OCI.

All resources in OCI have been exposed through REST APIs introduced earlier. Developers can also use several Software Development Kits (SDKs), which are all open source and available on GitHub. These include documentation, online sample code, and many useful tools for interfacing with OCI resources. As of this writing, there are OCI-related SDKs available for Java, Ruby, Python, and Go. Apache Hadoop applications can also use object storage resources through an HDFS connector. The Data Transfer Utility is a command-line tool for facilitating large data transfers and is detailed in Chapter 6. A noteworthy tool is the OCI command-line interface (CLI), which provides the same functionality as the web console and is available on the command line. As we proceed to explore several commonly used resources and their locations, it is instructive to do so using a combination of both the web console and the OCI CLI. The OCI CLI is discussed in detail in Chapter 7. It is not a requirement for you to have the CLI operational at this stage, but if you want to follow along with the examples, feel free to jump ahead to Chapter 7, set up the CLI on your machine, and then proceed with this chapter.

EXAM TIP While the OCI command-line interface tool is not an explicit topic in the exam, several questions do refer to this tool. It is important to understand the fundamental operation of the OCI CLI. Knowledge of the SDKs and HDFS is not measured in the exam.

Resource Locations

When a cloud tenancy is created, a default data region is chosen. As of this writing, you can choose APAC, EMEA, or North America as your default data region. You should choose the region based closest to your primary cloud users or primary on-premises data center locations. The tenancy is then created in one of the regions. When you log in to OCI, the top-right corner indicates your primary or home region. Choose Manage Regions from the region drop-down list and you see more details about your tenancy. Figure 2-9 shows a tenancy created with a North American default data region and allocated us-ashburn-1 as its Home Region. A home region is important for IAM resources.

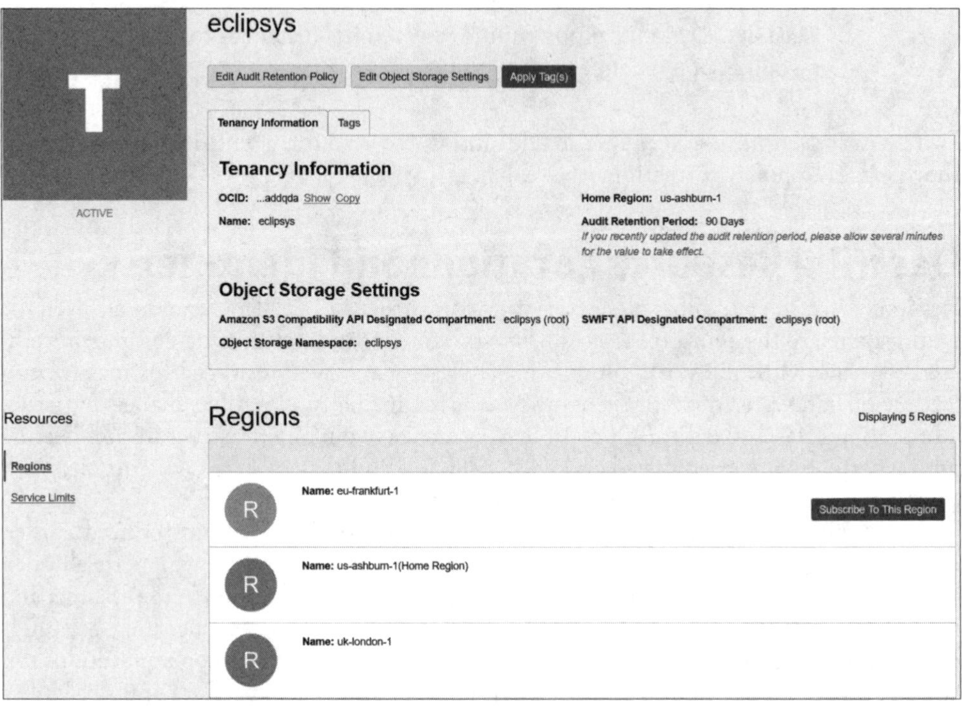

Figure 2-9 Tenancy and regions

Global Resources

IAM resources such as users, groups, compartments, and policies are considered global resources. A list of global resources is provided in Table 2-3. These resources exist in all regions and availability domains. However, they are initially created in the home region of the tenancy. Here, the master copy of their definition resides. When changes are made to IAM resources, they must be made in the home region and then these changes are automatically replicated to other regions. Changes to IAM resources in the home region typically take a few seconds, while it may take a few minutes for these changes to propagate to all regions. All API changes to IAM resources must use the endpoint for the home region.

Compartments	**Groups**	**Users**
Policies	dynamic groups	federation resources
API signing keys	encryption keys	key vaults
Tag namespaces	tag keys	

Table 2-3 Global IAM Resources

EXAM TIP IAM changes do not occur immediately across all regions. A user impacted by a policy change in the home region will experience a propagation delay before the changes are effected in all regions.

Many organizations have users spread across the globe. You may require OCI resources in other geographical locations, and this is supported by subscribing to one or more non-home regions. Figure 2-9 lists non-home regions with a Subscribe To This Region button. IAM resources are available in the new region but their master definitions always reside in the home region.

Exercise 2-1: Subscribe to Another Region

In this exercise, you will log in to your OCI tenancy, examine your tenancy home region, and subscribe to a new region. The OCI CLI is used in this and many other exercises throughout the book.

1. Navigate to http://cloud.oracle.com and choose Sign In. Select your account type (IDCS or Traditional), specify your cloud account name, authenticate your user, and you should be in the My Services dashboard.
2. Navigate to your compartment list and take note of the compartments. If you have a new cloud account, you should at least have the root and ManagedCompartmentForPaaS compartments.

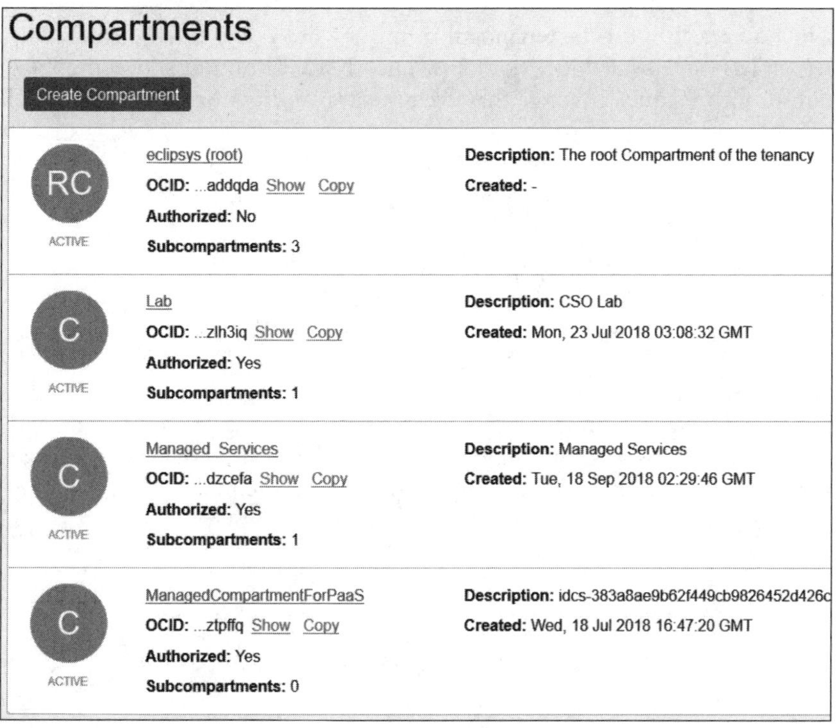

3. An OCI CLI listing of the ManagedCompartmentForPaaS compartment returns this JSON output. Take note that no metadata exists for the compartment that ties it back to a region. For the compartment-id key, a tenancy OCID is listed because compartments are global resources. Note also the OCID (id key value) for the compartment.

```
[root@sid ~]# oci iam compartment list -c $T
{"data": [{
      "compartment-id": "ocid1.tenancy.oc1...addqda",
      "description": "idcs-383...",
      "id": "ocid1.compartment.oc1...ztpffq",
      "lifecycle-state": "ACTIVE",
      "name": "ManagedCompartmentForPaaS",
      "time-created": "2018-07-18T16:47:20.361000+00:00"}],}
```

4. Access the OCI console, choose Administration | Tenancy details, and you should see your tenancy details similar to Figure 2-9. The list of available regions may also be retrieved with an OCI CLI command:

```
+-----+----------------+
| key | name           |
+-----+----------------+
| BOM | ap-mumbai-1    |
| FRA | eu-frankfurt-1 |
| IAD | us-ashburn-1   |
| ICN | ap-seoul-1     |
| LHR | uk-london-1    |
| NRT | ap-tokyo-1     |
| PHX | us-phoenix-1   |
| YYZ | ca-toronto-1   |
+-----+----------------+
```

5. The home region for the tenancy shown in Figure 2-9 is us-ashburn-1. This region has three availability domains. The OCI CLI output shows the JSON output for this query. Notice that even the availability domain has an OCID.

```
# oci iam availability-domain list{"data": [
{"compartment-id": "ocid1.tenancy.oc1...addqda",
 "id": "ocid1.availabilitydomain.oc1...wyohta",
 "name": "fFkS:US-ASHBURN-AD-1"},
{"compartment-id": "ocid1.tenancy.oc1...addqda",
  "id": "ocid1.availabilitydomain.oc1...jl2n3a",
  "name": "fFkS:US-ASHBURN-AD-2"},
{"compartment-id": "ocid1.tenancy.oc1...addqda",
  "id": "ocid1.availabilitydomain.oc1..mxsfdq",
  "name": "fFkS:US-ASHBURN-AD-3"}]}
```

6. In this exercise, you are going to subscribe to a region different from your home region. Choose a secondary region that is sensible for your architecture and click Subscribe To This Region. OCI prompts you if you are sure and once you say OK, your IAM global resources are propagated to the new region. After a few minutes, your new region should be available for use by your tenancy.

7. There is no additional financial implication but be aware that users are allowed to use the new region because they are allowed to use the home region resources unless you explicitly set preventative policies. In the top-right area of the OCI console, the region list of values should now reflect your new region. You may have to refresh your browser to see the updated list. Choose the new region. Navigate to the compartment, group, and policy lists in the new region, and note that they are identical to the views from the home region.

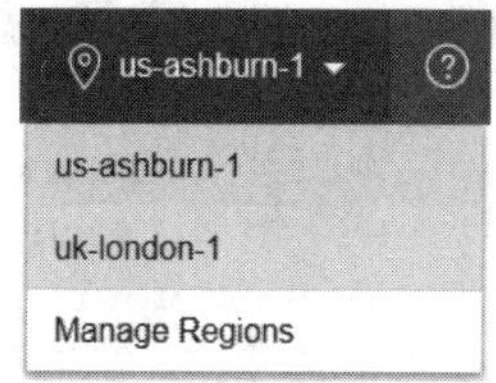

EXAM TIP The region subscriptions occur at the tenancy level. All IAM resources including policies are available in all regions to which your tenancy has subscribed.

Regional and Availability Domain–Level Resources

Non-IAM resources exist at a region level or at an availability domain level. Remember that a region consists of one or more ADs. An AD is a fault-tolerant data center. If you think about it, when you launch a compute instance, there is either a bare metal or virtual machine running in a data center. The compute instance is therefore an availability domain–specific resource. It exists in a single physical location. A virtual cloud network, however, spans all the ADs in a region and is therefore a regional resource. The following are some examples of region-specific resources:

- buckets
- images
- Internet Gateways (IG)
- Customer Premises Equipment (CPE)
- Dynamic Routing Gateways (DRGs)

- NAT Gateways
- route tables
- Local Peering Gateways (LPGs)
- repositories
- security lists
- volume backups

The ADs in a region are connected by a low-latency high-bandwidth network. It is not surprising that many of the regional resources are network resources. These networking resources are explored in Chapter 3.

NOTE OCI randomizes ADs by tenancy to ensure balanced utilization of available infrastructure. US-ASHBURN-AD-1 for tenancyA may be a different physical data center than the one labeled US-ASHBURN-AD-1 for tenancyB.

Exercise 2-2: Create a Compartment and a VCN

In this exercise, you will log in to your OCI tenancy and create a new compartment in your home region. The compartment in the exercise is called Lab, but you should provide a name that is meaningful in your environment.

1. Navigate to your compartment list (Identity | Compartments), and choose Create Compartment. Provide a name and a description, check that the parent for your new compartment is the root compartment, and choose Create Compartment. Tagging will be discussed in a subsequent section.

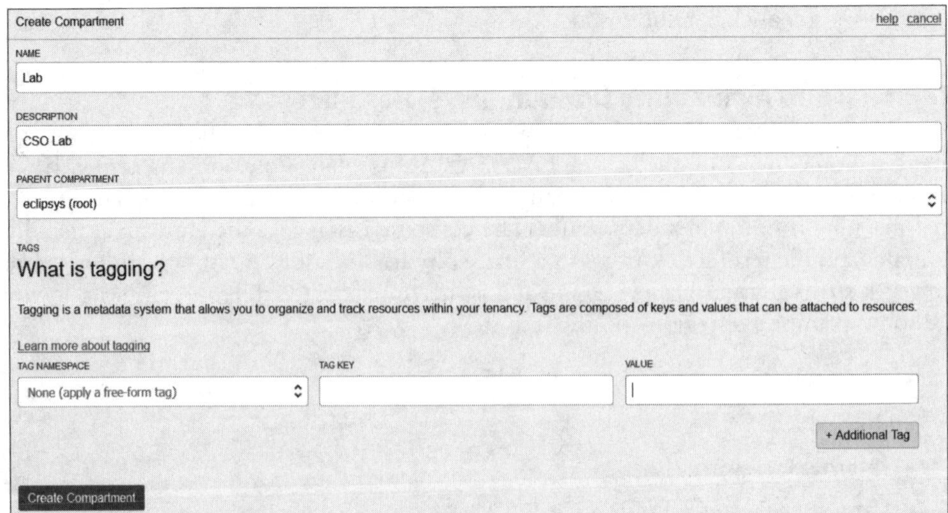

2. After a few seconds, your compartment should be ready. The replication of this IAM resource will begin, and, after a few minutes, this compartment will be visible in your non-home regions as well.

```
[root@sid ~]# oci iam compartment list -c $T
{...   "compartment-id": "ocid1.tenancy.oc1...addqda",
       "description": "CSO Lab",
       "id": "ocid1.compartment.oc1...zlh3iq",
       "lifecycle-state": "ACTIVE",
       "name": "Lab",
       "time-created": "2018-07-23T03:08:32.995000+00:00"}
```

3. Navigate to the VCN list (Networking | Virtual Cloud Networks). Ensure your new compartment is chosen under List Scope on the left, and choose Create Virtual Cloud Network.
4. Provide a name for the VCN. Choose the radio button: Create Virtual Cloud Network Plus Related Resources. The VCN details are explored in Chapter 3. For now, choose Create Virtual Cloud Network.

Create Virtual Cloud Network

Create Virtual Cloud Network

The Virtual Cloud Network was created: Lab

Create Internet Gateway

The Internet Gateway "Internet Gateway Lab" was created

Update Default Route Table

The Route Table was updated: Default Route Table for Lab

Create Subnet

Public Subnet fFkS:US-ASHBURN-AD-1 was created

Create Subnet

Public Subnet fFkS:US-ASHBURN-AD-2 was created

Create Subnet

Public Subnet fFkS:US-ASHBURN-AD-3 was created

Close

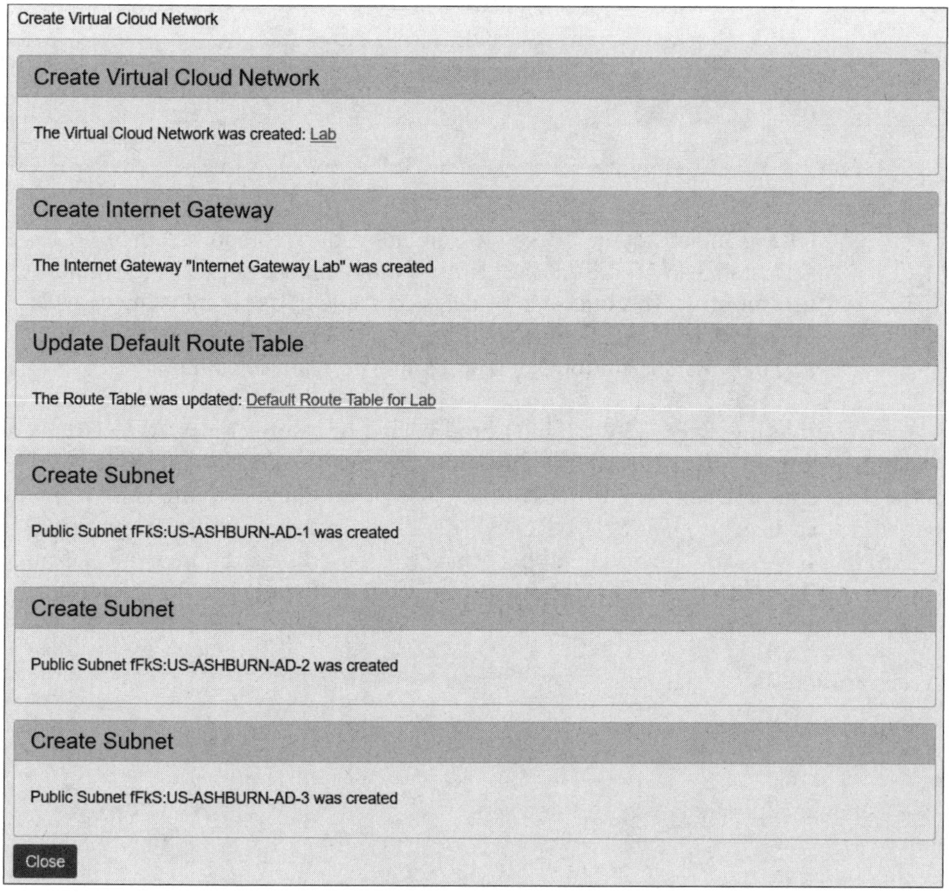

5. You have created a VCN. In addition, an Internet gateway, route table, and security list have been created in the Lab compartment. These network elements are regional resources. They are available for all ADs in the region to use.
6. Connect to a non-home region and navigate to the Lab compartment. There is no VCN in the Lab compartment in the uk-london-1 region because the VCN is a regional and not a global resource.
7. You can optionally clean up by connecting back to your home region, dropping the VCN in Lab compartment, and deleting the compartment. Bear in mind that after deleting the compartment, it remains visible as a deleted compartment for 60 days. It may be useful to retain a Lab or Sandbox compartment for testing purposes.

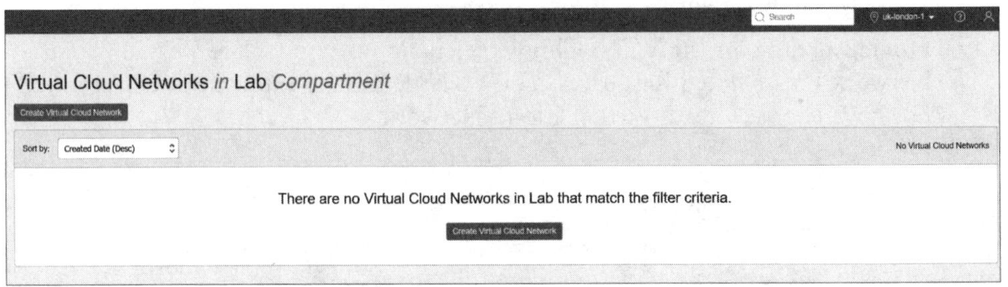

NOTE Object storage buckets are an interesting regional resource. An instance in AD: US-ASHBURN-AD-1 may access a bucket in the region: us-ashburn-1. This bucket is equally accessible by another instance in AD: US-ASHBURN-AD-2. Given the correct region-specific object storage URL and permissions, this bucket is accessible from any location.

After completing Exercise 2-2, you should have one subnet per AD. This is an availability domain–specific resource. Instances created in AD: US-ASHBURN-AD-1 in the Lab compartment (in this example) will be assigned IP addresses from the subnet created in AD: US-ASHBURN-AD-1. These instances will exist only in AD: US-ASHBURN-AD-1. Regional subnets may also be created. Subnets are resources that may be created at an AD or regional level. The following are some examples of AD-specific resources:

- volumes
- database systems
- instances
- ephemeral public IPs

Volumes are storage resources allocated to specific compute instances within the same availability domain.

Resource Identifiers

Tenancies, Regions, ADs, Compartments, Groups, Users, Policies, and every other OCI resource is assigned a unique identifier known as an Oracle Cloud Identifier or OCID (sometimes pronounced "o-sid"). OCIDs are required to use the API for OCI. OCIDs are unique across all tenancies.

The OCID is based on this format:

```
ocid1.<RESOURCE TYPE>.<REALM>.[REGION][.FUTURE USE].<UNIQUE ID>
```

The following are some examples:

```
ocid1.tenancy.oc1..aaaaaaaaaddqda
ocid1.availabilitydomain.oc1..aaaaaaaawyohta
ocid1.compartment.oc1..aaaaaaaazlh3iq
ocid1.vcn.oc1.iad.aaaaaaaahr6y4a
ocid1.routetable.oc1.iad.aaaaaaaapuwaa
ocid1.subnet.oc1.iad.aaaaaaaaqnyy2q
```

The resource-type component is a character string describing the resource. The realm is always oc1 for now and is meant to represent the set of regions that share OCI entities.

The region segment is blank for global resources such as tenancy and compartments but contains the region code for regional and AD-specific resources. As per Table 2-4, IAD represents the us-ashburn-1 region. Table 2-4 lists several provisioned OCI regions.

Key	Region Name	Location	Availability Domains
PHX	us-phoenix-1	Phoenix, Arizona, United States	3
IAD	us-ashburn-1	Ashburn, Virginia, United States	3
LHR	uk-london-1	London, United Kingdom	3
FRA	eu-frankfurt-1	Frankfurt, Germany	3
YYZ	ca-toronto-1	Toronto, Canada	1
NRT	ap-tokyo-1	Tokyo, Japan	1
ICN	ap-seoul-1	Seoul, South Korea	1
BOM	ap-mumbai-1	Mumbai, India	1

Table 2-4 OCI Regions

The future use segment is blank for now, while the unique alphanumeric string completes the OCID. As you have navigated the OCI console, you have inevitably noticed the OCID field alongside virtually every artifact. The OCID is partially displayed and is adjacent to hyperlinks that either Show or Copy the OCID.

Your tenancy OCID may be obtained by logging in to the console and either navigating to Administration | Tenancy Details or choosing Manage regions from the menu next to your home region and selecting the Show link.

Your tenancy OCID is required to access the OCI APIs through the CLI or the SDKs. For example, the following CLI command to delete a VCN takes its OCID as a parameter to the API to delete VCNs.

```
[root@sid ~]# oci network vcn delete --vcn-id ocid1.vcn.oc1.iad.aaaaaaaahr6y4a
Are you sure you want to delete this resource? [y/N]: N
```

Policy statements also use the OCID for IAM resources. Figure 2-10 shows an updated version of the NetPol1 policy created earlier. Here, the Show link has been clicked, exposing the OCID for the policy. Note that it has been replaced by a Hide link adjacent to the Copy link. A second policy statement has been added using OCIDs but these statements are equivalent because the NetworkAdmins group OCID and Lab compartment OCID are referenced in the second statement.

The OCI console search feature also uses OCIDs. For example, you can paste in the OCID of a compartment to see a list of all resources that belong to that compartment. Once you have used the search feature, you can select Advanced Search in the simple search results page. The advanced search option has a query language that also uses OCIDs. For example, this search query returns a list of subnets that belong to a specific compartment.

```
query subnet resources where compartmentId = 'ocid1.compartment.oc1..aazlh3iq'
```

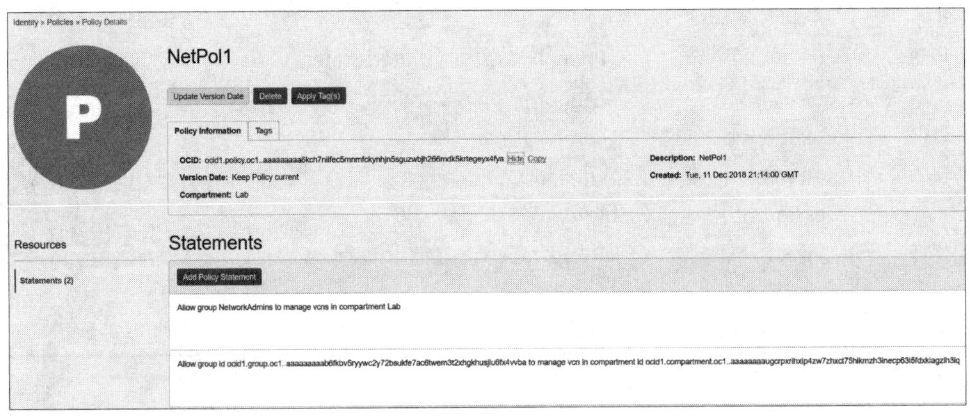

Figure 2-10 Policy statement using OCIDs

Managing Tags and Tag Namespaces

Tagging is a service available to all OCI tenants by default. Tagging in not an IAM concept but is being discussed here to encourage the best practice of tagging your resources in a planful manner. As your OCI estate expands, resource sprawl is inevitable and tagging from the beginning is a great way to remain organized and in control of your OCI resources.

A tag is simply a key-value pair that you associate with a resource. There are two types of tagging: free-form and defined tags.

Free-Form Tags

Free-form tags are limited and offer a pretty basic form of tagging. You can apply as many tags as you want to a resource, but there is a 5-kilobyte JSON limitation on all applied tags and their values per resource.

Figure 2-11 shows a free-form tag with a key called BusinessUnit (no spaces are permitted) and a value of Finance being added to a resource. This particular free-form tag was added to a parent compartment, its child compartment, and an object storage bucket used by the Finance business unit.

Free-form tags can be created, updated, or deleted by users with *use* permission on the resource. These tags are descriptive metadata about a resource, but they are not subject to any constraints. So typos could easily enter the metadata and affect the reliability of this tagging system. When adding a free-form tag, you cannot see a list of existing free-form tags. Most importantly, you cannot use free-form tags in IAM policies to control access to tag metadata of resources.

Free-form tagging is best used for demo, proof-of-concept, or tenancies with few resources. Searching for finance using the Search dialog in the console returns the three free-form tagged resources, as shown in Figure 2-12.

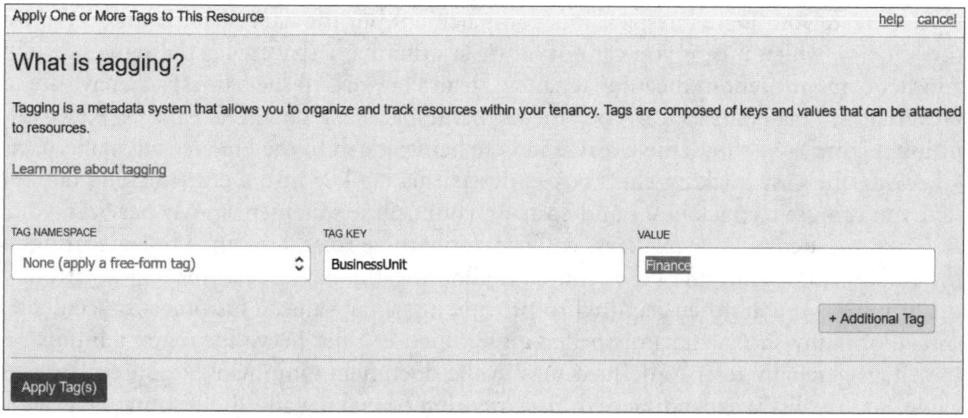

Figure 2-11 Creating a free-form tag

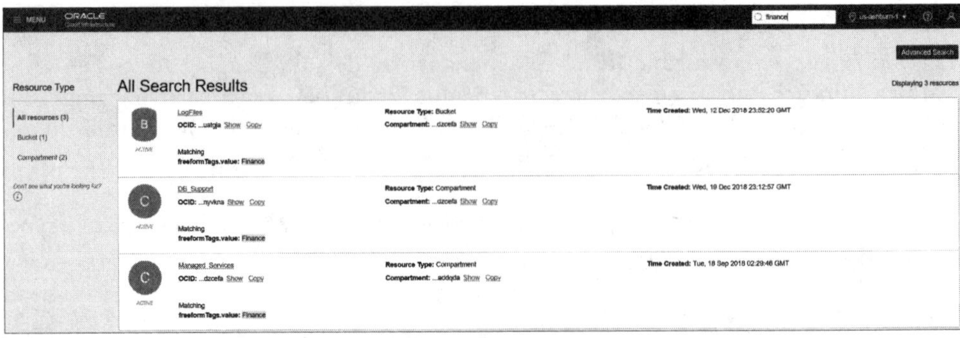

Figure 2-12 Search results of resources with free-form tags

Defined Tags

Defined or schema tagging is the recommended enterprise-grade mechanism for organizing, reporting, filtering, managing, and performing bulk actions on your OCI resources.

Defined tags rely on a tenant-wide unique namespace that consists of tag keys and tag values. The tag namespace serves as a container for use with IAM policies.

Consider your existing on-premises infrastructure tracking system. Chances are high that you have a system that factors in departments or lines of business or cost-centers for your infrastructure. You may also want to organize resources by project or team. There is a facility for enabling tags as cost-tracking tags that appear on your invoice, which is very useful for implementing a chargeback system. As of this writing there is a limit of ten tags that may be identified as cost-tracking tags, so factor this into your tag naming strategy.

To set up a defined tag schema, you must first create a tag namespace. In the console, navigate to Governance | Tag Namespaces, and choose Create Namespace Definition, as in Figure 2-13 where the Finance namespace is created in the Lab compartment.

You create your tag namespace in a compartment but the namespace is unique across the tenancy, which means you cannot create another namespace with the same name in another compartment in the same tenancy. To add tag keys to the namespace, navigate to Governance | Tag Namespaces, click the tag namespace, and choose Create Tag Key Definition. Figure 2-14 shows the CostCenter tag being added to the Finance tag namespace. Checking the cost-tracking checkbox converts this tag key into a cost-tracking tag key that you can use to track usage and costs on your online statement in My Services.

Once you define your tag keys, you can apply these to any resource by navigating to the resource, choosing the tag menu, and choosing the namespace and tag key from a list of values. You are then required to provide just a tag value. This prevents accidental sprawl of many similar but misspelled tags, which is a pet peeve for many administrators. Tags generally refer to defined tags in the documentation. Most resources are taggable, and the list is expanding with the intention of making all OCI resources taggable. You can apply tags with the console, CLI, or SDKs, but usually it is good practice to do so when creating resources. Applying tags does require authorization, and an IAM

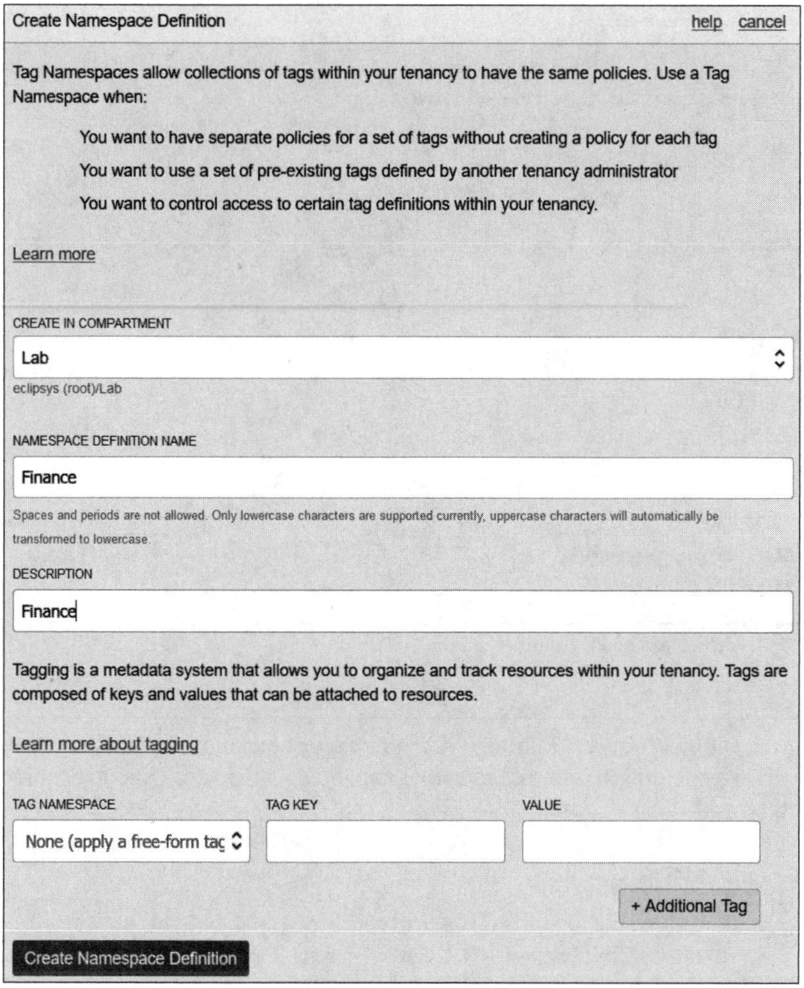

Create Namespace Definition help cancel

Tag Namespaces allow collections of tags within your tenancy to have the same policies. Use a Tag Namespace when:

You want to have separate policies for a set of tags without creating a policy for each tag

You want to use a set of pre-existing tags defined by another tenancy administrator

You want to control access to certain tag definitions within your tenancy.

Learn more

CREATE IN COMPARTMENT

Lab

eclipsys (root)/Lab

NAMESPACE DEFINITION NAME

Finance

Spaces and periods are not allowed. Only lowercase characters are supported currently, uppercase characters will automatically be transformed to lowercase.

DESCRIPTION

Finance

Tagging is a metadata system that allows you to organize and track resources within your tenancy. Tags are composed of keys and values that can be attached to resources.

Learn more about tagging

TAG NAMESPACE TAG KEY VALUE

None (apply a free-form tag

+ Additional Tag

Create Namespace Definition

Figure 2-13 Creating a defined tag namespace

policy must be created to permit non-administrator users to apply tags. A group can be explicitly given permissions to inspect or view the tag key definitions as follows:

```
Allow group NetworkAdmins to inspect tag-namespaces in tenancy
```

Use permission on both the tag and the resource allows tags to be added, removed, or edited.

Tag key definitions can only be retired, not reused. Resources with retired tags will retain the tag key definitions. These may be manually done per affected resource. The limit of ten cost-tracking tags per tenancy at a time includes both retired and active tags.

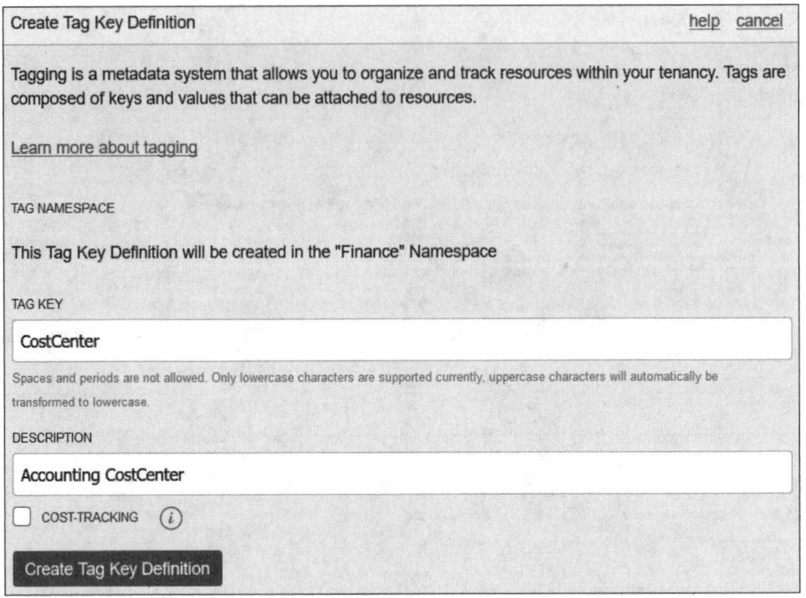

Figure 2-14 Create Tag Key Definition

CAUTION Only printable ASCII letters are allowed as tag namespace and tag key definition names. Tag values can, however, be any Unicode characters.

Advanced Policies

Armed with an understanding of OCIDs and resource-types, the full power of IAM policies can be expressed. This section discusses aggregate, or family, resource-types, policy location options, and how to use conditions in policies.

Family Resource-Types

Individual resources may be grouped into collections or families of related resources for ease of management. In Exercise 2-2, a VCN, route table, default security list, Internet gateway, and three subnets were created. All of these individual resource-types belong to the aggregate resource-type called virtual-network-family. Policy syntax can be applied to both individual and aggregate resource-types. Some examples of aggregate resource-types include:

- all-resources
- cluster-family
- database-family
- dns

- file-family
- instance-family
- object-family
- virtual-network-family
- volume-family

The all-resources aggregate resource-type refers to all OCI resources in your tenancy. The virtual-network, instance, and volume families each consist of many individual resource-types compared to the other aggregate groups. Figure 2-15 expands the virtual-network-family, instance-family, and volume-family aggregate resource-types into their individual resource-types.

Figure 2-16 lists the individual resource-types for the seven remaining aggregate resource-types: autonomous-transaction-processing-family (ATP), autonomous-data-warehouse-family (ADW), cluster-family, database-family, dns, file-family, and object-family. There may be several unfamiliar resource-types listed but all are covered in later chapters. These diagrams provide valuable context. When you encounter an unfamiliar resource-type, simply look up the family it belongs to in order to understand where it fits in the grander scheme. Figures 2-15 and 2-16 serve as useful reference lookups when designing IAM policies.

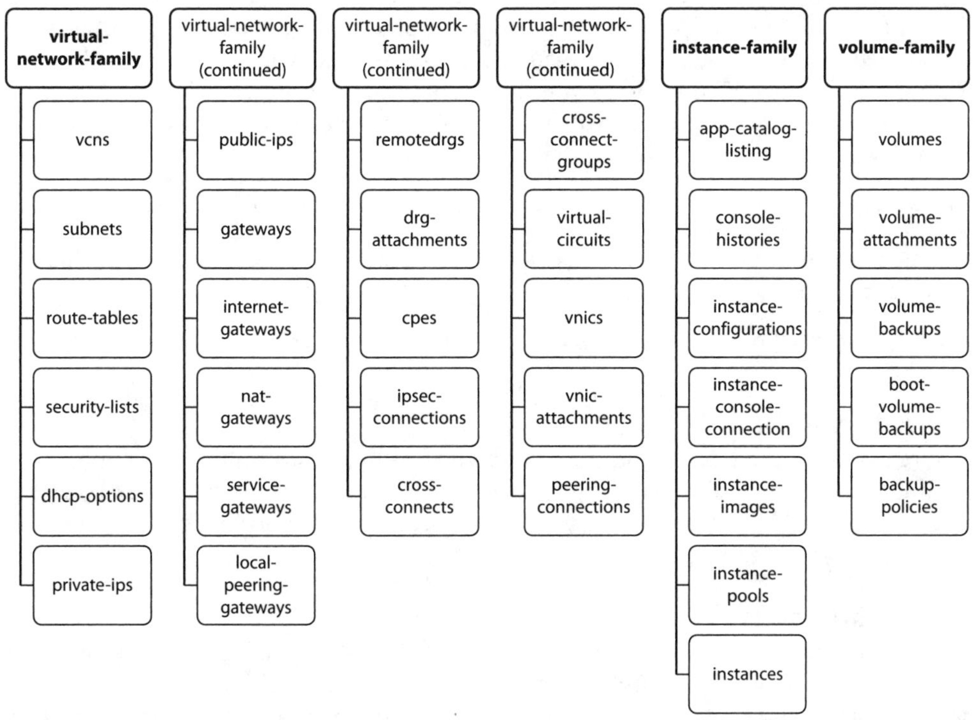

Figure 2-15 Virtual-network, instance, and volume family resource-types

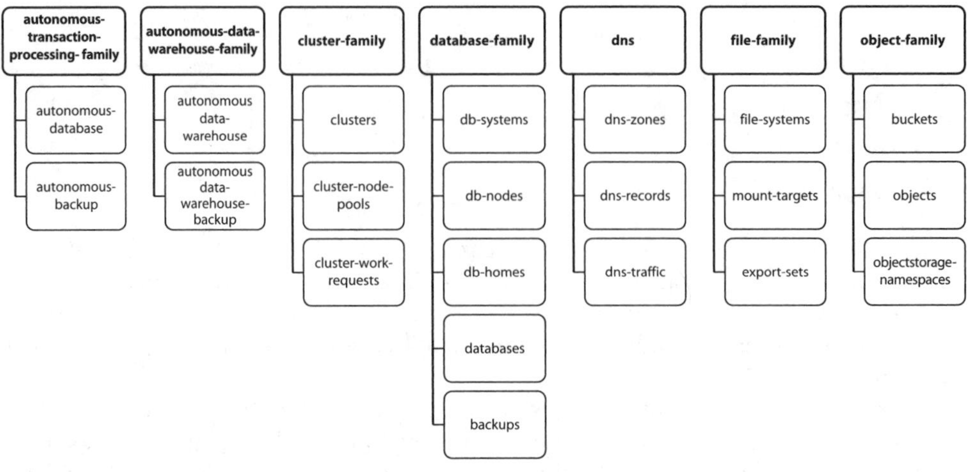

Figure 2-16 ATP, ADW, cluster, database, dns, file, and object family resource-types

The policy statement introduced earlier in this chapter followed this syntax:

```
Allow <subject> to <verb> <resource-type> in <location> where <condition>
```

The subjects and verbs are discussed in detail in the "Policies" discussion in the earlier "Explain IAM Concepts" section. The resource-type component of this syntax may be substituted by any individual or aggregate resource-type, as shown by the expanded syntax diagram in Figure 2-17. Instead of granting manage permissions to over 20 virtual network resources in the Lab compartment to the NetworkAdmins group, you can simply use a single statement:

```
Allow group NetworkAdmins to manage virtual-network-family in compartment Lab
```

You can permit your DBAs to manage all organizational databases with this policy statement:

```
Allow group DBAdmins to manage database-family in tenancy
```

Policy Locations

Figure 2-17 also extends the location component of the policy syntax to include compartment OCID in addition to compartment name and tenancy. An example of this was shown in Figure 2-10, where the Lab compartment is referenced in a policy statement using its OCID.

Policy Conditions

You may specify conditions on policy statements to have finer-grained control over your resources. Policy conditions use one or more predefined variables that you reference in the "where clause" of the policy statement. The following policy statement permits

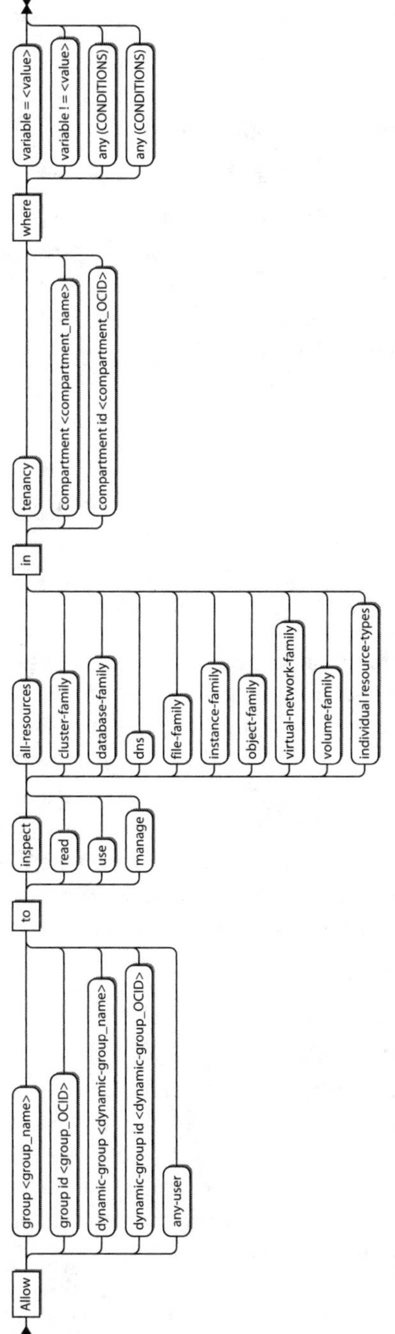

Figure 2-17 Policy syntax expansion for resource-type, location, and conditions

Name	Description
request.user.id	The OCID of the user making the resource request
request.groups.id	The OCIDs of all the groups to which the requesting user belongs
target.compartment.id	The OCID of the compartment to which the resource belongs
target.compartment.name	The name of the compartment to which the resource belongs
request.operation	The name of the OCI API service being requested
request.permission	The underlying permission or set of permissions being requested
request.region	The key of the region from which the request originates, for example: BOM, FRA, IAD, ICN, LHR, NRT, PHX, YYZ
request.ad	The name of the availability domain from which the request originates

Table 2-5 Variables Allowed in Policy Conditions

members of the US-DBAs group to manage all database resources in the US_ONLY compartment, as long as the group member makes a request from either the Ashburn or Phoenix regions.

```
Allow group US-DBAs to manage database-family in compartment US_ONLY where
ANY {request.region= 'ash', request.region= 'phx '}
```

Refer to the conditions "where clause" in Figure 2-17. The policy syntax allows conditions to test the equality or inequality of a variable or whether any of a set of conditions is true or whether all conditions in a set of conditions are true.

Table 2-5 summarizes the variables allowed in policy conditions.

EXAM TIP The topic of advanced policy statements using conditions is out of scope of the exam. It is a powerful feature essential to fine-grained policy administration and is included for completeness. A solid understanding of family resource-types as well as policy location options is, however, required for the exam.

Create IAM Resources

It is time to get your hands dirty with the IAM concepts introduced previously. This section is devoted to the practical tasks associated with creating IAM resources for a fictitious company, ES Corporation. You can play along in a trial or sandbox cloud account, or using your organization's OCI account. You just need a user in the Administrator group. Feel free to change the IAM resource names in the following exercises to align with your current naming standards and structures.

ES Corporation is an IT company with two primary lines of business: Infrastructure and Services. There are Sales, Services, and Operations business units. The Services business unit is further divided into Managed Services and Consulting Services, while the Operations business unit is divided into the HR, Finance, and IT departments. The business has offices in San Francisco (US) and London (UK). The IT department manages the infrastructure through a team of application, network, storage, systems, security, and database administrators based in each location working in local on-premises data centers. ES Corporation has decided to embrace Oracle Cloud Infrastructure and needs your help to design an efficient architecture that optimizes human and infrastructure resources. Learning from historical budget cycles, the new infrastructure must provide a mechanism to understand utilized infrastructure by respective departments.

Create Compartments

After careful business analysis, you conclude that all the departments should have a dedicated compartment to host resources specific to their needs. Shared resources will be located in the parent compartment at the organization-level compartment.

Exercise 2-3: Create Compartments for Organization

In this exercise, you will create compartments for the organization, each of the three business units, and their departments.

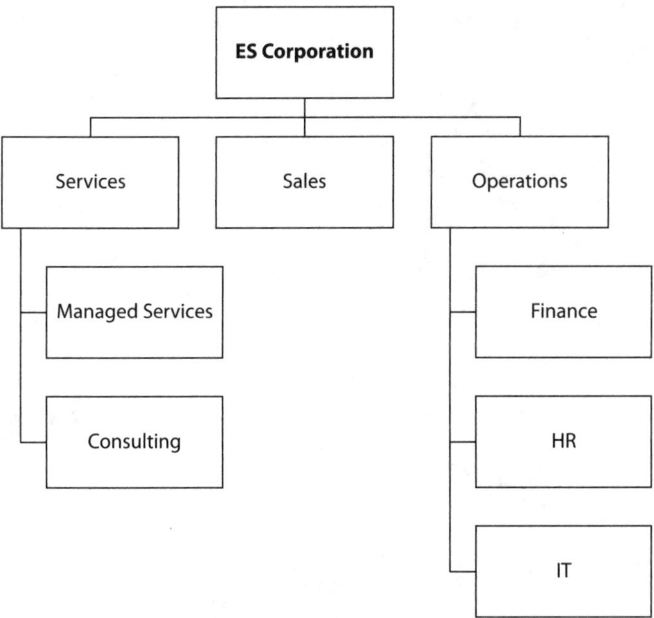

1. To ease management of these compartments but specifically to fulfill the mandate to track resource utilization by departments, a defined tagging schema should be configured. Navigate to Governance-Tag Namespaces and select

Create Namespace Definition. Ensure that the newly created ES_Corporation compartment is chosen. Provide a name, say ESC, and a description, and select Create Namespace Definition.

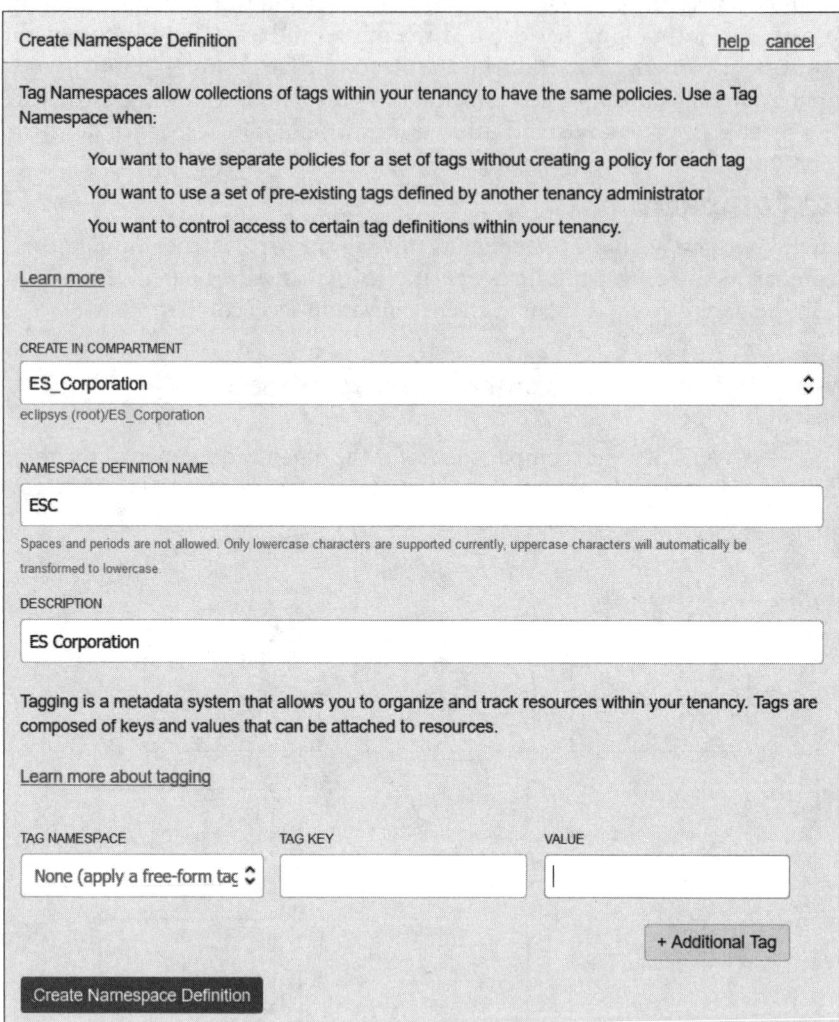

2. With a tag namespace in place, tag keys should be defined. Navigate to Governance-Tag Namespaces-ESC and select Create Tag Key Definition. Create a tag key called CostCenter with an appropriate description, check the cost-tracking checkbox, and select Create Tag Key Definition. Repeat this step to define two additional non-cost-tracking tag keys: Lifecycle and Project.

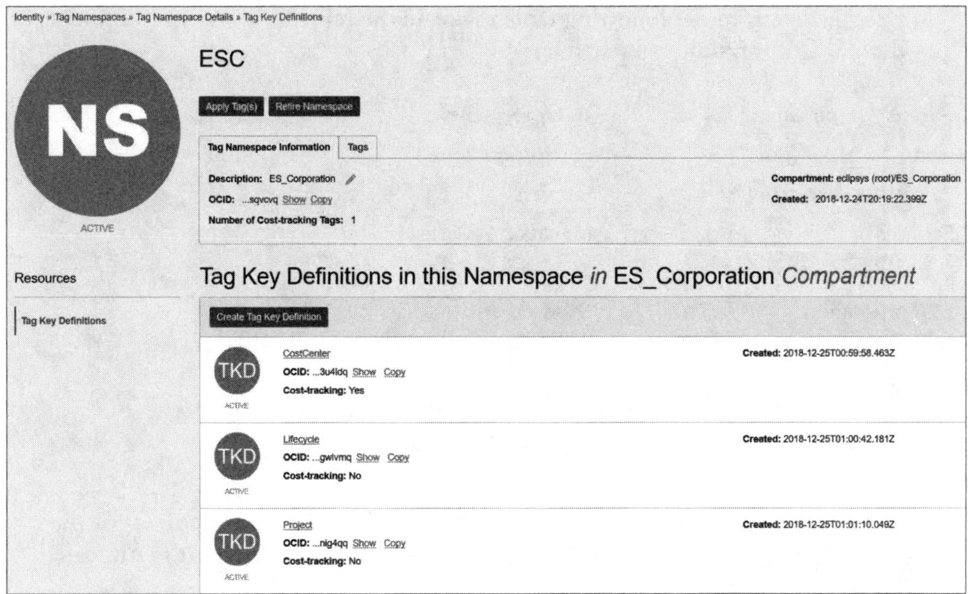

3. Navigate to Identity-Compartments. Choose Create Compartment. Provide a name for the organization, say ES_Corporation, and a description, and ensure that its parent compartment is the root compartment. Tag the compartment by choosing the ESC namespace, tag key CostCenter, and tag value 100, and then select Create Compartment.

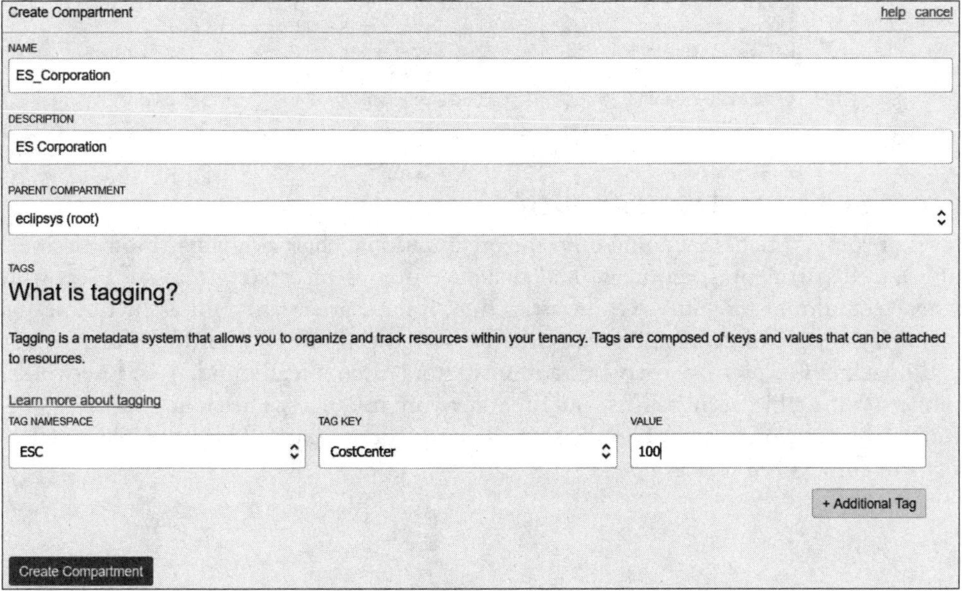

4. Use the details in the following table to create the remaining subcompartments of the ES_Corporation compartment.

Parent Compartment	Compartment	CostCenter
root	ES_Corporation	100
ES_Corporation	Services	110
Services	Managed Services	111
Services	Consulting	112
ES_Corporation	Sales	120
ES_Corporation	Operations	130
Operations	Finance	131
Operations	HR	132
Operations	IT	133

5. You have just created nine new compartments. Search your resources for the defined tag costcenter using the OCI CLI. The following output is truncated for brevity:

```
oci search resource structured-search --query-text
" query all resources where
 (definedTags.namespace = 'ESC' && definedTags.key ='costcenter') "
|grep -A5 defined-tags
{"ESC": {"CostCenter": "133"}},"display-name": "IT",
{"ESC": {"CostCenter": "132"}},"display-name": "HR",
{"ESC": {"CostCenter": "131"}},"display-name": "Finance",
{"ESC": {"CostCenter": "130"}},"display-name": "Operations",
{"ESC": {"CostCenter": "120"}},"display-name": "Sales",
{"ESC": {"CostCenter": "112"}},"display-name": "Consulting",
{"ESC": {"CostCenter": "111"}},"display-name": "Managed_Services",
{"ESC": {"CostCenter": "110"}},"display-name": "Services",
{"ESC": {"CostCenter": "100"}},"display-name": "ES_Corporation"
```

Create Groups, Users, Policies

A set of compartments mapping onto the organizational chart neatly partitions business unit and departmental resources. The challenge now is to create groups of users who manage or administer your OCI infrastructure. If there are existing infrastructure teams managing on-premises infrastructure, the path to the cloud is often more direct than you imagine. On-premises network administrators often already understand networks, subnets, route table, security lists, and other network resources. The cloud version of network resources closely resembles their on-premises counterparts. This principle is generally true for all OCI resources.

Exercise 2-4: Create Groups, Users, and Policies

In this exercise, you will create groups of administrators (local users) that parallel the on-premises teams. The IT department currently manages the infrastructure with a team of application, network, storage, systems, security, and database administrators based in each location working in local on-premises data centers.

1. Navigate to Identity-Groups and select Create Group. Provide a name and description and select the Project tag key from the ESC namespace, supply the appropriate key value, and click Submit. Create the five groups you see in the following table:

Group Name	Project
ESC_NetworkAdmins	Networks
ESC_StorageAdmins	Storage
ESC_SysAdmins	Systems
ESC_DBAs	Databases
ESC_SecAdmins	Security

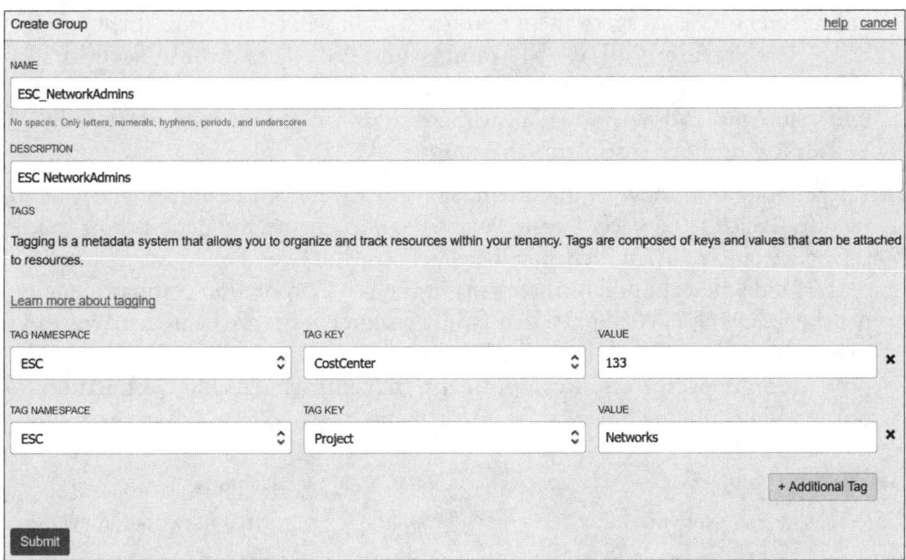

2. In this exercise, you have begun the construction of an IAM framework with compartments and groups. To illustrate the process of creating local users, a single user is created and added to the ESC_NetworkAdmins group. Feel free to substitute any meaningful username and to create additional local users in your environment. Navigate to Identity-Users and select Create User. Provide a name and description, select the CostCenter tag key from the ESC namespace, supply

the appropriate key value, and click Create. The user Jason was created with ESC.CostCenter=133.

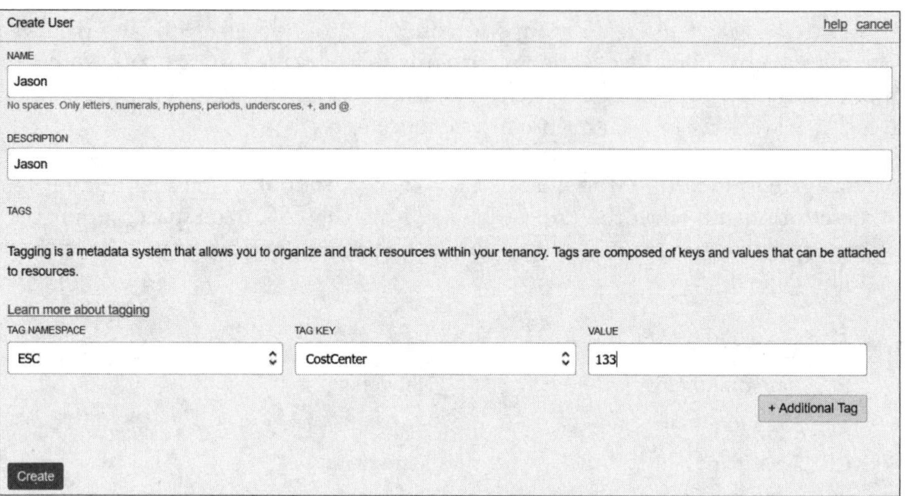

3. Jason is the lead network engineer and is often consulted with regard to operating systems hardening as well as network penetration testing. It is necessary that he has management level access to these resources. Jason will be added to three groups: ESC_NetworkAdmins, ESC_SysAdmins, and ESC_SecAdmins. Navigate to Identity-Groups-ESC_NetworkAdmins and select Add User To Group. Choose user Jason and choose Add. Repeat these steps for adding Jason to the ESC_SysAdmins and ESC_SecAdmins groups.
4. The admin groups now require permissions to access OCI resources. Navigate to Identity-Policies and select Create Policy. Provide a name and description. To keep the policy current as OCI changes occur, choose the Keep Policy Current radio button and add eight policy statements in the ES_Corporation compartment as per the following table. Notice that family resource-types are being used instead of many statements for each individual resource-type. Also, each group has manage privilege on respective resources for the parent compartment ES_Corporation. This policy will be inherited by all subcompartments.

Statement	Subject	Verb	Resource
1	ESC_NetworkAdmins	manage	virtual-network-family
2	ESC_StorageAdmins	manage	volume-family
3	ESC_StorageAdmins	manage	object-family
4	ESC_StorageAdmins	manage	file-family
5	ESC_SysAdmins	manage	instance-family
6	ESC_DBAs	manage	database-family
7	ESC_SecAdmins	read	virtual-network-family
8	ESC_SecAdmins	use	instance-family

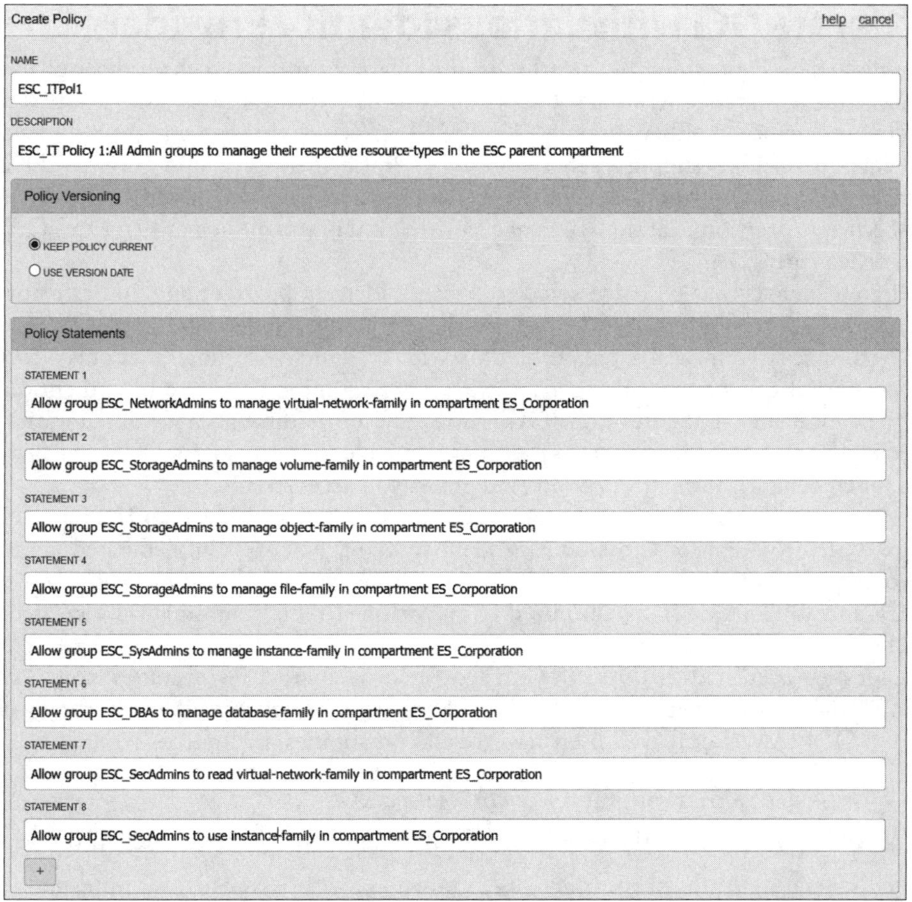

5. Your security design for infrastructure is now complete. You can log in as Jason and should be successful in managing network resources in the ES_Corporation compartment and all its child compartments.
6. Within the corporation there are usually one or more applications deployed, for example the HR application. It usually requires resources such as a network, web servers, databases, compute instances and block storage. If these resources are created and tagged in the HR compartment, the administration framework you just created supports the administration of the HR resources with no further modification because the policy ESC_ITPol1 is inherited by the HR compartment. It may be useful to group your applications and create compartments for infrastructure resources used by these applications.

Federate OCI with Various Identity Providers

The discussion concerning users earlier in this chapter introduced three types of users: local, federated, and provisioned. Usernames and passwords, groups, and group membership are managed either through OCI's IAM service or through an external identity provider (IdP). OCI supports federation with Oracle Identity Cloud Service (IDCS), Microsoft Active Directory (through AD Federation Services), and any IdP that supports the Security Assertion Markup Language (SAML) 2.0 protocol such as Okta and Oracle Access Manager (OAM).

If your tenancy has been federated to another identity provider and you attempt to access the OCI console, you will be prompted either to use a single sign-on (SSO) credential or to specify your local username and password. Figure 2-18 shows that once you try to access OCI using a tenancy federated with IDCS, you can choose to be authenticated through local user authentication (OCI IAM service) or through SSO authentication, which redirects your connection to the third-party identity provider (IDCS), challenges you for credentials, authenticates you, and grants you access to OCI.

To standardize user provisioning across discrete identity providers, an IETF protocol called SCIM (System for Cross-domain Identity Management) is implemented in OCI. A consequence of this standard is that users are synchronized automatically between IDCS and OCI IAM. A synchronized or provisioned user is automatically created in OCI's IAM for each federated user.

User Neo is created in IDCS in your federated tenancy. A few minutes later, a synchronized or provisioned user named oracleidentitycloudservice/neo is automatically created in OCI IAM. Local OCI users have several capabilities, including:

- Using a local password for direct console access
- Adding API keys to the user profile for programmatic access to OCI APIs
- Generating Auth tokens (previously known as Swift passwords) for third-party API authentication

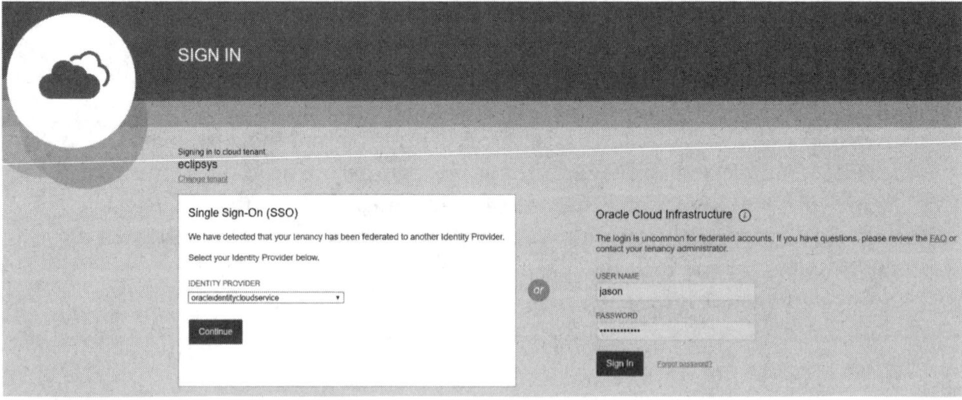

Figure 2-18 SSO sign-in for federated users

- Generating SMTP credentials to access the Email service
- Generating Customer secret keys (previously known as Amazon S3 Compatibility API keys)

Synchronized or provisioned users from non-OCI IAM providers have all the capabilities listed except for a local password for direct console access. Passwords for federated users are managed by the external identity provider. One of the benefits of federation is that users are managed in a single directory service and trust is established between the local and remote identity providers. Typical federated tenancies tend to not have many local users.

While users are directly synchronized, groups are not. In OCI IAM, an Administrators group is created during the tenancy setup process. When federating to IDCS, an OCI_Administrators group is mapped to the OCI IAM Administrators group. IDCS users appear in the IDCS OCI_Administrators group, but they are not listed in the OCI IAM Administrators group. If an IDCS user who belongs to the OCI_Administrators group signs in to OCI, they have full administrator access to the tenancy.

CAUTION In a federated tenancy, IDCS users may belong to IDCS groups mapped to OCI IAM groups. The OCI IAM groups only list local users and not provisioned or synchronized users. To make sure you understand the group membership of both local and federated users, examine the Identity provider group mappings.

Figure 2-19 shows the group mappings defined between OCI IAM and IDCS. There are two IDCS groups, OCI_Administrators and NetworkAdmins, that are mapped to the OCI IAM Administrators and NetworkAdmins groups respectively.

IDCS user Neo is a member of the IDCS NetworkAdmins group. His synchronized or provisioned OCI IAM user account, oracleidentitycloudservice/neo, is *not* a member

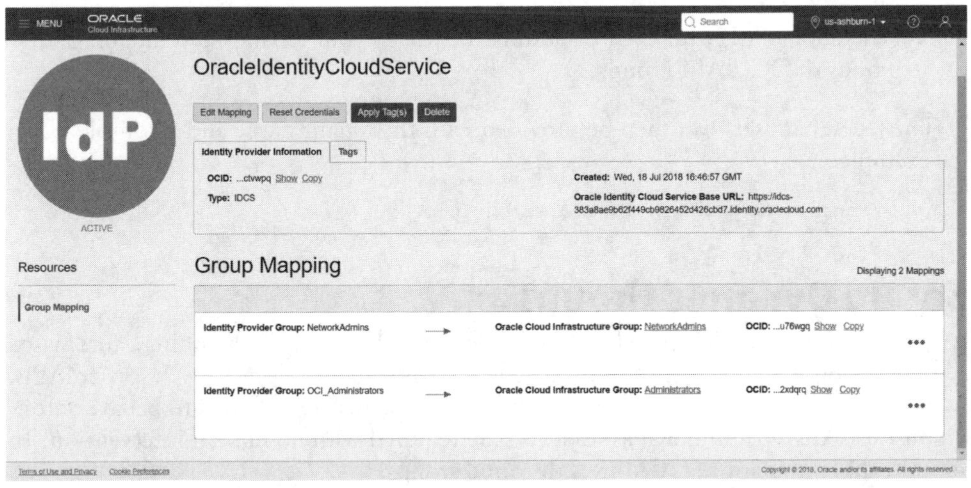

Figure 2-19 Map identity provider groups to OCI groups.

of the OCI IAM NetworkAdmins account…not directly anyway. Neo logs in to OCI, is authenticated by IDCS, and connects to the OCI console. A policy exists allowing members of the OCI IAM group NetworkAdmins to manage vcns in the Lab compartment. Neo attempts to create a vcn in the Lab compartment and is successful. This is due to the IDCS group mapping setup.

At the time of this writing, users who belong to more than 50 identity provider groups cannot be authenticated to sign in to the OCI console.

NOTE OCI tenancies created after December 20, 2018, are automatically federated with IDCS and configured to provision federated users in OCI. Tenancies created between December 18, 2017, and December 20, 2018, are automatically federated with IDCS but not configured to provision federated users in OCI to allow these users to have additional credentials such as API keys. This can be rectified with a few quick configuration steps. Earlier tenancies created before December 18, 2017, must be manually federated with IDCS.

A high-level description of the process an administrator follows to federate OCI IAM with a supported identity provider (IdP) is outlined next:

- Through the OCI console, obtain the federation metadata required to establish a trust relationship with the IdP. This typically involves downloading the federation metadata document by navigating to Identity | Federation and choosing the link named: Download this document.
- Configure OCI as a trusted application in the IdP.
- In the IdP, assign users and groups to use with the new OCI application.
- Through the IdP interface, obtain the federation metadata required to establish a trust relationship with OCI. This typically involves downloading the federation metadata document from the IdP.
- Federate the IdP with OCI by adding the IdP to your tenancy and mapping IdP groups to OCI IAM groups

The federated users can then be provided with the tenant name and a console URL; for example:

```
https://console.us-ashburn-1.oraclecloud.com
```

Set Up Dynamic Groups

A robust feature closely related to the notion of self-driving, self-tuning, automated systems involves granting compute instances permission to access OCI service APIs. Automation technologies are abundant and many systems are designed to behave autonomously, scaling up and down as resources are required with no human intervention. To support this automation, OCI offers dynamic groups.

Dynamic groups are a tenancy-wide construct and represent a collection of compute instances added to the group by one or more matching rules. A typical matching rule is to include all compute instances that belong to a certain compartment. The group becomes dynamic as instances in that compartment are launched or terminated. A single compute instance may belong to a maximum of ten dynamic groups.

Matching rules that determine the inclusion or exclusion of instances in dynamic groups are based on one or more of the following:

- Compartment OCID
- Compute instance OCID
- Tag namespace and tag key
- Tag namespace, tag key, and tag value

The following matching rule will include any instances that are running in either of the specified compartments with matching OCIDs.

```
ANY { instance.compartment.id = 'ocid1.compartment.oc1..aaaaaaazrguq',
instance.compartment.id = 'ocid1.compartment.oc1..aaaaaaaazlh3iq'}
```

The matching rules can be simple and use equality operators like the preceding example or the inequality operator (!=). The ANY keyword allows matching rules to add an instance to the dynamic group if any of the comma-separated criteria are true while the ALL keyword demands that all comma-separated criteria must be true before an instance is added to the group. The following matching rule uses a defined tag:

```
tag.Finance.CostCenter.value='12'
```

This defined tag with a value of 12 could be applied to any number of compute instances in your tenancy. These groups are dynamic because their membership is dynamic. Figure 2-20 shows how you create dynamic groups in the console by navigating to Identity | Dynamic Groups and selecting Create Dynamic Groups. You provide a name and description and one or more matching rules. You can type these in manually or launch the Rule Builder to help construct matching rules. The Rule Builder is quite limited as it cannot reference defined tags at the time of this writing

Once your dynamic rules are in place, IAM policies must be defined to authorize the dynamic group to interact with one or more resources. Figure 2-17 exposed the policy syntax diagram. Notice that dynamic groups may be referred to by their name or OCID in policy statements.

Consider a webstore application that is front-ended by a load balancer that directs traffic to a backend HTTP server running on a compute instance. During busy shopping days, administrators wait for the load on the webstore application to inevitably spike and bring down the system. Additional HTTP servers help with the load issue. So the following policy statements are implemented:

```
Allow dynamic-group RetailFrontEnd to manage instances in compartment Lab
Allow dynamic-group RetailFrontEnd to use load-balancers in compartment Webstore
```

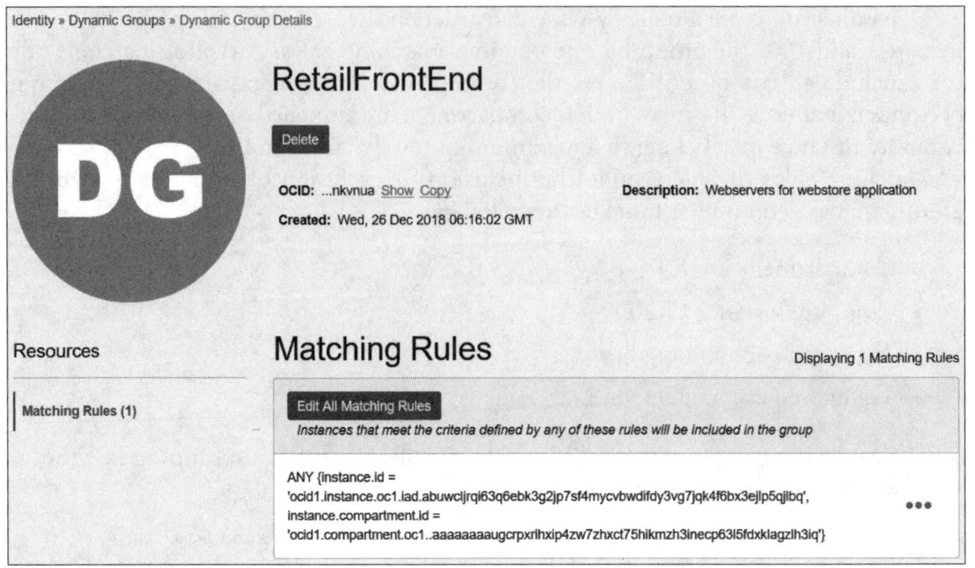

Figure 2-20 Create dynamic groups.

This policy authorizes compute instances that belong to a dynamic group called RetailFrontEnd to provision additional HTTP servers and load balancers automatically as required if unusual load conditions are encountered.

It is not the instances themselves that perform the provisioning but rather applications running on the instances. These applications use either the OCI CLI, Terraform, SDKs, or other interfaces to directly access the OCI APIs once the instance principal is enabled. The instance principal is the IAM service that authorizes instances (to behave as actors or principals) to interact with OCI resources. Each compute instance has a unique identity and it authenticates with OCI when making API calls by using certificates that are automatically added to the instance. These certificates are short-lived for security reasons and are frequently rotated automatically. This avoids the distribution of named credentials to your compute instances and is much safer. The current certificate may be queried from your instance using this command:

```
$ curl http://169.254.169.254/opc/v1/identity/cert.pem
-----BEGIN CERTIFICATE-----
<Certificate text>
-----END CERTIFICATE-----
```

OCI CLI scripts on instances in dynamic groups enable the instance principal authorization as follows:

```
oci os ns get --auth instance_principal
```

Once the required resources and policies are set up, an application running on an instance in a dynamic group can call OCI API services without requiring user credentials or configuration files.

CAUTION Any user who can connect to the instance (using SSH) automatically inherits the privileges granted to a compute instance that is authorized to act on service resources, so ensure that you carefully control access and that these users should be authorized with the permissions granted to the instance.

The following OCI services support access by instances:

- Compute
- Block volume
- Load balancing
- Object storage
- File storage

Because dynamic groups of instances operate in an application-driven manner, there are detailed audit logs captured that enable you to determine all resources accessed by instances in dynamic groups.

Chapter Review

Understanding OCI IAM is key to successful cloud adoption and forms the basis for the remainder of this book. In this chapter, the relationship between many IAM concepts were explored. At the core of OCI are resources grouped into resource family aggregations. Resources reside at a tenancy level or in a compartment. Compartments and their hierarchical nature were discussed as well as the consequential inheritance of policy from parent compartments to child compartments. IAM resources such as users, groups, dynamic groups, policies, and compartments are global and exist in all regions your tenancy is subscribed to, but are mastered in your home region. This means that changes to these global resources are made in the home region first, before being replicated to other regions.

Some resources exist at a region level while others exist at an availability domain level. Regardless of the resource location, they all have a unique identifier, the OCID. OCIDs are used in policy statements, in matching rules for dynamic groups, and in API calls.

The chapter introduced tagging, and although it is not examinable, it is a practical and useful mechanism for controlling and reporting on infrastructure utilization. Policies occupied a substantial chunk of this chapter. Policies are extremely powerful and have been implemented in OCI with a simple, clear syntax.

The chapter also explored federation with various identity providers. Because IDCS federation is standard with all new tenancies, this is likely to be the dominant identity provider you will encounter. The chapter wrapped up by introducing the mechanics of dynamic groups. Dynamic groups support a robust brand of automation and self-regulating systems that are likely to be the norm in the future.

Questions

1. Which IAM resources are global and span regions?
   A. Compartments
   B. Policies
   C. Compute instances
   D. DBAAS
2. Which policy verbs authorize groups to interact with resources with the highest level of permission?
   A. inspect
   B. read
   C. administer
   D. use
3. Which policy verbs authorize groups to interact with resources in order from lowest to highest level of permission?
   A. inspect, read, manage, use
   B. inspect, read, use, manage
   C. inspect, read, administer, use
   D. inspect, read, use, administer
4. Which is a capability of OCI users but not federated users?
   A. Can add API keys
   B. Can generate Auth tokens
   C. Can use a local password for console access
   D. Can generate customer secret keys
5. Which of the following statements is true?
   A. Region subscriptions occur at the AD level.
   B. Region subscriptions occur at the compartment level.
   C. Region subscriptions occur at the group level.
   D. Region subscriptions occur at the tenancy level.
6. Instances are added to dynamic groups based on what rules?
   A. Policy statements
   B. Matching rules
   C. Compartment OCID and Auth token
   D. Inheritance

7. Matching rules that determine the inclusion or exclusion of instances in dynamic groups are based on one of more of the following?
   - **A.** Compartment OCID, Instance OCID, tags
   - **B.** Instance shape, system load
   - **C.** Tenancy OCID, Region OCID, AD OCID
   - **D.** Policy syntax
8. Where is a federated user in your tenancy authenticated?
   - **A.** OCI IAM service
   - **B.** IDCS
   - **C.** The identity provider where it was created
   - **D.** Active Directory Federation Services
9. Which resource is not an availability domain–level resource?
   - **A.** Compute instance
   - **B.** Subnet
   - **C.** Block volume
   - **D.** Object storage
10. What is the name given to the location where the master copy of OCI IAM resources are located?
    - **A.** Home region
    - **B.** Primary IAM site
    - **C.** Identity provider
    - **D.** Tenancy

Answers

1. **A, B.** Compartments, users, groups, and policies are global resources and span regions. When you create these IAM entities, they exist in all regions to which your tenancy or cloud account has subscribed.
2. **D.** The verbs to authorize groups to interact with resources in order of lowest to highest levels of permission are inspect, read, use, and manage.
3. **B.** The verbs in order of lowest to highest levels of permission are inspect, read, use, and manage. There is no administer verb in the policy syntax.
4. **C.** Federated users have to use credentials from their identity provider to sign in.
5. **D.** The region subscriptions occur at the tenancy level. All IAM resources, including policies, are available in all regions to which your tenancy has subscribed.

6. **B.** Matching rules determine the inclusion or exclusion of instances in dynamic groups.
7. **A.** Matching rules that determine the inclusion or exclusion of instances in dynamic groups are based on one or more of the following: compartment OCID, compute instance OCID, tag namespace and tag key, and tag namespace, tag key, and tag value.
8. **C.** Federated users are authenticated in the IdP where they were created.
9. **D.** Object storage buckets are an interesting regional resource. An instance in AD: US-ASHBURN-AD-1 may access a bucket in the region: us-ashburn-1. This bucket is equally accessible by another instance in AD: US-ASHBURN-AD-2. Given the correct region-specific object storage URL and permissions, this bucket is accessible from any location.
10. **A.** IAM resources are available in all regions you have subscribed to but their master definitions always reside in the home region.

CHAPTER 3

OCI Networking

In this chapter, you will learn how to

- Describe OCI networking concepts
- Use virtual cloud networks
- Explain DNS concepts
- Create load balancers
- Design and secure OCI networks

Networking is the backbone of OCI and one of the components that significantly differentiates OCI from other mainstream cloud providers. OCI has virtualized its massive physical networking infrastructure to provide many recognizable classical network components, such as networks, subnets, route tables, gateways, DNS services, and load balancers, as well as several novel components, such as service and dynamic routing gateways.

It is important to take a step back and remind yourself that all IaaS clouds are hosted on physical equipment in several data centers that belong to the cloud provider. The physical servers, storage, and network infrastructure are partitioned into units of consumption presented as familiar patterns or resources that you lease.

You may add a compute instance to your cloud tenancy with two OCPUs and 15GB of memory, but this resource is physically located on a much more powerful server, and you subscribe to a partition or slice of this equipment. With bare-metal compute instances, you subscribe to the entire server, but the resource is still abstracted to a unit of consumption that you consume through your tenancy. Network resources are similarly partitioned in OCI. A networking background is not required as you begin to explore this fascinating realm, but even if you have a networking background, we recommend that you carefully read the following "Networking Concepts and Terminology" section as OCI networking has several unique components.

Networking Concepts and Terminology

Your traditional infrastructure estate may be hosted on-premises locally in the server room in your building or in one or more data centers. The on-premises infrastructure is interconnected through one or more networks. Your OCI infrastructure is interconnected through one or more virtual cloud networks, or VCNs.

NOTE You may connect an on-premises network to one or more VCNs in what is known as a hybrid cloud configuration. If a system is developed and deployed on cloud resources, it is anecdotally referred to as being born in the cloud. If it has no dependency on on-premises resources, it is said to run on cloud native infrastructure. These are anecdotal definitions because precise formal definitions of these terms are still evolving.

On-premises networking infrastructure usually includes physical devices such as routers/gateways, switches, and network interface cards (or NICs) on each connected device as well as a network segmented into subnets with route tables and security lists. OCI networking infrastructure includes access to gateways and virtualized NICs (vNICs), as well as VCNs divided or segmented into subnets with route tables and security lists. There are many direct parallels between on-premises and OCI networking.

Consider the example of a typical home network where you may have a router that connects to your Internet service provider (ISP). This router sets up a network by providing services to your devices, which may include laptops, TVs, and mobile devices, some of which may be connected wirelessly or through Ethernet cables from their NICs to the router. Each device that connects to your home network receives an IP address from a block of IP addresses that your router is configured to distribute by a service known as DHCP.

These addresses are unique in your home network. For example, your living room TV may get the IP address 192.168.0.10, while your laptop is assigned the address 192.168.0.11. Your next-door neighbor may have her router also configured to serve the same block of IP addresses and her mobile phone may be assigned the 192.168.0.11 IP address by the DHCP service on her router. There is no conflict, however, because these two networks are private and isolated from each other. These are private IP addresses. Unless you make an explicit configuration on your device, the IP address assignment is dynamic, and the next time your device connects to your home network, there is no guarantee that it will be assigned the same IP address as before. This scenario is sufficient for most home networks.

Your home router connects to the Internet. It actually connects to your ISP's network, which is connected to other networks and so on. Most home routers receive a DHCP-assigned public IP address from the ISP routers. This allows traffic to be routed from your ISP to your home router. As with your personal devices, your router's IP address could change once the DHCP lease is renewed by the ISP router. If you would like a consistent public IP address on the Internet, you have to specifically request a static IP address from your ISP. This usually adds an additional cost to your subscription.

The network created by your router connects devices on your home network to the broader Internet. These devices transmit and receive packets of data between devices on your network through your router according to a set of rules known as network protocols. The dominant network protocol in use today is Transmission Control Protocol/Internet Protocol (TCP/IP). This is the origin of the IP in IP address. When your device connects to your home network, the NIC on the device is assigned an IP address as well as a subnet mask and default gateway information. When your device accesses the Internet, TCP packets of data are sent to your default gateway (which usually is your home router), which then forwards the packet according to a set of routing rules. Routing rules stored in lists known as *route tables* specify what routing activities to perform with an incoming packet of data over the network.

An OCI VCN may have a virtual router known as an Internet gateway that connects the network to the Internet. VCNs are divided into subnets, some of which are private and isolated from each other. OCI networking services offer DHCP services that allocate IPs from the subnet ranges to instances. OCI offers two types of public IPs, a temporary one known as an ephemeral public IP and a static IP known as a reserved IP. Private IPs are available on OCI by default on all virtual network interface cards, or vNICs.

The home network example discussed in the preceding text serves to illustrate two fundamental points:

- There are direct parallels between on-premises networking and OCI networking.
- You are likely already using many of the components discussed next in your home network, including private and public IP addresses, NICs, networks, subnets, routers, route tables, firewall security lists, and DHCP services.

NOTE The OCI network is referred to as a full software-defined layer 3 network. The layers come from the seven-layer OSI model where layer 3 is the network layer sitting between the data link layer and the transport layer. In general terms, a layer 3 network facilitates segmented routing over Internet protocol (IP). It is software defined because the physical implementation is abstracted through OCI software and presents software-defined networking components.

CIDR

The dominant version of network addressing is Internet Protocol version 4 (IPv4). There is a growing prevalence of IPv6 addressing, but the de facto standard remains IPv4 addressing. In the early days of the Internet (1981–93), the 32-bit IPv4 address space was divided into address classes based on the leading four address bits and became known as classful addressing. The class A address space accommodated 128 networks with over 16 million addresses per network while the class B address space accommodated 16,384 networks with 65,536 addresses per network; finally, the class C address space accommodated over 2 million networks with 256 addresses per network. Class A network blocks are too large and class C network blocks are too small for most organizations so many class B network blocks were allocated although they were still too large in most cases. Classful addressing was wasteful and accelerated the consumption of available IP addresses. To buy time before the IP exhaustion problem manifests, a new scheme known as Classless Inter-Domain Routing (CIDR) was introduced in 1993.

EXAM TIP Your knowledge of CIDR blocks will be tested extensively in the exam so ensure you have a good understanding of how to derive a netmask from a CIDR block. Also note that the smaller the network prefix, the more bits are available for the host address space, which implies a larger IP address range.

CIDR notation is based on an IPv4 or IPv6 network or routing prefix separated by a slash from a number indicating the prefix length. OCI networking uses IPv4 addressing so the address length is 32 bits. Consider the block of IPv4 addresses specified with the following CIDR notation: 192.168.0.1/30.

CIDR notation may be divided into two components, a network identifier and a host address space. The network identifier is represented by the number of bits specified by the network prefix. The second part is the remaining bits that represent the available IP address space. The routing or network prefix is 30, which means that 30 of the 32 bits in this address space are used to uniquely identify the network while 2 bits are available for host addresses. In binary, 2 bits let you represent 00, 01, 10 and 11. Therefore, four addresses are available in the host address space.

Before the calculations and expansions are explored, note that one of the benefits of this notation is that a single line is required in a routing table to describe all the addresses in an address space and helps reduce the size of routing tables. The aggregation of the network address space as a single address using CIDR notation allows a combination of two or more networks or subnets to be formed into a larger network for routing purposes, also known as a supernet.

CIDR notation allows you to calculate the IP address range, the netmask, and the total number of addresses available for host addresses. The netmask, also known as a subnet mask, may be derived from the CIDR notation as follows:

1. Convert the IP address part to binary notation, with 8-bit parts (octets).
2. Take the leading bits from 1 to the network prefix and convert these bits to ones.
3. Convert the remaining bits to zeroes.
4. Convert the resultant binary string to decimal format.

The number of addresses available for host addresses may be derived using the formula 2^{32-n}, where n is the network prefix. In OCI, the networking service reserves the first IP, known as the network address; the last IP, known as the broadcast address; as well as the first host address in the CIDR range, known as the subnet default gateway address; so the actual usable number of addresses in a VCN is $2^{32-n}-3$. Consequently, when OCI assigns addresses, the first allocated address ends with .2 because the network and default gateway addresses end with a .0 and .1 respectively.

The first IP address in the range may be derived from the CIDR notation as follows:

1. Convert the IP address part to binary notation, with 8-bit parts (octets).
2. Convert the host identifier portion into zeroes.

3. Prefix the network identifier with the zeroed host identifier.
4. Convert the resultant binary string to decimal format.

The last IP address in the range may be derived from the CIDR notation as follows:

1. Convert the IP address part to binary notation, with 8-bit parts (octets).
2. Convert the host identifier portion into ones.
3. Prefix the network identifier with the converted host identifier.
4. Convert the resultant binary string to decimal format.

The CIDR block example mentioned earlier may therefore be expanded as follows:

```
CIDR: 192.168.0.0/30
Binary: 11000000.10101000.00000000.00000000
Network ID (First 30 bits): 11000000.10101000.00000000.000000
Host ID (Remaining 2 bits): 00
```

To calculate the netmask, convert the first 30 bits to ones because the network prefix is 30. The remaining 2 bits are zeroed. Convert the resultant string to decimal. Netmask=255.255.255.252.

```
Netmask in binary:  11111111.11111111.11111111.11111100
Netmask in decimal: 255     .255     .255     .252
```

Calculate the number of host addresses available. Remember that OCI networking service reserves three addresses, the first one and the last one in the range:

Number of host addresses = $2^{(32-30)}-3 = 2^2-3 = 4-3 = 1$

To calculate the first address available:

```
Network ID || ZERO (Host ID) = 11000000.10101000.00000000.00000000
First IP = 192.168.0.0
```

To calculate the last address available:

```
Network ID || ONES(Host ID) = 11000000.10101000.00000000.00000011
Last IP = 192.168.0.3
IPs: 192.168.0.0, 192.168.0.1, 192.168.0.2, 192.168.0.3
Reserved by Networking Service: 192.168.0.0, 192.168.0.1, 192.168.0.3
Usable IP: 192.168.0.2
```

Another example to illustrate this procedure considers a CIDR block recommended by Oracle for large VCNs:

```
CIDR: 172.16.0.0/12
Binary: 10101100.00010000.00000000.00000001
Network ID (First 12 bits): 10101100.0001
Host ID (Remaining 20 bits): 0000.00000000.00000001
```

To calculate the netmask, convert the first 12 bits to ones because the network prefix is 12. The remaining 20 bits are zeroed. Convert the resultant string to decimal. Netmask=255.240.0.0.

```
Netmask in binary:  11111111.11110000.00000000.00000000
Netmask in decimal: 255     .240     .0       .0
```

To calculate the number of host addresses available:

```
Number of host addresses = 2^(32-12)-3 = 2^20-3 = 1048576-3 =1048573
```

To calculate the first address available:

```
Network ID || ZERO (Host ID) = 10101100.00010000.00000000.00000000
First IP = 172.16.0.0
```

To calculate the last address available:

```
Network ID || ONES(Host ID) = 10101100.00011111.11111111.11111111
Last IP = 172.31.255.255
IP range: 172.16.0.0 - 172.31.255.255
Reserved by OCI Networking: 172.16.0.0, 172.16.0.1, 172.31.255.255
Usable IP range: 172.16.0.2 - 172.31.255.254
```

Exercise 3-1: Expand CIDR Notation

Given the CIDR block 10.1.0.0/24, answer the following questions.

1. What is the network prefix?

   ```
   24
   ```

2. What is the network identifier?

   First convert an address to 8-bit binary octets:

   ```
   00001010.00000001.00000000.00000000
   ```

   The first 24 bits are the network ID:

   ```
   00001010.00000001.00000000
   ```

3. What is the host identifier?

   ```
   00000000
   ```

4. Calculate the netmask. To calculate the netmask, convert the first 24 bits to ones because the network prefix is 24. The remaining 8 bits are zeroed. Convert the resultant string to decimal. Netmask=255.255.255.0.

   ```
   Netmask in binary:  11111111.11111111.11111111.00000000
   Netmask in decimal: 255     .255     .255     .0
   ```

5. Calculate the number of host addresses available for your instances in this address space. Remember that OCI networking service reserves three addresses, the first two and the last one in the range:

   ```
   Host addresses available = 2^(32-24)-3 = 2^8-3 = 256-3 =253
   ```

6. What is the IP address range represented by this CIDR block? Calculate the first and last IPs to determine the range.

   To calculate the first address available:

```
Network ID || ZERO (Host ID) = 00001010.00000001.00000000.00000000
First IP = 10.1.0.0
```

   To calculate the last address available:

```
Network ID || ONES(Host ID) = 00001010.00000001.00000000.11111111
Last IP = 10.1.0.255
IP range: 10.1.0.0 - 10.1.0.255
Reserved by OCI Networking: 10.1.0.0, 10.1.0.1, 10.1.0.255
Usable IP range: 10.1.0.2 - 10.1.0.254
```

CAUTION OCI has reserved the CIDR block 169.254.0.0/16 and it may not be assigned to your VCNs. These addresses are used by various OCI services, including instance metadata queries and iSCSI connections to storage volumes.

Virtual Cloud Networks

Figure 3-1 presents a shell architecture to contextualize various networking components and their interactions with other OCI and non-OCI entities discussed next.

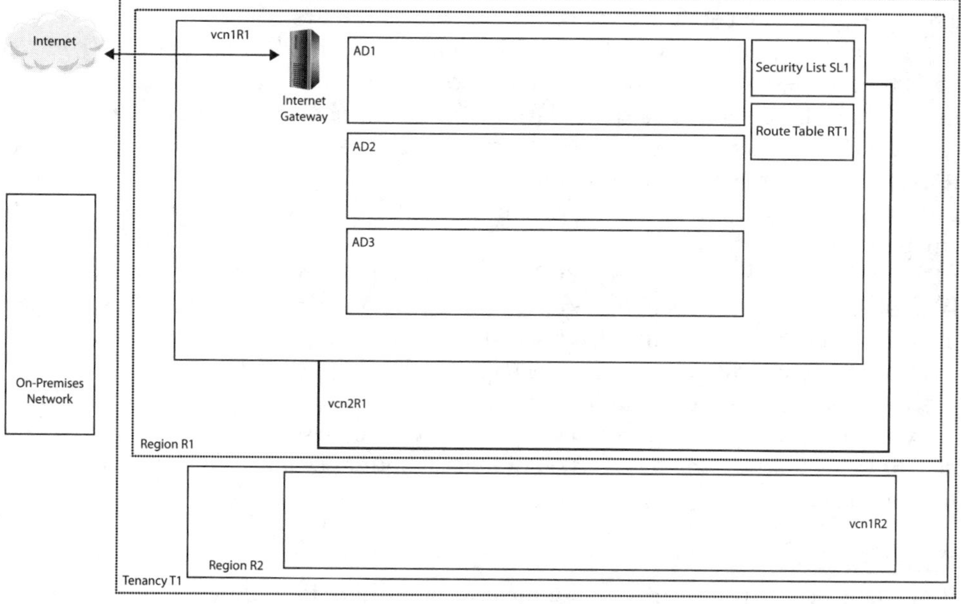

Figure 3-1 Networking concepts

First IP	Last IP	CIDR
10.0.0.0	10.255.255.255	10.0.0.0/8 or 10/8
172.16.0.0	172.31.255.255	172.16.0.0/12 or 172.16/12
192.168.0.0	192.168.255.255	192.168.0.0/16 or 192.168/16

Table 3-1 Private Address Space

At the highest level of abstraction, there are three entities: the Internet, your on-premises network, and your tenancy. Tenancy T1 is hosted in two regions, R1 and R2. These could be the us-ashburn-1 and uk-london-1 regions for example. Region R1 comprises three availability domains: AD1–3. These could be US-ASHBURN-AD-1, US-ASHBURN-AD-2, and US-ASHBURN-AD-3. Remember that ADs are physical data centers in geographically discrete locations connected by high-speed networks.

A virtual cloud network (VCN) is functionally equivalent to an on-premises network and is a private network running on Oracle networking equipment in several data centers. A VCN is a regional resource that spans all ADs in a single region and resides in a compartment. Multiple VCNs may be created in a given compartment.

Figure 3-1 shows three VCNs: vcn1R1 and vcn2R1 created in region R1, and vcn1R2 created in region R2. VCNs require several other networking resources, including subnets, gateways, security lists, and route tables in order to function. VCN resources may reside in different compartments from the VCN.

When a VCN is created through the console, one of the first decisions to be made is to specify a single contiguous IPv4 CIDR block. If you elect to create a VCN plus related resources through the console, the CIDR block of 10.0.0.0/16 is assigned by default. This specifies a range of over 65,000 addressable IP addresses.

The network prefix of the VCN CIDR block is permitted to range from /16 (over 65,000 addresses) to /30 (four host addresses, but three are reserved so only one is usable). Oracle recommends using one of the private IP address ranges specified in IETF RFC1918, section 3, where the Internet Assigned Numbers Authority (IANA) has reserved three IP blocks for private internets as per Table 3-1. This is to guarantee that this private address space is unique within your enterprise and these are not assigned to any public routable hosts.

The CIDR block assigned to a VCN represents a range of continuous or contiguous IP addresses. If you connect your VCN to other networks such as other VCNs (the act of connecting them is called *VCN peering*) or to your on-premises network, you must ensure that the CIDR blocks do not overlap. In other words, OCI will disallow network peering if there is a risk of IP address collisions.

When a VCN is created, three mandatory networking resources are created. You get a default route table, security list, and set of DHCP options created. The following subsections offer summaries of these resources.

Route Tables

Route tables contain rules that determine how network traffic coming in or leaving subnets in your VCN is routed via OCI gateways or specially configured compute instances. The default route table created when you create a VCN has no routing rules. You can add rules to the empty default route table or add your own new route tables.

Security Lists

Security lists contain firewall rules for all the compute instances using the subnet. Ingress and egress rules specify whether certain types of traffic are permitted into and out of the VCN respectively. The traffic type is based on the protocol and port and a rule can be either stateful or stateless. Stateful rules allow connection tracking and are the default, but stateless is recommended if you have high traffic volumes. Stateful rules with connection tracking allow response traffic to leave your network without the need to explicitly define an egress rule to match an ingress rule. Stateless rules, however, do not permit response traffic to leave your network unless an egress rule is defined. One of the ingress rules in the default security list allows traffic from anywhere to instances using the subnet on TCP port 22. This supports incoming SSH traffic and is useful for connecting to Linux compute instances.

DHCP Options

DHCP services provide configuration information to compute instance at boot time. You can influence only a subset of the DHCP service offerings by setting DHCP Options. These operate at a subnet level but in the absence of multiple subnet-level DHCP Options, the default set applies to all compute instances created in the VCN.

Subnets

A subnet is a portion of your network or VCN that comprises a contiguous CIDR block that is a subset of the VCN CIDR block. When a VCN plus related resources is created through the console in a region with three ADs, three subnets are also automatically created, one per AD with the default non-overlapping CIDR blocks of 10.0.0.0/24, 10.0.1.0/24, and 10.0.2.0/24. These blocks specify a range of 256 addresses per subnet. This leaves over 64,000 addresses from the VCN CIDR block that may be allocated to new subnets in your VCN. The CIDR blocks allocated to subnets must not overlap with one another. Regional subnets are also available and span all ADs in a region.

Figure 3-2 shows a new subnet that will be created in the Lab VCN in the Lab compartment, in the US-ASHBURN-AD-1 AD with the CIDR block 10.0.5.0/28. This is acceptable because this is a subset of the CIDR block 10.0.0.0/16 assigned to the VCN. If the CIDR block format is invalid, some validation checking is performed and you are informed if there are problems. If the CIDR validation check passes, you see the IP range listed below the CIDR block you entered, similar to this: Specified IP addresses: 10.0.5.0–10.0.5.15 (16 IP addresses).

If you try to create a subnet with a CIDR block that overlaps with an existing subnet CIDR block in the same VCN, you get a message similar to this:

```
InvalidParameter - The requested CIDR 10.0.4.0/24 is invalid:
subnet ocid1.subnet.oc1.iad.aaaaaaa…j3axq with
CIDR 10.0.4.0/24 overlaps with this CIDR.
```

Another key decision to be made when creating a subnet is whether it will be private or public. Public IP addresses are prohibited for instances using private subnets, while public subnets allow instances with public IP addresses. Use public subnets if you require resources using the subnet to be reachable from the Internet; otherwise, use private subnets.

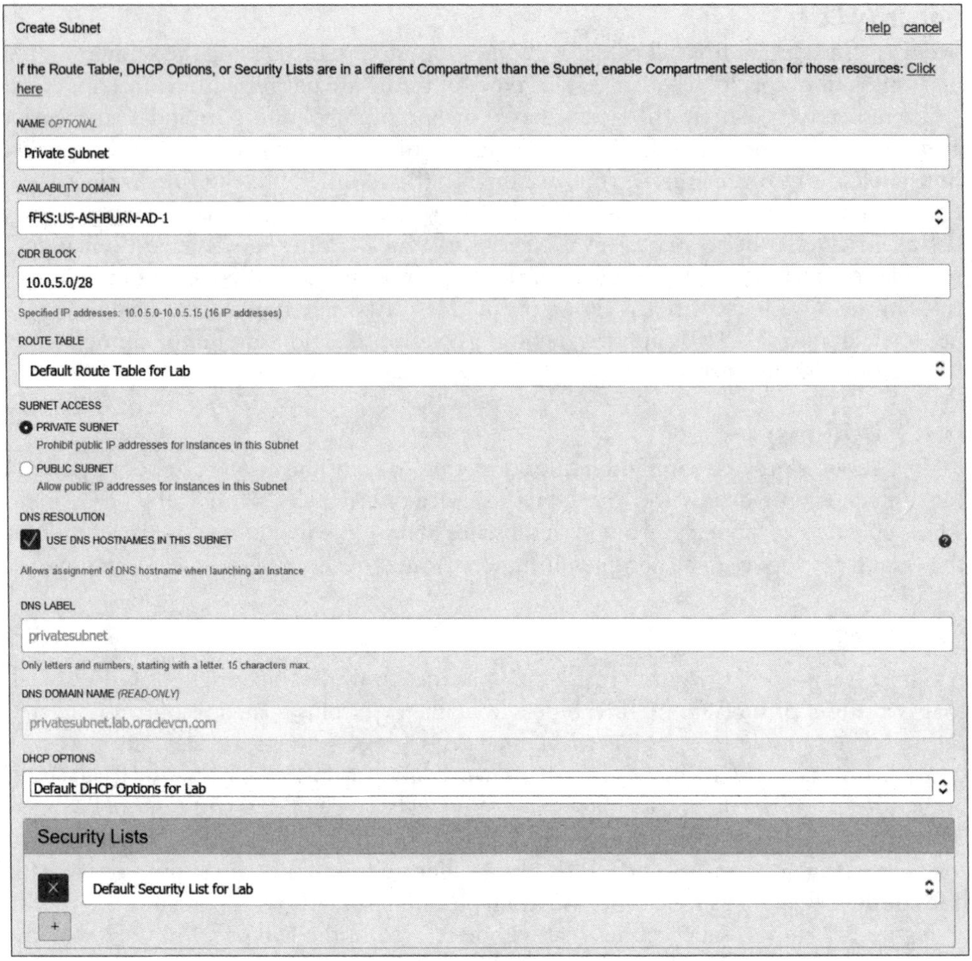

Create Subnet help cancel

If the Route Table, DHCP Options, or Security Lists are in a different Compartment than the Subnet, enable Compartment selection for those resources: Click here

NAME *OPTIONAL*

Private Subnet

AVAILABILITY DOMAIN

fFkS:US-ASHBURN-AD-1

CIDR BLOCK

10.0.5.0/28

Specified IP addresses: 10.0.5.0-10.0.5.15 (16 IP addresses)

ROUTE TABLE

Default Route Table for Lab

SUBNET ACCESS

PRIVATE SUBNET
Prohibit public IP addresses for Instances in this Subnet

PUBLIC SUBNET
Allow public IP addresses for Instances in this Subnet

DNS RESOLUTION

USE DNS HOSTNAMES IN THIS SUBNET

Allows assignment of DNS hostname when launching an Instance

DNS LABEL

privatesubnet

Only letters and numbers, starting with a letter. 15 characters max.

DNS DOMAIN NAME *(READ-ONLY)*

privatesubnet.lab.oraclevcn.com

DHCP OPTIONS

Default DHCP Options for Lab

Security Lists

Default Security List for Lab

Figure 3-2 Creating a subnet

NOTE A discussion of private and public IP addresses as well as vNICs straddles the realms of both networking and compute instances. The physical servers in OCI data centers have physical NICs that are assigned IP addresses. The OCI hypervisor software creates and manages virtual NICs (vNICs), which may be thought of as residing in a subnet rather than belonging to a compute instance. A compute instance receives a primary vNIC from the subnet in which the compute instance is created and that vNIC is allocated a private IP address that is associated with the instance until the instance is terminated. Secondary vNICs may be added to the compute instance and public and private IP addresses may be associated with these vNICs.

vNICs

The OCI networking service manages the association between virtual NICs (vNICs) and physical NICs on servers in OCI data centers. A vNIC resides in a subnet and is allocated to a compute instance, thus allowing the instance to connect to the subnet's VCN. Upon launch of a compute instance, a private, unremovable vNIC is assigned to the instance and allocated a private IP address (discussed next). Secondary vNICs can be assigned to and removed from an existing instance at any time. A secondary vNIC may reside in any subnet in the VCN as long as it is in the same AD as the primary vNIC. Each vNIC has an OCID, resides in a subnet, and includes the following:

- A primary private IP address from the vNIC's subnet, automatically allocated by OCI network services or specified by you upon instance creation.
- A maximum of 31 optional secondary private IPv4 addresses from the vNIC's subnet, chosen either automatically or by you. For each of these optional secondary private vNICs, you can choose to have OCI network services create and assign a public IPv4 address.
- An optional DNS hostname for each private IP address (discussed later in this chapter).
- A media access control (MAC) address, which is a unique device identifier assigned to a NIC.
- A VLAN tag optionally used by bare metal instances.
- A flag to enable or check the source and destination listed in the header of each network packet traversing the vNIC, dropping those that do not conform to the accepted source or destination address.

vNIC metadata may be queried from within a compute instance using this URL: http://169.254.169.254/opc/v1/vnics/. The following example shows the vNIC metadata returned by this URL query from a compute instance with a primary private vNIC as well as details on the IP addresses assigned to all its network interfaces:

```
$ curl http://169.254.169.254/opc/v1/vnics/
[ {"vnicId" : "ocid1.vnic.oc1.iad…ph6yjq",
  "privateIp" : "10.0.0.2",
  "vlanTag" : 1413,
  "macAddr" : "02:00:17:00:68:79",
  "virtualRouterIp" : "10.0.0.1",
  "subnetCidrBlock" : "10.0.0.0/24"} ]

$ ip addr
1: lo: <LOOPBACK,UP,LOWER_UP> mtu 65536
qdisc noqueue state UNKNOWN group default qlen 1000

    link/loopback 00:00:00:00:00:00 brd 00:00:00:00:00:00
    inet 127.0.0.1/8 scope host lo
       valid_lft forever preferred_lft forever
2: ens3: <BROADCAST,MULTICAST,UP,LOWER_UP> mtu 9000 qdisc mq state UP group
default qlen 1000
    link/ether 02:00:17:00:68:79 brd ff:ff:ff:ff:ff:ff
    inet 10.0.0.2/24 brd 10.0.0.255 scope global dynamic ens3
       valid_lft 75336sec preferred_lft 75336sec
```

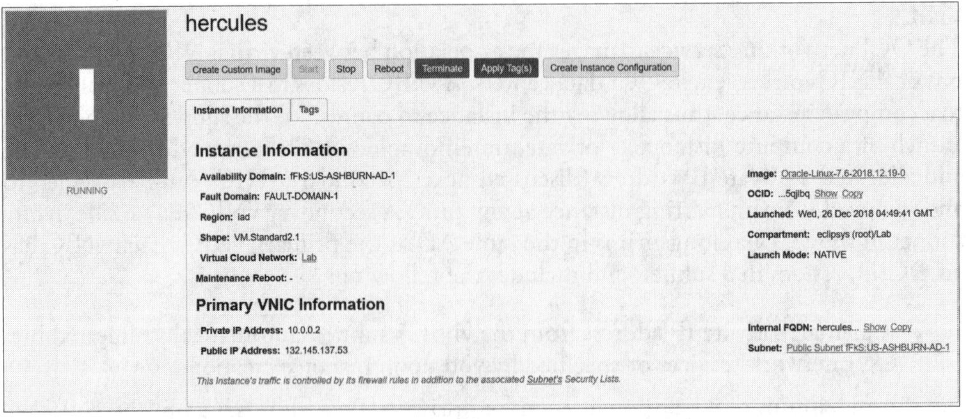

Figure 3-3 Compute instance network information

The vNIC has an OCID. The private IP address is 10.0.0.2. There are two network devices listed, a standard loopback adapter and the vNIC labeled ens3 to which the private IP address has been attached. Note the MAC address of ens3 is identical to the macAddr field returned by the metadata query. The private IP address is also in the subnet CIDR block.

Figure 3-3 shows the instance information from the console for this example compute instance. While the private IP address matches the private IP field returned by the earlier metadata query, the console also shows the public IP address: 132.145.137.53. This is the IP address used to SSH to the instance over the public Internet, yet it does not appear to be part of the local networking setup of the instance. The public IP object is actually assigned to a private IP object on the instance.

Private IP Addresses

An OCI private IP address object has an OCID and consists of a private IPv4 address and an optional DNS hostname. Each compute instance is provided a primary private IP object upon launch via the DHCP service. The private IP address cannot be removed from the instance and is terminated when the instance is terminated. As discussed in the earlier section on vNICs, you may choose to add secondary vNICs to your instance, each of which has a primary private IP object to which you can optionally assign a public IP object as long as that vNIC belongs to a public subnet.

A secondary private IP may be optionally added after an instance has launched and must come from the CIDR block of the subnet of the respective private vNIC. A secondary private IP may be moved from its vNIC on one compute instance to a vNIC on another instance as long as both vNICs belong to the same subnet. Any public IP assigned to the secondary private IP moves with it.

Public IP Addresses

A public IP address is an IPv4 address that is accessible or routable from anywhere on the Internet. Direct communication from the Internet to an instance is enabled by assigning a public IP address to a vNIC in a public subnet. An OCI public IP is defined as an object that consists of a public IPv4 address assigned by OCI Networking service, an OCID, and several properties depending on the type. There are two types of public IP addresses:

- *Ephemeral addresses* are transient and are optionally assigned to an instance at launch or afterwards to a secondary vNIC. These persist reboot cycles of an instance and can be unassigned at any time resulting in the object being deleted. Once the instance is terminated, the address is unassigned and automatically deleted. Ephemeral public IPs cannot be moved to a different private IP. The scope of an ephemeral IP is limited to one AD.
- *Reserved addresses* are persistent and exist independently of an instance. These may be assigned to an instance, unassigned back to the tenancy's pool of reserved public IPs at any time, and assigned to a different instance. The scope of the reserved public IP is regional and can be assigned to any private IP in any AD in a region.

EXAM TIP Several prerequisites must be met before an instance can be accessed from the Internet. The subnet it is created in must be a public subnet, with appropriately configured route tables and security lists, located in a VCN with an Internet gateway.

Public IP addresses in your VCNs are allocated from several CIDR blocks in each region. Table 3-2 lists the CIDR blocks that should be whitelisted on your on-premises or virtual networks in other clouds to support connectivity. This table is not exhaustive and lists CIDR blocks of public IPs for five OCI regions.

us-ashburn-1	us-phoenix-1	uk-london-1	ca-toronto-1	eu-frankfurt-1
129.213.8.0/21	129.146.0.0/21	132.145.8.0/21	132.145.96.0/21	130.61.8.0/21
129.213.16.0/20	129.146.8.0/22	132.145.16.0/20	132.145.104.0/22	130.61.16.0/20
129.213.32.0/19	129.146.16.0/20	132.145.32.0/19		130.61.32.0/19
129.213.64.0/18	129.146.32.0/19	132.145.64.0/23		130.61.64.0/19
129.213.128.0/18	129.146.64.0/18			130.61.96.0/23
129.213.192.0/21	129.146.128.0/19			130.61.104.0/21
132.145.128.0/19	129.146.160.0/20			130.61.112.0/20
132.145.160.0/20	129.146.208.0/21			

Table 3-2 OCI Public IP CIDR Blocks

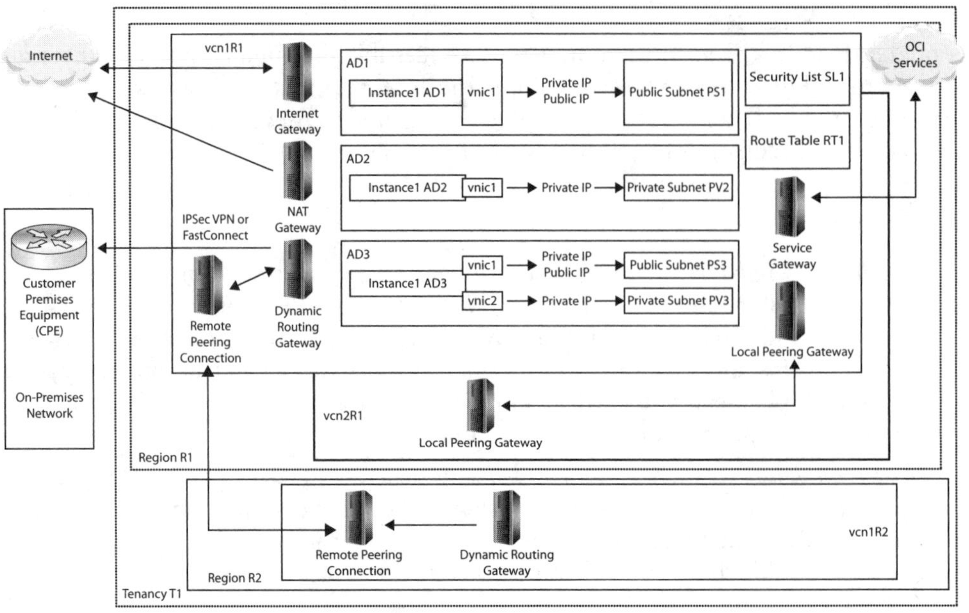

Figure 3-4 OCI networking components

Figure 3-4 adds some detail to Figure 3-1 to illustrate the interactions between the primary OCI networking components. Instance1 AD1 is a compute instance running in AD1. It has a single vNIC with a private IP from the public subnet PS1, which has also been allocated a public IP address. Instance1 AD2 has a single vNIC with a private IP from the private subnet PV2. No public IP can be assigned to this vNIC because it is on a private subnet. Instance1 AD3 has two vNICs. The primary vNIC (vnic1) belongs to public subnet, PS3, and has both a private and public IP. The secondary vNIC(vnic2) has a private IP from the private subnet PV3. All subnets—PS1, PV2, PS3, and PV3—are non-overlapping and contained within the CIDR block of the VCN called vcn1R1. The security list SL1 and route table RT1 belong to the VCN and may be used by all networking resources within the VCN. The next section discusses the various OCI gateways shown in Figure 3-4.

EXAM TIP A vNIC on a public subnet is automatically assigned a public IP. It is not mandatory and may be removed or de-assigned.

Gateways

OCI uses the terminology of virtual routers and gateways interchangeably and has created several novel virtual networking components.

Internet Gateway

An Internet gateway is attached to any new VCN. It allows instances with public IP addresses to be reached over the Internet and for these instances to connect to the Internet. There is very limited configuration of this virtual router and your control is limited to the `create`, `delete`, `get`, `list`, and `update` commands. Here is an example of the OCI CLI `get` command on the Internet gateway. Internet access at a VCN level may be disabled by updating the `is-enabled` property of the Internet gateway to false.

```
# oci network internet-gateway get --ig-id
ocid1.internetgateway.oc1.iad...wwgyra{
  "data": {"compartment-id": "ocid1.compartment.oc1...zlh3iq",

    "display-name": "Internet Gateway Lab",
    "id": "ocid1.internetgateway.oc1.iad...wwgyra",
    "is-enabled": true,
    "lifecycle-state": "AVAILABLE",
    "vcn-id": "ocid1.vcn.oc1.iad...hr6y4a"}

(output truncated for brevity)
```

NAT Gateway

A network address translation (NAT) gateway allows instances with no public IP addresses to access the Internet while protecting the instance from incoming traffic from the Internet. When an instance makes a request for a network resource outside the VCN, the NAT gateway makes the request on behalf of the instance to the Internet and forwards the response back to the instance.

NOTE Instances with no public IP addresses may still be accessed directly from other internal instances or bastion hosts that have a route to the private IP address of the instance.

When a gateway is created in a specific compartment, a public IP address is assigned to it. This is the IP address that resources on the Internet see as the address of the incoming request.

```
$ oci network nat-gateway list
--compartment-id ocid1.compartment.oc1..zlh3iq
{"data": [{
      "block-traffic": false,
      "compartment-id": "ocid1.compartment.oc1..zlh3iq",
      "display-name": "NatGateway1",
      "id": "ocid1.natgateway.oc1.iad..zwccqya",
      "lifecycle-state": "AVAILABLE",
      "nat-ip": "129.213.180.128",
      "vcn-id": "ocid1.vcn.oc1.iad..hr6y4a"}]}

(output truncated for brevity)
```

A rule must be added to the NAT gateway in the route table of a specific subnet, which is typically private. In this example, a rule is added to route table RT_PV2 to route traffic to the NAT gateway. This route table is attached to a private subnet named pv2.

```
$ oci network route-table get --rt-id
cid1.routetable.oc1.iad..127biq
{"data": { "compartment-id": "ocid1.compartment.oc1..zlh3iq",

    "display-name": "RT_PV2",
    "id": "ocid1.routetable.oc1.iad..27biq",
    "lifecycle-state": "AVAILABLE",
    "route-rules": [{
        "cidr-block": "0.0.0.0/0",
        "destination": "0.0.0.0/0",
        "destination-type": "CIDR_BLOCK",
        "network-entity-id": "ocid1.natgateway.oc1.iad..wccqya"}],
    "vcn-id": "ocid1.vcn.oc1.iad..hr6y4a"}

(output truncated for brevity)
```

With a NAT gateway and route rule in place, instances created in the private subnet can access resources on the Internet, even though they have private IP addresses.

NOTE If there are overlapping rules in a route table, the more selective rules take precedence over the non-selective 0.0.0.0/0 CIDR block.

Dynamic Routing Gateway

Remember that when working with any cloud infrastructure you are simply connecting from your office or home computers to cloud resources through some network connection. There are several ways to connect on-premises networks to OCI, including the following:

- Direct connection over the public Internet
- Connection through customer-premises equipment (CPE) over an IPSec VPN tunnel over the public Internet
- Connection through CPE over a FastConnect private connection

Consider Instance1 AD1 in Figure 3-4. You could connect to this instance directly over the public Internet from your on-premises network using an encrypted connection. OCI instances run either Linux or Windows operating systems. You can connect to Instance1 AD1 from your on-premises network using SSH or RDP protocols depending on whether your instance is running Linux or Windows and the security list's ingress rules permit SSH or RDP connections from your location. Your commands are encrypted before leaving the on-premises network, transmitted over public Internet connections, decrypted, and executed on the instance.

There are several concerns with this approach. Primarily, the security concern is that sensitive data should not be transported over public Internet connections, and the performance concern is that network latency over the public Internet can be erratic and unpredictable.

To alleviate these concerns, you may set up a connection between your on-premises network's edge router (CPE or customer-premises equipment) and an OCI component known as a Dynamic Routing Gateway (DRG). A DRG is a VCN-level device that extends your on-premises network into your VCN. It is important to think of a DRG as a gateway that provides a private path between discrete networks. Figure 3-4 shows a DRG in vcn1R1 in region R1 connecting to the CPE at the edge of the on-premises network.

Instance1 AD2 has only a private IP address and is reachable by other instances in the same private subnet or in other subnets in your region and tenancy, assuming appropriate security lists are in place, but it is not reachable over the Internet. Instance1 AD3 can connect to Instance1 AD1 through either a public or private IP address. If the connection is through the public IP, then traffic will flow from Instance1 AD3 to the Internet gateway, which routes it to Instance1 AD1 without sending the traffic over the Internet. The shorter and more secure route would be for these instances to communicate with each other over their private IP addresses.

The network path between the CPE and DRG can be a set of redundant IPSec VPN tunnels or over FastConnect. IPSec VPNs offer end-to-end encrypted communications thereby improving security. The tunnels still run over public networks, which makes them more affordable but less secure than using FastConnect. When an IPSec VPN is set up, two tunnels are created for redundancy.

OCI provides FastConnect as a means to create a dedicated high-speed private connection between on-premises networks and OCI. FastConnect provides consistent, predictable, secure, and reliable performance. FastConnect supports the following uses:

- Private peering extends your on-premises network into a VCN and may be used to create a hybrid cloud. On-premises connections can be made to the private IP addresses of instances as if they were coming from instances in the VCN as in the connection between Instance1 AD1 and Instance1 AD3 described earlier. Private peering can also occur between instances in VCNs in other regions.
- Public peering allows you to connect from resources outside the VCN, such as on-premises network, to public OCI services, such as object storage, without traversing the Internet over FastConnect.

FastConnect is actualized using several connectivity models:

- Colocation with Oracle allows direct physical cross-connects between your network and Oracle's FastConnect edge devices.
- Using an Oracle Network Provider or Exchange Partner, you can set up a FastConnect connection from your network to the provider or partner network that has a high bandwidth connection into Oracle's FastConnect edge devices.
- Using a third-party provider that is not a FastConnect partner but is typically an MPLS VPN provider who sets up a private or dedicated circuit between your on-premises network and Oracle's FastConnect edge devices.

EXAM TIP Border Gateway Protocol (BGP) is supported with FastConnect but not IPSec VPN connecting external networks to your VCN.

When a DRG object is created, it is assigned an OCID. DRGs may be attached to or detached from a VCN. A VCN can have only one DRG attached at a time. A DRG can be attached to only one VCN at a time, but may be detached from one VCN and attached to another. A DRG may also be used to provide a private path that does not traverse the Internet between VCNs in different regions. Once a DRG is attached to a VCN, the route tables for the VCN or specific subnets must be updated to allow traffic to flow to the DRG.

NOTE An IPSec VPN may be used to connect to your OCI-Classic IP network, or you may open a service request (SR) with Oracle to provision a connection between your OCI-C IP network's private gateway and the DRG attached to your VCN. Support of the OCI-C to OCI connection has several limitations, including the use of only private IP addresses and non-overlapping CIDR blocks, and the fact that this connection is not available in all regions. An IPSec VPN may also be used to connect to another cloud provider using a Libreswan VM as the CPE.

Service Gateway

A service gateway allows OCI instances to access OCI services (which are not part of your VCN) using a private network path on OCI network fabric without needing to traverse the Internet. A service gateway gets an OCID and is a regional resource providing access to OCI services to the VCN where it resides without using an Internet or NAT gateway.

NOTE Service gateways initially allowed access to the object storage service discussed in detail in Chapter 5. Private access for PaaS was added next and, as OCI evolves, new services will be accessible via service gateways. If an instance with a public IP belongs to a VCN with an Internet gateway, and OCI services are accessed, the request is routed through the OCI fabric by the Internet gateway and not over the public Internet. The object storage service in each region is labeled using the region prefix. For example, the us-ashburn-1 and uk-london-1 regions are named OCI IAD Object Storage and OCI LHR Object Storage, respectively.

The steps to set up a working service gateway are as follows:

1. Create the service gateway in a VCN and compartment, and choose the services that will be accessed through the service gateway. For example, you may create a service gateway named SG1, which accesses the OCI Object Storage service in that region. The storage gateway is open for traffic by default upon creation but can be set to block traffic at any time.

Edit Route Rules help cancel

Important: For a route rule that targets a Private IP, you must first enable "Skip Source/Destination Check" on the VNIC that the Private IP is assigned to.

TARGET TYPE: Internet Gateway
DESTINATION CIDR BLOCK: 0.0.0.0/0
COMPARTMENT: Lab
eclipsys (root)/Lab
TARGET INTERNET GATEWAY: Internet Gateway Lab

TARGET TYPE: Service Gateway
DESTINATION SERVICE: OCI IAD Object Storage
COMPARTMENT: Lab
eclipsys (root)/Lab
TARGET SERVICE GATEWAY: SG1

+ Another Route Rule

Save

Figure 3-5 Route table rule for service gateway

2. Add a route table rule to direct traffic for a destination service to the target service gateway. For example, you can add a rule with the target type Service Gateway in the Lab compartment for all traffic to the destination: OCI Object Storage service to go through the SG1 gateway as per Figure 3-5. Prior to deleting the service gateway, you must first delete this route rule to avoid errors.
3. You may have to update the security list in your VCN to allow traffic associated with the chosen service. For example, the object storage service requires a stateful egress rule to allow HTTPS traffic.
4. The previous three steps will allow access to all resources in the VCN to access object storage. It is prudent to use IAM policies (discussed in Chapter 2) to limit access to specific object storage buckets. The following rule permits members of the ESC_DBAs group to manage the object storage bucket named DB_Backups.

```
Allow group ESC_DBAs to manage objects
in compartment Lab
where target.bucket.name='DB_Backups'
```

CAUTION The default security list created when a VCN is created contains a stateful egress rule that allows TCP traffic for all ports with destination type CIDR. When setting up a service gateway for object storage, an additional stateful rule is required with destination type service.

A good use case for the service gateway relates to reading and writing database backups to object storage from private networks. A database typically resides on a compute instance in a private subnet. You could back up the database to an object storage bucket without needing public IP addresses or access to the Internet by using a service gateway.

In the following example, an object storage bucket named DB_Backups has been created in the Lab compartment. Using the OCI CLI tool, the bucket is listed here:

```
$ oci os bucket list --compartment-id
ocid1.compartment.oc1..zlh3iq
{"data": [{"compartment-id": "ocid1.compartment.oc1..zlh3iq",
 "name": "DB_Backups",
 "namespace": "eclipsys",
 "time-created": "2019-01-03T06:51:01.394000+00:00"}
```

A 30GB file is created and copied to the bucket using the OCI CLI. The OCI instance has a public IP address and is on a VCN with functional Internet access through an Internet gateway but with no service gateway:

```
$ dd if=/dev/zero of=30GB_FILE count=30720 bs=1048576
30720+0 records in
30720+0 records out
32212254720 bytes (32 GB) copied, 579.236 s, 55.6 MB/s
$ ls -lrth
total 30G
-rw-rw-r--. 1 opc opc 30G Jan  6 02:10 30GB_FILE

$ time oci os object put --namespace eclipsys
-bn DB_Backups --file /home/opc/30GB_FILE
Upload ID: 5a3a233c-4024-2153-2104-528c9bd8a147
Split file into 240 parts for upload.
Uploading object  [####################################]  100%
real    10m41.131s
user    5m21.307s
sys     2m46.607s
```

The file upload operation takes just over ten minutes. The same test is performed with an instance with only a private IP in a private subnet in the same VCN with a service gateway named SG1:

```
$ oci network service-gateway list
--compartment-id ocid1.compartment.oc1..zlh3iq {
  "data": [{"block-traffic": false,
      "compartment-id": "ocid1.compartment.oc1..zlh3iq",
      "display-name": "SG1",
      "id": ocid1.servicegateway.oc1.iad..jzn3u2a",
      "lifecycle-state": "AVAILABLE",
      "services": [{"service-id": "ocid1.service.oc1.iad..yl3eaq",
                   "service-name": "OCI IAD Object Storage"}],
      "vcn-id": "ocid1.vcn.oc1.iad..hr6y4a"}]}

$ time oci os object put --namespace eclipsys
-bn DB_Backups --file /home/opc/30GB_FILE
(output truncated for brevity)
real    10m39.073s
```

Two interesting observations emerged from this test. First, the instance with the private IP successfully accessed the object storage bucket through the service gateway.

Second, the IO performance was almost identical, which makes sense because the Internet gateway in the first test routed the file transfer from the instance over internal OCI networks and not the public Internet, which is a similar path that the file traveled through the service gateway. Remember that without the service gateway, the instance with the private IP cannot see the object storage, but its IO performance is not negatively impacted by the service gateway.

Local Peering Gateway

You may create multiple VCNs with non-overlapping CIDR ranges in a region. Using the reserved IP blocks in Table 3-1, you may have vcn1R1 with CIDR 10.0.0.0/8 and vcn2R1 with CIDR 192.168.0.0/16, for example. Each VCN has zero or more public or private subnets per AD with zero or more compute instances with private IP addresses and possibly some with public IPs. An instance in one VCN can connect to another instance in the same VCN using either a public or private IP, but can connect only to the public IP of instances in different VCNs (as long as an Internet gateway, relevant route table entries, and security lists are in place).

A local peering gateway (LPG) allows VCNs in the same region, regardless of tenancy, to act as peers and supports instances in one VCN connecting to instances in another VCN using private IP addresses. This is known as local VCN peering and requires the following:

- Two VCNs in the same region with non-overlapping CIDR ranges
- A connected local peering gateway in each VCN
- Route table rules enabling traffic flow over the LPGs between specific subnets in each VCN
- Security lists egress and ingress rules controlling traffic between instances from each VCN

Figure 3-6 shows the VCN vcn1R1 in the Lab compartment with local peering set up with CIDR block: 192.168.0.0/16. This VCN is peered using LPG vcn1R1_LPG to another VCN with an advertised CIDR block: 10.0.0.0/16.

Remote Peering Connection

While local peering connects VCNs in the same region even across tenancy, remote peering connects VCNs in the same tenancy across regions. Remote peering allows instances in regionally separated VCNs to communicate using their private IP addresses. A DRG must be attached to each remote VCN to be peered. A remote peering connection (RPC) is created on the DRG in both regionally separated VCNs. One VCN is designated a requestor role while the other is the acceptor. The requestor initiates the

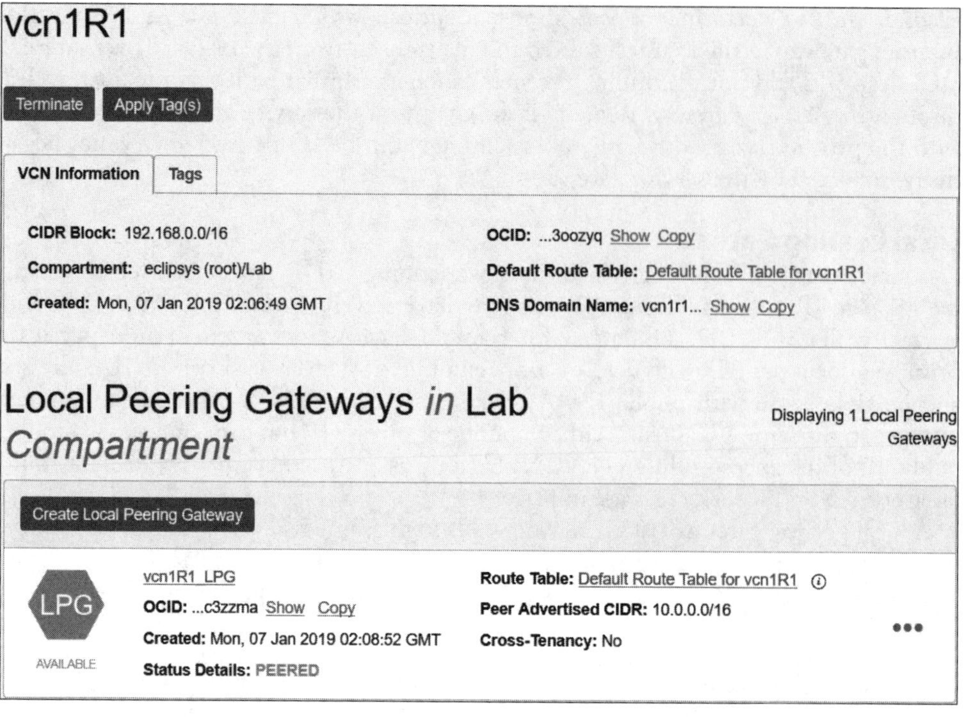

Figure 3-6 Local peering gateway

peering request and specifies the OCID of the RPC that belongs to the acceptor. You can have a maximum of ten RPCs per tenancy, as of this writing. Remote VCN peering requires the following:

- Two VCNs in the same tenancy that reside in different regions with non-overlapping CIDR ranges.
- A DRG attached to each VCN that will participate in the remote peering connection.
- A remote peering connection (RPC) component created on each DRG. The connection is enabled by the requesting VCN by supplying the OCID of the RPC of the accepting VCN.
- Route table rules enabling traffic flow over the DRGs between specific subnets in each VCN.
- Security lists with egress and ingress rules to control traffic between instances from each VCN.

Figure 3-7 shows the requesting RPC named RPC_vcn1R1-vcn1R2 with status: PEERED. This RPC is created as a component on the DRG named DRG_VCN1R1.

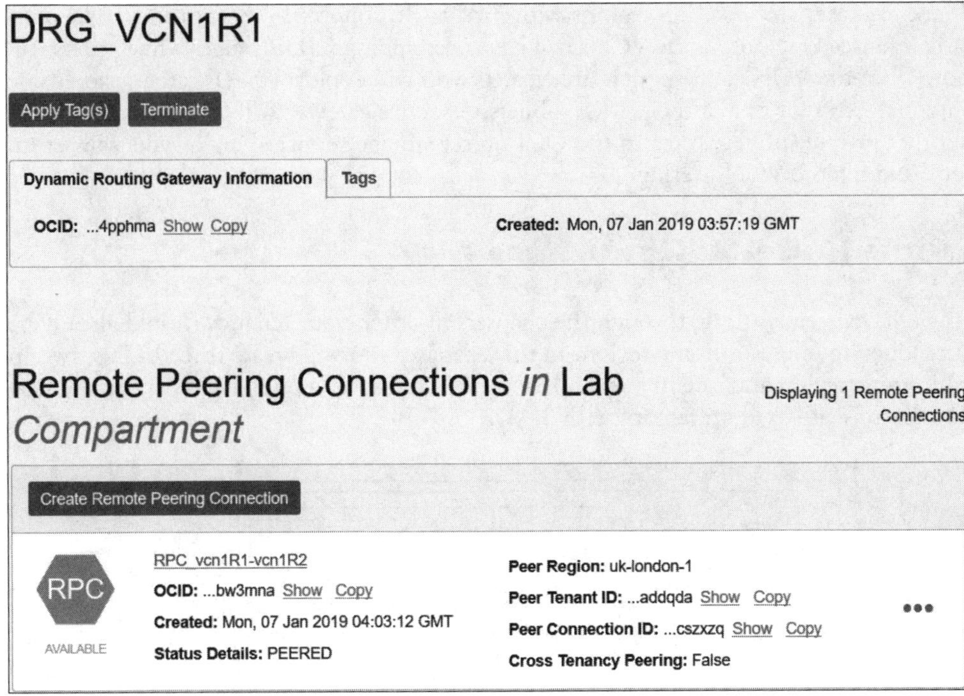

Figure 3-7 Remote peering connection

This configuration permits instances in vcn1R1 to communicate with instances in vcn1R2 using their private IP addresses.

CAUTION VCNs in a peering setup must have non-overlapping CIDR block ranges. In a local peering setup, a VCN may be peered with several other VCNs within the region. For example, vcn1R1 may be peered with vcn2R1 and vcn3R1. It is acceptable if vcn2R1 and vcn3R1 have overlapping CIDRs as long as the route table rules for the subnets in vcn1R1 route traffic to the intended peered VCN. In a remote peering setup, a VCN may be peered with multiple VCNs as long as there are no overlapping CIDRs. For example, vcn1R1 may be peered with vcn1R2 and vcn1R3 as long as there is no CIDR range overlap between vcn1R2 and vcn1R3.

Use Virtual Cloud Networks

The previous section provided a theoretical basis for VCN-related components. It is time to get your hands dirty. This section consists of five exercises designed to get you familiar with using virtual cloud networks. You will start by creating a number of VCNs with several private and public subnets in both your home and another region in your tenancy.

These exercises are based on regions with 3 ADs. To follow along, try to use two similarly resourced regions. Some VCNs will have overlapping CIDR ranges while others will not. Once the VCNs and subnets are created, you will deploy a NAT gateway to enable Internet access for one of the private subnets. A service gateway will be deployed to allow another private subnet access to the OCI object storage service. Finally, you will set up local and remote VCN peering.

Exercise 3-2: Create VCNs and Subnets

If you have been working through the chapters in order, your tenancy should already be subscribed to one non-home region. In this exercise, you will create three VCNs, two in your home region and one in a secondary region, and several public and private subnets. This exercise is based on regions with 3 ADs.

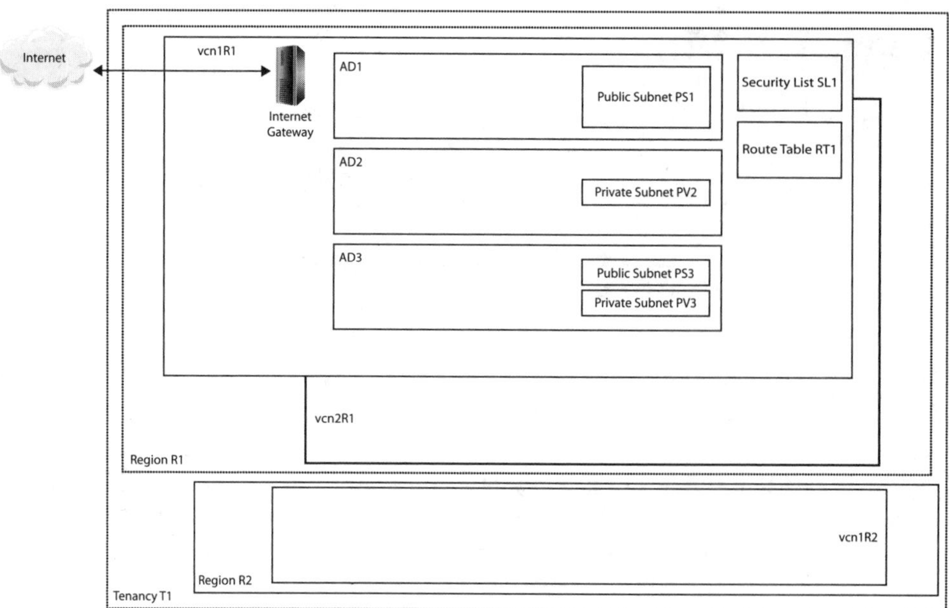

1. Sign in to the OCI console.
2. In your home region, navigate to Networking | Virtual Cloud Networks. Choose Create Virtual Cloud Network. Choose the compartment in your tenancy that will hold these networking components. The compartment used in the exercise is called Lab, but you should use a compartment that is meaningful in your environment. Provide a VCN name: vcn1R1. Choose Create Virtual Cloud Network Only. Provide a CIDR block for the VCN: 192.168.0.0/16. Leave the DNS options at the defaults, apply any relevant tags, and choose Create Virtual Cloud Network. After a few moments, your new barebones VCN is provisioned.

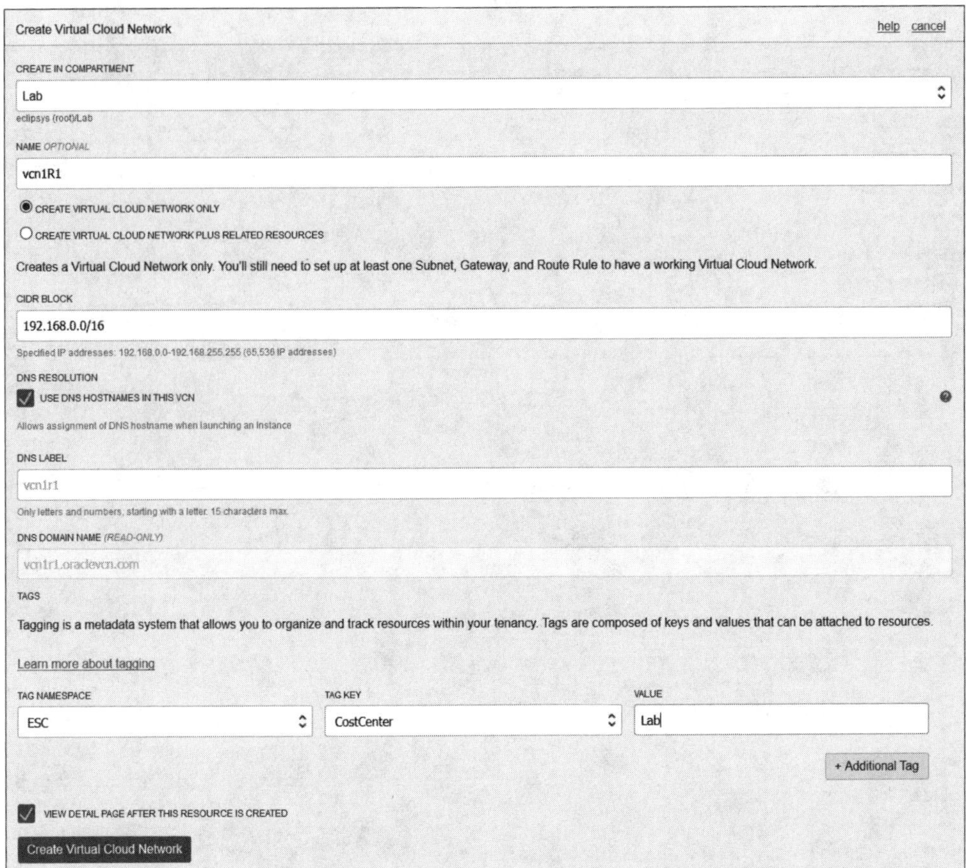

3. Choose the newly created VCN from Networking | Virtual Cloud Networks and choose Create Subnet. Provide a name: vcn1R1ps1. Choose the first AD in your region for this subnet—for example, fFkS:US-ASHBURN-AD-1. Provide a CIDR block for this subnet that must be a subset of the VCN CIDR range but must also not overlap with other subnets in the VCN—for example, 192.168.1.0/24. Choose the default route table for vcn1R1. For subnet access, choose Public Subnet. This is an important choice that cannot be updated later. The only subnet options that may be updated later are the subnet name, the DHCP options, route table, security lists, and tags. Leave the DNS, DHCP options, and security lists at defaults; apply any relevant tags; and choose Create. After a few moments, your subnet is provisioned. The fFks prefix to the AD is a tenancy-specific prefix allocated by OCI to keep track of which AD corresponds to which data center for each tenancy. This is required because OCI load balances tenancies across the ADs in a region randomly. In the same region, the data center that is called AD1 in your tenancy may be different from AD1 in another tenancy.

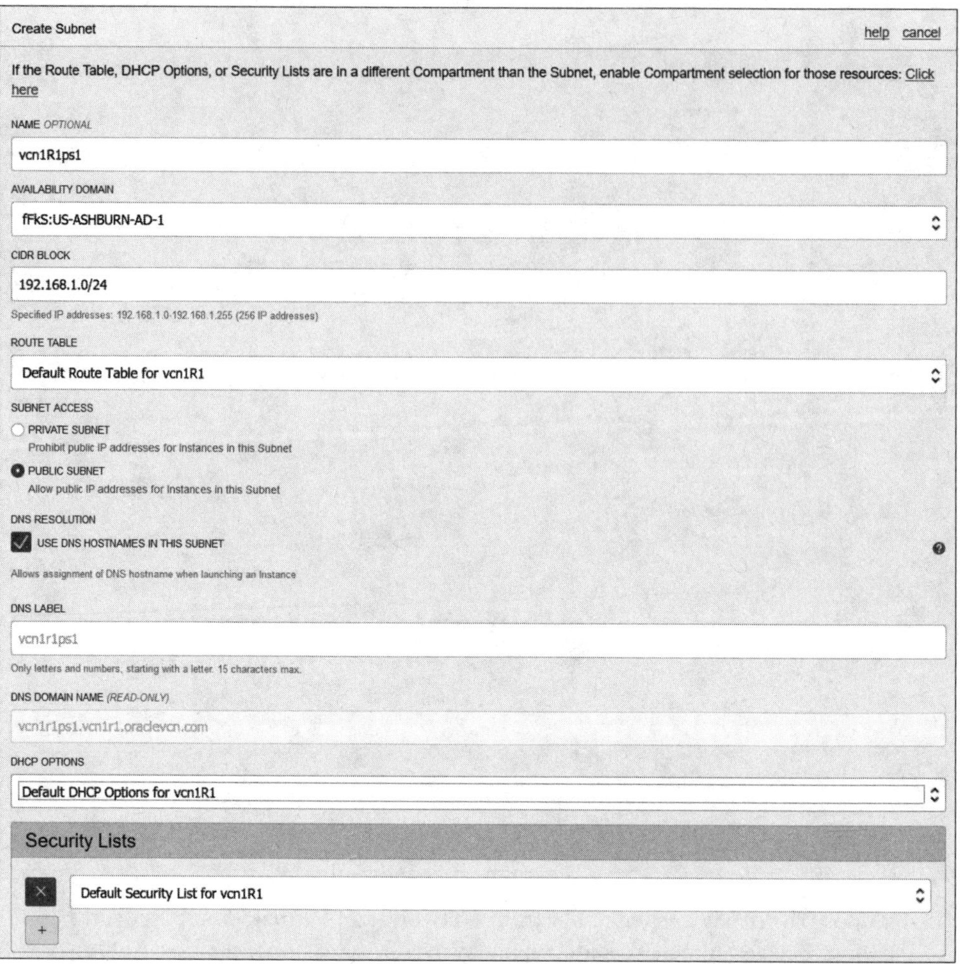

4. Repeat Steps 2 and 3 using the adjacent table data to create the three remaining subnets for vcn1R1, using the default route table, DHCP options, and security list. For vcn2R1 and vcn1R2, choose Create Virtual Cloud Network Plus Related Resources. Create vcn1R2 in your non-home region—for example, uk-london-1. The naming convention employed for subnets in this exercise references the AD number to which the subnet belongs.

VCN	CIDR Block	Subnet	Subnet CIDR Block	Subnet Access	AD
vcn1R1	192.168.0.0/16	vcn1R1ps1	192.168.1.0/24	Public	AD1
		vcn1R1pv2	192.168.2.0/24	Private	AD2
		vcn1R1ps3	192.168.3.0/24	Public	AD3
		vcn1R1pv3	192.168.5.0/24	Private	AD3

VCN	CIDR Block	Subnet	Subnet CIDR Block	Subnet Access	AD
vcn2R1	10.0.0.0/16	fFkS:<home region>-<AD-1>	10.0.0.0/24	Public	AD1
		fFkS:<home region>-<AD-2>	10.0.1.0/24	Public	AD2
		fFkS:<home region>-<AD-3>	10.0.2.0/24	Public	AD3
vcn1R2	10.0.0.0/16	fFkS:<non-home region>-<AD-1>	10.0.0.0/24	Public	AD1
		fFkS:<non-home region>-<AD-2>	10.0.1.0/24	Public	AD2
		fFkS:<non-home region>-<AD-3>	10.0.2.0/24	Public	AD3

5. Notice that with vcn2R1 and vcn1R2, because you chose Create Virtual Cloud Network Plus Related Resources, the CIDR block defaults to 10.0.0.0/16 and cannot be changed. Additionally, three public subnets (one in each AD) with CIDR blocks 10.0.0.0/24, 10.0.1.0/24, and 10.0.2.0/24 are provisioned.
6. In your home region, create an Internet gateway for vcn1R1. Navigate to Networking | Virtual Cloud Networks. Choose vcn1R1. Then click Internet Gateways in the Resources list on the left and choose Create Internet Gateway. Provide a name: Internet Gateway vcn1R1 and then optionally tag the resource and select Create Internet Gateway.

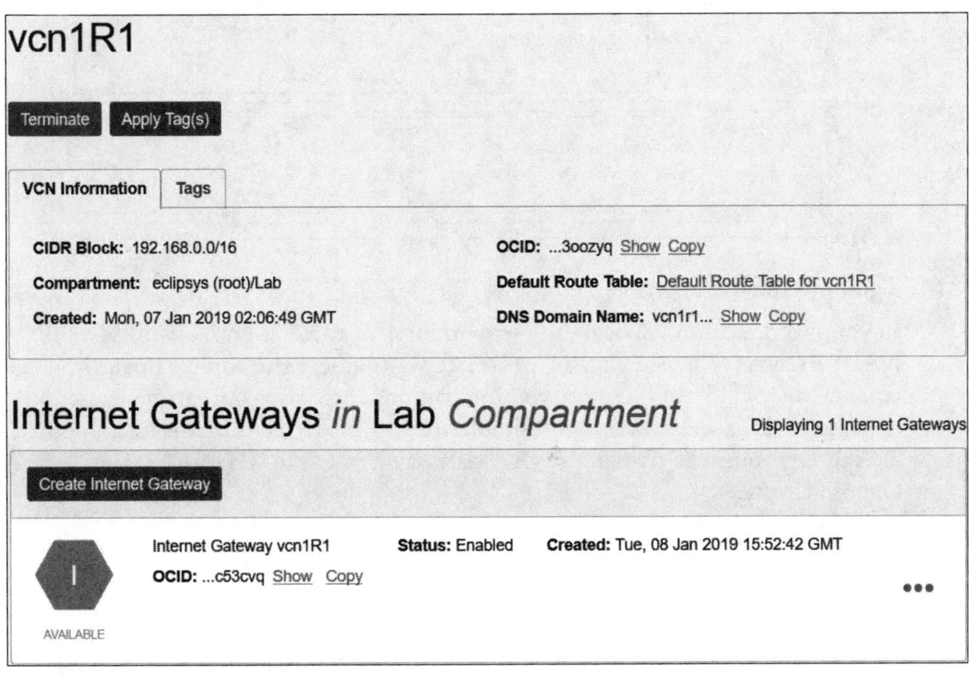

7. You should now have three VCNs, each with default route tables, security lists, and DHCP options. Each VCN created with related resources (vcn2R1 and vcn1R2) has three public subnets and one Internet gateway provisioned. The manually provisioned VCN (vcn1R1) has two private and two public subnets and one manually created Internet gateway.

Exercise 3-3: Deploy a NAT Gateway

This exercise builds on the infrastructure you created in Exercise 3-2. In this exercise, you will deploy a NAT gateway in VCN, vcn1R1, to enable outgoing Internet access for instances created in a private subnet: vcn1R1pv2.

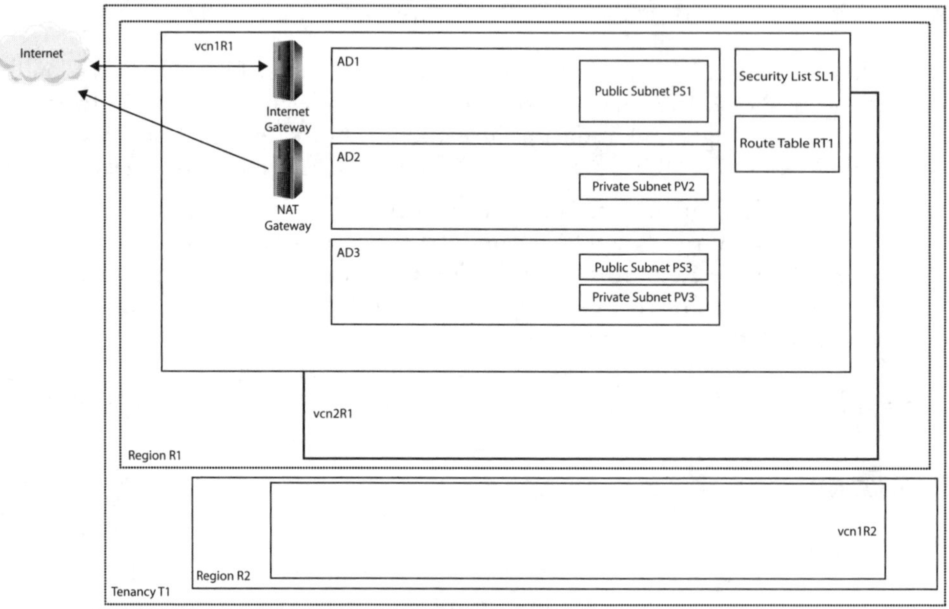

1. Sign in to the OCI console.
2. In your home region, navigate to Networking | Virtual Cloud Networks | vcnR1 | NAT Gateways. Choose Create NAT Gateway. Choose the compartment in your tenancy that will hold these networking components. The compartment used in the exercise is called Lab, but you should use a compartment that is meaningful in your environment. Provide a NAT Gateway name: vcn1R1-NAT-GW1. Choose Create.

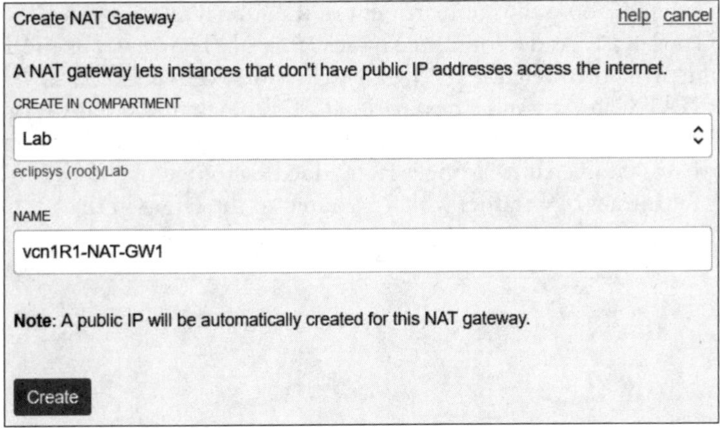

3. After a few moments, your gateway is created. A notification reminds you to add a route rule for any subnet that needs to use this NAT gateway and to ensure that the NAT gateway is in the AVAILABLE state. Note that once the NAT gateway is available, you can stop all traffic going to the Internet from private networks in the VCN by choosing the Block Traffic option on the NAT gateway. Also note the public IP address that has been allocated to the NAT gateway allowing it to access the Internet.

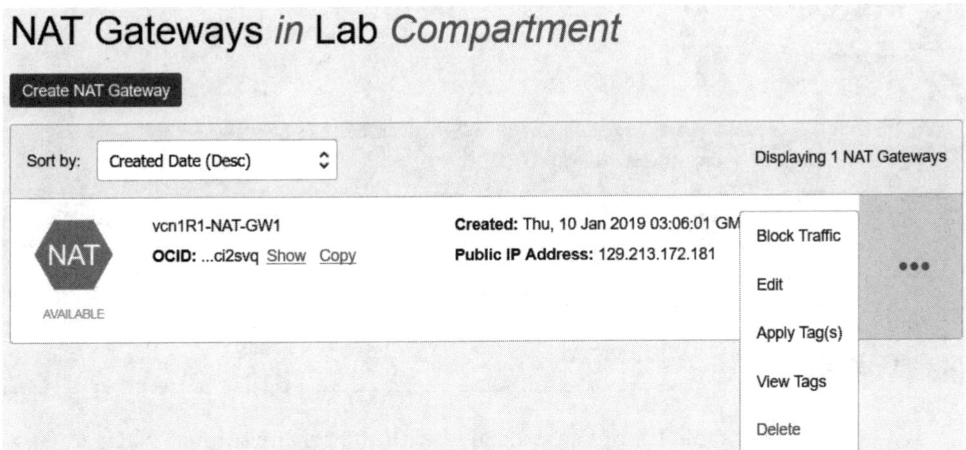

4. For instances in a subnet to actually use the NAT gateway, route rules must be added to the route table associated with the subnet. When the private subnet vcn1R1pv2 was created, the default route table of the VCN was chosen as its route table. You will create a new route table, add a route rule, and update the private subnet to use the new route table. In your home region, navigate to Networking | Virtual Cloud Networks | vcnR1 | Route Tables. Choose Create

Route Table. Choose the compartment of the subnet and provide a name: vcn1R1pv2-RT1. Add a route rule by selecting NAT Gateway as the Target Type, the compartment where the NAT gateway resides, vcn1R1-NAT-GW1 as the Target NAT Gateway, and a destination CIDR block of 0.0.0.0/0. Any subnet traffic with a destination that matches the rule (and not handled by a more selective route table entry if one is later added) is routed to the NAT gateway except for intra-VCN traffic, which is routed to the target in the VCN. Select Create Route Table.

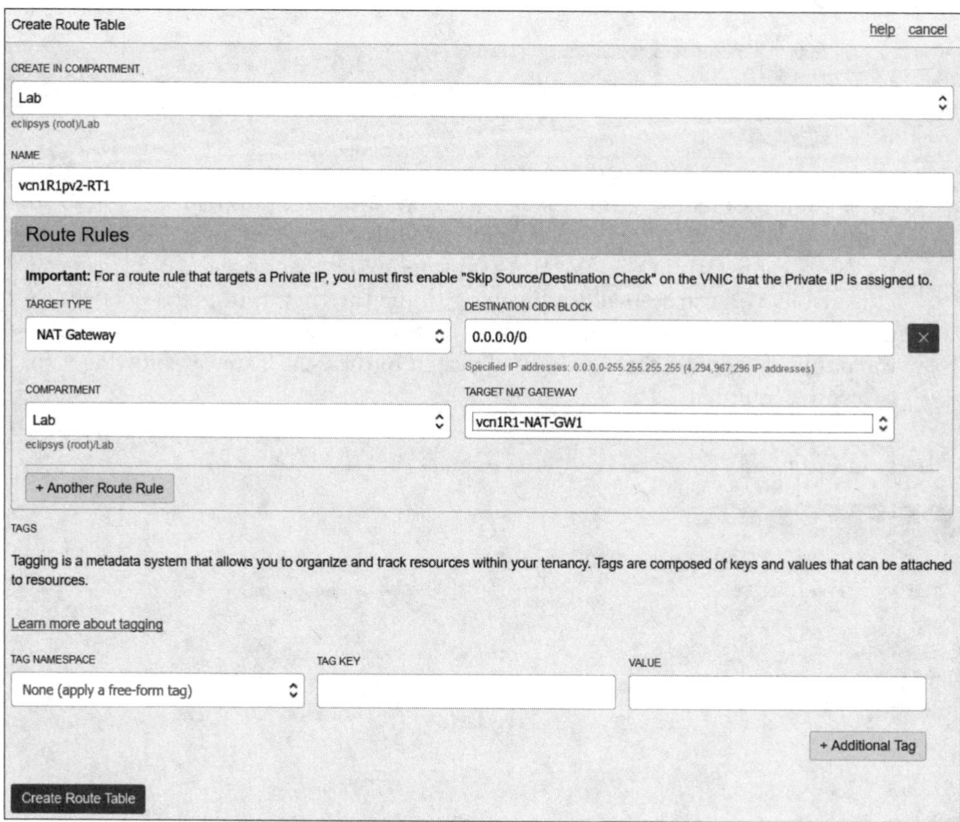

5. The new route table is not yet associated with the private subnet. Navigate to Networking | Virtual Cloud Networks | vcnR1-Subnets and choose the Edit option adjacent to subnet vcn1R1pv2. Choose the new route table, vcn1R1pv2-RT1, in the Route Table section as the new route table for this subnet and select Update.

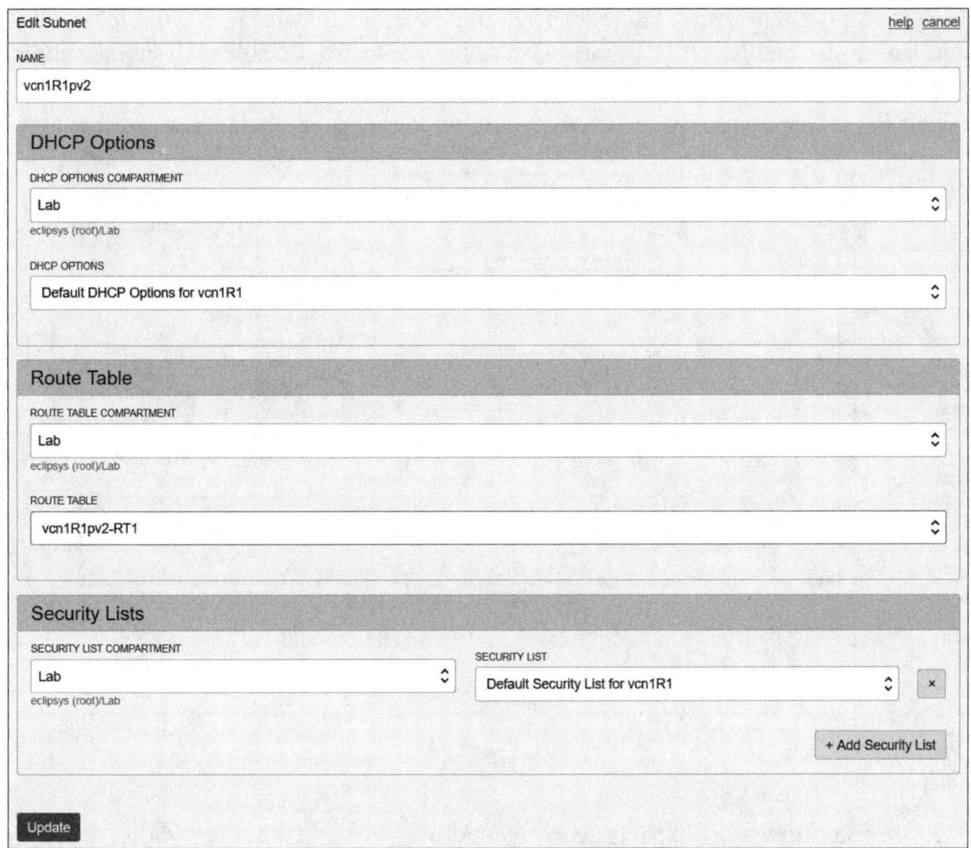

6. Instances created in subnet vcn1R1pv2 will receive private VNICs and private IPs from the CIDR block of the subnet. The NAT gateway, route table, and route rule created previously (plus the egress rule from the default security list) will allow these instances to connect to the Internet.

Exercise 3-4: Deploy a Service Gateway

This exercise builds on the infrastructure you created in Exercise 3-3. In this exercise, you will deploy a service gateway in VCN vcn1R1, to enable OCI object storage access for instances created in private subnet vcn1R1pv3. Instances in this subnet do not have Internet access because it is private, so the VCN's Internet gateway cannot be used. Although the NAT gateway created in Exercise 3-3 exists at the VCN level, there are no route rules in the VCN's default route table currently used by this subnet to allow

Internet-bound traffic out of the subnet. In this exercise, you will create a service gateway and a new route table (vcnR1pv3-RT1), and update the route table used by the subnet: vcnR1pv3.

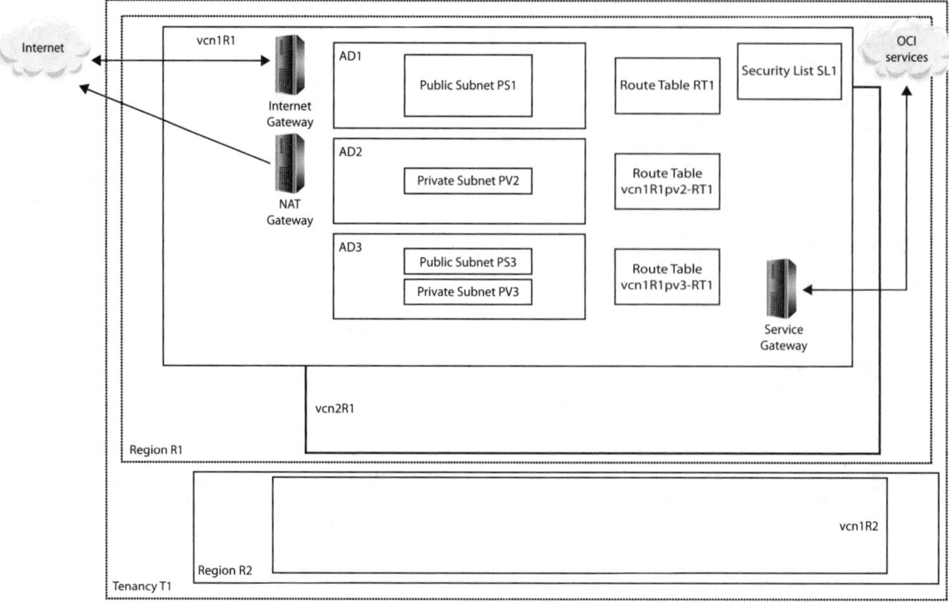

1. Sign in to the OCI console.
2. In your home region, navigate to Networking | Virtual Cloud Networks | vcnR1 | Service Gateways. Choose Create Service Gateway. Choose the compartment in your tenancy that will hold these networking components. The compartment used in the exercise is called Lab, but you should use a compartment that is meaningful in your environment. Provide a service gateway name: vcn1R1-Service-GW1. Choose the OCI services to which this gateway will allow access, such as OCI IAD Object Storage, and select Create.

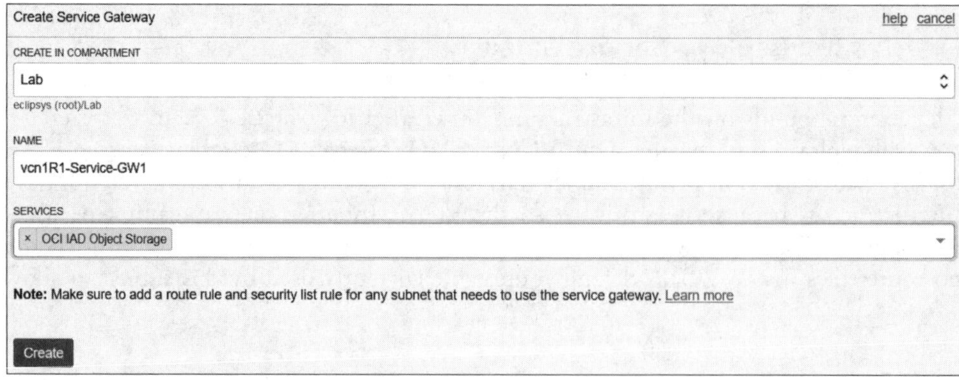

3. After a few moments, your gateway is created. A notification reminds you to add a route rule and security list rule for any subnet that needs to use this service gateway and to ensure that it is AVAILABLE. Similar to the NAT gateway, you can stop all traffic going to the OCI service selected from instances using the gateway by choosing the Block Traffic option.
4. For instances in subnet vcnR1pv3 to access object storage through the service gateway, route rules must be added to the route table associated with the subnet. You will create a new route table with a route rule for the service gateway and update the private subnet to use the new route table. In your home region, navigate to Networking | Virtual Cloud Networks | vcnR1 | Route Tables. Choose Create Route Table. Choose the compartment of the subnet and provide a name: vcn1R1pv3-RT1. Add a route rule by selecting Service Gateway as the Target Type, the compartment where the service gateway resides, vcn1R1-Service-GW1 as the Target Service Gateway, and a destination service like OCI IAD Object Storage. Select Create Route Table.

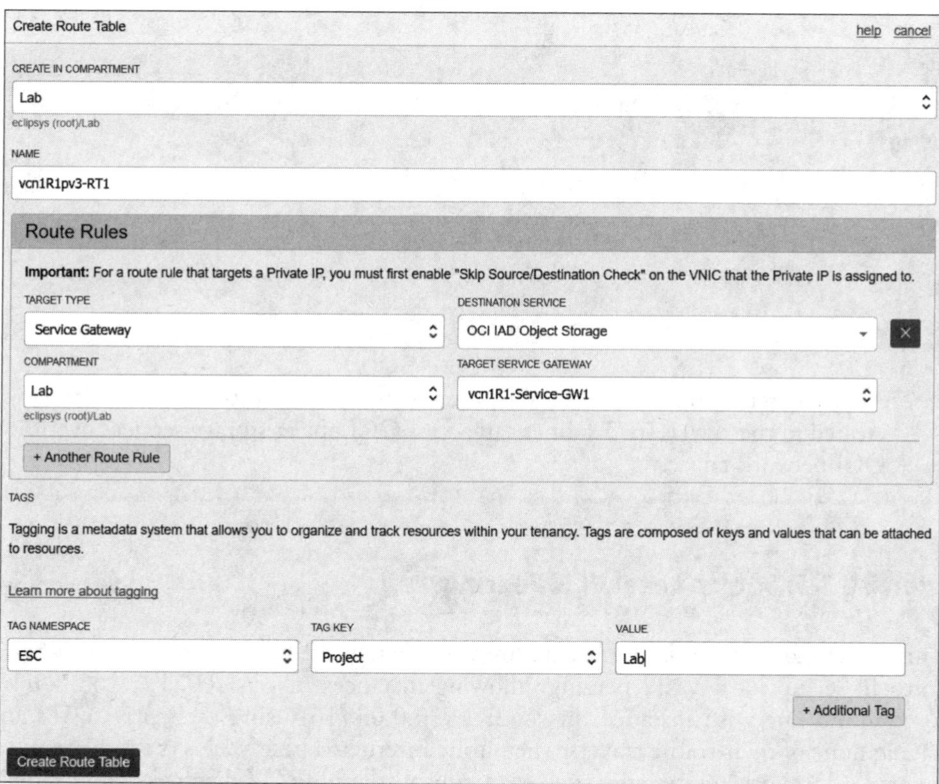

5. The new route table is not yet associated with the private subnet. Navigate to Networking | Virtual Cloud Networks | vcnR1 | Subnets and choose the Edit option adjacent to subnet vcn1R1pv3. Choose the new route table, vcn1R1pv3-RT1, in the Route Table section as the new route table for this subnet and select Update.
6. Any traffic from instances in this subnet trying to access OCI object storage will be routed through the storage gateway provided the security list allows the outgoing or egress traffic. Navigate to Networking | Virtual Cloud Networks | vcnR1 | Security Lists and choose the View Security List Details option adjacent to the default security list. Choose Edit All Rules. Scroll to the Allow Rules for Egress section. Choose Service as the destination type and the OCI service, such as OCI IAD Object Storage, as the destination service. To allow only HTTPS secure calls to be made to object storage, choose TCP as the IP protocol and set the destination port range to 443. The source port range can be optionally specified or left as All. Select Save Security List Rules.

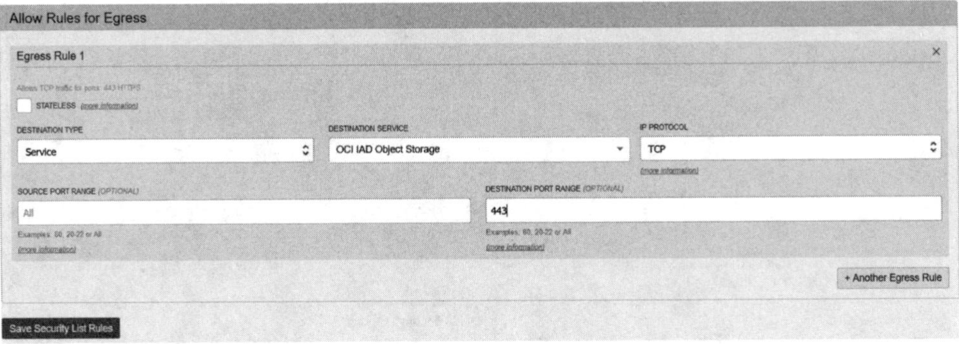

7. After you set up the service gateway, route table, and security list rule, instances created in the vcn1R1pv3 subnet can access OCI object storage services over the OCI network fabric.

Exercise 3-5: Set Up Local VCN Peering

This exercise builds on the infrastructure you created in Exercise 3-4. In this exercise, you will set up local VCN peering, allowing instances in vcn1R1 (192.168.0.0/16) to communicate with instances in vcn2R1 (10.0.0.0/16) using their private IPs and having none of their traffic traverse the public Internet. These VCNs meet the requirements for local peering because they have non-overlapping CIDR blocks and reside in the same region.

Peering relies on the agreement between the administrators of both VCNs. In this example, you are the administrator of both local VCNs. One VCN administrator is designated as the requestor while the other is the acceptor. The requestor initiates the peering request, while the acceptor permits the requestor to connect to the local peering gateway. IAM policies, routing rules, and security list rules are also required to complete the setup.

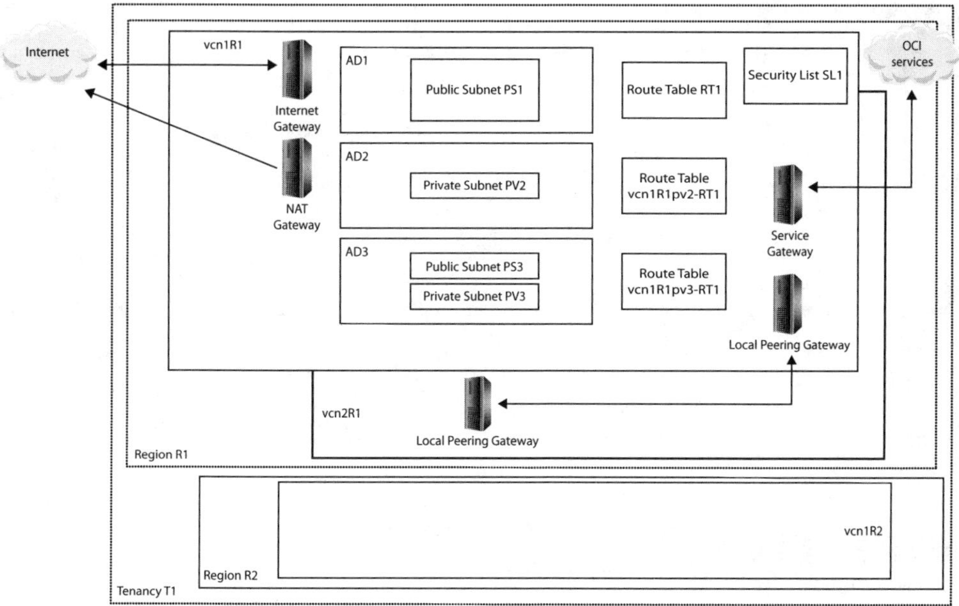

1. Sign in to the OCI console.
2. Both the requestor and acceptor must create a local peering gateway in each VCN. For this exercise, vcn1R1 will be the requesting side while vcn2R1will be the accepting side.
3. In your home region, navigate to Networking | Virtual Cloud Networks | vcn1R1 | Local Peering Gateways. Choose Create Local Peering Gateway. Provide a name: vcn1R1_LPG1. Choose the compartment in your tenancy that will hold this networking component. Leave the route table options at default values and select Create Local Peering Gateway. Repeat these steps in vcn1R2 to create the accepting side LPG called vcn2R1_LPG1.

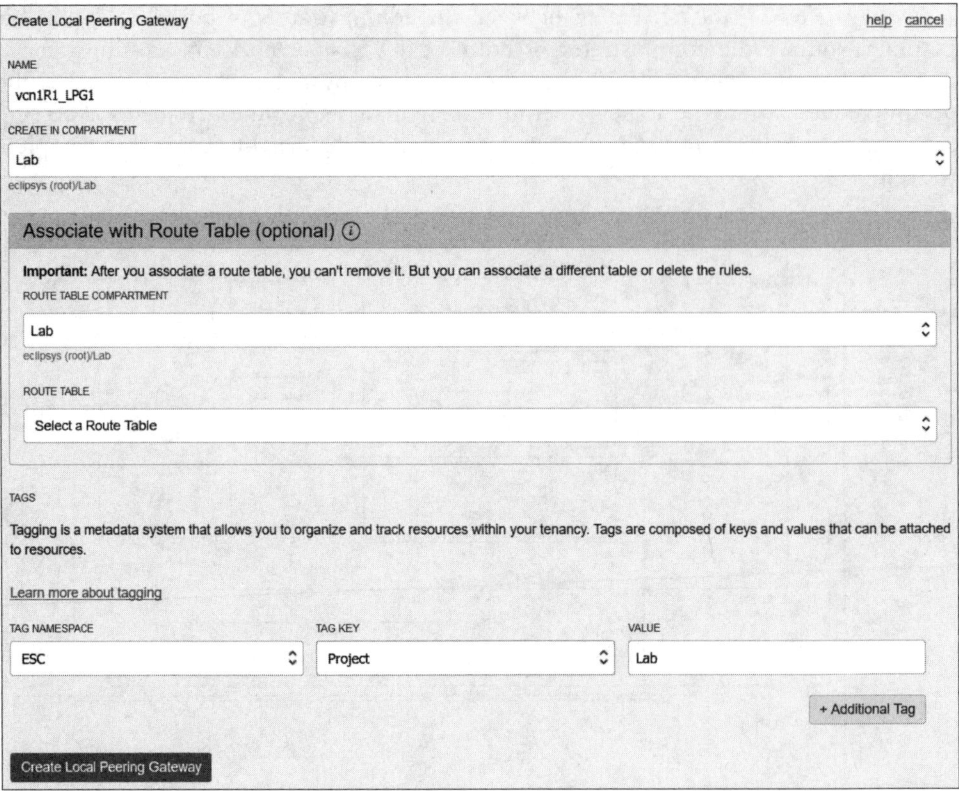

4. Once vcn2R1_LPG1 is created, take note of its OCID. Because this peering is between VCNs in the same tenancy, the LPGs of both the acceptor and requestor can be chosen from a list of values. For cross-tenancy peering in the same region, you will require the OCID, which may resemble this format:

```
ocid1.localpeeringgateway.oc1.iad...mjcpq
```

5. For local peering between VCNs in the same tenancy, an IAM policy must be created to allow users from the requestor side to initiate a connection from the LPG in the requestor's compartment. An IAM policy on the acceptor's side must be created to allow the requestor's LPG to establish a connection to the acceptor's LPG.

6. IAM policies for cross-tenancy peering are slightly more complex, requiring additional policy statements endorsing requestor groups to manage LPGs in the acceptor's tenancy and to associate LPGs in the requestor's compartment with LPGs in the acceptor's tenancy. Corresponding policy statements on the acceptor's side admit the requestor's group to manage LPGs in the acceptor's compartment and to associate LPGs in the requestor's compartment with LPGs in the acceptor's compartment.

7. In this exercise, you will forego the IAM policy creation. In practice, while this step is relatively important for local peering between VCNs in the same tenancy, it is essential for cross-tenancy local peering.
8. The requestor must perform the task of establishing the connection between the two LPGs. Navigate to Networking | Virtual Cloud Networks | vcn1R1 | Local Peering Gateways | vcn1R1_LPG1, and choose Establish Peering Connection. You are peering two VCNs in the same tenancy so leave the radio button at its default setting, allowing LPGs to be browsed. Choose the acceptor VCN compartment (Lab), the requestor VCN name (vcn2R1), the compartment name where the acceptor's LPG resides, as well as the name of the acceptor's LPG (vcn2R1_LPG1) and choose Establish Peering Connection.

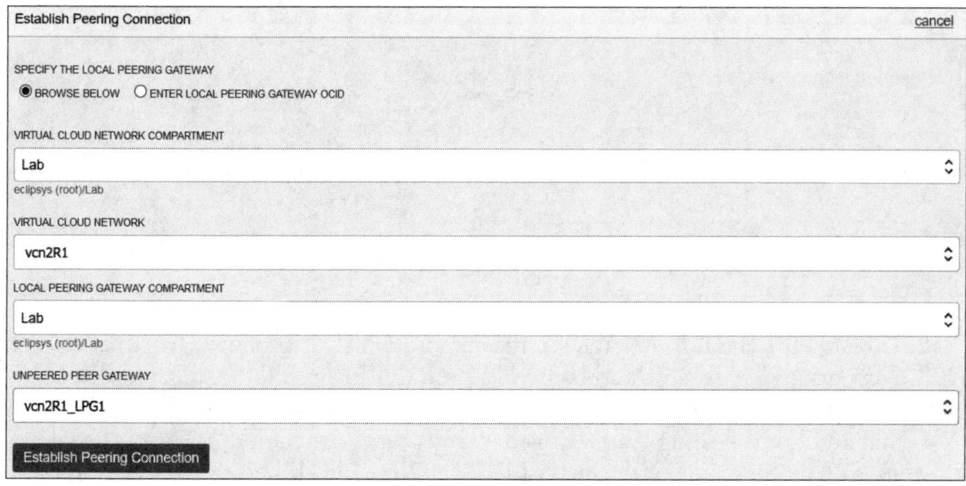

9. After a few moments, the peering status on the requestor and acceptor LPGs changes from PENDING to PEERED. The requestor's LPG, vcn1R1_LPG1, has information about the requestor's VCN, CIDR Block:192.168.0.0/16, and the acceptor's VCN, Peer Advertised CIDR:10.0.0.0/16.

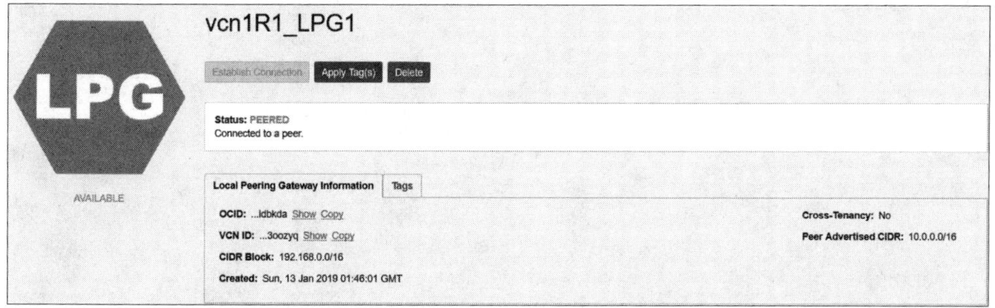

10. The acceptor's LPG: vcn2R1_LPG1 has information about the acceptor's VCN, CIDR Block: 10.0.0.0/16, and the acceptor's VCN, Peer Advertised CIDR, 192.168.0.0/16.

11. The peer-advertised CIDR blocks above must be added to the route tables of each VCN to direct requestor traffic to the acceptor's VCN and vice versa. Navigate to Networking | Virtual Cloud Networks | vcn1R1 | Route Tables | Default Route Table for vcn1R1 and choose Edit Route Rules. Choose +Another Route Rule. Choose Local Peering Gateway as the target type; the compartment of the target LPG, Lab; the name of the target LPG, vcn1R1_LPG1, and the destination CIDR block, 10.0.0.0/16; and select Save. This rule will allow traffic from instances in vcn1R1 with private IP addresses from the CIDR range: 192.168.0.0/16 trying to access instances with private IP addresses from the 10.0.0.0/16 range to connect through the LPG.

12. Update the default route table on the acceptor's VCN as follows: Navigate to Networking | Virtual Cloud Networks | vcn2R1 | Route Tables | Default Route Table for vcn2R1 and choose Edit Route Rules. Choose +Another Route Rule and add Local Peering Gateway as the target type; the compartment of the target LPG, Lab; the name of the target LPG, vcn2R1_LPG1; and the destination CIDR block, 192.168.0.0/16, and select Save.

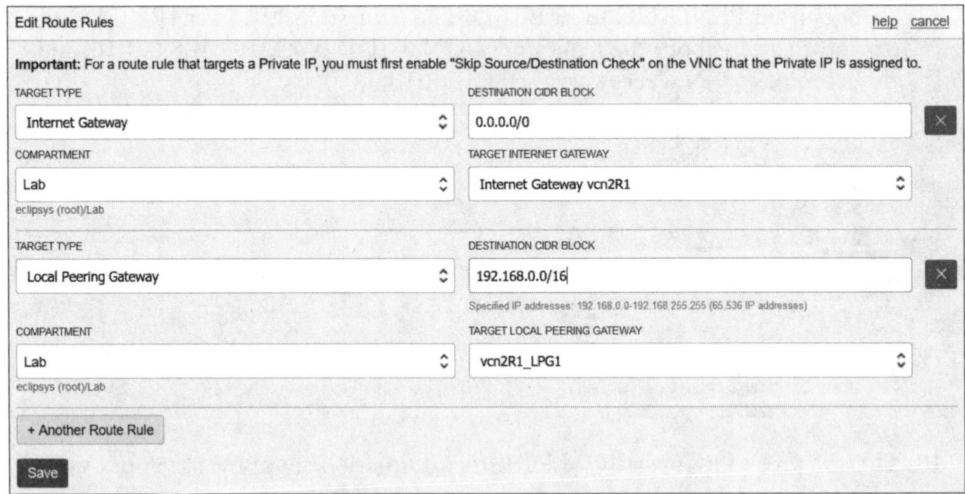

13. The last configuration step required is to set up ingress and egress rules if necessary to allow instances from each VCN to connect to each other. In this exercise, SSH access on TCP port 22 is sufficient but you may want to allow access to database listener ports or HTTPS ports. The requestor's default security list should be updated by navigating to Networking | Virtual Cloud Networks | vcn1R1 | Security Lists | Default Security List for vcn1R1 and choosing Edit All Rules. There is already an ingress rule allowing incoming traffic from any IP address (0.0.0.0/0) to TCP port 22, so you only need to add an egress rule. Choose +Another Egress Rule, and select CIDR as the destination type with any IP address (0.0.0.0/0) as the destination CIDR, TCP as the protocol, and 22 as the destination port range.

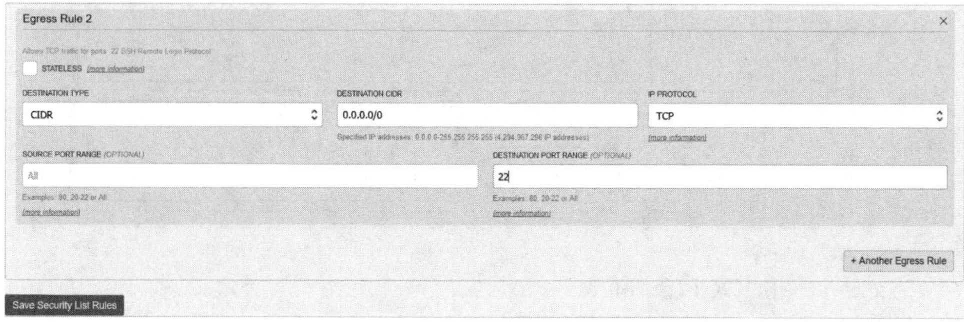

14. The default security list for vcn2R1 already has default ingress and egress rules that permit instances to SSH externally and to accept incoming SSH traffic.
15. With local VCN peering enabled, instances in vcn1R1 are thus able to communicate with instances in vcn2R1 using their private IPs over SSH.

Exercise 3-6: Set Up Remote VCN Peering

This exercise builds on the infrastructure you created in Exercise 3-5. In this exercise, you will set up remote VCN peering, allowing instances in vcn1R1(192.168.0.0/16) to communicate with instances in vcn1R2 (10.0.0.0/16) using their private IPs and having none of their traffic traverse the public Internet despite these VCNs residing in different regions. These VCNs meet the requirements for remote peering because they have non-overlapping CIDR blocks and reside in different regions.

Like local peering, remote peering relies on the agreement between the administrators of both VCNs, one designated the requestor while the other is the acceptor. The requestor initiates the peering request while the acceptor permits the requestor to connect to the peering mechanism.

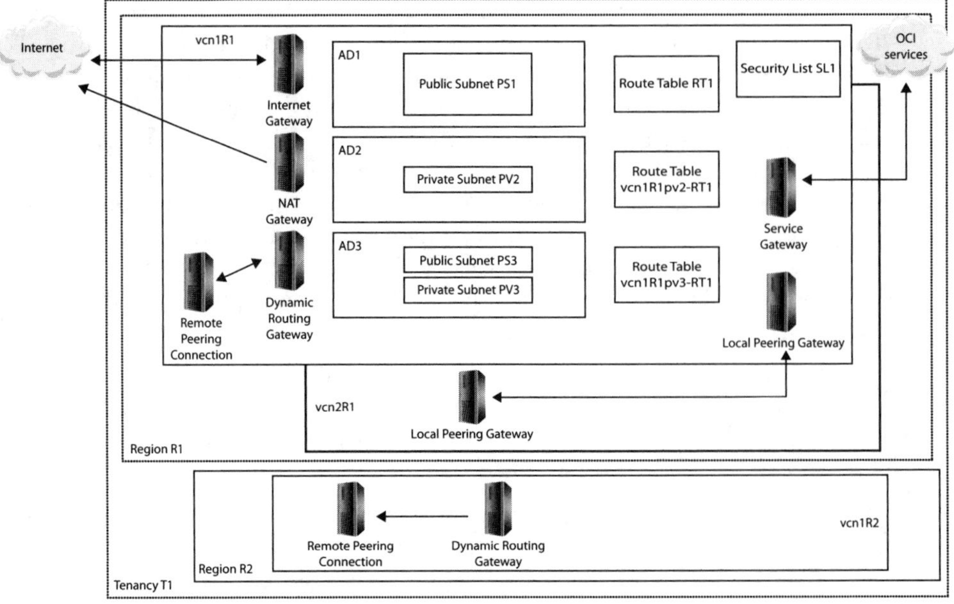

1. Sign in to the OCI console
2. Both the requestor and acceptor must create a dynamic routing gateway (DRG) in each VCN. For this exercise, vcn1R1 will be the requesting side while vcn1R2 will be the accepting side.
3. In your home region, navigate to Networking | Dynamic Routing Gateways, and choose Create Dynamic Routing Gateway. Choose the compartment in your tenancy that will hold the networking component Lab, provide the name DRG_VCN1R1, and choose Create Dynamic Routing Gateway. Repeat this step in your non-home region and create a DRG named DRG_VCN1R2.

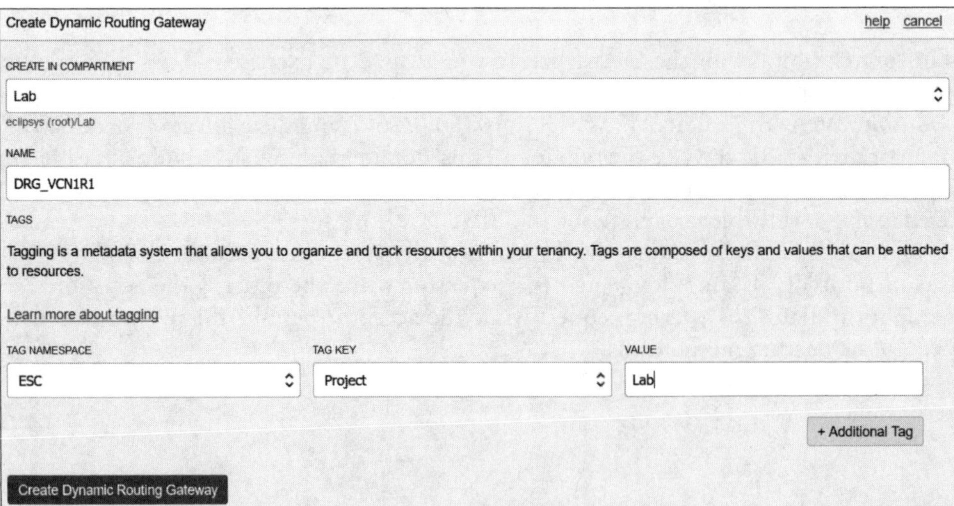

4. Attach the DRGs to your VCNs. Navigate to Virtual Cloud Networks | vcn1R1 | Dynamic Routing Gateways, and choose Attach Dynamic Routing Gateway. Choose the DRG's compartment and the DRG_VCN1R1, and select Attach. Repeat this step in your non-home region and attach DRG_VCN1R2 to vcn1R2.

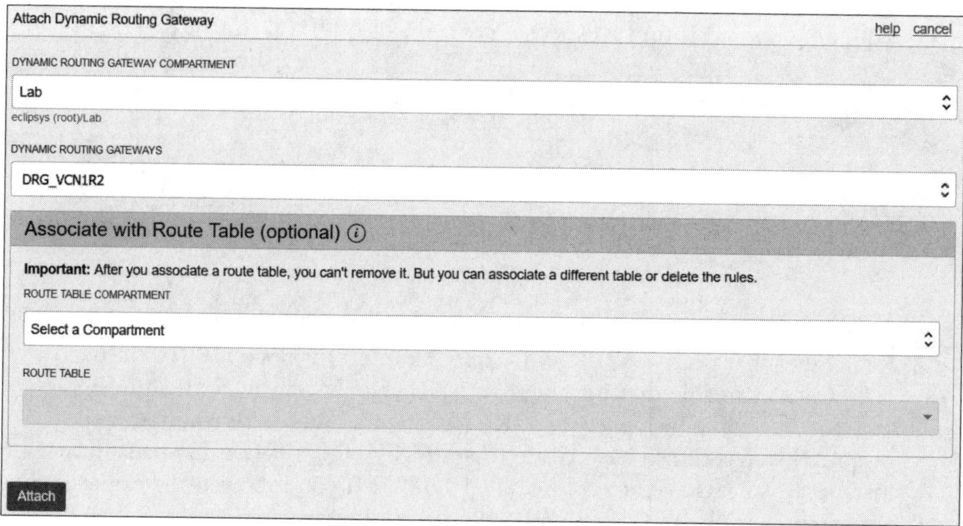

5. Remote peering connections (RPCs) must also be created in each DRG. Navigate to Virtual Cloud Networks | vcn1R1 | Dynamic Routing Gateways | DRG_VCN1R1 | Remote Peering Connections, and choose Create Remote Peering Connection. Provide a name, RPC_vcn1R1-vcn1R2, and the compartment, Lab, and select Create Remote Peering Connection. Repeat this step in your non-home region and create RPC_vcn1R2-vcn1R1 in DRG_VCN1R2. Take note of the OCID of the acceptor's RPC, which should resemble the following:

```
ocid1.remotepeeringconnection.oc1.uk-london-1...xyxfa
```

Create Remote Peering Connection
cancel
NAME
RPC_vcn1R2-vcn1R1
CREATE IN COMPARTMENT
Lab
eclipsys (root)/Lab
Create Remote Peering Connection

6. Similar to the LPG setup, IAM policies must be set up. The requestor should have a policy permitting connections from the requestor's compartments to be initiated from the RPC, while the acceptor permits the requestor's group to connect to the acceptor's RPC. Once again, this step is skipped, although in practice, this is important for network security.

7. The requestor must establish the connection between the RPCs. Navigate to Networking | Dynamic Routing Gateways | DRG_VCN1R1 | Remote Peering Connections | RPC_vcn1R1-vcn1R2 and choose Establish Connection. Choose the acceptor's region, uk-london-1; provide the OCID of the acceptor's RPC; and select Establish Connection. After a few moments, the state of both the requestor's and acceptor's RPCs changes from PENDING to PEERED.

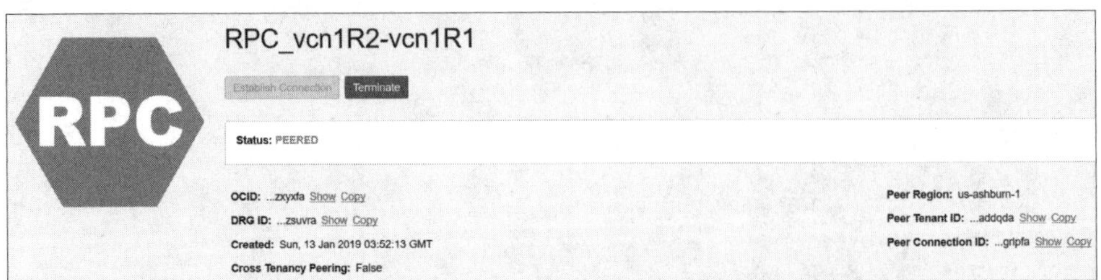

8. Remember that both vcn2R1 and vcn1R2 use CIDR block (10.0.0.0/16). It is entirely possible that instance1_vcn1R1 may have private IP address 192.168.0.5 while instance2_vcn2R1 has private IP address 10.0.0.4, and instance3_vcn1R2 also has private IP address 10.0.0.4. What happens if instance1_vcn1R1 tries to connect to 10.0.0.4? If you followed the exercises in sequence, then the LPG route rule will direct the traffic to instance2_vcn2R1. With remote peering, it becomes more complicated. You have to decide which subnets in vcn1R1 need to access vcn1R2 and configure routing accordingly. If you try to add a rule to the default route table that points to the same destination CIDR block as another rule, you get an error stating that you cannot add multiple rules with the same destination.

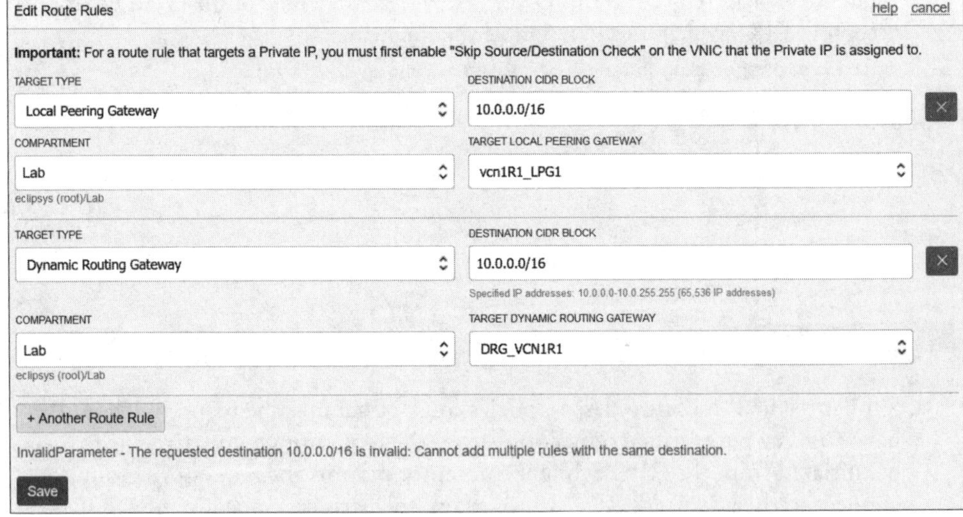

9. To correctly route traffic between the remotely peered VCNs, you decide that only traffic from subnet vcn1R1pv2 will access the remote VCN, so you update the route table for this subnet on the requestor's VCN as follows: Navigate to Networking | Virtual Cloud Networks | vcn1R1 | Route Tables | vcn1R1pv2-RT1, and choose Edit Route Rules. Choose +Another Route Rule and add Dynamic Routing Gateway as the target type; the compartment of the target DRG, Lab; the name of the target, DRG: DRG_VCN1R1; and the destination CIDR block, 10.0.0.0/16. Select Save.

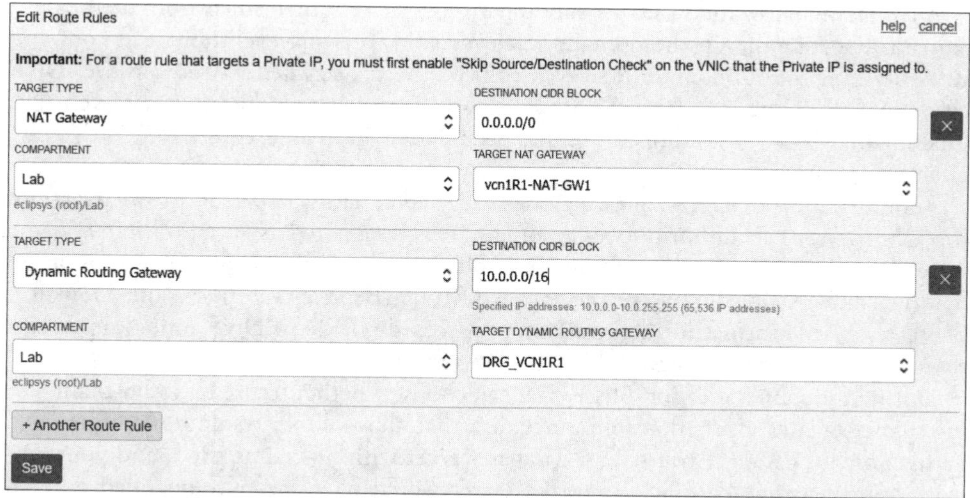

10. The last configuration step required is to set up ingress and egress rules if necessary to allow instances from each VCN to connect to one another. In the previous exercise, the requestor's default security list was updated, permitting ingress and egress traffic on any IP address (0.0.0.0/0) on TCP port 22, but tweak this as necessary.

11. The default security list for vcn1R2 already has default ingress and egress rules that permit instances to SSH externally and to accept incoming SSH traffic.

12. With remote VCN peering enabled, instances in subnet vcn1R1pv2 are thus able to communicate with instances in vcn1R2 using their private IPs over SSH.

DNS in OCI

A hostname is a name provided to a computer or host either explicitly or through the DHCP service discussed earlier. The Domain Name System (DNS) is a directory that maps hostnames to IP addresses. The OCI DNS service is a regional service. This section describes DNS concepts and features in OCI as well as several advanced DNS topics, including zone management and creating and managing DNS records.

DNS Concepts and Features

DNS evolved from a centralized text file that mapped hostnames to IP addresses to computers on the early Internet to a decentralized hierarchy of name servers, each responsible for assigning domain names and mapping these to Internet resources. The DNS server hierarchy starts with top-level domains (TLDs) like com and org, most of which are administered by ICANN (Internet Corporation for Assigned Names and Numbers), which operates IANA (Internet Assigned Numbers Authority), which is responsible for maintaining the DNS root zone, which contains the TLDs.

All domains below the TLDs are subdomains that inherit their suffix from their parent domain. For example, in the domain oraclevcn.com, the top-level domain is com and authority over the subdomain oraclevcn.com has been delegated to a lower-level DNS server. A DNS zone is a distinct part of a domain namespace, like the oraclevcn.com subdomain, where the administration has been delegated to an organization, in this case Oracle Corporation.

Administration of DNS zones may be delegated to either a person or organization. If a DNS server has authority over a domain, it is designated as an authoritative name server, and it maintains copies of domain resource records for that zone. The application that runs on virtually all DNS servers is called BIND (Berkeley Internet Name Domain). BIND uses a file format for defining resource records (RRs) in DNS zones known as a *zone file*. DNS zones are discussed in the next section.

During the subnet creation phase, you can choose whether to use DNS hostnames in the subnet or not. Hosts that join a network that allows DNS resolution are provided with a domain name. If you have a database server with hostname prod, and your network domain is named oracle.com, the server would have the fully qualified domain name (FQDN) prod.oracle.com. A domain like oracle.com is sometimes referred to as a DNS suffix, as this is appended onto a hostname to form the FQDN. Figure 3-8 shows the OCI console interface for creating a public subnet named ps3 in AD-3 with CIDR block 10.0.6.0/24. Note the DNS resolution section where the option to Use DNS Hostnames In This Subnet is checked. The DNS label is copied from the subnet name but can be overridden while the DNS domain name is derived from the DNS label and VCN domain name.

DNS labels are validated for compliance and uniqueness during instance launch and should adhere to these guidelines:

- VCN domain name: <VCN DNS label>.oraclevcn.com. The VCN DNS label should preferably be unique across your VCNs but is not mandatory.
- Subnet domain name: <subnet DNS label>.<VCN DNS label>.oraclevcn.com. The subnet DNS label must be unique in the VCN.
- Instance FQDN: <hostname>.<subnet DNS label>.<VCN DNS label>.oraclevcn .com. The hostname must be unique within the subnet.

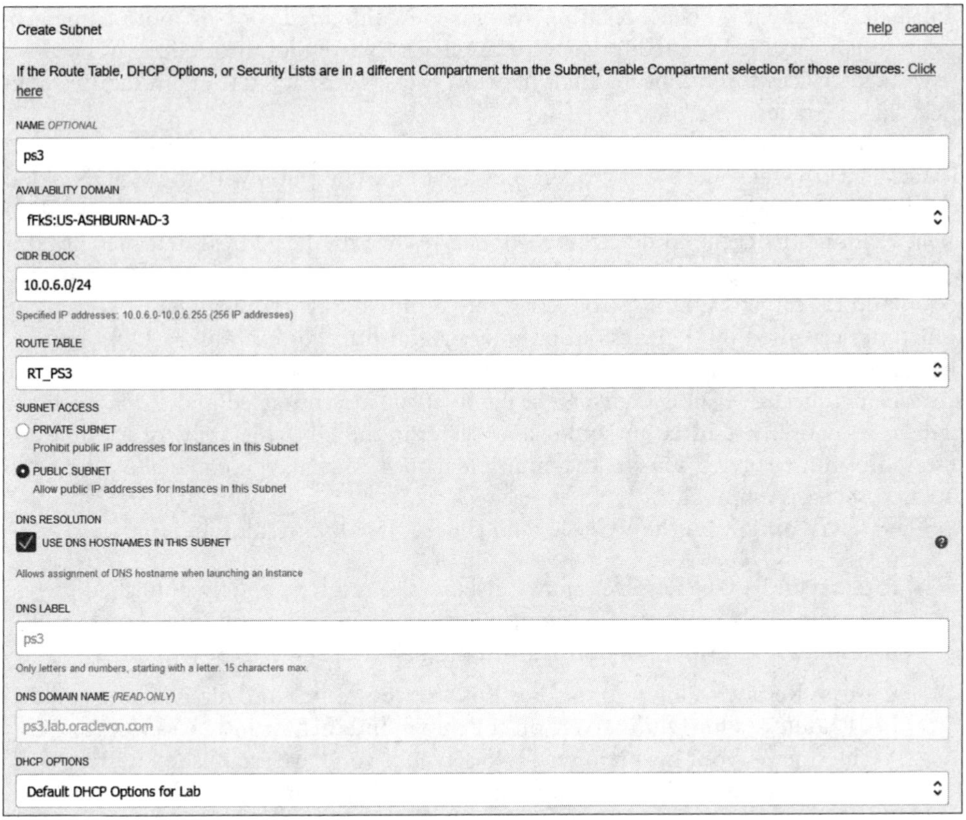

Create Subnet help cancel

If the Route Table, DHCP Options, or Security Lists are in a different Compartment than the Subnet, enable Compartment selection for those resources: Click here

NAME *OPTIONAL*

ps3

AVAILABILITY DOMAIN

fFkS:US-ASHBURN-AD-3

CIDR BLOCK

10.0.6.0/24

Specified IP addresses: 10.0.6.0-10.0.6.255 (256 IP addresses)

ROUTE TABLE

RT_PS3

SUBNET ACCESS

PRIVATE SUBNET
Prohibit public IP addresses for instances in this Subnet

PUBLIC SUBNET
Allow public IP addresses for instances in this Subnet

DNS RESOLUTION

USE DNS HOSTNAMES IN THIS SUBNET

Allows assignment of DNS hostname when launching an instance

DNS LABEL

ps3

Only letters and numbers, starting with a letter. 15 characters max.

DNS DOMAIN NAME *(READ-ONLY)*

ps3.lab.oraclevcn.com

DHCP OPTIONS

Default DHCP Options for Lab

Figure 3-8 Setting DNS options while creating a subnet

NOTE You can use different DHCP options per subnet and not the default set used by all subnets in the VCN. If you choose different DHCP options, such as different search domains at a subnet level, you lose the flexibility of instances in the VCN communicating with hostnames. Instead, they have to use FQDNs to communicate.

DNS supports communication between devices on a network using hostnames, which are resolved into IP addresses through a process known as DNS resolution. DNS resolution requires two components: a DNS client and a DNS server known as a nameserver because it manages a namespace. Modern computer operating systems usually have a built-in DNS client. When operating systems are configured, one or more nameservers are often specified for redundancy to provide DNS resolution services. When two networked devices communicate, their network packets are routed using the addresses in their packet headers.

For example, say you are browsing the URL cloud.oracle.com from your personal device. The browser routes your request message to the computer with the FQDN cloud .oracle.com by first engaging the DNS resolution services on your computer. The DNS client examines its cache to determine if it can resolve the IP address that matches this FQDN. If not, the nameservers specified on your device are systematically contacted to look up the target FQDN to convert it into a routable IP address. DNS resolvers are sometimes classified by their resolution query algorithm. For example, a DNS resolver that uses a recursive query method would first check if local nameservers contain the entry being queried. If not, their parent nameservers are contacted and so on until the name is successfully resolved by some name server in the DNS hierarchy or it cannot be resolved. While resolving a hostname, multiple nameservers may be contacted. The DNS lookup process is essentially a DNS zone check.

The DHCP options in the VCN let you choose the DNS resolution type:

- Internet and VCN Resolver allows instances to resolve publicly published hostnames on the Internet without requiring them to have Internet access and to also resolve hostnames of other instances in the same VCN.
- Custom Resolver allows up to three DNS servers to be configured. These could be IP addresses for DNS servers on the public Internet, or instances in your VCN, or even your on-premises DNS server, if you have established routing to your on-premises infrastructure through a DRG using either IPSec VPN or FastConnect.

The compute instance Instance1AD3 is running in the subnet created in Figure 3-8. Here are several Linux commands that pertain to how DNS interacts with this instance.

```
$ hostname
instancelad3
$ dnsdomainname
ps3.lab.oraclevcn.com
$ hostname -d
ps3.lab.oraclevcn.com
$ hostname --fqdn
instancelad3.ps3.lab.oraclevcn.com
```

The `hostname` command returns the instance's hostname, instancelad3, while both the `dnsdomain` and `hostname -d` commands return the domain name ps3.lab .oraclevcn.com. The DNS search domain lab.oraclevcn.com provided to the VCN in this compartment by the DHCP options is appended to the ps3 DNS label provided when the subnet was created.

Three of the configuration files that influence how DNS resolution works on a Linux client are /etc/resolv.conf, /etc/nsswitch.conf, and /etc/hosts. Consider the extracts from these files:

```
$ cat /etc/hosts
127.0.0.1   localhost localhost.localdomain localhost4 localhost4.localdomain4
::1         localhost localhost.localdomain localhost6 localhost6.localdomain6
10.0.6.2 instance1ad3.ps3.lab.oraclevcn.com instance1ad3
```

This /etc/hosts file contains the localhost loopback IPv4 address 127.0.0.1 and IPv6 address ::1. It also lists the private IP address 10.0.6.2, allocated from the subnet ps3, as well as the FQDN and hostname (in any order).

```
$ cat /etc/resolv.conf
; Any changes made to this file will be overwritten whenever the
; DHCP lease is renewed. To persist changes you must update the
; /etc/oci-hostname.conf file. For more information see
;[https://docs.cloud.oracle.com/iaas/
Content/Network/Tasks/managingDHCP.htm#notes]
; generated by /usr/sbin/dhclient-script
search lab.oraclevcn.com ps3.lab.oraclevcn.com
nameserver 169.254.169.254
```

This /etc/resolv.conf file specifies the DNS search domains lab.oraclevnc.com and ps3.lab.oraclevcn.com, as well as the nameserver IP address 169.254.169.254.

```
$ grep hosts /etc/nsswitch.conf
hosts:      files dns myhostname
```

This /etc/nsswitch.conf file specifies the DNS resolution order, which in this case is to resolve the target hostname by first looking in local files such as /etc/hosts and, if unsuccessful, to query the DNS nameserver listed in /etc/resolv.conf. The IP addresses configured on this instance may be queried on Linux using the `ip address` command:

```
$ ip address
1: lo: <LOOPBACK,UP,LOWER_UP> mtu 65536 qdisc noqueue
state UNKNOWN group default qlen 1000
    link/loopback 00:00:00:00:00:00 brd 00:00:00:00:00:00
    inet 127.0.0.1/8 scope host lo
       valid_lft forever preferred_lft forever
2: ens3: <BROADCAST,MULTICAST,UP,LOWER_UP> mtu 9000 qdisc mq
state UP group default qlen 1000ddd
    link/ether 02:00:17:02:9f:54 brd ff:ff:ff:ff:ff:ff
    inet 10.0.6.2/24 brd 10.0.6.255 scope global dynamic ens3
       valid_lft 82545sec preferred_lft 82545sec
```

This shows the localhost loopback IP as well as the private IP. Remember that there is an ephemeral public IP associated with this private IP, although it is not shown by the OS `ip addr` command. You may obtain the public IP address with the following OCI CLI command using the OCID of the private IP object.

```
$ oci network public-ip
get --private-ip-id ocid1.privateip.oc1.iad...tlqtq
{"data": {
    "ocid1.privateip.oc1.iad...tlqtq",
    "assigned-entity-type": "PRIVATE_IP",
```

```
    "availability-domain": "fFkS:US-ASHBURN-AD-3",
    "compartment-id": "ocid1.compartment.oc1...zlh3iq",
    "display-name": "publicip20190104044905",
    "id": "ocid1.publicip.oc1.iad...s7ssjq",
    "ip-address": "129.213.138.238",
    "lifecycle-state": "ASSIGNED",
    "lifetime": "EPHEMERAL",
    "private-ip-id": "ocid1.privateip.oc1.iad...tlqtq",
    "scope": "AVAILABILITY_DOMAIN",

(output truncated for brevity)
```

Consider the output from the `nslookup` command (available in most Linux and Windows distributions) as it performs various nameserver lookups:

```
$ nslookup instance1ad3
Server:         169.254.169.254
Address:        169.254.169.254#53
Non-authoritative answer:
Name:   instance1ad3.ps3.lab.oraclevcn.com
Address: 10.0.6.2
```

The `nslookup` command queries the name server specified in /etc/resolv.conf and returns the IP address 10.0.6.2. The message indicating that this is a non-authoritative answer means that the DNS server that resolved the lookup request is not the DNS server that manages the zone file where the primary DNS record is defined. Rather, it was satisfied by another nameserver that recognized the hostname from its lookup cache and returned the matching IP address.

By querying an IP address, the `nslookup` command is smart enough to understand that you are requesting a reverse DNS lookup. It is similar to looking up an owner of a telephone number in a directory service to identify the account holder. In this case, the reverse DNS lookup of the private IP address 10.0.6.2 returns the FQDN instance1ad3.ps3.lab.oraclevcn.com.

```
$ nslookup 10.0.6.2
Server:         169.254.169.254
Address:        169.254.169.254#53
Non-authoritative answer:
2.6.0.10.in-addr.arpa    name = instance1ad3.ps3.lab.oraclevcn.com.
Authoritative answers can be found from:
0.10.in-addr.arpa        nameserver = vcn-dns.oraclevcn.com.
vcn-dns.oraclevcn.com    internet address = 169.254.169.254
```

Finally, querying a nonexistent name with `nslookup` yields the message that this domain cannot be found.

```
opc@instance1ad3 ~]$ nslookup garbage-nonexistent-name.com
Server:         169.254.169.254
Address:        169.254.169.254#53
** server can't find garbage-nonexistent-name.com: NXDOMAIN
```

Creating and Managing DNS Records

A DNS zone stores DNS records for a DNS domain. OCI offers a DNS service, which is useful for many scenarios including the following:

- Exposing domains and zones via the Internet for DNS resolution
- Resolving DNS queries for domains and zones that reside in on-premises, OCI, and other third-party hosted environments by centralizing DNS management
- Providing a predictable, reliable, and secure DNS resolution for global DNS queries

The OCI DNS service is highly available, performant, and secure, and includes built-in security measures, such as protection against Distributed Denial of Services (DDoS) attacks. The service uses a network routing methodology well suited to cloud vendors known as anycast, which supports multiple routing paths to multiple endpoint destinations for a single destination address. This routing scheme calculates the shortest and most efficient path for a network packet to traverse, which is key when consumers may be located anywhere in the world. DNS services are part of the Networking Edge services that reduce network traffic while serving a global audience by providing DNS services at edge locations, close to where end users access OCI services.

The DNS services allow you to manage your corporate DNS records, which are domain names mapped to IP addresses for both on-premises and cloud resources. The OCI console provides access to the DNS services by navigating to Networking | DNS Zone Management, as shown in Figure 3-9.

When you create a DNS zone, you may choose to manually define resource records or to import these from an existing zone file in a compatible format. RFCs 1034 and 1035 from the IETF describe Concepts and Facilities as well as Implementation and Specification of domain names respectively. A valid zone file must be in RFC 1035 master file format as exported by the BIND method. A DNS zone typically comprises either a primary zone that controls modification of the master zone file or a secondary zone that hosts a read-only zone file copy that is kept in sync with the primary DNS server.

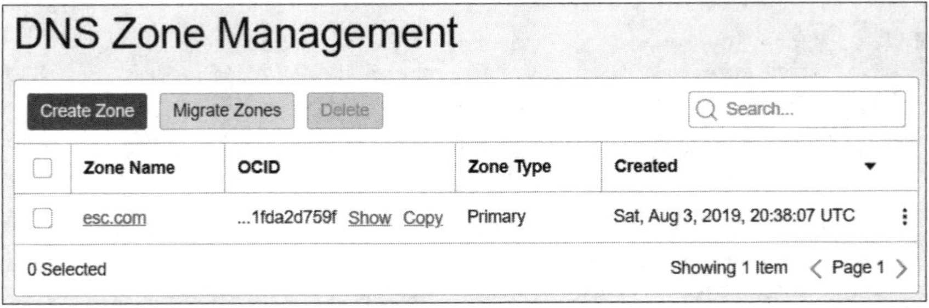

Figure 3-9 DNS zone management

DNS Record Types

A DNS zone contains a set of resource records (RRs) for each domain being administered. Resource records are divided into various record types. The data held in each RR is called record data or RDATA. Resource records have the following components:

- **NAME** An owner name or the name of the node to which this RR pertains.
- **TYPE** The RR type code.
- **CLASS** The RR class code.
- **TTL** The time to live interval specifies the time interval that an RR may be cached before the authoritative name server is consulted.
- **RDLENGTH** Specifies the length of the RDATA field.
- **RDATA** The resource data, the format of which varies based on TYPE and CLASS.

Table 3-3 lists a subset of the RR types available for you to define for a domain being managed through the OCI DNS services. Detailed information about the various RRs may be located by consulting the RFCs adjacent to the description in the table.

NOTE OCI normalizes all RDATA into a consistent and standardized format as per RFC 1034, so be aware that the RDATA displayed in the DNS zone records may differ slightly from the RDATA you submitted. A common normalization is to append a trailing dot (the DNS root zone) to the given name of a domain if one does not already exist. For example, *cloud.oracle .com* is normalized to *cloud.oracle.com.* by appending a dot.

Record Type	Description	RFC
A	An address record used to match an IPv4 address to a hostname.	1035
AAAA	An address record used to match an IPv6 address to a hostname.	3596
CNAME	The domain name that specifies the canonical name for the owner. The owner name is an alias.	1035
ALIAS	A private pseudo-record that allows CNAME functionality at the zone apex. OCI DNS does not allow the creation of ALIAS records, only the viewing and reading of them.	
DNAME	A delegation name record allows the mapping of an entire subtree beneath a label to another domain.	6672
MX	Mail exchanger records specify an incoming mail server for a domain.	1035
NS	A nameserver record stores the authoritative nameservers for a zone. NS records are automatically created by OCI DNS at the top level or apex of each new primary zone.	1035
PTR	Pointer records provide for reverse IP lookups.	1035
SOA	Exactly one SOA RR is generated by OCI DNS at the zone apex, providing authoritative information, including the primary nameserver and the domain administrator's email address.	1035

Table 3-3 Common DNS Resource Record Types

Exercise 3-7: Set Up a DNS Zone and Resource Records

In this exercise, you will set up a DNS zone and create several resource records. You may want to import an existing bind-compatible zone file or use a different domain name that is meaningful in your organization. Existing domain names cannot be used or you receive the message, "Authorization failed or requested resource already exists." The DNS zone management in this exercise is completed using the OCI console.

1. Sign in to the OCI console.
2. Navigate to Networking | DNS Zone Management and select Create Zone. Explore the Method drop-down list, which varies between Manual or Import. Choose Manual. The zone type may be Primary or Secondary (for high availability). Choose Primary. Provide a zone name in the form *<your-domain-name>*, and select Submit.

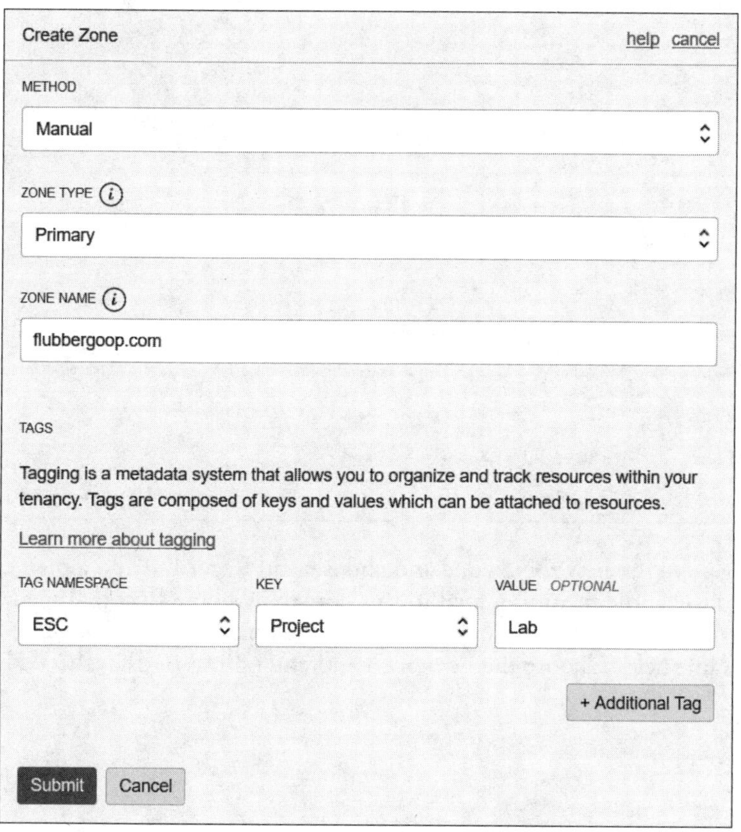

3. The OCI DNS server creates a new DNS primary zone and autogenerates several NS and exactly one SOA record.

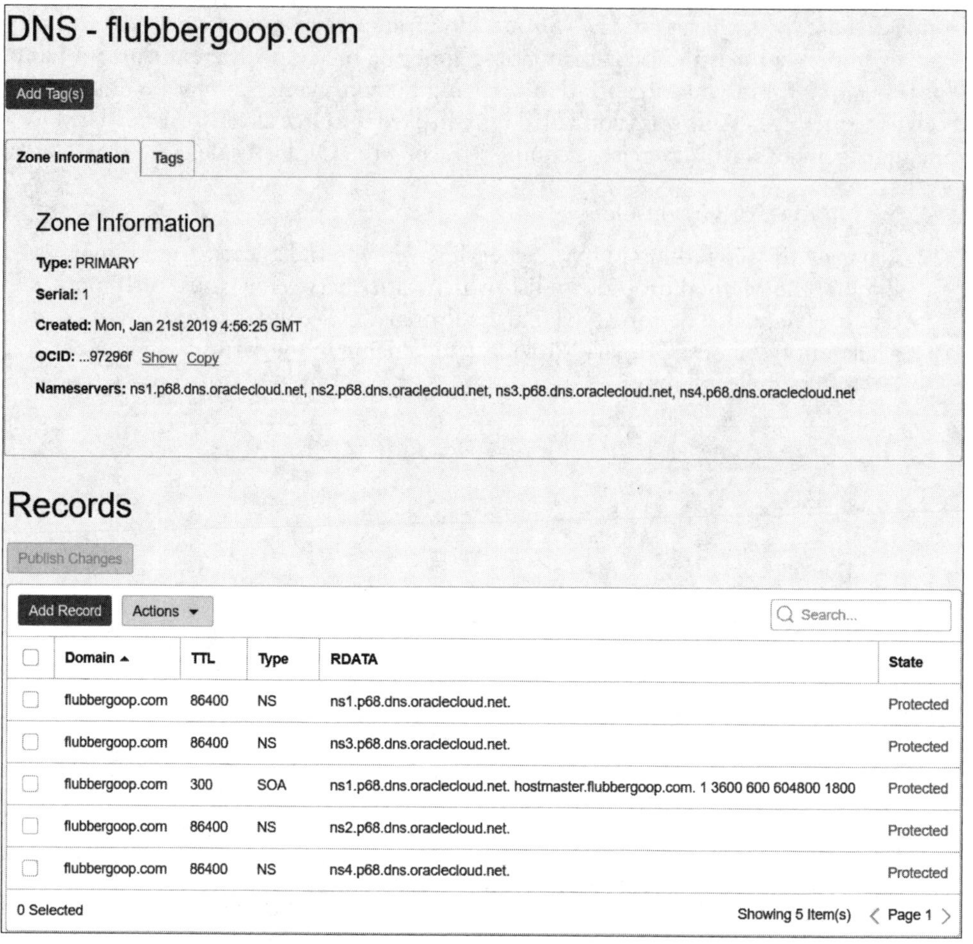

4. Navigate to the new DNS zone and choose Add Record to add a mail exchange record to handle incoming mail to this domain. Choose Record Type MX – Mail Exchanger and provide a domain name in the form *<mail.your-domain-name>* in the Name field. Choose the Lock icon and enter 30 seconds as the TTL value.

Choose Basic mode for the RDATA. Enter 1 for the Preference field. Valid values for the Preference field is any 16-bit integer, and the field specifies the priority given to this RR among others at the same owner. Finally, specify the FQDN of the host running a mail server and select Submit.

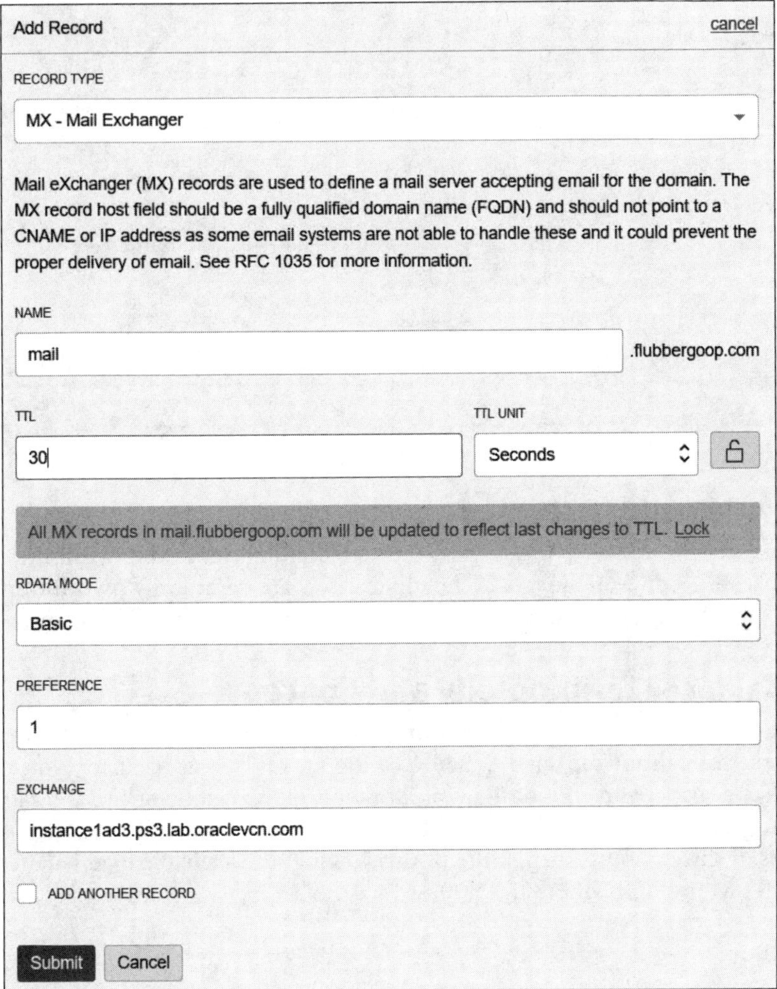

5. Notice the extra record added to the zone. To add your new MX record to the OCI DNS service, choose Publish Changes. The new MX record is now available for DNS lookup to any device using the OCI DNS service for name resolution.

Records

Publish Changes

Add Record   Actions ▾   Search...

Domain ▲	TTL	Type	RDATA	State
flubbergoop.com	86400	NS	ns1.p68.dns.oraclecloud.net.	Protected
flubbergoop.com	86400	NS	ns3.p68.dns.oraclecloud.net.	Protected
flubbergoop.com	300	SOA	ns1.p68.dns.oraclecloud.net. hostmaster.flubbergoop.com. 2 3600 600 604800 1800	Protected
flubbergoop.com	86400	NS	ns2.p68.dns.oraclecloud.net.	Protected
flubbergoop.com	86400	NS	ns4.p68.dns.oraclecloud.net.	Protected
mail.flubbergoop.com	30	MX	1 instance1ad3.ps3.lab.oraclevcn.com.	Unmodified

Load Balancers in OCI

A load balancer is a network device that accepts incoming traffic and distributes it to one or more backend compute instances. Load balancers are commonly used for optimizing the utilization of backend resources as well as to provide scaling and high availability.

Load Balancer Terminology and Concepts

A load balancer may be public or private and is defined based on a shape that determines its network throughput capacity. When creating an OCI load balancer, you provide a name, select a shape, and choose the visibility type, either public or private. Figure 3-10 shows the specification of a public load balancer named LB1, which can support up to 100 Mbps of throughput. At the time of this writing, the available load balancer shapes include 100 Mbps, 400 Mbps, and 8000 Mbps.

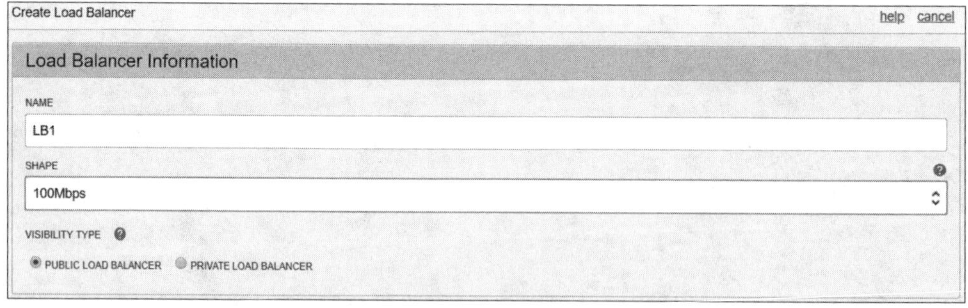

Figure 3-10 Load balancer visibility and shape

Public and Private Load Balancers

A load balancer accepts incoming TCP or HTTP network traffic on a single IP address and distributes it to a backend set that comprises one or more compute instances. In this context, the compute instances are known as backend servers. Each of these compute instances resides in either a public or private subnet. When a private load balancer is created in a compartment, you specify the VCN and private subnet to which it belongs. Figure 3-11 shows an active (primary) private load balancer that obtains a private IP address from the CIDR range of the private subnet S1.

A passive (standby) private load balancer is created automatically for failover purposes and also receives a private IP address from the same subnet. A floating private IP address serves as a highly available address of the load balancer. The active and passive private load balancers are highly available within a single AD. If the primary load balancer fails, the listener directs traffic to the standby load balancer and availability is maintained. Security list rules permitting, a private load balancer is accessible from instances within the VCN where the subnet of the load balancer resides.

EXAM TIP A private load balancer requires three IP addresses from the associated subnet for the primary and standby load balancers as well as the floating private IP.

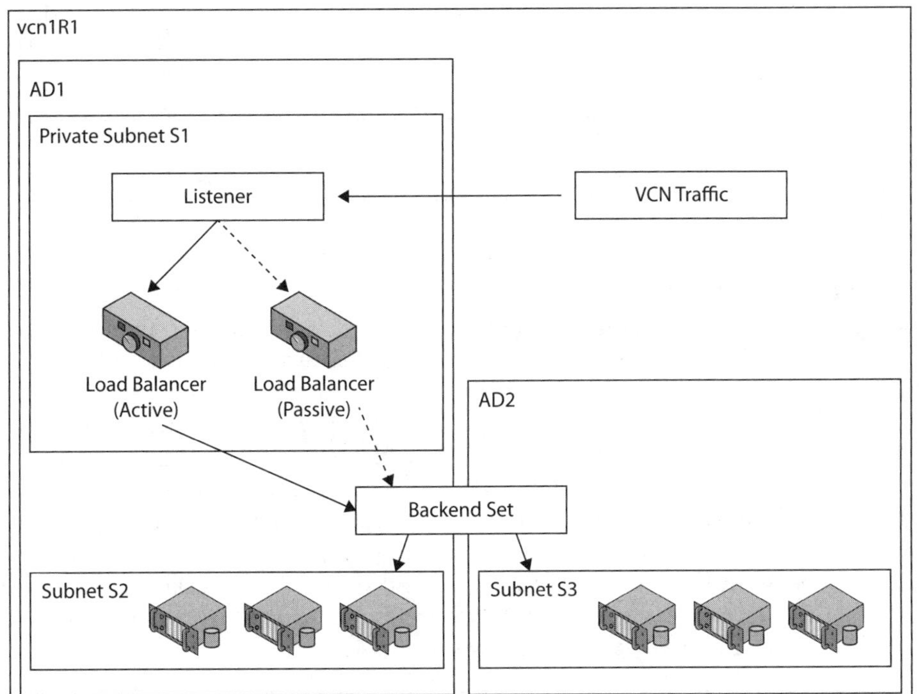

Figure 3-11 Private load balancer

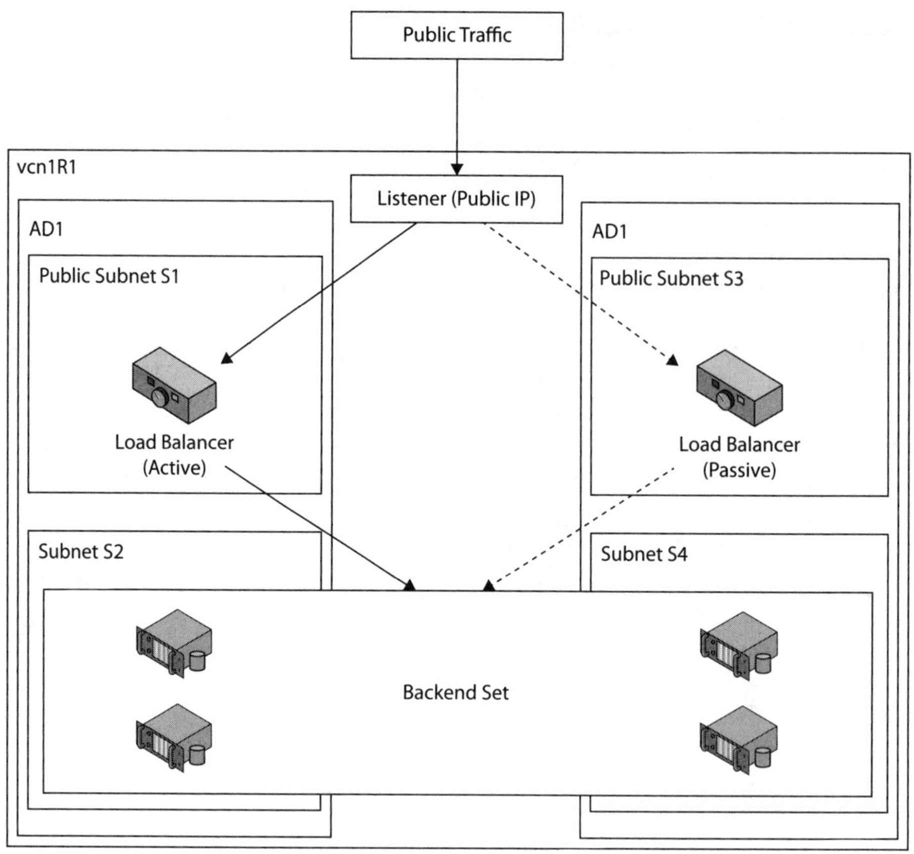

Figure 3-12 Public load balancer

Public Load Balancer

A public load balancer is allocated a public IP address that is routable from the Internet. Figure 3-12 shows the active (primary) public load balancer in subnet S1 in AD1 in vcn1R1.

Incoming traffic from the public Internet on allowed ports and protocols is directed to the floating public IP address associated with the active load balancer. If the load balancer in subnet S1 fails, the passive device in subnet S3 is automatically made active.

The public load balancer is a regional resource as opposed to a private load balancer, which is an AD-level resource. In regions with multiple ADs, it is mandatory to specify public subnets in different ADs for the active and passive load balancers. Figure 3-13 shows a load balancer in the Phoenix region being defined. This region has multiple ADs. Two subnets in different ADs must be chosen.

NOTE New OCI regions are being initially provisioned with a single AD. In these regions, you are only required to specify a single public subnet in your VCN when creating a public load balancer.

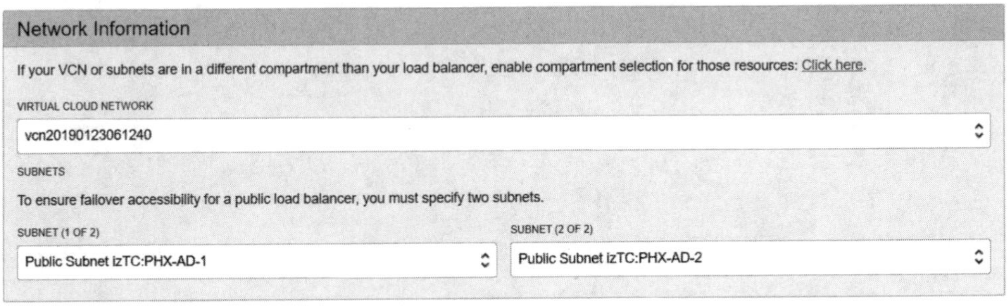

Network Information

If your VCN or subnets are in a different compartment than your load balancer, enable compartment selection for those resources: Click here.

VIRTUAL CLOUD NETWORK

vcn20190123061240

SUBNETS

To ensure failover accessibility for a public load balancer, you must specify two subnets.

SUBNET (1 OF 2)

Public Subnet izTC:PHX-AD-1

SUBNET (2 OF 2)

Public Subnet izTC:PHX-AD-2

Figure 3-13 Failover accessibility for a public load balancer

Listener

At least one listener is created for each load balancer, and as of this writing, up to 16 listeners may be created. Each listener in a load balancer defines a set of properties that include a unique combination of protocol (HTTP or TCP) and port number. Web traffic (HTTP) is also known as application layer or layer 7 (from the OSI model) traffic while TCP traffic is known as transport layer or layer 4 traffic. Figure 3-14 shows the listener properties that may be defined. At a minimum, a listener requires a protocol and a port.

Your load balancer can handle incoming SSL traffic if you check the Use SSL checkbox and provide the relevant certificate information. SSL traffic may be handled with the following three mechanisms:

- **SSL termination** SSL traffic is terminated at the load balancer. Traffic between the load balancer and the backend set is unencrypted.
- **SSL tunneling** Available for TCP load balancers, SSL traffic is passed through to the backend set.
- **End-to-end SSL** Incoming SSL traffic is terminated at the load balancer and a new SSL connection to the backend set is created.

You may also specify an idle timeout duration that will disconnect a connection if the time between two successive send or receive network I/O operations is exceeded during the HTTP request-response phase.

Once a load balancer is provisioned through the console, additional listeners may be defined as well as these additional properties that reduce the number of load balancers and listeners required:

- **Hostname or virtual hostname** You define this property and assign to an HTTP or HTTPS (SSL enabled) listener. As of this writing, up to 16 virtual hostnames may be assigned to a listener and often correspond to application names. Hostnames may also be backed by DNS that resolve to the load balancer IP address.
- **Path Route Rules** Used to route HTTP traffic to different backend sets based on matching the URL pattern in an incoming request. For example, requests with the pattern /login may be routed to the identity management backend set while requests with the pattern /apex may be routed to the application server backend set.

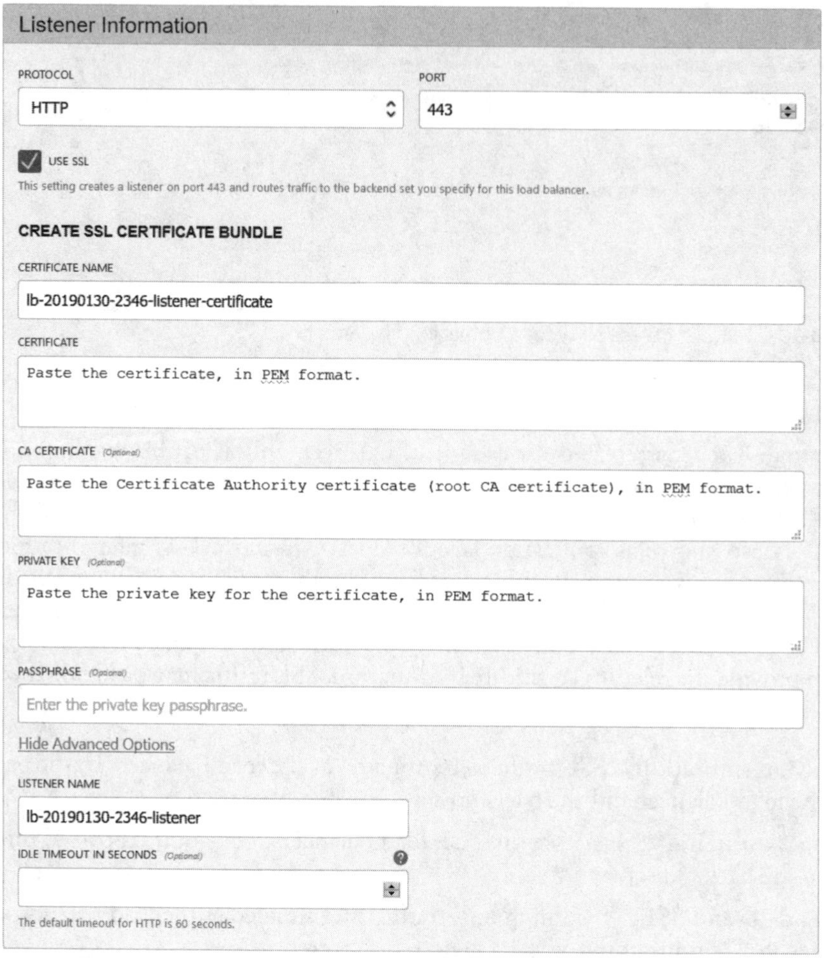

Listener Information
PROTOCOL
HTTP
PORT
443
USE SSL
This setting creates a listener on port 443 and routes traffic to the backend set you specify for this load balancer.
CREATE SSL CERTIFICATE BUNDLE
CERTIFICATE NAME
lb-20190130-2346-listener-certificate
CERTIFICATE
Paste the certificate, in PEM format.
CA CERTIFICATE (Optional)
Paste the Certificate Authority certificate (root CA certificate), in PEM format.
PRIVATE KEY (Optional)
Paste the private key for the certificate, in PEM format.
PASSPHRASE (Optional)
Enter the private key passphrase.
Hide Advanced Options
LISTENER NAME
lb-20190130-2346-listener
IDLE TIMEOUT IN SECONDS (Optional)
The default timeout for HTTP is 60 seconds.

Figure 3-14 Listener information

- **Rule sets** Defined at the load balancer level and may be used by multiple listeners of the load balancer. Rule sets add, alter, or remove incoming HTTP request headers. Examples of how rule sets enhance security include stripping debug headers from requests and preventing external domains from embedding your site in an iframe. Backend servers may also be notified of SSL termination by adding application-specific information to a request header at the load balancer listener.

Backend Set

A load balancer is a network device that ultimately routes traffic to one or more reachable backend compute instances (called backend servers) that reside in any subnet in the VCN. A backend set is a logical grouping of backend servers and a traffic distribution policy. Figure 3-15 shows a backend set with two compute instances (webserver1 and webserver2) and their compartments, IP addresses, local listening ports

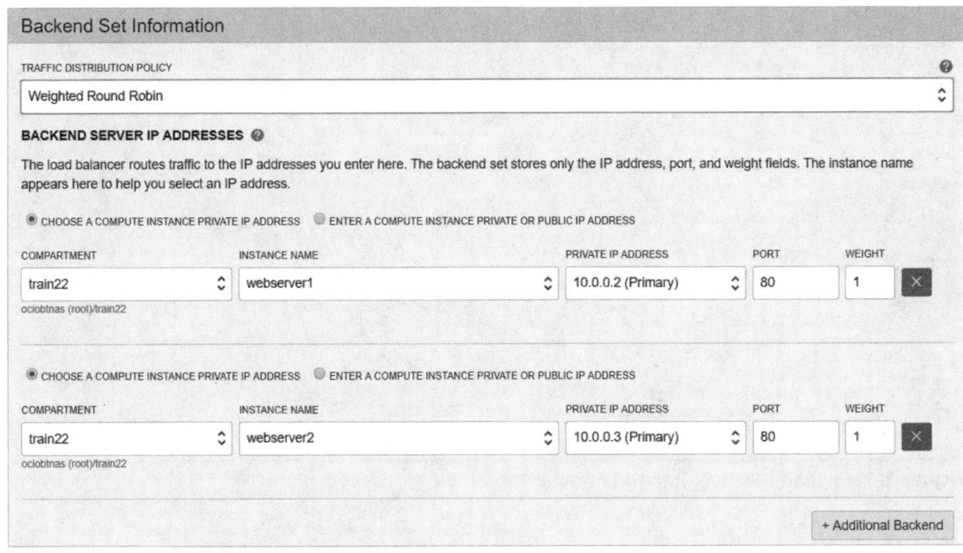

Figure 3-15 Backend set information

(which may be different from the load balancer listener port), and a weight. It is good practice to spread backend set instances across multiple ADs to support high availability.

You choose a traffic distribution policy and the compute instances that comprise the backend set. Additional properties of a backend set include the following:

- Configuring a Health Check that determines the status of backend compute instances and their eligibility to accept incoming requests.
- Choosing whether SSL is to be used between the load balancer and backend instances.
- Enabling session persistence, also known as stickiness, to route traffic from a single client to a specific backend instance when multiple requests are made, such as in the context of a shopping cart application running on a website. This option provides support for cookies.

TCP and non-sticky HTTP incoming traffic is distributed to the compute instances in a backend set based on the instance's weight and traffic distribution policies. Cookie-based persistent HTTP requests additionally forward the cookie's session information. The three traffic distribution policies are

- **Weighted Round Robin** The default policy. Allocates connections to backend servers in a sequential manner based on the weight fields. Traffic to the load balancer front-ends the backend set with webserver1 and webserver2 in Figure 3-15 will be evenly distributed because each instance has an identical weight. If the weight of webserver1 was updated to 2, it would receive two requests for every one request that was sent to webserver2.

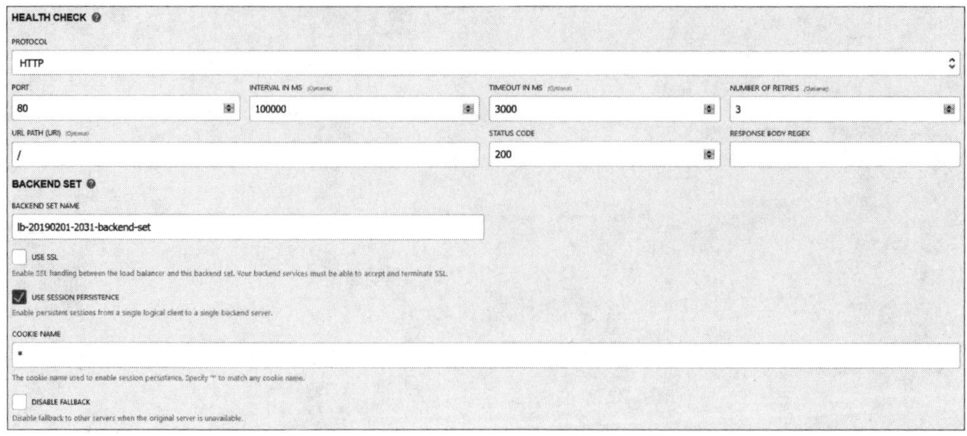

Figure 3-16 Load balancer health check

- **IP Hash** Applies a hashing function to the IP address of the incoming request to route non-sticky traffic to the same backend server.
- **Least Connections** Routes non-sticky incoming requests to the backend instance with the least active connections.

CAUTION The Least Connections distribution policy works better with HTTP rather than TCP traffic because TCP connections can be active on an instance but have no activity.

The Health Check API caters to four health status values including OK, warning, critical, or unknown. Figure 3-16 shows an HTTP health check on port 80 that connects to each of the instances in the backend set every 100000 milliseconds. HTTP works with request and response pairs. An HTTP request is made from the load balancer to an HTTP listener on a compute instance, which replies with an HTTP response. The response contains a status code like 200, which means OK, as well as an HTTP response body, which may be evaluated using a regular expression to identify success or potential problems with the backend instances. You can specify the number of retries the health check attempts before flagging a problem with a backend instance.

EXAM TIP OCI load balancers support many protocols, including TCP, HTTP/1.0, HTTP/1.1, HTTP/2, and WebSocket.

Exercise 3-8: Set Up a Load Balancer

In this exercise, you will set up a public load balancer with a backend set with no compute instances. In Chapter 4, you will create several compute instances and add some of these to the backend set in a new load balancer.

1. Sign in to the OCI console.
2. Navigate to Networking – Load Balancers, choose a compartment, and select Create Load Balancer. Explore the Shape drop-down list, which varies between 100 Mbps, 400 Mbps, and 8000 Mbps. Choose 100 Mbps. Provide a name, such as public-lb1, and choose the visibility type to be public.
3. The Network Information section may display multiple subnets or a single subnet depending on the number of ADs in your region. Choose a VCN and one or two public subnets.
4. Choose HTTP as the protocol and port 80 in the Listener Information section. Expand the Advanced Options and specify a listener name, such as public-lb1-listener, and update the idle timeout to 30 seconds.

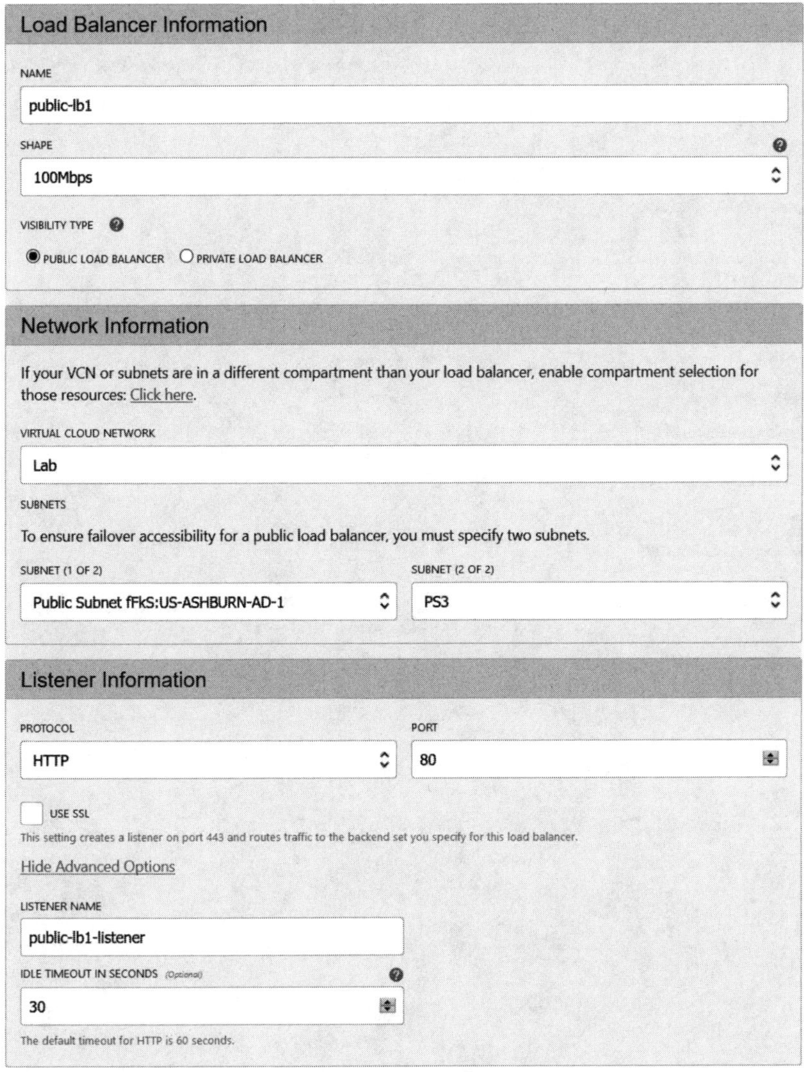

5. Choose Weighted Round Robin as the traffic distribution policy. Expand the Advanced Options to configure the Health Check. Update the URL path to /healthcheck.html and provide a name for the backend set, such as public-lb1-backendset, and choose Create. On each backend compute instance, you may now define a customized healthcheck.html file to respond to health check requests from the load balancer.

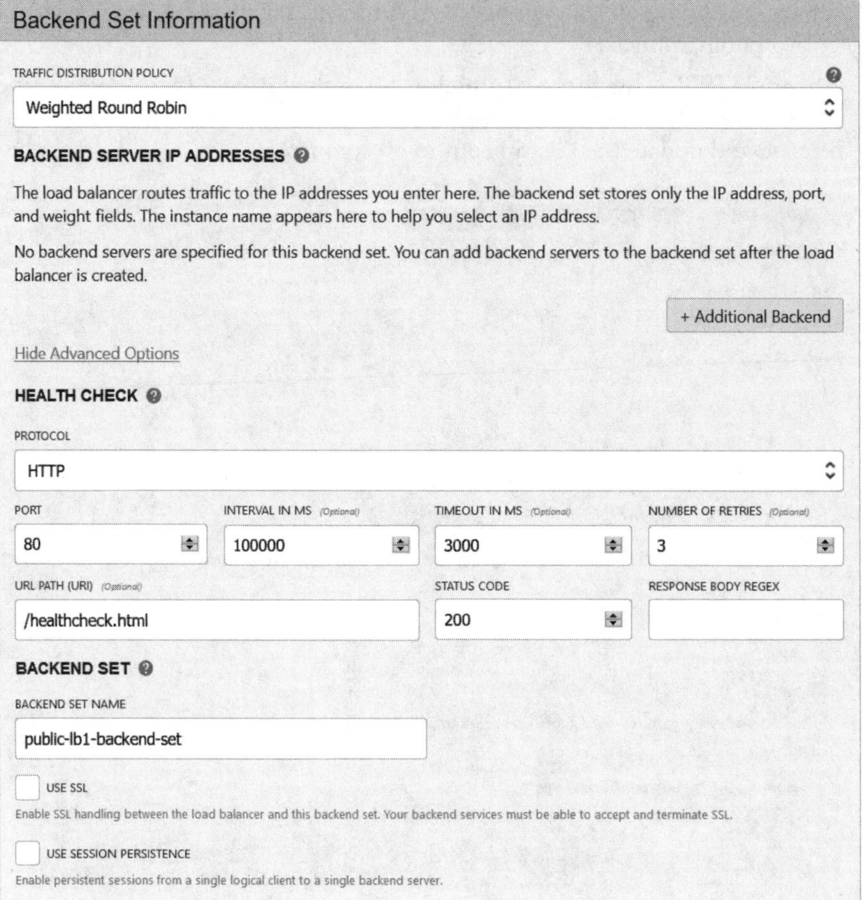

6. After a few minutes, a public load balancer is provisioned with an ephemeral floating public IP address.

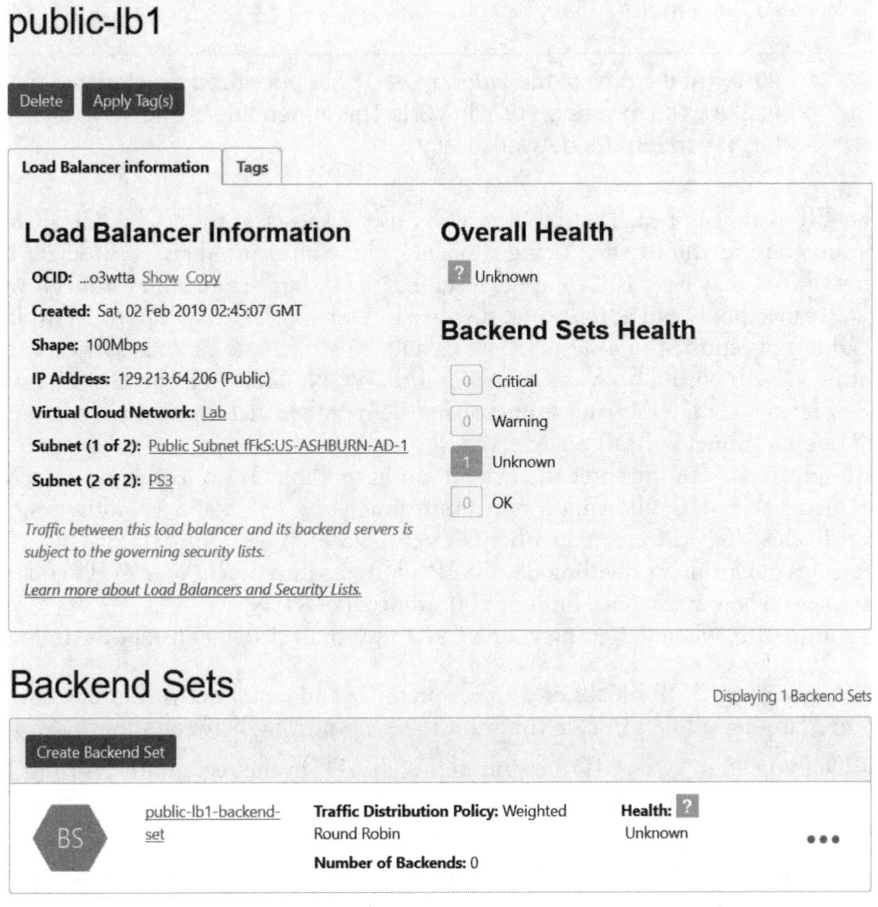

Design and Secure OCI Networks

This section reviews the interaction between key VCN components and discusses best practices for VCN design and edge security.

VCN Design

A VCN is allocated an unmodifiable contiguous IPv4 CIDR range from /16 to /30, so when designing VCNs, ensure that the range is sufficiently large. Many customers use VCNs with a /16 netmask and subnets with /24 netmasks, primarily selecting smaller VCNs and subnet ranges to avoid overlapping with existing networks. This is also the default VCN and subnet sizing provided when you create a VCN plus related resources through the console. A VCN spans all ADs in a region and may contain subnets in any AD in the region. Regional subnets allow for a subnet to span all ADs in a region and may simplify your design. You may, however, want to use AD-specific subnets to isolate networks by AD in a multi-AD region.

NOTE At the time of this writing, Oracle has prioritized development efforts to allow OCI to support IPv6 in VCNs. This impending change will offer further options for network design.

The CIDR range of each subnet in a VCN uses a subset of the VCN's CIDR block. Common considerations when sizing subnets include ensuring there is sufficient room for growth. You may have 100 compute instances today, but design with future growth in mind. Instance pools and autoscaling, discussed in Chapter 4, may lead to an explosion of IP addresses required in a subnet. The balance to strike is to provide sufficient room for future growth within both the subnet and the VCN. Table 3-4 provides an example frame of reference for VCN and subnet sizing. Remember that the first two IPs and the last IP in each subnet's CIDR are reserved.

A simplistic way to interpret the default sizing in Table 3-4 is as follows. The VCN CIDR netmask is /16, allowing a maximum range size of 65,488 IP addresses. If all subnets in this VCN are created with a /24 netmask, each will support 256–3 = 253 IP addresses. Segmenting or dividing 65,488 IP addresses into blocks of 253 IPs equates to 258 subnets. There is a service limit of 300 subnets per VCN.

To summarize, when designing your VCN and subnet sizing, consider the following:

- Segregating CIDR blocks of your on-premises and cloud networks to avoid overlapping subnets in case you want to set up peering between these networks.
- Dividing your VCN CIDR evenly across all ADs in the region into *n*+1 blocks where *n* is the number of ADs in your region, keeping one block for future expansion.
- Whether you are likely to need larger ranges for private subnets rather than public subnets and partition accordingly.

VCN Size	Netmask	Subnet Size	IPs/Subnet	Subnets/VCN	IPs in VCN
X-Small	/24	/27	29	8	232
Small	/21	/24	253	8	2024
Medium	/20	/24	253	16	4048
Large	/19	/22	1021	8	8168
X-Large	/18	/21	2045	8	16360
XX-Large	/16	/20	4093	16	65488
Default	/16	/24	253	258	65488

Table 3-4 VCN and Subnet Sizing Frame of Reference

Architecting for high availability is discussed in Chapter 8, but when designing VCNs, try to maximize the use of multiple ADs for high-availability and to make use of fault domains in single AD regions.

Edge Security

When designing security for your VCN, many OCI networking components are available out of the box to support good practice, starting with private and public subnets. It is usually permissible to expose a public load balancer to the Internet for HTTP traffic to your public website or web applications. These points of entry need to be secured and protected. Sensitive databases should be located in private subnets. NAT gateways may be used for instances in private networks to gain one-way access to Internet resources and still be protected. Use the route table infrastructure to ensure that Dynamic Routing Gateways only route allowed traffic between your VCN and your on-premises network or other cloud networks.

Each subnet can have one route table comprising rules that route traffic to one or more targets. It is good practice for hosts that have similar routing requirements to use the same route tables across multiple ADs. It is also recommended that private subnets have individual route tables to control traffic flow. Traffic between all compute instances within a VCN is routable but the VCN route table limits routing of traffic into and out of the VCN.

Each subnet may have multiple security lists (up to a hard limit of 5, as of this writing), each of which supports multiple stateful and stateless ingress and egress rules. You must ensure that security lists behave like firewalls, managing traffic into and out of the VCN (known as *North–South* traffic) as well as managing internal VCN traffic between multiple subnets (known as *East–West* traffic).

Oracle also recommends the use of OCI IAM policies to allow only authorized groups of users to manage VCN resources. As with all security policies, it is usually best to provide the minimum set of privileges to groups.

CAUTION If access to compute resources is required from the public Internet, it is good practice to create a Bastion host. A Bastion host, or server, is colloquially known as a jump-box designed and configured to withstand attacks. Oracle provides a whitepaper to configure OCI compute access through a Bastion host.

Chapter Review

Understanding OCI networking is a fundamental skill for architecting and securing your OCI environment. This chapter explored the relationship between many generic networking concepts. Many on-premises physical network components are virtualized in OCI but are essentially functionally equivalent. This chapter assumed no prior networking experience, explaining CIDR blocks before introducing virtual cloud networks. The speed at which you can provision a VCN and create subnets, route tables, and security lists is astonishing in OCI. A detailed discussion of subnets, both public and private, ensued by defining how public and private IP objects are assigned to vNICs from your subnets.

Internet gateways extend your VCN by providing Internet access to public subnets while NAT gateways provide a mechanism for instances in private subnets to access the Internet. Service gateways extend the reach of instances in your VCN to other OCI services, notably object storage, without needing to route traffic through the DRG. Local peering gateways link up VCNs in the same region, while remote peering across regions is facilitated by running a remote peering connection through your DRG.

We turned our focus to the DNS edge services as well as how to create and manage DNS records and zones. The chapter explored private and public load balancers and explained the underlying listeners, backend sets, path route rules, and rule sets. The chapter closed with a discussion of best practices when designing VCNs and sizing subnets as well as considerations for edge security. With your VCN and subnets in place, you are ready to start creating compute instances, the subject of Chapter 4.

Questions

1. Choose the CIDR range with the largest IP address block?
   - A. 192.168.1.1/30
   - B. 192.168.1.1/255
   - C. 10.1.0.0/16
   - D. 255.255.255.0
2. Which statement regarding the scope of a VCN is true?
   - A. A VCN is a regional construct.
   - B. A VCN is a global construct.
   - C. A VCN is an AD-level construct.
   - D. All of the above.
3. Which of the following network components facilitates access to the Internet?
   - A. Local peering gateway
   - B. Service gateway
   - C. Internet gateway
   - D. Remote peering connection
4. Which set of prerequisites must be met before an instance can be accessed from the Internet? Choose one or more options.
   - A. The instance must be in a public subnet.
   - B. The instance must be in a private subnet.
   - C. The route table must be configured appropriately.

D. The security list must be configured appropriately.

E. The VCN must contain a functional Internet gateway.

F. The VCN must contain a functional NAT gateway.

5. Which of the following statements is true?

A. BGP is supported with IPSec VPN but not FastConnect when connecting external networks to your VCN.

B. BGP is supported with FastConnect but not IPSec VPN when connecting external networks to your VCN.

C. BGP is supported with FastConnect but not IPSec VPN when connecting subnets within your VCN.

D. BGP is supported with IPSec VPN but not FastConnect when connecting subnets within your VCN.

6. How many IP addresses does a private load balancer require?

A. One

B. Two

C. Three

D. Four

7. A VCN is defined with the CIDR 192.168.0.0/30. How many IP addresses from this CIDR block are reserved by OCI?

A. 1

B. 2

C. 3

D. 4

8. A VCN is defined with the CIDR 192.168.0.0/30. How many IP addresses from this CIDR block are available for host addresses?

A. 1

B. 30

C. 192

D. 168

9. Which protocols are supported by OCI load balancers?

A. HTTP/1.0, HTTP/1.1, HTTP/2.0

B. HTTP/1.0, HTTP/1.1, HTTP/2.0, TCP

C. WebSocket, HTTP/1.0, HTTP/1.1, HTTP/2.0, TCP

D. WebSocks, TCP, HTTPS

E. WebSocks, SSL, TCP, HTTP

10. Which are three load balancer traffic distribution policies?
    - A. Weighted Round Robin, IP Hash, Coin Toss
    - B. Weighted Round Robin, IP Hash, Random
    - C. Round Robin, Coin Toss, Most Connections
    - D. Weighted Round Robin, IP Hash, Least Connections

Answers

1. **C.** The lower the netmask in the CIDR notation, the larger the addressable IP range.
2. **A.** A VCN spans all ADs in a region and is therefore a regional construct.
3. **C.** An Internet gateway is required to facilitate Internet access in a VCN.
4. **A, C, D, E.** Several prerequisites must be met before an instance can connect to the Internet. The subnet it is created in must be a public subnet, with appropriately configured route tables and security lists, located in a VCN with an Internet gateway.
5. **B.** BGP is supported with FastConnect but not IPSec VPN when connecting external networks to your VCN.
6. **C.** A private load balancer requires three IP addresses from the associated subnet for the primary and standby load balancers as well as the floating private IP.
7. **C.** OCI networking service reserves the first IP known as the network address, the last IP known as the broadcast address, as well as the first host address in the CIDR range known as the subnet default gateway address.
8. **A.** This CIDR block specifies four IPs: 192.168.0.0–192.168.0.3. After OCI networking services takes the three it requires, only one remains for host addressing.
9. **C.** OCI load balancers support many protocols, including TCP, HTTP/1.0, HTTP/1.1, HTTP/2.0, and WebSocket.
10. **D.** The three traffic distribution policies available for load balancers are Weighted Round Robin, IP Hash, and Least Connections.

CHAPTER

Compute Instances

In this chapter, you will learn how to

- Describe compute service components
- Create and manage compute instances
- Explain advanced compute concepts

All roads in cloud computing lead to the compute instances. These are the actual computers or servers that run system and application software. This is a huge driver for the existence of public clouds. Instead of managing your own equipment, you pay for just the equipment you need while it is managed by a cloud vendor in one or more data centers.

Compute instances are used for desktop and server class machines. Some organizations no longer provide desktop PCs or laptops to employees. Instead, they have opted to provide staff with dumb terminal access via web browsers to PC desktops that are actually compute instances running in a cloud. The flexibility of this offering is staggering. When staff leave, their VM access needs only to be terminated. If they require more computing resources, these VMs can be upgraded on-the-fly. Backups, upgrades, patching, and corporate software management of end-user PCs may be orchestrated through a common set of commands and processes, ensuring a secure and consistent desktop ecosystem.

This flexibility extends to larger compute instances often used as file, database, middleware, and directory servers. In fact, there is no distinction based on the size of the compute instances. There are just different shapes, either running as bare-metal or virtual compute instances on either a predefined or custom image. It is a very compelling proposition that you can right-size your compute footprint based on your actual requirements and scale as your organizational needs change, without needing to prophesy your requirements over the next five years in terms of both hardware infrastructure and human capital.

This chapter discusses shapes, images, and custom images before exploring the administrative tasks of creating and managing instances. The notions of BYOI (Bring Your Own Image) and BYOH (Bring Your Own Hypervisor) are described before the chapter closes with a discussion on boot volumes and fault domains.

Compute Service Components

The compute service fundamentally provides compute instances as a service, which means you interact with OCI through APIs or the console to provision a computing host or instance. OCI provides a hypervisor layer that accepts API calls from the console, CLI, and other SDKs. A hypervisor is the lowest-level operating system software that is installed on bare-metal servers. A compute instance runs on top of the hypervisor layer and interacts with the physical hardware through the hypervisor.

A compute instance resides in a single availability domain (AD). Instances are either virtual machines (VMs) or bare-metal machines (BMs). VMs and BMs reside on physical equipment localized in a data center or AD. A VM is defined as an independent computing environment executing on physical hardware. Multiple VMs may share the same physical hardware. BM instances execute on dedicated hardware, providing strong isolation and highest performance. In other words, the hypervisor on a particular x86 server may host multiple VMs or a single BM instance. Both machine types are available in many shapes and are based on x86 hardware, and so are capable of running a variety of Linux and Windows operating systems.

When a new compute instance is created, many options may be specified, including a name, the AD it resides in, the boot volume (which may be an Oracle-provided image such as Oracle Linux 7.7), and the shape.

CAUTION Within OCI, when the word "instance" is used without additional description, it is almost always referring to compute instances and not Oracle database instances.

Compute Shapes

A compute shape is a predefined bundle of computing resources, primarily differentiated by Oracle Compute Units (OCPUs), memory, network interfaces, network bandwidth, and support for block and NVMe local storage. An OCPU is equivalent to a hyper-threaded core. Therefore, each OCPU corresponds to two hardware execution threads, known as vCPUs. Table 4-1 lists a subset of available compute shapes across both VM and BM instance types. New compute shapes are added as new hardware is added to availability domains.

Shape names contain several useful identifiers. VM and BM refer to the broad category of instance type. Standard means that only block storage is available, while DenseIO means local NVMe drivers are present to support NVMe SSD disk drives. GPU shapes are based on servers with NVIDIA GPUs (Graphical Processing Units) while HPC shapes offer supercomputer high performance compute power. The two numbers at the end of the shape name refer to the generation of the hardware and the number of OCPUs.

Consider the shapes VM.Standard1.8 and VM.Standard2.8, described in Table 4-1. Both have eight OCPUs, but they are based on first- and second-generation hardware (in this case, X5 and X7). Other differences between these two VM shapes are the available

Shape	Instance Type	OCPU	Memory (GB)	Local Disk (TB)	Bandwidth (Gbps)	Max vNICs
BM.Standard1.36	Standard compute	36	256	Block storage	10	Linux: 36, Windows: 1
VM.Standard1.8		8	56	Block storage	2.4	Linux: 8, Windows: 1
VM.Standard2.8		8	120	Block storage	8.2	Linux: 8, Windows: 8
VM.Standard.E2.8		8	64	Block storage	5.6	Linux: 4, Windows: 4
BM.DenseIO2.52	X7-based dense I/O compute	52	768	51.2 TB NVMe SSD	2 x 25 Gbps	Linux: 52, Windows: 27
BM.GPU3.8	X7-based GPU: 8xV100 NVIDIA GPUs	52	768	Block storage	2 x 25 Gbps	Linux: 52, Windows: 27
VM.GPU2.1 (GPU: 1xP100)		12	72	Block storage	8	Linux: 12, Windows: 12
BM.HPC2.36	X7-based high frequency compute	36	384	6.7 TB NVMe SSD (1 drive)	1 x 25 Gbps 1 x 100 Gbps RDMA	Linux: 50, Windows: 1

Table 4-1 VM and BM Compute Shapes

memory (56GB vs 120GB), the network bandwidth supported (2.4 Gbps vs. 8.2 Gbps), and the support for multiple network interfaces when running Windows operating systems (1 vs. 8).

CAUTION Not all shapes are available in all regions. For example, the first-generation shapes are only available to certain tenancies in the Phoenix, Ashburn, and Frankfurt regions. When you create a compute instance, there may already be service limits imposed on your account. These may be elevated but require a service request to be opened by an administrator through the OCI console.

Consider the shapes VM.Standard2.8 and VM.Standard.E2.8, described in Table 4-1. These shapes are almost identically named, except for the additional ".E" in the latter shape. This identifies the underlying CPU as an AMD E-series microprocessor (EPYC CPU) as opposed to the standard Intel Xeon–based microchips found in other shapes. Other differences between the VM.Standard2.8 and VM.Standard.E2.8 shapes include the available memory (120GB vs. 64GB), the network bandwidth supported (8.2 Gbps vs. 5.6 Gbps), and the number of available network interfaces (8 vs. 4). Similarly, the GPU3 and GPU2 shapes are based on NVIDIA P100 and V100 chipsets respectively.

NOTE The underlying physical server that hosts multiple VMs or a single BM instance is an Oracle bare-metal server like an X7-2 x86 machine you could purchase for your on-premises data center. VMs share the physical infrastructure, whereas BM instances have dedicated access to the CPU cores, memory, and network interfaces (NICs) on the physical hosts. A wide range of compute shapes is currently available, and the variety will continue to increase as demand grows. It is important to know your options to understand the costs and benefits of each shape. Unsurprisingly, bare-metal shapes cost more than their VM counterparts, and larger machines cost more than smaller machines. This will inform prudent decision-making that balances scalability and performance requirements with financial constraints.

Compute Images

When creating compute instances, a key decision is to determine the operating system image. You may choose from the following:

- **Platform images** Pre-built OCI-provided images with an operating system
- **Oracle images** Pre-built OCI images with applications pre-installed as well
- **Partner images** Trusted pre-built third-party images published by partners
- **Custom images** Images you have generated from other OCI instances or imported into OCI
- **Boot volumes** Previously created boot volumes
- **Image OCID** A specific version of an image (example: an image location provided from the OCI Marketplace)
- **BYOH** Bring Your Own Hypervisor

These image types are discussed next.

Platform Images

OCI offers several pre-built Linux and Windows images complete with the appropriate drivers to rapidly provision your instance. Available OCI preconfigured images include these operating systems in various shape-related editions. Table 4-2 shows several images for several Windows Server images.

Using the CLI, you may also list the current set of images:

```
$ oci compute image list
--compartment-id ocid1.compartment.oc1..zlh3iq |
grep -i display|grep Oracle-Linux-7.6|
sed  's/"display-name": "//' | sed 's/",//'
      Oracle-Linux-7.6-Gen2-GPU-2019.02.20-0
      Oracle-Linux-7.6-Gen2-GPU-2019.01.17-0
      Oracle-Linux-7.6-Gen2-GPU-2018.12.19-0
      Oracle-Linux-7.6-2019.02.20-0
      Oracle-Linux-7.6-2019.01.17-0
      Oracle-Linux-7.6-2018.12.19-0
```

Operating System	Edition	Shape
Windows Server 2016	Standard Edition	VM Gen2
Windows Server 2016	Datacenter Edition	BM Gen2 E2
Windows Server 2016	Datacenter Edition	BM Gen2 DenseIO
Windows Server 2016	Datacenter Edition	BM Gen2
Windows Server 2012 R2	Standard Edition	VM Gen2 E2
Windows Server 2012 R2	Standard Edition	VM
Windows Server 2012 R2	Datacenter Edition	BM Gen2 E2
Windows Server 2012 R2	Datacenter Edition	BM Gen2 DenseIO
Windows Server 2012 R2	Datacenter Edition	BM Gen2
Windows Server 2012 R2	Datacenter Edition	BM
Windows Server 2008 R2	Enterprise Edition	VM Gen2
Windows Server 2008 R2	Enterprise Edition	VM

Table 4-2 Several Preconfigured Windows Images and Supported Shape Type

This list shows six builds of the Oracle Linux 7.6 image. The Gen2-GPU images are specific to the second-generation GPU shapes. When creating an instance, the console shows the latest builds for all preconfigured images. Other available builds are visible through the Advanced Options section discussed later in the chapter or through the CLI and API. Figure 4-1 shows a typical list of platform images available through the console. This list evolves as newer versions are released and older versions are desupported.

Oracle Images

Oracle has published images with preinstalled applications known as Oracle images. Figure 4-2 shows how applications, including the Oracle E-Business Suite Demo environment, Oracle Enterprise Manager, or PeopleSoft Cloud Manager, can be deployed by simply selecting an image from a list of prebuilt applications.

CAUTION Not all Oracle images are available in all regions. The repository of canned images is expanding and images are released to different regions at different times.

When you create a compute instance from an Oracle image, you have to accept some legal terms and conditions before the instance is provisioned.

Partner Images

OCI provides a cloud marketplace where third-party vendors proffer their application software to OCI users. Partner images are pre-built images that include an operating system and application deployment from a third-party provider. These images have been vetted by Oracle and are considered trusted images. Upon choosing a partner image on which to base your compute instance, you are required to accept legal terms and conditions from both Oracle and the third-party vendor that governs your use of the image.

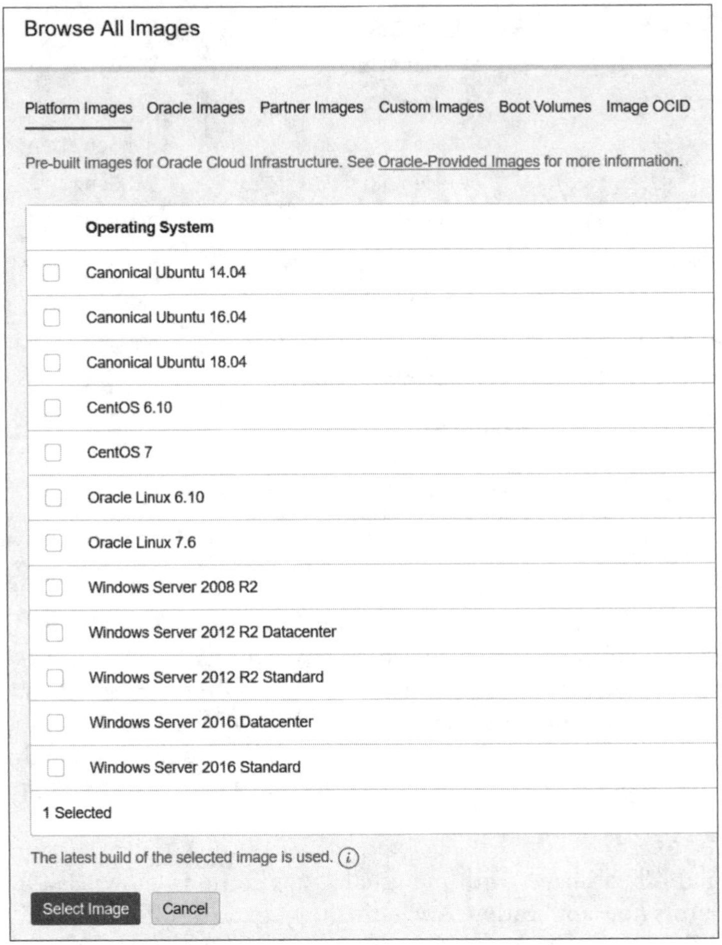

Figure 4-1 A variety of pre-built platform images

Custom Images

OCI provides an interface for you to create your own images from existing compute instances and save these as custom images to be used as the basis for future compute instance deployments. Custom images may be based on OCI platform, oracle, or partner images that have been customized in some way, or they may be imported from an external image that meets several requirements.

Some organizations create a master image, sometimes known as a gold image, that is rolled out to a specific user community. You can create a custom image, ensuring that all security, network, and antivirus settings are in place with appropriate patches. These could be desktop images preloaded with office productivity applications or pretty much any software.

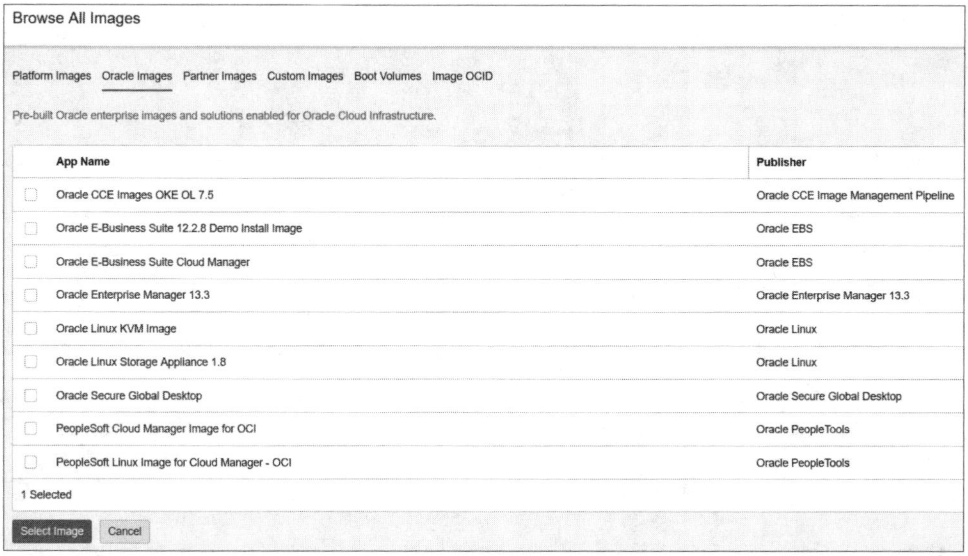

Browse All Images

Platform Images Oracle Images Partner Images Custom Images Boot Volumes Image OCID

Pre-built Oracle enterprise images and solutions enabled for Oracle Cloud Infrastructure.

App Name	Publisher
Oracle CCE Images OKE OL 7.5	Oracle CCE Image Management Pipeline
Oracle E-Business Suite 12.2.8 Demo Install Image	Oracle EBS
Oracle E-Business Suite Cloud Manager	Oracle EBS
Oracle Enterprise Manager 13.3	Oracle Enterprise Manager 13.3
Oracle Linux KVM Image	Oracle Linux
Oracle Linux Storage Appliance 1.8	Oracle Linux
Oracle Secure Global Desktop	Oracle Secure Global Desktop
PeopleSoft Cloud Manager Image for OCI	Oracle PeopleTools
PeopleSoft Linux Image for Cloud Manager - OCI	Oracle PeopleTools

1 Selected

Select Image Cancel

Figure 4-2 Enterprise images pre-built for OCI

Another situation that lends itself to custom images is related to autoscaling, discussed later in this chapter. Imagine a website hosted on a single compute instance running an HTTP server. You can create a custom image from this compute instance and use it as the basis for automatically provisioning additional preconfigured web server compute instances when your website is overloaded.

Figure 4-3 shows the OCI console interface used for importing pre-existing external images as custom images.

Existing virtual machines may be exported as OCI, VMDK, or QCOW2 format images. These exports are uploaded to object storage (discussed in Chapter 5). For example, you may have a legacy Oracle 10*g* database on Oracle Enterprise Linux 5.5 hosting a production system on-premises in a virtualized environment. You could lift and shift this environment to OCI by exporting the virtualized image as a VMDK or QCOW2 format image type, uploading the exported image files to object storage, importing the image as a custom image in OCI, and creating a compute instance based on this image.

As Figure 4-3 shows, custom images must be launched in one of three modes:

- **Native mode** Drivers in the image communicate directly with underlying hypervisor.
- **Paravirtualized mode** The guest image is modified to hook directly to the underlying hypervisor for certain tasks.
- **Emulated mode** The guest image is fully virtualized and runs without modification on the OCI hypervisor.

Import Image help cancel

CREATE IN COMPARTMENT

Lab

eclipsys (root)/Lab

NAME

10g DB on OEL 5.5

OPERATING SYSTEM

Linux

OBJECT STORAGE URL

See Object Storage URLs for more information. See instructions for creating a pre-authenticated request.

IMAGE TYPE

VMDK

QCOW2

OCI

Select OCI for .oci files exported from Oracle Cloud Infrastructure. The launch mode setting is specified in the .oci file and cannot be changed in the Console.

LAUNCH MODE

PARAVIRTUALIZED MODE

Select this option for virtual machines that support paravirtualized drivers, created outside of Oracle Cloud Infrastructure.

Show Launch Options

EMULATED MODE

Select this option for virtual machines that do not support paravirtualized drivers, created outside of Oracle Cloud Infrastructure from your older on-premise physical or virtual machines.

Show Launch Options

NATIVE MODE

Select this option for images exported from Oracle Cloud Infrastructure.

Show Launch Options

Figure 4-3 Import custom images for compute instances.

The launch mode is determined by the compatibility of the underlying image with the hardware hosting the virtual machines. Custom images imported from OCI format exports may be launched in native mode because these images already have system drivers for the underlying hardware. Images created outside of OCI may be launched in either emulated mode or paravirtualized mode, depending on whether the operating systems in these images have support for the underlying hardware. Older operating systems typically do not have drivers for modern hardware and are likely to launch in emulated mode only.

NOTE The performance of virtual machines is related to its launch mode. If the compute shapes are the same, a VM launched in native mode performs better than one launched in paravirtualized (PV) mode. An instance launched in PV mode will perform better than one in emulated mode. It is therefore preferable to migrate older systems to newer natively supported images.

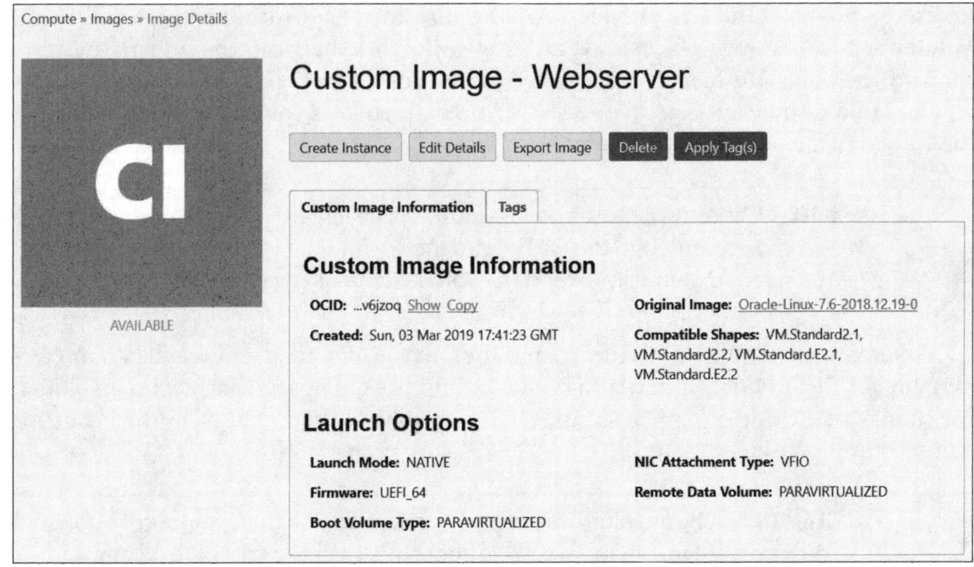

Figure 4-4 Custom image created from a running compute instance

You may create a custom image from an existing compute instance. The compute instance is stopped (though a manual shutdown beforehand is usually advisable) for the duration of the image creation and started up automatically once the imaging is completed. Figure 4-4 shows a custom image created from an existing instance. This image has an OCID and is compatible with several compute shapes. It may be launched in native mode and is based on an Oracle Linux 7.6 image.

Boot Volumes

When you create a compute instance, you may configure the boot volume for the instance. This is a special block volume that stores the operating system and boot loader required to launch the compute instance. Figure 4-5 shows several optional boot volume configuration options.

The boot volume size may be increased to provide headroom for future growth of the boot volume. The default boot volume size depends on the image chosen. Linux images usually require a significantly smaller boot volume than Windows images.

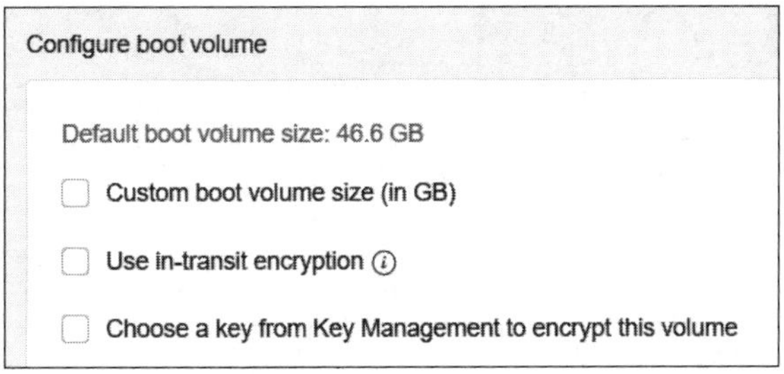

Figure 4-5 Boot volume sizing and encryption configuration options

Configure boot volume

Default boot volume size: 46.6 GB

☐ Custom boot volume size (in GB)

☐ Use in-transit encryption ⓘ

☐ Choose a key from Key Management to encrypt this volume

Access to boot volumes is provided to compute instances through the OCI Block Volume service. Storage blocks traverse a network fabric between the underlying storage and the compute instance. You may choose to encrypt the data in-transit. Boot volumes may also be encrypted at rest using predefined keys you have configured using the Key Management vault.

NOTE Choosing a custom boot volume size increases the size of the block volume presented to the OS but not the size of the file systems built upon it. You need to manually extend the volume to take advantage of the larger size.

A boot volume is attached to the instance but may be detached and retained upon termination of the instance. It may also be cloned and backed up. A detached boot volume, which may be a clone or previously attached boot volume, may be used as the image for a new compute instance.

EXAM TIP A boot volume used as the image source for a compute instance must be available in the same AD chosen to host the compute instance.

Figure 4-6 lists six boot volumes in the Lab compartment. Three are attached to compute instances, one is terminated, and two are not attached. It is these detached volumes that are available to reuse as boot volumes in new compute instances. Notice that each boot volume has an OCID and resides physically in storage in a particular AD. Therefore, to create a new compute instance in AD1 in the Ashburn region (for this tenancy), only the OEM boot volume is available for reuse as a boot volume for compatible shapes.

Boot Volumes *in* Lab *Compartment*

Sort by: Created Date (Desc) | Displaying 6 Boot Volumes < Page 1 >

instance-20190128-2132 (Boot Volume) **OCID:** ...h6tiwa Show Copy **Availability Domain:** fFkS:US-ASHBURN-AD-2 **Size:** 46.6 GB	**Attached Instance:** instance-20190128-2132 **Attachment Access:** Read/Write **Attachment Type:** Boot Volume **Date Attached:** Tue, 29 Jan 2019 02:38:28 GMT	**Encryption Key:** None **Created:** Tue, 29 Jan 2019 02:38:28 GMT **Backup Policy:** – **Source:** –
Instance1AD2 (Boot Volume) **OCID:** ...j5h6pa Show Copy **Availability Domain:** fFkS:US-ASHBURN-AD-2 **Size:** 46.6 GB	**Attached Instance:** None in this compartment.	**Encryption Key:** None **Created:** Sun, 06 Jan 2019 22:15:15 GMT **Backup Policy:** – **Source:** –
Instance1AD3 (Boot Volume) **OCID:** ...fkyorq Show Copy **Availability Domain:** fFkS:US-ASHBURN-AD-3 **Size:** 46.6 GB	**Attached Instance:** Instance1AD3 **Attachment Access:** Read/Write **Attachment Type:** Boot Volume **Date Attached:** Fri, 04 Jan 2019 04:49:04 GMT	**Encryption Key:** None **Created:** Fri, 04 Jan 2019 04:49:04 GMT **Backup Policy:** – **Source:** –
instance-20190103-2336 (Boot Volume) **OCID:** ...vuhooa Show Copy **Availability Domain:** fFkS:US-ASHBURN-AD-2 **Size:** 46.6 GB		**Encryption Key:** None **Created:** Fri, 04 Jan 2019 04:37:04 GMT **Source:** –
hercules (Boot Volume) **OCID:** ...zufpla Show Copy **Availability Domain:** fFkS:US-ASHBURN-AD-1 **Size:** 46.6 GB	**Attached Instance:** hercules **Attachment Access:** Read/Write **Attachment Type:** Boot Volume **Date Attached:** Wed, 26 Dec 2018 04:49:45 GMT	**Encryption Key:** None **Created:** Wed, 26 Dec 2018 04:49:45 GMT **Backup Policy:** – **Source:** –
oem (Boot Volume) **OCID:** ...lhi3fq Show Copy **Availability Domain:** fFkS:US-ASHBURN-AD-1 **Size:** 46.6 GB	**Attached Instance:** None in this compartment.	**Encryption Key:** None **Created:** Wed, 19 Dec 2018 23:30:59 GMT **Backup Policy:** – **Source:** –

Figure 4-6 Attached and detached boot volumes

Apart from imaging compute instances, a boot volume clone may be taken when troubleshooting a problematic instance that cannot boot up or to recover data. A useful technique is to clone the boot volume of the problematic instance and attach the clone to another instance as another block volume (discussed in Chapter 5). By mounting the cloned volume as a secondary volume, you can expose the file systems on the cloned volume for further investigation.

Image OCID

Custom and platform images are storage resources with OCIDs. You can create a compute instance by referencing an available image by its OCID. This image is then used to clone a new boot volume for your compute instance. Figure 4-7 shows an older-platform image (Oracle Linux 6.8) that is no longer available through the platform images list, being referenced using its OCID.

The Oracle-Provided Image Release Notes link on the Image OCID page in the OCI console takes you to the online documentation where families of operating system images and their OCIDs are listed. Custom images may also be created using their image OCID.

CAUTION An important distinction must be made between images and boot volumes. Platform, Oracle, Partner, and Custom images as well as images referenced by their OCIDs are templates that are cloned onto new boot volumes when a compute instance is created. Boot volumes and boot volume clones are actually attached to new compute instances. These may be cloned to instantiate a new boot volume to attach to another new compute instance.

Bring Your Own Hypervisor

Strictly speaking, BYOH follows the same principles as Oracle and custom images discussed earlier. These offer significant value so are covered discretely. Moving existing virtualized infrastructure becomes a simple lift and shift exercise because BYOH allows you to use a wide range of operating systems, including many legacy systems. OCI provides

Platform Images Oracle Images Partner Images Custom Images Boot Volumes Image OCID

Create an instance using a specific version of an image using the image OCID. See Oracle-Provided Image Release Notes to determine the image OCID for Oracle-provided images.

Image OCID

ocid1.image.oc1.iad.aaaaaaaazuvdeqsufjlme3otnulbqpofwlmvplj6lhk6qaxvcptkam7rxgga

Image name: Oracle-Linux-6.8-2017.03.02-0

Boot volume size (in GB): 46.6

Select Image Cancel

Figure 4-7 Create a compute instance using an image OCID

support for installing several hypervisors on bare-metal instances. Supported hypervisors include the following:

- **Kernel-based VM (KVM)** This entails imaging a bare-metal instance with an Oracle Linux image and installing the KVM server software. After configuring the networking on the bare-metal instance to leverage multiple vNICs and provisioning additional block storage, KVM guests may be imported from existing images or installed from ISO images. You may choose an Oracle Linux KVM Image from the Oracle image list in the OCI console.
- **Oracle VM (OVM)** You set up OVM Manager on a VM or BM instance and OVM Server on bare-metal instances using Image OCIDs provided by Oracle. OVM may be used as on-premises for hosting guest VMs. OVM manager behaves as a bastion host to the guest VMs.
- **Hyper-V** Older Windows operating system images may be deployed as guest VMs of Hyper-V deployed on bare-metal instances.

Instance Management

It is about time we get into the thick of things and create some compute instances. Prerequisites include having a VCN in place and deciding on an architecture. If you have worked through exercises in the earlier chapters, you should have several VCNs in place in your OCI tenancy and should be good to go. This section consists of several exercises geared to producing a solution based on the architecture in Figure 4-8. The second part in this section discusses management of these compute instances.

NOTE While the console is great for deploying relatively small solutions, it does not scale well to large solutions. Treating infrastructure as a service and deploying hundreds or thousands of compute instances, network, storage, and security infrastructure is only practical by leveraging automation tools such as Terraform, OCI CLI scripts, or the APIs through the SDKs. Automation tools are discussed in Chapter 7.

Create Compute Instances

This section consists of five exercises that entail

- Creating an SSH key pair to use to connect to the Linux compute instances
- Creating a compute instance to use as a web server to serve a simple Hello World static HTML page
- Creating a custom image based on this compute instance and using this to spawn a new compute instance

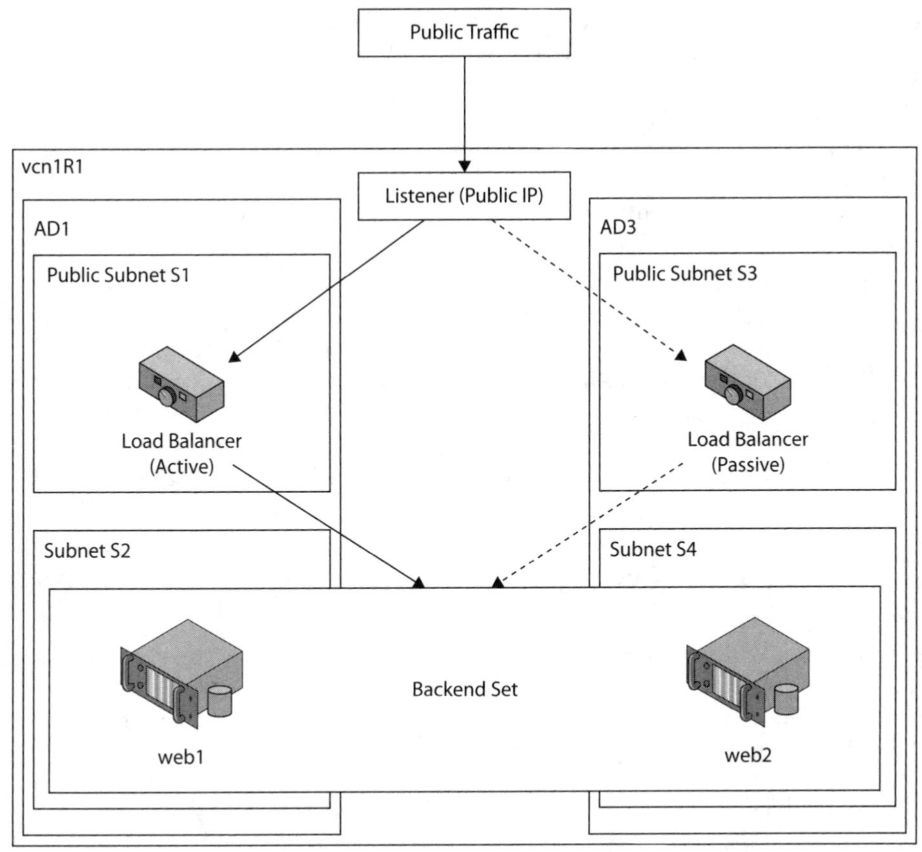

Figure 4-8 Two compute instances serving as web servers as part of a backend set

- Creating a public load balancer to round robin HTTP traffic to these web servers
- Creating a Windows instance

To connect securely to your Linux compute instances, you need an SSH key pair. Basically, you generate a key pair consisting of a private key and a public key. You keep the private key safe and do not share or post publicly. You provide the public key at compute instance create time.

When OCI provisions a new Oracle Linux or CentOS compute instance, a user named opc is created. This is the initial user used to connect to the instance. The opc (Oracle Public Cloud) user has privileges to gain root access through the `sudo` command.

The public key is added into the authorized_keys file in a hidden subdirectory in the opc users home directory (/home/opc/.ssh). For Ubuntu Linux, the initial user created is named ubuntu.

When you try to connect to the public IP address of the instance using the SSH protocol on port 22 (open by default in the firewall), you provide the private key. Through a series of encrypted message exchanges between your SSH client and the compute instance, the client is authenticated and a connection is established.

NOTE SSH key pairs may be created using a variety of encryption formats including RSA, DSS, and DSA and may be created using tools such a ssh-keygen from the UNIX OpenSSH package or the PuTTY Key Generator on Windows. Key pairs may be used multiple times, but this presents the same risk as setting the same root password on multiple systems. Whether the key pair is used only once or used in multiple situations, the private key must be kept secret. It is good practice to rotate these keys periodically.

Exercise 4-1: Create an SSH Key Pair

If you are using Windows, download a tool that is capable of generating SSH keys, such as PuTTY Key Generator, and follow Steps 1–6. If you are using a Unix-style system (including MacOS), ensure that a tool such as ssh-keygen is available and follow Step 7 or 8 in this exercise.

1. Launch PuTTY Key Generator (sometimes labeled as PuTTYgen).
2. Choose SSH2-RSA as the key type and specify 2048 as the number of bits in this key.
3. Choose Generate and move your mouse cursor over the blank area to generate some random seed that will be used to generate the keys.
4. Provide a key passphrase as an additional security measure.
5. Copy the public key in OpenSSH authorized_keys file format and paste it into a text file, typically saved with a .pub extension. In this exercise, the file with the public key is named rsa-key.pub.
6. Choose Save Private Key and save the PuTTY format private key as rsa-key.ppk. It is usually advisable to export the private key via Conversions | Export OpenSSH key into RSA format if you intend to use the same key pair on a Unix-style computer (including MacOS). Alternatively, the PuTTY format private key can later be converted using PuTTYgen on Windows or Linux via the putty-tools package.

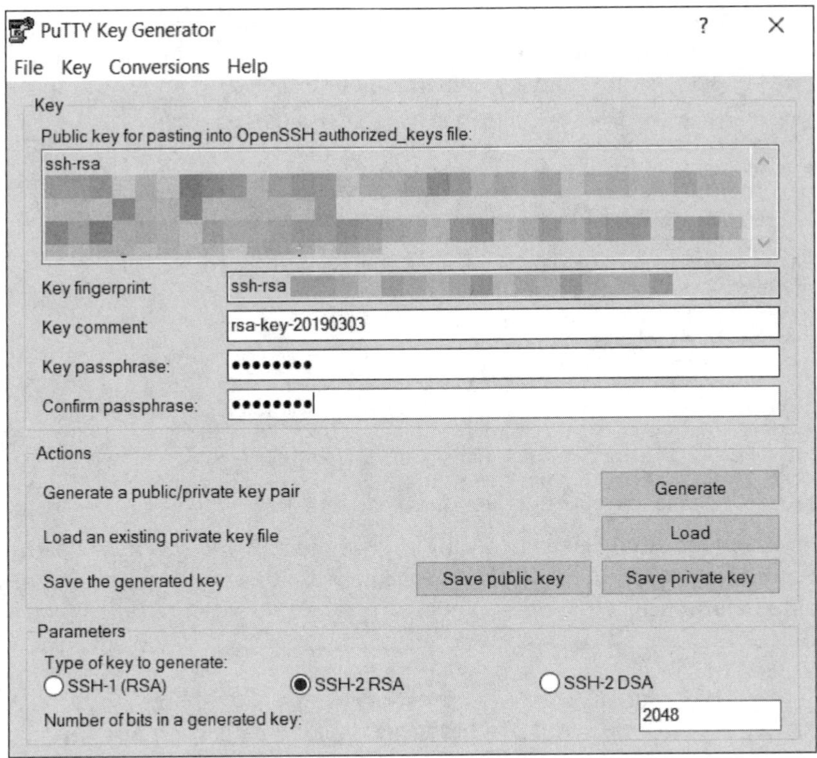

7. You can run ssh-keygen in interactive mode or through a single command. In interactive mode, simply run ssh-keygen at the Unix prompt. You will be prompted to provide a filename (/home/sid/.ssh/rsa-key) and a passphrase.

```
$ ssh-keygen
Generating public/private rsa key pair.
Enter file in which to save the key
(/home/sid/.ssh/id_rsa): /home/sid/.ssh/rsa-key
Enter passphrase (empty for no passphrase):
Enter same passphrase again:
Your identification has been saved in /home/sid/.ssh/rsa-key.
Your public key has been saved in /home/sid/.ssh/rsa-key.pub.
The key fingerprint is:SHA256xx
The key's randomart image is:
+---[RSA 2048]----+
+----[SHA256]-----+
sid$ ls -l /home/sid/.ssh
-rw-------. 1 sid sid  398 Jan  4 04:51 authorized_keys
-rw-r--r--. 1 sid sid  911 Jan  7 01:40 known_hosts
-rw-------. 1 sid sid 1766 Mar  4 02:48 rsa-key
-rw-r--r--. 1 sid sid  398 Mar  4 02:48 rsa-key.pub

$ cat /home/sid/.ssh/rsa-key.pub
ssh-rsa AAAAB3NzaC1yc2EAAAADAQABAAABAQ...
```

8. To run `ssh-keygen` as a single command, you are required to specify several parameters including -t <key type>, -N <passphrase>, -b <number of bits in key>, -C <key name>, and -f <filename>. For example:

```
$ ssh-keygen -t rsa -N "admin123" -b 2048 -C "RSA-KEY"
-f /home/sid/.ssh/RSA-KEY
Generating public/private rsa key pair.
Your identification has been saved in /home/sid/.ssh/RSA-KEY.
Your public key has been saved in /home/sid/.ssh/RSA-KEY.pub.
The key fingerprint is:
SHA256:V8wW/zO5zZ4XvDG8BJy6N6X8ofWOFwb2VtWl/D2vVgg RSA-KEY
The key's randomart image is:
+---[RSA 2048]----+
+----[SHA256]-----+
$ ls -l /home/sid/.ssh
-rw-------. 1 sid sid  398 Jan  4 04:51 authorized_keys
-rw-r--r--. 1 sid sid  911 Jan  7 01:40 known_hosts
-rw-------. 1 sid sid 1766 Mar  4 02:46 RSA-KEY
-rw-r--r--. 1 sid sid  389 Mar  4 02:46 RSA-KEY.pub
$ cat /home/sid/.ssh/RSA-KEY.pub
ssh-rsa AAAAB3NzaC1yc2EAAAADAQABAAABAQ...RSA-KEY
```

9. You have successfully generated your SSH key pair. If you specified a passphrase, keep this safe as it will be required in the next exercise when connecting to your compute instance.

Exercise 4-2: Create a Compute Instance to Use as a Web Server

In this exercise, you will create a compute instance in your home region in a VCN with at least two subnets. If you completed all the exercises in Chapter 3, you should have a VCN similar to VCN1R1. A security ingress rule allowing TCP traffic in through port 80 must be added to the relevant security list used by the public subnet you plan to use for your web server compute instance.

1. Sign in to the OCI console and choose your compartment.
2. Navigate to Compute | Instances and choose Create Instance.
3. Name your instance (for example, web1) and select an AD for your instance (for example, AD1).
4. For operating system or image source, choose Change Image Source, navigate to Platform Images, and select an operating system (for example, Oracle Linux 7.*x*).

Create Compute Instance

Help Close

Oracle Cloud Infrastructure Compute lets you provision and manage compute hosts, known as instances. You can launch instances as needed to meet your compute and application requirements.

Name your instance

web1

Select an availability domain for your instance

AD 1
fFkS:US-ASHBURN-AD-1

AD 2
fFkS:US-ASHBURN-AD-2

AD 3
fFkS:US-ASHBURN-AD-3

Choose an operating system or image source

ORACLE LINUX

Oracle Linux 7.6
Image Build: 2019.02.20-0

Change Image Source

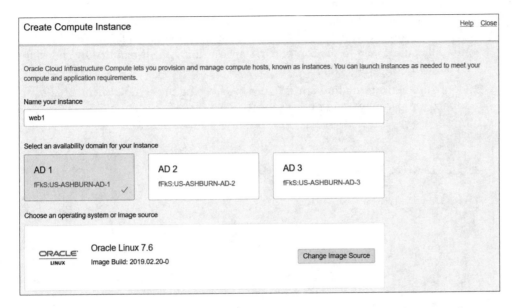

5. Select a virtual machine instance type, click Change Shape, and choose a shape (for example, VM.StandardE2.1). Change any boot volume configuration options as required or accept the default settings.

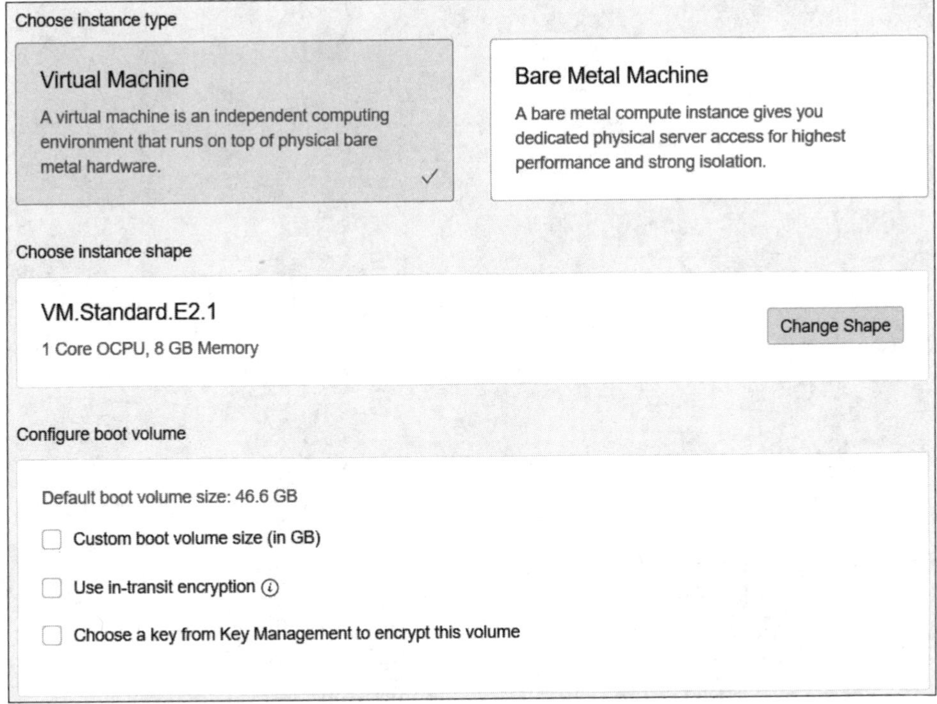

6. Add the public SSH key file you generated in the previous exercise. You may choose the key file or paste the SSH key from the public key file. You may add multiple public keys to the compute instance at this stage if required by choosing to paste multiple public SSH keys.
7. Configure networking for your instance by choosing the compartment, VCN, subnet compartment, and public subnet.

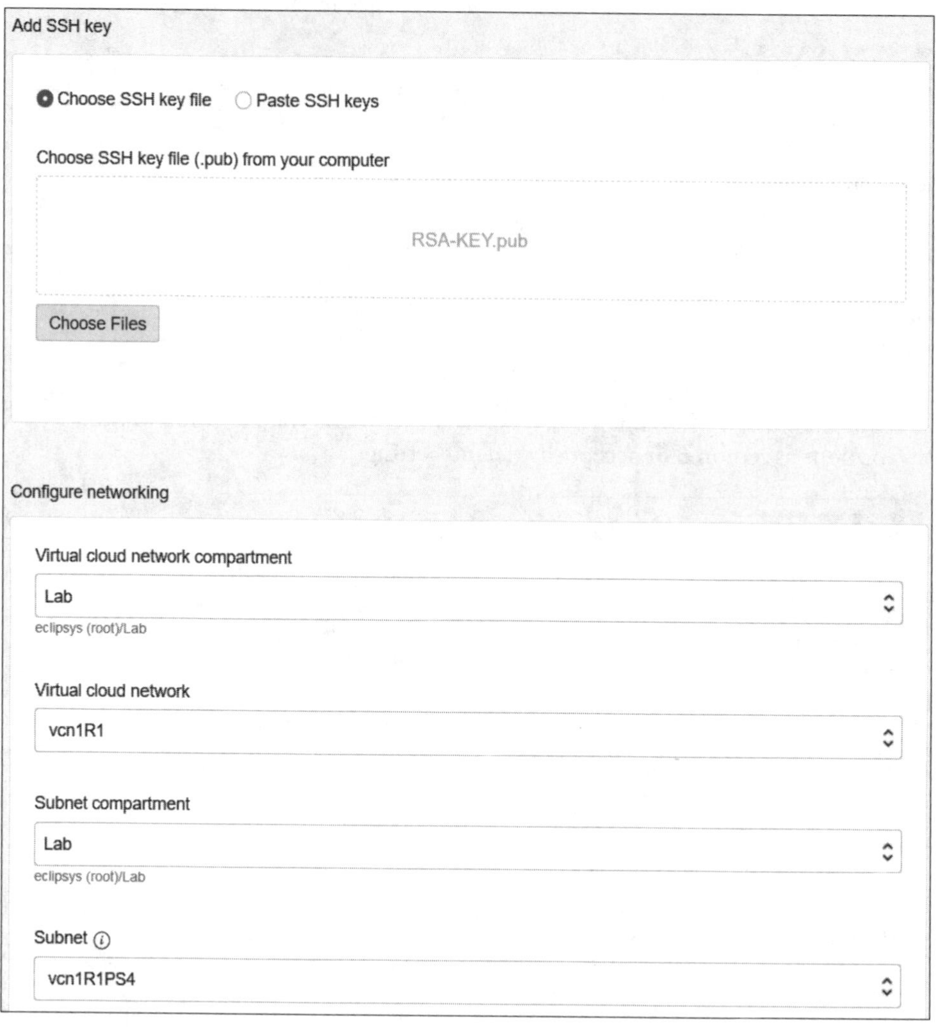

8. Click Show Advanced Options. Ensure that your compartment is correct. Choose a fault domain (FAULT-DOMAIN-1). Fault domains are sets of fault-tolerant isolated physical infrastructure within an AD. By choosing different fault domains for two VM instances, you ensure these are hosted on separate physical hardware, thus increasing your intra-availability domain resilience.

9. Insert the following commands into the User data cloud-init script area. This script will run when the newly provisioned compute instance boots up. The following script updates the package repository.

```
sudo yum -y update
```

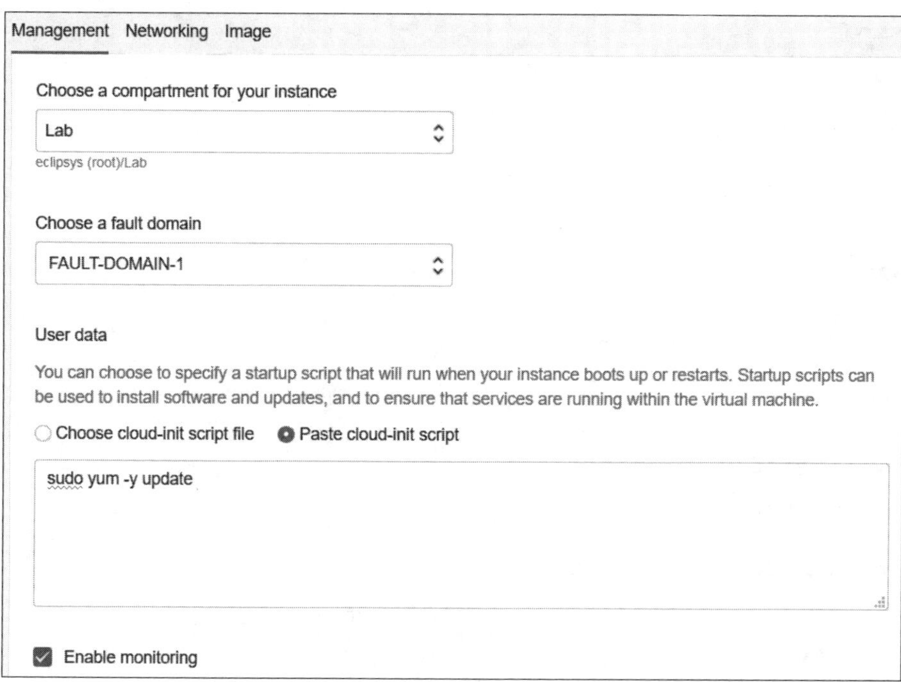

10. Choose the Networking menu in the Advanced options and confirm the VCN and subnet settings. Additionally, check that the Assign Public IP Address option is checked. Finally, enter a hostname, for example, web1 and click Create.

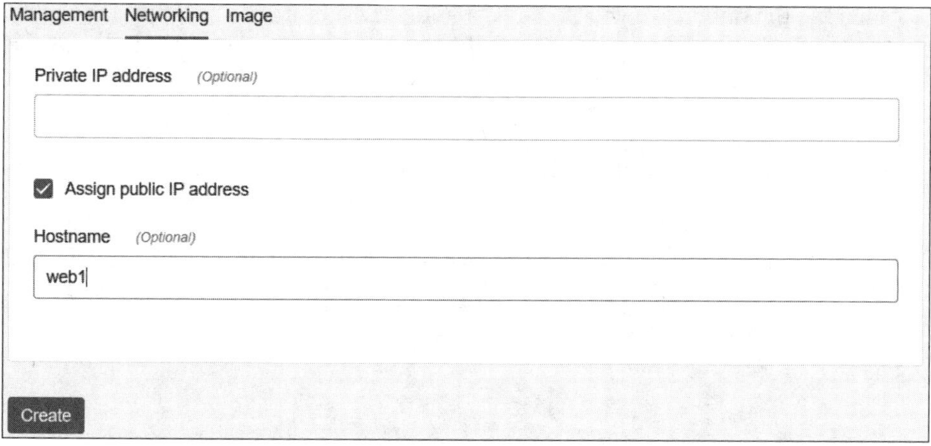

11. After a few minutes, the status of your new compute instance will change from PROVISIONING to RUNNING. RUNNING does not mean the instance has fully booted up. You may have to wait a few minutes for the instance to boot up and run the cloud-init startup script.

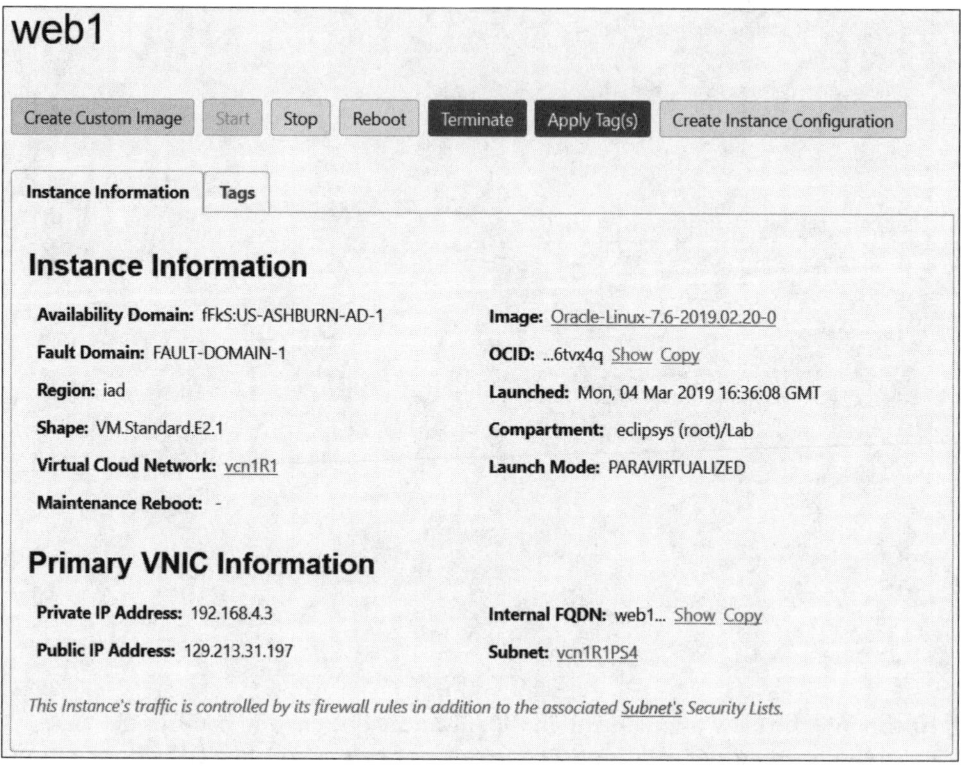

12. You may connect to the compute instance using `ssh` and the private key, which matches the public key you provided when provisioning the instance. If you are using a Unix-style system, ensure that the `ssh` program is available and connect to the instance as follows: ssh -i <*path to private key file*> opc@<*public IP address of compute instance*>. For example:

```
$ ssh -i /home/opc/.ssh/RSA-KEY opc@129.213.31.197
Enter passphrase for key '/home/opc/.ssh/RSA-KEY':
Last login: Mon Mar 4 20:27:08 2019 from 129.213.138.238
[opc@web1 ~]$
```

13. If you are using a Windows system, launch a terminal emulator such as PuTTY, provide the public IP address in the Session category, and choose SSH as the connection type.

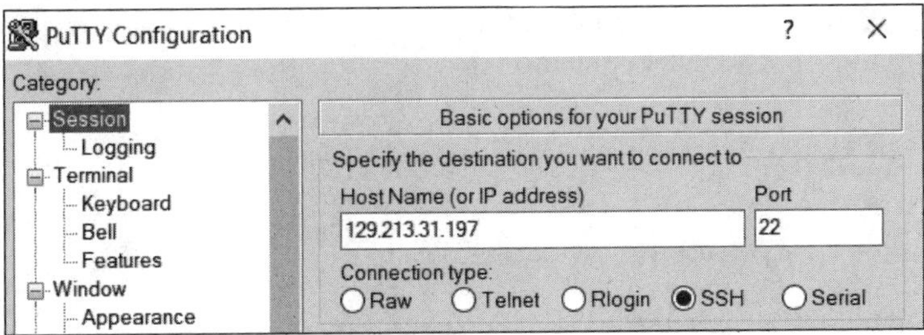

14. In PuTTY, navigate to the Connection | Data section and provide opc as the auto-login username. Navigate to the Connection | SSH | Auth section, and browse to the private key file created earlier.

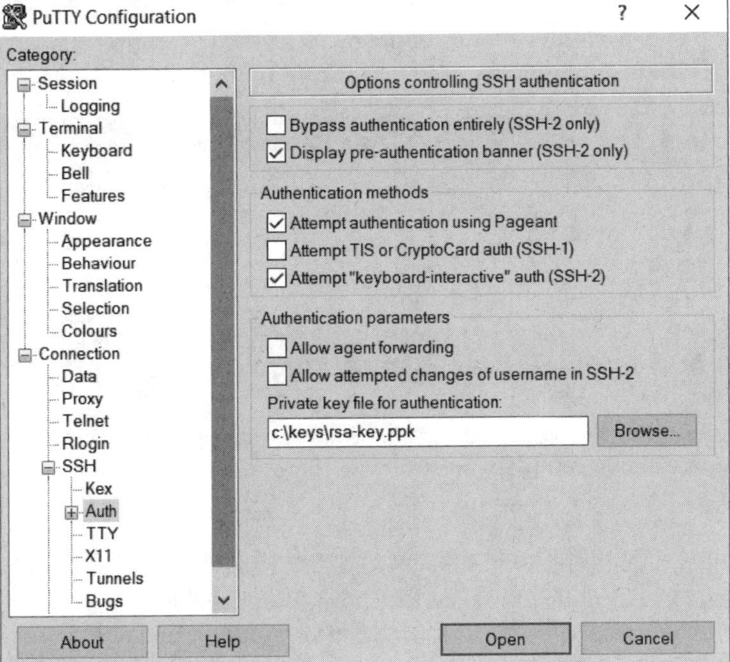

15. Navigate to the Session category and provide a name for this connection, such as web1, and choose Save. Choose Open to connect to the instance.

16. You should now be at the linux prompt connected as the opc user to your new web1 instance. Ensure that you can connect to the Internet, specifically the yum.oracle.com server. If you have difficulties with network connectivity, ensure that an Internet gateway is attached to your VCN and that there are no security list or route table rules preventing the connection.

17. The following commands install the Apache web server (httpd), add a firewall rule to allow incoming traffic on TCP port 80, reload the firewall daemon, create

a simple index.html file with the message Hello World from *<hostname>*, and start up the Apache HTTP daemon.

```
[opc@web1 ~]$ sudo yum install httpd -y
...
Installed:httpd.x86_64 0:2.4.6-88.0.1.el7
...
Complete!
[opc@web1 ~]$ sudo firewall-cmd --permanent --add-port=80/tcp
success
[opc@web1 ~]$ sudo firewall-cmd --reload
success
[opc@web1 ~]$ sudo sh -c "echo 'Hello World from:'
 `hostname` >/var/www/html/index.html"
[opc@web1 ~]$ cat /var/www/html/index.html
Hello World from: web1
[opc@web1 ~]$ sudo systemctl enable httpd
[opc@web1 ~]$ sudo systemctl start httpd
```

18. In a browser, navigate to your website by using the URL http://*<public IP address of web1>* and you should see the Hello World from: web1 message.

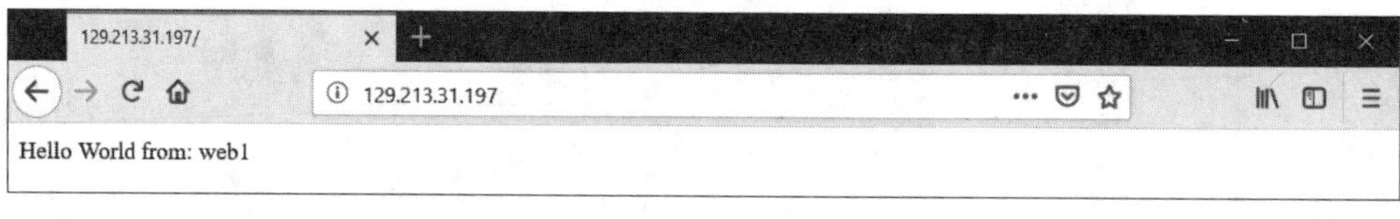

Exercise 4-3: Create and Use a Custom Image

In this exercise, you will create a custom image from the web1 compute instance created in the previous exercise. You then create a new compute instance named web2 using the custom image.

1. Sign in to the OCI console and choose your compartment.
2. Navigate to Compute | Instances and hover over the ellipsis adjacent to the web1 compute instance, and choose Create Custom Image. An alternative navigation path is to choose the Create Custom Image button on the Instance Details page.

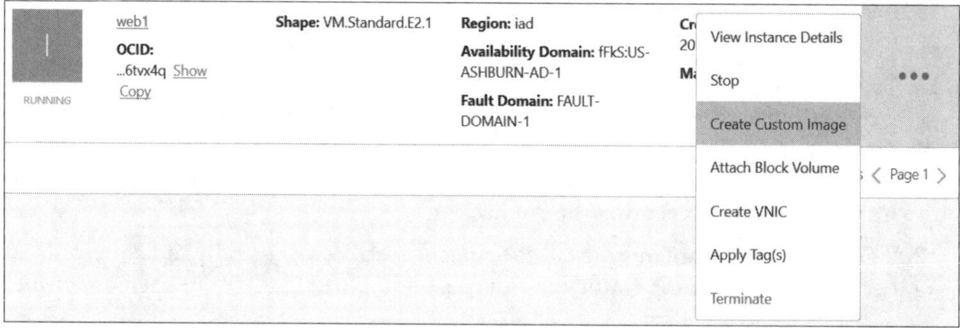

3. Name your custom image (for example, webserver), select a compartment for this resource, and choose Create Custom Image. The compute instance is offline during image creation and its status changes to Creating Image. It is good practice to properly shut down the instance before using it to create a custom image. This ensures data consistency when it is used to build future instances. If you do not stop the instance prior to creating a custom image, OCI shuts it down cleanly or forcibly if necessary, risking data corruption, before creating the custom image and rebooting the source instance.

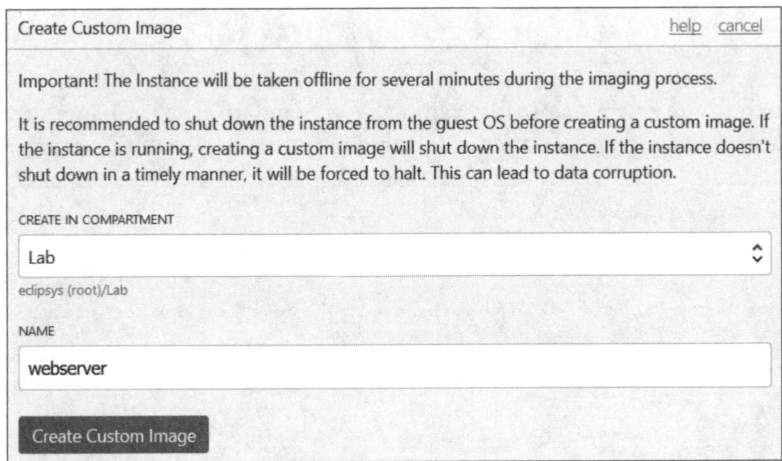

4. Once the custom image is created, navigate to Compute | Custom Images to see the list of custom images including the web server image you have just created.

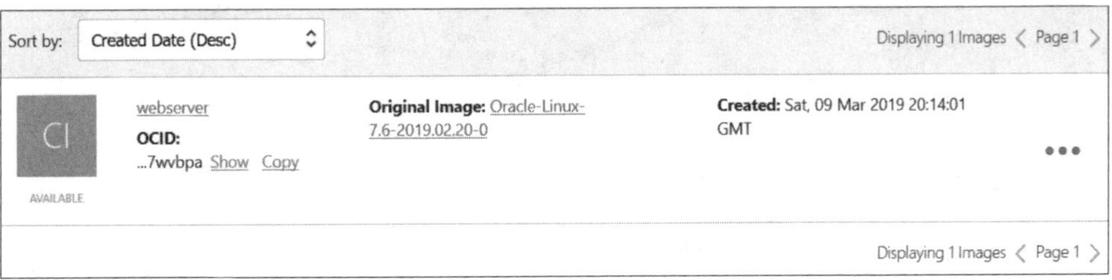

5. Before using this custom image to create a new instance, ensure that your VCN has two separate public subnets.

6. Navigate to Compute | Instances and choose Create Instance. Name your instance (for example, web2) and select an AD for your instance (for example, AD3).

7. For operating system or image source, choose Change Image Source, navigate to Custom Images, select webserver, and choose Select Image.

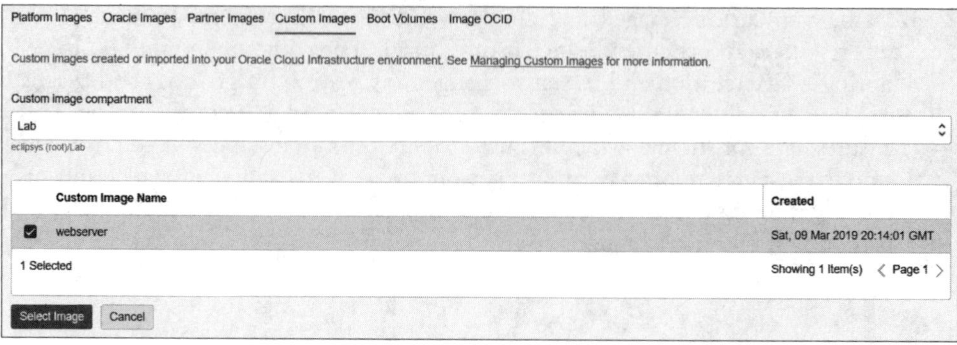

8. Choose an instance shape (for example, VM.Standard.E2.1). Change any boot volume configuration options as required or accept the default settings.

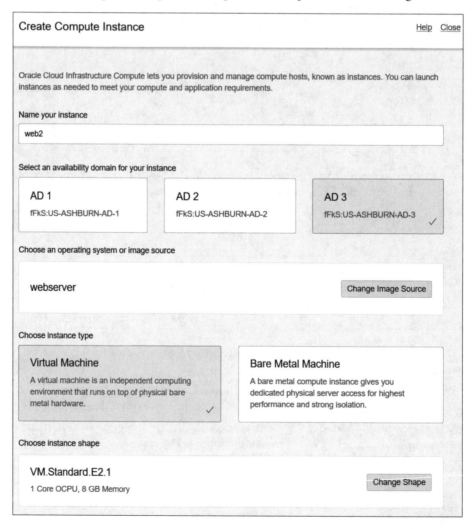

Create Compute Instance Help Close

Oracle Cloud Infrastructure Compute lets you provision and manage compute hosts, known as instances. You can launch instances as needed to meet your compute and application requirements.

Name your instance

web2

Select an availability domain for your instance

AD 1
fFkS:US-ASHBURN-AD-1

AD 2
fFkS:US-ASHBURN-AD-2

AD 3
fFkS:US-ASHBURN-AD-3

Choose an operating system or image source

webserver Change Image Source

Choose instance type

Virtual Machine
A virtual machine is an independent computing environment that runs on top of physical bare metal hardware.

Bare Metal Machine
A bare metal compute instance gives you dedicated physical server access for highest performance and strong isolation.

Choose instance shape

VM.Standard.E2.1
1 Core OCPU, 8 GB Memory Change Shape

9. Because you are creating this instance from a custom image, the public key used when creating the web1 instance is already present in the .ssh/authorized_hosts file. You need only add a public key here if you generate a new key pair.

10. Configure networking for your instance by choosing the compartment, VCN, Subnet compartment, and public subnet. Choose a different subnet from the one being used by the web1 compute instance.

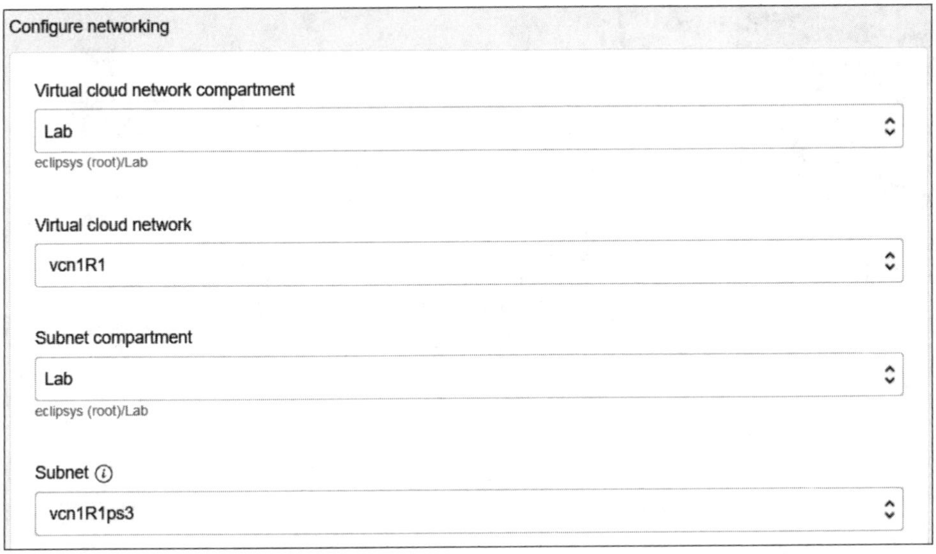

Configure networking

Virtual cloud network compartment

Lab

eclipsys (root)/Lab

Virtual cloud network

vcn1R1

Subnet compartment

Lab

eclipsys (root)/Lab

Subnet

vcn1R1ps3

11. Click Show Advanced Options. Ensure that your compartment is correct. If your web2 instance resides in the same AD as web1, choose a fault domain (for example, FAULT-DOMAIN-3) that is different from the fault domain being used by web1. Choose Create to build the instance.

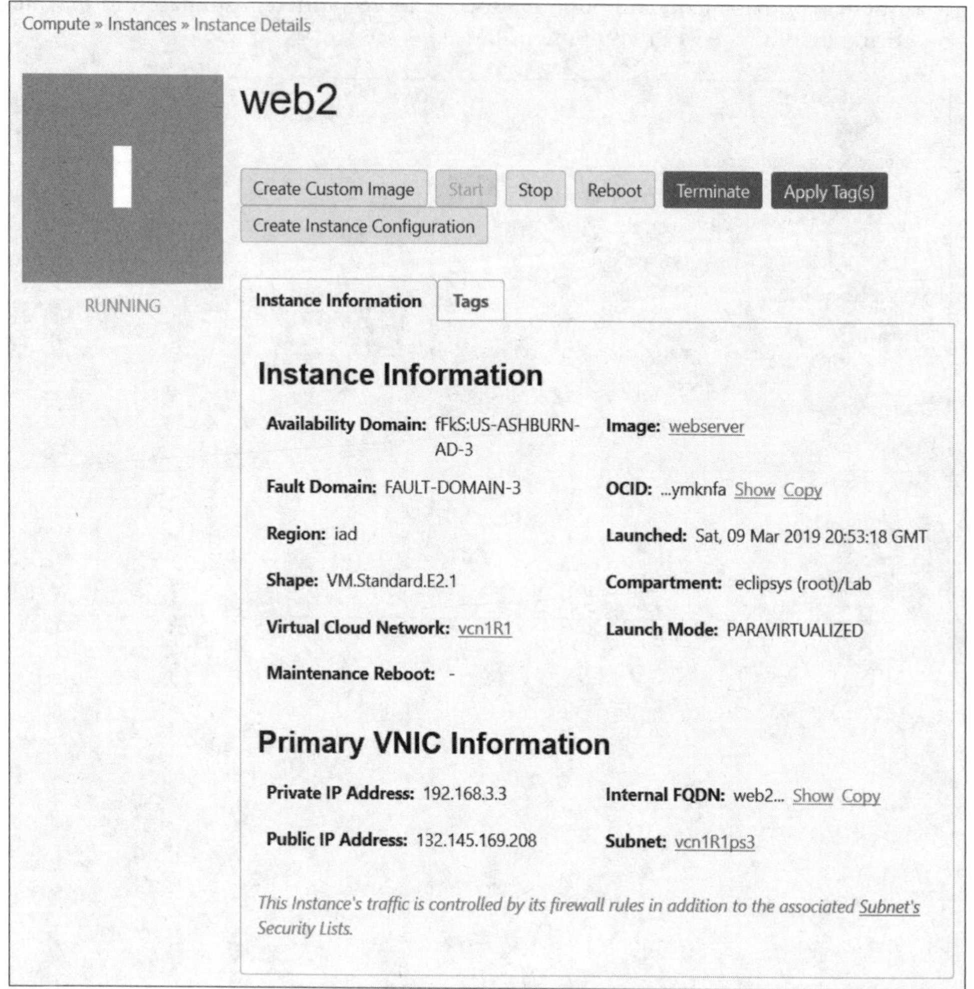

12. Because the web2 instance is based on your web server custom image, the index .html file must be updated. Once the instance is up and running, connect using ssh and the matching private key, and run the following commands.

```
[opc@web2 ~]$ cat /var/www/html/index.html
Hello World from: web1
[opc@web2 ~]$ sudo sh -c "echo 'Hello World from:' `hostname`
>/var/www/html/index.html"
[opc@web2 ~]$ cat /var/www/html/index.html
Hello World from: web2
```

13. In a browser, navigate to your web page by using the URL http://<*public IP address of web2*>, and you should see the Hello World from: web2 message.

NOTE There seems to be a shift in thinking about compute instances and treating them as disposable commodities rather than as individuals. For example, if a web server like web2 has errors or failures, a system administrator may decide that instead of investing several hours in troubleshooting the error, it may be simpler and faster to clone a new web server from a custom image.

Exercise 4-4: Create a Load Balancer to Route Traffic to Web Servers

In this exercise, you will create a public load balancer to direct HTTP traffic to a backend set comprising the web1 and web2 compute instances.

1. Sign in to the OCI console, and choose your compartment.
2. Navigate to Networking | Load Balancer, and choose Create Load Balancer.
3. Provide a load balancer name (for example, website) as well as a shape. Choose Public Load Balancer and select the VCN where compute instances web1 and web2 reside (for example, vcn1R1). If the region this is being created in has multiple ADs, choose two subnets in different ADs or choose a single regional subnet in a single AD region. Choose HTTP and port 80 for the listener.

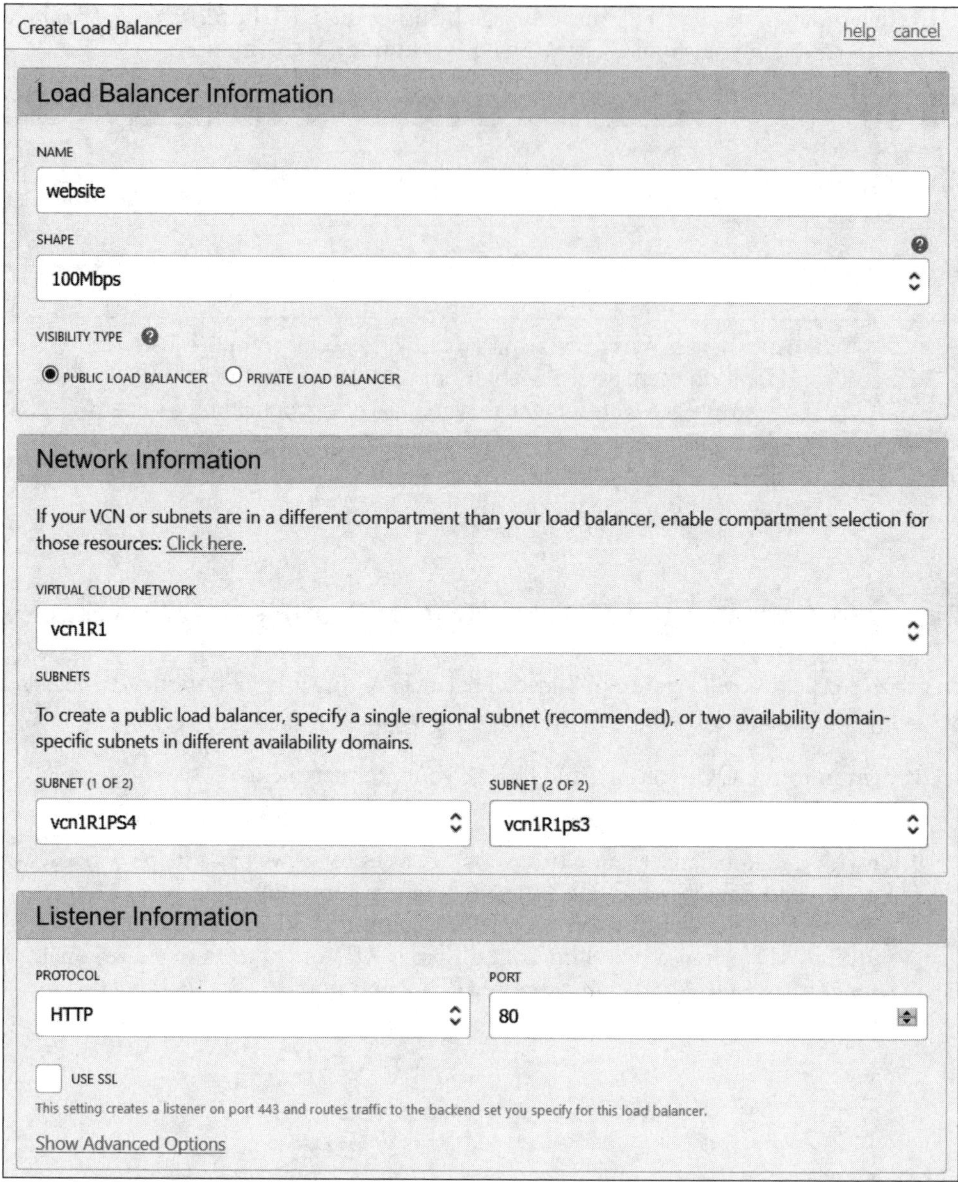

4. Select Weighted Round Robin as the traffic distribution policy. Choose Enter A Compute Instance Private Or Public IP Address, and specify the public IP for web1. Add an additional backend server and specify the public IP for web 2. Both web1 and web2 are added as equally weighted backend servers. Choose Create to provision the load balancer.

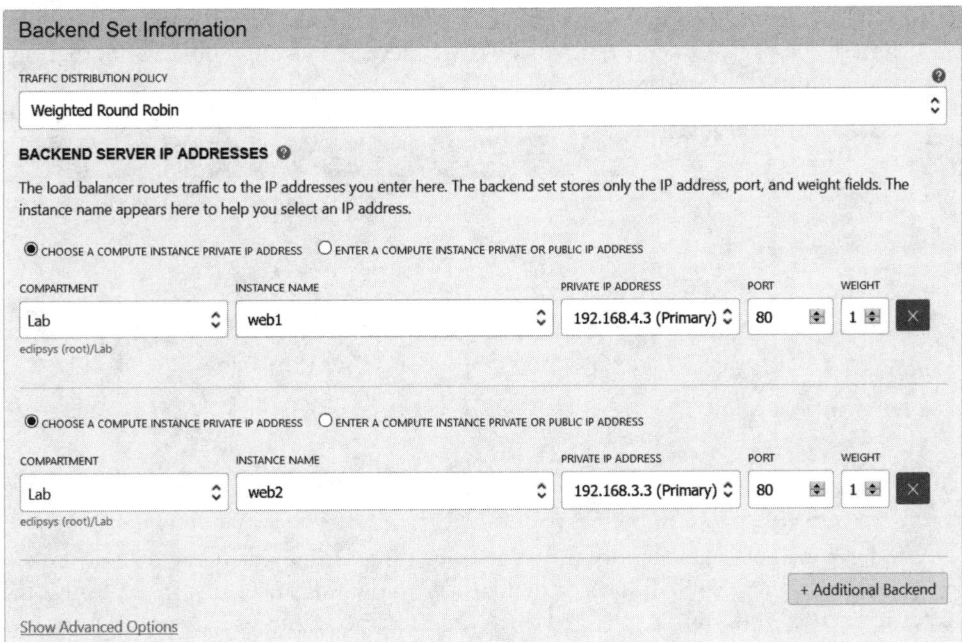

5. Once the load balancer is active, you may have to wait several minutes while the health check completes, and the Backend Sets Health shows up as OK.

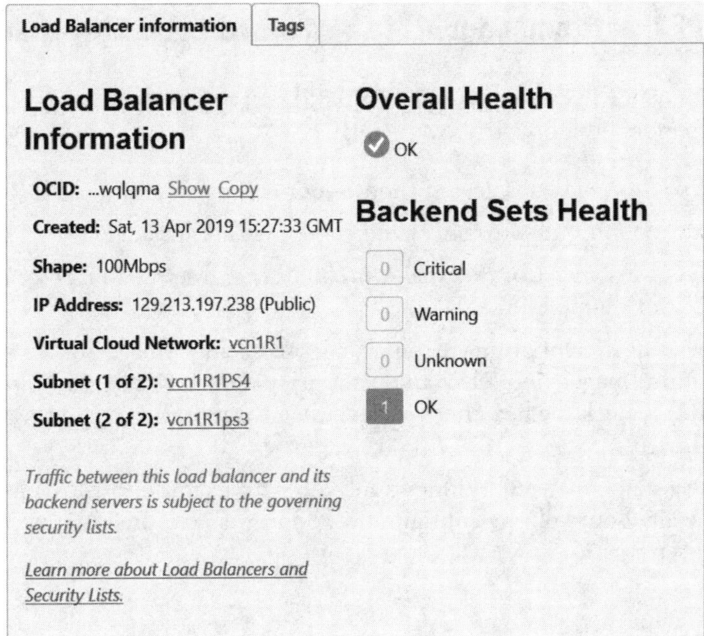

6. Navigate to the load balancer's public IP address in your browser and repeatedly refresh the page. On consecutive HTTP requests, you should observe alternating traffic from web1 and web2.

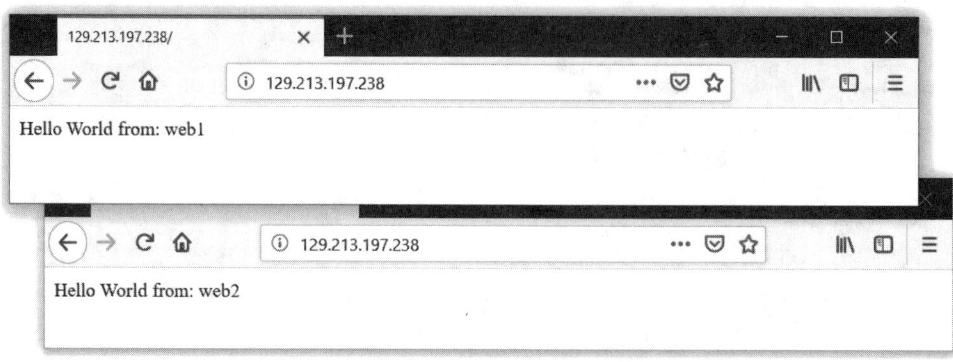

Windows instances are slightly different from Linux instances. They do not use ssh key pairs, but rather use Windows credentials. Windows instances require an additional software license, and you are charged a runtime fee each time you use your Windows instance. You connect to the Windows instance using remote desktop protocol (RDP) on port 3389 as opposed to SSH on port 22, so the RDP port must be open for ingress traffic on the security list in the relevant VCN.

Exercise 4-5: Create and Connect to a Windows Compute Instance

In this exercise, you will create a Windows 2008 R2 server compute instance and connect to it using a remote desktop client over RDP.

1. Sign in to the OCI console and choose your compartment.
2. Navigate to Compute | Instances and choose Create Instance.
3. Name your instance (for example, win2008R2) and select an AD for your instance (for example, AD1).
4. For operating system or image source, choose Change Image Source and navigate to Platform Images, and select an operating system (for example, Windows Server 2008 R2). Check the box after you review and accept the terms of use and choose Select Image.
5. Choose a shape for your Windows instance (for example, VM.Standard2.1). Change any boot volume configuration options as required or accept the default settings.

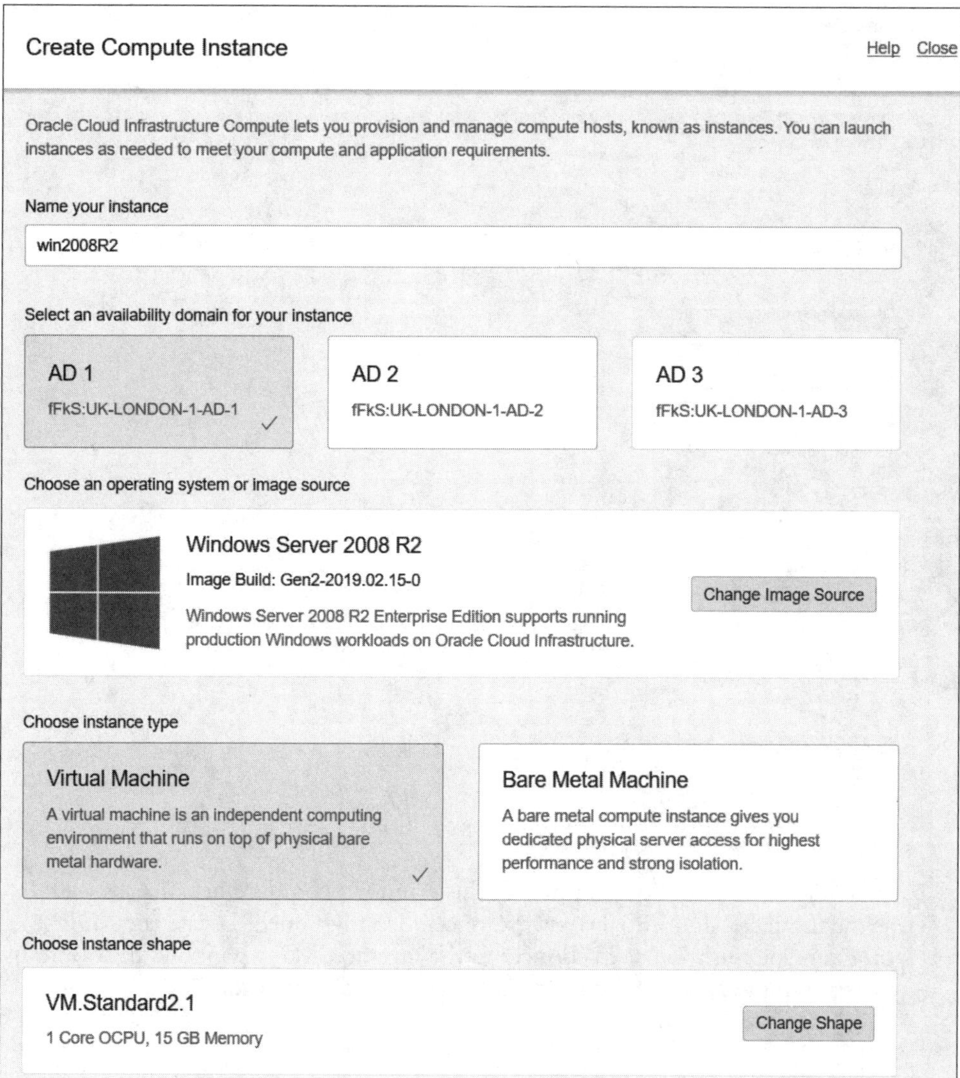

6. Take note that upon creation of the Windows instance, both a username and an initial password are generated. Choose your VCN compartment, VCN, Subnet compartment, and Subnet, and click Create.

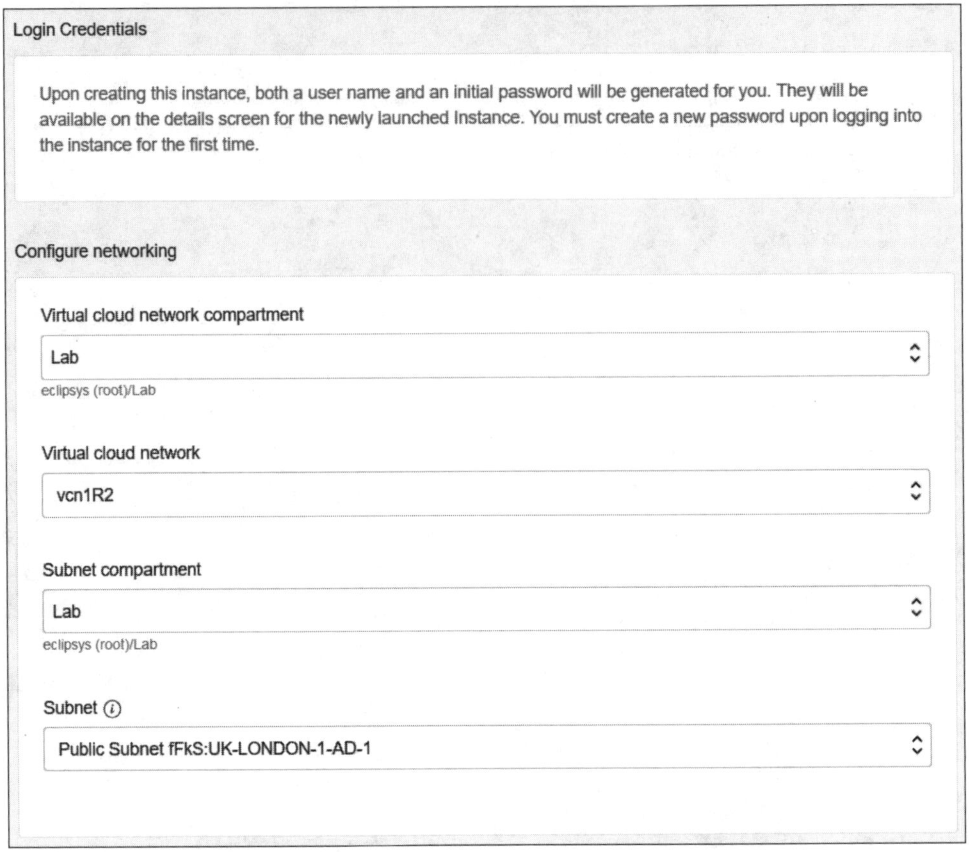

Login Credentials

Upon creating this instance, both a user name and an initial password will be generated for you. They will be available on the details screen for the newly launched Instance. You must create a new password upon logging into the instance for the first time.

Configure networking

Virtual cloud network compartment

Lab

eclipsys (root)/Lab

Virtual cloud network

vcn1R2

Subnet compartment

Lab

eclipsys (root)/Lab

Subnet ⓘ

Public Subnet fFkS:UK-LONDON-1-AD-1

7. Take note of the public IP address of the Windows compute instance, as well as the username and initial password once it is provisioned. Locate the RDP program you wish to use to connect to the instance. Many windows distributions have a Remote Desktop Connection program, and similar tools exist on Linux and Mac systems as well.

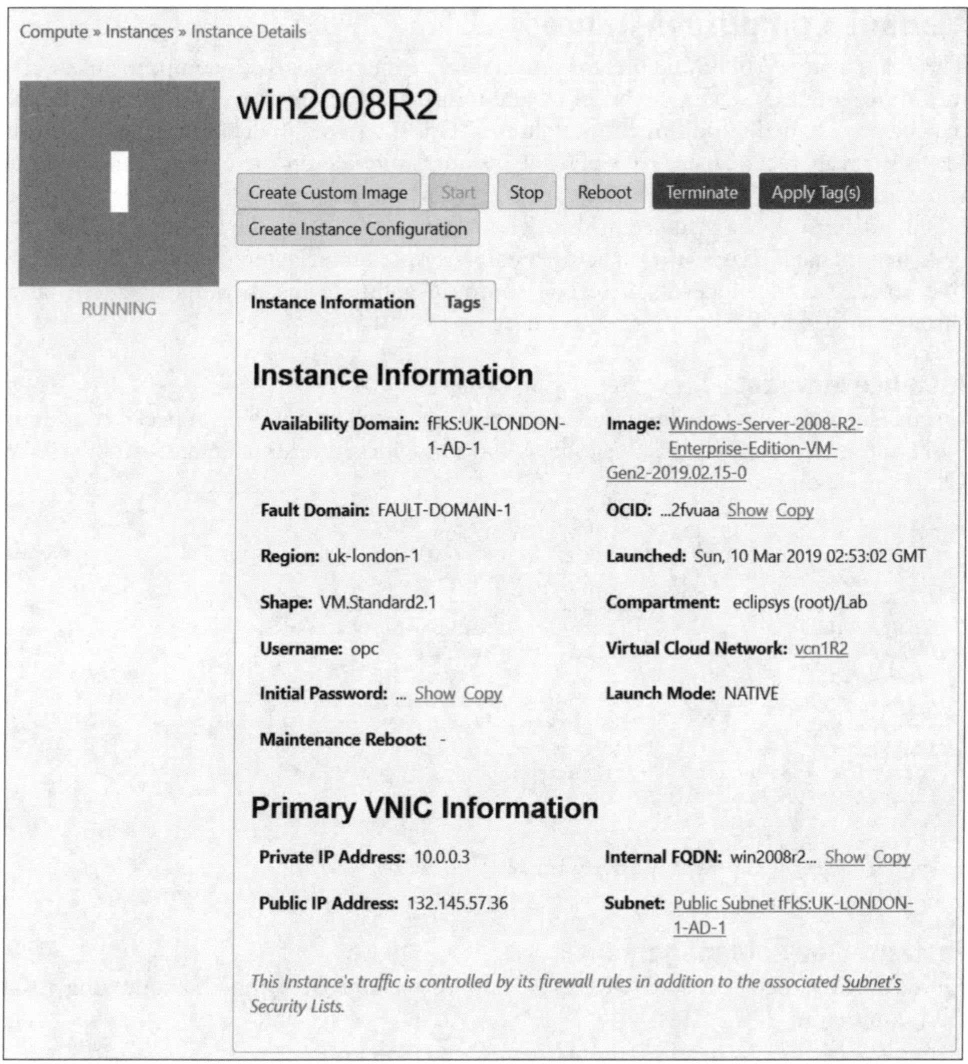

8. Launch the RDP software and specify the public IP address of the Windows compute instance, and click Connect. If you are warned because the identity of the remote computer cannot be verified, choose to connect anyway. Choose the opc user and initial password. You are prompted to change your password and are now connected to your Windows instance.

Once created, compute instances require care and feeding just like regular on-premises compute instances. The next section discusses common management activities associated with compute instances.

Manage Compute Instances

There are many APIs available for managing various aspects of compute instances, including stopping, starting, rebooting, and terminating the instance. Additional storage may be provisioned by adding block volumes. This is covered in detail in Chapter 5. You may also create secondary vNICs in some instances if it is supported by the chosen shape and platform. The APIs mentioned earlier are available through the console by using the menus adjacent to the instance or through scripts written using the CLI and SDKs.

When managing large infrastructure estates, scripted management is often more effective, so this section focuses on several common compute instance management tasks through the CLI.

Instance Metadata

Instance metadata on Oracle-provided images is retrieved by querying a special IP address while connected to an instance as follows. This provides instance metadata similar to the OCI console output.

```
# curl -L http://169.254.169.254/opc/v1/instance/
{ "availabilityDomain" : "fFkS:US-ASHBURN-AD-1",
  "faultDomain" : "FAULT-DOMAIN-1",
  "compartmentId" : "ocid1.compartment.oc1..zlh3iq",
  "displayName" : "web1","id" : "ocid1.instance.oc1.iad.h6tvx4q",
  "image" : "ocid1.image.oc1.iad. axah5a",
  "metadata" : {
    "ssh_authorized_keys" : "ssh-rsa AAAABAABAQCusCufnol64a5r RSA-KEY",
    "user_data" : "c3VkbyB5dW0gLXkg"},
  "region" : "iad",
  "canonicalRegionName" : "us-ashburn-1",
  "shape" : "VM.Standard.E2.1",
  "state" : "Running",
  "timeCreated" : 1551717368710,
  "agentConfig" : {"monitoringDisabled" : false}
```

Instance Power Management

Compute instance management tasks may be performed using the following OCI CLI command:

```
oci compute instance action
--instance-id ocid1.instance.oc1.XX
--action <ACTION>
```

ACTION commands relate to power management for the instance and include the following:

- **START** Power on
- **STOP** Power off
- **RESET** Power off and power on
- **SOFTRESET** Graceful shutdown and power on
- **SOFTSTOP** Graceful shutdown

Multiple vNICs

Secondary vNIC management is also supported through the OCI CLI. Current vNICs may be listed with the `list-vnics` command:

```
oci compute instance list-vnics --instance-id ocid1.instance.oc1.iad.6tvx4q
      "availability-domain": "fFkS:US-ASHBURN-AD-1",
      "compartment-id": "ocid1.compartment.oc1..zlh3iq",
      "display-name": "web1", "hostname-label": "web1",
      "id": "ocid1.vnic.oc1.iad.abuwcljrcxkqia",
      "is-primary": true, "lifecycle-state": "AVAILABLE",
      "mac-address": "02:00:17:00:80:07",
      "private-ip": "192.168.4.3",
      "public-ip": "129.213.31.197",
      "skip-source-dest-check": false,
      "subnet-id": "ocid1.subnet.oc1.iad.aaaaaaaazvdnxeaktaisq",
      "time-created": "2019-03-04T16:36:18.249000+00:00"}]}
```

An additional vNIC may be added with the `attach-vnic` command:

```
oci compute instance attach-vnic --instance-id XX --subnet-id YY
```

Use the `list-vnics` command, searching only for display-name, mac-address, and IPs:

```
oci compute instance list-vnics --instance-id XX |
  grep -E "display-name|mac-address|private-ip|public-ip"
      "display-name": "web1",
      "mac-address": "02:00:17:00:80:07",
      "private-ip": "192.168.4.3",
      "public-ip": "129.213.31.197",
      "display-name": "vnic20190310062339",
      "mac-address": "02:00:17:00:0F:08",
      "private-ip": "192.168.4.7",
      "public-ip": "132.145.192.246",
```

Use the `detach-vnic` command to remove a vNIC:

```
oci compute instance detach-vnic --vnic-id ocid1.vnic.XX
  --compartment-id ocid1.compartment.oc1.YY
Are you sure you want to delete this resource? [y/N]: y
```

Use the `list-vnics` command to confirm the detachment of the vNIC:

```
oci compute instance list-vnics --instance-id ocid1.instance.XX |
grep -E "display-name|mac-address|private-ip|public-ip"
      "display-name": "web1",
      "mac-address": "02:00:17:00:80:07",
      "private-ip": "192.168.4.3",
      "public-ip": "129.213.31.197",
```

Instance Configurations, Pools, and Autoscaling

Instance configurations provide a system for creating configuration templates from existing compute instances. Figure 4-9 shows an instance configuration created from the web1 instance documenting a set of configuration information including boot volume type and size, operating system, and compute shape.

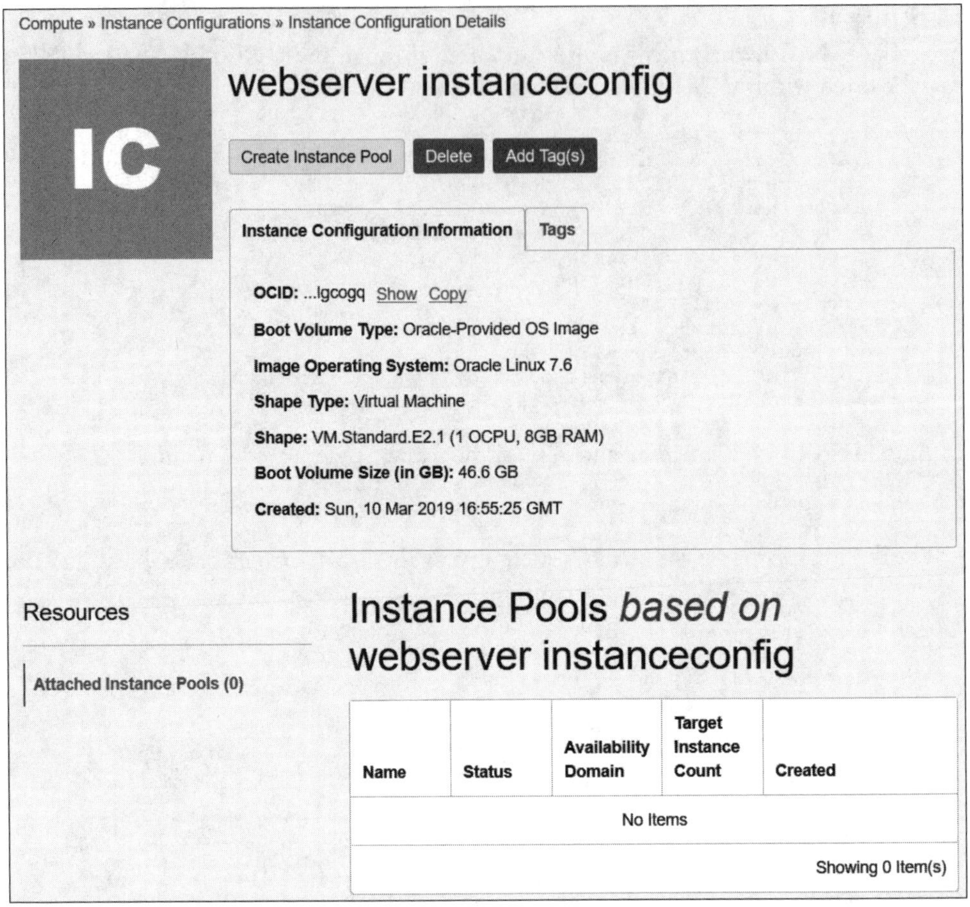

Compute » Instance Configurations » Instance Configuration Details

IC

webserver instanceconfig

Create Instance Pool | Delete | Add Tag(s)

Instance Configuration Information | Tags

OCID: ...lgcogq Show Copy

Boot Volume Type: Oracle-Provided OS Image

Image Operating System: Oracle Linux 7.6

Shape Type: Virtual Machine

Shape: VM.Standard.E2.1 (1 OCPU, 8GB RAM)

Boot Volume Size (in GB): 46.6 GB

Created: Sun, 10 Mar 2019 16:55:25 GMT

Resources

Attached Instance Pools (0)

Instance Pools *based on* webserver instanceconfig

Name	Status	Availability Domain	Target Instance Count	Created
No Items				
Showing 0 Item(s)				

Figure 4-9 Instance configuration information

Instance configurations form the basis for instance pools. These are pools of compute instances created using the instance configuration templates in a particular region. Instance configurations are different from custom images. Custom images are operating system images used as boot volumes for new instances whereas instance configurations contain a set of parameters to be used for instance pools. Figure 4-10 shows how you can spawn many compute instances in a pool based a common instance configuration. In this example, up to four compute instances may be provisioned with a standardized instance configuration in this pool.

EXAM TIP Instances in an instance pool are provisioned in the same region but can be in multiple availability domains.

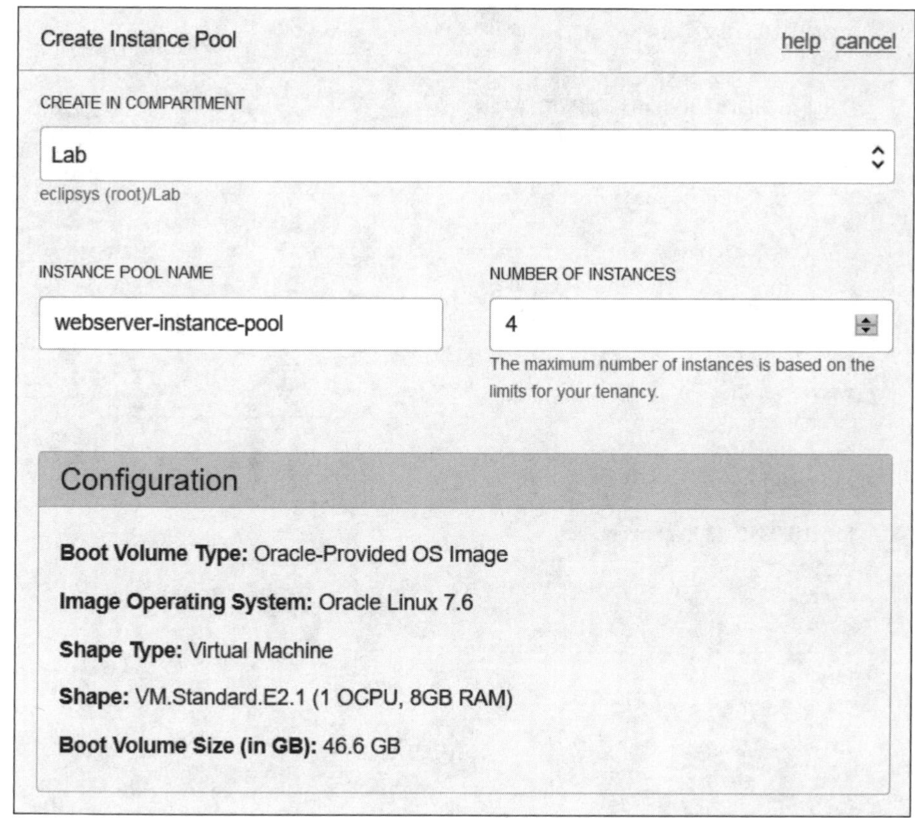

Figure 4-10 Instance pool configuration

Load balancers may be attached to instance pools. Figure 4-11 shows how provisioned instances in the pool may be added to the backend set associated with the load balancer. You may also specify multiple availability domains for the instance pool. As new instances are provisioned, these are created in the instance pool–specified ADs.

Instances in a pool may be managed together (or individually). For example, all instances in a pool may be reset with a single ResetInstancePool API operation. Other pool-level management APIs include StartInstancePool, StopInstancePool, and TerminateInstancePool. An instance pool may be in one of several states, including the following:

- **Provisioning** Initial creation of instances in the pool based on the instance configuration.
- **Starting** Instances are being launched.
- **Running** Instances are running.

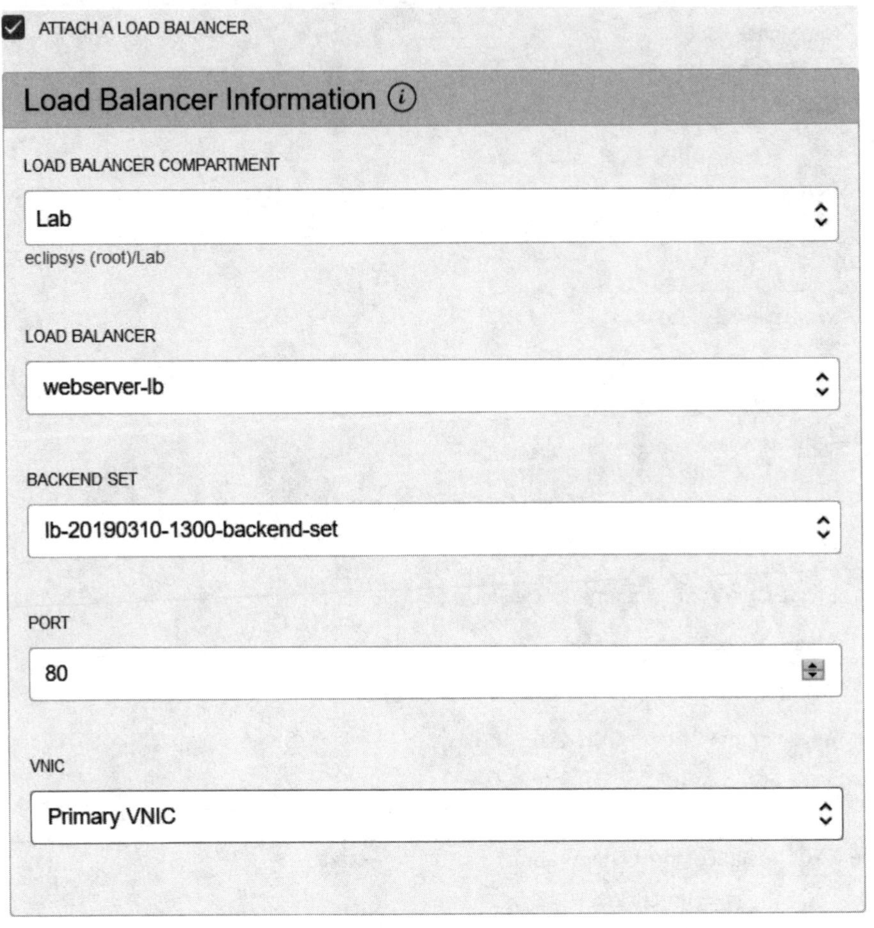

Figure 4-11 Attach a load balancer to the instance pool.

- **Stopping** Instances are being shut down.
- **Stopped** All instances in the pool are shut down.
- **Terminating** All instances in the instance pool and their associated resources are being deprovisioned.
- **Terminated** The instance pool and its associated resources have been terminated.
- **Scaling** The instance pool is being updated. Instances are being added or terminated.

Instance configuration and pools provide the basis for Autoscaling. Autoscaling refers to the dynamic addition or removal of instances from an instance pool based on an autoscaling policy. Figure 4-12 shows an autoscaling configuration being created in a compartment for a specific instance pool.

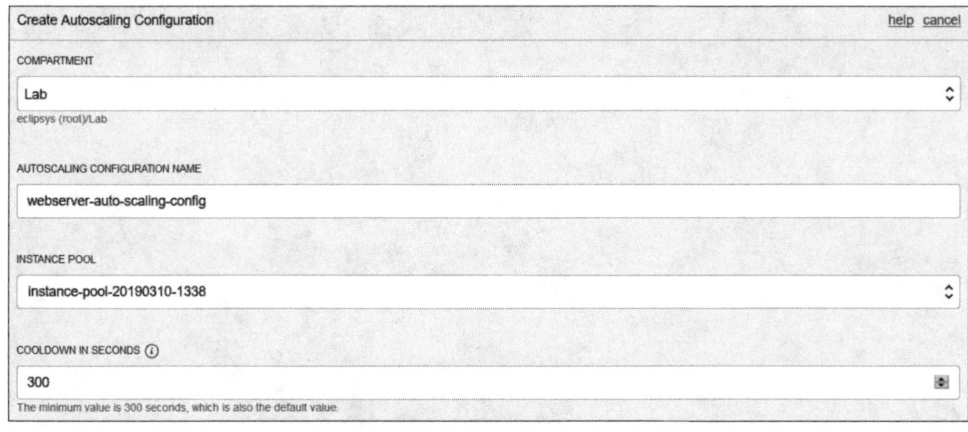

Figure 4-12 Autoscaling configuration for an instance pool

The autoscaling adjustment is triggered by thresholds set in the autoscaling policy such as CPU or memory utilization. In Figure 4-13, an autoscaling policy is defined based on the CPU utilization. Scaling limits and a scaling rule determine the autoscaling behavior.

Scaling limits define the minimum and maximum number of compute instances that may be automatically spawned in the instance pool, as well as the initial number of instances to start. The scaling rule defines the thresholds for scale-out, or adding instances, and for scale-in, or removing instances from the instance pool. The performance metrics of all instances in the pool are aggregated into one-minute intervals and averaged across the instance pool. When the average performance metric exceeds the given threshold in three consecutive one-minute intervals, an autoscaling event is triggered.

The cooldown period in Figure 4-12 refers to the time spent evaluating the autoscaling thresholds after an adjustment is made. For example, the policy in Figure 4-13 states that when the average CPU utilization across all instances in the pool exceeds 90 percent for three minutes in a row, then add one instance to the pool. Once the newly added instance is up and running, the pool must run for the cooldown period (300 seconds by default) before the averaged performance metrics are considered for another autoscaling event.

EXAM TIP Autoscaling requires an instance pool. An instance pool requires an instance configuration. An autoscaling policy specifies scale-out and scale-in limits as well as the initial number of instances to start. The scaling rule defines the thresholds for scale-out and scale-in.

Instance Console Connections

Compute instances are incarnated on servers in racks in data centers across the globe. There is no KVM (keyboard-video-mouse device) or monitor attached to the instance to see the console activity as you would if you were physically plugged into the server. Sometimes, an instance may not boot up properly or the SSH daemon on the operating

Autoscaling Policy

AUTOSCALING POLICY NAME

webserver-auto-scaling-policy

PERFORMANCE METRIC

CPU Utilization

Scaling Limits

MINIMUM NUMBER OF INSTANCES	MAXIMUM NUMBER OF INSTANCES	INITIAL NUMBER OF INSTANCES
1	8 The maximum number of instances is based on the limits for your tenancy	1

Scaling Rule

SCALE-OUT OPERATOR	THRESHOLD PERCENTAGE	NUMBER OF INSTANCES TO ADD
Greater than (>)	90	1
SCALE-IN OPERATOR	**THRESHOLD PERCENTAGE**	**NUMBER OF INSTANCES TO REMOVE**
Less than (<)	60	1

Figure 4-13 Autoscaling policy defining the scaling metric, limits, and rule

system does not start so regular SSH access to the instance stops working. Troubleshooting is the most common reason you may wish to access the console. OCI provides a secure mechanism to connect to the instance console. For both Windows and Linux instances, you establish a secure SSH tunnel between your client machine and the compute instance. Your client machine can be running a Windows or Linux or Mac operating system. Once the tunnel is established, you make an SSH or VNC connection to the console of the compute instance. The VNC connection uses port forwarding to redirect a VNC connection to localhost:5900 to the compute instance.

To create a console connection to the web1 compute instance using the OCI console, navigate to Compute | Instances and choose the web1 instance. Choose Console Connections from the Resources area and select Create Console Connection. Provide an SSH public key you previously created and choose Create Console Connection. Figure 4-14 shows the console connection resource that establishes the SSH tunnel to the console.

You may connect over this tunnel with SSH or VNC to the compute instance. Choosing to Connect with SSH returns an interface, as shown in Figure 4-15.

CAUTION The connection string provided assumes that the matching private key to the public key you provided when setting up the tunnel is available in the default location on your client machine. You may have to alter the provided connection string to reference your private key.

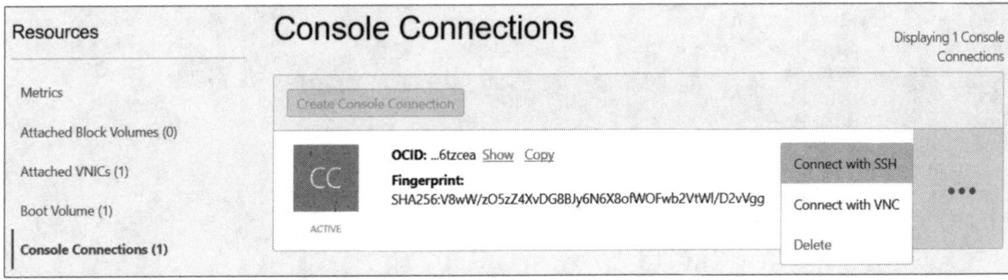

Figure 4-14 Console connection

Notice that you may connect from a Linux, Mac, or Windows platform. You may copy the provided connection string to establish the console connection. If Windows is chosen as the client platform, the provided connection string consists of Powershell commands. Here is an excerpt from a Linux client connecting to the console of the web1 compute instance.

```
$ ssh -i .ssh/RSA-KEY -o
ProxyCommand='ssh -i .ssh/RSA-KEY -W %h:%p -p 443
ocid1.instanceconsoleconnection.oc1.iad.XX@
instance-console.us-ashburn-1.oraclecloud.com'
ocid1.instance.oc1.iad.YY
Enter passphrase for key '.ssh/RSA-KEY':
The authenticity of host 'ocid1.instance.oc1.iad.ZZ
(<no hostip for proxy command>)' can't be established.
RSA key fingerprint is SHA256:fUQVrcZPMzVvtQXPkLizy6qsFD1a/Y9
RSA key fingerprint is MD5:f6:27:95:3b:07:d3:62:38:3a:f8:ff.
Are you sure you want to continue connecting (yes/no)? yes
Warning: Permanently added 'ocid1.instance.XZ' (RSA)
to the list of known hosts.
```

Figure 4-15 Console connection – Connect with SSH

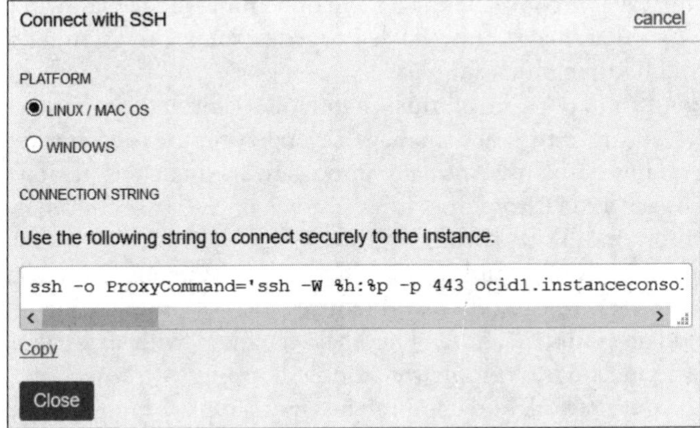

```
Enter passphrase for key '.ssh/RSA-KEY': *****
Oracle Linux Server 7.6
Kernel 4.14.35-1844.2.5.el7uek.x86_64 on an x86_64
web1 login: opc
Password:
Last login: Sun Mar 10 21:13:21 from 129.213.138.238
[opc@web1 ~]$ ps
  PID TTY          TIME CMD
18466 ttyS0    00:00:00 bash
18509 ttyS0    00:00:00 ps
```

On Linux instances, you typically connect with SSH and work in a pseudo terminal session. In the previous excerpt from an SSH session, the `ps` (process) command is run, displaying, among other information, the PIDs of processes being run by the current user and the terminal associated with the process. Note that the terminal (TTY) is ttyS0. This means this is a serial console connection.

Consider the following excerpt taken when connected to the web1 compute instance using SSH and not using the console connection.

```
[root@web1 opc]# ps
  PID TTY          TIME CMD
 5925 pts/0    00:00:00 sudo
 5927 pts/0    00:00:00 su
 5928 pts/0    00:00:00 bash
18511 pts/0    00:00:00 ps
```

Here, all four listed processes run by the root user on the web1 compute instance are associated with the pseudo terminal pts/0.

Chapter Review

Compute instances are the quintessential IaaS components and OCI has done a great job simplifying the provisioning and management of these resources. This chapter discussed virtualized and bare-metal compute types and their associated shapes. The ever-expanding variety of available compute images will only improve the platform further. As the marketplace for partner images and Oracle images expands, provisioning once-complex software stacks will become much simpler.

A significant portion of this chapter is dedicated to hands-on practical exercises enabling you to create and manage several compute VM instances. This chapter also explored fault domains, especially important in single AD regions, as well as the ability to run legacy and custom operating systems on OCI through BYOH (Bring Your Own Hypervisor) and BYOI (Bring Your Own Image).

Autoscaling is a valuable feature for scaling systems through peak loads and downscaling during off-peak times, and reduces costs of provisioning for the worst days along with reducing human effort. The chapter closed with a discussion on using instance console connections, typically for troubleshooting.

With your network and compute instances in place, you are ready to explore the available storage options, which is the subject of Chapter 5.

Questions

1. List the compute instance types available for provisioning on OCI.
   - **A.** Virtual machines
   - **B.** Paravirtualized machines
   - **C.** Bare-metal machines
   - **D.** OVM, KVM, and Hyper-V
2. Which of the following compute images may be used to create a compute instance?
   - **A.** Oracle and Platform images
   - **B.** Boot volumes and Partner images
   - **C.** Paravirtualized machines
   - **D.** OVA format images
3. A boot volume has been detached from an instance in AD1. Which of the following statements are true?
   - **A.** A compute instance can be created in AD2 using the boot volume in AD1.
   - **B.** A compute instance cannot be created in AD2 using the boot volume in AD1.
   - **C.** The boot volume can be backed up in A1 and restored in AD2 and used to create a compute instance in AD2.
   - **D.** The boot volume cannot be moved.
4. A compute instance is not starting up. You suspect a problem with the boot volume. Which of the following options may be used to troubleshoot this further?
   - **A.** There is nothing further to do. The compute instance must be cloned and recreated.
   - **B.** A console connection may be created to see if there is more information available on the console.
   - **C.** The compute instance must just be reimaged from the same source image.
   - **D.** The boot volume may be detached and attached to another working instance as a regular volume to access log files and examine configuration.
5. Which of the following statements is true?
   - **A.** Instances in an instance pool may be provisioned across multiple VCNs.
   - **B.** Instances in an instance pool may be provisioned across multiple regions.
   - **C.** Instances in an instance pool are provisioned in the same AD.
   - **D.** Instances in an instance pool are provisioned in the same region.

6. Instance metadata on Oracle-provided Linux images are retrieved by querying which special IP address while connected to an instance?
   A. http://169.254.169.254/opc/v1/instance/
   B. http://127.0.0.1/opc/v1/instance/
   C. http://255.255.255.0/opc/v1/instance/
   D. There is no such thing. Use the OCI console or CLI to get instance metadata.
7. Autoscaling requires which of the following resources in order to work? Choose all dependent resources.
   A. Multiple vNICs
   B. Instance pool
   C. Instance configuration
   D. Autoscaling policy
8. Which of the following statements is true?
   A. When autoscaling is enabled, OCI provisions as many compute instances as required, with no limit when scale-out thresholds are exceeded.
   B. When autoscaling is enabled, OCI provisions as many compute instances as required, limited by the autoscaling policy.
   C. When autoscaling is enabled, OCI provisions an equal number of compute instances as there currently are in the instance pool to ensure even load balancing.
   D. When autoscaling is enabled, OCI provisions zero compute instances. The cloud administrator must authorize the provisioning of new instances.
9. Which instance management ACTION commands are supported by the OCI CLI command: oci compute instance action --instance-id ocid1.instance.oc1.XX --action ACTION?
   A. TERMINATE
   B. CREATE
   C. STOP
   D. SOFTRESET
   E. HARDSTOP
10. Which hypervisors are supported by OCI on bare-metal instances?
   A. Kernel-based VM (KVM)
   B. Oracle VM (OVM)
   C. Oracle Virtual Box
   D. Oracle Solaris containers
   E. Hyper-V

Answers

1. **A, C.** VM and BM are the only available compute types.
2. **A, B.** Oracle, Platform, and Partner images and Boot volumes may be used to create a compute instance.
3. **B, C.** A boot volume used as the image source for a compute instance must be available in the same AD chosen to host the compute instance. A boot volume may be backed up and restored in a different AD.
4. **B, D.** Using a console connection to see if more information is available on the instance console is usually helpful as is detaching the boot volume from the problematic instance and attaching it to a working instance as a regular volume to access log files and examine configuration.
5. **D.** Instances in an instance pool are provisioned in the same region.
6. **A.** Instance metadata on Oracle-provided Linux images are retrieved by querying http://169.254.169.254/opc/v1/instance/.
7. **B, C, D.** Autoscaling requires an instance pool, instance configuration, and an autoscaling policy.
8. **B.** When autoscaling is enabled, OCI provisions as many compute instances as required, limited by the autoscaling policy.
9. **C, D.** ACTION commands relate to power management for the instance and include: START, STOP, RESET, SOFTRESET, and SOFTSTOP.
10. **A, B, E.** OCI provides support for installing several hypervisors on bare-metal instances, including KVM, OVM, and Hyper-V.

CHAPTER 5

Storage

In this chapter, you will learn how to

- Create and manage block storage volumes
- Use object storage
- Explain file storage service

Storage is an essential ingredient in the cloud computing puzzle and unsurprisingly a comprehensive array of storage options is available on OCI. Instead of relying on teams of storage engineers to prepare SAN (storage area network), NAS (network attached storage), DAS (direct attached storage), and other storage types for your enterprise, you can rapidly provision equally diverse storage options on OCI with ease. Each storage option serves a different purpose.

The fastest, most expensive storage options available in OCI are NVMe SSD storage drives attached locally to a compute instance. This storage is typically used in high performance computing where high IO speeds are required, such as an important transactional database, and provides terabyte scale capacity. This is not durable storage because it is not replicated to other ADs, unlike block volumes that are durable and fast as they are based on NVMe SSD storage in a storage server and provide petabyte scale storage. The slowest and cheapest storage option is OCI object storage, also providing petabyte scale storage. Archive tier object storage buckets are appropriate for long-term storage when some data must be kept safely but IO speeds are not important, such as keeping several years of financial record backups for audit or compliance purposes. The File Storage Service (FSS) provides network file systems (NFSv3) that provide shared storage to instances in the same region and offers exabyte scale storage.

Figure 5-1 contextualizes the most common OCI storage offerings within a tenancy spanning two regions.

Region 1 consists of two ADs, each hosting two compute instances. Instance1 AD1 has block volume and NVMe SSD storage attached. As discussed in Chapter 4, when a compute instance is provisioned a boot volume is chosen. This boot volume resides on OCI block volume storage and behaves like a regular disk volume in your PC or server. If this was a database server, the Oracle binary files ($ORACLE_HOME) could be placed on the block volume, while the database files would reside on the high-speed local NVMe SSD disk drives attached to Instance1 AD1. Instance2 AD1 has only a block volume attached. Instance1 On-Prem also has a block volume (regular disk drives) and local NVMe SSD storage.

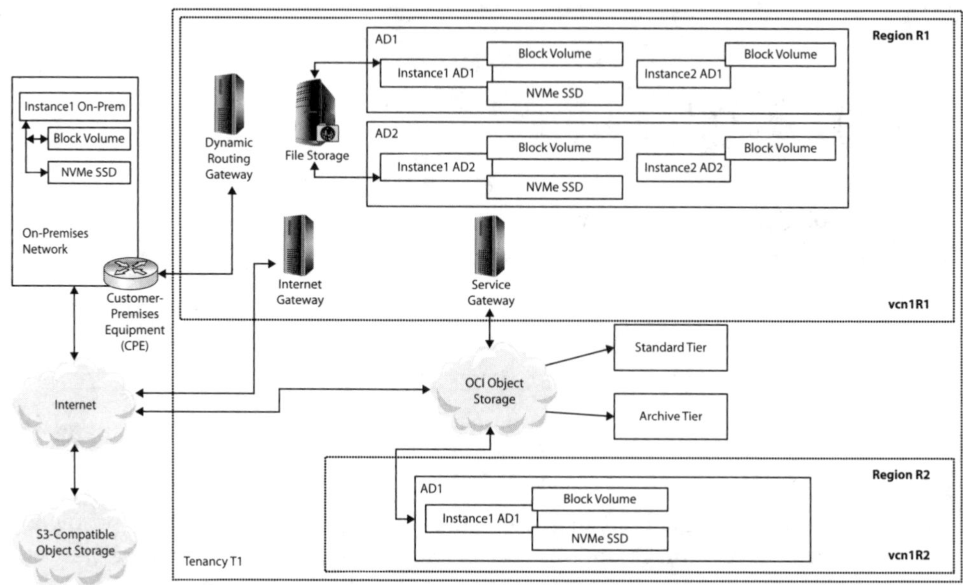

Figure 5-1 OCI storage topology

Instance1 AD1 and Instance1 AD2 can concurrently mount network attached storage over NFS (network file system protocol) through the File Storage Service (FSS). FSS is versatile shared storage that is slower than block volumes but faster than object storage. FSS is typically used for file server type applications. Through the CPE-DRG bridge, Instance1 On-Prem may access the file storage service if the correct permissions are in place.

Object storage is a relatively new construct based on tiered storage buckets. These are akin to folders or directories in a typical file system but there is no hierarchy. Object storage is accessible over the Internet. A bucket may be either standard or archive tier. These tiers are differentiated by performance and cost. Instance1 On-Prem may access the same object storage bucket over the Internet as Instance2 AD2 through an OCI service gateway.

With this 10,000-foot view of the primary storage options, you are ready to dive deeper into the storage intricacies available on OCI.

Block Storage

Block volumes are provided to your compute instances by the OCI block volume service. This service manages and carves out block storage volumes as per your requirement. Block volumes may be created, attached, connected, or detached from compute instances. In fact, a block volume may be detached from one compute instance and attached to another instance in the same AD, thereby moving the volume. They may be grouped with other block volumes to form a logical entity known as a volume group.

Volume groups may be backed up together to form a consistent point-in-time, crash-consistent backup that is also useful for cloning.

A boot volume is a special type of block volume because it contains a boot image. OCI differentiates between boot volumes and block volumes. When you create a compute instance, you may either create a new boot volume, which hosts the operating system boot image, or use an existing available unused boot volume. Boot volumes are discussed in Chapter 4. Additional block volumes may be created and attached to your instances to expand available storage. Block volumes may be used for database storage or for hosting general purpose file systems.

EXAM TIP There are two types of block storage volumes. A boot volume is used as the image source for a compute instance while a block volume allows dynamic expansion of storage capacity of an instance.

When you create a block volume, you specify several attributes, including the following:

- **Name** This is the block volume description.
- **Compartment** The logical container to which the block volume belongs.
- **AD** Only instances in the same AD can use this volume.
- **Size** Can be between 50GB and 32TB, at the time of this writing.
- **Backup Policy** OCI offers three optional block volume backup policies: bronze, silver, and gold.
- **Encryption** All block volumes are encrypted using either Oracle-managed keys or customer-managed keys stored in an OCI key management vault.

This section describes typical block volume administration activities including creating, listing, using, deleting, and backup options.

Create Block Volumes

The following OCI CLI command creates a 50GB block volume in AD1 in a specific compartment.

```
$ oci bv volume create --size-in-gbs 50
--availability-domain fFkS:US-ASHBURN-AD-1
--compartment-id ocid1.compartment.oc1..zlh3iq
{"data": {"availability-domain": "fFkS:US-ASHBURN-AD-1",
"compartment-id": "ocid1.compartment.oc1.. zlh3iq",
"display-name": "abuwcljrocjwsdsjdyfipugzfzugp7jy4o5twydv7zvaaqalxxv66qq6g5ba",
"id": "ocid1.volume.oc1.iad.q6g5ba",
    "is-hydrated": null,
    "kms-key-id": null,
    "lifecycle-state": "PROVISIONING",
    "size-in-gbs": 50,
    "size-in-mbs": 51200,
    "time-created": "2019-03-22T04:04:50.264000+00:00",
    "volume-group-id": null},"etag": "-2110775474"}
```

The system-generated block volume display-name property may be updated, for example to bv1, with the following command:

```
$ oci bv volume update --volume-id ocid1.volume.oc1.iad.6g5ba
--display-name bv1
{
"data": {
"availability-domain": "fFkS:US-ASHBURN-AD-1",
"compartment-id": "ocid1.compartment.oc1..zlh3iq",
"display-name": "bv1",
"id": "ocid1.volume.oc1.iad.q6g5ba",
   "is-hydrated": true,
    "lifecycle-state": "AVAILABLE",
    "size-in-gbs": 50,
    "size-in-mbs": 51200,
    "time-created": "2019-03-22T04:04:50.264000+00:00",
    "volume-group-id": null}, "etag": "91504310"}
```

One of the block volume attributes to note is lifecycle-state, which may have one of the following values:

- **PROVISIONING** Block volume is being created.
- **AVAILABLE** Block volume is ready to be attached, detached, connected, or disconnected.
- **TERMINATING** Block volume is being deleted.
- **TERMINATED** Block volume has been deleted and is no longer available.
- **FAULTY** Block volume requires diagnosis.
- **RESTORING** Block volume is being restored from a backup.

NOTE A block volume belongs to a specific AD. This makes sense if you consider that it is physically manifested across several disk drives in a data center somewhere.

Exercise 5-1: Create a Block Volume

In this exercise, you will create a block volume in the same AD as compute instance web1. If you completed all the exercises in Chapter 4, you should have the required instance.

1. Sign in to the OCI console and choose your compartment.
2. Navigate to Compute | Instance and choose the web1 instance. Take note of the AD in which it resides.
3. Navigate to Block Storage | Block Volumes and choose Create Block Volume.

4. Provide a name (for example bv1), choose the compartment to which it will belong, and choose the same AD as compute instance web1. Specify a size—for example, 50GB. Leave the backup policy and encryption options at their default settings. Provide a tag as desired, and choose Create Block Volume.

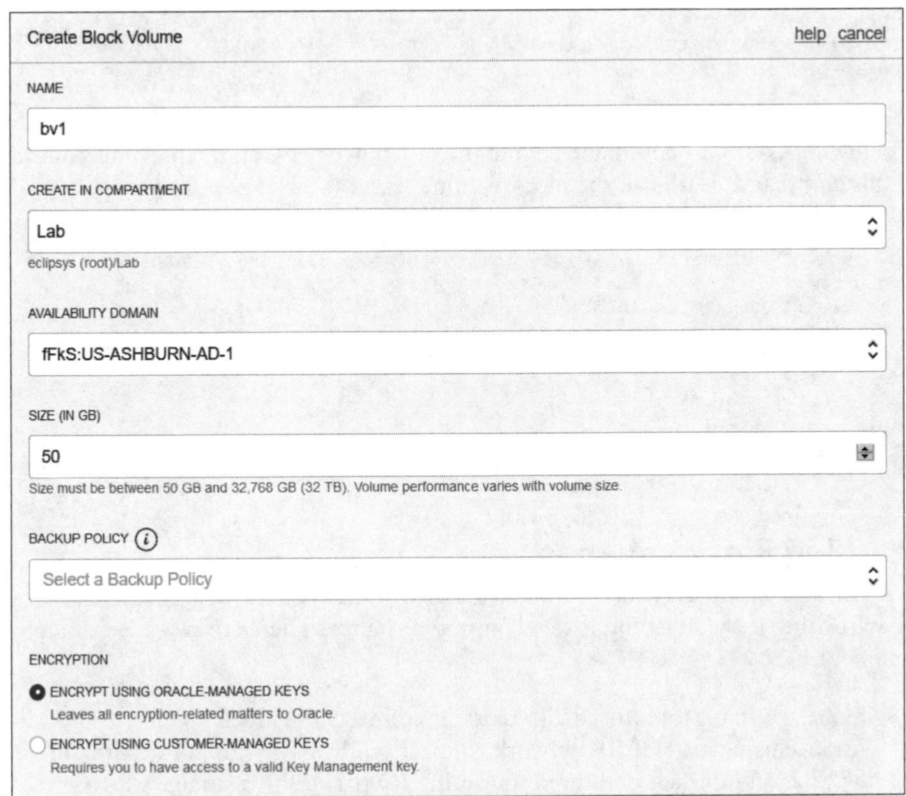

5. The block volume provisioning process begins and after a few minutes its status changes to AVAILABLE.

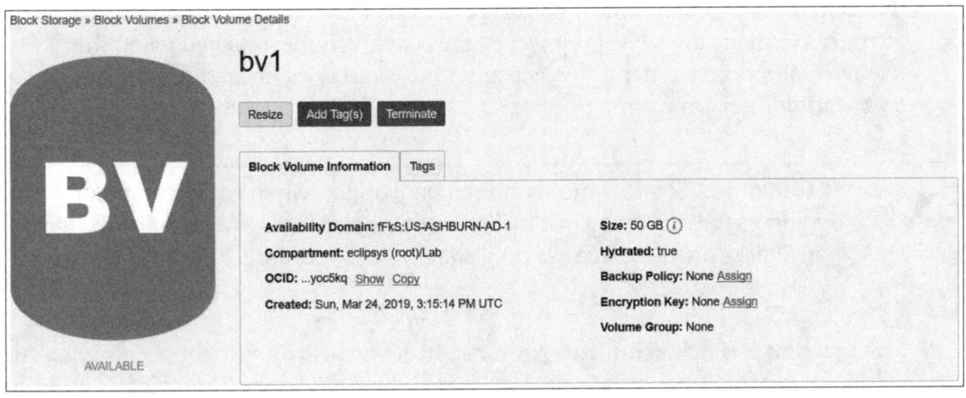

You may list all block volumes in an AD that belong to a compartment with the following OCI CLI command:

```
$ oci bv volume list  --availability-domain fFkS:US-ASHBURN-AD-1
--compartment-id X | egrep '(display-name)|
(lifecycle-state)|(size-in-gbs)'
"display-name": "bv1",
"lifecycle-state": "AVAILABLE",
"size-in-gbs": 50,
```

Boot volumes in the same AD may be listed by querying the block volume service with the following OCI CLI commands. Note the difference between the previous command and this command. Both call the block volume server (`oci bv`) but block volumes use the `volume` API while boot volumes use the `boot-volume` API.

```
$ oci bv boot-volume list  --availability-domain fFkS:US-ASHBURN-AD-1
--compartment-id X | egrep '(display-name)|
(lifecycle-state)|(size-in-gbs)'
"display-name": "hercules (Boot Volume)",
"lifecycle-state": "AVAILABLE",
"size-in-gbs": 47,

"display-name": "web1 (Boot Volume)",
"lifecycle-state": "AVAILABLE",
"size-in-gbs": 47
```

Attaching Block Volumes

Once a block volume has been provisioned and is at the AVAILABLE lifecycle-state, you may start using it by attaching it to a compute instance. There are two types of volume attachments:

- **iSCSI** Often pronounced "i-scuzzy," it connects the block volume to the instance using an TCP/IP network connection. It may be useful to think of iSCSI as an interface dedicated to routing IO packets to a storage subsystem over TCP/IP. iSCSI is an established storage communications protocol and is supported on bare-metal and VM instances. Once a block volume is attached with iSCSI, it must be connected to the instance.
- **Paravirtualized** This attachment type is available only on VMs and adds an extra IO virtualization layer. However, the block volume attached using the paravirtualized attachment type is ready to use and does not require further connection intervention.

CAUTION iSCSI attachments are the only option when connecting block volumes to bare-metal instances, Windows and Linux VM instances based on Oracle-provided images published before February 2018 and December 2017 respectively.

When attaching a block volume to your instance, you also choose the access type. An attached block volume may be accessed in read/write or read-only modes. Read/write mode is the default access type, allowing instances to change data on the volume, while read-only attached volumes are protected from modification. To change the access type of a block volume, you need to detach the volume and reattach it with the new access type. You may also require that iSCSI-attached block volumes be authenticated using CHAP (Challenge Handshake Authentication Protocol) when connecting the attached volumes to the instance.

EXAM TIP Boot volumes are always attached with read/write access. To obtain information from the boot volume—for example, while troubleshooting an instance boot-up issue—the boot volume may be detached from an instance and attached with read-only access to another instance as a regular block volume.

Figure 5-2 shows the Attach Block Volume console interface where you specify the attachment type (iSCSI or paravirtualized), the block volume compartment, the volume to be attached, whether CHAP credentials are required or not, and the access type (read/write or read-only).

Some instances created using Oracle-provided Linux images support consistent device paths. When attaching the volume to an instance, you may have an additional option to choose a consistent device path—for example, /dev/oracleoci/oraclevdb. Consistent device paths remain constant between instance reboots. This enables you to refer to a consistent path when performing several operations on a volume, including partitioning, creating file systems, mounting file systems, and specifying automatic mounting options

Attach Block Volume
help cancel
Choose how you want to attach your block volume.
ISCSI
PARAVIRTUALIZED
BLOCK VOLUME COMPARTMENT
Lab
eclipsys (root)/Lab
SELECT VOLUME
ENTER VOLUME OCID
BLOCK VOLUME
bv1
REQUIRE CHAP CREDENTIALS
ACCESS
READ/WRITE
READ-ONLY
Attach

Figure 5-2 Attach a read/write block volume using iSCSI

in the Linux /etc/fstab file. These operations are possible with instances that do not support consistent device paths by referencing the volume by its unique block identifier.

NOTE iSCSI-attached volumes have higher IOPS performance than paravirtualized-attached volumes, which have additional overheads due to IO virtualization.

Exercise 5-2: Attach a Block Volume to a Linux Instance

In this exercise, you will attach the previously created block volume to the web1 compute instance.

1. Sign in to the OCI console, and choose your compartment.
2. Navigate to Compute | Instance and choose the web1 instance.
3. Choose Attached Block Volumes and click Attach Block Volumes.
4. Choose iSCSI as the attachment type.
5. Choose the relevant compartment and newly created block volume.
6. Check the Require CHAP Credentials checkbox.
7. Ensure that read/write access is selected and choose Attach.

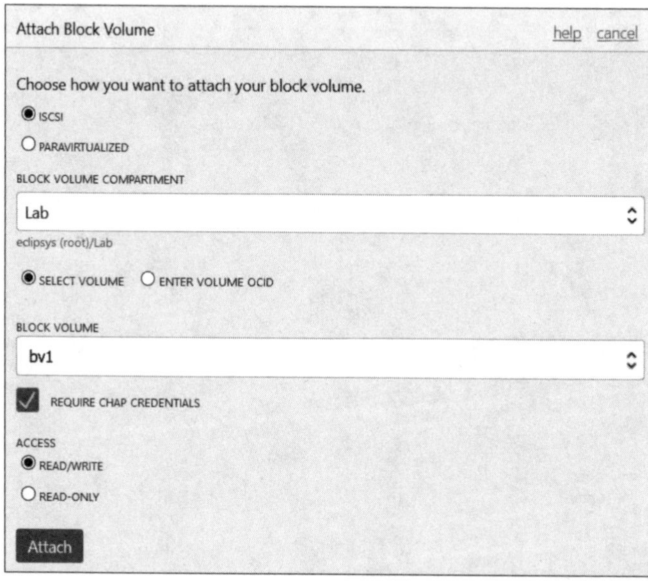

8. As the attachment process begins, the console notifies you to run the block volume's iSCSI commands to connect and enable the volume. There is also information of mounting options required when specifying this volume in the Linux /etc/fstab file. This is discussed in the next section.

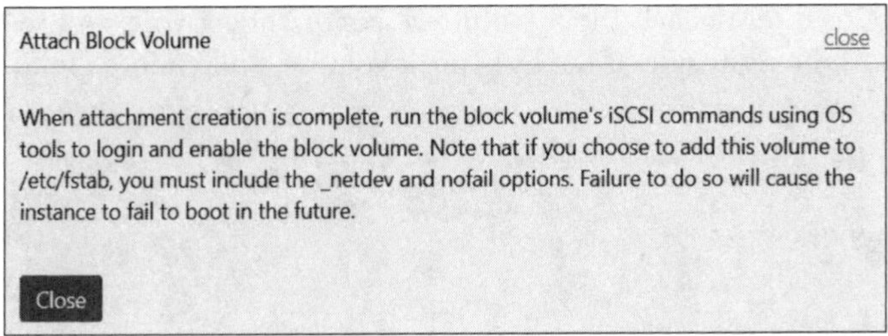

9. When the block volume is attached, the instance information page in the console shows the newly attached block volume.

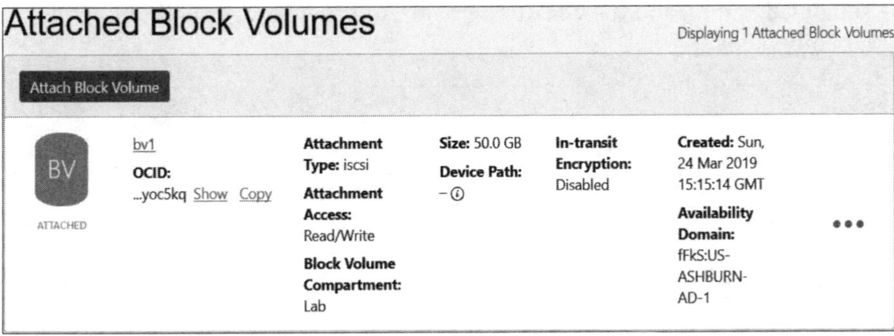

Connecting Block Volumes

Once a block volume is attached to an instance using iSCSI, it must be connected to the instance. The connection procedure varies based on two fundamental criteria:

- **Operating system image** Block volume connection procedure is different on Windows and Linux.
- **CHAP requirements** Additional connection steps are required if CHAP credentials are required to connect the block volume to the instance.

Exercise 5-3: Connect a Block Volume to Your Linux Volume Using iSCSI and CHAP

In this exercise, you will connect the previously attached block volume to the web1 compute instance.

1. Sign in to the OCI console, navigate to Compute | Instance, choose the web1 instance, and click Start it if it is not yet started.

2. Navigate to the Attached Block Volumes section, hover your mouse over the ellipses on the right side of the bv1 block volume, and choose iSCSI Commands & Information.

BV
ATTACHED
bv1
OCID:
...yoc5kq Show Copy
Attachment Type: iscsi
Attachment Access:
Read/Write
Block Volume
Compartment: Lab
Size: 50.0 GB
Device Path: –
In-transit Encryption:
Disabled
View Block Volume Details
iSCSI Commands & Information
Detach

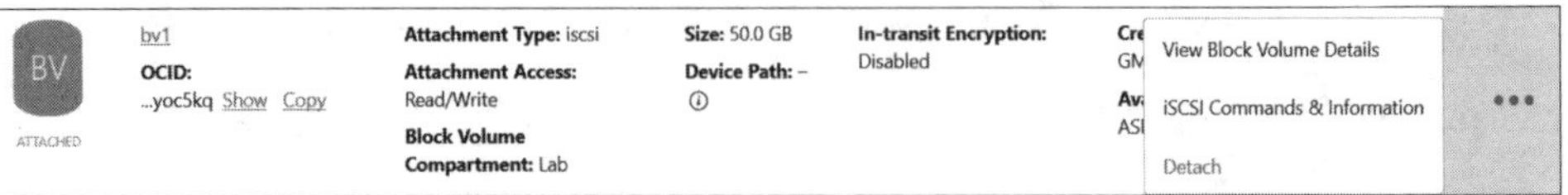

3. Copy the `attach` commands to a text editor. You will need this to connect the volume to the instance from the Linux shell. Note that the `attach` commands include the block volume IP address and port number, the volume IQN (iSCSI qualified name), and the CHAP username and password. These commands are used in Steps 5–10.

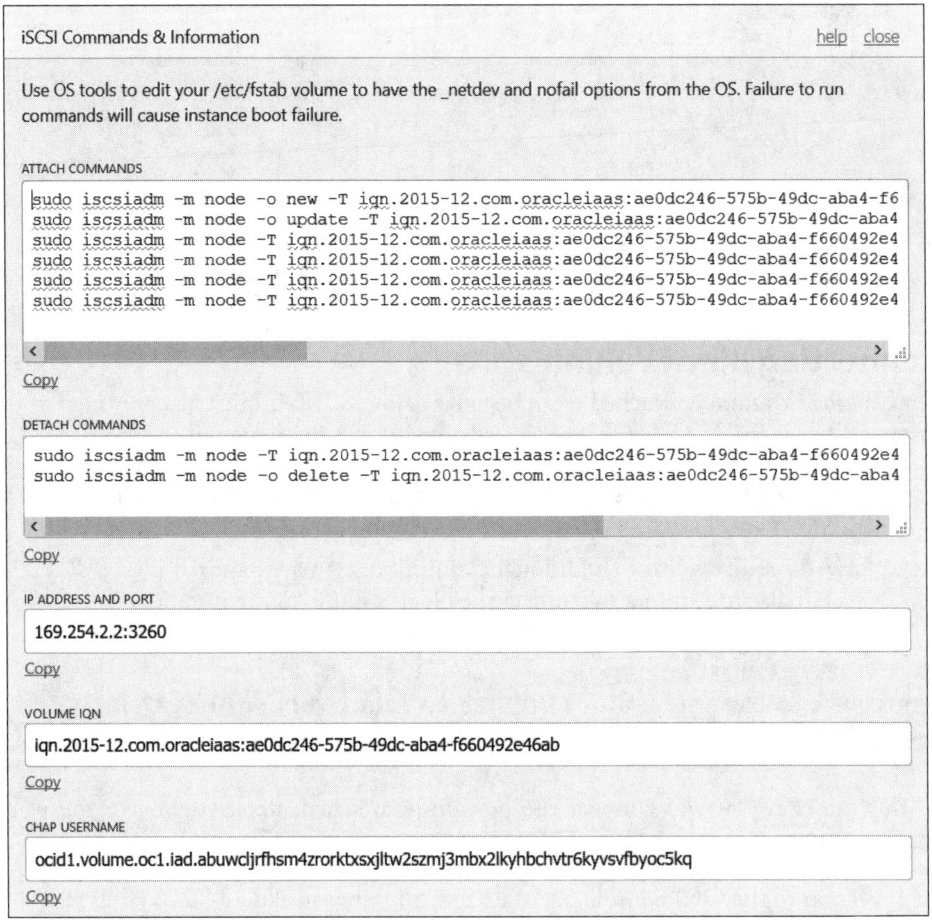

iSCSI Commands & Information
help close
Use OS tools to edit your /etc/fstab volume to have the _netdev and nofail options from the OS. Failure to run commands will cause instance boot failure.
ATTACH COMMANDS
sudo iscsiadm -m node -o new -T iqn.2015-12.com.oracleiaas:ae0dc246-575b-49dc-aba4-f6
sudo iscsiadm -m node -o update -T iqn.2015-12.com.oracleiaas:ae0dc246-575b-49dc-aba4
sudo iscsiadm -m node -T iqn.2015-12.com.oracleiaas:ae0dc246-575b-49dc-aba4-f660492e4
sudo iscsiadm -m node -T iqn.2015-12.com.oracleiaas:ae0dc246-575b-49dc-aba4-f660492e4
sudo iscsiadm -m node -T iqn.2015-12.com.oracleiaas:ae0dc246-575b-49dc-aba4-f660492e4
sudo iscsiadm -m node -T iqn.2015-12.com.oracleiaas:ae0dc246-575b-49dc-aba4-f660492e4
Copy
DETACH COMMANDS
sudo iscsiadm -m node -T iqn.2015-12.com.oracleiaas:ae0dc246-575b-49dc-aba4-f660492e4
sudo iscsiadm -m node -o delete -T iqn.2015-12.com.oracleiaas:ae0dc246-575b-49dc-aba4
Copy
IP ADDRESS AND PORT
169.254.2.2:3260
Copy
VOLUME IQN
iqn.2015-12.com.oracleiaas:ae0dc246-575b-49dc-aba4-f660492e46ab
Copy
CHAP USERNAME
ocid1.volume.oc1.iad.abuwcljrfhsm4zrorktxsxjltw2szmj3mbx2lkyhbchvtr6kyvsvfbyoc5kq
Copy

4. Make an SSH connection to the web1 instance and describe the attached disks with the `fdisk -l` command. There is a single disk, the boot volume, that was attached when the instance was created.

```
$ sudo fdisk -l
...
Disk /dev/sda: 50.0 GB, 50010783744 bytes, 97677312 sectors
Units = sectors of 1 * 512 = 512 bytes
Sector size (logical/physical): 512 bytes / 4096 bytes
I/O size (minimum/optimal): 4096 bytes / 1048576 bytes
Disk label type: gpt
Disk identifier: 24B3008A-713C-4A61-9EF0-709312E028D4
#         Start          End    Size  Type            Name
 1         2048       411647    200M  EFI System      EFI System Partition
 2       411648     17188863      8G  Linux swap
 3     17188864     97675263   38.4G  Microsoft basic
```

5. Use the following `attach` command to register the newly attached volume with the instance:

```
sudo iscsiadm -m node -o new -T <volume IQN> -p <iSCSI IP address>:<iSCSI port>
```

6. When the newly attached volume is registered, the output should resemble the following:

```
$ sudo iscsiadm -m node -o new -T iqn.2015-12.com.
oracleiaas:ae0dc246-575b-49dc-aba4-f660492e46ab
-p 169.254.2.2:3260

New iSCSI node [tcp:[hw=,ip=,net_if=,iscsi_if=default]
169.254.2.2,3260,-1 iqn.2015-12.com.oracleiaas:
ae0dc246-575b-49dc-aba4-f660492e46ab] added
```

7. For the registration to persist reboots, issue the following command, which returns nothing when it completes successfully.

```
sudo iscsiadm -m node -T <volume IQN> -o update
-n node.startup -v automatic
```

8. Because you chose that CHAP credentials were required to connect to the volume when creating the block volume attachment, issue the following commands. Notice there is no output when the `iscsiadm` commands complete successfully.

```
iscsiadm -m node -T <volume IQN> -p <iSCSI IP address>:<iSCSI port>
-o update -n node.session.auth.authmethod -v CHAP

iscsiadm -m node -T <volume IQN> -p <iSCSI IP address>:<iSCSI port>
-o update -n node.session.auth.username -v <CHAP user name>

iscsiadm -m node -T <volume's IQN> -p <iSCSI IP address>:<iSCSI port>
-o update -n node.session.auth.password -v <CHAP password>
```

9. Log in to iSCSI using this command:

```
iscsiadm -m node -T <volume's IQN> -p <iSCSI IP Address>:<iSCSI port> -l
```

10. When you are successfully connected, the output resembles the following:

```
$ sudo iscsiadm -m node -T iqn.2015-12.com.oracleiaas:
ae0dc246-575b-49dc-aba4-f660492e46ab -p 169.254.2.2:3260 -l

Logging in to [iface: default, target: iqn.2015-12.com.oracleiaas:
ae0dc246-575b-49dc-aba4-f660492e46ab,
portal: 169.254.2.2,3260] (multiple)

Login to [iface: default, target: iqn.2015-12.com.oracleiaas:
ae0dc246-575b-49dc-aba4-f660492e46ab,
portal: 169.254.2.2,3260] successful.
```

11. You may run `fdisk -l` again to confirm the new block volume is listed as follows:

```
[opc@web1 ~]$ sudo fdisk -l
...
Disk /dev/sdb: 53.7 GB, 53687091200 bytes, 104857600 sectors
Units = sectors of 1 * 512 = 512 bytes
Sector size (logical/physical): 512 bytes / 4096 bytes
I/O size (minimum/optimal): 4096 bytes / 1048576 bytes
```

Once a block volume is connected and visible to an instance, it may be used for ASM disk storage for databases (discussed in Chapter 6) or for file systems, or for pretty much anything you would use a disk volume for on a regular on-premises server to which a disk has been presented.

Exercise 5-4: Format a Block Volume, Create a File System, and Mount the Volume

In this exercise, you use the previously connected block volume in the web1 compute instance. A directory (/app) is created to mount the block volume. The volume is partitioned with `fdisk`. An ext4 file system is created and the volume is mounted on the /app directory. To persist this mapping through reboots, the /etc/fstab file is updated with the UUID of the block volume mapped to the /app directory. The web1 instance used in this exercise does not support consistent device paths.

1. Make an SSH connection to the web1 instance.
2. Use the `fdisk` command with the device path (for example, /dev/sdb) for the newly connected block volume.

```
[opc@web1 ~]$ sudo fdisk /dev/sdb
Welcome to fdisk (util-linux 2.23.2).
Changes will remain in memory only, until you decide to write them.
Be careful before using the write command.
Device does not contain a recognized partition table
Building a new DOS disklabel with disk identifier 0x420b13d2.
The device presents a logical sector size that is smaller than the
physical sector size. Aligning to a physical sector (or optimal I/O)
size boundary is recommended, or performance may be impacted.
```

3. Choose n to create a new partition and choose p for primary partition type.

```
Command (m for help): n
Partition type:
   p   primary (0 primary, 0 extended, 4 free)
   e   extended
Select (default p): p
```

4. Accept the default partition number 1 and the default settings for the first and last sectors because you are allocating all the space on this disk to this partition.

```
Partition number (1-4, default 1): 1
First sector (2048-104857599, default 2048):
Using default value 2048
Last sector, +sectors or +size{K,M,G} (2048-104857599, default
104857599):
Using default value 104857599
Partition 1 of type Linux and of size 50 GiB is set
```

5. Choose p to print the configuration to the screen.

```
Command (m for help): p
Disk /dev/sdb: 53.7 GB, 53687091200 bytes, 104857600 sectors
Units = sectors of 1 * 512 = 512 bytes
Sector size (logical/physical): 512 bytes / 4096 bytes
I/O size (minimum/optimal): 4096 bytes / 1048576 bytes
Disk label type: dos
Disk identifier: 0x420b13d2
   Device Boot      Start         End      Blocks   Id  System
/dev/sdb1            2048   104857599    52427776   83  Linux
```

6. Choose w to write or save the configuration.

```
Command (m for help): w
The partition table has been altered!
Calling ioctl() to re-read partition table.
Syncing disks.
```

7. Create an ext4 file system on this new partition.

```
[opc@web1 ~]$ sudo mkfs.ext4 /dev/sdb1
…Allocating group tables: done
Writing inode tables: done
Creating journal (32768 blocks): done
Writing superblocks and filesystem accounting information: done
```

8. Create a directory to mount the file system.

```
[opc@web1 ~]$ sudo mkdir /app
```

9. Mount the file system to the /app directory and confirm that it has been mounted.

```
[opc@web1 ~]$ sudo mount /dev/sdb1 /app
[opc@web1 ~]$ df -h | grep /app
/dev/sdb1          50G    53M    47G    1% /app
```

10. Your block volume is ready to be used. However, once the compute instance restarts, the partition must be manually mounted again unless you configure automounting by adding an entry into the /etc/fstab file. Because this instance does not support consistent device paths like /dev/oracleoci/oraclevdb, you have to use the disk partition unique identifier (UUID), which you get from the `blkid` command.

```
[opc@web1 ~]$ sudo blkid | grep /dev/sdb1
/dev/sdb1: UUID="91042f7d-1ff1-4cee-a620-2fa3367bdf86" TYPE="ext4"
```

11. An entry must be placed in the /etc/fstab to mount the /app mount point to the UUID along with the mount type (ext4 in this case) and several mount options to ensure the instance does not hang because of this volume mount. The `nofail` option basically lets the operating system know that it should ignore any failures associated with this mount, whereas the `_netdev` option indicates there is a dependency on the networking services that should be started on the instance prior to mounting this volume. These options allow the instance startup routine to get services started in the correct sequence and to proceed with the startup routine even if there are errors when mounting this volume.

```
$ echo "UUID=91042f7d-1ff1-4cee-a620-2fa3367bdf86 /app ext4
defaults,nofail,_netdev  0 2" | sudo tee -a  /etc/fstab

$ grep /app  /etc/fstab
UUID=91042f7d-1ff1-4cee-a620-2fa3367bdf86 /app                    ext4
defaults,nofail,_netdev  0 2
```

12. Test the persistence of this setting by rebooting the instance. You should find the /app volume when the instance restarts.

```
$ uptime
01:26:56 up 0 min,  1 user,  load average: 1.37, 0.40, 0.14
$ df -h | grep app
/dev/sdb1        50G   53M   47G   1% /app
```

The steps to create and attach a block volume to Linux and Windows compute instances are identical. Connecting the volume to the instance is different because of the different operating system tools required for iSCSI and disk management.

Exercise 5-5: Present a Block Volume to a Windows Instance

To complete this exercise, you need a Windows compute instance—for example, one based on the Oracle-provided Windows 2016 image.

1. Create a 50GB block volume in the same AD as your Windows instance.

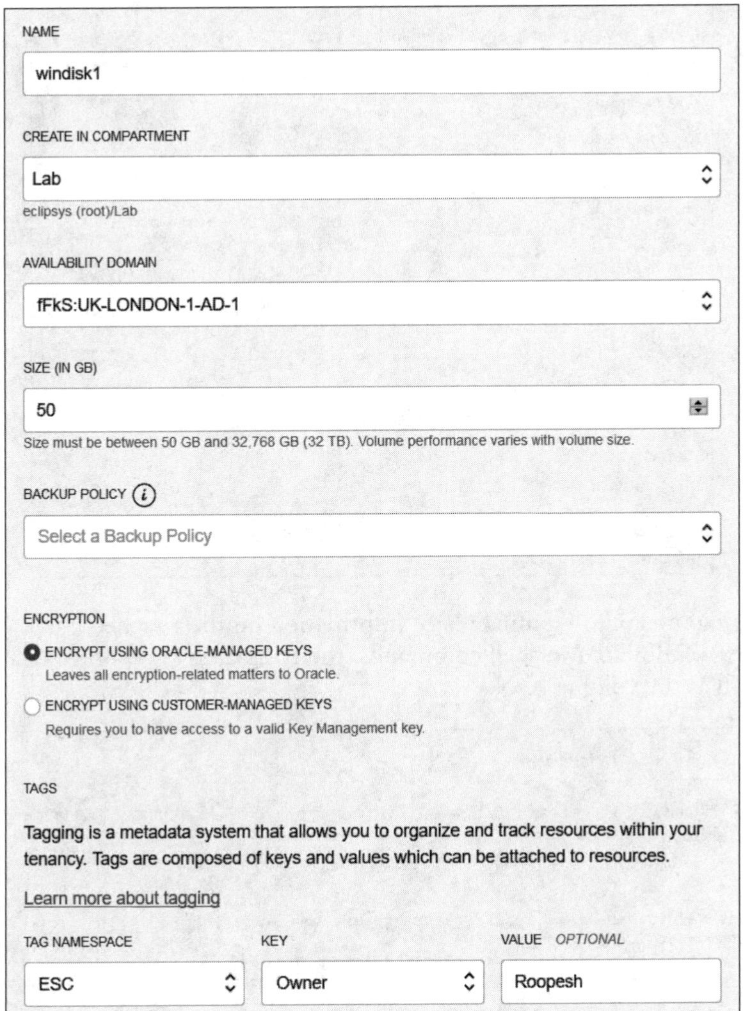

2. Attach the block volume to your instance using iSCSI. Choose a read/write access mode and select Attach. You will be reminded to run the block volume's iSCSI commands to log in and enable the volume once the attachment is created.

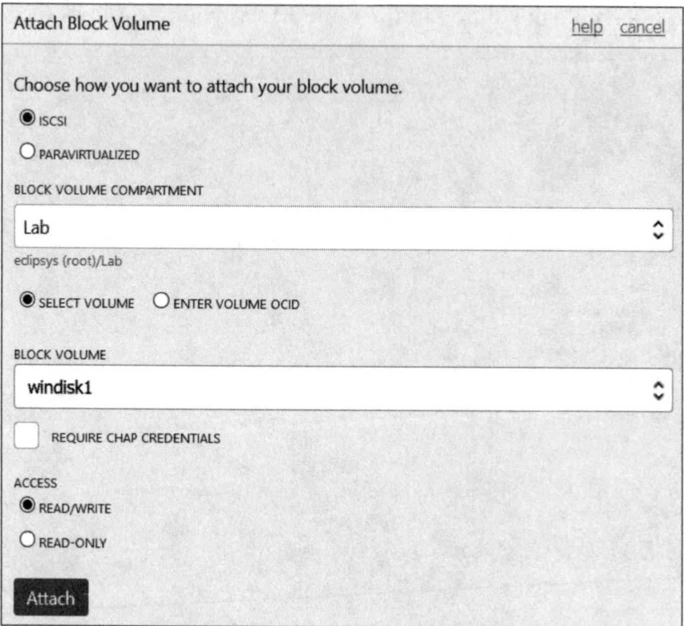

3. Viewing the iSCSI Commands & Information on the attached block volume yields Windows Powershell commands, the IP address and port for the volume, as well as the volume IQN.

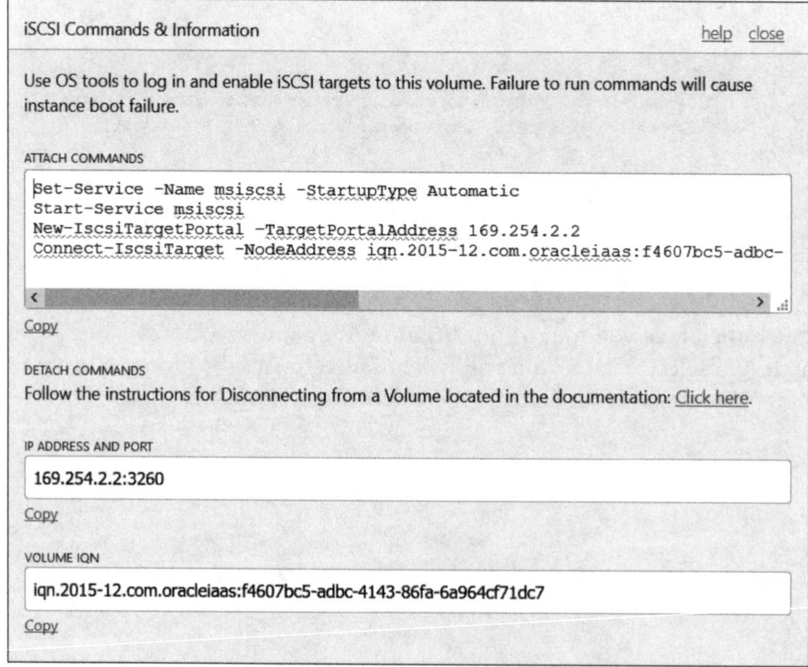

4. Connect to the Windows instance with a remote desktop tool, search the Windows menu for iSCSI Initiator, and launch the tool. Navigate to the Discovery tab, choose Discover Portal, specify the IP address and port number, and select OK.

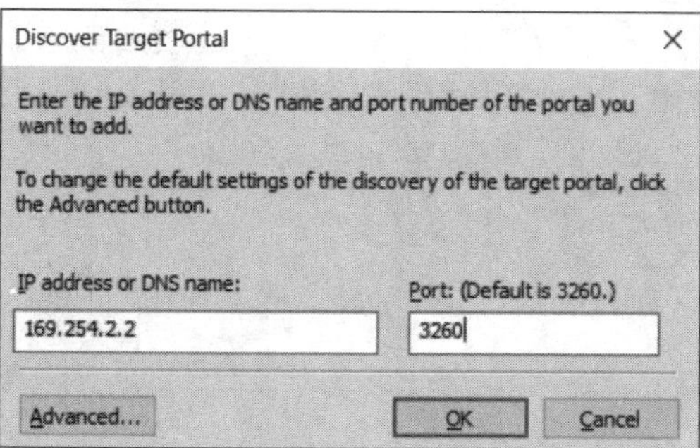

5. Navigate to the Targets tab, and the discovered volume should be listed under discovered targets (though marked as inactive). Highlight the new target and then choose Connect.

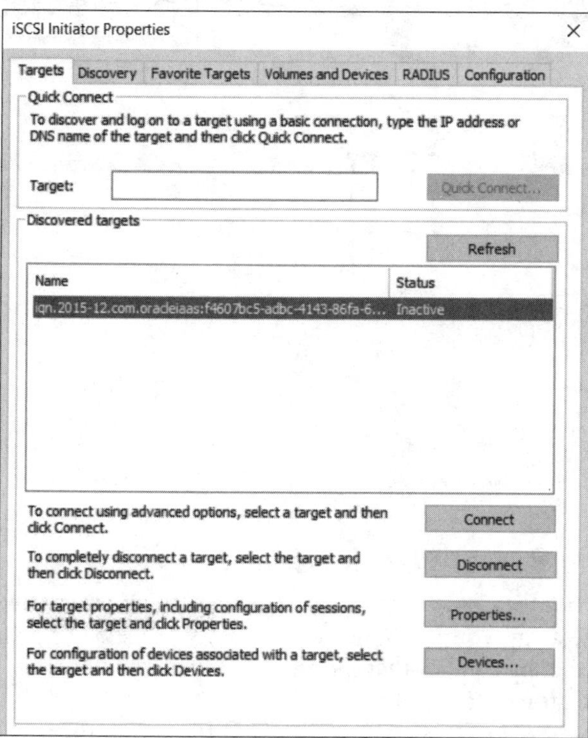

6. Ensure that the Add This Connection To The List Of Favorite Targets checkbox is selected before choosing OK. The volume is now connected to the instance.

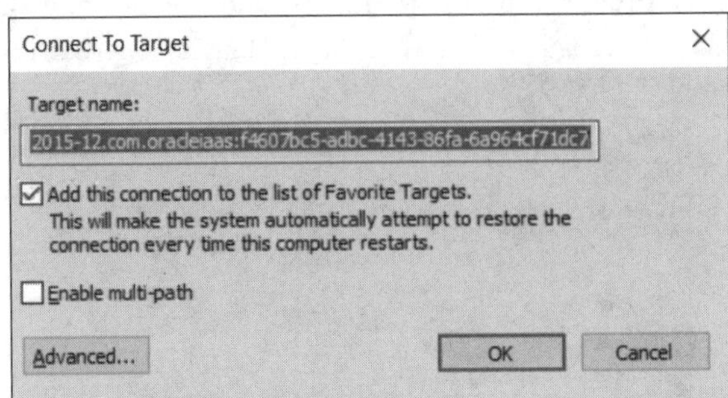

7. In Windows Server Manager, use the File And Storage Services | Volumes | Disks interface to mount the newly added volume.

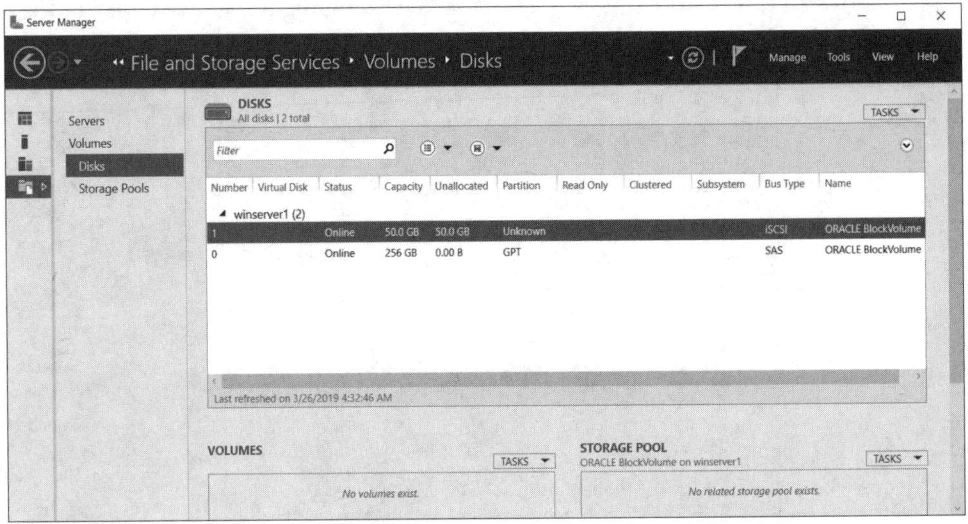

Block Volume Backup Options

Backups protect your data and are an essential component of any business continuity and disaster recovery strategy. Point-in-time backups of data on a block volume may be taken manually or by assigning a policy that specifies a backup schedule. Block volume backups are encrypted and stored in object storage buckets (discussed later in this chapter) and may be restored as new volumes to any AD within the region they are stored.

	Daily Incremental	Weekly Incremental	Monthly Incremental	Annual Full Backup
Bronze	N	N	Y	Y
Silver	N	Y	Y	Y
Gold	Y	Y	Y	Y
Backup start day	Everyday	Sunday	First day of the month	January 1
Retention period	7 days	4 weeks	12 months	5 years

Table 5-1 Volume Backup Policies

Block volume backups may be either

- **Full** All changes since the volume was created are backed up.
- **Incremental** Only changes since the last backup are saved.

The rate of changes on the block volume determines the size of the incremental backup, but it is generally smaller and faster than a full backup.

Block Volume Backup Policies

A block volume may be backed up manually or be assigned one of the automatic backup policies listed in Table 5-1. These policies specify an increasingly aggressive backup and retention schedule as they progress from Bronze to Silver to Gold.

A block volume may be assigned a policy at any time in its lifecycle. A volume assigned a Silver policy is incrementally backed up weekly on a Sunday, monthly on the first day of the month, and annually on January 1. Once a policy-based backup expires (the backup is older than the policy retention period), it is automatically deleted. If you want to retain a backup for longer than its retention period, a manual backup must be performed.

Manual Block Volume Backups

You may back up block volume using the OCI CLI, the API, or the console. Figure 5-3 shows the console interface used to create a manual backup of a volume or to assign a backup policy to a volume.

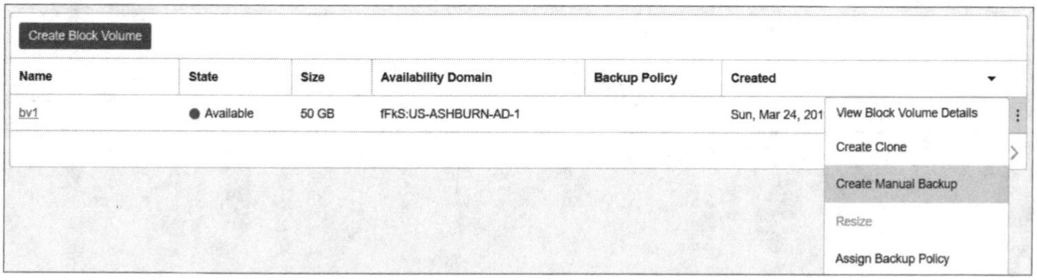

Figure 5-3 Block volume backup options

The following OCI CLI command lists the block volumes in a specific compartment. Note that some of the OCI CLI output has been removed for brevity.

```
$ oci bv volume list  --availability-domain fFkS:US-ASHBURN-AD-1
--compartment-id ocid1.compartment.oc1..zlh3iq
    { "availability-domain": "fFkS:US-ASHBURN-AD-1",
      "compartment-id": "ocid1.compartment.oc1.. zlh3iq",
      "display-name": "bv1",
      "id": "ocid1.volume.oc1.iad.abuwc...yoc5kq",
      "lifecycle-state": "AVAILABLE",
      "size-in-gbs": 50,
      "volume-group-id": null }]}
```

Using the `volume_id`, you can create a manual backup using the OCI CLI as follows:

```
$  oci bv backup create --volume-id ocid1.volume.oc1.iad...vtr6k
{"compartment-id": "ocid1.compartment.oc1.. zlh3iq",
    "display-name": "abuwcl..33jy6q",
    "expiration-time": null,
    "id": "ocid1.volumebackup.oc1.iad.abuwcl..33jy6q",
    "lifecycle-state": "REQUEST_RECEIVED",
    "size-in-gbs": 50,
    "source-type": "MANUAL",
    "source-volume-backup-id": null,
    "time-created": null,
    "type": "INCREMENTAL",
    "unique-size-in-gbs": 0,
    "volume-id": "ocid1.volume.oc1.iad.abuwcl..yoc5kq" }
```

CAUTION If you do not specify the backup type to either incremental or full, the OCI CLI defaults to an incremental backup.

Figure 5-4 lists the block volume backup made with the earlier OCI CLI command.

Block Volume Backups *in* Lab *Compartment*

Name	State	Backup Source	Backup Type	Backup Size / Volume Size (in GB)	Source Type	Expiration	Created
abuwcljrbj3dcfzq5qk3mriw47fdntfyeh2aydjsu6owntgqe4ahpl33jy6q	Available	bv1	Incremental	1 / 50	Manual		Wed, Mar 27, 2019, 2:17:50 AM UTC

Showing 1 Item(s) < Page 1 >

Figure 5-4 Block volume backup list

Exercise 5-6: Create a Full Backup of a Block Volume

You may use the console, the CLI, or the API to back up a volume. Unless you use a predefined policy, you may want to create backup scripts that run on your preferred schedule. Hence, this exercise focuses on backups using the CLI and assumes there is a block volume available to be backed up like the one created in Exercise 5-1.

1. List the available block volumes in your compartment with the CLI command, taking note of the `volume-id` for the block volume you wish to back up.

```
oci bv volume list  --compartment-id <compartment OCID>
```

2. Create a FULL backup by specifying the `-type` parameter, and provide a display name if desired. The CLI command to create a block volume backup requires the `volume-id` returned by the previous command.

```
oci bv backup create --type full --display-name bv1_full
--volume-id <volume OCID>
```

3. The volume backup begins with the life-cycle property being set to "REQUEST_RECEIVED" before changing to "AVAILABLE".
4. To take a manual backup using the console, navigate to Block Storage | Block Volume, choose the ellipses menu adjacent to the block volume, and choose Create Manual Backup (see Figure 5-3). This menu also lets you assign a backup policy (Bronze, Silver, or Gold) to the volume.
5. To view the available block volume backups, navigate to Block Storage | Block Volume Backups. The full backup created earlier in the exercise should be listed.

Block Volume Backups *in* Lab *Compartment*

Name	State	Backup Source	Backup Type	Backup Size / Volume Size (in GB)	Source Type	Expiration	Created
bv1_full	Available	bv1	Full	1 / 50	Manual		Fri, Mar 29, 2019, 9:07:55 PM UTC
bv1_backup_20190329_210244	Available	bv1	Full	1 / 50	Manual		Fri, Mar 29, 2019, 9:02:55 PM UTC
abuwcljrbj3dcfzq5qk3mriw47fdntfyeh2aydjsu6owntgqe4ahpl33jy6q	Available	bv1	Incremental	1 / 50	Manual		Wed, Mar 27, 2019, 2:17:50 AM UTC

Showing 3 Item(s) < Page 1 >

Volume Groups

Multiple volumes including boot and block volumes may be grouped together as a volume group. Volume groups may be backed up and restored as a consistent point-in-time set or cloned to create new consistent environments.

Exercise 5-7: Create and Back Up a Volume Group

1. In the console, navigate to Block Storage | Volume Groups, and choose Create Volume Group.
2. Provide a volume group name like vg1, and choose the compartment and AD for the volume group. Add multiple blocks or boot volumes to the volume group. These volumes usually belong to the same instance or have some dependency on one another for data consistency. The bv1 block volume attached to the web1 instance and its boot volume are chosen. Use the +Volume button to add additional volumes to the group, and choose Create Volume Group.

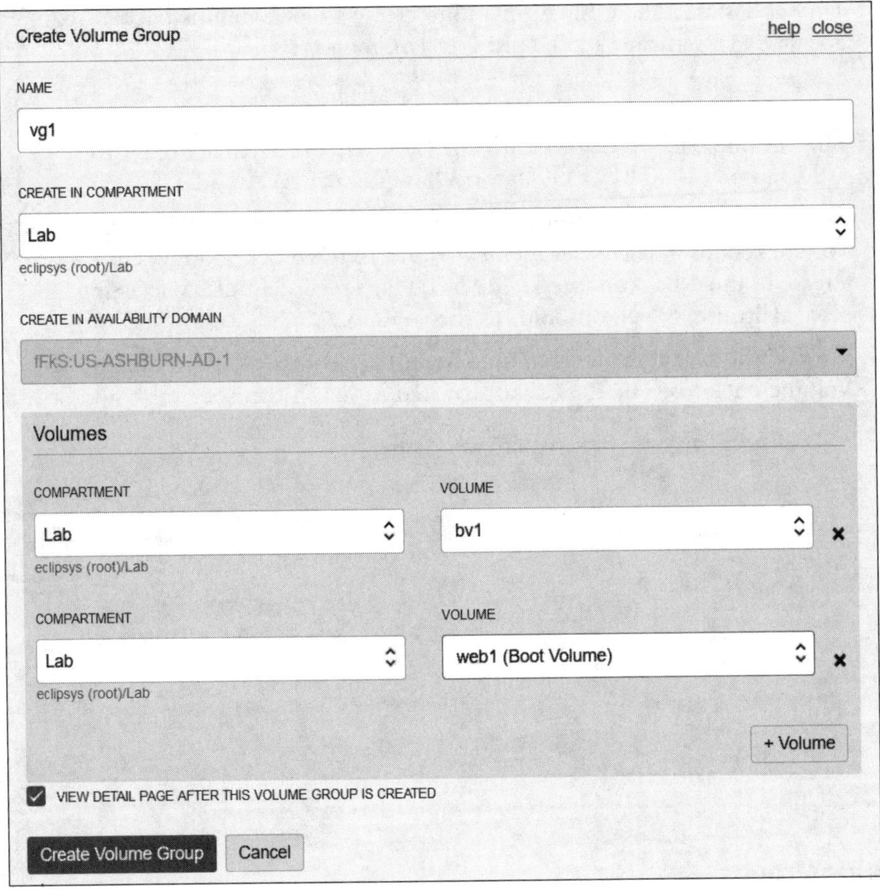

3. Seconds later the volume group detail page should appear. The volume group is a logical grouping of volumes. It has no data but is rather a metadata description of the volumes it comprises. Navigate to Block Storage | Volume Groups and choose the ellipses menu adjacent to the new volume group.

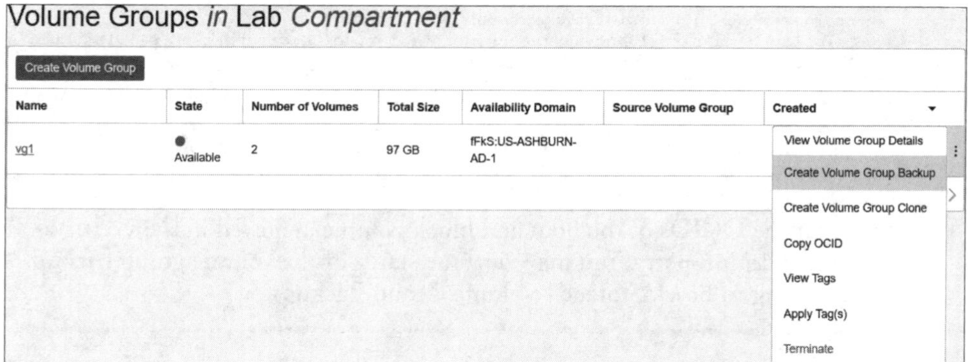

4. You can create a volume group backup or a clone in another compartment. Choose Create Volume Group Backup, specify a volume group backup name like vg1_backup, and choose Full Backup (the other type is Incremental).
5. Navigate to Block Storage | Volume Group Backups to see the list of volume group backups.

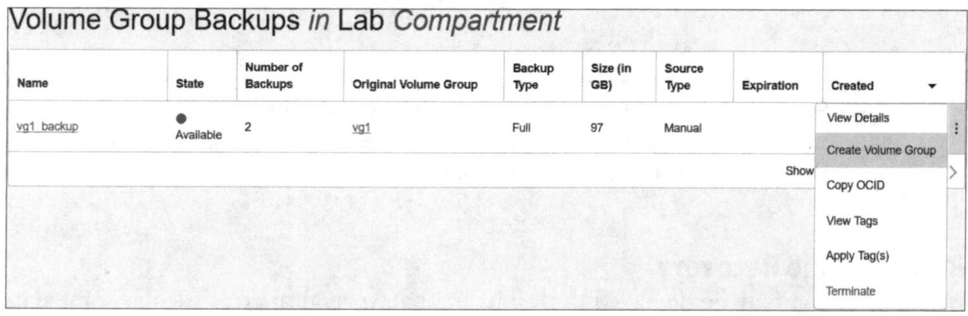

6. This volume group backup is a group of boot and block volume backups. These backups are also accessible through the listings of individual boot and block volume backups with display names like web1 (Boot Volume)_backup_20190329_210244 and bv1_backup_20190329_210244 respectively. Note the identical suffix backup_20190329_210244 between them indicating they are part of a volume group backup set.

7. It is likely to be more practical to back up volume groups using scripts with an OCI CLI command like the following:

```
$ oci bv volume-group-backup
create --type INCREMENTAL --display-name vg1_backup_inc
--volume-group-id ocid1.volumegroup.oc1.iad.abuwc..jmksna

    "compartment-id": "ocid1.compartment.oc1..zlh3iq",
    "display-name": "vg1_backup_inc","id": "ocid1.volumegroupbackup.oc1.iad.kxfq",
    "lifecycle-state": "CREATING",
    "size-in-gbs": 97,
    "type": "INCREMENTAL",
    "volume-backup-ids": [
      "ocid1.bootvolumebackup.oc1.iad.abuwcl..4r3p2ptgqq",
      "ocid1.volumebackup.oc1.iad.abuwcl..wxwarq"],
    "volume-group-id": "ocid1.volumegroup.oc1.iad.abuwcl..kjmksna"}
```

8. Note that the OCIDs of the boot and block volume are listed in the `volume-backup-ids` property. You may view the status of the volume group backup by navigating to Block Storage | Volume Group Backups.

Delete and Recover Block Volumes

When instances are no longer required, you may reclaim the block storage by detaching block volumes from instances. Detached block volumes may be deleted or terminated. The following OCI CLI command deletes a block volume no longer required.

```
$ oci bv volume delete --volume-id ocid1.volume.oc1.iad.abuwclj..quf2a
Are you sure you want to delete this resource? [y/N]: y
$
```

NOTE You always pay for OCI block storage, whether it is attached to a running or stopped instance. To avoid unnecessary costs, block volumes that are no longer required should be deleted.

Block Volume Recovery

A block volume may be damaged during its lifespan. A logical error such as some data corruption, or data being accidentally removed or overwritten, may have damaged the volume. If a backup is available, it may be restored to a new block volume.

Remember this new block volume has the data as of the time the last backup was taken. You can attach this new block volume to an instance to recover lost data or use it as a replacement volume if the original volume must be replaced. In this case, detach the original volume from its instance and attach the new volume created from the backup.

Exercise 5-8: Restore a Block Volume Backup to a New Block Volume

1. In the console, navigate to Block Storage | Block Volume Backups, choose the ellipses menu adjacent to one of your block volumes, and choose Create

Block Volume. Provide a name like bv-created-from-backup, a compartment and AD for the new block volume, a backup policy if required, and encryption options, and choose Create Block Volume.

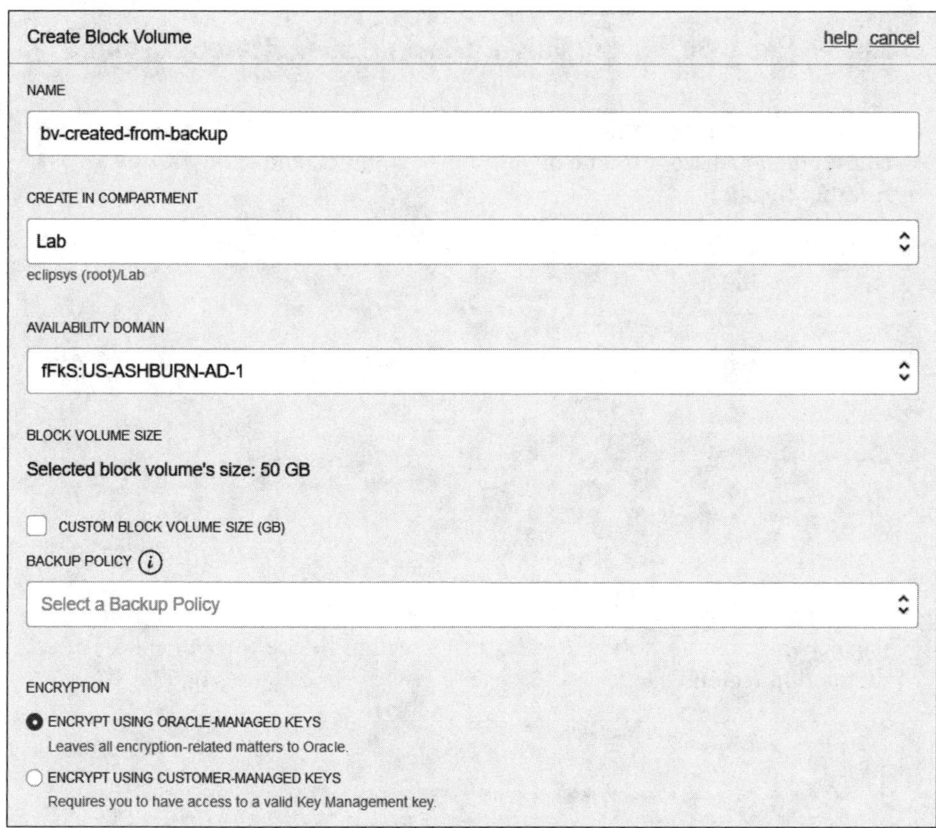

2. You can view the newly created block volume restored from the backup in the console by navigating to Block Storage | Block Volumes.

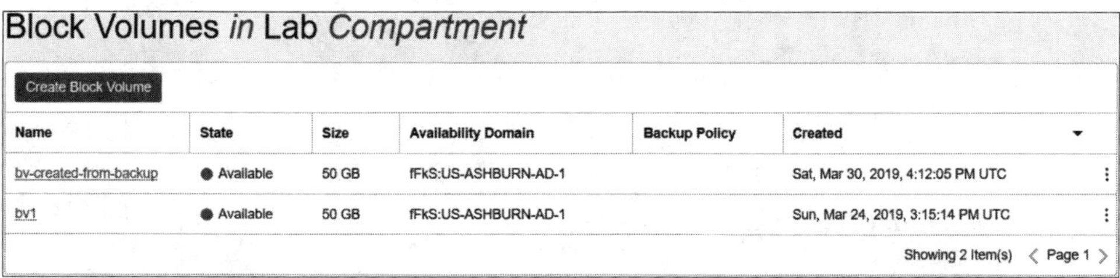

Name	State	Size	Availability Domain	Backup Policy	Created
bv-created-from-backup	Available	50 GB	fFkS:US-ASHBURN-AD-1		Sat, Mar 30, 2019, 4:12:05 PM UTC
bv1	Available	50 GB	fFkS:US-ASHBURN-AD-1		Sun, Mar 24, 2019, 3:15:14 PM UTC

3. This block volume is ready to be attached to an instance or to be cloned and used like a regular block volume.

Copy Block Volume Backup to Another Region

Volume backups may be copied to other regions. This may be useful to clone environments in other OCI regions.

Exercise 5-9: Recover a Block Volume Backup in a Different Region

1. In the console, navigate to Block Storage | Block Volume Backups, choose the ellipses menu adjacent to one of your block volumes, and choose Copy To Another Region.

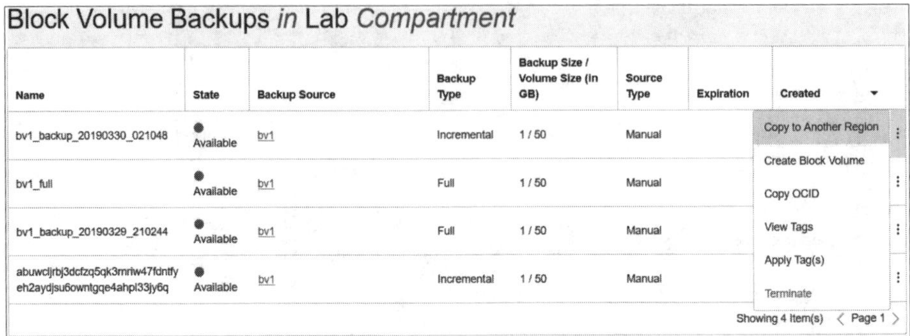

Block Volume Backups in Lab Compartment
Name
State
Backup Source
Backup Type
Backup Size / Volume Size (in GB)
Source Type
Expiration
Created
bv1_backup_20190330_021048
Available
bv1
Incremental
1 / 50
Manual
bv1_full
Available
bv1
Full
1 / 50
Manual
bv1_backup_20190329_210244
Available
bv1
Full
1 / 50
Manual
abuwcljrbj3dcfzq5qk3mriw47fdntfy eh2aydjsu6owntgqe4ahpl33jy6q
Available
bv1
Incremental
1 / 50
Manual
Copy to Another Region
Create Block Volume
Copy OCID
View Tags
Apply Tag(s)
Terminate
Showing 4 Item(s)
Page 1

2. Provide a destination region and choose Copy Block Volume Backup. Your tenancy must be subscribed to at least two regions before you can choose a destination region.

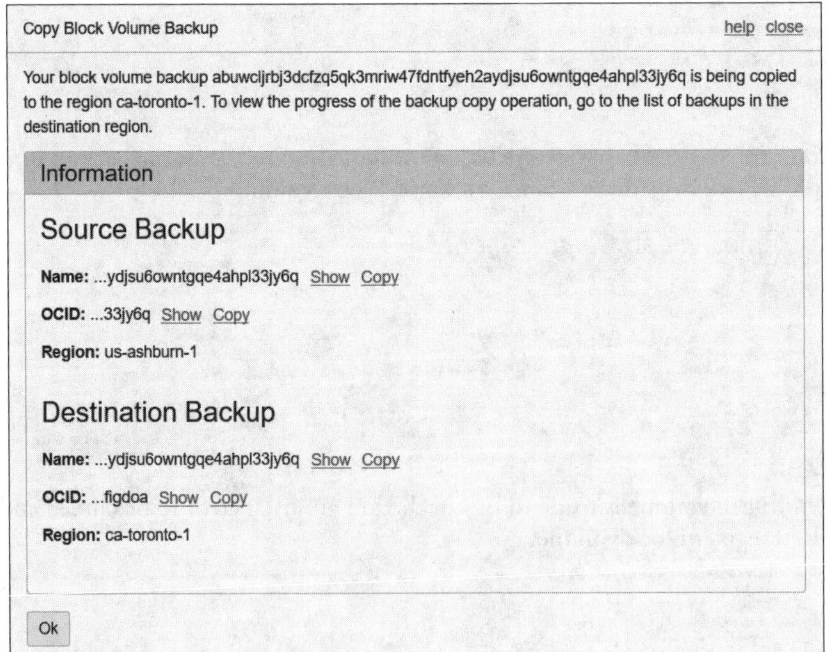

3. Once the backup has been copied, you can change your region and navigate to Block Storage | Block Volume Backups to locate the foreign backup. Note that the Backup Source column describes the source region.

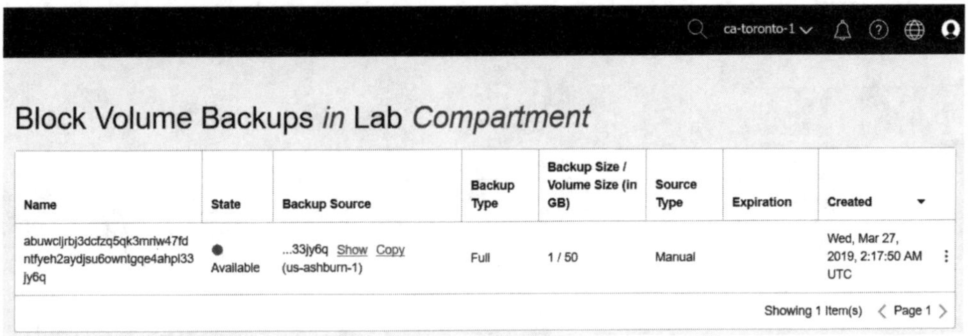

ca-toronto-1

Block Volume Backups *in* Lab *Compartment*

Name	State	Backup Source	Backup Type	Backup Size / Volume Size (in GB)	Source Type	Expiration	Created
abuwcljrbj3dcfzq5qk3mriw47fdntfyeh2aydjsu6owntgqe4ahpl33jy6q	Available	...33jy6q Show Copy (us-ashburn-1)	Full	1 / 50	Manual		Wed, Mar 27, 2019, 2:17:50 AM UTC

Showing 1 Item(s) < Page 1 >

4. You may create block volumes in the new region from this backup as in the previous exercise.

Object Storage

Object storage is a relatively new resilient storage type that has become a standard for general purpose file storage in the cloud. The object storage system is Internet accessible, and you control the permissions and whether a bucket is publicly accessible or not. OCI object storage integrates with OCI's Identity and Access Management (IAM) to control permissions on object storage.

Object storage is not suitable for high-speed computing storage requirements (such as those required to run databases) but provides flexible and scalable options for unstructured data storage and sharing as well as being great for big data and content repositories, backups and archives, log data, and other large datasets. Object storage is also not bound to an instance or an AD but is a region-level construct that resides in a compartment. Figure 5-5 situates OCI object storage within a tenancy. Instances in your tenancy may read and write to object storage through a service gateway. Instances on-premises connect either through the VCN (if this connection is set up) or through the Internet to object storage if sufficient permissions have been granted. Both OCI and on-premises instances connect to non–OCI S3–compatible object storage through the Internet.

Buckets and Objects

A bucket is a logical container for objects that reside in a compartment. As the name suggests, you store objects of any data type in a bucket. You may create up to 1,000 buckets per compartment per region and store an unlimited number of objects in a bucket, as of this writing. Buckets may not be nested. This is different from traditional file systems. A bucket may not contain other buckets. A single uneditable namespace is provided to

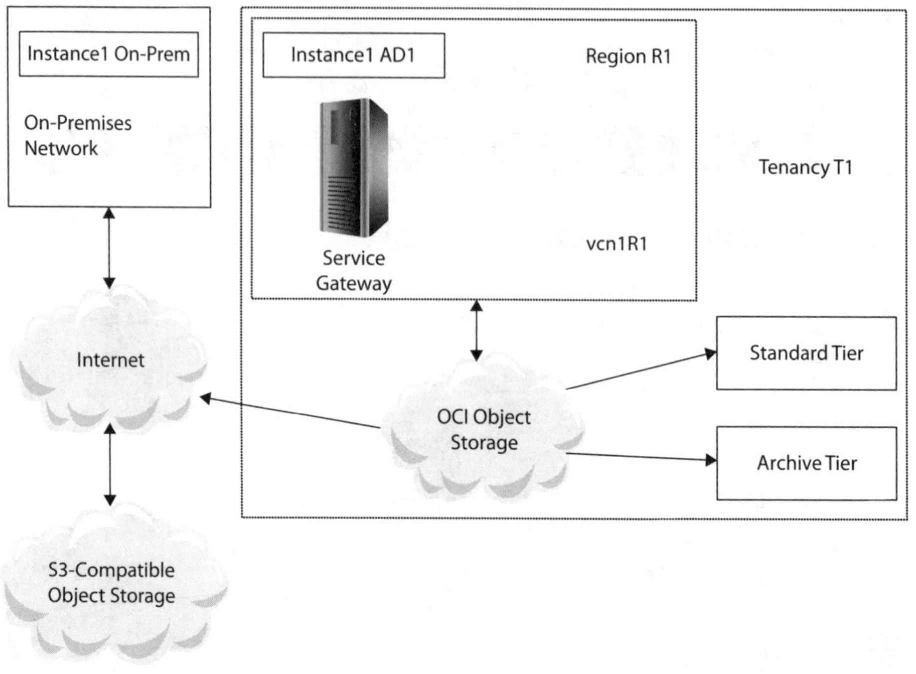

Figure 5-5 Object storage location within a tenancy

a tenancy that serves as the top-level root container for all buckets and objects. This is a system-generated string and may be queried with this CLI command:

```
$ oci os ns get
```

For some older tenancies, the namespace string may be a lowercase version of the tenancy name, but this is now a system-generated string.

EXAM TIP Bucket names must be unique within a namespace. The same bucket name may be used in a separate tenancy, unlike several other mainstream cloud object storage vendors. Bucket names are case sensitive, may not be longer than 256 characters, and may only contain letters, numbers, hyphens, underscores, and periods.

A bucket may exist at one of two tiers:

- **Standard tier** Objects stored in a standard tier bucket may be accessed frequently, and your data is immediately available. This tier of storage has good performance but is more expensive than archive tier storage.

- **Archive tier** Objects that are infrequently accessed but that must be retained and preserved for a long time are well suited to this tier. There is a longer lead time to access objects in archive tier buckets than in standard tier buckets.

Objects in buckets are encrypted automatically using either keys from your key management system or with OCI-provided keys. Object storage is also replicated across multiple storage servers in a region providing high data durability.

Object storage may be accessed in several ways including the following:

- **OCI console** This is a simple browser-based interface well suited to working with a relatively small number of object storage artifacts.
- **CLI** This is a fully functional command-line interface that is easily integrated into scripts and well suited for working with a relatively large number of object storage artifacts. Most API calls are wrapped by the CLI simplifying the interaction with object storage without the need for programming.
- **REST APIs and SDKs** These offer the most functionality but require some programming expertise.

When objects are placed in a bucket, they are uploaded. When they are retrieved, they are downloaded. You may upload and download objects to a bucket using the mechanisms listed previously. If a bucket is designated as a public bucket or if a bucket or object is shared with a pre-authenticated request, users may interact with object storage, performing reads and writes based on the sharing permissions, using HTTPS-based tools including web browsers and the curl and wget utilities. These mechanisms are discussed later in the chapter.

When an object is downloaded, the most recently written copy of the object is served by the object storage service, ensuring strong data consistency.

EXAM TIP An object storage bucket can exist in only one compartment but can also be moved between compartments.

Using the following CLI command, you may list the bucket names in your compartment:

```
$ oci os bucket list --compartment-id
ocid1.compartment.oc1.. zlh3iq | grep  \"name\"
       "name": "DB_Backups",
       "name": "Documents",
       "name": "Tax-Compliance-Records",
```

Archive Tier Buckets

Objects in standard tier buckets may be downloaded immediately, whereas objects in archive tier buckets must be restored before they are downloadable. The restore time can take several hours so it is important to store appropriate data in archive tier buckets.

Exercise 5-10: Upload, Restore, and Download Using an Archive Tier Bucket

In this exercise, you will create an archive tier bucket named Tax-Compliance-Records, upload a file, restore the object, and download it to your local machine.

1. Sign in to the OCI console and choose your compartment.
2. Navigate to Object Storage | Object Storage, and choose Create Bucket.
3. Name the bucket Tax-Compliance-Records, choose the archive storage tier, provide appropriate tag and encryption information, and choose Create Bucket.

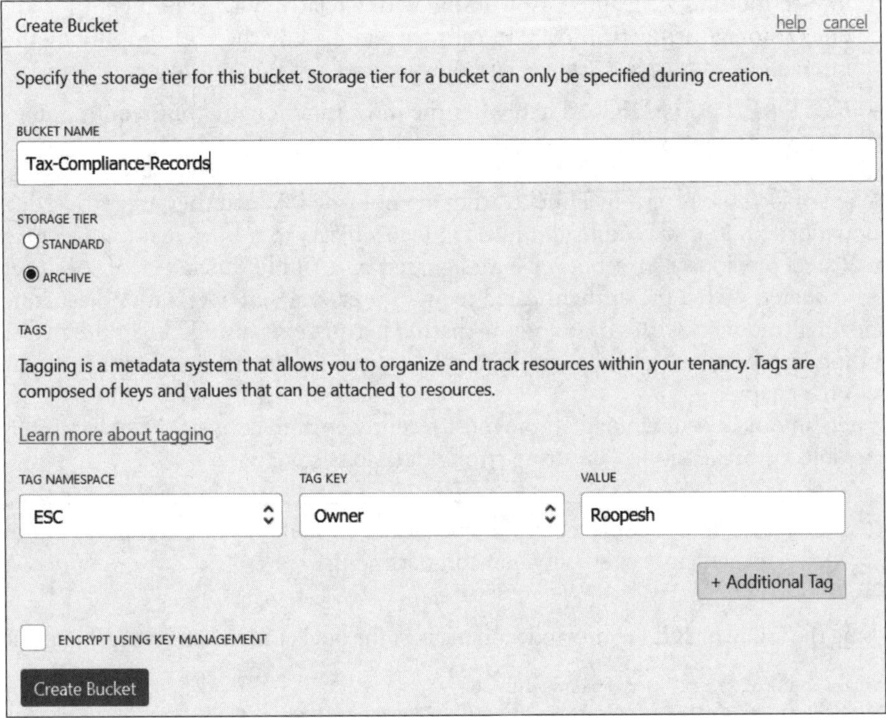

4. Navigate to the Tax-Compliance-Records bucket and choose Upload Object. Browse your local machine and choose a file less than 2GB in size. The file upload process begins, and after a short while, your file is stored in archive storage. You can use the console, API, or the following CLI command to list the file uploaded into this bucket as follows:

```
$ oci os object list --bucket-name Tax-Compliance-Records
```

5. To retrieve the file uploaded to this archive tier bucket, you must first initiate an object restore request. Using the console, navigate to the bucket and choose Restore Object from the ellipses menu adjacent to the object name. You are asked to optionally specify the time available to download the object once it is restored. It is available for download by default for 24 hours, but you may specify a download availability time from 1 to 240 hours. The following CLI command requests a restore of an object named EXACM.pdf from the Tax-Compliance-Records bucket.

```
$ oci os object restore --bucket-name Tax-Compliance-Records
--name EXACM.pdf
```

6. You may check the progress of the restore request using the CLI as follows:

```
$ oci os object restore-status --bucket-name Tax-Compliance-Records
--name EXACM.pdf

Restoring, this object is being restored and will be available for
download in about 4 hours from the time you issued the restore command.
```

7. Once the restore is complete, you may download the object. If you try to download the object using the CLI before the restore is completed, you will receive an error similar to the following:

```
$ oci os object get --bucket-name Tax-Compliance-Records
--name EXACM.pdf  --file /home/opc/EXACM.pdf

ServiceError:{
    "code": "NotRestored",
    "message": "Archived object is being restored.",
    "opc-request-id": "6fcf904b-5ee3-fbd8-119b-50a29dbf45f6",
    "status": 409}
```

NOTE The object storage service uses the 134.70.0.0/17 CIDR block IP range for all regions.

Standard Tier Buckets

Standard tier buckets are created by default and are often referred to as object storage while archive tier buckets are often known as archive storage. These are general purpose and support fast uploads and immediate downloads with no delays as you wait for data to be restored. Oracle is continuously improving the underlying physical storage infrastructure supporting the object storage service to provide a high performing storage option at a lower cost than block storage. Standard tier buckets are resilient and durable and are a good option for storing recent backups, big data repositories, images, videos, log files, and other content. OCI provides an HDFS connector enabling Apache Spark and Hadoop jobs to run against data in the OCI object storage service. Internet of Things (IoT) data and other large application data sets are good candidates for standard tier buckets.

Exercise 5-11: Upload, Restore, and Download Using a Standard Tier Bucket

In this exercise, you will create a standard tier bucket named Documents, upload a file, and download it to your local machine.

1. Sign in to the OCI console and choose your compartment.
2. Navigate to Object Storage | Object Storage, and choose Create Bucket.
3. Name the bucket Documents, choose the standard storage tier, provide appropriate tag and encryption information, and choose Create Bucket.
4. Once the bucket is created choose Upload Object on the Document bucket details page, browse your local machine, and choose a file less than 2GB in size. The file upload process begins, and after a short while, your file is stored in an object storage bucket.
5. To retrieve the file uploaded to this standard tier bucket using the console, navigate to the bucket and choose Download from the ellipses menu adjacent to the object name. You are prompted to choose a destination location and filename on your local machine for this object. The following CLI command requests a download of an object named apex_18.1_en.zip from the Documents bucket to a file named /home/opc/ apex_18.1_en.zip.

```
$ oci os object get --bucket-name Documents
--name apex_18.1_en.zip  --file /home/opc/apex_18.1_en.zip
Downloading object  [####################################]  100%
$ ls -lrth /home/opc/apex_18.1_en.zip
-rw-rw-r--. 1 opc opc 90M Mar 30 22:13 /home/opc/apex_18.1_en.zip
```

6. In the following example, the downloaded file is renamed apex.zip and uploaded to this bucket using the CLI:

```
$ cp apex_18.1_en.zip apex.zip
$ oci os object put --bucket-name Documents
--name apex.zip --file /home/opc/apex.zip
Uploading object  [####################################]  100%...
```

Pseudo-Hierarchies in Object Storage

The flat structure in a bucket may simulate a traditional hierarchical file system by naming objects with a trailing slash (/). Consider the following hierarchical structure on a typical Linux system:

```
$ find root_dir/
root_dir/
root_dir/file_in_root_dir
root_dir/subdir1
root_dir/subdir1/subdir1.1
root_dir/subdir1/subdir1.1/file1_in_subdir1.1
root_dir/subdir1/subdir1.1/file2_in_subdir1.1
root_dir/subdir1/subdir1.2
root_dir/subdir1/subdir1.2/file1_in_subdir1.2
```

```
root_dir/subdir1/file_in_subdir1
root_dir/subdir2
root_dir/subdir2/file1_in_subdir2
```

The entire directory may be uploaded to an object storage bucket using the CLI bulk-upload command. The etag, last-modified, and opc-content-md5 attributes have been omitted for brevity.

```
$ oci os object bulk-upload --bucket-name Documents
--src-dir /home/opc/upload2os/

Uploaded root_dir/subdir2/file1_in_subdir2  100%
{ "skipped-objects": [],
 "upload-failures": {},
"uploaded-objects": {
    "root_dir/file_in_root_dir": {"etag":"last-modified": "opc-content-md5"},
    "root_dir/subdir1/file_in_subdir1":
    "root_dir/subdir1/subdir1.1/file1_in_subdir1.1":
    "root_dir/subdir1/subdir1.1/file2_in_subdir1.1":
    "root_dir/subdir1/subdir1.2/file1_in_subdir1.2":
    "root_dir/subdir2/file1_in_subdir2"}
```

These objects are actually all files in the same flat bucket with names that make them appear like a traditional hierarchical directory. To manage these as if they were hierarchical, you can use matching patterns. For example, to delete all the objects with names beginning with root_dir/subdir1, you may use the CLI `bulk-delete` command with the prefix option. This command also allows you to perform a dry-run to ensure you delete what you mean to delete.

```
$ oci os object bulk-delete --bucket-name Documents
--prefix root_dir/subdir1 --dry-run
{ "delete-failures": {}, "deleted-objects": [
    "root_dir/subdir1/file_in_subdir1",
    "root_dir/subdir1/subdir1.1/file1_in_subdir1.1",
    "root_dir/subdir1/subdir1.1/file2_in_subdir1.1",
    "root_dir/subdir1/subdir1.2/file1_in_subdir1.2"]}
```

Run the command without the `dry-run` option to remove these objects.

```
$ oci os object bulk-delete --bucket-name Documents --prefix root_dir/subdir1
WARNING: This command will delete 4 objects.
Are you sure you wish to continue? [y/N]: y
Deleted root_dir/subdir1/subdir1.2/file1_in_subdir1.2  100%
{"delete-failures": {},
 "deleted-objects": [
    "root_dir/subdir1/subdir1.1/file1_in_subdir1.1",
    "root_dir/subdir1/file_in_subdir1",
    "root_dir/subdir1/subdir1.2/file1_in_subdir1.2",
    "root_dir/subdir1/subdir1.1/file2_in_subdir1.1"]}
```

Multipart Uploads for Large Objects

Objects may be uploaded to buckets using the console, but there is a 2GB limit per object. The CLI, SDKs, or API may be used to upload larger objects up to 10TB by performing a multipart upload and parallelizing the upload to reduce the overall upload time. Using the

API, you are required to split the object into multiple parts, upload the parts, and commit the upload, which allows the object storage service to reconstruct the large object from its constituent parts. When using the CLI, you are not required to split the object into parts manually as the splitting, upload, and commit are done automatically by the utility. You can choose the size of the component parts and the maximum number of parts to be uploaded in parallel (the default is three). The following CLI command allows you to initiate the multipart upload. A worked example shows a 10GB file being split into 2GB parts and uploaded using five parallel threads.

```
oci os object put -ns <object_storage_namespace>
-bn <bucket_name> --file <file_location> --name <object_name>
--part-size <upload_part_size_in_MB>
--parallel-upload-count <maximum_number_parallel_uploads>

$ oci os object put -ns eclipsys
-bn DB_Backups --file /home/opc/10GB_FILE --name 10GB_FILE
--part-size 2048 --parallel-upload-count 5
Upload ID: b446223d-5e42-9daa-398c-a3b1b742b120
Split file into 5 parts for upload.
Uploading object  [####################################]  100% {
  "etag": "379fb993-a795-45c3-a98a-e2c8fcef745f",
  "last-modified": "Sun, 31 Mar 2019 16:55:22 GMT",
  "opc-multipart-md5": "T1i89Sg+PzJi8w4/jAPIfA==-5"}
```

To list the progress of the upload and to abort the upload, you may use the following CLI commands:

```
oci os multipart list -ns <object_storage_namespace>
-bn <bucket_name>

oci os multipart abort -ns <object_storage_namespace>
-bn <bucket_name> --object-name <object_name> --upload-id <upload_ID>
```

Pre-Authenticated Requests

OCI provides several options to share objects or buckets. You can designate a bucket's visibility as public, which allows anyone to access your bucket without requiring authentication. You should use this option cautiously and carefully evaluate whether you need to make a bucket publicly visible. A safer option is to set up a pre-authenticated request (PAR) that exposes a bucket or an object for a limited time.

A pre-authenticated request may be created for a bucket or an object as follows:

- **Bucket** PARs permit writes.
- **Object** PARs permit either reads or writes or both reads and writes.

Using the console to create PARs illustrates the options, as shown in Figure 5-6. Navigate to the object storage bucket list and choose Create Pre-Authenticated Request from the ellipsis menu adjacent to a bucket or object. Provide a name for the PAR and choose whether you wish to expose a bucket or a specific object, the access type, and the expiration date and time after which the PAR is no longer valid.

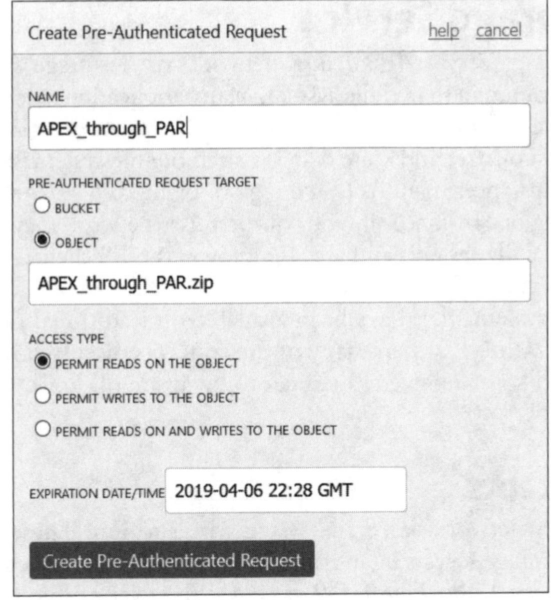

Figure 5-6 Create pre-authenticated request on an object

Once the PAR is created, a request URL is provided, as shown in Figure 5-7. This URL must be saved as it is not shown again by the console. You may use commands such as `wget` and `curl` on Linux to access the bucket or objects exposed through the PAR. The following command reads the apex.zip file through the PAR with no authentication required:

```
wget "https://objectstorage.us-ashburn-1.oraclecloud.com
/p/sUmTmsdfwKW_VB3S0/n/eclipsys/b/Documents/o/apex.zip"
```

The following command writes a file to the object storage bucket using a PAR:

```
curl -X PUT -d 'APEX_through_PAR.zip' -v
https://objectstorage.us-ashburn-1.oraclecloud.com
/p/soLNPdfwKW_VB3S0/n/eclipsys/b/Documents/o/APEX_through_PAR.zip
```

Pre-Authenticated Request Details
close
NAME
APEX_through_PAR
PRE-AUTHENTICATED REQUEST URL
https://objectstorage.us-ashburn-1.oraclecloud.com/p/pHyfYSal
Copy
Copy this URL for your records. It will not be shown again.
Close

Figure 5-7 Pre-authenticated request details

File Storage Service

The file storage service (FSS) is a network-based storage system that allows multiple instances to mount a shared file system. Many applications such as Oracle EBS (E-Business Suite) require a shared file system and many organizations use NFS (network file system) mountpoints to share and store data on a remote file system. The FSS is a regional service available to instances in all ADs in a region. Figure 5-8 situates the file storage service in a VCN in a region. Instances in your on-premises network may be permitted to use the file storage service file systems and are also known as NFS clients.

FSS provides NFSv3–compatible file systems supporting full POSIX semantics similar to NFS file systems that have been available on traditional networks for decades. If you are familiar with NFS, then many of the concepts discussed in the following section will be familiar. There are several nuances to be aware of, however, so this is well worth the read.

FSS Concepts

FSS provides network-based file systems in a region. These file systems are physically located on storage servers in an AD and are replicated to other ADs or fault domains providing high durability. Figure 5-9 expresses the relationship between three FSS concepts and instances in your region.

A mount target is an NFS endpoint that resides in a subnet in an AD or region and is given three IP addresses from that subnet by the file storage service. The mount target provides network access for file systems.

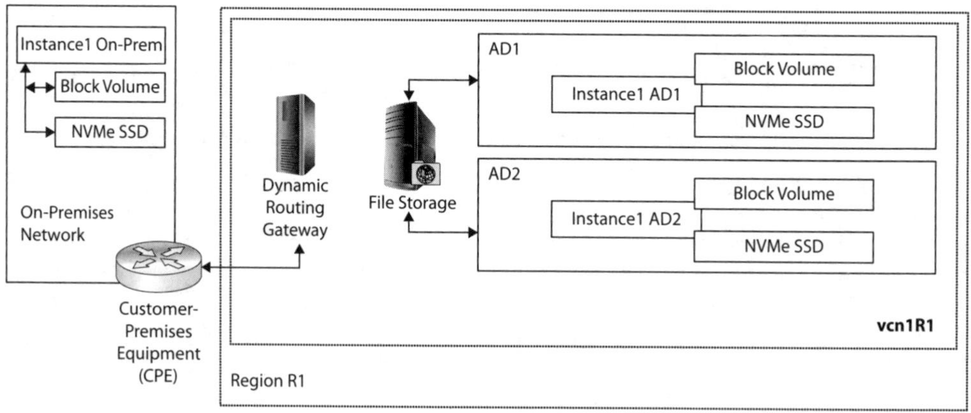

Figure 5-8 File storage as a regional service

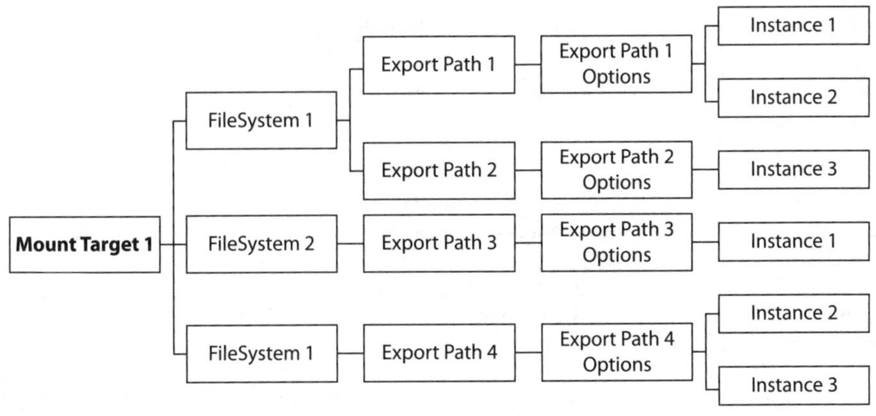

Figure 5-9 Relationships between mount targets, file systems, exports, and instances

CAUTION Locate the mount target in a subnet that has a CIDR range larger than /30 as each mount target requires three private IP addresses. NFS clients connect to the mount target. To avoid potential IP conflicts, it is good practice to place mount targets and subnets into dedicated subnets.

A file system is the primary resource for storing files in FSS. A file system is AD-specific and could be accessed via multiple export paths. Each export path is associated with a set of export options that determine which instances or NFS clients have access to the export path. Export options may specify the allowed source IP addresses and ports, whether access is read/write or read-only, and how Unix-style user and group access rights are reduced or squashed for the mounted network file system.

Multiple file systems may use the same mount target. The default soft limit is 100 file systems per mount target. Multiple export paths may be created for each file system to configure different export options for different NFS clients, on condition that the export paths in each file system are unique and non-overlapping. In Figure 5-9, both FileSystem 1 and FileSystem 2 use the same mount target. FileSystem 1 exports three paths to the mount target. This is allowed on condition that these are unique and non-overlapping paths. For example, the export paths /exp1 and /exp1/p1 are overlapping and are not allowed to be exported to the same mount target.

Several network-related prerequisites must be met before using the file storage service. The security list associated with the subnet that contains the mount target must allow ingress TCP and UDP traffic on ports 111 and ports 2048, 2049, and 2050. Figure 5-10

Source: 0.0.0.0/0	**IP Protocol:** UDP	**Source Port Range:** All	**Destination Port Range:** 111	**Allows:** UDP traffic for ports: 111
Source: 0.0.0.0/0	**IP Protocol:** UDP	**Source Port Range:** All	**Destination Port Range:** 2048-2050	**Allows:** UDP traffic for ports: 2048-2050
Source: 0.0.0.0/0	**IP Protocol:** TCP	**Source Port Range:** All	**Destination Port Range:** 2048-2050	**Allows:** TCP traffic for ports: 2048-2050
Source: 0.0.0.0/0	**IP Protocol:** TCP	**Source Port Range:** All	**Destination Port Range:** 111	**Allows:** TCP traffic for ports: 111

Figure 5-10 Stateful ingress security list rules required for mount target subnet

shows an example of four stateful ingress rules that allow traffic from any source IP address (0.0.0.0/0). You may wish to restrict the source range to specific CIDR ranges or even IP addresses, although it may become tedious to manage these virtual firewall rules at an IP address level for individual NFS clients. In a multitenant environment where multiple NFS clients access file systems through the same mount target, you can limit a client's ability to connect to the file system and view or write data using export path options.

There are four layers of security to limit access to FSS:

- **IAM service** This uses OCI users, groups, and policies to permit OCI users to create and manage infrastructure for FSS, including creating instances (NFS clients), VCNs, and subnets; updating security lists; and creating OCI mount targets and file system objects.
- **Security list** This uses CIDR ranges to limit which instances can connect to the mount target.
- **Export options** This uses IP addresses, CIDR block ranges, access permissions, and root squash options to control access on a per-file system basis.
- **NFSv3 Unix security** This controls which Unix users can mount file systems and update or view files on the FSS file system.

CAUTION Typical NFS mount options you may be used to may not be appropriate for mounting FSS file systems. Avoid specifying mount options such as nolock, rsize, or wsize when mounting FSS file systems to avoid performance and file locking issues.

Create, Configure, and Mount a File Storage Service

It is about time to get hands-on with the file storage service. In the upcoming exercise, you will complete the following steps:

- Set up security list prerequisites. Set up stateful ingress rules, opening TCP and UDP ports 111 and 2048–2050, and egress rules allowing all traffic out in the security list used by the subnet where the mount target resides.
- Create a file system and associate it with a new or existing mount target. If this is a new mount target, you choose the AD and subnet where this mount target resides.
- Connect to an NFS client, mount the exported file system, and confirm it is mounted with read/write access.

Exercise 5-12: Create a File System, Mount Target, and Mount with NFS Clients

In this exercise, you will first set up the networking prerequisites that FSS depends on to expose the mount target to instances in your network. The exercise uses the virtual cloud network named vcn1R1, and a public subnet named PS1 in AD1 in the Ashburn region. Once the FSS artifacts are created, the web1 and web2 instances created in Chapter 4 are used to mount the shared network file system.

1. Sign in to the OCI console and choose your compartment.
2. Navigate to Networking | Virtual Cloud Networks, and choose vcn1R1 or a suitable VCN. Choose a subnet for your mount target and choose its security list. In this exercise, the subnet vcn1R1ps1 is chosen. It is a public subnet. You can choose a private subnet for the mount target; in fact, it's good practice to do so, but additional configuration is required in that case.
3. Edit the security list rules, adding four stateful ingress rules opening TCP and UDP destination ports 111 and 2048–2050, and an egress rule allowing all traffic out (if none exists). You can set the source CIDR range to limit the NFS client IP range, if desired. If you set the source CIDR range to 0.0.0.0/0, your ingress rules should resemble those listed in Figure 5-10.

4. Navigate to File Storage | File Systems and choose Create File System. Default file system, export information, and mount target information are provided. Choose Edit Details and provide a name for the file system, like NFS1. Choose an AD for the file system. The export path in the export information section defaults to /NFS1.

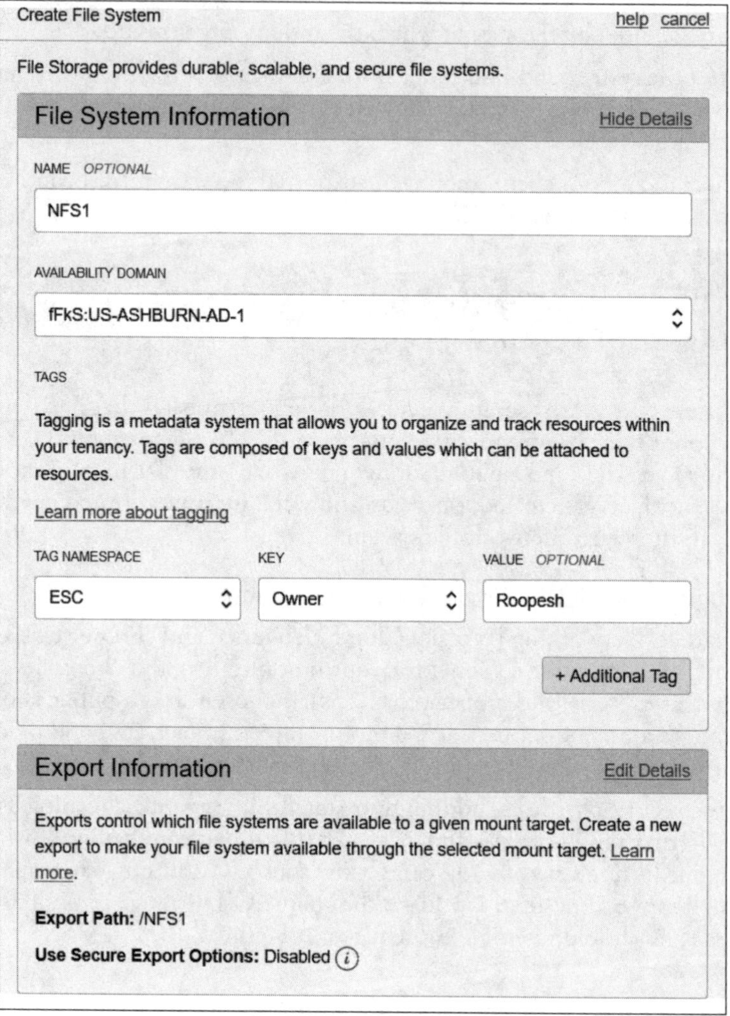
Create File System
help cancel
File Storage provides durable, scalable, and secure file systems.
File System Information
Hide Details
NAME OPTIONAL
NFS1
AVAILABILITY DOMAIN
fFkS:US-ASHBURN-AD-1
TAGS
Tagging is a metadata system that allows you to organize and track resources within your tenancy. Tags are composed of keys and values which can be attached to resources.
Learn more about tagging
TAG NAMESPACE
KEY
VALUE OPTIONAL
ESC
Owner
Roopesh
+ Additional Tag
Export Information
Edit Details
Exports control which file systems are available to a given mount target. Create a new export to make your file system available through the selected mount target. Learn more.
Export Path: /NFS1
Use Secure Export Options: Disabled

5. In the mount target section, you may choose to associate the file system you are about to create with an existing mount target or create a new mount target. Choose Create New Mount Target and provide a name, like MT1. Choose a VCN, like vcn1R1, and a subnet, like vcn1R1ps1, and choose Create.

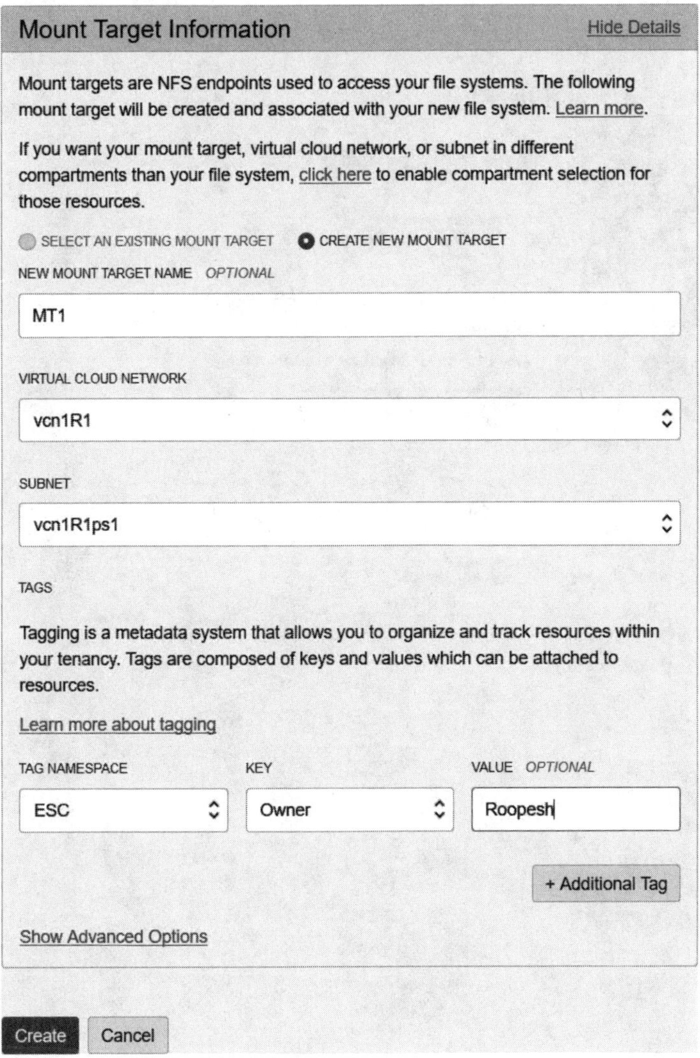

6. Once the file system is created, examine the details page listing the OCID, AD, compartment, and utilization data. In the Exports section, note there is an active export path named /NFS1 associated with mount target MT1. You may add additional export paths to this file system as long as the export paths are unique and non-overlapping.

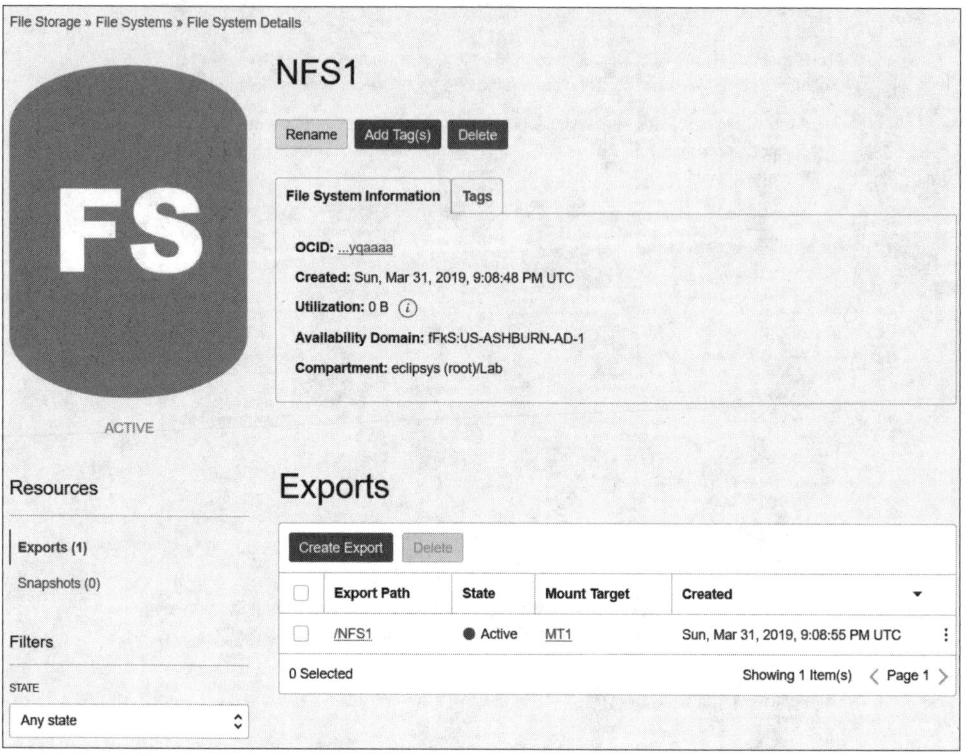

7. Choose mount target MT1 and note the OCID, AD, compartment, reported size, and number of inodes in gibibytes, which is a decimal unit closely related to gigabyte. The subnet and IP address of the mount target is also listed, along with a facility to set a hostname. You may set the hostname and the fully qualified domain name (FQDN) field is updated, or you can use the IP address to mount the target, as discussed in subsequent steps.

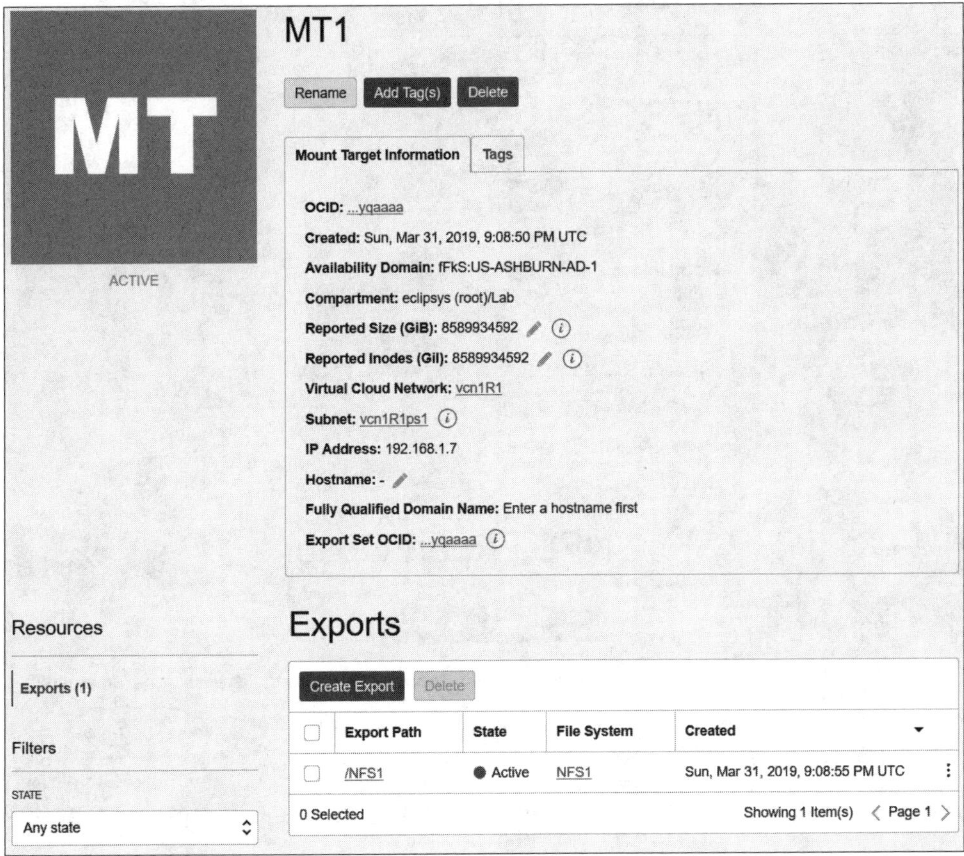

8. Choose the /NFS1 export path to view the default NFS export options. The default options allow any instances (0.0.0.0/0) mounting this file system through this mount target to access the file system with read/write privilege. You may edit the NFS export options to restrict the CIDR range for NFS clients and to configure whether privileged source ports (1–1023) are required, whether the access is read-only or read/write, and whether identity squash or remapping of user IDs (UIDs) and group IDs (GIDs) to anonymous IDs is required.

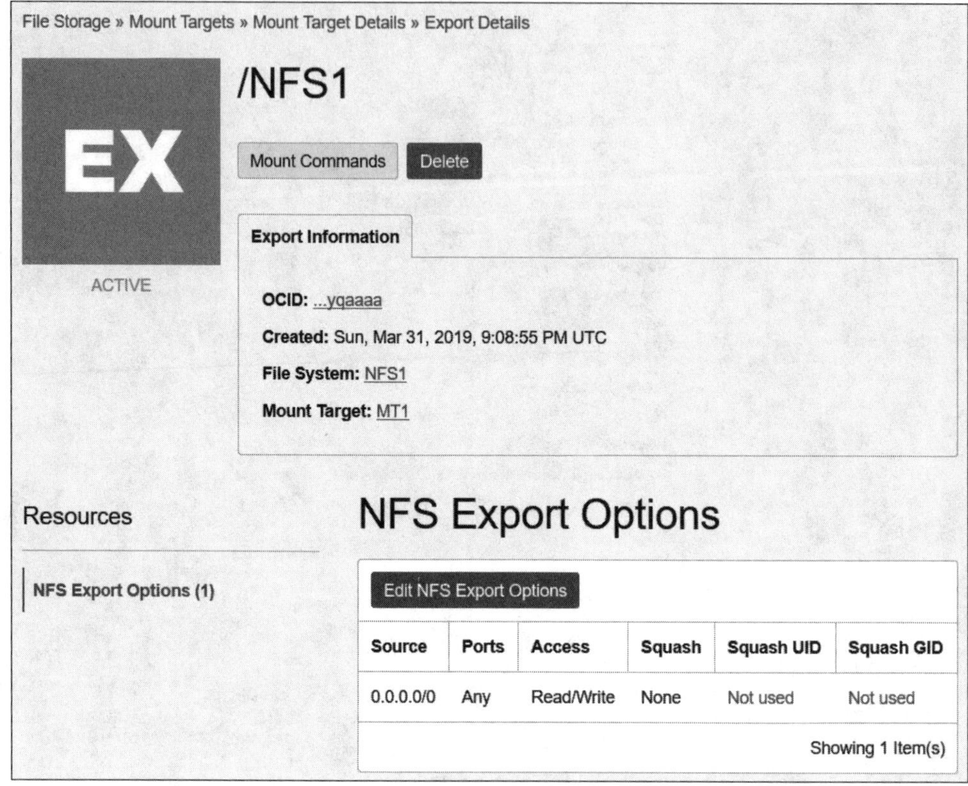

9. Navigate to the File Storage | Mount Targets page and choose MT1. Choose the ellipses menu adjacent to the /NFS1 export path in the Exports section and choose mount commands. Choose the image used to create your NFS client. Choose the appropriate OS image for your NFS client to get the mount commands. In this exercise, the web1 instance is designated as the NFS client and it uses Oracle Linux. Steps 10–12 are based on these mount commands.

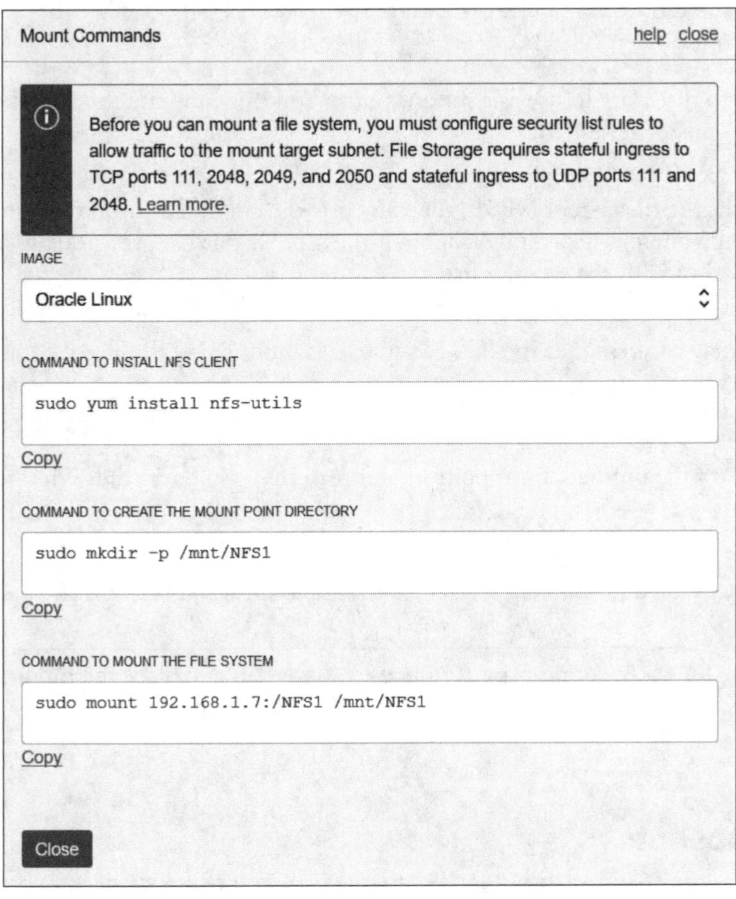

10. SSH to the compute instance that is your NFS client, such as the web1 instance, and install the NFS client library by copying the command from the mount command list provided in the console in the previous step. In this case, the nfs-util package is already installed.

```
$ sudo yum install nfs-utils
Loaded plugins: langpacks, ulninfo
ol7_UEKR5…
Package 1:nfs-utils-1.3.0-0.61.0.1.el7.x86_64
already installed and latest version
Nothing to do
```

11. Make a directory to use as a mount point. You can copy the command from the OCI console if desired.

```
$ sudo mkdir -p /mnt/NFS1
```

12. Mount the file system NFS1. You can copy the command from the console if desired. There is no acknowledgment message. If this hangs, it usually indicates a problem with the security list.

```
$ sudo mount 192.168.1.7:/NFS1 /mnt/NFS1
```

13. You may confirm that the FSS file system is mounted with the `df` command.

```
$ df -h | head -1 && df -h | grep NFS1
Filesystem          Size  Used Avail Use% Mounted on
192.168.1.7:/NFS1   8.0E     0  8.0E   0% /mnt/NFS1
```

14. Create a file on the mount point to confirm that you have read/write permission.

```
$ sudo vi /mnt/NFS1/test.txt
$ cat /mnt/NFS1/test.txt
Update 1 from web1
```

NOTE For optimal performance, it is advisable to place the mount targets in the same AD as the instances using the mount point.

FSS Snapshots

FSS offers a convenient snapshot facility that takes a point-in-time backup of an FSS file system. Snapshots are read-only and are located in a hidden directory named .snapshot in the root directory of the FSS file system. Snapshots are incremental and are consequently very space efficient, backing up only files that have changed since the last snapshot. By default, you can take up to 10,000 snapshots per file system.

You can create snapshots through the console, API, or CLI. In this section, the CLI is used. Use the following CLI command to identify the file systems in an AD and compartment. Assuming you completed the previous exercise, you should see your file system listed here.

```
$ oci fs file-system list  --availability-domain fFkS:US-ASHBURN-AD-1
--compartment-id ocid1.compartment.oc1…zlh3iq
{"data": [{
      "availability-domain": "fFkS:US-ASHBURN-AD-1",
      "compartment-id": "ocid1.compartment.oc1…zlh3iq",
      "display-name": "NFS1",
      "id": "ocid1.filesystem.oc1.iad.yqaaaa",
      "lifecycle-state": "ACTIVE",
      "metered-bytes": 17920,
      "time-created": "2019-03-31T21:08:48.353000+00:00"}]}
```

Take note of the file system OCID. The following CLI command creates a snapshot of the NFS1 file system called SNAP1_NFS1.

```
$  oci fs snapshot create --file-system-id ocid1.filesystem.oc1.iad.yqaaaa
--name SNAP1_NFS1
"data": {
    "file-system-id": "ocid1.filesystem.oc1.iad.yqaaaa",
    "id": "ocid1.snapshot.oc1.iad.qwiljr",
    "lifecycle-state": "ACTIVE",
    "name": "SNAP1_NFS1",
    "time-created": "2019-04-02T03:55:25.323000+00:00"}
```

You may use the following command to list the snapshots available for your file system:

```
oci fs snapshot list --file-system-id < file-system-id >
```

To test the snapshot, delete the /mnt/NFS1/test.txt file created in the previous exercise through the web1 instance.

```
[root@web1 ~]# cd /mnt/NFS1/
[root@web1 NFS1]# ls
test.txt
[root@web1 NFS1]# rm *
rm: remove regular file test.txt? y
[root@web1 NFS1]# ls -l
total 0
```

Check for hidden files in the root directory:

```
[root@web1 ~]# ls -al /mnt/NFS1/
total 1
drwxr-xr-x. 2 root root  0 Apr  2 04:02 .
drwxr-xr-x. 3 root root 18 Mar 31 21:25 ..
drwxr-xr-x. 3 root root  1 Apr  2 04:07 .snapshot
```

Explore the contents of the snapshot:

```
[root@web1 ~]# find  /mnt/NFS1/.snapshot/
/mnt/NFS1/.snapshot/
/mnt/NFS1/.snapshot/SNAP1_NFS1
/mnt/NFS1/.snapshot/SNAP1_NFS1/test.txt
```

Restore the deleted file by copying the backup in the snapshot back to the original location. The `rsync` command may be used for restoring multiple missing files.

```
[root@web1 ~]# cp /mnt/NFS1/.snapshot/SNAP1_NFS1/test.txt /mnt/NFS1/test.txt
[root@web1 ~]# ls -l /mnt/NFS1/test.txt
-rw-r--r--. 1 root root 38 Apr  2 04:08 /mnt/NFS1/test.txt
```

Chapter Review

This chapter discussed five OCI storage services, each suitable for different use cases.

Local NVMe SSD storage is temporary and has no durability. You have to ensure redundancy and protect against disk failures by creating RAID sets with adequate mirroring or set up other high-availability mechanisms. These are, however, the fastest storage available to bare-metal and VM instances as they are directly attached. Local NVMe SSD storage is suitable for high-performance workloads, including transactional databases.

Block storage provides boot volumes and block volumes and is most akin to classical on-premises SAN storage. Block volumes are durable, with multiple data block copies being made across multiple ADs or fault domains. Block volumes scale to petabytes of capacity and are well suited for databases and general-purpose storage offering good IO performance.

Object storage is exposed through buckets at either an archive tier or a standard tier. Archive tier buckets are often just referred to as archive storage while standard tier buckets are frequently referred to as object storage. Archive storage is suitable for long-term data retention and is highly durable and affordable. However, restoring data from archive storage can be a lengthy process requiring a restore operation before the data may be downloaded.

Standard tier buckets are the default object storage option and are suitable for most types of data, including backups, logfiles, photos, videos, and even big data and content repositories. Object storage scales to petabytes of capacity and is an attractive option for offloading legacy data sets from more expensive storage.

A significant portion of this chapter is dedicated to hands-on practical exercises enabling you to create and manage block storage, object storage, and file storage services.

The chapter closed with a discussion of the file storage service, an NFSv3-compatible shared network storage offering. FSS is durable and scales to exabytes of capacity and is critical for systems and applications that require a shared file system. FSS snapshots offer a convenient and simple option for incrementally backing up and restoring your FSS file systems.

With your network, compute instances, and storage options in place, you are ready to explore Oracle database options available in OCI, which is the subject of Chapter 6.

Questions

1. List the storage types available for provisioning on OCI VMs.
   - A. Block storage
   - B. NVMe SSD
   - C. Object storage
   - D. Flash storage
2. Which of the following are types of block storage?
   - A. NVMe SSD
   - B. Boot volumes
   - C. Block volumes
   - D. Object storage
3. When an instance starts up, what are the possible access options for attaching the boot volume?
   - A. Read-only
   - B. Read/write
   - C. Copy-on-write (COW)
   - D. Write-only
4. What are the different storage tiers available for buckets in object storage?
   - A. Gold
   - B. Archive
   - C. Silver
   - D. Standard
   - E. Bronze
5. Which of the following statements are true?
   - A. OCI bucket names must be unique within a namespace.
   - B. OCI bucket names must be unique across all tenancies.
   - C. OCI bucket names are not case-sensitive.
   - D. OCI bucket names are case-sensitive.
6. When provisioning or configuring a block volume, you may specify which categories of backup policies?
   - A. Gold
   - B. Archive
   - C. Silver
   - D. Standard
   - E. Bronze

7. Which of the following statements is true?
   A. An object storage bucket can only exist in one compartment.
   B. An object storage bucket can exist in multiple compartments.
   C. An object storage bucket is an AD-level resource.
   D. An object storage bucket is a regional-level resource.
8. Which of the following statements are true?
   A. Object storage has a flat structure.
   B. Object storage has a hierarchical structure.
   C. Multipart uploads can only be done for standard tier buckets.
   D. Multipart uploads are possible for all types of object storage.
9. File storage service snapshots are useful for making file system backups. What type of backup is taken with an FSS snapshot?
   A. FULL
   B. ROLLING
   C. INCREMENTAL
   D. CLONE
   E. NFSv3
10. An important production system with a boot volume and two block volumes must be moved from the Ashburn (IAD) region to the Toronto (YYZ) region. Choose which options are feasible?
    A. Copy block storage to FSS file systems and mount on a new instance in Toronto.
    B. Copy a snapshot to the Toronto region and mount on a new YYZ instance.
    C. Use pre-authenticated requests to move the data without complex authentication.
    D. Create a volume group backup of the boot and block volumes, copy each of these volume backups to the YYZ region, and mount on a new YYZ instance.

Answers

1. **A, B, C.** Block storage, NVMe SSD, and object storage, as well as file storage services, may be provisioned on OCI.
2. **B, C.** Boot and block volumes are types of block storage.
3. **B.** Boot volumes are always attached with read/write access.
4. **B, D.** Object storage buckets are available at the standard and archive tiers.
5. **A, D.** OCI bucket names must be unique within a namespace and are case-sensitive.

6. **A, C, E.** Bronze, Silver, and Gold level backup policies may be configured for a block volume.
7. **A, D.** An object storage bucket can exist in only one compartment and is a regional-level resource.
8. **A, D.** Object storage has a flat structure, and multipart uploads are possible for all types of object storage.
9. **C.** A snapshot makes an incremental backup of an FSS file system.
10. **D.** The instance may be relocated by creating a consistent volume group backup of the boot and block volumes. These volume backups may be copied to the YYZ region and mounted on a new YYZ instance.

CHAPTER 6

Databases

In this chapter, you will learn how to

- Create and manage databases
- Use advanced database features
- Use the autonomous database services
- Migrate databases to the Cloud

Oracle Cloud Infrastructure (OCI) offers a wide selection of database services. You could provision compute instances to set up a database on OCI the same way traditional on-premises database administrators (DBAs) have always done it, by fulfilling the prerequisites such as deploying a certified operating system, security hardening and patching the OS, downloading and staging the Grid Infrastructure (GI) and database install media and any patches, preparing the operating system kernel parameters, setting up GI and then the database binaries, and finally creating a database. Or you could use Database Cloud Services (DBCS) to choose the compute shape, storage, and GI and DB versions, and let OCI's cloud automation complete the tedious heavy lifting behind the scenes while you grab a coffee, and then come back later and connect to your brand-new database.

Figure 6-1 contextualizes the OCI database services that are discussed in this chapter. DBCS is a PaaS offering that provides you with a fully functional and deployed Oracle database platform on a virtual machine (VM), bare metal (BM), or Exadata server. Exadata is Oracle's flagship engineered systems platform explicitly designed for hosting clustered highly available and high-performance Oracle databases. DBCS significantly simplifies database instance management, including taking backups, performing restores, and applying patches.

Once you get started with DBCS, this chapter covers several advanced topics, including licensing, disaster recovery, encryption, and clustering options before it tackles the often daunting task of migrating your non-OCI databases to the Cloud. It is not complicated and many migration options are available.

This chapter aims to demystify the available cloud database options and recommend appropriate use-cases for the different database services. It closes with a detailed examination of the leading-edge Autonomous Data Warehouse (ADW) and Autonomous Transaction Processing (ATP) services. ADW and ATP are truly next-generation cloud database services leveraging machine learning to automate previously manual tuning tasks performed by DBAs to optimize performance.

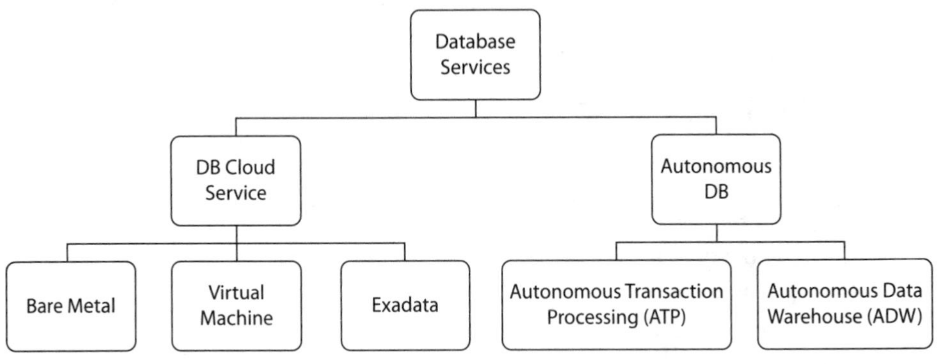

Figure 6-1 OCI storage topology

NOTE Oracle sometimes updates the abbreviations it uses in its documentation. For example, OCI was previously known as BMCS (Bare Metal Cloud Services), so be warned that the abbreviations referenced in this book are subject to future change. Autonomous Data Warehouse is inconsistently abbreviated as ADW as well as ADWC (Autonomous Data Warehouse Cloud). In this book, the abbreviation ADW will be used to refer to the Autonomous Data Warehouse Cloud service.

You do not have to be an experienced Oracle database professional to get through this chapter, but if you are, buckle up, because the database services offered by OCI are a radical departure from the complexity typically associated with setting up traditional Oracle database environments.

Database Cloud Service

DBCS is available on VM, BM, and Exadata servers. Each hosting environment serves a different use.

Before this chapter explores the differences in the hosting environments, here is a quick refresher on parlance for folks less familiar with Oracle databases:

- The Oracle server consists of a database instance and a set of database files. The database instance is a set of memory structures and background processes. The Oracle server is usually just referred to as the Oracle database.
- When you license the database, you have access to some core features. Many additional options and packs may be enabled on Enterprise Edition (discussed later), and these are usually licensed additionally. For example, to use partitioned tables in your database, you must enable the Partitioning option. Other options include Multitenant, Advanced Compression, Advanced Security, Advanced Analytics, Database Vault, and Real Application Clusters (RAC).

- Real Application Clusters (RAC) is an option that allows a set of database files to be mounted by multiple database instances concurrently. RAC relies on shared storage accessible by each instance participating in the cluster. The RAC option provides high availability for a database because an instance on a node may fail, but the database remains accessible through the instances running on the remaining nodes in the cluster. RAC also provides horizontal scaling. RAC is included with all Exadata Cloud services and is optional on VM-based DBCS. But you cannot build your own RAC deployment using OCI IaaS.
- Oracle Enterprise Manager (OEM) is a powerful monitoring and management suite widely used to manage Oracle environments.
- Many core OEM features are available at no cost, but there are additional management packs that may be enabled that require additional licenses.
- The Oracle database software has traditionally been available in either a Standard Edition (SE2 hereafter SE) or Enterprise Edition (EE). EE has many features and options that are not available on SE, notably the physical replication option known as Data Guard. OCI offers two additional editions: EE High Performance (EE-HP) and EE Extreme Performance (EE-EP).
- EE-HP bundles additional database options on top of EE as well as several OEM management packs. The additional database options include Multitenant, Partitioning, Advanced Compression, Advanced Security, Label Security, Database Vault, OLAP, Advanced Analytics, and Spatial and Graph, while the additional OEM packs include Database Lifecycle Management Pack and Cloud Management Pack for Oracle Database.
- EE-EP adds the In-Memory Database, Active Data Guard, and RAC database options to EE-HP.
- The ORACLE HOME is a file system location where the Oracle database software is installed. The executable programs and all supporting software residing in the ORACLE HOME are collectively and colloquially referred to as Oracle binaries.
- ASM, or Automatic Storage Management, is a volume manager used to manage disk storage that runs as a specialized Oracle instance. Storage LUNs are carved into ASM disks, which make up ASM disk groups. Disk groups are not visible externally from the OS. Database files, including data files, redo logfiles, and control files, usually reside in ASM disk groups. DBCS creates two disk groups: DATA and RECO, and optionally a SPARSE disk group on Exadata. The DATA disk group is typically used for datafiles, redo logfiles, and control files, while the RECO disk group typically stores recovery-related files such as archive logfiles, flashback logs, and sometimes RMAN backups. The optional SPARSE disk group on Exadata is used for snapshot databases, which are essentially thin-provisioned database clones. ASM may be used to provide shared storage for RAC instances.
- GI, or Grid Infrastructure, is specialized Oracle software used for supporting databases that use ASM for storage and provides cluster services used by RAC databases and the Oracle Restart feature that improves database availability by automatically restarting various Oracle components.

- ASM File System (ACFS) is a general purpose file system mounted on ASM that is accessible by standard OS tools. Database files may also be stored on ACFS.
- ASM redundancy refers to the number of copies of data maintained by ASM across the available ASM disks. Three redundancy levels are supported: EXTERNAL, NORMAL, and HIGH, mapping to 0, 1, and 2 additional copies of data maintained respectively. DBCS only supports NORMAL and HIGH ASM redundancy levels.
- RMAN, or Recovery Manager, is an Oracle database utility used for performing backup, restore, and recovery operations.

EXAM TIP Transparent Data Encryption (TDE) is a feature of the Advanced Security option. However, on DBCS, all database editions include TDE.

Bare metal shapes are single-node servers and support only single-instance databases, whereas you can run a Real Application Clusters (RAC) database on a two-node VM environment or on an Exadata environment. All single-node database systems such as DBCS on bare metal or DBCS on a single VM node support the following database editions:

- Standard Edition (SE)
- Enterprise Edition (EE)
- Enterprise Edition—High Performance (EE-HP)
- Enterprise Edition—Extreme Performance (EE-EP)

NOTE RAC database systems on DBCS require Enterprise Edition—Extreme Performance. While Standard Edition is the cheapest database edition, there are restrictions in terms of the shapes it supports—no more than eight OCPUs on bare metal shapes and a maximum of VM.Standard.*x*.8 (where *x* is the hardware generation number) for VMs.

The database versions supported by DBCS will change over time. As of this writing, the supported versions range from Oracle database 11g Release 2 to 19c. As new versions become available and older versions are deprecated, the range of supported versions will change.

DBCS on Bare Metal

A bare metal database system consists of a single bare metal server preinstalled with Oracle Linux (6.8 as of writing), with locally attached NVMe storage. Earlier bare metal servers with limited availability are Oracle X5-2 servers providing the BM.DenseIO1.36 shape, while the current bare metal servers available at the time of this writing are Oracle X7-2 servers providing the BM.DenseIO2.52 shape. As hardware refreshes occur, the

Shape	CPU Cores	Memory	Raw Storage
BM.DenseIO1.36	Up to 36	512GB	9 × 3.2 TB = 28.8TB
BM.DenseIO2.52	Up to 52	768GB	8 × 6.4 TB = 51.2TB

Table 6-1 DBCS Bare Metal Shapes

available bare metal hardware will be updated. Table 6-1 summarizes some key features of these bare metal shapes.

Note the raw storage listed in Table 6-1 for each of the DBCS bare metal shapes. The raw storage forms the basis for two ASM disk groups, named DATA and RECO respectively. Database files typically reside in the DATA disk group while recovery-related files typically reside in the RECO disk group. Table 6-2 shows the usable storage is less than the raw storage due to ASM redundancy. DBCS supports Normal (two-way mirroring) and High (three-way mirroring) ASM redundancy settings. There is a significant trade-off to be made with regard to usable storage when choosing a HIGH redundancy level, but the benefit is that there are three copies of each ASM segment and your database is strongly protected against disk failures, tolerating the loss of two disks simultaneously, whereas NORMAL redundancy allows the database to transparently tolerate the loss of one disk with no impact to availability.

The NVMe disks present in a bare metal DBCS instance are locally attached. These are not part of a SAN and have no external mirroring or striping configured. Therefore, you have no choice but to use at least the NORMAL level of ASM redundancy.

When you install Oracle database software, the binaries are located in a directory structure known as an Oracle home. The software in an Oracle home may be used to create a database. You may have many Oracle home directories each with an independent set of binary files. Traditionally, different versions of the database software are installed into different Oracle homes, while one or more databases are created and run using the software from the same Oracle home.

However, DBCS on bare metal deploys an Oracle home on a node and allows you to create only a single database per Oracle home. You may have multiple Oracle homes, but each one may drive only a single database. At first glance, this may appear restrictive, but constraining the Oracle home to run a single database exposes only a single database at a time to service restrictions caused by software failure or patching activities.

Shape	Raw Storage	Disk Group	Usable Storage with Normal Redundancy	Usable Storage with High Redundancy
BM.DenseIO1.36	28.8TB	DATA	9.4TB	5.4TB
BM.DenseIO1.36	28.8TB	RECO	1.7TB	1TB
BM.DenseIO2.52	51.2TB	DATA	16TB	9TB
BM.DenseIO2.52	51.2TB	RECO	4TB	2.3TB

Table 6-2 Impact of ASM Redundancy Level on Usable Disk Group Storage

The console, CLI, and SDKs may be used to perform the following actions on DBCS databases:

- Create a new database with no user data
- Create a new database from a pre-existing backup
- Delete a database
- Patch a database
- Create a database backup
- Restore database from a backup
- Set up a Data Guard standby database

Enabling these common DBA tasks through reliable Cloud automation is an extremely compelling factor behind the success of DBCS.

Let us walk through some of the options available when creating a DBCS bare metal database. Using the OCI console, navigate to the Bare Metal, VM, and Exadata option in the Database section of the menu and choose Launch DB System. Figure 6-2 shows a guided template for setting up your new DB system on bare metal.

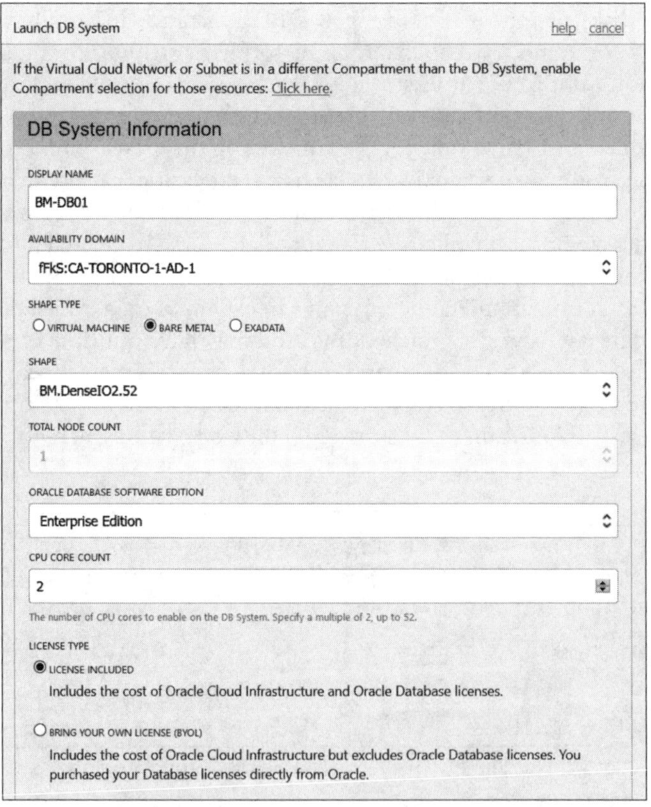

Figure 6-2 Create a bare metal DB system.

A display name for the DB system is required as well as the Availability Domain (AD). Database systems are AD-specific resources as they require a physical server in an AD on which to run. The bare metal shape type exposes two options: BM.DenseIO2.52 and BM.DenseIO1.36 (as of this writing). The total node count is grayed out and defaults to 1 for bare metal systems, so RAC databases are not an option. One of the four DB software editions must be chosen. This determines the edition for all databases that may be created on this system. Adjust the CPU core count in multiples of 2 up to 52 (in this case) depending on your requirements and budget. The wizard further prompts you to specify two storage attributes, as shown in Figure 6-3.

You may specify either 40% or 80% of the available storage to assign to the DATA disk group for database files and user data. The remaining storage is assigned to the RECO disk group for recovery-related files including online and archive redo logs and RMAN backups. One of the ASM disk group redundancy levels, High or Normal, is also specified. These two settings have a dramatic impact on available storage. The fault domain is important if you plan to set up another bare metal DBCS instance as a Data Guard standby in the same AD. The primary and standby systems should reside in different fault domains in the same AD to improve resilience to rack failures.

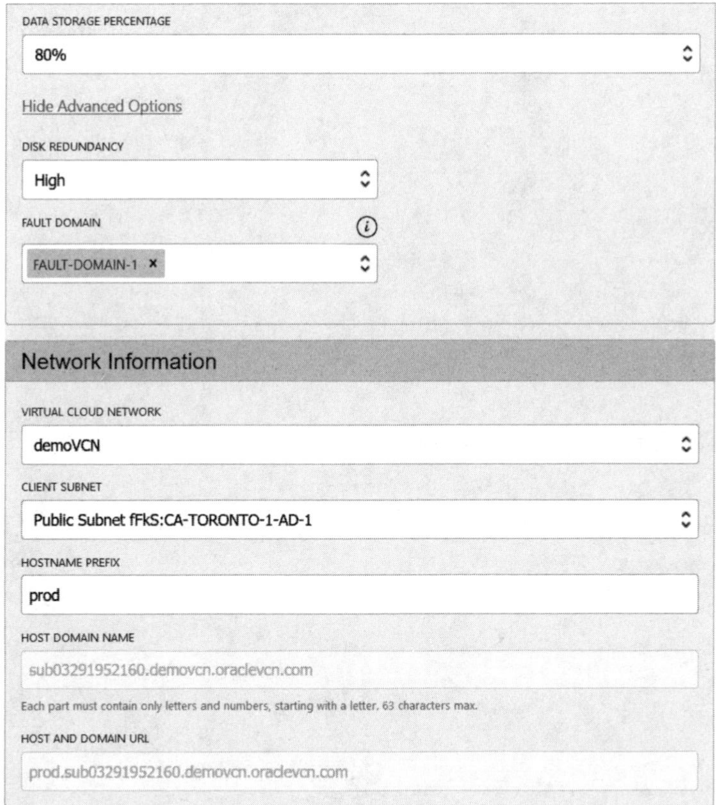

Figure 6-3 Storage and network specification for a bare metal DB system

DBCS will deploy a specialized compute node in a VCN you specify that is attached to a client subnet. An IP address from this subnet pool is allocated to the DB system. A hostname prefix, up to 16 characters and unique within the specified subnet, may be chosen if the subnet uses the OCI VCN resolver for DNS resolution. The last section under consideration while provisioning a DB system on bare metal pertains to the actual database. Figure 6-4 shows the specification of a DB named prod.

You may choose a currently supported database version. If the DB software version supports multitenant databases, you may optionally provide a pluggable DB (PDB) name. The strong DB admin password you provide is used for the SYS and SYSTEM users as well as the TDE wallet and PDB Admin. The database workload options influence the starter database's initialization parameters to favor either OLTP or DSS workloads. Finally, you may specify the character set and national character set for your database. Choosing Launch DB System kicks off an orchestration process that serves you up a fully operational deployed database system on a bare metal server a few hours later.

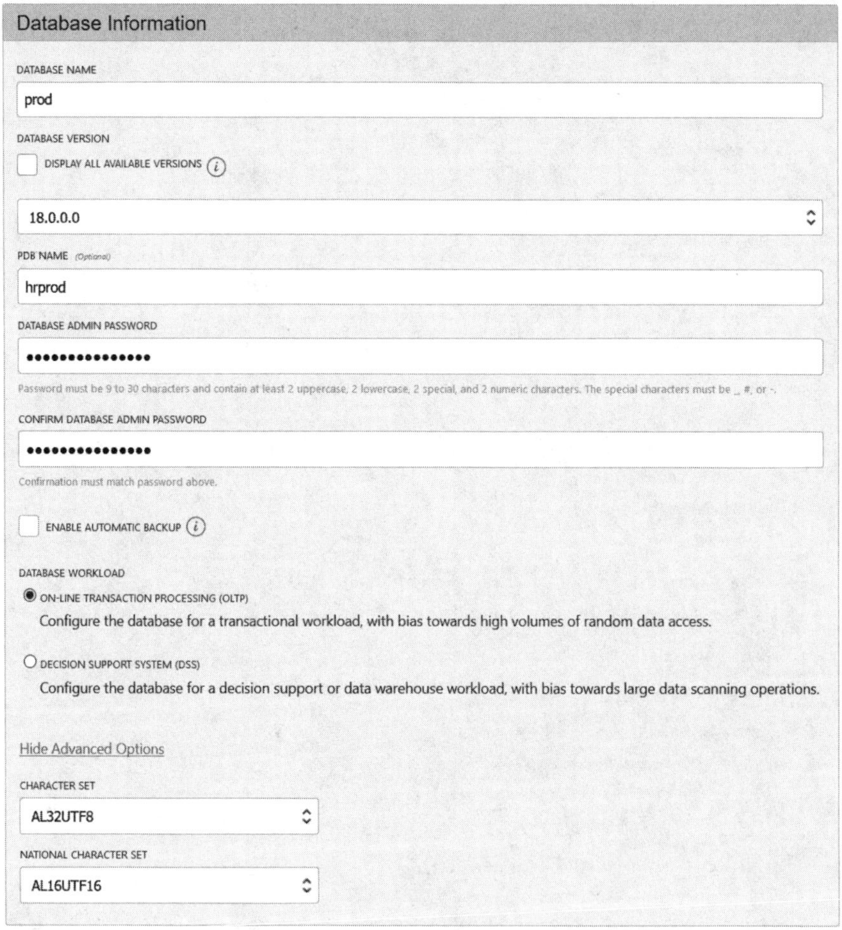

Figure 6-4 Database specification for a bare metal DB system

DBCS on Exadata (Exadata Cloud Service)

Exadata is a uniquely Oracle offering that is not available on any other public cloud platform. DBCS places Exadata within reach of many more customers than ever before. The Exadata platform is stable and mature and is the Oracle flagship engineered systems product built with redundancy and high-performance components at its core. An Exadata system consists of compute nodes, storage cells and networking infrastructure (all three core IaaS components) preconfigured and tested to host database workloads. Exadata system software unlocks several unique database software optimizations that are not available in non-Exadata systems that include SmartScan and Storage Indexes. Other features such as Hybrid Columnar Compression, while not unique to Exadata, are only available on OCI through the Exadata Cloud Service.

Exadata systems are well suited for clustered (RAC) databases. Each system has at least two compute nodes and three storage cells. These serve as clustered database instances, one per node making the system tolerant to a compute node failure. Each compute node and storage cell in the system is connected using Infiniband network infrastructure providing high-performance internode cluster communication and high IO bandwidth to the storage cells. Each compute node is an x86 computer with dual socket multicore CPUs, memory, and some local storage. Each storage cell is a full-blown computer, unlike traditional storage arrays. They have multicore CPUs, memory, and two types of storage, PCIe flash cards to support the flash cache and serial attached SCSI (SAS) disks available in either high capacity (HC) or high performance (HP) configurations.

Three Exadata configurations are available on DBCS:

- Quarter rack consisting of 2 compute nodes, 3 storage servers
- Half rack consisting of 4 compute nodes, 6 storage servers
- Full rack consisting of 8 compute nodes, 12 storage servers

When an Exadata is deployed on premises, you choose to deploy a bare metal or virtualized software image. You have full control and access to all hardware infrastructure.

Exadata on DBCS (commonly referred to as ExaCS) is deployed with a virtualized image and when you create an Exadata system. You choose the shape of your Exadata VM (Quarter, Half, or Full rack) and you specify the number of CPU cores to enable. You may dynamically scale the CPU cores allocated to your Exadata VM up to the limit allowed by the Exadata shape you chose. If you wish to move to a larger shape, an SR must be opened with Oracle to assist with this request. You have root access to the VM but you have no access to the networking and storage infrastructure.

Depending on the OCI region, you may have access to both generation 1 (X6) or 2 (X7) Exadata systems. Third-generation Exadata, based on X-8 hardware, is generally available and will be used to refresh the Exadata servers in OCI ADs.

When deploying an Exadata system on DBCS, you have similar options to bare metal deployments but there are a few nuances. Figure 6-5 shows the shape chosen as Exadata.Full2.368.

This system uses a full rack, second-generation (X7-8) Exadata system with eight compute nodes. You choose to enable CPU cores (up to 368 with this shape) and provide a RAC cluster name. When this database is created, there will be eight RAC instances

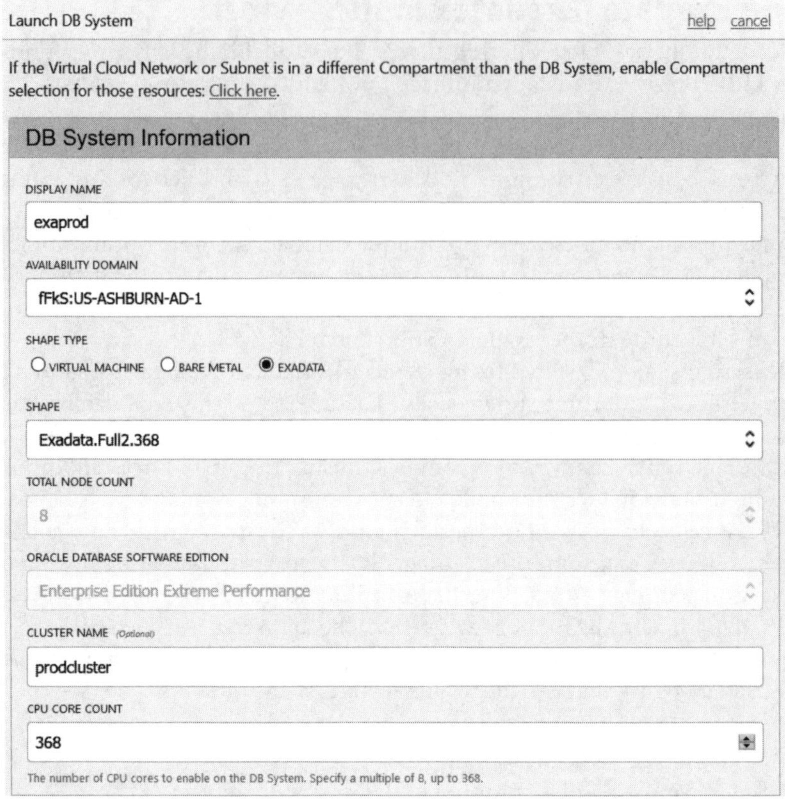

Figure 6-5 Create an Exadata DB system.

mounting and opening the database stored across the twelve storage servers. Notice that you cannot change the Oracle database software edition. On Exadata, the only option is to use Enterprise Edition—Extreme Performance (EE-EP) edition.

Two other main configuration differences between deploying a database system and bare metal relate to storage and network configuration. The storage allocation to ASM disk groups DATA, RECO, and SPARSE is a function of whether you choose to store backups on Exadata storage and whether you want a SPARSE disk group configured. Table 6-3 summarizes the impact these choices have on Exadata disk group storage allocation as a percentage of total available storage, which depends on the shape you choose.

In Figure 6-6, the disk group storage allocations are indicated as a function of choosing both to store backups on the Exadata storage and to configure a SPARSE disk group. Notice that the ASM disk group redundancy is set to high (three-way mirroring), and this cannot be changed on Exadata. Remember—this system is engineered for redundancy.

The network settings for an Exadata system on DBCS provide for two subnet specifications. The client subnet refers to the network to be used for client connections such as from your applications like SQL Developer. The backup subnet specifies the network dedicated for traffic related to IO intensive backup and restore operations.

DB Backups on Exadata Storage	Sparse Disk Group	DATA	RECO	SPARSE
Yes	Yes	35%	50%	15%
Yes	No	40%	60%	0%
No	Yes	60%	20%	20%
No	No	80%	20%	0%

Table 6-3 Exadata Disk Group Storage Allocation Based on Backup and SPARSE Disk Group Configuration

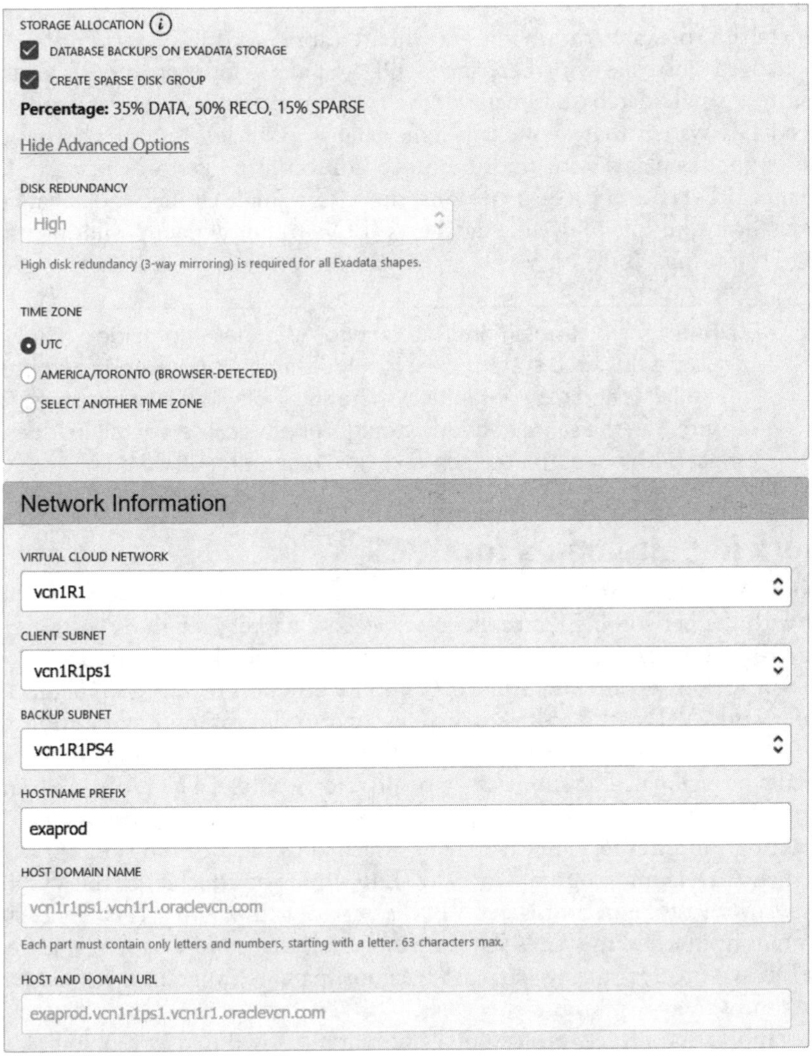

Figure 6-6 Storage and network specification for an Exadata DB system

EXAM TIP Usable storage for database files on Exadata is impacted by whether you choose to keep backups on the storage. Configuring SPARSE disk groups also reduces the storage available for database files.

DBCS on VM

DBCS systems on VMs offer very flexible options with many underlying compute shapes and the ability to scale the storage allocated to your VM dynamically. Both single-instance and two-node RAC databases are supported on a 1-node and 2-node VM DB system respectively. OCI is the first PaaS platform to support Oracle RAC databases on VM and Exadata systems.

The database software edition chosen when creating a DBCS system on a VM cannot be changed, just like with bare metal DB systems. However, DBCS on a VM is restricted to a single database Oracle Home that can host only one database, unlike a bare metal DB system that allows multiple database Oracle Homes. The multitenant database option, available with the Enterprise Edition High Performance and Extreme Performance (EE-HP and EE-EP) editions, supports a single container database (CDB), which may host multiple pluggable databases (PDBs), thus allowing multiple databases (PDBs) to run using DBCS on VM.

CAUTION If you implement RAC on two VM nodes to provide a highly available clustered system, bear in mind that the underlying compute nodes are still VMs and may potentially share some physical infrastructure. To ensure that the same network, storage, or physical server failure does not affect both nodes, place each node in a different fault domain.

Network Requirements for DBCS

DBCS on VM and bare metal systems require several network resources. You should be familiar with the networking concepts described in Chapter 3. This discussion does not apply to DBCS on Exadata, which has a very specific network configuration.

DBCS provisions a compute instance. Compute instances require a subnet in a Virtual Cloud Network (VCN). IP addresses are allocated to the compute node from the subnet. Therefore, a DB system requires a VCN with at least one subnet, which is either AD-specific or regional. The subnet may be private or public. The route table and security list used by the subnet also requires some configuration to support secure database traffic routing. An Internet gateway may be attached to the VCN to support access over the Internet. A Dynamic Routing Gateway (DRG) may be attached to the VCN to support access over FastConnect or IPSec VPN. A service gateway to access object storage is also commonly attached to VCNs. Object storage, described in Chapter 5, is frequently used in DB systems for storing database backups, patches, migration-related data files, and other software repositories.

This combination of network resources supports many different topologies, but two common architectures are described next.

Public Subnet with Internet Gateway

Database systems that must be accessible over the Internet require the following resources:

- **Public subnet** Oracle recommends a regional subnet but an AD-specific subnet works as well.
- **Internet gateway** Used for routing traffic between the subnet and the Internet.
- **Service gateway** Used for routing traffic between the object storage service and the subnet.
- **Route table** Two rules are required. One for egress 0.0.0.0/0 and targeting the Internet gateway and the second for the object storage service in your region targeting the service gateway.
- **Security list** Two security lists are recommended but you could customize one. Oracle recommends the default security list in your VCN with basic rules required by the DB system, like ingress SSH and general egress from the DB system as well as a custom security list catering to SQL*NET traffic if DB clients are allowed to connect, and recommends a rule to allow Oracle Notification Services (ONS) and Fast Application Notification (FAN) Event traffic. ONS and FAN are Oracle database services. For monitoring your database, ports for Oracle Enterprise Manager Database Control or EM Express may also need to be opened.

CAUTION It is unusual to place a database on a publicly accessible server so be wary of unintentionally exposing your databases.

Private Subnet with Dynamic Routing Gateway

Database systems that must be not be accessible over the Internet require the following resources:

- **Private subnet** Allocated private IP addresses to the DB system nodes.
- **Dynamic routing gateway** This is required if you are connecting to another network, such as your on-premises network to allow other clients or systems to connect to the database.
- **Service gateway** To reach object storage.
- **NAT gateway** Required to access public endpoints not supported by the service gateway.
- **Route table** Several rules may be required. One for egress 0.0.0.0/0 and targeting the NAT gateway, another for the object storage service in your region targeting the service gateway, another for the on-premises network CIDR targeting the DRG.
- **Security list** As for the previous option, two security lists are recommended but you could customize one. Rules may include ingress SSH on port 22 and SQL*NET on port 1521 and general egress from the DB system. Oracle recommends a rule to allow ONS and FAN Event traffic on port 6200.

Exercise 6-1: Configure a Public Subnet with Internet Gateway for Your DB System

In this exercise, you create a new VCN with a public subnet; you then create a service gateway and configure your default route table and security list. You may use an existing VCN and adapt the exercise accordingly.

1. Sign in to the OCI console and choose your compartment.
2. Navigate to Networking | Virtual Cloud Networks and choose Create Virtual Cloud Network. Specify a name, like demoVCN, and a compartment, and choose to create a VCN only. Specify a CIDR block, like 10.0.0.0/16, check Use DNS Hostnames In This VCN, and choose Create Virtual Cloud Network.

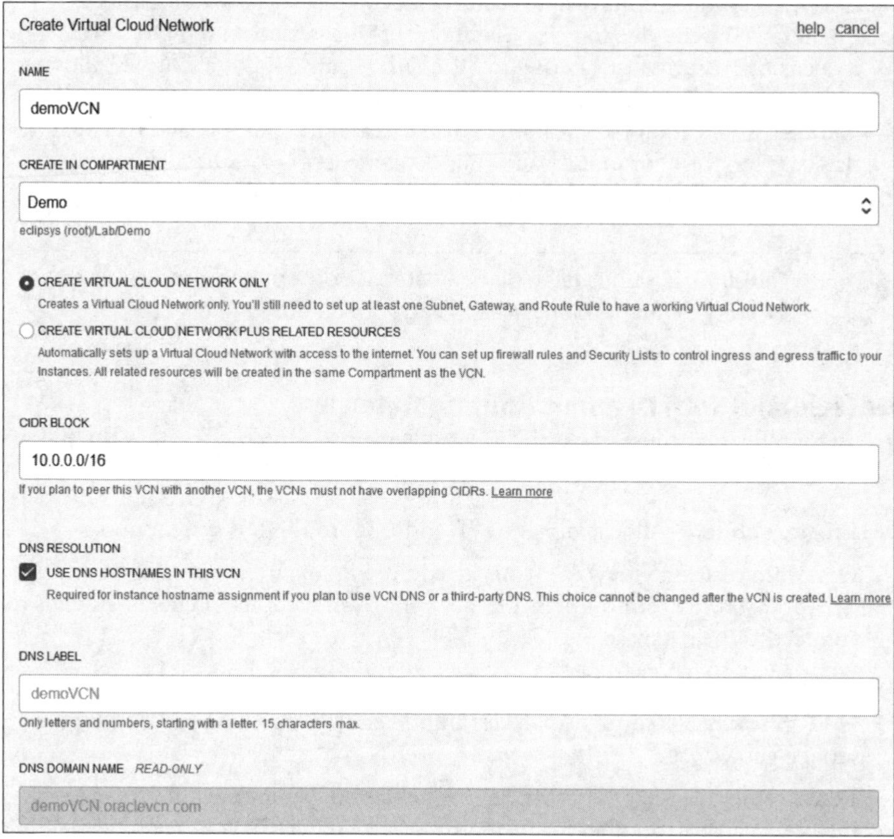

3. Navigate to Networking | Virtual Cloud Networks | demoVCN and choose Create Subnet. Specify a name, subnet type (regional or AD-specific), and a CIDR block that is part of the VCN CIDR chosen earlier, like 10.0.0.0/24. Choose the VCN's default route table, security list, and DHCP options. Ensure that the subnet is public, check Use DNS Hostnames In This Subnet, and choose Create Subnet.

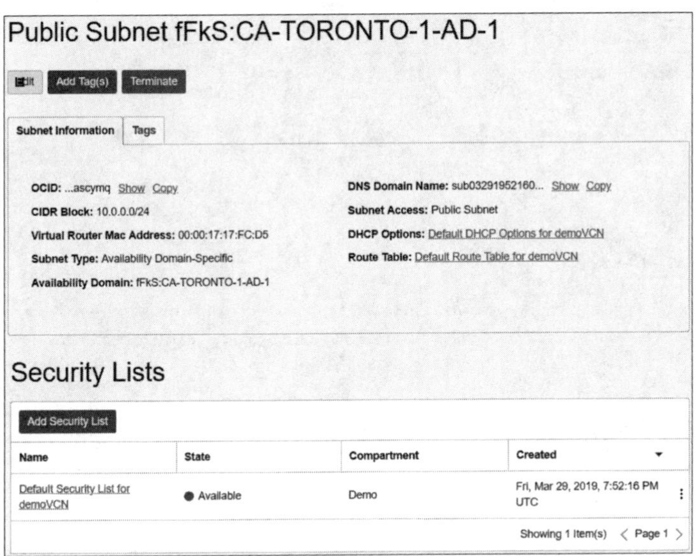

4. Navigate to Networking | Virtual Cloud Networks | demoVCN | Service Gateways and choose Create Service Gateway. Specify a name, like SG1, and a compartment, and choose the region-specific object storage service. Then choose Create Service Gateway.

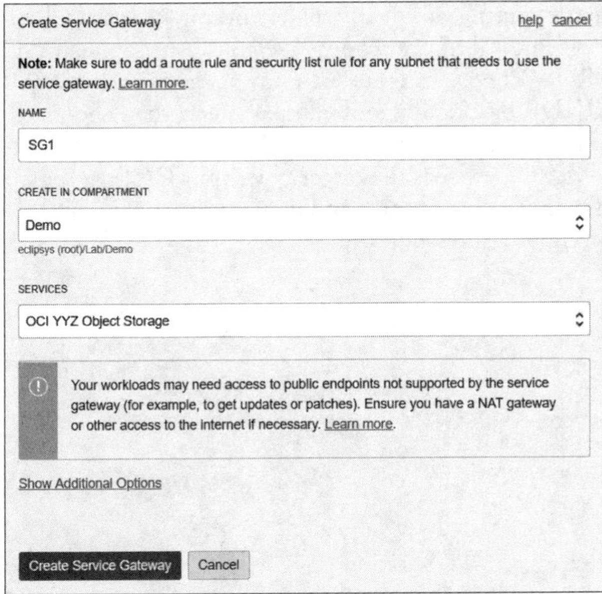

5. Navigate to Networking | Virtual Cloud Networks | demoVCN | Internet Gateways, and choose Create Internet Gateway. Specify a name, like Internet Gateway demoVCN, and a compartment, and choose Create Internet Gateway.

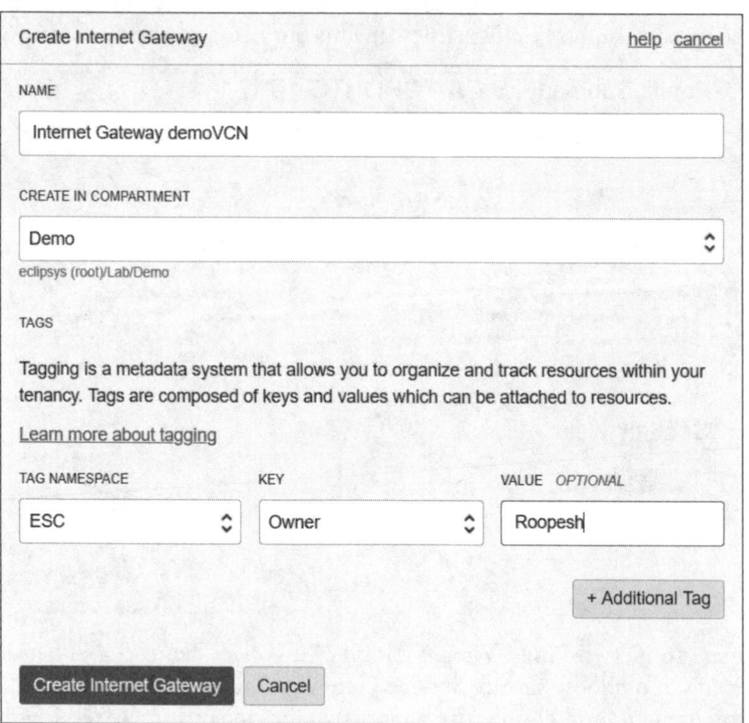

6. You now have a VCN, a subnet and service, and Internet gateways. It's time to configure the routing. Navigate to Networking | Virtual Cloud Networks | demoVCN | Route Tables and choose Default Route Table for demoVCN. Select Add Route Rule. Choose Internet Gateway as the target type, 0.0.0.0/0 as the destination CIDR block, and your compartment; then choose the target Internet gateway created previously and select Add Route Rules. Add another route rule, selecting Service Gateway as the target type, your OCI region-specific object storage as the destination service, and your compartment, and select the service gateway and choose Add Route Rules.

7. Next you add an ingress rule for incoming SQL*NET traffic to the security list. Navigate to Networking | Virtual Cloud Networks | demoVCN and choose Default Security List for demoVCN. Select Add Ingress Rules and specify a stateful rule that allows incoming traffic to TCP port 1521. You may restrict the source CIDR range to specific IP addresses or expose this to the public Internet, which is not something typically done on production environments. Select Add Ingress Rules.

Ingress Rules

Add Ingress Rules

Stateless	Source	IP Protocol	Source Port Range	Destination Port Range	Type and Code	Allows
No	0.0.0.0/0	TCP	All	22		TCP traffic for ports: 22 SSH Remote Login Protocol
No	0.0.0.0/0	ICMP			3, 4	ICMP traffic for: 3, 4 Destination Unreachable: Fragmentation Needed and Don't Fragment was Set
No	10.0.0.0/16	ICMP			3	ICMP traffic for: 3 Destination Unreachable
No	0.0.0.0/0	TCP	All	1521		TCP traffic for ports: 1521

Showing 4 Item(s) 〈 Page 1 〉

8. The last networking prerequisite to be met is to add an egress rule allowing instances in the VCN to access the object storage service. Navigate to Networking | Virtual Cloud Networks | demoVCN | Default Security List for demoVCN | Egress Rules. Select Add Egress Rules, choose Service as the Destination Type, and specify a stateful rule that allows outgoing traffic to your regional object storage service on secure TCP port 443. Select Add Egress Rules.

Egress Rules

Add Egress Rules

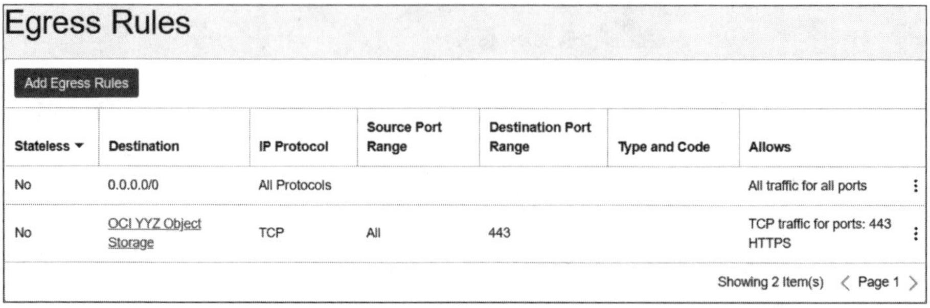

Stateless ▾	Destination	IP Protocol	Source Port Range	Destination Port Range	Type and Code	Allows
No	0.0.0.0/0	All Protocols				All traffic for all ports
No	OCI YYZ Object Storage	TCP	All	443		TCP traffic for ports: 443 HTTPS

Showing 2 Item(s) < Page 1 >

You are all set to create a new DB system on a VM in this VCN.

IP Address Space and DNS Requirements for Bare Metal and VM DB Systems

DB systems must conform to several network guidelines.

- Always specify a VCN domain DNS label, a subnet domain DNS label, and a hostname prefix when creating a DB system. When combined, these values constitute the node's fully qualified domain name (FQDN).
- On clustered RAC systems, the node number is appended to the hostname prefix automatically to create unique, numbered FQDNs for each RAC node.
- FQDN resolution is provided by the default Internet and VCN Resolver along with resolution of important resources including SCAN names for databases and the Oracle YUM repository endpoints.
- When creating a RAC system, Oracle Clusterware on each node communicates over a private interconnect using the CIDR range 192.168.16.16/28. Ensure that your subnet does not overlap with this CIDR block as this will cause problems with the interconnect.
- Ensure that the IP address space of VCNs in multiple regions do not overlap to simplify communication between DB systems in different VCNs.
- Single-node bare metal or VM database systems require at least four IP addresses in a subnet, so the minimum subnet size is /30. Three IP addresses are reserved for each subnet by OCI networking services and one IP address is required for the DB node.
- A two-node RAC VM cluster requires ten IP addresses. Each node requires two IP addresses. The SCAN listener requires three IP addresses and three IP addresses are reserved for each subnet by OCI networking services. For ten IP addresses, the minimum subnet size is /28, which can allocate sixteen IP addresses.

Exercise 6-2: Create a DB System on a VM

In this exercise, you create a DBCS system on a VM using the OCI console. Note that database licensing is discussed later in this chapter. However, here are some basics to get you through this exercise. If your organization has unused licenses, you may choose the BYOL option. If not, be prepared to be charged for the license. Bearing this in mind, the cheapest options are recommended in this exercise.

1. Sign in to the OCI console and choose your compartment.
2. Navigate to Bare Metal, VM, and Exadata and choose the Launch DB System.
3. Provide a display name, like DEMODB, and choose an AD where resources such as the VM compute instance underlying the database will be created.
4. Explore the relationships between shapes and edition. Notice that if you choose bare metal or Exadata as the shape type, your shape options change accordingly. If you choose a shape that supports RAC, such as VM.Standard2.2, you may increase the node count to 2, causing database software edition to automatically move to EE-EP. If you set the software edition to SE, your choice of available VM shapes is reduced to those with eight OCPUs or less.
5. Choose a VM shape type and an appropriate shape, like VM.Standard2.1. Notice, the total node count is 1. You may not create a RAC database system using this VM shape.

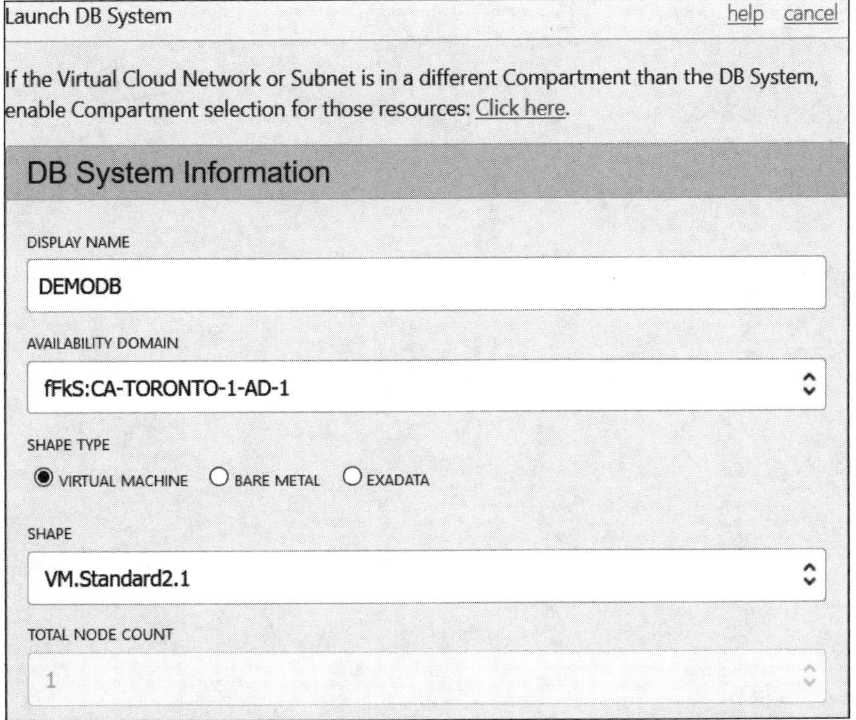

6. Choose a software edition, such as Standard Edition, and your license type—either with the license included (OCI cost is higher) or bring your own license (BYOL). When the instance is not in use, you may stop it and you will be charged only for the total storage allocated, so keep this in mind when choosing the initial storage allocation. For an initial available storage request of 256GB, you will be charged for total storage (grayed-out) of 712GB. DBCS on VM storage is block storage, and once the node is created you may investigate exactly how the total storage is allocated. The primary components are two 256GB ASM disks for the DATA and RECO disks and about 200GB for the /u01 filesystem. Specify an SSH public key as you would for any compute instance.

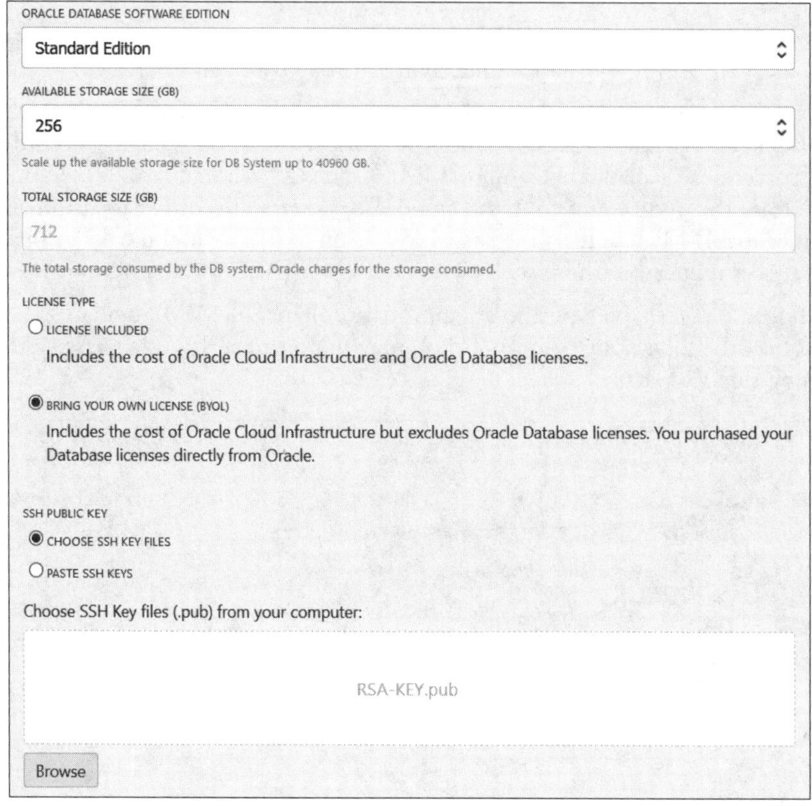

7. Expand the Advanced Options and optionally choose a fault domain. In a RAC database system, it is important to specify multiple fault domains. Specify the network information for this DB system. In this example, a public subnet is chosen, but databases would typically reside in a private subnet. Specify a hostname prefix. This will be resolvable by the default Internet and VCN Resolver.

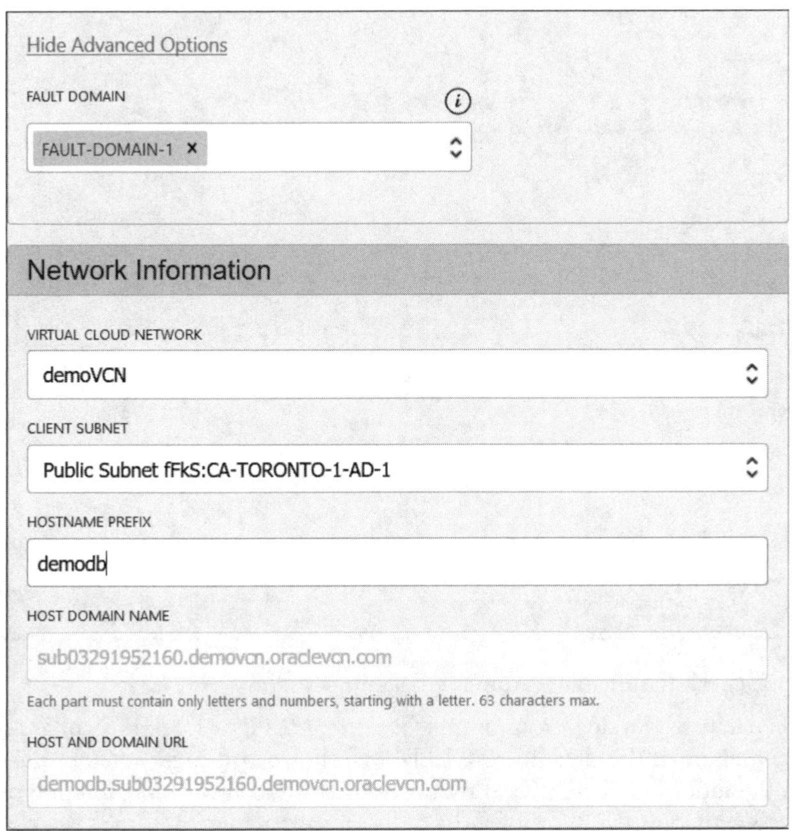

8. Specify a database name and choose a version, for example demodb and 18.3.0.0. By default, only the base releases are listed. Checking the Display All Available Versions checkbox expands the list to also include versions that have been patched or updated.

9. Optionally, specify a PDB name. By default, unless the version chosen is 11.2.0.4, the database will be created as a CDB. Specify the DB admin password that is set for the SYS and SYSTEM users as well as the TDE wallet and PDB Admin.

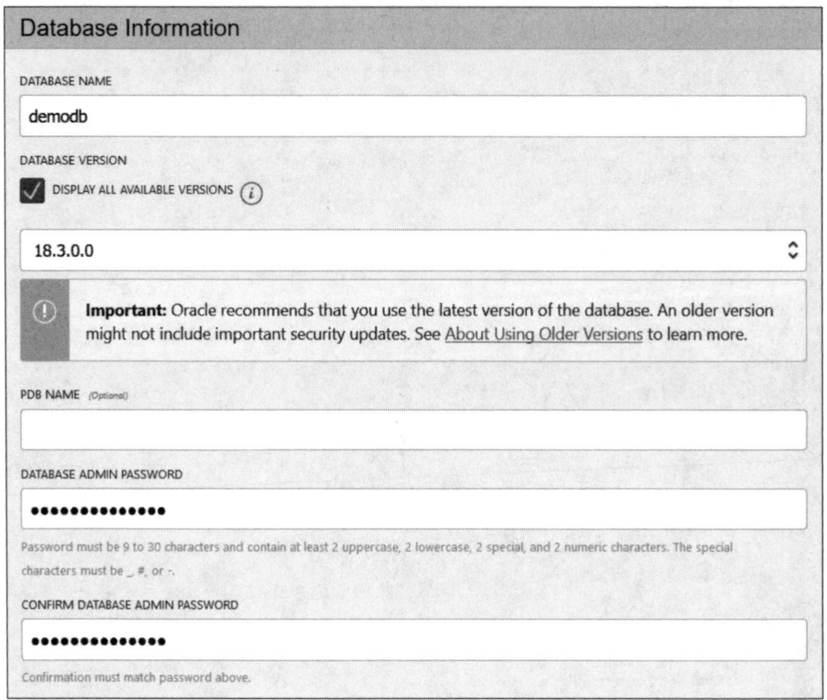

10. Don't check the Enable Automatic Backup checkbox.
11. The database workload section may be either OLTP or DSS. If Standard Edition is chosen, then this defaults to OLTP. This choice influences whether the database configuration is biased toward transactional workload with lots of random data access activity (OLTP) or toward a decision support system (DSS) workload that typically has large scanning activity.

12. The Advanced options enable you to specify the database character set and national character set. Choose Launch DB System to begin the provisioning process. This takes a while and timing varies.

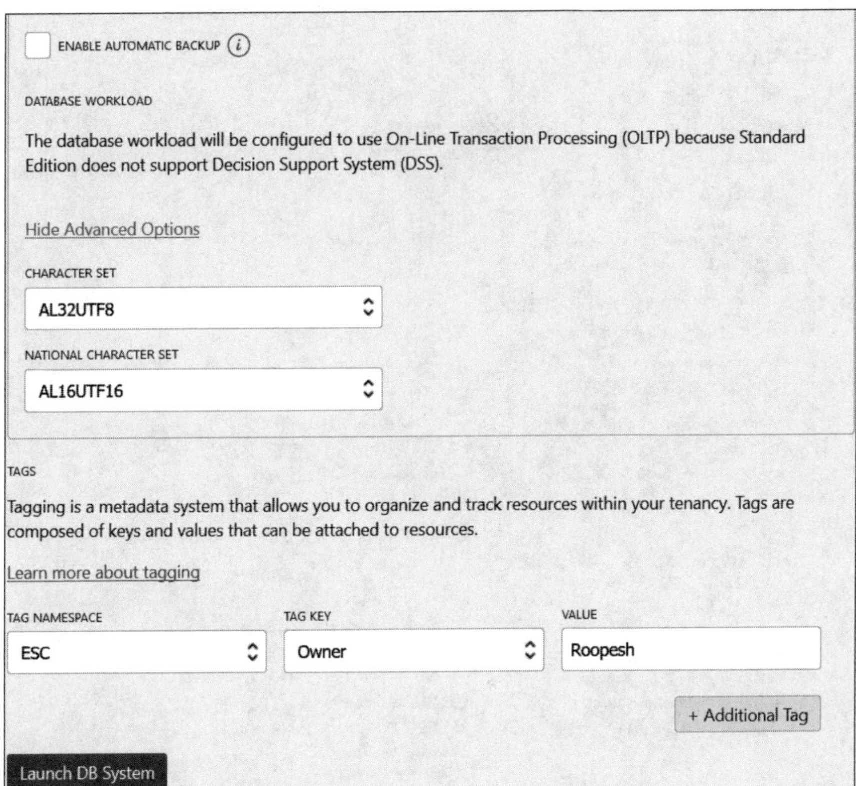

13. The provisioning usually completes in under an hour. DBCS creates a compute instance, known as a database node, based on the shape you choose and lays out an Oracle Linux operating system, with packages and configuration required for a database system. Block storage is allocated as per your storage specification and attached to this instance. This block storage is not visible through the Block Storage | Block Volumes console interface or through the API. Grid Infrastructure is deployed. A database is created as per your choices.

14. Navigate to Bare Metal, VM, and Exadata, and Choose DEMODB. The resources deployed include one node, one database, and any patches that are tested and available for you to apply. The DB system information is summarized and the demodb is listed here.

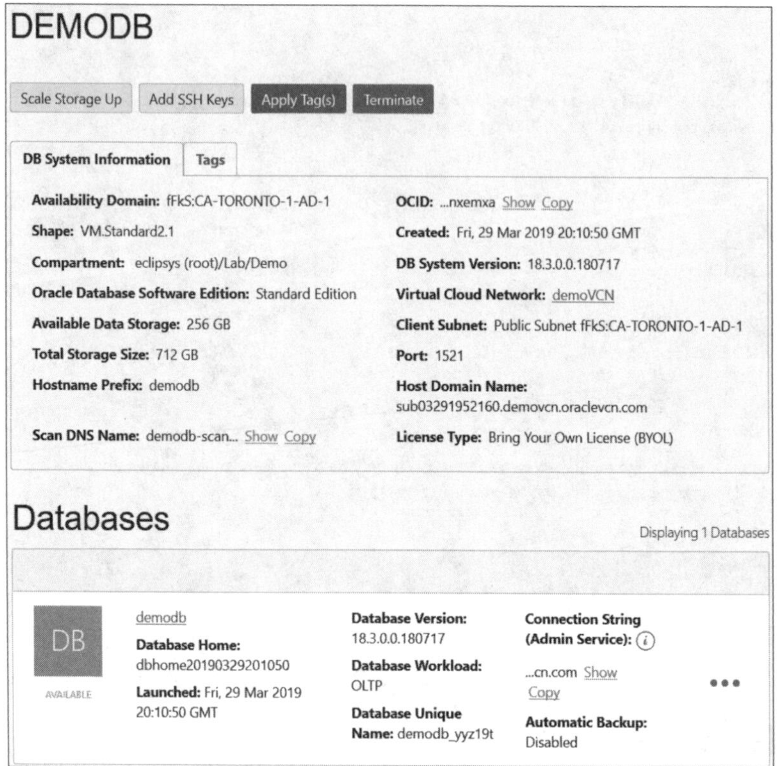

EXAM TIP You cannot run a clustered database (RAC) using DBCS on bare metal. RAC databases are supported on two-node VM systems and on Exadata.

Exercise 6-3: Connect to the Database System with SSH, SQL*Plus, and asmcmd

In this exercise, you connect to the database node and connect to the database using the SQL*Plus utility.

1. Sign in to the OCI console and choose your compartment.
2. Navigate to Bare Metal, VM, and Exadata | DEMODB | Nodes and take note of the public IP address of the host.

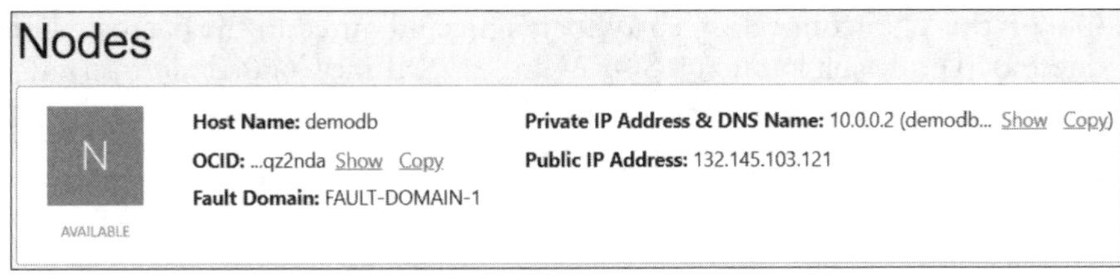

3. Using the private key paired with the public key you provided when creating the DB system, initiate an SSH connection to this server using an SSH client like PuTTY.
4. Once connected as user opc, confirm the hostname and the operating system version, examine the filesystem layout, check for any Oracle PMON processes, and get familiar with your new database server.

```
[opc@demodb ~]$ hostname
demodb
[opc@demodb ~]$ cat /etc/oracle-release
Oracle Linux Server release 6.10
[opc@demodb ~]$ df -h
Filesystem              Size  Used Avail Use% Mounted on ...LogVolRoot
                         35G   23G   11G  69% /
tmpfs                   7.3G  1.4G  5.9G  19% /dev/shm
/dev/sda2               1.4G   46M  1.3G   4% /boot
/dev/sda1               486M  276K  485M   1% /boot/efi
/dev/sdi                197G   27G  161G  15% /u01
/dev/asm/commonstore-236
                        5.0G  319M  4.7G   7% /opt/oracle/dcs/commonstore
[opc@demodb ~]$ ps -ef | grep pmon
grid      7278     1  0 Apr14 ?        00:01:40 asm_pmon_+ASM1
grid      9967     1  0 Apr14 ?        00:01:53 apx_pmon_+APX1
oracle   10758     1  0 Apr14 ?        00:01:44 ora_pmon_demodb
opc      43063 42085  0 20:47 pts/0    00:00:00 grep pmon
```

5. Notice that there are PMON background processes for the ASM instance +ASM1, the ASM proxy instance +APX1, and the demodb database instance. This is the database instance we wish to connect to so switch the user from opc to oracle, confirm if the ORACLE_SID variable is set correctly, and connect using SQL*Plus.

```
[opc@demodb ~]$ sudo su - oracle
[oracle@demodb ~]$ env | grep -i sid
ORACLE_SID=demodb
[oracle@demodb ~]$ sqlplus / as sysdba
SQL*Plus: Release 18.0.0.0.0 - Production on Sun May 5 20:50:23 2019
Version 18.3.0.0.0
Copyright (c) 1982, 2018, Oracle.  All rights reserved.
Connected to:
Oracle Database 18c Standard Edition 2 Release 18.0.0.0.0 - Production
Version 18.3.0.0.0
SQL> select host_name, instance_name, version from v$instance;
HOST_NAME   INSTANCE_NAME    VERSION
---------   -------------    ----------
demodb      demodb           18.0.0.0.0
SQL> exit
```

6. Obtain the TNS connection entry that is preconfigured in the database home directory. The default location is $ORACLE_HOME/network/admin/tnsnames.ora.

```
[oracle@demodb ~]$ cat $ORACLE_HOME/network/admin/tnsnames.ora
# tnsnames.ora Network Configuration File:
/u01/app/oracle/product/18.0.0.0/dbhome_1/network/admin/tnsnames.ora
# Generated by Oracle configuration tools.
DEMODB_YYZ19T =(DESCRIPTION =
(ADDRESS =
 (PROTOCOL = TCP)(HOST = demodb)(PORT = 1521))
(CONNECT_DATA =
 (SERVER = DEDICATED)
 (SERVICE_NAME =
   demodb_yyz19t.sub03291952160.demovcn.oraclevcn.com)))
LISTENER_DEMODB =(ADDRESS =
(PROTOCOL = TCP)(HOST = demodb)(PORT = 1521))
```

7. Notice in Step 4 that the ASM instance runs as the Linux user named grid. Switch the user back to opc; then switch user to grid, and figure out the directory location of the grid ORACLE home.

```
oracle@demodb ~]$ exit
logout
[opc@demodb ~]$ sudo su - grid
[grid@demodb ~]$ grep +ASM1 /etc/oratab
# nothing returned means this is not set
[grid@demodb ~]$ ps -ef | grep LISTENER
# identify directory that spawns the LISTENER
grid      9343     1  0 Apr14 ?        00:01:09
/u01/app/18.0.0.0/grid/bin/tnslsnr LISTENER -no_crs_notify -inherit
```

8. Set the required environment variables and run the asmcmd list disk groups command. Notice that 256GB is allocated to both the DATA and RECO ASM disk groups. Your output may differ if you chose a larger storage allocation when you created the DB system.

```
[grid@demodb ~]$ . oraenv  # set the ASM environment
ORACLE_SID = [+ASM1] ? +ASM1
ORACLE_HOME = [/home/oracle] ? /u01/app/18.0.0.0/grid
The Oracle base has been set to /u01/app/grid
[grid@demodb ~]$ asmcmd lsdg # output truncated for brevity
State    Type    Total_MB  Free_MB  Usable_file_MB   Name
MOUNTED  EXTERN  262144    252900   252900           DATA/
MOUNTED  EXTERN  262144    249692   249692           RECO/
```

Exercise 6-4: Connect to the Database System with SQL Developer

In this exercise, you connect to the database instance using the SQL Developer tool from your PC across the Internet to this database. SQL Developer is freely downloadable from Oracle and this exercise assumes you have already installed SQL Developer or a similar Oracle client.

1. In SQL Developer, choose File | New | Database Connection, and select OK.

2. Provide a connection name, like demodb. Supply a database username. The default administrator accounts SYS and SYSTEM may be used. If using SYS, change the role from default to SYSDBA.
3. If you add a TNS entry to your client's TNS resolution mechanism, usually a local tnsnames.ora file, you can change the connection type from Basic to TNS and select the network alias from a drop-down list. With a Basic connection type, you are required to provide a hostname, port number, and SID or service name.
4. You will need to resolve the TNS connection string obtained in Step 6 of the previous exercise in order to successfully connect to your database. If your client PC can resolve the FQDN hostname in the tnsnames.ora file, then this may be used; otherwise, use the public IP address for the database node used for your SSH connection as the hostname. The default port is 1521 and the service name is obtained from the tnsnames.ora file.
5. Choose Test and look for the Success status on the bottom left of the window.

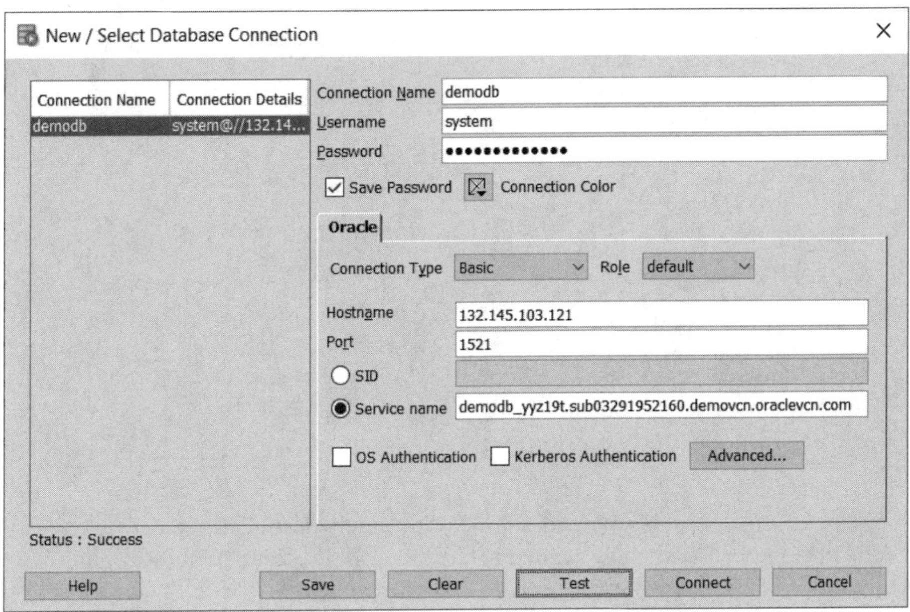

6. Save the connection by selecting Save, and launch a connection by choosing Connect. You are now connected to your DBCS database.

dbcli

DBCS nodes on VM and bare metal are preinstalled with the database CLI or dbcli. This is an OCI-specific utility not available with on-premises installations. The dbcli must be run as the root user and is located in the /opt/oracle/dcs/bin directory. The dbcli operates on all Oracle software homes, and reports, lists, configures, and executes many operations, including the following:

- Creating backups and recovering databases
- Rotating and managing TDE keys
- Managing database storage
- Performing upgrades
- Configuring Swift object storage
- Creating, executing, and scheduling jobs

Here is the output of the `dbcli describe-system` command run on the `demodb` system created in an earlier exercise.

```
[root@demodb ~]# dbcli describe-system
DbSystem Information
----------------------------------------------------------------
                    ID: 3e21d43d-5f72-4090-8dfe-60352429793e
              Platform: Vmdb
       Data Disk Count: 8
        CPU Core Count: 1
               Created: March 29, 2019 1:25:21 PM UTC
System Information
----------------------------------------------------------------
                  Name: zfnxemxa
           Domain Name: sub03291952160.demovcn.oraclevcn.com
             Time Zone: UTC
            DB Edition: SE
           DNS Servers:
           NTP Servers: 169.254.169.254
Disk Group Information
----------------------------------------------------------------
DG Name                   Redundancy                Percentage
------------------------- ------------------------- ------------
Data                      External                  100
Reco                      External                  100
```

Logs from dbcli are maintained in the /opt/oracle/dcs/log directory. The dbcli is occasionally updated with new features. It is good practice to periodically update the dbcli, using the `cliadm update-dbcli` command, and check the progress of the update with the `dbcli describe-job --jobid` command:

```
[root@demodb ~]# cliadm update-dbcli
Job details
----------------------------------------------------------------
                    ID:  13144651-4239-4fe0-bb53-759e189cfbb6
           Description:  DcsCli patching
                Status:  Created
               Created:  May 6, 2019 5:03:29 AM UTC
               Message:  Dcs cli will be updated
[root@demodb ~]# dbcli describe-job
--jobid 13144651-4239-4fe0-bb53-759e189cfbb6
```

```
Job details
----------------------------------------------------------------
                     ID:  13144651-4239-4fe0-bb53-759e189cfbb6
            Description:  DcsCli patching
                 Status:  Success
                Created:  May 6, 2019 5:03:29 AM UTC
```

Use `dbcli -h` for a full list of available commands.

DBCS Backups

DBCS backups may be unmanaged or managed. Unmanaged backups are standalone backups taken independently using either RMAN or dbcli. DBCS provides several managed options for backing up databases. Exadata DB backups are taken in a different manner to VM and bare metal DB systems and are discussed later. DBCS backups are encrypted using the key used for Transparent Data Encryption (TDE) in the database. It is important to back up the TDE wallet separately because the backup cannot be restored unless you have the correct TDE key. Although DBCS restore and recovery are not discussed explicitly, these are converse operations and once your backups are configured, the restore and recovery approach must be consistent with the backup approach. For example, if you use dbcli to create a backup, it is best to use dbcli to restore and recover the database or TDE wallet.

EXAM TIP High-level knowledge of DBCS backup options is measured in the exam. The DBCS backups discussion goes into much greater detail, but it is my belief that understanding, using, and testing backup and recovery are critical for adoption of DBCS.

Unmanaged Database Backup Using dbcli

When a standalone backup is taken with dbcli, you may store the resulting backup in the FRA disk group or in an object storage bucket. The interface to the object storage bucket is an OpenStack Swift object storage bucket. This allows you to store backups in any Swift object store and for on-premises and other Cloud infrastructure to store data in the OCI object store using an open, uniform interface.

The database must be in archivelog mode. When backing up to disk with dbcli, the backups are stored by default in the Fast Recovery Area (FRA) that resides in the RECO disk group, but you may configure your disk backups to point to other locations. The following are the high-level steps for taking backups to disk using dbcli:

1. Create a backup configuration resource with a disk backup destination.
2. Associate the backup configuration with the database to be backed up.
3. Create the backup.

These are the high-level steps required to back up a DBCS database to object storage using dbcli:

1. Create an object storage bucket to store backups.
2. Generate an Auth token using the console or API and retain the password.

3. Create an OCI user with privileges limited to the bucket.
4. Create an object store swift using the OCI username, the Auth token password, and the swift endpoint (one per region of the format https://swiftobjectstorage.<REGION NAME>/v1—for example, https://swiftobjectstorage.ca-toronto-1.oraclecloud.com/v1).
5. Create a backup configuration resource with an object storage backup destination using the object store swift name.
6. Associate the backup configuration with the database to be backed up.
7. Create the backup.

CAUTION When you use dbcli or RMAN to back up a database, a backup configuration is created and associated with the database. When you use the console or the API to back up the database, a different backup configuration is created and associated with the database. This may cause previously configured unmanaged backups to fail.

Exercise 6-5: Make a Disk-Based Database Backup Using dbcli

In this exercise, you configure and take a disk backup of the demodb database created in an earlier exercise. Several less descriptive dbcli output rows and columns, like time-stamps, have been removed for brevity.

1. Obtain details about the database to be backed up using dbcli.

```
[root@demodb ~]# dbcli list-databases
ID                          DB Name     DB Type  DB Version
--------------------------- ---------- -------- ---------------
489ea179-...-9a9d92be70b0    demodb      Si       18.3.0.0.180717
```

2. Create a backup configuration using the `dbcli create-backupconfig` command, providing a backup name, destination type of disk, and a recovery window or backup retention period of 1 day. Using the `list-backupconfigs` command lists the available backup configurations.

```
[root@demodb ~]# dbcli create-backupconfig --name demodb_backups
 --backupdestination disk --recoverywindow 1
{ "jobId" : "a72802c8-471d-48c3-87c1-947a7ac23161",
  "status" : "Created",
  "message" : "backup config creation",
  "resourceList" : [ {
    "resourceId" : "97dd38d1-231e-466e-96d1-5c792e01c73b",
    "resourceType" : "BackupConfig",
    "jobId" : "a72802c8-471d-48c3-87c1-947a7ac23161"],
  "description" : "create backup config:demodb_backups"}
[root@demodb ~]#  dbcli list-backupconfigs
ID      Name              Recovery Crosscheck Backup
                          Window   Enabled    Destination
97...73b demodb_backups    1        true       Disk
```

3. The backup configuration must be associated with a database using the `dbcli update-database` command, specifying either the database name or database ID and the backup configuration ID.

```
[root@demodb ~]# dbcli update-database --dbName demodb
--backupconfigid 97dd38d1-231e-466e-96d1-5c792e01c73b
{ "jobId" : "6a485c25-8540-4e31-85d9-0936b6f5dcaf",
  "status" : "Created",
  "message" : "update database",
  "resourceList" : [ {
    "resourceId" : "489ea179-eefb-4acf-bd5f-9a9d92be70b0",
    "resourceType" : "DB",
    "jobId" : "6a485c25-8540-4e31-85d9-0936b6f5dcaf"],
  "description" : "update database : demodb"}
```

4. Associating the backup configuration with the database updates metadata in the database configuration so it is advisable to check on the progress of this association job before taking the backup using the `dbcli describe-job` command. This handy command can be used for any task created with a job ID.

```
[root@demodb ~]# dbcli describe-job
--jobid 6a485c25-8540-4e31-85d9-0936b6f5dcaf
Job details
----------------------------------------------------------------
                     ID:  6a485c25-8540-4e31-85d9-0936b6f5dcaf
            Description:  update database : demodb
                 Status:  Success
                Created:  May 6, 2019 4:21:23 AM UTC
                Message:  update database
Task Name                                  Start    End       Status
------------------------------------       ------- -------    -------
Validate OMF parameter values              4:21:38 4:21:40    Success
update db with backupconfig attributes     4:22:11 4:22:33    Success
Backup Current Control file                4:22:39 4:23:01    Success
update metadata for database:demodb        4:23:01 4:23:01    Success
```

5. Once the database update completes successfully, you are ready to run the backup. If you take future backups to disk, you are not required to create new backup configurations or to associate the configuration with your database. If you create a new configuration, say to back up to a object storage or to use the OCI console or API, that new configuration must be associated with the database. Only one configuration may be associated with a database at a time. To initiate a level 0 backup, you may use the `dbcli create-backup` command, providing the backup type, component to be backed up, database ID, and, optionally, a descriptive backup tag.

```
[root@demodb ~]# dbcli create-backup --backupType Regular-L0
--component Database --dbid 489ea179-eefb-4acf-bd5f-9a9d92be70b0
-t pre-patch-backup
{ "jobId" : "dd476fc2-f322-4db5-a9a4-dd559334e81a",
  "status" : "Created",
  "description" : "Create Regular-L0 Backup with
   TAG-pre-patch-backup for Db:demodb in FRA"}
```

6. Describe the backup job using its job ID to determine the progress of the backup. You may also query the backup status using the `get-status-backup` command and schedule the backup using the `schedule-backup` command.

```
[root@demodb ~]# dbcli describe-job
--jobid dd476fc2-f322-4db5-a9a4-dd559334e81a
Job details
----------------------------------------------------------------
                     ID:  dd476fc2-f322-4db5-a9a4-dd559334e81a
            Description:  Create Regular-L0 Backup with
TAG-pre-patch-backup for Db:demodb in FRA
                 Status:  Success
                Created:  May 6, 2019 4:25:27 AM UTC
                Message:
Task Name                                     End Time    Status
Validate backup config                        4:25:32 AM Success
Backup Validations                            4:25:55 AM Success
Recovery Window validation                         4:26:07 AM  Success
Archivelog deletion policy configuration 4:26:13 AM Success
Database backup                                    4:33:38 AM  Success
```

CAUTION The dbcli utility exposes and relies on many identifiers, including job IDs and database IDs. These should not be confused with Oracle Cloud IDs (OCIDs). Also be mindful that at the time of this writing, backups taken with the dbcli utility do not appear with the listings of backups taken using the web console.

Exercise 6-6: Back Up Your TDE Wallet to Object Storage Using dbcli

In this exercise, you create an object storage bucket for DB backup files. To connect dbcli on your DBCS node to the object storage and to also allow non-DBCS instances to place files in an object storage bucket, an objectstoreswift resource is created and used to set up a backup configuration. The backup configuration is associated with a DB instance and then any type of backup (DB or TDE wallet) may be taken and stored in your object storage bucket. Several less descriptive dbcli rows and columns, such as timestamps, have been removed from the command output for brevity.

1. In the OCI console, navigate to Object Storage | Object Storage and choose Create Bucket. Provide a name like db-backups, choose a standard storage tier, choose your preferred encryption setting, and click Create Bucket.
2. In order for dbcli on the DBCS compute node to access object storage, it must first authenticate with OCI. An authentication token is created in OCI and credentials provided to dbcli. You may use any OCI account for this exercise, but in your organization, you may want to set up IAM users and limited privileged groups with

permissions only on backup-related object storage buckets and use these accounts for backup configurations. To create an authentication token using the console, navigate to Identity | Users and choose a user with privileges on the db-backups bucket.

3. Choose Auth Tokens from the list of resources and select Generate Token. Provide a description, such as "backups," and click Generate Token. The token is a string of characters that behaves like a password. Copy the string to a safe location. Once the dialog displaying the token is closed, it will not be shown again.

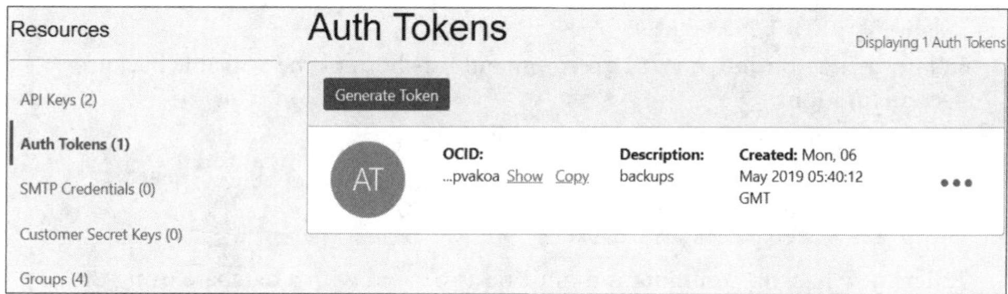

4. An objectstoreswift resource must be created by providing the `dbcli create-objectstoreswift` command with a name, your OCI tenancy, username and password (authentication token), and a Swift endpoint URL. The `dbcli list-objectstoreswifts` command may be used to list your objectstoreswift resources.

```
[root@demodb ~]#  dbcli create-objectstoreswift
-n db-obj_store-backups -t MyTenancy -u orabackups
-e https://swiftobjectstorage.ca-toronto-1.oraclecloud.com/v1
-p object store swift password: <auth token>
{ "jobId" : "c049ae4e-7ab6-48fc-8ac5-313d6dc9ffc5",
  "status" : "Created",
  "message" : "Create object store swift",
  "resourceList" : [ {
    "resourceId" : "9ccb5cc5-4b3e-4649-a026-a8fdfe7dfa0b",
    "resourceType" : "ObjectStoreSwift",
    "jobId" : "c049ae4e-7ab6-48fc-8ac5-313d6dc9ffc5" } ],
  "description" : "create object store:db-obj_store-backups"}
```

5. Create a backup configuration using the `dbcli create-backupconfig` command, providing a backup name, the destination type of object store, and a recovery window or backup retention period of 1 day. Describe the job to view the tasks required to create the object storage backup configuration.

```
[root@demodb ~]# dbcli create-backupconfig --name backups
--backupdestination ObjectStore --container db-backups
--objectstoreswiftName db-obj_store-backups --recoverywindow 1
{ "jobId" : "df539e7f-ec91-4ea9-b45d-1591dcf8e211"}
[root@demodb ~]# dbcli describe-job --jobid df539e7f-ec91-4ea9-b45d-
1591dcf8e211
Job details
```

```
--------------------------------------------------------------
                     ID:  df539e7f-ec91-4ea9-b45d-1591dcf8e211
            Description:  create backup config:backups
                 Status:  Success
                Message:  backup config creation
Task Name
libopc existence check
Installer existence check
Database container validation
ObjectStoreSwift directory creation
Install object store swift module
Backup config metadata persist
```

6. The `list-backupconfigs` command lists both of the available backup configurations.

```
[root@demodb ~]# dbcli list-backupconfigs
ID                      Name            BackupDestination
----------------------  --------------  -----------------
97dd38d1-...5c792e01c73b  demodb_backups  Disk
d7a71597-...3cbdb8cc8e63  backups         ObjectStore
```

7. The new backup configuration must be associated with a database using the `dbcli update-database` command, specifying either the database name or database ID and the backup configuration ID.

```
[root@demodb ~]# dbcli update-database --dbName demodb
--backupconfigid d7a71597-cebd-4cbe-94ac-3cbdb8cc8e63
```

8. Once the database update completes successfully, you are ready to run the backup. If you wish to take future backups to disk, you need only update the database to use the disk-based configuration. To create a backup of the TDE wallet, use the `dbcli create-backup` command, providing the backup type, component to be backed up, database ID, and, optionally, a descriptive backup tag.

```
[root@demodb ~]# dbcli create-backup  --component TdeWallet
--dbName demodb -t pre-patch-wallet-backup
{ "jobId" : "45ad8bbb-6fa1-468a-a652-6db0603049d3",
  "status" : "Created",
  "description" : "Create  TdeWallet Backup for Db:
                  demodb in OSS:db-backups"}
[root@demodb ~]# dbcli describe-job
--jobid 45ad8bbb-6fa1-468a-a652-6db0603049d3
Job details
--------------------------------------------------------------
                     ID:  45ad8bbb-6fa1-468a-a652-6db0603049d3
            Description:  Create  TdeWallet Backup for Db:
demodb in OSS:db-backups
                 Status:  Success
```

9. You may encounter a DCS-10045 validation error, which is usually accompanied by a more descriptive message. Several iterations of testing have yielded inconsistent results. All testing results in successful backups, most completed without any validation errors. It may be that there is a delay in finalizing the backup configuration, which results in a validation error when the backup is initiated.

10. Using the console, navigate to Object Storage | Object Storage | db-backups and confirm that your backup has been written to the correct bucket.

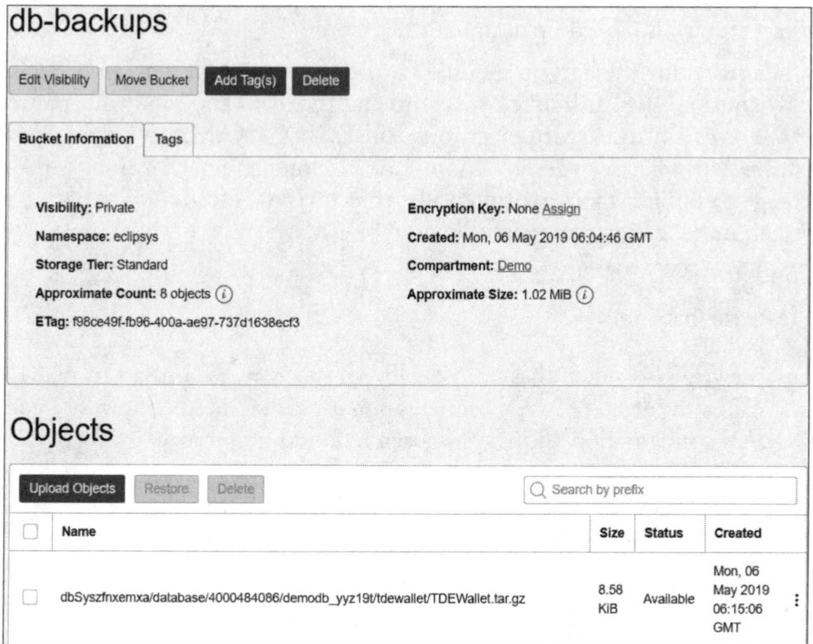

Unmanaged Database Backup Using RMAN

Using Oracle Recovery Manager (RMAN) for taking database backups is probably familiar to most DBAs. RMAN is widely used and trusted for backup and recovery of Oracle databases. The dbcli backups used in the previous sections make use of RMAN under the wrapper as well.

The database must be in archivelog mode. When backing up to disk with RMAN, just like unmanaged backups with dbcli, by default backups are stored in the Fast Recovery Area (FRA) in the RECO disk group but may be stored in other locations. The following are the high-level steps for taking backups to disk using RMAN:

1. Set RMAN configuration parameters.
2. Create the backup with RMAN.

These are the high-level steps required to back up a DBCS database to object storage using RMAN:

1. Create an object storage bucket to store backups.
2. Generate an Auth token using the console or API, and retain the password.
3. Create an OCI user with privileges limited to the bucket.

4. Install the backup module opc_install.jar file. This step is similar to creating an object store swift resource as done previously for use with dbcli. In fact, these steps do the same thing, and the previous configuration done for dbcli backups to object storage is picked up automatically.
5. When installing the backup module for the first time, you must provide an OCI username and the Auth token password and the Swift endpoint (one per region of the format https://swiftobjectstorage.<REGION NAME>/v1—for example, https://swiftobjectstorage.ca-toronto-1.oraclecloud.com/v1), as well as the object storage container, an encryption wallet directory, the location of the SBT library, and an initialization parameter file used by RMAN.
6. Configure RMAN.
7. Create the backup.

When a new DBCS system has been deployed, you may SSH to a DB node, sudo to oracle, and review the default RMAN configuration using the RMAN `show all` command. Several RMAN configuration settings have been removed from the following output.

```
[oracle@dborcl]$ rman target /
Recovery Manager: Release 18.0.0.0.0 - Production on Fri May 10 17:10:44 2019
Version 18.3.0.0.0
connected to target database: ORCL (DBID=1527314999)
RMAN> show all;
using target database control file instead of recovery catalog
RMAN configuration parameters for database with db_unique_name ORCL_YYZ1FC
are:
CONFIGURE RETENTION POLICY TO REDUNDANCY 1; # default
CONFIGURE BACKUP OPTIMIZATION OFF; # default
CONFIGURE DEFAULT DEVICE TYPE TO DISK; # default
CONFIGURE DATAFILE BACKUP COPIES FOR DEVICE TYPE DISK TO 1; # default
CONFIGURE ARCHIVELOG BACKUP COPIES FOR DEVICE TYPE DISK TO 1; # default
CONFIGURE ENCRYPTION FOR DATABASE OFF; # default
CONFIGURE ARCHIVELOG DELETION POLICY TO NONE; # default
```

You may create an RMAN backup to disk as you would have done with your non-DBCS databases using the default disk channel to write backups to the FRA to other file systems.

```
RMAN>  backup spfile format '/tmp/spfileorcl.ora';
Starting backup at 10-MAY-19
using channel ORA_DISK_1
channel ORA_DISK_1: starting full datafile backup set
channel ORA_DISK_1: specifying datafile(s) in backup set
including current SPFILE in backup set
channel ORA_DISK_1: starting piece 1 at 10-MAY-19
channel ORA_DISK_1: finished piece 1 at 10-MAY-19
piece handle=/tmp/spfileorcl.ora tag=TAG20190510T172120 comment=NONE
channel ORA_DISK_1: backup set complete, elapsed time: 00:00:01
```

The next exercise describes the steps to create backups to object storage buckets using RMAN. If you completed the previous exercise, you may create a backup to the same object storage bucket as before with no further configuration changes. Note the RMAN channel used is SBT_TAPE_1, indicating the use of the backup module. Listing the backups shows the media location prefixed with `swiftobjectstorage`.

```
RMAN> backup spfile;
Starting backup at 10-MAY-19
using channel ORA_SBT_TAPE_1
channel ORA_SBT_TAPE_1: starting compressed full datafile backup set
channel ORA_SBT_TAPE_1: specifying datafile(s) in backup set
including current SPFILE in backup set
channel ORA_SBT_TAPE_1: starting piece 1 at 10-MAY-19
channel ORA_SBT_TAPE_1: finished piece 1 at 10-MAY-19
piece handle=DEMODB_4000484086_0lu16v7m_1_1_20190510_1007910134
tag=TAG20190510T150213 comment=API Version 2.0,MMS Version 12.2.0.2
channel ORA_SBT_TAPE_1: backup set complete, elapsed time: 00:00:01
Finished backup at 10-MAY-19
Starting Control File and SPFILE Autobackup at 10-MAY-19
piece handle=c-4000484086-20190510-02
comment=API Version 2.0,MMS Version 12.2.0.2
Finished Control File and SPFILE Autobackup at 10-MAY-19
RMAN> list backup of spfile;
List of Backup Sets
===================
BS Key  Type LV Size       Device Type Elapsed Time Completion Time
------- ---- -- ---------- ----------- ------------ ---------------
19      Full    256.00K    SBT_TAPE    00:00:00     10-MAY-19
        BP Key: 20   Status: AVAILABLE  Compressed: YES  Tag:
TAG20190510T150213
        Handle: DEMODB_4000484086_0lu16v7m_1_1_20190510_1007910134
Media: swiftobjectstorage.ca-tor..raclecloud.com
/v1/eclipsys/db-backups
  SPFILE Included: Modification time: 06-MAY-19
  SPFILE db_unique_name: DEMODB_YYZ19T
```

Exercise 6-7: Back Up Your Database to Object Storage Using RMAN

In this exercise, you create an object storage bucket for DB backup files, and an authentication token for a relevant OCI user with appropriate permissions to access the object storage bucket.

1. In the OCI console, navigate to Object Storage | Object Storage, and choose Create Bucket. Provide a name like rman-backups, choose a standard storage tier and your preferred encryption setting, and select Create Bucket.
2. Create an authentication token using the console, navigate to Identity | Users, and choose a user with privileges on the rman-backups bucket.
3. Choose Auth Tokens from the list of resources and select Generate Token. Provide a description, such as "backups," and click Generate Token. The token is a string of characters that behaves like a password. Copy the string to a safe location. Once the dialog displaying the token is closed, it will not be shown again.

4. Install the backup module. SSH to the DB node, sudo to the oracle user, and navigate to the directory that contains the backup module opc_install.jar file. To back up on-premises databases to object storage, this module must be downloaded separately. The backup module requires several parameters, including an OCI username and password (token), the object storage bucket name (container), pre-created directories for the Oracle wallet, the backup module library, the RMAN config file, and the Swift endpoint URL for your region. In this exercise, the /u01/app/oracle/admin/rman/wallets and the /u01/app/oracle/admin/rman/config directories were pre-created to store the Oracle wallet, RMAN library, and configuration files.

```
$ cd /opt/oracle/oak/pkgrepos/oss/odbcs
$ ls
libopc.so  opc_install.jar
$ java -jar opc_install.jar -opcId orabackup
-opcPass '&token' -container rman-backups
-walletDir /u01/app/oracle/admin/wallets/
-libDir  /u01/app/oracle/admin/rman/config/
-configfile /u01/app/oracle/admin/rman/config/rman.conf
-host https://swiftobjectstorage.ca-toronto-1.oraclecloud.com
/v1/eclipsys

Oracle Database Cloud Backup Module Install Tool,
build 12.2.0.1.0DBBKPCSBP_2018-06-12
Oracle Database Cloud Backup Module credentials are valid.
Backups would be sent to container rman-backups.
Oracle Database Cloud Backup Module wallet created in directory
/u01/app/oracle/admin/wallets.
Oracle Database Cloud Backup Module initialization file
/u01/app/oracle/admin/rman/config/rman.conf created.
Downloading Oracle Database Cloud Backup Module Software Library
from file opc_linux64.zip.
Download complete.
```

5. Connect to RMAN after setting the environment variables for your DB instance, and set several RMAN configuration defaults. Setting the default device type to channel SBT_TAPE associated with the backup module library allows future RMAN backups for this database to be taken to the object storage by default. Backups stored in the Cloud must be encrypted so database backup encryption must be enabled and an encryption password must be set (it is set to "password" in this example for illustrative purposes, but a strong password is recommended).

```
RMAN> CONFIGURE CHANNEL DEVICE TYPE 'SBT_TAPE' PARMS
'SBT_LIBRARY=/u01/app/oracle/admin/rman/config/libopc.so,
 SBT_PARMS=(OPC_PFILE=/u01/app/oracle/admin/rman/config/rman.conf)';
RMAN> CONFIGURE DEFAULT DEVICE TYPE TO SBT_TAPE;
RMAN> CONFIGURE CONTROLFILE AUTOBACKUP FORMAT FOR
DEVICE TYPE SBT_TAPE TO '%F';
RMAN> SET ENCRYPTION IDENTIFIED BY "password" ONLY;
RMAN> CONFIGURE ENCRYPTION FOR DATABASE ON;
```

6. Create a backup of the system datafile. Notice that the control file and spfile are automatically backed up to object storage as well each time an RMAN backup completes.

```
RMAN> backup datafile 1;
Starting backup at 10-MAY-19
using channel ORA_SBT_TAPE_1
channel ORA_SBT_TAPE_1: starting full datafile backup set
channel ORA_SBT_TAPE_1: specifying datafile(s) in backup set
input datafile file number=00001
name=+DATA/ORCL_YYZ1FC/DATAFILE/system.261.999534143
channel ORA_SBT_TAPE_1: starting piece 1 at 10-MAY-19
channel ORA_SBT_TAPE_1: finished piece 1 at 10-MAY-19
piece handle=09u17dmb_1_1 tag=TAG20190510T190859 comment=API
Version 2.0,MMS Version 12.2.0.2
channel ORA_SBT_TAPE_1: backup set complete, elapsed time: 00:00:35
Finished backup at 10-MAY-19
Starting Control File and SPFILE Autobackup at 10-MAY-19
piece handle=c-1527314999-20190510-02 comment=API
Version 2.0,MMS Version 12.2.0.2
Finished Control File and SPFILE Autobackup at 10-MAY-19
```

7. Using the console, navigate to Object Storage | Object Storage | rman-backups and confirm that your backup has been written to the correct bucket.

EXAM TIP DBCS backups may be stored in both local and object storage. Local backups use FRA space and are fast and optimized, but durability is low because the backup is not available if the DB system is down. Storing backups in object storage is recommended for high durability, availability, and performance. An ideal solution may be a hybrid approach where backups are kept locally for fast point-in-time recovery and a backup copy also resides in object storage.

Managed Database Backup Using the Console

The OCI console provides a powerful interface for creating full backups on demand, enabling automatic backups. Both automatic incremental and standalone backups created through the console are known as managed backups and may be listed, deleted, and used to restore, recover, and even create new database systems from backups with a few clicks.

When you create a DBCS system, you may enable automatic backups, which have the following convenient characteristics.

- Daily incremental backups are taken to object storage within a backup window.
- The backup window is between midnight and 6:00 AM, in the time zone of the DB system's region or UTC for older DBCS systems created before November 21, 2018.
- A level zero backup is initially created, followed by daily incremental level 1 backups until the weekend, when the cycle repeats, starting with a fresh level zero backup.
- Automatic backups are retained in object storage for 30 days, unless the database is terminated, which results in the automatic incremental backups being removed as well.

You may create on-demand backups at any time, which are retained until they are explicitly deleted.

Exercise 6-8: Create a Standalone Managed Backup Using the Console

In this exercise, you create a full standalone backup using the console.

1. Sign in to the OCI console and choose your compartment.
2. Navigate to Bare Metal, VM, and Exadata and choose one of your databases. In the databases section for that database, hover on the ellipses and choose Create Backup.

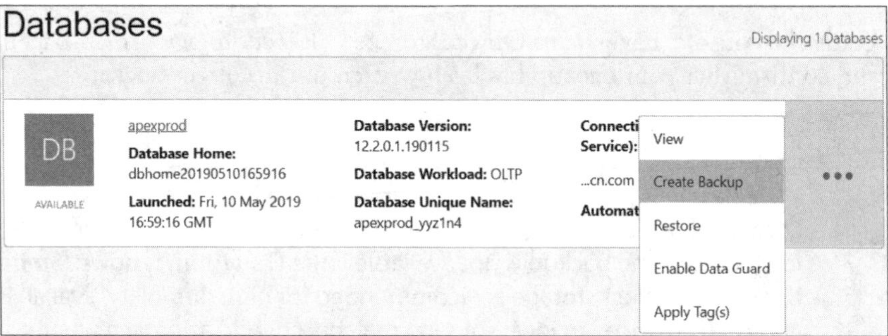

3. Provide a descriptive name for the backup and choose Create Backup. In this example, a full standalone backup is being taken prior to applying a patch. This is a typical DBA activity. The backup runtime depends on the size of the database.

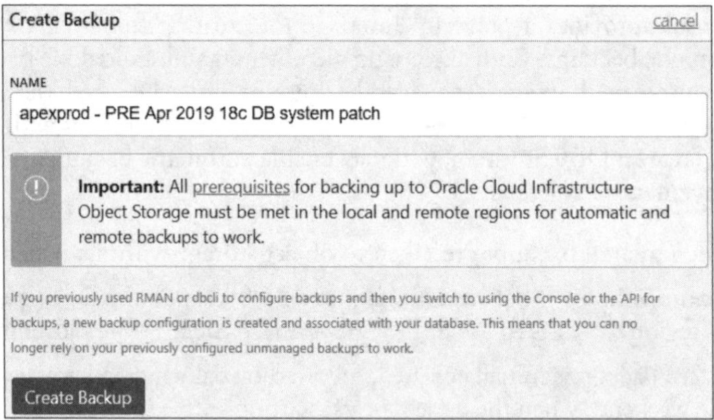

4. Navigate to Bare Metal, VM, and Exadata | Standalone Backups and view the list of explicit full backups. If you hover on the ellipses adjacent to the standalone backup, you may either delete the backup or create a new database system using this backup. If your current DBCS system is a VM, then the new DB must reside on a new system. If your current DBCS system is bare metal, you may choose to create another database on the bare metal system based on this backup.

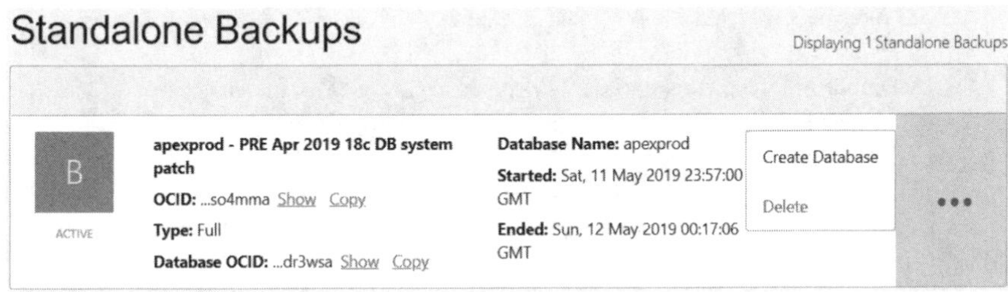

Exercise 6-9: Enable Automatic Incremental Backups Using the Console

In this exercise, you enable automatic backups for an existing database using the console.

1. Sign in to the OCI console and choose your compartment.
2. Navigate to Bare Metal, VM, and Exadata | DB Systems | DB System Details | Database, and choose Enable Automatic Backup.

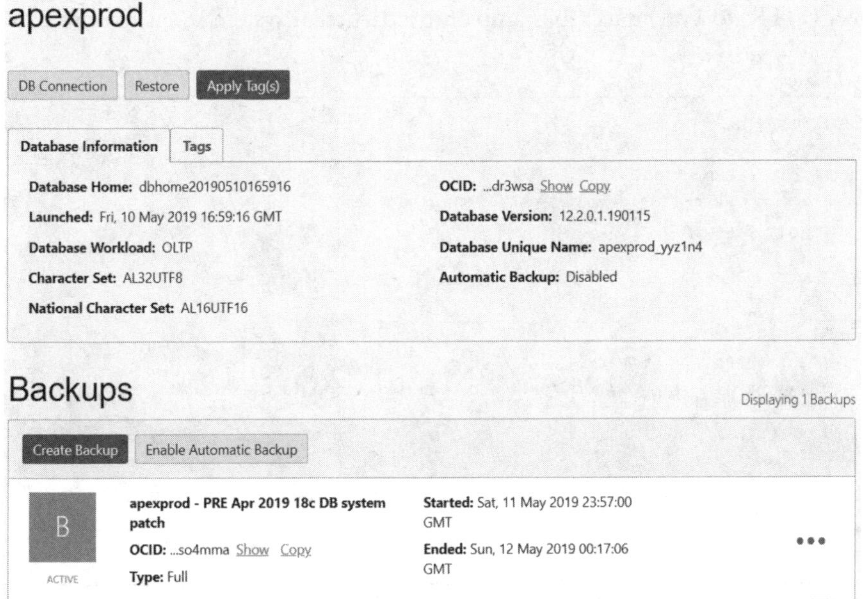

3. You should receive a prompt when enabling automatic backups reminding you that a new backup configuration will be created and that any unmanaged backups using other backup configurations may no longer be reliable. Choose OK to confirm and enable automatic backups.

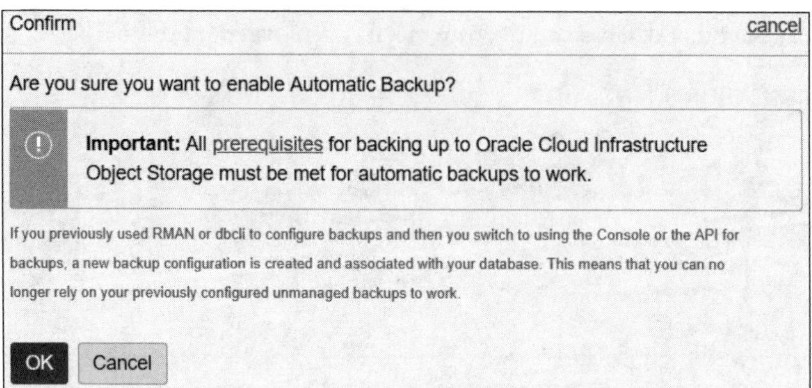

4. Navigate to Bare Metal, VM, and Exadata | DB Systems | DB System Details | Database | Backups to see the new automatic backups being created.

Database recovery using managed backups is performed by navigating to the database to be repaired through the console—Bare Metal, VM, and Exadata | DB Systems | DB System Details | Database—and choosing Restore. Figure 6-7 shows three options available when restoring a database through the console.

You may restore to the latest backup, minimizing data loss, or perform point-in-time recovery (PITR) to a previous timestamp or to a particular system change number (SCN).

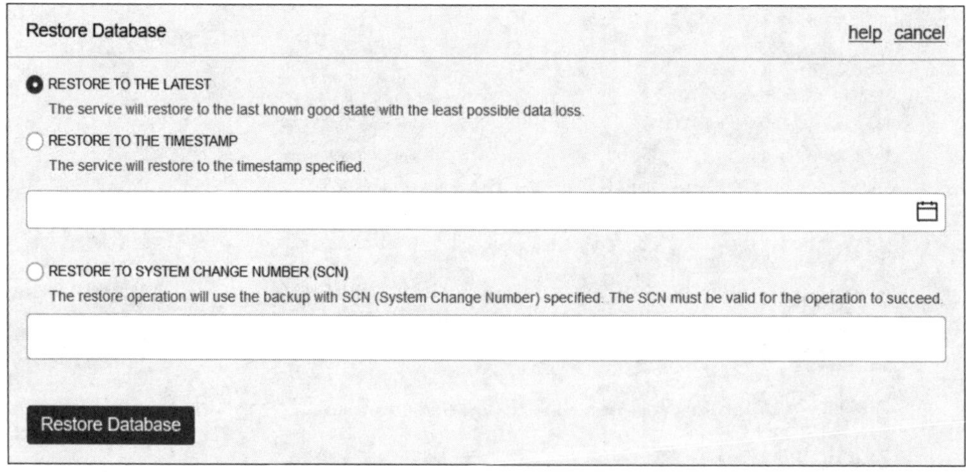

Figure 6-7 Restore database using managed backups.

Explaining system change numbers is beyond the scope of this discussion. Simply stated, an SCN functions like an internal clock marking the passage of time in a database. There are many ways of correlating SCNs with available backups, including creating an RMAN backup report.

Creating an RMAN backup report with dbcli is straightforward. Connect to a database node, switch user to root, and run the `dbcli create-rmanbackupreport` command to create the report and then the `dbcli describe-rmanbackupreport` command to identify the log file location. Viewing the file shows various RMAN commands used to report on the backups.

```
# dbcli create-rmanbackupreport --dbname apexprod -w summary -rn rpt1
{ "jobId" : "39a68caf-8ec2-4944-8f54-6f4df6791f82",
  "status" : "Created",
  "message" : "Rman BackupReport creation.",
    "resourceId" : "8977fe50-2c5a-4856-99e1-8bca74ce8872",
    "resourceType" : "Report" } ],
  "description" : "Create summary Backup Report "}
# dbcli describe-rmanbackupreport -i 8977fe50-2c5a-4856-99e1-8bca74ce8872
Backup Report details
----------------------------------------------------------------
                     ID: 8977fe50-2c5a-4856-99e1-8bca74ce8872
            Report Type: summary
               Location: Node apexprod: /opt/oracle/dcs/log/apexprod/rman/
bkup/apexprod_yyz1n4
/rman_list_backup_summary_2019-05-12_01-42-48-540…491.log
            Database ID: b2b5b328-07a2-4503-954f-945c7b890b2c
# cat /opt/oracle/dcs/log/apexprod/rman/bkup/apexprod_yyz1n4
/rman_list_backup_summary_2019-05-12_01-42-48-540…491.log
connected to target database: APEXPROD (DBID=3264559290)
RMAN> set echo on;
2> set echo on;
3> list db_unique_name all;
4> report schema;
5> show all;
6> list incarnation of database;
7> list copy;
8> list backup by file;
<output truncated for brevity>
```

Exadata Database Backups

DBCS backups on Exadata are conceptually identical to DBCS backups on VMs and bare metal. Both local FRA and object storage are also available for backups. Backup configurations and Swift object storage setup are required as well. So, what is different? Essentially, a different set of tools and some additional infrastructure setup are required to configure DBCS backup on Exadata. Remember that an Exadata system is associated with several networks. There is a private infiniband network as well as a management network between all compute nodes and storage cells. There is a public client–facing subnet and a private backup subnet used for backup-related traffic. The infrastructure prerequisites include the following:

- A service gateway is required for the VCN where the Exadata VMs reside for access to object storage. Apart from storing backups, object storage access is used for patch and tooling updates.

- A static route must be added to each Exadata compute node to direct traffic over the backup network to object storage to reduce network traffic on the client data network.
- An egress security list rule may be required to allow traffic to the object storage service from the backup subnet.
- An object storage bucket is used to store backups.
- An OCI user and associated Auth token. I recommended that the user belong to a group with limited privileges to access backup-related object storage buckets.

Once the infrastructure prerequisites are in place, a backup configuration file is created that specifies the backup destination, schedule, and retention period. The backup configuration file is created by the root user connected to the first compute node in the Exadata DB system. The node may be identified by using the `olsnodes -n` command while connected as the grid user. The backup configuration file, named exadb1_backup .conf for example, should be placed in the directory /var/opt/oracle/ocde/assistants/ bkup/ and is used to schedule backups to local storage as well as to a pre-created object storage bucket. The `bkup` command, also located in directory /var/opt/oracle/ocde/ assistants/bkup/, is used to associate the configuration file with a database and create a crontab entry to schedule the backup:

```
[root@EXA1]# ./bkup -cfg bkup.cfg -dbname=<database_name>
```

The default backup configuration adheres to Oracle DBCS backup best practices. A weekly full backup (level 0) is accompanied by daily incremental (level 1) backups. All backups to cloud storage are encrypted. Backups are retained based on the destination:

- **Local FRA storage only** Backups are retained for seven days.
- **Object storage only** Backups are retained for 30 days.
- **Both local and object storage** The most recent backups are retained locally for seven days and on object storage for 30 days.

DBCS on Exadata provides the bkup_api tool for management of backups. Located in the /var/opt/oracle/bkup_api/ directory, the bkup_api tool provides access to the backup API and includes options to query the status of an Exadata scheduled backup, list available backups, delete local backups, initiate an on-demand backup, and to create long-term backups. The backup configuration file is associated with a database, which may be backed up accordingly

DBCS Patching

Relevant patches for your DBCS system are automatically discovered and listed in the OCI console. If a new patch is released, previous patches are still available through the console. You are not forced to apply the latest available patch, but you cannot downgrade

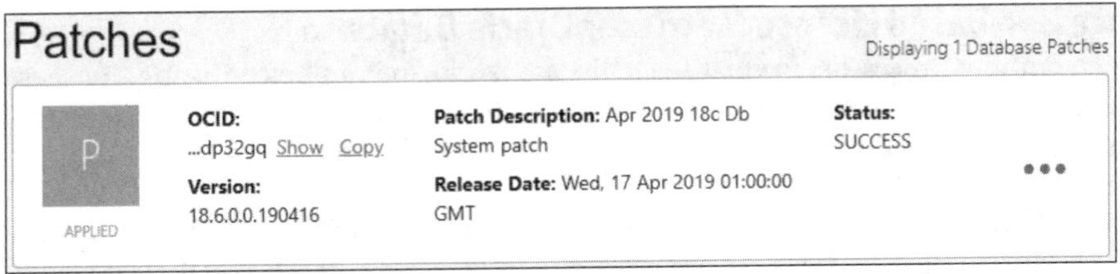

Figure 6-8 Pre-check completed and applying a patch to a DBCS database

to a previous patch. You may pre-check a patch before applying to identify any potential downstream issues.

The two categories of patching are DB system and Databases patches. These correspond to Grid Infrastructure and Database patches. Both must be patched independently. Both have a pre-check option. The sequence of patch application is important because there may be dependencies between them. For example, a specific database patch may only be successfully applied if a dependent DB system patch has already been applied.

Navigate to Bare Metal, VM, and Exadata | DB Systems | DB System Details | Database | Patches to view a list of database patches applicable to your database version. Hovering over the ellipses menu adjacent to a listed patch reveals the patch Pre-check and Apply options. Figure 6-8 shows a DB system patch that has been successfully pre-checked and applied. During a suitable maintenance window, a backup is typically taken before applying a patch.

When patching single-node database systems, downtime may be incurred while the relevant patch steps execute. RAC databases on VM and Exadata are usually available during patching because most patches are rolling, which means they may be applied in a rolling manner on each node in the cluster.

Advanced Database Features

Cost, security, and availability are key factors to consider when choosing a database system. Although there are tons of advanced database options and features available, this section concentrates on the following topics related to these key factors. Database licensing, data encryption, and two high-availability options, RAC and Data Guard, are discussed within the context of DBCS.

Database Licensing

Oracle database software license costs are non-trivial. In general, the database software license is often significantly more expensive than the infrastructure required to host a database system. There are currently two metrics used for licensing database software: named user plus (NUP) and processor-based. A named user is essentially an individual or device that connects to the database. There are many legacy licensing metrics, which are not discussed here.

Processor-Based License Metric for Oracle Database

Understanding processors in the Oracle license landscape can be confusing, but here are several facts to try to distinguish the Oracle processor license metric among terms like CPUs, sockets, cores, threads, OCPUs, and database editions.

- Modern servers have one or more CPU sockets on their motherboards.
- Modern CPUs have multiple physical cores.
- One physical core may have hyperthreading enabled. On Intel Xeon cores, it is common for hyperthreading to be enabled, providing two threads per core.
- Oracle license rules specify a table of core processor licensing factors depending on the underlying hardware architecture. For x86-based systems (all OCI servers), there is a core processor licensing factor, often called a core multiplier of 0.5. For several non-Oracle hardware vendors, the core multiplier is 1.
- The processor licenses required is the product of the number of cores, the number of threads per core, and the core processor licensing factor. A server with two sockets occupied by four-core Intel Xeon CPUs with hyperthreading enabled requires eight (2 sockets × 4 cores × 2 threads × 0.5 core factor) processor licenses.
- An OCPU is an Oracle Compute Processing Unit equivalent to 1 hyperthreaded core of an x86 CPU. OCI guarantees that both threads are dedicated to your compute shape and not shared among other VMs that may share the server.
- Oracle Standard Edition (SE2) may only be licensed on servers with a maximum of two sockets. Two-node RAC databases on SE2 are allowed on-premises but each node must have at most one socket. Additionally, SE2 RAC database instances may use a maximum of sixteen threads per instance.
- A vCPU, or virtual CPU, is a measure used by several other Cloud providers, including AWS and Azure. On AWS and Azure VMs, vCPUs refer to threads that are not guaranteed to be dedicated to your VM. This implies that in the best-case scenario, where no threads are shared at that moment, then AWS and Azure VMs with two vCPUs are equivalent to one OCPU on an OCI VM.
- If hyperthreading is enabled on AWS (RDS and EC2) and Azure, for non–Standard Edition software, then two vCPUs (two threads) require one processor license. If hyperthreading is not enabled, the one vCPU requires one processor license.

Compute infrastructure varies from standard VM shapes with one OCPU to bare metal and Exadata servers with tens to hundreds of OCPUs. OCPUs are important because they are directly linked to the metrics used for licensing Oracle database software. Table 6-4 shows a few OCI shapes as well as several non-OCI servers and the processor licenses required. Note that the core factors for processors on non-OCI Cloud infrastructure are subject to change. The processor licenses required value is calculated using this formula:

Processor Licenses Required = Sockets × Cores × Core factor × Threads

Location	Shape	Sockets	Cores Allocated/ Socket	Core Processor Licensing Factor	OCPU or vCPU	Threads Per Core	Processor Licenses Required
OCI	VM.Standard.2.1	1	1	0.5	1 OCPU	2	$1 \times 1 \times 0.5 \times 2 = 1$
OCI	BM.Standard.2.52	2	26	0.5	52 OCPUs	2	$2 \times 26 \times 0.5 \times 2 = 52$
On-premises	AMD, single socket, 8-core, no HT	1	8	0.5	8 vCPUs	1	$1 \times 8 \times 0.5 = 4$
On-premises	IBM Power 9, dual socket, SMT8 (8-way multithreading)	2	24	1	384 vCPUs	8	$2 \times 24 \times 1 \times 8 = 384$
AWS (EC2)	m5.4xlarge	1	2	0.5	4 vCPUs	2	$1 \times 2 \times 0.5 \times 2 = 2$
OCI	Exadata ¼ Rack – X7-2. Two compute nodes each with 2 sockets.	4	23	0.5	92 OCPUs	2	$4 \times 23 \times 0.5 \times 2 = 92$

Table 6-4 Processor Licenses Required by Various Cloud Shapes and On-Premises Servers

Named User Plus (NUP) License Metrics for Oracle Database

If you have a relatively low number of named database users, it may be more cost-effective to license the database software using the NUP metric. NUP licenses are subject to certain minimums per processor and are also dependent on the database edition being licensed. Here are several NUP-related facts to consider.

- An EE license requires the greater of the total number of users, or a minimum of 25 NUPs per processor.
- An SE2 license requires the greater of the total number of users, or a minimum of 10 NUPs per processor.

For example, if you want to license EE on the BM.Standard.2.52 OCI shape, as shown in Table 6-4, 52 processor licenses are required. If you have 1,000 named users using the databases on this server and this number is not going to change much in the future, you may benefit from licensing using the NUP metric. As there are 52 licensable processors and you need to license a minimum of 25 named users per processor, you will need 25 × 52 = 1,300 NUP licenses. Because 1,300 is greater than 1,000, you will need to purchase 1,300 NUP licenses. It is then up to you to determine if 1,300 NUP licenses is more affordable than 52 processor licenses.

DBCS Licensing

DBCS systems on OCI comprise network, storage, and compute infrastructure as well as Oracle database software. Oracle offers two models for licensing a database system on DBCS and also offers Pay As You Go and Monthly Flex pricing options.

- **Bring your own license (BYOL)** This model includes the infrastructure cost but not the database software license costs. This model is suitable for migrating existing on-premises systems to OCI and allows the pre-existing license investment to be reused. Only like-for-like licenses may be used. If you have four Enterprise Edition (EE) processor-based licenses on-premises, you may use these for EE databases on DBCS.
- **License included** This model includes both the infrastructure cost and the database software license costs. Using the online pricing calculator, you can easily estimate the cost of DBCS with included licenses.

As discussed earlier in this chapter, OCI offers several additional database software editions, including EE-HP and EE-EP, that do not exist as on-premises offerings. EE licenses cannot be used for EE-HP and EE-EP database editions.

For database systems on VMs, you are charged for each OCPU hour that the system uses, rounded up to the nearest hour. If your DBCS on VM system is stopped, you do not pay for OCPU, just for storage and any other infrastructure being used.

For database systems on bare metal, you are charged hourly for the hosted environment regardless of whether it is running or not. When scaling up by adding additional OCPUs (in multiples of two, limited to a maximum of eight OCPUs for DB SE), you are charged for each OCPU using a per-hour metric, rounded up to the nearest hour.

Pricing for DBCS on Exadata works in the same way as bare metal except there is an additional upfront cost, which varies depending on the shape of the Exadata system chosen.

Data Encryption

Security is baked into the OCI platform and DBCS is no exception. Transparent data encryption (TDE) on premises is an additionally licensed component of the Advanced Security Option available for Oracle DB Enterprise Edition. All DBCS database software editions, including Standard Edition, are available with TDE.

TDE offers encryption at several layers of the database stack. Within the database, user tablespaces as well as temporary and UNDO tablespaces, tables, and columns may be encrypted. All data stored in encrypted tablespaces is automatically encrypted. Backups and Data Pump exports may be encrypted before being transmitted over networks. Standby databases built with Data Guard work seamlessly with encrypted datafiles. Basically, TDE works transparently with other complementary database options and features.

When you use TDE, there is a low performance impact, as additional CPU cycles are required to encrypt and decrypt data. Hardware-based encryption and decryption acceleration is available on Exadata and many new CPUs, including Intel Xeon CPUs widely used in the OCI infrastructure, reducing the performance impact.

TDE relies on master encryption keys that are stored by default in an Oracle PKCS12 file-based keystore known as an Oracle wallet. You may optionally store your TDE master encryption keys in Oracle OCI or Key Vault or an external key management system (KMS).

When a DBCS system is created, a database administrator password is required. This password initially serves as the password for the TDE wallet, which, of course, should be changed periodically. All user tablespaces are encrypted by default using TDE. The TDE master encryption keys should be rotated periodically. You may use the `dbcli update-tdekey` command to rotate keys for your databases.

CAUTION The same TDE encryption key used to encrypt an RMAN backup or Data Pump export must be used for decryption. Before rotating keys, ensure that you back up your TDE wallet and that you understand the implications for previously encrypted backups and exports. Resist the temptation to keep the TDE wallet backup with your database backup so you have it on-hand if you need to restore in an emergency, as this defeats the point of using TDE. Keep the lock separate from the key. Ensure that you back up the TDE wallet and tag the backup appropriately.

High Availability

While Oracle databases are renowned for their reliability, performance, and scalability, they do, however, run on physical infrastructure that may occasionally fail. Infrastructure failure scenarios may be grouped into three broad categories: node failure, rack failure, and data center failure.

A node failure occurs when infrastructure internal to a server or compute node malfunctions, leading to a node being rebooted or shut down in an unplanned manner. Examples of root causes of node failures include faulty boot devices, bad memory modules, and power supply interruption. Rack failure occurs when an outage affects all servers in a specific rack or cage. This is uncommon but may occur when there is loss of power to a particular rack or overheating in the cage prompts an emergency unplanned shutdown of all servers in the rack. A data center comprises many server racks, and when there is a data center outage, it is usually associated with a catastrophic disaster like a flood or earthquake that has damaged or severed power or network access to an entire data center.

Fortunately, OCI has been architected with high availability (HA) as one of its core design objectives, and many mitigating strategies have been implemented to support HA during a failure event. All OCI servers have many redundant components that tolerate failure of a power supply, network interface, and disk drives. OCI VMs may be created in separated infrastructure known as fault domains within a data center or availability domain to tolerate rack failure. There are also many regions with multiple ADs and strong high-speed networks between ADs and regions. These mitigating strategies lend themselves to two powerful software-based HA solutions, RAC and Data Guard.

RAC

To understand RAC, first a quick refresher for non-Oracle DBAs about the Oracle Server. An Oracle Server is composed of a database instance and a set of database files. A database instance is a collection of memory structures and operating system background processes. When an Oracle Server is shut down, the database files are closed and the instance is stopped. The database files persist. They occupy disk space, and they contain the tables and rows of data that will be accessed the next time the database files are opened. When the instance stops, its memory structures are deallocated and all its background processes are stopped. The compute power (CPU and memory resources mainly) used by the instance are released and may be used by other programs. When the instance starts on a node, memory structures are created, background processes are started, and the instance attempts to mount the database files and open the database.

A Real Application Cluster (RAC) allows multiple instances, each running on its own compute nodes, to simultaneously mount and open the same set of database files that are stored on shared storage. RAC depends on Oracle Grid Infrastructure (GI) software to coordinate the communication between the RAC nodes and the shared storage.

OCI makes RAC available on DBCS through a two-node VM cluster and on Exadata. RAC databases can tolerate the complete loss of one compute node in the cluster with no interruption to the database availability. RAC also supports HA during patching and node maintenance exercises. When setting up RAC on a two-node VM, ensure that each RAC node resides in a separate fault domain.

When GI is configured, a set of listeners, known as scan listeners, are configured to provide highly available database client network traffic management services. Scan listeners route incoming connections to available local listeners based on algorithms that consider the load profile of specific instances to ensure even load distribution. In the event of a RAC node failure, the scan listeners direct traffic to the operational node.

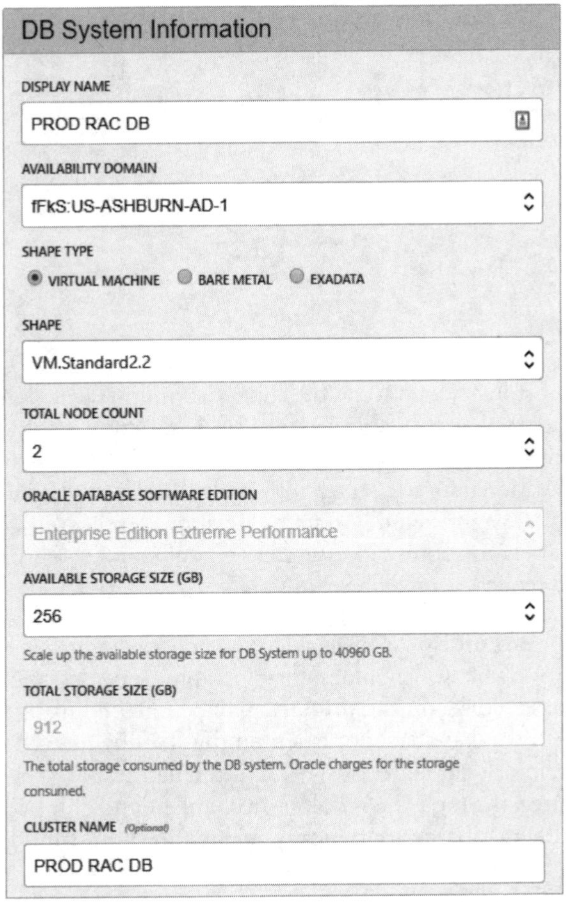

Figure 6-9 Create a two-node RAC database on VM.

RAC on OCI is available only with EE-EP edition. To create a RAC system on DBCS using the console, navigate to Bare Metal, VM, and Exadata, and choose Launch DB System. Figure 6-9 shows the familiar DB System Information dialog screen.

Provide a display name, choose an AD, and choose a VM or Exadata shape. The VM shape must have at least two OCPUs. Choose two nodes to enable RAC, and the Oracle database software edition will default to EE-EP. Choose available storage to be allocated to your database. Both RAC nodes will access the same shared storage to be allocated. Provide an optional cluster name. As shown in Figure 6-10, ensure that at least two fault domains are chosen.

The remaining options have been discussed previously, so supply the required information and choose Launch DB System. After a short while, incredibly, a fully functional highly available RAC database system is provisioned and ready for business.

Exadata has been engineered with RAC and HA in mind as discussed earlier. Notably, to facilitate high-speed cluster internode communications, a high-speed, redundant infiniband network fabric is implemented.

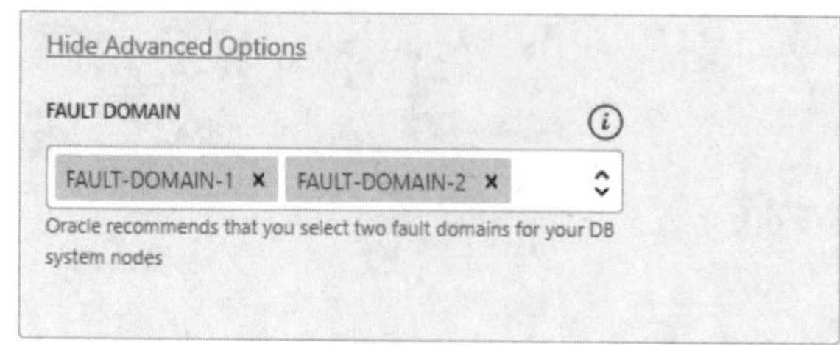

Figure 6-10 Choose two fault domains for resilience of RAC node VMs to node failure.

Data Guard

While RAC mitigates against node failure and ensures HA, Data Guard mitigates against node, shared storage, and even AD failure in multi-AD regions. Data Guard is a mature replication technology available with all Oracle Enterprise Edition versions. All Data Guard configurations consist of a primary database and at least one standby database. Each system is a fully operational Oracle server with nodes, instances, and independent sets of database files. The primary and standby systems are almost exclusively on separate infrastructure to provide business continuity in case there is a failure of the primary system. Two modes of Data Guard replication may be configured:

- **Physical standby** This is the most pervasive form of Data Guard. Primary and standby databases are block-for-block physical copies of one another. Damaged database blocks on the primary may be repaired using blocks from the standby. RMAN database backups taken on the standby may be used to restore and recover the primary database as they are interchangeable. Changes in the primary are captured through the redolog mechanism and shipped to the standby. Physical standby databases are typically opened in mount mode while changes (in the form of redolog entries) are applied through a process known as *managed recovery*. Basically, the standby database is in a constant state of being recovered using the latest changes being made to the primary ("perpetual recovery"). Physical standbys support many advanced features including Active Data Guard (where the standby is open in read-only mode) and snapshot standby databases.
- **Logical standby or SQL Apply** The less popular, seriously understated little sibling of physical Data Guard. Primary and logical standby databases start off being physically identical. Instead of block replication by applying the redo stream directly onto the standby database, the redo is mined, and SQL transactions are extracted and applied using SQL Apply, a process that runs SQL changes in the correct sequence to maintain primary data integrity between the primary and standby. Logical replication replicates only a subset of the databases that includes user-specified schemas and objects. The logical standby can be opened read-write. Indexes, which do not exist on the primary, can be created on the logical standby, and writes are tolerated as long as primary data is not impacted.

Each database in a Data Guard architecture is designated a role. One database occupies the primary role while one or more databases occupy the standby role. Logical standby databases are not discussed further and the rest of this section is pertinent to physical standby databases. These are most pervasive and offered out-of-the-box with all the automation prebuilt on DBCS.

Data Guard replication may be configured in one of three modes, which determines how the redo stream of changes from the primary database is shipped and applied on the standby:

- **Maximum Performance** Optimized for performance. Replication is asynchronous and the primary database does not wait for confirmation that the captured redo stream has been successfully shipped or applied on the standby. Replication interruptions or issues do not impact the primary database.
- **Maximum Availability** Optimized for availability and protection. Under normal operation, changes are not committed on the primary database until all changes are written to the redo logs and confirmation that the captured redo stream has been successfully shipped or applied on the standby has been received. Issues with the replication cause the system to operate as if in maximum performance mode and the availability of the primary database is not impacted.
- **Maximum Protection** Optimized for data protection and integrity of the standby. No data loss is possible. Replication is synchronous and the primary database waits for confirmation that the captured redo stream has been successfully shipped or applied on the standby. Replication interruptions or issues cause the primary database to shut down.

A role transition occurs when one of the standby databases assumes the primary role. The following are two types of role transitions:

- **Switchover** A planned role transition often to perform OS patching or hardware maintenance on the primary. No data loss is incurred during a switchover because the primary and standby databases are completely synchronized when the roles are transitioned. There is a small window (a few minutes at most, usually less than a minute) of unavailability during a switchover. The "old" standby database is now the primary (open read-write) while the "old" primary acts in a standby role. Managed recovery is paused, while maintenance is performed without interruption to the business. This provides HA in a planned manner.
- **Failover** This is an unplanned role transition and, as the name suggests, a failure has occurred. One of the standby databases is designated as the new primary. Point-in-time recovery (PITR) occurs. Depending on the Data Guard configuration discussed earlier, minimal (max performance or max availability) or no data loss (max protection) may occur during failover. Max protection mode ensures that any last in-flight transactions are only committed on the primary if they are committed on the standby, so no data loss occurs.

Ideally, each database system resides in separate availability domains in a multi-AD region, but at the very least each system should reside in separate fault domains.

In a two-system Data Guard configuration, one is designated the primary role while the other takes on the standby role. Applications and users connect to the primary database and, as changes are made on the primary database, they are captured and shipped over the network to the standby database, where they are applied. This is a classical physical standby configuration.

DBCS automates the configuration of Data Guard. If you choose any EE database, you can easily enable Data Guard by choosing Enable Data Guard from the Databases options menu, as shown in Figure 6-11. This prompts you for a set of responses for the creation of the standby database system that are almost identical to those provided when the primary database was created.

Several important considerations for Data Guard systems include setting up a regional subnet in multi-AD regions. This simplifies networking configuration, and primary and standby database systems can be placed in different ADs. Data Guard also provides a monitoring agent known as an observer that ideally runs on different infrastructure from both the primary and secondary DB systems. The observer can be configured to determine when a failover is required and to automatically perform the failover. This provides a huge HA advantage as no human involvement is required.

Enabling Data Guard with DBCS masks the configuration complexity required in a manual Data Guard setup. Here, OCI takes care of creating the new system, installing the same binaries, duplicating the database and configuring the broker. Note that both the primary and standby database systems must be on the same VCN. For more advanced Data Guard scenarios such as having a third standby database or spanning

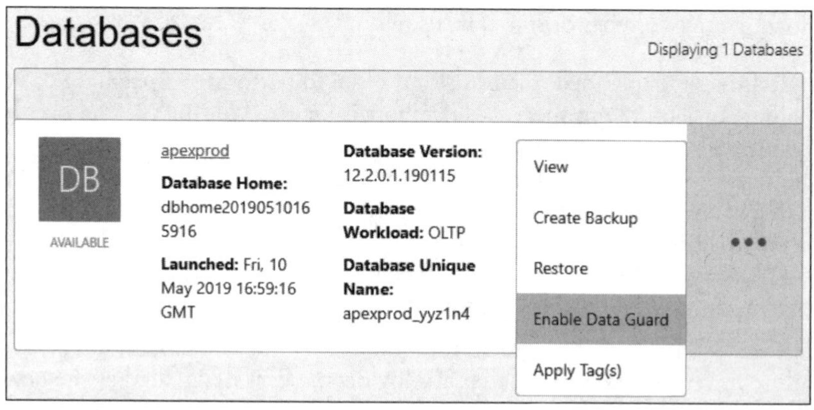

Figure 6-11 Enable Data Guard for a DBCS system.

multiple VCNs, Data Guard must be set up manually. In this case, the DBA has to do all of the setup work for provisioning the infrastructure and database and for configuring Data Guard.

Data Guard may be enhanced by licensing the additional Active Data Guard (ADG) option. ADG allows standby databases to be opened in read-only mode, supporting the offloading of expensive queries and read-intensive activities such as exports and backups to the standby. ADG in 19c and later supports limited read-write operations on the standby database, which opens up some exciting HA possibilities.

NOTE Consider the us-ashburn-1 region, which has at least three ADs. A best-practice HA architecture may include a primary RAC database system in AD1 with each RAC node in a separate fault domain, with a standby RAC database system in AD2, again with both standby nodes in separate fault domains. Active Data Guard has been implemented for backup and query offloading. A Data Guard observer has been configured in AD3 to orchestrate a fast-start-fail-over (FSFO) if issues with the primary RAC database system are detected.

Autonomous Databases

Oracle autonomous database (ADB) systems offer a hosted and managed option with an underlying Exadata service and the ability to dynamically scale up and scale down both the CPUs and storage allocated to your VM. This single feature unlocks a great number of possibilities, chief among them the game-changing idea of sizing your environment for average workload, scaling up during peak periods, and scaling back down once the workload normalizes. ADB is a pluggable database and is available on a shared or dedicated Exadata infrastructure.

Relying on decades of internal automation, ADB uses advanced machine learning algorithms to balance performance and availability with cost, automating many tasks including indexing, tuning, upgrading, patching, and backing up the database. HA is achieved through the use of a RAC database (when scaling to more than 16 OCPUs), triple-mirrored disk groups, redundant compute and network infrastructure, and nightly backups.

The following are two autonomous database variants:

- **Autonomous Transaction Processing** The ATP workload type targets OLTP databases, and configuration parameters are biased toward high-volume random data access typical of OLTP systems. ATP databases are also suitable for mixed workloads, including some batch processing reporting, IoT, and machine learning, as well as transaction processing.

- **Autonomous Data Warehouse** The ADW workload type targets analytic systems including data warehouses and marts, data lakes, and large machine learning data databases with configuration parameters biased toward high-volume ordered data scanning operations.

Autonomous Transaction Processing (ATP) and Autonomous Data Warehousing (ADW) each support a different workload type but they share the underlying infrastructure and tooling. Essentially, they differ in database initialization parameters and automation options. ADW stores data in a columnar format while ADB uses a traditional row store. The following sections discuss the autonomous database service, which encompasses the ATP and ADW cloud services.

Create an Autonomous Database

While the CLI and API may be used for creating ADBs, the console is used to exemplify the underlying principle of autonomous databases: It should be easy for anyone to provision a secure, powerful database system that is largely self-managing.

When you create an ADB, you choose the initial CPU cores and storage allocation. At the time of this writing, the minimums are one OCPU and 1TB of storage charged on an hourly basis. There is also a free-tier single serverless ADB with one OCPU and 0.2TB of storage available to each tenancy. Be mindful of the licensing model you intend to use. The more CPU cores you choose, the more processor licenses you will use. If you choose the BYOL model, allocate your licenses accordingly. If you subscribe to new database software licenses at database create time, be prepared to be charged accordingly. Regardless of the licensing model you choose, you are implicitly charged for the DBCS infrastructure and storage allocated and used by your ADB.

You cannot choose the Oracle software version used in your ADB. As of this writing, ATP and ADW databases are provisioned with Oracle database version 18c with the 19c release planned for general availability in due course. While you can choose your ADB region and compartment, other options are limited. For example, you do not have the option to specify the AD or VCN in which to provision these databases and all ADBs are exposed to the Internet.

Exercise 6-10: Create an ATP Database Using the Console

In this exercise, you create an ATP database using the OCI console. If you have not provisioned the free tier ADB in your tenancy, this may be a good time to try it.

1. Sign in to the OCI console and choose your compartment.

2. Navigate to Autonomous Transaction Processing and choose Create Autonomous Database. Choose an ATP workload type, a compartment, a display name like ATP Demo, and a database name. Select an initial CPU core count and an initial amount of storage to allocate.

Create Autonomous Database help cancel

Workload Type

AUTONOMOUS DATA WAREHOUSE
Configures the database for a decision support or data warehouse workload, with a bias towards large data scanning operations.

AUTONOMOUS TRANSACTION PROCESSING
Configures the database for a transactional workload, with a bias towards high volumes of random data access.

Database Information

COMPARTMENT
Demo

DISPLAY NAME
ATP Demo

DATABASE NAME
ATPDEMODB
The name must contain only letters and numbers, starting with a letter. 14 characters max.

CPU CORE COUNT
1
The number of CPU cores to enable. Available cores are subject to your tenancy's service limits.

STORAGE (TB)
1
The amount of storage to allocate.

Database Version: Oracle Database 18c

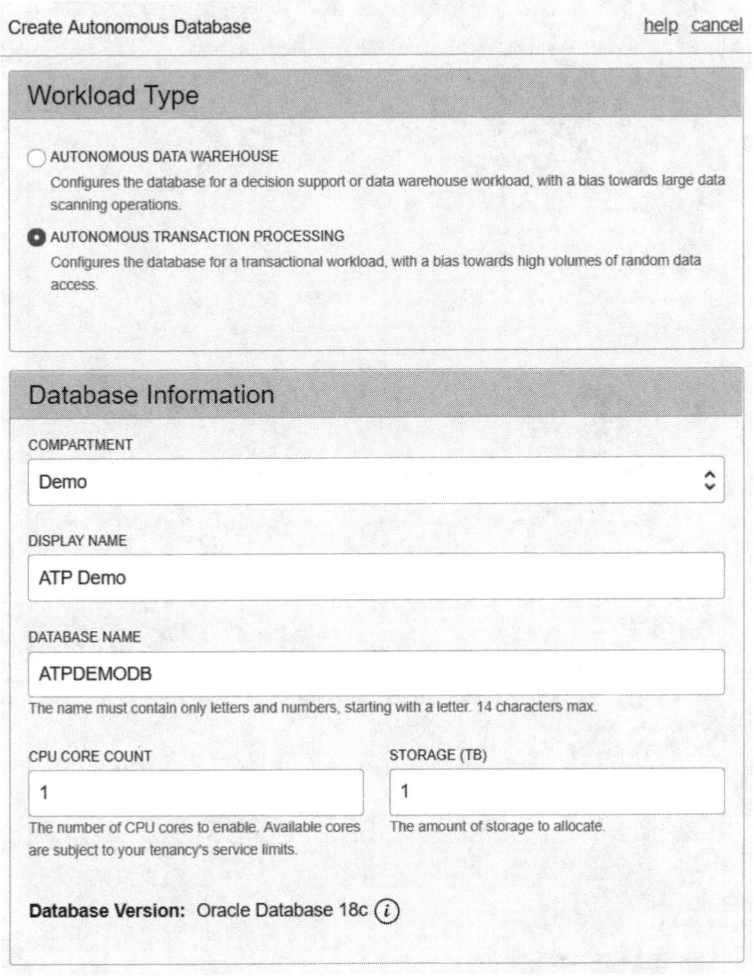

3. Provide a password for the administrator account. This is probably the toughest part as the password must conform to strict password rules. Select a license type, optionally specify tags, and choose Create Autonomous Database.

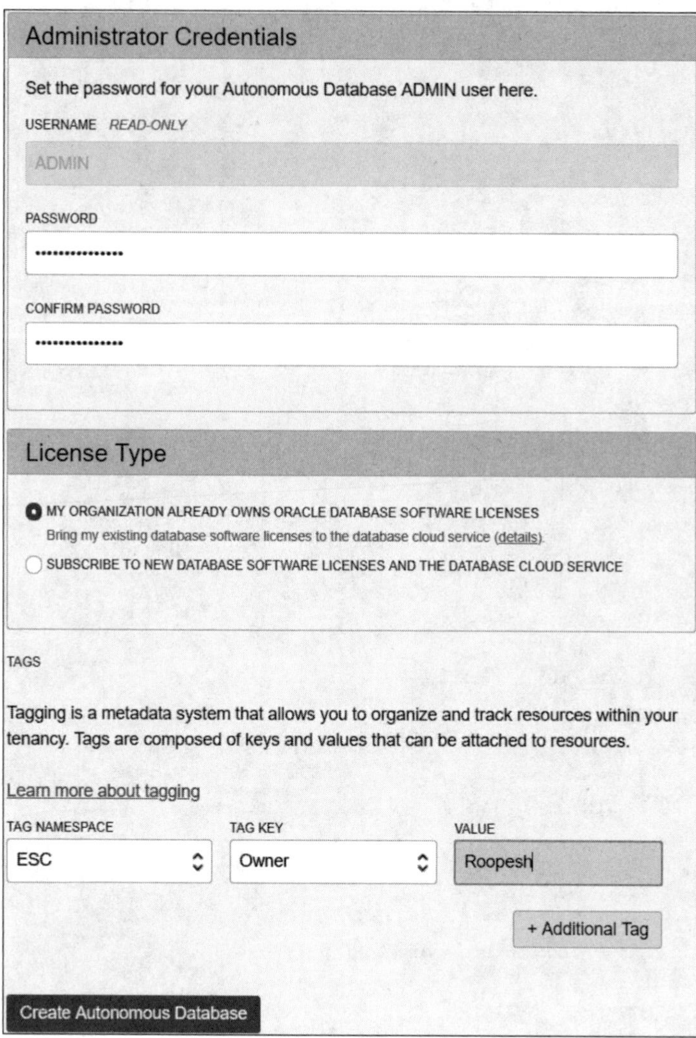

4. Navigate to Autonomous Transaction Processing | ATP Demo and review your newly provisioned database after a few minutes.

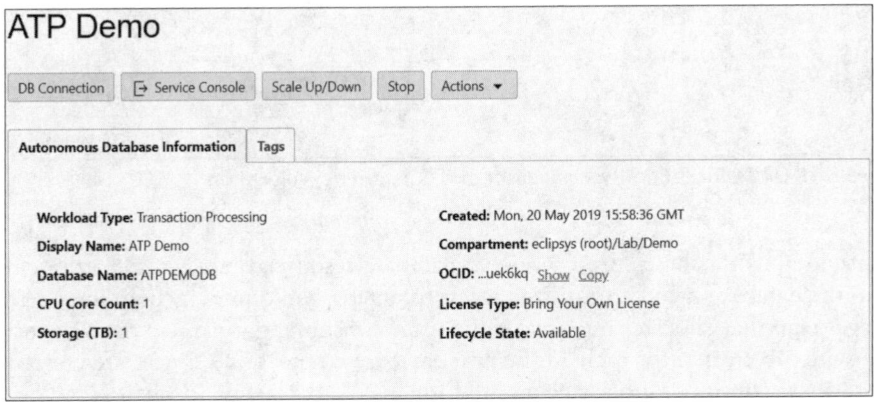

Connecting to an Autonomous Database

Autonomous databases are hosted on OCI infrastructure that is not accessible to you. You have access to the database through a SQL*Net, OCI, or JDBC thin connection through the default listener port 1521. You cannot SSH to the compute node and no operating system access is permitted. Oracle Cloud Operations maintains the infrastructure. There are two connectivity options, through the public Internet or through FastConnect with public or private peering (or both), which provides private connections from on-premises networks. Databases in your VCN in private subnets can use service gateways to access ADB instances in the same region without routing data through the public Internet. ADBs maintain access control lists (ACLs) that may be used to "whitelist" IP addresses, preventing access to those IP addresses not on the list.

Your ADB is highly secure, encrypting all data. When connecting to your ADB, certificate-based authentication and Secure Sockets Layer (SSL) are utilized, allowing only authenticated connections to access the database. When the ADB is created, an encrypted key is stored in a wallet on the server. This key is also required on each client that needs to connect to the ADB. Clients using Oracle Call Interface, including ODBC and JDBC OCI as well as "thin" JDBC, use credential wallets to connect to the ADB.

A new privileged user called ADMIN is the default user created. When creating an ADB in the previous exercise, you provided a password for the ADMIN user. Once you connect to the ADB as the ADMIN user, you may create other users. Once the ADB has been provisioned, you may download the wallet credentials file, either through the console or using the API.

Service	ADB	Parallelism	RM Shares	Concurrency
TPURGENT	ATP	MANUAL	12	Unlimited
TP	ATP	1	8	Unlimited
HIGH	ADW, ATP	CPU_COUNT	4	3 Queries
MEDIUM	ADW, ATP	4	2	1.25 × CPU_COUNT Queries
LOW	ADW, ATP	1	1	2 × CPU_COUNT Queries

Table 6-5 ADB Services Priority, Parallelism, and Concurrency Allocation

Autonomous databases make use of a database resource manager, a feature embedded in the database, which prioritizes access to database resources by defining a resource manager plan that allocates resources to resource consumer groups. Up to five consumer groups are pre-created for each ADB. Five database connection services are created that map to these consumer groups using the format <ADB NAME>_<CONSUMER GROUP>. Two OLTP-specific services, TPURGENT and TP, are available for ATP only. Users must choose the appropriate database service based on their performance and concurrency requirements. The administrator manages available resources for users by assigning connection options to each user. The five consumer groups and, consequently, associated application connection services may be described as follows:

- **TPURGENT** Highest priority for time-critical transaction processing operations, supporting manual parallelism on ATP databases.
- **TP** Typical for OLTP, non-parallel operations on ATP databases.
- **HIGH** High priority for batch and reporting parallel operations that are subject to queuing.
- **MEDIUM** Typical for batch and reporting parallel operations that are subject to queuing.
- **LOW** Lowest priority for non-parallel batch and reporting operations.

ADB resources are broadly allocated to these services to control parallelism and concurrency as well as priority using resource manager plan shares that define the proportion of the CPU and IO resources allocated to each consumer group, as shown in Table 6-5. You may update the resource manager plan shares using the service console.

Exercise 6-11: Connect to an ATP Database Using the SQL Developer

In this exercise, you connect to the ATP database created in the previous exercise using SQL Developer.

1. Sign in to the OCI console and navigate to Autonomous Transaction Processing | ATP, and choose DB Connection. Notice the five Connection Strings that may be used for your connections.

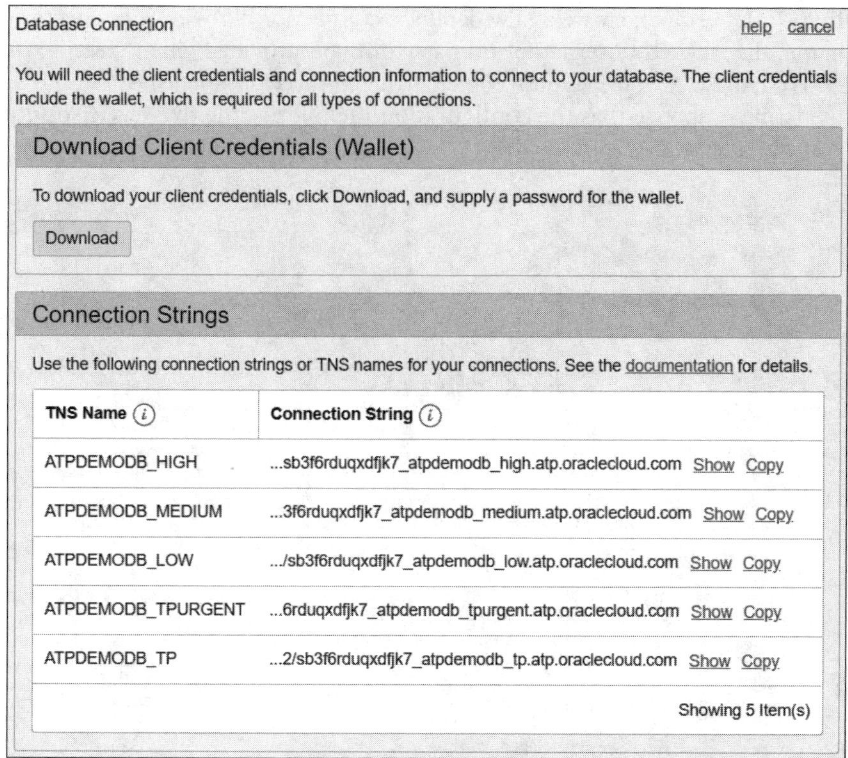

2. Choose Download, provide a password, and save the zip file that contains several files including the client wallet in a secure location.

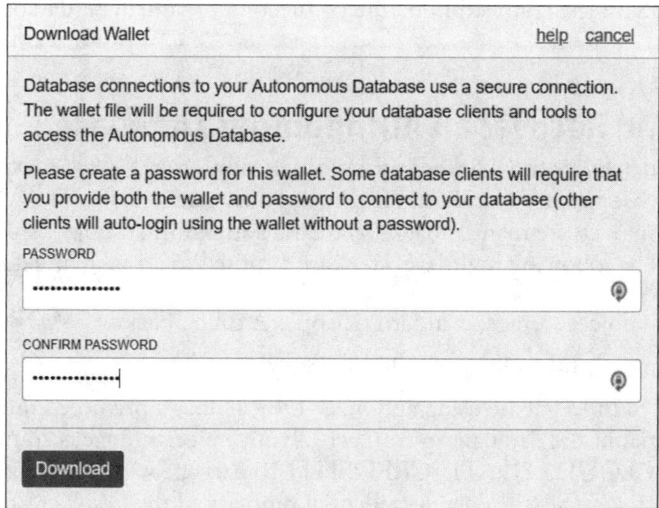

3. In SQL Developer, create a new database connection. Provide a connection name, the ADMIN username and password you provided when creating the ATP database. Choose Cloud Wallet as the connection type, specifying the zip file (still compressed) as the configuration file. Notice the five service options you can select.

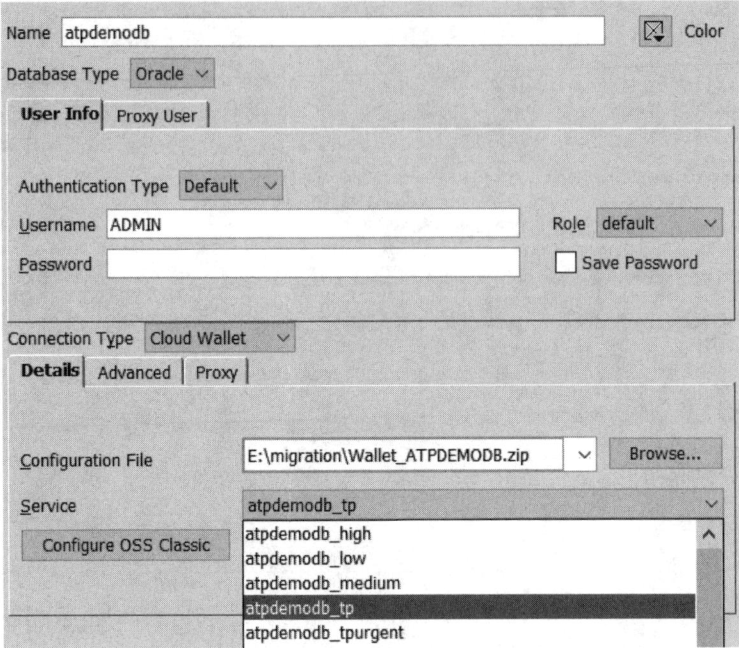

4. Test and Save the connection before connecting to your ATP database.

Back Up and Recover an Autonomous Database

Autonomous databases are backed up automatically at night as encrypted backups using the database backup cloud service. Backups are retained for 60 days before being removed. You may create manual backups that are stored in an object storage bucket in your tenancy. The following high-level steps are required to create manual ADB backups:

1. Create an object storage, standard tier bucket called backup_<ADB Name>.
2. Create an auth token for your OCI tenancy.
3. Connect to the database using an Oracle DB client as a privileged user, and create a credential in the database to connect to your object storage account using the DBMS_CLOUD.CREATE_CREDENTIAL package with your tenancy credential and auth token. Set the default credential property to the newly created credential.
4. Set the default bucket property to your object storage tenancy URL using the format: https://swiftobjectstorage.<region>.oraclecloud.com/v1/<object_storage_namespace>.

Once these steps are done, manual backups may be taken through the console or through the API.

ADB restore and recovery may be initiated using the API or through the console by navigating to Autonomous Database | <ADB> | Actions | Restore. You may specify an exact timestamp for point in time recovery (PITR) to restore the database to a previous point in time (if there are sufficient backups), or you may search your backups and choose a specific backupset to restore and recover.

ADB clones may be initiated using the API or through the console by navigating to Autonomous Database | <ADB> | Actions | Create Clone. You can make a full clone or a metadata clone that creates a new database with all source database schema metadata but with no source data. This is very useful for test and development scenarios.

Operating an Autonomous Database

ADB operations have many unique features. Several operational topics related to CPU and storage scaling, tuning, patching, and monitoring are discussed in this section.

ADB CPU and Storage Scaling

Sizing database servers for peak load is no longer required with autonomous databases. With APIs or the console, it is a trivial matter to scale up both your CPU count and storage allocation. The ADB in Figure 6-12 may be significantly updated to 128 CPUs from 1 CPU and to 128TB of storage from 1TB. This is an extreme example to demonstrate the sheer power of this feature.

You have an ace up your sleeve with this feature, for the inevitable 2:00 AM pager alert, indicating the system is overloaded while processing a business-critical workload. Preauthorizing scale-up parameters with your management can help you literally brute force your way out of a crisis. Perhaps a better way to pitch this is to consider the case of many organizations that run overprovisioned servers in anticipation of the busy periods, such as Black Friday for retailers or student registration week for universities. These databases may now run with just the CPU cores (and licenses) they require and burst during busy times and scale down during quiet times.

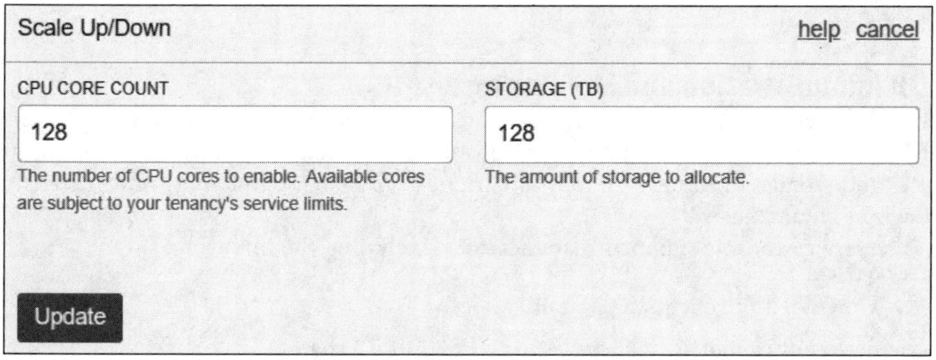

Figure 6-12 CPU core and storage scaling with ADB

ADB Tuning Considerations

Many traditional database tuning tasks have been automated in ADB. The following list is presented as a subset of topics traditional DBAs may need to be aware of as they move to ADB.

- Optimizer statistics are gathered automatically during direct-path loading operations. However, manual gathering of statistics is still possible, if required.
- Optimizer hints and parallel hints in SQL statements are disabled by default when you migrate to ADB, but these may be explicitly re-enabled if required.
- Schema tuning is highly automated with regular enhancements and improvements being released. Tables are automatically partitioned, compressed, configured for in-memory, and tablespaces are automatically created as required. However, manual schema tuning is still possible but should only be used with careful consideration.
- Automatic indexing simplifies tuning significantly and is based on an expert system that automatically generates and validates candidate indexes before implementing them.
- All tuning is auditable, so you can keep track of tuning changes being automatically implemented in the database.

ADB Patching and Security

Oracle Cloud Operations support and maintain the Exadata systems that underlie autonomous databases in each region. The Oracle Cloud Operations support team are responsible for patching, which occurs as a quarterly full stack rolling patch of the equipment firmware, operating systems, VM, clusterware, and database using a pretested gold image. As of this writing, you are informed about upcoming patches but you cannot influence the patching schedule.

There is a strict isolation so your data is only accessed by authorized users. Unified Audit is enabled, which tracks login failures, user modifications, and database structural changes. All data is encrypted at rest and with SSL over the wire. In exceptional circumstances, you may grant Cloud operations access to your system using a "Break Glass" function.

ADB Administration and Monitoring

The ADB Service Console provides an increasingly complex set of features geared specifically for administering and monitoring your autonomous database. You may monitor CPU and storage utilization as well as current SQL statement activity and metrics, as shown in Figure 6-13.

The service console supports many features, including the following:

- Download the client credentials (wallet).
- Set resource management rules for CPU and IO shares

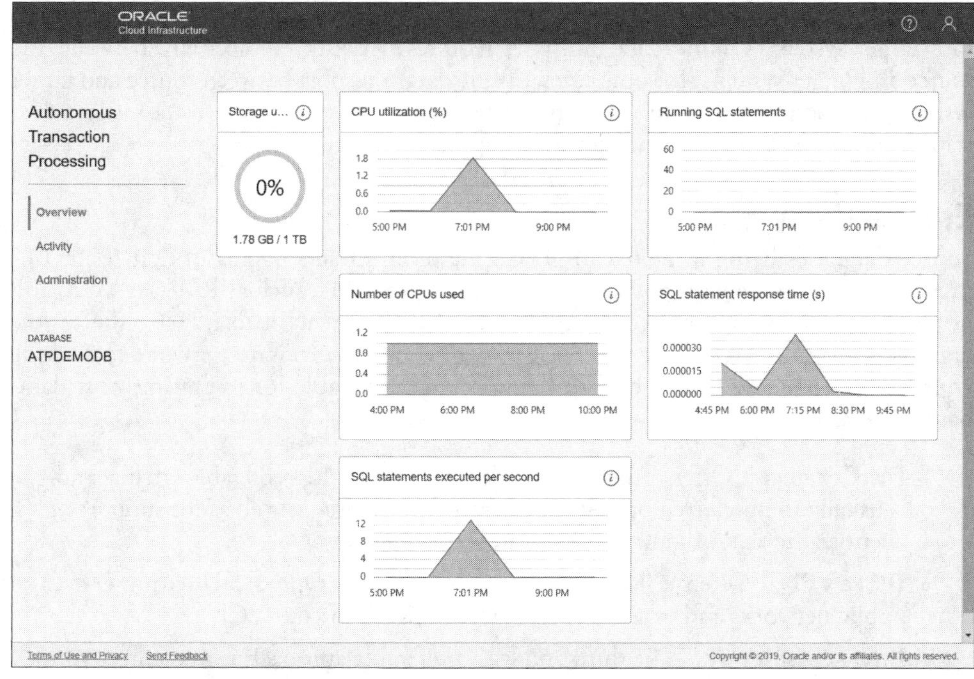

Figure 6-13 ADB service console for monitoring and administration

- Set run-away criteria for each consumer group to limit query run times and query IO.
- Download the Oracle instant client, which includes a free set of tools for developing and migrating data to Oracle ADB.
- Manage Oracle machine learning (ML) users.

EXAM TIP It is important to understand the differences between the ADB OCI Console and the ADB Service Console. Specifically, you may be asked about what activities are done from the ADB OCI Console versus the ADB Service Console.

Database Migration

Migrating your on-premises databases to the Cloud is a daunting prospect for many organizations. As cloud platforms mature and the concerns related to data security on cloud infrastructure morph into an understanding and appreciation for the implicit implementation of security best practices by the major cloud vendors, more organizations are embracing the shift to hosting their databases in the Cloud. The benefits are numerous, ranging from agile, scalable compute shapes to push automation for backups, patching, building RAC systems, and setting up Data Guard on DBCS to name a few.

Database migration fundamentally involves transporting data from a source system to a target system. Online data transport requires network connectivity between the source and target systems. In some cases, offline data transport between source and target systems may be preferable. In the sections that follow, I outline online and offline data transport options before discussing various migration approaches.

Connectivity

Source databases being migrated to DBCS are often Oracle databases that reside on-premises. Oracle databases hosted by other cloud providers, such as RDS on AWS, and non-Oracle databases may be migrated to DBCS. If you wish to transfer the source database over the network, it is typical to extend your corporate network to include your VCN. There are three network-based options available for migrating your database to DBCS.

- **FastConnect** Offers private network extension with predictable latency and is usually the preferred option for migrating databases as well as for supporting client traffic that originates from your source network.
- **IPSec VPN** Offers a slower-than-FastConnect, encrypted, secure tunnel over public networks and extends your source network to your VCN.
- **Internet Gateway** The third and least preferable approach is to connect your source network with your VCN through an Internet gateway, passing network traffic over the less secure, unpredictable public Internet.

For very large databases or when migrating to DBCS from a source environment with poor network infrastructure, OCI offers a Data Transfer Service.

Data Transfer Service

Consider a 500TB database on-premises that you wish to migrate to DBCS. You may set up a VCN with a DRG and a 10 Gbps FastConnect connection (fastest available as of this writing) to your on-premises network. Regardless of the migration strategy selected, moving 500TB of data over the 10 Gbps infrastructure takes almost five days. This duration gets worse as the database size increases or the network throughput decreases.

Oracle offers an offline, secure data transfer service to upload data to your designated object storage bucket at no additional cost. The approximate, rounded-up time required to transport databases of various sizes, using various presumed sustained network throughput rates, is compared with the data transfer service throughput in Table 6-6. FastConnect (10 Gbps) is preferred in most cases when it is available.

Using the data transfer service to transport data to OCI object storage entails several steps:

1. A transfer job is created through the OCI console by navigating to Object Storage | Data Transfer | Create Transfer Job. Provide a descriptive job name and select the object storage upload bucket that will ultimately contain the transferred data.

Database Size	10 Mbps	100 Mbps	1 Gbps	10 Gbps	Data Transfer Service
1TB	10 days	1 day	2.3 hours	14 minutes	1 week
5TB	48.5 days	5 days	11.5 hours	69 minutes	1 week
10TB	3 months	9 days	23 hours	2 hours	1 week
50TB	1.4 years	48.5 days	5 days	11.5 hours	1 week
100TB	2.8 years	3 months	9 days	23 hours	1 week
500TB	14 years	1.4 years	48.5 days	5 days	1 week
1PB	28 years	2.8 years	3 months	9 days	2 weeks

Table 6-6 Comparison of Wired Data Transport with Offline Data Transfer Service

2. Data Transfer Appliances are Oracle-owned equipment capable of storing up to 150TB of data but are not available in all regions. Oracle ships the appliance to you. You transfer your data onto the appliance and send it back to Oracle.
3. The default Data Transfer Disk option entails that you purchase hard drives, which are returned once the data has been uploaded. The Disk option is available in all regions. Select Create Transfer Job.
4. When using the disk option, determine the storage required and attach a hard disk drive (HDD) to a host with access to the data to be transferred.
5. Download and use the Data Transfer Utility (DTU) to create an encrypted transfer disk.
6. Copy data to be transferred to the hard drives to the mount point created by the DTU.
7. Generate a Manifest file to create an inventory of all files to be transferred. A Dry Run report may be generated to review the transfer results to ensure there are no duplicate files or naming collision issues.
8. Use the DTU to lock the transfer disk. This step unmounts the disk and deletes the encryption passphrase from the host.
9. If additional HDDs are required, repeat the previous steps after attaching the HDD to the host.
10. The OCI console or DTU may be used to create a transfer package which consists of one or more transfer disks created by DTU. Figure 6-14 shows a Data Transfer Job in the OCI console.
11. Initiate the shipment of the package. Once the shipment is received by Oracle, the data is uploaded to your designated object storage bucket, before the HDDs are returned to you.

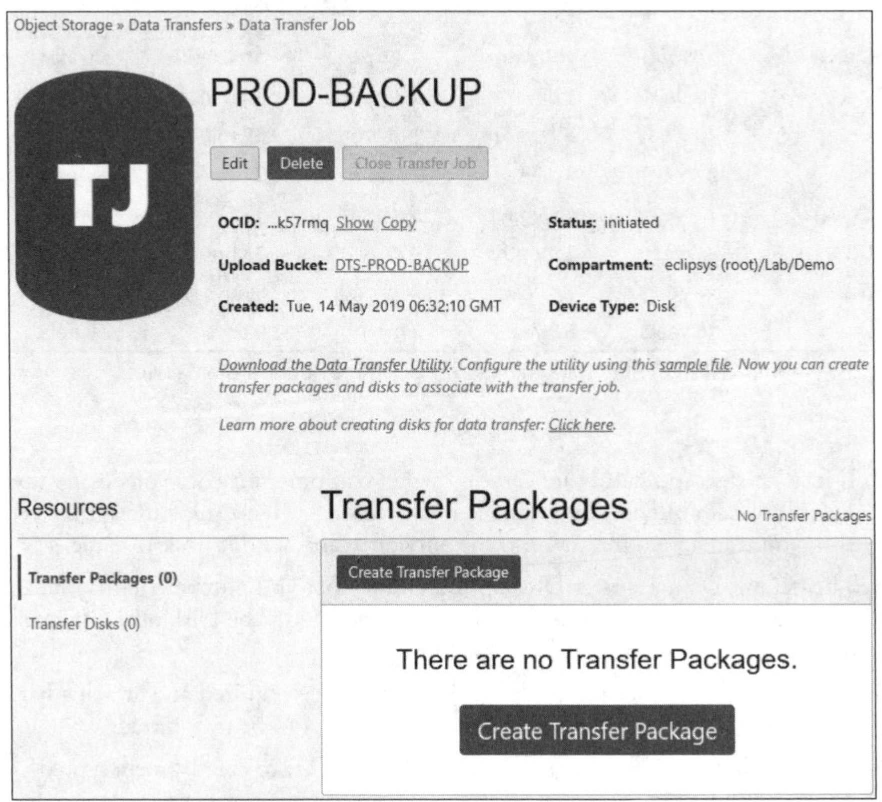

Figure 6-14 Create a transfer job to use offline data transfer service.

Approaches to Migration

The conversation now turns to determining which migration method is best suited for moving your source databases to target databases hosted on Oracle Cloud. While you may provision OCI infrastructure to install and host a database using traditional on-premises methods, you do not benefit from the tooling and automation offered for databases on DBCS. The converse of this is that you are not restricted by the limitations of DBCS. This section focuses on migrating to DBCS, ExaCS, ATP, and ADW. The following are the primary factors that inform the migration approach:

- **Source database version** Only 11.2.0.4 and later versions of Oracle databases are supported on DBCS. Generally, the later the version of the source database, the wider the choice of migration options.
- **Special one-off patches** If your database requires any specialty patches ("one-off" patches), this may prevent the use of DBCS.

- **Source database platform** DBCS infrastructure resides on x86 servers supporting a byte ordering system known as little-endian. Platforms such as Solaris on Sparc and AIX on IBM Power use a big-endian byte order. When migrating big-endian platforms to DBCS, a byte order conversion is required, either on the source or target environment.
- **Source database size** It may take an unacceptably long time to migrate extremely large databases over networks, especially when network conditions are poor and FastConnect options are limited. OCI provides a free data transfer service that may solve this problem. Smaller databases lend themselves to network-based migration techniques.
- **Database options** You may have EE licenses on premises with the RAC option. If you plan to implement RAC on OCI, an EE-EP license is required. If you end up using an EE-EP license for your DBCS database, you may implicitly acquire additional options that should be factored into your migration strategy. EE-EP includes many powerful software options that may be used to reduce storage and improve performance and availability.
- **Source database character sets** Not all database character sets are available on DBCS. Incompatible character sets may limit your migration options.
- **Source database block size** All DBCS databases use a standard 8K default block size. Migrating databases with non-8K default block sizes may limit your migration options.
- **Multitenancy** The option to use a single container database (CDB), with multiple pluggable databases (PDB), has been available since database version 12c and is a separately licensable option on-premises if your CDB has more than one tenant (PDB). When migrating to DBCS on VM, you may want to consider using the multitenant option (available with EE-HP and EE-EP) to host multiple databases (PDBs), as DBCS on VM only supports a single database (which could be a CDB) in a single Oracle Home.

CAUTION Oracle DBA knowledge is required when performing migrations. The migration methods discussion assumes the reader is familiar with Data Pump, RMAN, PDBs, SQL Developer, and SQL*Loader.

Database migrations usually occur within a framework of competing objectives:

- **Cost** Often the single largest determinant of the migration strategy. While using change data capture and logical replication solutions may provide zero downtime migrations, these come with a hefty price tag that may be difficult to justify for migrating a low-impact database where long migration windows are possible.
- **Complexity** Simple is usually better. To avoid costs and sometimes increase migration speeds, custom scripts and tweaks may be introduced, increasing non-standardization, introducing more room for error, and requiring more testing.

- **Speed** Fastest is usually expensive. See the earlier connectivity discussion. High-speed online data transport solutions may be used to reduce migration times but are usually more costly.
- **Reliability** To migrate many databases in what is known as "lift and shift" migrations, it is common practice to cluster source database systems with similar characteristics and build reusable templates or recipes. Reliability is increased when tasks are repeatable with predictable outcomes. Introduce some automation and you may improve reliability. Go too far and you tip the scales and complexity begins to damage reliability.
- **Availability** When migrating non-production databases, maintenance windows tend to be longer since more downtime is tolerated than for production databases. Migration strategies that reduce or completely eliminate downtime increase availability of systems being migrated but are usually costly and complex.

There are many Oracle and third-party tools and solutions that may be used to migrate Oracle databases to DBCS. It is prudent to balance the often-competing objectives listed earlier to find an appropriate migration strategy for your databases. The tools and techniques discussed in the material that follows are a subset of the Oracle toolset and are well suited for migrating Oracle databases across a wide spectrum of differences. Some techniques and tools are version agnostic, while others have strict version and platform requirements.

Database migration to support cloud adoption is an area of constant innovation. Oracle is aggressively updating its tooling and automation to drive adoption of DBCS and OCI. Instead of focusing only on what is currently supported and automated, this section takes a broader view and discusses migration concepts. Implementation steps using each approach are varied and regularly updated. A presentation of the primary techniques is provided within the context that the detailed implementation steps are evolving.

Oracle automated migration solutions may be grouped into the following categories: Zero Downtime Migration (ZDM), Maximum Availability Architecture (MAA), Data Transfer Service (discussed earlier), SQL Developer, RMAN, Data Pump, Plug/Unplug, and Remote Cloning.

- Zero Downtime Migration (ZDM) makes use of logical replication tools such as Oracle GoldenGate or Active Data Guard to minimize downtime, achieving near-zero actual downtime during migration.
- Maximum Availability Architecture (MAA) is composed of several high-availability tools and approaches, including a simple Data Guard migration as well as an advanced migration approach that performs an upgrade, as well as a TDE conversion from both on-premises and AWS EC2 sources. The MAA solution also includes cross-platform DB migration using the Zero Data Loss Recovery Appliance (ZDLRA), which supports minimal downtime while migrating across platform endianness. GoldenGate may be used to migrate to ADW and ATP with zero downtime.

- Oracle SQL Developer is a freely downloadable, feature-rich, integrated development environment that supports SQL and PL/SQL development, database management, and a powerful wizard-driven migration platform geared to move Oracle databases and an increasing number of third-party databases to Oracle Cloud databases.
- Data Pump supports the export and import of data out of and into Oracle databases. Except for network mode Data Pump, exported data is unloaded from your Oracle tables into dump files. Dump files may be imported into any Oracle target database. The destination database may even be the source database if you wish to restore a table to previous time or create a new table or schema based on the contents of an export dump file. Data Pump is commonly used as an additional logical backup mechanism and individual objects are easily restored in case of any user errors. Data Pump evolved from the legacy Oracle export and import utilities, which are still available, and is scalable and resilient and supports many data types and parallel loading and unloading. You may export your on-premises database schemas using a specific SCN to create a consistent export backup, copy into object storage, and import into any existing DBCS or ATP or ADW database. For DBCS databases, the export dump files could additionally be placed on the DB node file system or even into the FRA and ASM storage.
- RMAN full backups of source databases may be restored on target cloud databases. Iterative incremental backups of the primary and restores and recovery on the target may be used to considerably reduce migration downtimes. RMAN forms the basis for duplicating databases from active databases or backups as well as for cross-platform transportable tablespace backup sets and PDBs and transportable tablespaces when used with Data Pump for handling metadata exports and imports.
- Oracle Cloud multitenant target databases (12c and later) support two migration procedures known as Unplug/Plug and remote cloning. These are further differentiated into Unplug/Plug for PDBs or non-CDB and remote cloning for PDBs and non-CDBs.
- Unplug/Plug for PDBs involves unplugging a source PDB from its parent container and plugging it into a cloud-based CDB. A non-CDB source database may also be plugged into a cloud-based CDB as a new PDB.
- Remote cloning refers to migrating a PDB or non-CDB to a target CDB over the network.

NOTE Exadata Cloud at Customer (ExaCC) is mentioned in this chapter as a cloud migration target using the Oracle recommended solutions but this hybrid cloud on-premises solution is beyond the scope of this book. In a nutshell, an ExaCC is based on an Exadata engineered system with a control plane that runs software that abstracts the lower-level machine infrastructure and limits user interaction with the machine to APIs and a cloud UI. The infrastructure is also supported by Oracle Cloud operations support.

Solution	Source DB	Target DB
ZDM	CDB/PDB ≥ 12c Non-CDB ≥ 11g	DB ≥ 11g on: DBCS VMs ExaCS, ExaCC
MAA Data Pump	CDB/PDB ≥ 12c Non-CDB ≥ 11g Oracle DB on AWS EC2	DB ≥ 11g on: DBCS VMs and Bare Metal ExaCS, ExaCC ATP, ADW
SQL Developer	CDB/PDB ≥ 12c Non-CDB ≥ 11g AWS RDS AWS Redshift	DB ≥ 11g on: DBCS VMs and Bare Metal ExaCS, ExaCC ATP, ADW
RMAN Remote Cloning	CDB/PDB ≥ 12c Non-CDB ≥ 11g Oracle DB on AWS EC2	DB ≥ 11g on: DBCS VMs and Bare Metal ExaCS, ExaCC
Unplug/Plug	CDB/PDB ≥ 12c Non-CDB ≥ 11g Oracle DB on AWS EC2	DB ≥ 12c on: DBCS VMs and Bare Metal ExaCS, ExaCC

Table 6-7 Migration Solutions and Applicable Source and Target Versions and Systems

These migration solutions are appropriate under different and sometimes overlapping circumstances. Table 6-7 outlines these migration solutions appropriate for moving a source database to a target database system.

For example, if you have an 11.2.0.4 production database on AIX on-premises and you wish to migrate it to an Exadata cloud service database, you could use several of these solutions. Data Guard is not an option because there is no AIX on Oracle Cloud. ZDM is possible with GoldenGate, which does require additional software licenses. SQL Developer is an option, but for production databases, especially very large databases, there may be faster options that will reduce downtimes. Data Pump is an option, but again may take a long time, which leads to long migration windows. RMAN is probably a good solution, if GoldenGate is unavailable, as it supports cross-platform conversion and may be used to minimize the migration downtime window.

You may alternatively use any number of tools and techniques to migrate a subset or your entire database to an Oracle Cloud system. The following topics describe several tools and techniques at a conceptual level. These approaches are not exhaustive and represent a subset of available migration options.

SQL*Loader

SQL*Loader is an Oracle utility used to load data in external formatted files into a database. Data from the source system is extracted into flat files. A SQL*Loader control file is configured to specify the source flat files and mappings between flat file data and pre-existing schema tables and columns. SQL*Loader, also known as a bulk loader, uses rules and mappings specified in the control file to read flat files and write the data into database objects. Rows not conforming with the rules are placed in either discard files or bad files (errors were encountered while trying to load these rows).

SQL*Loader prerequisites include the following:

- Data in an external text file to be loaded must be formatted consistently.
- Target tables must be in place before the data loading begins.

Pros include the following:

- Data source can be any system where text may be extracted.
- No constraints on source and target Oracle software versions.
- Supports direct-path loading for faster row inserts.
- Sophisticated control file specification language supports a wide variety of input file layouts.

Cons include the following:

- Bulk loading with SQL*Loader effectively rebuilds all tables.
- Migration durations may be lengthy.
- Relational constraints and indexes must be enforced and built post loading.
- Usually unsuitable if source system continues to process data changes during the migration.

Export and Import

Although, the Oracle export and import utilities have been available from the early versions of Oracle, these legacy tools are still widely used more than 30 years after their introduction. Each database installation, regardless of the version, contains the exp and imp binary executable programs. Export is used to unload data, which includes tables, indexes, stored procedures, grants, and most database objects into a proprietary formatted dump file that is readable by the Import utility to load all or subsets of the dump file into an Oracle database.

Like SQL*Loader, these legacy utilities have their place, allowing the migration of older database systems to Oracle Cloud. For example, instead of upgrading an old Oracle 7.3.4 database running on outdated, outmoded, and possibly failing equipment to a later version, through multiple versions, to end up with an 11.2.0.4 database as a source for migration, it may be much simpler to export the required schemas and objects, transfer the dump file to your cloud database, and import the required objects into a new shiny database.

Pros include the following:

- Most database objects can be exported, so tables, constraints, indexes, grants, stored procedures, database links, and their dependent objects can be easily migrated.

- All Oracle databases have these utilities, ensuring wide compatibility and unlimited version migration potential.
- You may export the entire database (full), one or more schemas (owner), or a specific table and optionally choose the dump file to be compressed or even span multiple files of a certain volume size.
- Utilities may be driven through a parameter file, run interactively, or scripted.
- Dump files are platform-independent.

Cons include the following:

- These utilities have been deprecated since version 11g so no new feature enhancements are being added, but they are backward compatible so the 18c import utility can read a dump file exported from an Oracle 7 database using that server's version of the export utility.
- Not all data types may be exported—for example, tables with long and raw (pre-blob) columns cannot be exported using exp.
- Migration durations may be lengthy because the utilities were not designed to efficiently process very large volumes so performance does not scale very well.
- Usually unsuitable if the source system continues to process data changes during the migration.

Data Guard

Data Guard in DBCS is discussed earlier in this chapter. This discussion describes a scenario using Data Guard physical standby databases to migrate an on-premises database to DBCS. Remember that the primary and standby databases must be on the same version of the database software with the same platform endianness.

- Configure your VCN to connect to the network where the source database is located.
- Create a backup of the source database and copy or ship it to an OCI object storage bucket.
- Create a new DBCS system with the same database name as the source database and shape and drop the database that is automatically created using DBCA, thereby preserving the Oracle Home.
- Register the backup that was copied to object storage and restore the backup to instantiate the standby database.
- Configure the network parameters and test that logs are being shipped between the primary and standby databases.
- Switchover, or role transition to activate the cloud database in the primary role.

RMAN

RMAN offers many options for migration, including the following:

- **Cross-platform Transportable PDB** A 12c or later PDB on an endian and character set compatible source system may be easily migrated to a PDB on an existing DBCS deployment using this method. You have to unplug the source PDB to generate an XML file with the datafile metadata and use the RMAN command: `backup for transport pluggable database`. Both the XML file and backup set must be securely copied to the DBCS compute node where the RMAN `restore all foreign datafiles` command extracts the datafiles. The SQL command `create pluggable database` creates a new PDB on DBCS ready to be opened.
- **Cross-platform Transportable Tablespace Backup Sets** Tablespaces from a 12c or later database on an endian and character set compatible source system may be easily migrated to an existing DBCS deployment using this method. The user tablespaces on the source databases must be placed in read-only mode before an RMAN tablespace backup is taken with the TO PLATFORM or FOR TRANSPORT clause along with the DATAPUMP clause to create a backupset and export dump file that must be securely copied to the DBCS compute node. The target DBCS system must be prepared by creating schemas required by objects from the tablespaces that were exported before using RMAN to restore the backupset with the foreign file specification clause.
- **Transportable Tablespace with Data Pump** Create a transportable tablespace set using the RMAN command, `transport tablespace <tablespaces> tablespace destination '/dest' auxiliary destination '/auxdest'`, which must be securely copied to the DBCS compute node. The target environment may require further preparations by creating schemas required by objects from the tablespaces that were exported before using the Data Pump import command with the TRANSPORT_DATAFILES option to import the source data.

Data Pump

The Data Pump utilities are a modernized replacement of the venerable Export (exp) and Import utilities (imp) and was introduced in version 10g. Data Pump utilities Export (expdp) and Import (impdp) are very powerful, supporting exports and imports of entire databases, schemas, and objects, in addition to providing the backbone driver for external tables, supporting network mode data transfer as well as supporting transportable tablespaces and transportable databases. Dump files are platform-independent, support encryption and compression, and may contain data, metadata, or both content types. The utilities are architected to be resilient, supporting interruption and continuation of tasks, very large data volumes, and sophisticated logging features. Both imports and exports may be done in parallel to speed up migration times.

Data Pump offers several migration options, including the following:

- **Full export and import** Source databases may be easily exported and imported into target databases. Dump files are platform-independent so an 11.2.0.3 database on AIX could be exported with Data Pump and imported into a target database on Linux using version 18c.
- **Schema and object export and import** Schemas and even specific objects may be exported and potentially be remapped into different schemas during import.
- **Network mode export and import** This is a particularly powerful mechanism that uses database links to export data from one database and import into another without creating dump files.
- **Transportable tablespaces** Entire tablespaces are exported in one go. The mechanics involve setting the source tablespaces to read-only mode, exporting some metadata with Data Pump, securely copying the datafiles to the compatible (little endian) target database, setting the source tablespaces back to read-write mode, and importing the metadata dump file into the target database. This approach is much faster than exporting all your source objects in from tablespaces and then importing them because you are physically copying the underlying datafiles to a new database.
- **Full Transportable** This technique works very much like transportable tablespaces but instead of transporting a subset of the tablespaces, all user tablespaces are exported from the source database, datafiles are securely copied, and the tablespaces are imported into the target. Full Transportable was designed with 12c target databases, including PDBs, in mind and is a fast, powerful method for migrating endian-compatible databases.

Multitenant Migration Approaches

The multitenant option allows several novel approaches to migrate 12c or higher PDBs and non-CDBs to 12c or higher PDB targets in the Cloud. These migration techniques leverage the architectural segregation of administration and user tablespaces in multitenant databases. Source and target platforms must be endian compatible (little endian) and have compatible character sets.

- **Unplugging and plugging a PDB** Close and unplug the source PDB, generating an XML metadata file. Securely copy the datafiles to be plugged into the target CDB as well as the XML file to a compute node of the target system. Create a new PDB in the target CDB by referencing the source PDB files.
- **Unplugging and plugging a non-CDB** Set the source non-CDB to read-only mode and generate an XML metadata file using the DBMS_PDB.DESCRIBE procedure. Securely copy the datafiles to be plugged into the target CDB, as well as the XML file to a compute node of the target system. Create a new PDB in the target CDB by referencing the source PDB files. Execute the noncdb_to_pdb.sql script to clean up the SYSTEM tablespace of the new PDB.

- **Cloning a remote PDB or non-CDB** This method conceptually works almost identically to the previous two techniques, but instead of securely copying datafiles to the target, data is transferred using a database link between the source and target databases. Once the prerequisites are in place, the following SQL statement is all that is required to create a clone PDB pdbclone from the remote source PDB or non-CDB dbsrc:

```
create pluggable database pdbclone from dbsrc@dblink2dbsrc;
```

SQL Developer

SQL Developer is in a state of constant evolution with many recent features geared toward Oracle Cloud adoption. This is evident from the ease of connecting to Oracle ATP, ADW, DBCS, and other third-party databases both in the Cloud and on-premises. Having a single tool with simultaneous connectivity to multiple databases is very handy for data migration. SQL Developer has a multitude of features and wizards geared toward migration including tools that enable you to create Data Pump exports and even automate script generation by capturing changes from several non-Oracle databases to reduce the migration effort. SQL Developer also has specific cloud migration wizards that include the following:

- **AWS Redshift to ADW Cloud** The AWS Redshift to ADW Cloud database migration tool connects to both your Redshift and ADW databases and simplifies the migration process.
- **SQL Developer Carts** The familiar online shopping cart concept is available in SQL Developer, providing a framework to pick and choose objects from your databases and add these to a cart. SQL Developer connections must be established to all source databases. The cart is an XML file with references to the source objects. You may have many carts. When you are ready to migrate the contents of a cart, you choose whether DDL or data or both are to be exported for each object in the cart, and specify export options, an export file data format and an output file or file set. The output files are either database object metadata or actual row data in scripts that may be run on the target database to complete the migration.

A popular data export format, as shown in Figure 6-15, generates INSERT statements for the objects in the cart chosen for data export. These options also generate the DDL required for the cart objects. The output SQL script may be run against a target database, where tables are created, rows are inserted, constraints are enforced, and referential integrity is maintained with minimal DBA effort. Clearly, however, this is an option that is only practical for very small databases.

Another interesting SQL Developer cart export format is loader, which generates a set of SQL*Loader-compatible control files and data files. These may be securely copied to a target database compute node, where SQL*Loader may be invoked to load the exported data.

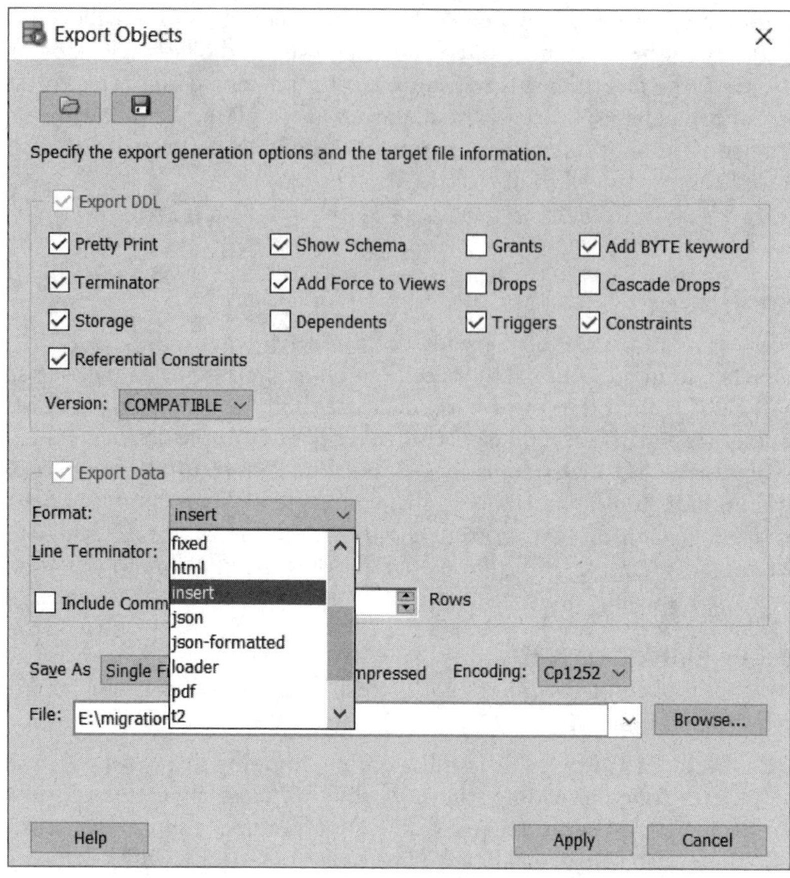

Figure 6-15 Exporting SQL Developer cart objects for migration

Chapter Review

This chapter discussed various formats for using Oracle databases on OCI. Creating and managing databases using DBCS exposed you to the automation Oracle has developed to simplify administration on VM, bare metal, and Exadata cloud services. Typically time-consuming tasks such as setting up RAC and Data Guard or configuring backups are available as API commands or a few clicks in the console.

Oracle database processor-based and NUP metrics were introduced along with the license cost implications when using DBCS compared to other platforms. An in-depth discussion of the RAC and Data Guard high availability features was also provided.

Autonomous databases are a game-changing offering. ADBs were explored indicating that ATP and ADW are just differently configured ADBs. While there are some limitations and restrictions with ADBs, there are very compelling reasons for adopting ADB, especially the CPU core and storage scaling as well as the AI-driven automations.

Migrating databases to the Cloud is a complex topic and a significant chunk of this chapter is dedicated to this topic. Connectivity options as well as the data transfer service were discussed before a general discussion of approaches to migration was undertaken. Source database properties are a key determinant of the migration strategy. Source and target software versions, platform endianness, and database service-level objectives further inform the approach taken when planning a migration.

The chapter concluded with a discussion of several cloud migration approaches, including legacy utilities such as SQL*Loader and the original Oracle Export and Import tools that were discussed to showcase available options for moving off legacy Oracle databases. Modern approaches to database migration using Data Guard, RMAN, Data Pump, unplugging and plugging PDBs and non-CDBs as well as using remote PDB cloning techniques were also discussed. An exploration of several SQL Developer tools rounded off the migration conversation. Oracle is constantly innovating to drive Cloud adoption, so stay updated with the latest automated migration solutions.

With your network, compute instances, storage options, and databases in place, you are ready to automate the deployment of the infrastructure components available in OCI, which is the subject of Chapter 7.

Questions

1. List the Oracle Cloud database solutions that support CPU core and storage scaling.
   - **A.** DBCS–VM
   - **B.** ExaCS
   - **C.** ADB
   - **D.** DBCS–Bare metal
2. List the Oracle Cloud database solutions that support storage scaling.
   - **A.** DBCS–VM
   - **B.** ExaCS
   - **C.** ADB
   - **D.** DBCS–Bare metal
3. List the Oracle Cloud database solutions that include Transparent Data Encryption (TDE).
   - **A.** DBCS–VM
   - **B.** ExaCS
   - **C.** ADB
   - **D.** DBCS–Bare metal

4. When configuring a DB using Exadata Cloud Service, you may elect to configure a SPARSE disk group. Choose any statements that are true about configuring a SPARSE disk group.
   A. SPARSE disk groups are mandatory.
   B. SPARSE disk groups reduce available storage for database files.
   C. SPARSE disk groups enable snapshot standby databases.
   D. SPARSE disk groups may be used for Exadata snapshot databases.
5. When configuring a DB using Exadata Cloud Service, you may elect to store backups in the FRA on disk. Which statement is true regarding usable storage?
   A. Space allocated for backups in the FRA has no impact on storage available for database files.
   B. ExaCS backups are stored in an ACFS volume.
   C. Space allocated for backups in the FRA reduces the space available for the DATA disk group.
   D. ExaCS backups are stored in object storage.
6. Which of the following statements are true?
   A. Oracle database licenses are free in OCI.
   B. On-premises Oracle database licenses may be used on OCI.
   C. Oracle database licenses are not required on Oracle Cloud.
   D. DBCS and ADB systems may be procured with a license-included option.
7. Which is not a valid Data Guard configuration mode?
   A. Maximum Performance
   B. Maximum Security
   C. Maximum Protection
   D. Maximum Availability
8. Which of the following statements are true?
   A. A two-node RAC database consists of two copies of the database files.
   B. A two-node RAC database consists of one shared copy of the database files.
   C. A two-node RAC Data Guarded database consists of two copies of the database files.
   D. A two-node RAC Data Guarded database consists of four copies of the database files.

9. Which of the following statements is false?
   A. ATP and ADW are types of autonomous databases.
   B. ADBs use DB Resource Manager for defining differentiated services.
   C. TPURGENT and TP are services available only for ADW.
   D. TPURGENT and TP are services available only for ATP.
10. Which benefits are associated with autonomous databases?
   A. Automatic Migration
   B. Automatic Indexing
   C. Automatic Tuning
   D. Automatic Backups

Answers

1. **C.** CPU and storage may be scaled up on autonomous databases.
2. **A, C.** Storage may be scaled up and down on autonomous databases but scaled up on DBCS on VM.
3. **A, B, C, D.** Transparent Data Encryption (TDE) is a feature of the Advanced Security option. However, on OCI, all database editions include TDE.
4. **B, D.** While configuring SPARSE disk groups does reduce the storage available for database files, they are required for hosting Exadata snapshot databases.
5. **C.** Usable storage for database files on Exadata is impacted by whether you choose to keep backups on the storage.
6. **B, D.** The practice of using on-premises Oracle database licenses in the Cloud is known as "Bring Your Own License" or BYOL. License-included and BYOL are the two methods for licensing Oracle databases in the Cloud.
7. **B.** Data Guard may be configured in Maximum Performance, Availability, and Protection modes.
8. **B, C.** RAC databases share one copy of the database files. Data Guarded databases have two sets, one for the primary and another for the standby.
9. **C.** TPURGENT and TP are services available only for ATP.
10. **B, C, D.** Automatic Indexing, Tuning, and Backups are benefits associated with autonomous databases.

CHAPTER 7

Automation Tools

In this chapter, you will learn how to

- Install and use Oracle Cloud Infrastructure CLI
- Install, configure, and use Terraform

While most OCI tasks may be performed through the OCI console, the real power of cloud infrastructure computing is realized through automation tools that allow you to deploy Infrastructure as Code (IaC). Treating infrastructure as code changes the deployment paradigm by supporting massive, yet consistent, infrastructure architectures to be programmatically deployed.

OCI is accessed through REST APIs. Infrastructure orchestration is based on calling these APIs to create, update, or destroy OCI resources. The OCI web console, CLI, and SDKs interact with OCI resources through these APIs. The CLI and SDKs extend the functionality of the console by supporting scripting and programmatic interfaces to OCI. Additional developer tools provided by Oracle include a Toolkit for Eclipse and an HDFS connector for object storage. Several DevOps automation tools are provided, such as a Terraform provider and Ansible modules as well as many plugins for Chef Knife, Jenkins, and Grafana. These are just a few from a constantly evolving list. The taxonomy presented in Figure 7-1 shows several popular IaC tools categorized into tools for scripting, configuration management, templates, and infrastructure provisioning.

Terraform is a generic declarative tool designed by HashiCorp to provision infrastructure through code. Oracle provides a freely downloadable Terraform provider for OCI that exposes OCI services to Terraform. While many automation tools enable you to orchestrate infrastructure on OCI, this short chapter focuses on getting you started with using the OCI CLI and Terraform.

OCI CLI

The OCI CLI operates in a similar manner to many other Oracle command-line interfaces. It is simple and powerful and lends itself to easy integration into shell scripts. The CLI is based on Python and makes use of JSON input and output formats. The Python code is a wrapper around OCI REST APIs. OCI CLI commands call these APIs that

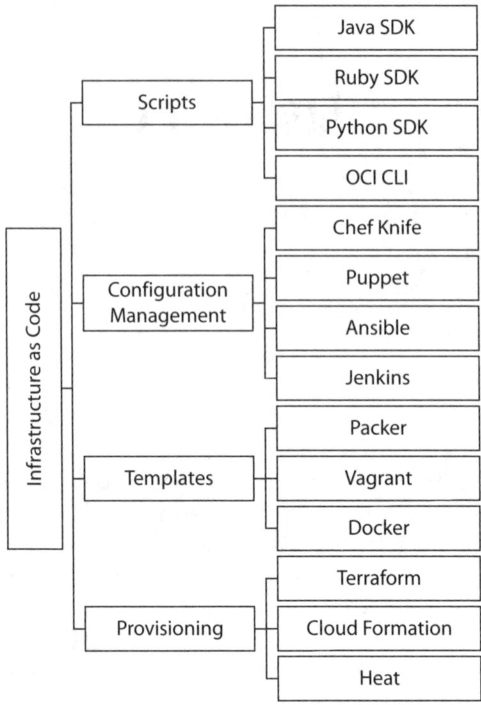

Figure 7-1 Popular groups of IaC tools

implement the required functionality. These are the same APIs called by the SDKs and the console.

Many examples throughout this book are illustrated using OCI CLI commands. In this section, you will install the OCI CLI and use it to interact with several OCI resources.

Install and Configure OCI CLI

The OCI CLI runs on Mac, Windows, and Linux machines and is built on Python. Refer to the relevant online documentation for updated installation instructions. The following prerequisites must be met before installing and configuring OCI CLI:

- An OCI account
- An OCI user with sufficient permissions
- An SSH key pair
- A compatible version of Python
- FIPS-validated libraries if FIPS compliance is required

The CLI may be installed automatically on Linux, Unix, and Mac OS with a single command, or you can perform a manual installation.

Automated Installation of the OCI CLI

Using the QuickStart installation script provided by Oracle is the simplest and quickest way to get started with the CLI. Refer to the online documentation for the latest installation procedure as this may vary slightly as the tool evolves.

Exercise 7-1: Install the OCI CLI Using the Quickstart Installation Script

In this exercise, you install the OCI CLI on Linux, Unix, or Mac OS using an installation script provided by Oracle. Your output may differ depending on your operating system and the packaging of the CLI at the time of installation.

1. Log on to the machine where the OCI CLI is to be installed. This may be your personal workstation or a shared OCI VM to be used for automation and orchestration. In this exercise, a VM with Oracle Linux 6.8 is used and the OCI CLI is installed by the Oracle user.
2. At the shell prompt, run the Quickstart installation script as per the documentation. At the time of this writing, the installation script is downloaded and executed through the bash command shell with the following command:

```
$ bash -c "$(curl -L https://raw.githubusercontent.com
/oracle/oci-cli/master/scripts/install/install.sh)"
```

3. The initial shell script is downloaded and the OCI CLI Installer is started in interactive mode. Provide responses to the installation script prompts. On Linux, for example, the script verifies prerequisites, such as a compatible version of Python and any other platform-specific packages like virtualenv, and downloads and installs missing dependencies.

```
System version of Python must be either a Python 2
version >= 2.7.5 or a Python 3 version >= 3.5.0.
Running install script.
python3 /tmp/oci_cli_install_tmp_4D1B
-- Verifying Python version.
-- Python version 3.6.0 okay.
```

4. You must provide directories where the install, `oci` executable, and OCI scripts must be placed.

```
===> In what directory would you like to place the install?
(leave blank to use '/home/oracle/lib/oracle-cli'):
-- Creating directory '/home/oracle/lib/oracle-cli'.
-- We will install at '/home/oracle/lib/oracle-cli'.
===> In what directory would you like to place the 'oci' executable?
(leave blank to use '/home/oracle/bin'):
-- The executable will be in '/home/oracle/bin'.
===> In what directory would you like to place the OCI scripts?
(leave blank to use '/home/oracle/bin/oci-cli-scripts'):
-- The scripts will be in '/home/oracle/bin/oci-cli-scripts'.
```

5. Once the packages are installed and built, you have the option to have the PATH environment variable updated in your profile to include the path to the `oci` executable, allowing the executable to be invoked without providing the full path. You are also given the option to enable shell/tab completion, which allows OCI commands to be autocompleted when you partially enter an OCI command and press the TAB key to complete the command. Respond with Y if you want these two options enabled.

```
===> Modify profile to update your $PATH and
 enable shell/tab completion now? (Y/n): Y
===> Enter a path to an rc file to update
(leave blank to use '/home/oracle/.bashrc'):
-- Backed up '/home/oracle/.bashrc' to
'/home/oracle/.bashrc.backup'
-- Tab completion set up complete.
```

6. If all goes well, the install script completes with the following message:

```
-- You can run this installation of the CLI with '/home/oracle/bin/oci'.
-- ** Run `exec -l $SHELL` to restart your shell. **
-- Installation successful.
-- Run the CLI with /home/oracle/bin/oci --help
```

Manual Installation of the OCI CLI

If you prefer to install the OCI CLI manually instead of using the Quickstart script, the steps vary depending on your platform. At a high level, the manual installation involves these steps:

1. Install a compatible version of Python. On Oracle Linux 7.3, for example, the following packages are required for Python and several additional components before installing the CLI.

```
yum install gcc libffi-devel python-devel openssl-devel
easy_install pip
```

2. Install and configure virtualenv, which is a virtual environment builder for isolating Python environments. If you choose to not use virtualenv, the system-wide Python execution environment is used and package conflicts may occur. On Linux, virtualenv is often packaged separately from Python and may be downloaded from GitHub or the Python Package Index (PyPI). The virtualenv environment may be installed using the following `pip` and `pip3` commands for Python 2 and Python 3 respectively.

```
pip install virtualenv
pip3 install virtualenv
```

3. Download the CLI from GitHub or PyPI and install using `pip`. For example, you can download and unzip oci-cli.zip from GitHub and install using the following:

```
pip install oci_cli-*-py2.py3-none-any.whl
```

You can check if the CLI is successfully installed by running the tool with the help option. This option describes the commands and capabilities of the OCI CLI tool. The output has been truncated for brevity.

```
$ oci -help
Usage: oci [OPTIONS] COMMAND [ARGS]...
  Oracle Cloud Infrastructure command line interface, with support for
  Audit, Block Volume, Compute, Database, IAM, Load Balancing, Networking,
  DNS, File Storage, Email Delivery and Object Storage Services.
  Most commands must specify a service, followed by a resource type and then
  an action. For example, to list users (where $T contains the OCID of the
  current tenant):
    oci iam user list --compartment-id $T
  Output is in JSON format.
```

Once the OCI CLI is installed it must be configured before use.

NOTE The OCI CLI is constantly being updated so it is good practice to regularly upgrade the CLI. You may use the Quickstart installation script to upgrade the CLI. During the script's execution, you are prompted to upgrade the CLI if a new version is available. You may then choose to overwrite the existing installation.

Configure the OCI CLI

Configuring the CLI includes saving the Oracle Cloud IDs (OCIDs) for your OCI user and tenancy as well as RSA key references in a configuration file that you create manually or let the CLI configuration process automatically create for you. A pair of RSA public and private keys is needed to authenticate your CLI user with OCI. You keep the private key safe and do not share or post publicly. You add the public key to your designated OCI user. This creates an API signing key. This process supports the OCI CLI user authentication. Once the configuration in complete, OCI CLI commands are run using the user and tenancy specified in the configuration file.

You may also use token-based authentication allowing users to authenticate sessions interactively without an API signing key. This section focuses on configuring the OCI CLI to use API signing keys.

Exercise 7-2: Configure OCI CLI

In this exercise, you will configure the OCI CLI on Linux, Unix, or Mac OS. Before you configure the OCI CLI, you will need the Oracle Cloud ID (OCID) values for both the OCI users and the tenancy.

1. Obtain the OCID for the username that will interact with OCI through the CLI. Connect to Oracle Cloud using the console. Navigate to Identity | Users and choose a username. Choose the Copy link next to OCID in the User Information section to copy the OCID to your clipboard. Paste this OCID in a safe location.

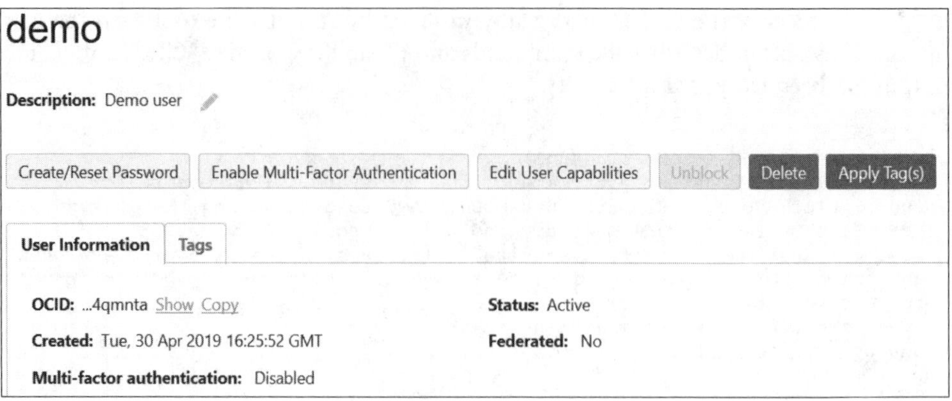

2. Obtain the OCID for the tenancy you will interact with through the CLI. Navigate to Administration | Tenancy Details and choose the Copy link next to OCID in the Tenancy Information section to copy the OCID to your clipboard. Paste this OCID in a safe location. Take note of the Home Region of your tenancy. In this example, the Home Region is us-ashburn-1.

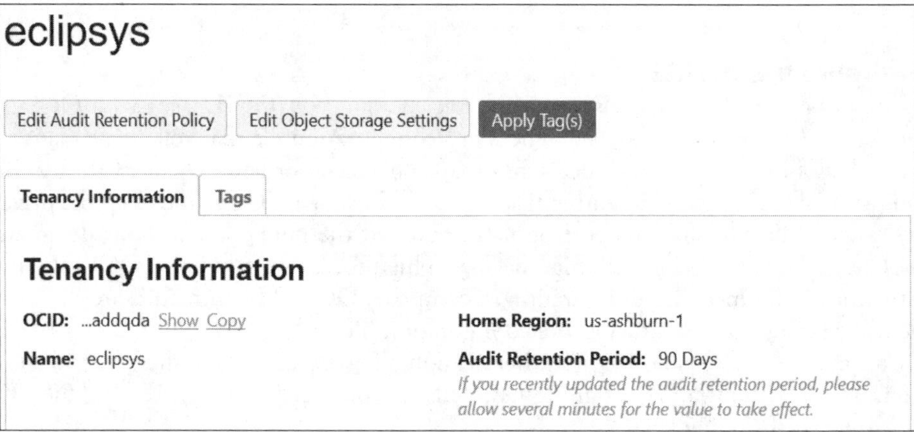

3. Log on to the machine as the user that installed the OCI CLI.
4. At the shell prompt, run the `oci setup config` command, which guides you through the setup of a valid CLI configuration file.

```
$ oci setup config
This command provides a walkthrough of creating a valid
CLI config file.
```

5. You are prompted to enter a location for the config file.

```
Enter a location for your config [/home/oracle/.oci/config]:
```

6. You are prompted for the user OCID and tenancy OCID and region.

```
Enter a user OCID: ocid1.user.oc1..4qmnta
Enter a tenancy OCID: ocid1.tenancy.oc1..addqda
Enter a region (e.g. ap-seoul-1, ap-tokyo-1, ca-toronto-1,
eu-frankfurt-1, uk-london-1, us-ashburn-1, us-gov-ashburn-1,
us-gov-chicago-1, us-gov-phoenix-1, us-langley-1, us-luke-1,
us-phoenix-1): us-ashburn-1
```

7. At this stage in the configuration, you may choose to provide your own RSA keys or to generate a new pair. Keys are then written to various locations you choose.

```
Do you want to generate a new RSA key pair? (If you decline you
will be asked to supply the path to an existing key.) [Y/n]: Y
Enter a directory for your keys to be created [/home/oracle/.oci]:
Enter a name for your key [oci_api_key]:
Public key written to: /home/oracle/.oci/oci_api_key_public.pem
Enter a passphrase for your private key (empty for no passphrase):
Repeat for confirmation:
Private key written to: /home/oracle/.oci/oci_api_key.pem
Fingerprint: 06:b3:07:59:2b:7a:
Do you want to write your passphrase to the config file?
(if not, you will need to supply it as an argument to the CLI) [y/N]: y
Config written to /home/oracle/.oci/config
```

8. The public key must be added to the OCI user. View the public key in a text editor and copy the contents to your clipboard. The key output has been truncated for brevity.

```
$ cat /home/oracle/.oci/oci_api_key_public.pem
-----BEGIN PUBLIC KEY-----
MIIBIjANBgkqhkiG9w0BAQEFAAOCAQ8AMIIBCgKCAQEAqupIAPy8MqKnbyVw51Dt...
-----END PUBLIC KEY-----
```

9. In the console, navigate to Identity | Users and choose your designated user. Scroll to the API Keys section and choose Add Public Key. Paste the public key referenced in the previous step and choose Add.

10. You should be all set to test the OCI CLI from your workstation. Run the `oci iam region list` command to report on all OCI regions available to you.

```
$ oci iam region list

{"data": [
 { "key": "BOM","name": "ap-mumbai-1"},
 { "key": "FRA","name": "eu-frankfurt-1"},
 { "key": "GRU","name": "sa-saopaulo-1"},
 { "key": "IAD","name": "us-ashburn-1"},
```

```
{ "key": "ICN","name": "ap-seoul-1"},
{ "key": "LHR","name": "uk-london-1"},
{ "key": "NRT","name": "ap-tokyo-1"},
{ "key": "PHX","name": "us-phoenix-1"},
{ "key": "SYD","name": "ap-sydney-1"},
{ "key": "YYZ","name": "ca-toronto-1"},
{ "key": "ZRH","name": "eu-zurich-1"}]}
```

Use OCI CLI

The previous exercise showed how the OCI CLI output is returned in JSON format. You may also create JSON format input files to pass to OCI CLI commands. This is beyond the scope of this book. The CLI output may alternatively be displayed in a tabular format by appending `--output table` to the command.

```
$ oci iam region list --output table
+-----+----------------+
| key | name           |
+-----+----------------+
| BOM | ap-mumbai-1    |
| FRA | eu-frankfurt-1 |
| GRU | sa-saopaulo-1  |
| IAD | us-ashburn-1   |
| ICN | ap-seoul-1     |
| LHR | uk-london-1    |
| NRT | ap-tokyo-1     |
| PHX | us-phoenix-1   |
| SYD | ap-sydney-1    |
| YYZ | ca-toronto-1   |
| ZRH | eu-zurich-1    |
+-----+----------------+
```

After configuring the CLI, the config file may include the following fields:

```
$ cat /home/oracle/.oci/config
[DEFAULT]
user=ocid1.user.oc1..4qmnta
fingerprint=06:b3:07:59:2b:7a
key_file=/home/oracle/.oci/oci_api_key.pem
tenancy=ocid1.tenancy.oc1..addqda
region=us-ashburn-1
pass_phrase=secret
```

You may generate a new RSA key pair and update the configuration file accordingly. Remember to add the new public key to the user profile through the console or through the CLI. The profile header [DEFAULT] in the configuration file refers to the default settings used whenever the CLI is invoked. You may add your preferred compartment or namespace as default values to avoid explicitly specifying these in CLI commands. You may also add other non-default profiles and use those associated key-value pairs by providing the `--profile` parameter to the `oci` command.

The CLI usage syntax is based on service, type, action, and options.

```
oci <service> <type> <action> <options>
```

Table 7-1 lists a subset of an ever-growing set of OCI services exposed to the CLI, including Block volume, Compute, and Database services. As OCI services are added, APIs to interact with these services are built and exposed to the CLI, SDKs, and other interfaces.

The following examples demonstrate the basic usage principles of the OCI CLI. Just type `oci` and press ENTER and the full usage manual page scrolls by. Drill into the different types of Networking Service CLI commands with `oci network`. If you are interested in the virtual cloud network (VCN) resource type, you need only issue the `oci network vcn` command to see the available actions to perform on this resource type.

```
$ oci network vcn
Usage: oci network vcn [OPTIONS] COMMAND [ARGS]...
A virtual cloud network (VCN). For more information, see
[Overview of the Networking Service]
Options:
  -?, -h, --help  For detailed help on any of these individual
commands, enter <command> --help.
Commands:
  create  Creates a new virtual cloud network (VCN).
  delete  Deletes the specified VCN.
  get     Gets the specified VCN's information.
  list    Lists the virtual cloud networks (VCNs) in...
  update  Updates the specified VCN.
```

Service	Description
announce	Announcements service
bv	Block volume service
ce	Container engine for Kubernetes
compute	Compute service
compute-management	Compute management service
db	Database service
dns	Domain Name Service
fs	File storage service
health-checks	Health checks
iam	Identity and Access Management service
lb	Load balancing
monitoring	Monitoring
network	Networking service
os	Object storage service
resource-manager	Resource manager
search	Search service
streaming	Streaming service

Table 7-1 Subset of OCI Services Accessible Through the CLI

The actions available through the `oci network vcn` command is this example are `create`, `delete`, `get`, `list`, and `update` and are a fairly consistent set of action commands available for most resource types. The `oci bv backup` command lists these same actions for backups through the Block volume service in addition to specific actions such as `copy` and `change-compartment`.

The options for individual commands vary and usually limit the scope of the command to a specific OCID or compartment. For example, the `oci network vcn list --compartment-id <compartment OCID>` command returns a JSON format listing of the VCNs in the specified compartment, assuming the CLI user has IAM permissions to list the VCNs.

```
$ oci network vcn list
  --compartment-id ocid1.compartment.oc1..4rdv4q
{"data": [
 {"cidr-block": "10.0.0.0/16",
  "compartment-id": "ocid1.compartment.oc1..4rdv4q",
  "default-dhcp-options-id": "ocid1.dhcpoptions.oc1.iad.2vz4l6a",
  "default-route-table-id": "ocid1.routetable.oc1.pghekq",
  "default-security-list-id": "ocid1.securitylist.oc1.iad.g54m4novfma",
  "display-name": "demoVCN",
  "dns-label": "demovcn",
  "id": "ocid1.vcn.oc1.iad. ye22ba",
  "lifecycle-state": "AVAILABLE",
  "vcn-domain-name": "demovcn.oraclevcn.com"}}
```

You may list all block volumes in an AD that belongs to a compartment with the following OCI CLI command:

```
$ oci bv volume list
--availability-domain fFkS:US-ASHBURN-AD-1
--compartment-id X |
egrep '(display-name)|(lifecycle-state)|(size-in-gbs)'
"display-name": "bv1",
"lifecycle-state": "AVAILABLE",
"size-in-gbs": 50,
```

Boot volumes in the same AD may be listed by querying the Block volume service with the following OCI CLI commands. Note the difference between the previous command and this command. Both call the Block volume service (oci bv) but block volumes use the bv api while boot volumes use the boot-volume api.

```
$ oci bv boot-volume list
--availability-domain fFkS:US-ASHBURN-AD-1
--compartment-id X |
egrep '(display-name)|(lifecycle-state)|(size-in-gbs)'
"display-name": "hercules (Boot Volume)",
"lifecycle-state": "AVAILABLE",
"size-in-gbs": 47,

"display-name": "web1 (Boot Volume)",
"lifecycle-state": "AVAILABLE",
"size-in-gbs": 47
```

Exercise 7-3: Use the OCI CLI to List Supported Oracle Databases

In this exercise, you create a block volume in the same AD as compute instance web1. If you completed all the exercises in Chapter 4, you should already have this compute instance.

1. Obtain the OCID of a compartment to which your CLI user has been granted at least read access. Sign in to the OCI console and navigate to Identity | Compartments and choose a compartment accessible to your CLI user. Copy the compartment OCID to your clipboard. You will need this OCID in the next step.

2. Log on to the machine as the user that installed the OCI CLI.
3. At the shell prompt, run the `oci db version list --output table --compartment-id` command, providing the compartment OCID.

```
$ oci db version list --output table
--compartment-id ocid1.compartment.oc1..rdv4q
+-----------------------------+--------------+----------+
| is-latest-for-major-version | supports-pdb | version  |
+-----------------------------+--------------+----------+
| True                        | False        | 11.2.0.4 |
| True                        | True         | 12.1.0.2 |
| True                        | True         | 12.2.0.1 |
| True                        | True         | 18.0.0.0 |
+-----------------------------+--------------+----------+
```

4. Your output may differ as new database versions are supported by the OCI DB service and older versions are deprecated.

You could architect and script the creation, management, and removal of infrastructure using the OCI CLI with great efficiency. Indeed, treating infrastructure as code (IaC) is the only feasible scalable model for future infrastructure management. The following section describes the creation, listing, and removal of a VCN using three simple OCI CLI commands. It is followed by a simple example of creating a VCN using a JSON formatted input file. It is likely that you will use the JSON input file approach for more complex and repetitive tasks. The following CLI command creates a network VCN in the specified compartment using the CIDR block 10.0.0.0/22. In this example, the CIDR range is a subset of the CIDR block allocated to the root compartment to which this compartment belongs. Navigating to Networking | Virtual Cloud Networks and choosing the appropriate compartment through the OCI console will list the newly created VCN.

```
$ oci network vcn create --cidr-block 10.0.0.0/22
--compartment-id ocid1.compartment.oc1..4rdv4q
{"data": {
 "cidr-block": "10.0.0.0/22",
 "compartment-id": "ocid1.compartment.oc1..4rdv4q",
 "default-dhcp-options-id": "ocid1.dhcpoptions.oc1.iad.dnhmq",
 "default-route-table-id": "ocid1.routetable.oc1.iad.hrkrq",
 "default-security-list-id": "ocid1.securitylist.oc1.iad.gf3p3a",
 "display-name": "vcn20190701163235",
    "id": "ocid1.vcn.oc1.iad.lczcq",
    "lifecycle-state": "AVAILABLE"}}
```

You may alternatively list the VCNs in the compartment using the following:

```
$ oci network vcn list --compartment-id ocid1.compartment.oc1..rdv4q
```

When the VCN is no longer needed, it may be easily deleted using the following:

```
$ oci network vcn delete --vcn-id ocid1.vcn.oc1.iad.lczcq
Are you sure you want to delete this resource? [y/N]: y
```

As mentioned previously, the CLI output is in JSON format. You may also pass commands to the CLI using a JSON input file that is in a specific format. The CLI provides the `--generate-full-command-json-input` option to generate the JSON code to use as input for CLI commands. The following command generates the JSON code to use as input for the CLI to create a VCN.

```
$ oci network vcn create --generate-full-command-json-input
{ "cidrBlock": "string",
  "compartmentId": "string",
  "definedTags":
   {"string1": {"string1": {"string1": "string","string2": "string"},
     "string2": {"string1": "string","string2": "string"}},
    "string2": {"string1": {"string1": "string","string2": "string"},
     "string2": {"string1": "string","string2": "string"}}},
  "displayName": "string",
  "dnsLabel": "string",
  "freeformTags": {"string1": "string","string2": "string"},
  "maxWaitSeconds": 0,
  "waitForState": "PROVISIONING|AVAILABLE|TERMINATING|TERMINATED",
  "waitIntervalSeconds": 0}
```

Many of these variables are optional. For this example, a JSON file is created with these name-value pairs:

```
$ cat demovcn1.json
{
  "cidrBlock": "10.0.0.0/22",
  "compartmentId": "ocid1.compartment.oc1..rdv4q",
  "displayName": "demovcn1",
  "dnsLabel": "demovcn1.oraclevcn.com"
}
```

This input file is provided to the CLI using the `--from-json file` option:

```
[oracle@sid ~]$ oci network vcn create --from-json file://demovcn1.json
{"data": {"cidr-block": "10.0.0.0/22",
"compartment-id": "ocid1.compartment.oc1..rdv4q",
    "default-dhcp-options-id": "ocid1.dhcpoptions.oc1.iad.hoena",
    "default-route-table-id": "ocid1.routetable.oc1.iad.nu3ja",
    "default-security-list-id": "ocid1.securitylist.oc1.iad.d44xhq",
    "display-name": "demovcn1",
    "dns-label": "demovcn1",
    "id": "ocid1.vcn.oc1.iad.k5yyq",
    "lifecycle-state": "AVAILABLE",
    "vcn-domain-name": "demovcn1.oraclevcn.com"},"etag": "ff3f0e24"}
```

Terraform

Terraform is a declarative tool used to automate the full infrastructure lifecycle from the provision stage to updates and maintenance to the destroy stage. Terraform is developed by HashiCorp and is integrated into OCI through the Terraform provider for OCI. Terraform uses text configuration files with HashiCorp Configuration Language (HCL), which is simple to understand and edit, providing a self-documenting infrastructure provisioning solution. Terraform can also read JSON configurations. HCL code is used to specify infrastructure provisioning directives that are agnostic. Terraform files may be used by multiple cloud and on-premises infrastructure providers. The Terraform provider for OCI handles the interaction between Terraform and OCI, allowing OCI credentials to be configured, and translates the Terraform directives into OCI API calls, effectively exposing OCI resources to Terraform code.

Follow these steps to get started using Terraform on OCI:

1. Download and install Terraform and the provider for OCI.
2. Collect OCIDs and API and SSH keys for Terraform.
3. Prepare your provisioning environment for Terraform.
4. Create terraform configuration files.
5. Use Terraform commands such as `plan`, `graph`, `apply`, and `refresh`.
6. Use the Terraform `destroy` command to purge resources no longer required.

This section is designed to get you started with Terraform and the provider for OCI. It is an introduction and in no way a comprehensive treatment of the subject.

Install and Configure Terraform and the Provider for OCI

Terraform may be installed on a variety of platforms. When using Windows, it is useful to have access to a bash shell through a tool like Git-bash. Several packages need to be managed during the installation and, on Windows, tools like the Chocolately package manager ease this process. Basic knowledge of git is useful as well to clone the Terraform OCI provider repository. For more details on how to set up Terraform and the OCI provider on Windows, refer to the online documentation.

Exercise 7-4: Install and Configure Terraform and the Provider for OCI on Linux

In this exercise, you will download and install both Terraform and the Terraform provider for OCI on a Linux host. Several prerequisites are required for setting up the Terraform provider for OCI. These include the OCIDs for the tenancy and an OCI user whose account is used for the OCI interaction through Terraform on your host. A PEM format private key and public key are required as well.

1. You may reuse an existing PEM key pair or generate a new pair of keys on your Linux host using the following commands:

```
$ openssl genrsa -out ~/.oci/ocidemo_api_key.pem 2048
Generating RSA private key, 2048 bit long modulus
$ ls -l  ~/.oci/ocidemo_api_key.pem
-rw-rw-r--. 1 opc opc /home/opc/.oci/ocidemo_api_key.pem
$ chmod go-rwx  ~/.oci/ocidemo_api_key.pem
$ ls -l  ~/.oci/ocidemo_api_key.pem
-rw-------. 1 opc opc /home/opc/.oci/ocidemo_api_key.pem
$ openssl rsa -pubout -in ~/.oci/ocidemo_api_key.pem
-out ~/.oci/ocidemo_api_key_public.pem
writing RSA key
```

2. Obtain the OCID of the tenancy. Sign in to the OCI console and navigate to Administration | Tenancy Details and copy the OCID to your clipboard. You will need this OCID later. You can use Terraform to orchestrate infrastructure in any region to which your tenancy is subscribed. Take note of your preferred region for this exercise.
3. Obtain the OCID of the designated user. This user will be used by Terraform and the provider to interface with OCI, so ensure that adequate IAM privileges are granted to the user. Navigate to Identity | Users in the console, choose the user, and copy the OCID to your clipboard.
4. Navigate to the API Keys section if a new PEM key is to be added to the user. Choose Add Public Key and paste the public key created in the first step of this exercise, and then choose Add. Copy the fingerprint associated with the public key to your clipboard.
5. Download Terraform for your platform from the HashiCorp download page (https://www.terraform.io/downloads.html) and copy the zip file to your Linux machine where you plan to install and configure Terraform and the provider for OCI.

6. Unzip the Terraform archive in your preferred location. At the time of this writing, the Terraform archive contains a single executable. You may wish to add this location to your default PATH. Confirm the executable works by checking the version.

```
$ ./terraform -version
Terraform v0.12.3
```

7. Using the data in your clipboard, set the following environment variables in your shell.

```
$ export TF_VAR_tenancy_ocid=ocid1.tenancy.oc1..ddqda
$ export TF_VAR_user_ocid=ocid1.user.oc1..4qmnta
$ export TF_VAR_fingerprint=b5:1d:48:9c:13:fb:45
$ export TF_VAR_private_key_path=/home/opc/.oci/ocidemo_api_key.pem
$ export TF_VAR_region=us-ashburn-1
```

8. Create a Terraform file to instantiate the Terraform provider for OCI. You may embed other Terraform commands in this file, but at the very least, you need to specify references to the environment variables set in the previous step. As Terraform versions evolve, slight variations in the file formats may be required. The tool will let you know if any upgrades or modifications are required for your Terraform files.

```
$ cat oci.tf
variable "tenancy_ocid" {}
variable "region" {}
variable "user_ocid" {}
variable "fingerprint" {}
variable "private_key_path" {}
provider "oci" {
  tenancy_ocid = "${var.tenancy_ocid}"
  region = "${var.region}"
  user_ocid = "${var.user_ocid}"
  fingerprint = "${var.fingerprint}"
  private_key_path = "${var.private_key_path}"}
```

9. Initialize Terraform.

```
$ terraform init
Initializing the backend...
Initializing provider plugins...
- Checking for available provider plugins...
- Downloading plugin for provider "oci"
(terraform-providers/oci) 3.31.0...
The following providers do not have any version constraints
in configuration, so the latest version was installed.
To prevent automatic upgrades to new major versions that may
contain breaking changes, it is recommended to add version = "..."
constraints to the corresponding provider blocks in configuration,
with the constraint strings suggested below.
* provider.oci: version = "~> 3.31"
Terraform has been successfully initialized!
```

10. Confirm that both Terraform and the provider for OCI have been installed and configured.

```
$ terraform -version
Terraform v0.12.3
+ provider.oci v3.31.0
```

Use Terraform

You can describe and manage your infrastructure as code using Terraform configuration files written in either human-readable HCL files ending with the .tf extension or machine-readable JSON format files ending with the .tf.json file extension. Terraform configuration files specify provider definitions, like the oci.tf file used in the previous exercise when initializing the provider for OCI, as well as for defining OCI resources, variables, and data sources. Terraform converts these configurations into a set of API calls against the OCI API endpoints.

Terraform configuration files reside in a specific directory on your file system. When Terraform commands are run, all .tf and .tf.json files in a directory are loaded. By default, Terraform expects each configuration file to define a distinct set of objects and returns an error if multiple files attempt to define the same object. Overriding this behavior is possible by using a special override file, but this is rare and not encouraged as it hurts readability. Refer to the online Terraform documentation for syntax description. HCL is a complex command language that is being updated constantly and is out of scope for this chapter. It is common to see the following HCL configuration language elements in these configuration files:

- **variable** Both input and output variables are supported, enabling data to be sent to and received by OCI through the API.
- **resource** These are the primary constructs in Terraform configurations and typically consist of resource blocks describing one or more infrastructure resource objects.
- **provider** A provider offers a set of resource types that determine the behaviors of the resources. Providers expose IaaS resource types to Terraform. For example, the OCI provider exposes the virtual cloud network resource type. Resource constructs can then interact with this type by defining, creating, managing, and destroying elements of this resource type.

Terraform creates state files to store information about your managed infrastructure and configuration. This is primarily used to map real-world resources to your configuration and is located by default in a local file named terraform.tfstate.

EXAM TIP The Terraform `init` and `apply` commands appear similar, but each performs a very different function. Use `terraform init` to initialize new or existing configurations and use `terraform apply` to execute a Terraform plan.

Once the Terraform configuration files are created, use the Terraform commands to load and process these. The following popular Terraform commands are briefly described:

- **`init`** Initializes new or changes existing Terraform configurations.

- **`plan`** Generates and displays an execution plan that helps you validate your script before you apply it to your environment.
- **`apply`** Runs the Terraform scripts using the variables passed in with the `terraform plan` command to build or change infrastructure.
- **`graph`** Builds a visual graph of Terraform resources.
- **`refresh`** Synchronizes the local state file with real-world resources.
- **`taint`** Marks a resource for recreation. The next time the Terraform apply runs, the resource is destroyed and rebuilt.
- **`untaint`** Updates the resource state metadata so it is no longer marked as tainted and remains unchanged at the next Terraform apply.
- **`destroy`** Deletes the Terraform managed infrastructure resource.

There are hundreds of examples of Terraform configurations on the Oracle maintained GitHub site so you have to start from scratch. At the time of this writing, this GitHub repo resides at https://github.com/terraform-providers/terraform-provider-oci/tree/master/examples.

Exercise 7-5: Use Terraform to Create and Remove an OCI VCN

In this exercise, you will create a VCN and then delete it by using Terraform and the provider for OCI. You are guided through creating a single Terraform configuration file that defines the variables for the OCI environment to be impacted, the provider to use, and the resource to manage. Terraform commands are used to validate the configuration file and build the resource defined before finally removing the VCN. This exercise is dependent on your successful completion of the previous exercise.

1. Obtain the OCID of the compartment that will contain the new VCN. Navigate to Identity | Compartments in the console, choose the compartment, and copy the OCID to your clipboard.
2. Using the data in your clipboard, set the following environment variables in your shell. If you are working in the same shell session you used for the previous exercise, some of these variables may already be set, but it does not hurt to set them anyway.

```
$ export TF_VAR_tenancy_ocid=ocid1.tenancy.oc1..ddqda
$ export TF_VAR_user_ocid=ocid1.user.oc1..4qmnta
$ export TF_VAR_fingerprint=b5:1d:48:9c:13:fb:45
$ export TF_VAR_private_key_path=/home/opc/.oci/ocidemo_api_key.pem
$ export TF_VAR_region=us-ashburn-1
$ export TF_VAR_compartment_ocid=ocid1.compartment.oc1rdv4q
```

3. Create a Terraform configuration file named demovcn.tf in the same directory as the provider configuration file oci.tf. This file references the OCID of the compartment where the VCN named demovcn1 is to be created.

```
$ cat demovcn.tf
variable "compartment_ocid" {}
resource "oci_core_virtual_network" "vcn1" {
  cidr_block     = "10.0.0.0/22"
  dns_label      = "demovcn1"
  compartment_id = "${var.compartment_ocid}"
  display_name   = "demovcn1"
}
```

4. Run the `terraform plan` command to generate an execution plan.

```
$ terraform plan
Refreshing Terraform state in-memory prior to plan...
The refreshed state will be used to calculate this plan,
but will not be persisted to local or remote state storage.
------------------------------------------------------------
An execution plan has been generated and is shown below.
Resource actions are indicated with the following symbols:
  + create
Terraform will perform the following actions:
  # oci_core_virtual_network.vcn1 will be created
  + resource "oci_core_virtual_network" "vcn1" {
      + cidr_block               = "10.0.0.0/22"
      + compartment_id           = "ocid1.compartment.oc1.. 4rdv4q"
      + default_dhcp_options_id  = (known after apply)
      + default_route_table_id   = (known after apply)
      + default_security_list_id = (known after apply)
      + defined_tags             = (known after apply)
      + display_name             = "demovcn1"
      + dns_label                = "demovcn1"
      + freeform_tags            = (known after apply)
      + id                       = (known after apply)
      + state                    = (known after apply)
      + time_created             = (known after apply)
      + vcn_domain_name          = (known after apply)}
Plan: 1 to add, 0 to change, 0 to destroy.
```

5. Review the generated plan and verify the planned changes are aligned with your expectations. Until you apply the planned changes, no changes are made in OCI. You may want to connect to the OCI console and navigate to Networking | Virtual Cloud Networks and confirm there is no demovcn1 in the specified compartment. When you are ready, apply the plan. The output has been truncated for brevity and the generated execution plan output that is identical to the output in the previous step has been removed.

```
$ terraform apply
<same as terraform plan output>
Plan: 1 to add, 0 to change, 0 to destroy.
Do you want to perform these actions?
  Terraform will perform the actions described above.
  Only 'yes' will be accepted to approve.
  Enter a value: yes
oci_core_virtual_network.vcn1: Creating...
oci_core_virtual_network.vcn1:
Creation complete after 1s [id=ocid1.vcn.oc1.iad. 6f2uq]
Apply complete! Resources: 1 added, 0 changed, 0 destroyed.
```

6. A new VCN should appear in the OCI console.

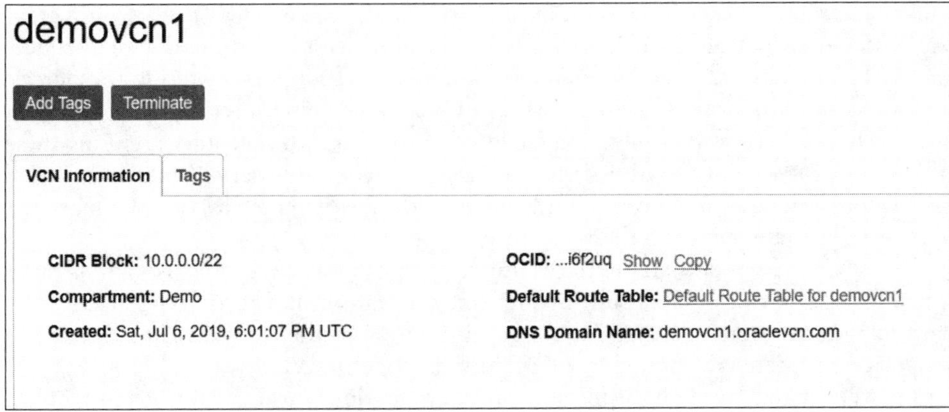

7. You could update the demovcn.tf configuration file with new elements to specify subnets, route tables, or other resources, or create new configuration files defining other resources to be managed.
8. When you are ready to decommission a resource, it is easily removed with the `terraform destroy` command.

```
$ terraform destroy
oci_core_virtual_network.vcn1: Refreshing state...
[id=ocid1.vcn.oc1.iad.6f2uq]
An execution plan has been generated and is shown below.
Resource actions are indicated with the following symbols:
- destroy
Terraform will perform the following actions:
# oci_core_virtual_network.vcn1 will be destroyed
- resource "oci_core_virtual_network" "vcn1" {
 - cidr_block = "10.0.0.0/22" -> null
 - compartment_id = "ocid1.compartment. x" -> null
 - default_dhcp_options_id  = "ocid1.dhcpoptions. x" -> null
 - default_route_table_id   = "ocid1.routetable. x" -> null
 - default_security_list_id = "ocid1.securitylist. x" -> null
 - defined_tags             = {} -> null
 - display_name             = "demovcn1" -> null
 - dns_label                = "demovcn1" -> null
 - freeform_tags            = {} -> null
 - id                       = "ocid1.vcn.oc1.x" -> null
 - state                    = "AVAILABLE" -> null
 - vcn_domain_name          = "demovcn1.oraclevcn.com" -> null}
Plan: 0 to add, 0 to change, 1 to destroy.
Do you really want to destroy all resources?
  Terraform will destroy all your managed infrastructure,
  as shown above.
  There is no undo. Only 'yes' will be accepted to confirm.
  Enter a value: yes
oci_core_virtual_network.vcn1: Destroying... [id=ocid1.vcn.oc1.iad.x]
oci_core_virtual_network.vcn1: Destruction complete after 1s
Destroy complete! Resources: 1 destroyed.
```

Chapter Review

This chapter introduced the concept of Infrastructure-as-Code. IaC is key to automating large-scale infrastructure architectures. OCI is designed with IaC in mind with a service-based API interface wrapped around all OCI resources. To interact with OCI resources, tools need only access the API endpoints. The OCI console, which is the official graphical face of OCI, uses these API calls. You could write your own console interface using these APIs if so desired, and the SDKs provided facilitate your applications interacting with OCI through these APIs. The OCI CLI and Terraform with a provider for OCI make use of these APIs to interact with OCI.

The OCI CLI presents an interface familiar to most Oracle technologists and is easily suited for shell scripting or ad-hoc maintenance. Terraform has become a de facto standard in infrastructure automation and treating infrastructure as code, and Oracle has supported this standard through the Terraform provider for OCI.

You were guided through the installation, configuration, and some introductory usage examples in this chapter to not only whet your appetite but to familiarize you with the OCI CLI, which is used throughout this book.

Questions

1. List the supported interfaces for programmatically interacting with OCI.
   A. Java, Python, Ruby, Go SDKs
   B. OCI CLI
   C. C++ SDK
   D. Terraform with the provider for OCI
2. Which of the following formats are acceptable input and output when using the OCI CLI?
   A. Terraform .tf configuration files
   B. HCL commands
   C. JSON
   D. CamelCase
3. Which command displays the VCNs in a compartment using the OCI CLI?
   A. `oci network vcn list --compartment-id <compartment-id >`
   B. `oci vcn list --compartment-id <compartment-id >`
   C. `oci network list --compartment-id <compartment-id >`
   D. `oci compartment list --vcn-id <vcn-id >`
4. Which of the following are acceptable input formats when using Terraform and the provider for OCI?
   A. Terraform .tf configuration files
   B. CLI commands

C. Terraform .tf.json configuration files

D. CamelCase

5. Which of the following statements are true?

   A. Terraform may only be used to manage OCI resources.

   B. Terraform is an Oracle technology.

   C. Terraform may be used to manage infrastructure from many providers.

   D. Terraform manages infrastructure as code.

6. What are commonly used HCL elements found in Terraform configuration files?

   A. variable

   B. resource

   C. apply

   D. plan

7. Which of the following statements is true?

   A. You can only interact with OCI resources using the CLI and Terraform.

   B. You can only interact with OCI resources using the CLI, Terraform, and SDKs.

   C. You can only interact with OCI resources using the CLI, Terraform, SDKs, and the OCI console.

   D. You can interact with OCI using any tool through the OCI API endpoints.

8. Which of the following statements are true?

   A. Only input variables are supported in Terraform configuration files.

   B. Only output variables are supported in Terraform configuration files.

   C. Both input and output variables are supported in Terraform configuration files.

   D. Common HCL elements found in Terraform configuration files include variable, resource, and providers.

9. What are commonly used Terraform commands?

   A. `init`, `plan`, `apply`, `graph`, `refresh`, `destroy`, `taint`, `untaint`

   B. `variable`, `resource`, `provider`

   C. `oci <service> <type> <action> <options>`

   D. `create`, `delete`, `get`, `list`, `update`

10. Which Terraform commands can potentially change OCI infrastructure resources?

    A. `apply`

    B. `plan`

    C. `init`

    D. `destroy`

Answers

1. **A, B, D.** Java, Python, Ruby, Go SDKs, the OCI CLI, and Terraform with the provider for OCI are supported interfaces for programmatically interacting with OCI.

2. **C.** JSON format is acceptable input and output when using the OCI CLI.

3. **A.** `oci network vcn list --compartment-id <compartment-id>` is the correct command to display the VCNs in a specified compartment using the OCI CLI.

4. **A, C.** Terraform .tf and .tf.json configuration files are acceptable input formats when using Terraform and the provider for OCI.

5. **C, D.** Terraform may be used to manage infrastructure from many providers as code.

6. **A, B.** Both variable and resource are commonly used HCL elements found in Terraform configuration files.

7. **D.** You can interact with OCI using any tool through the OCI API endpoints. You are not confined to using any specific tools.

8. **C, D.** Both input and output variables are supported in Terraform configuration files, and common HCL elements found in Terraform configuration files include variable, resource, and providers.

9. **A.** Commonly used Terraform commands include `init`, `plan`, `apply`, `graph`, `refresh`, `destroy`, `taint`, `untaint`.

10. **A, D.** The `apply` command runs Terraform scripts using the variables passed in with the `terraform plan` command to build or change infrastructure, and the `destroy` command deletes managed infrastructure resources.

CHAPTER 8

OCI Best Practice Architectures

In this chapter, you will learn how to

- Design Highly Available Disaster Recovery (HADR) OCI solutions
- Leverage OCI security features to protect your cloud infrastructure

High Availability (HA) and Disaster Recovery (DR) are interrelated concepts and go hand-in-hand with each other. A robust design that is fault tolerant, uses redundant components, and ensures application or system availability in a manner that is transparent to end users is considered an HADR architecture. The best HADR is when users do not even know that anything has failed because they experienced zero downtime and no loss of service. Disaster Recovery refers to the ability for systems to continue operating after an outage with zero or minimal loss of data. We define HA as availability in relation to service while DR is defined as availability in relation to data. These concepts represent availability and recovery goals. Their definitions overlap as technology converges, resulting in the hybrid term HADR used to collectively describe design for both HA and DR.

Good examples of HADR are Oracle RAC databases with Data Guard standby databases. A RAC database is a single set of database files concurrently accessed by more than one database instance running on more than one node. If a RAC node fails, database availability is not affected, and applications being serviced by the RAC database continue uninterrupted, oblivious to the fact that a node failure just occurred. If the entire primary site where all RAC instances reside is lost, a Data Guard failover occurs to the standby database at a secondary site. Service is temporarily impacted while the failover and data recovery complete following a disaster.

HADR designs include eliminating single points of failure by leveraging redundant components. In the previous example, RAC protects availability against loss of database nodes or instances while Data Guard protects against loss of the entire primary database because it effectively keeps a redundant copy of the database at the standby location. This configuration is usually further protected using database backups. If a database server experiences a catastrophic failure and a database is lost, you may have to restore the server and database from backups, which are yet other redundant offline copies of the database. Service is often interrupted while data is being restored and recovered.

This chapter covers OCI design principles in relation to HADR. A discussion of good security practices in OCI follows later in the chapter. Security in OCI must be considered when designing cloud-based solutions. Understanding the deceptively powerful security features available in OCI allows you to leverage these features in designing secure cloud architectures. OCI gives many organizations an opportunity for a fresh start when designing their security posture. You may have inherited archaic security policies that are no longer working, exposing your systems to unnecessary risk, and now is the time to learn from past mistakes and design secure architectures with the wisdom of hindsight based on learning from your on-premises security approach. Contrary to early security-related fears that may have led to slow cloud adoption, the technology industry recognizes that cloud vendors have invested heavily in securing their offerings to the point that public clouds today ironically have security that is superior to many on-premises systems.

As you read through this chapter, you will encounter familiar OCI terms and concepts introduced in earlier chapters but described here through an HADR lens.

Design Highly Available Disaster Recovery (HADR) OCI Solutions

The basic design principle behind HADR is to eliminate single points of failure by leveraging redundant components. HADR is associated with two additional terms that reflect the organizational context within which these technical architectures are situated: RPO (Recovery Point Objective) and RTO (Recovery Time Objective).

RPO refers to how much data loss is tolerable for the organization in the event of a disaster. Ideally, you should strive for a zero data loss architecture. This ideal is accompanied by increased costs for redundant components and advanced software that reduces or eliminates data loss. The financial realities of an organization often dictate the RPO. It is common to see financial systems with zero data loss architectures, whereas non-production systems or systems where data can be recreated from downstream sources have less stringent RPO requirements.

RTO refers to the duration of a service outage. If the organizational requirement is to have zero downtime for some systems, this has implications for the underlying design and cost of the solution. Many systems can tolerate short outages. It is not ideal but can reduce the implementation costs significantly. Critical systems, usually governing life support and other high-risk environments, require zero downtime, and implementation costs for these designs tend to be material.

CAUTION Understanding RPO and RTO for various systems in your organization is crucial and forms the basis for your solution. It is your duty to gather the input realities, design the most optimal HADR architecture given these realities, and highlight the risks and points of failure. It is equally important to present alternative (usually more costly) options where risks are mitigated to key stakeholders and to get written acceptance of the final solution and consequent service level agreement.

Any infrastructure resource is at risk of failure. It is your task to mitigate that risk by architecting a solution that is fault tolerant while meeting RPO and RTO requirements. This is an art that requires a solid understanding of the fault-tolerant options available in OCI.

Regions and Availability Domains

Fault tolerance may be found along the entire spectrum of OCI resources. At the highest level of the OCI resource hierarchy are regions. Your cloud account is your tenancy and upon creation is designated a home region. Your tenancy may subscribe to multiple regions. This permits you to create OCI resources in data centers across the globe. Consider a website serving customers on opposite ends of the earth. It is entirely conceivable to register your website domain name with a DNS provider that resolves to IP addresses of load balancers or compute instances in the Phoenix region in the United States and in the Bombay region in India, providing both HADR for your website and shorter network distance that requesting clients closer to these host regions need to traverse, leading to superior website access performance.

Regions comprise one or more availability domains. Regions with a single AD are less fault tolerant than regions with multiple ADs. Figure 8-1 describes a tenancy subscribed to two regions. Region R1 has two ADs while region R2 has one AD.

Figure 8-1 Tenancy, regions, availability, and fault domains

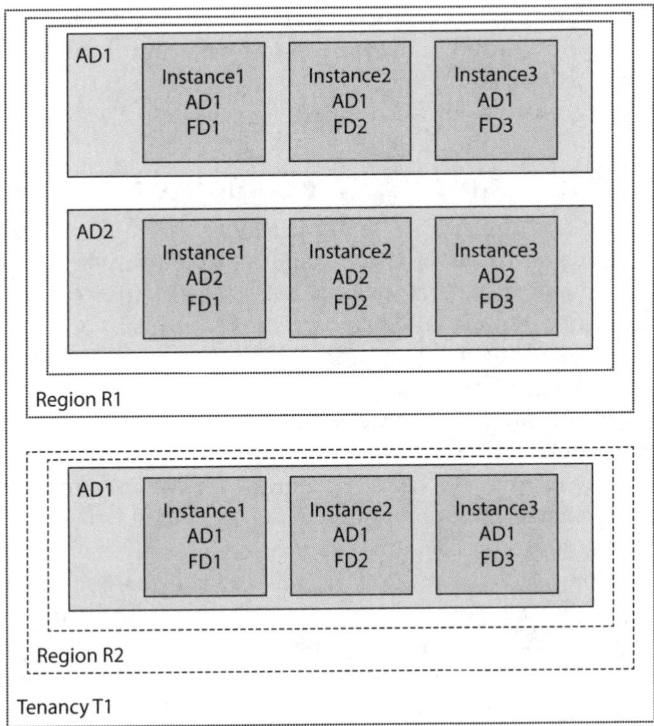

Loss of the AD in region R2 equates to the loss of an entire region while in the multi-AD region R1; loss of an AD does not bring down the entire region. The relative seriousness of losing an AD must be placed in context. While losing an AD is a big deal, it is extremely uncommon and a low probability event. For many organizations, their current on-premises infrastructure still resides in a single data center. Loss of an entire data center or AD is usually the result of a large-scale disaster or wide-reaching sustained power outage. The nature of multi-AD regions is such that they are located relatively close to one another. This physical proximity is needed to sustain low network latency between the ADs in the region. Therefore, a disaster that knocks out an AD in a region could be large enough to wipe out all the ADs in that region. If there are multiple ADs in your region, you should architect your infrastructure in such a way that critical systems are protected from an AD failure. A common use case involves a regional load balancer distributing traffic to middleware webservers or application servers located in separate ADs within a region to ensure HA.

Single AD regions are not without protection. Redundancy has been engineered into the ADs through the provision of fault domains. Three fault domains exist per AD. A fault domain is a set of fault-tolerant isolated physical infrastructure within an AD. By choosing different fault domains for VM instances, you ensure these are hosted on separate physical hardware, thus increasing your intra-availability domain resilience. It is a good HADR DBaaS solution to use the Oracle RAC option and place RAC compute nodes in separate fault domains. In Figure 8-1, three instances are shown in the single AD region R2. Instancel in AD1 in FD1 could be one RAC node, and Instance2 in AD1 in FD2 could be the second node of a two-node DBaaS RAC cluster. Instance3 in AD1 in FD3 could be a single-instance Data Guard standby database system. Each instance is isolated from hardware failure by placing them in separate fault domains. Architecting redundant instances across fault domains, availability domains, and regions provides a multi-tiered approach to HA.

VCNs, Load Balancers, and Compute Instances

Your tenancy may subscribe to multiple regions. A VCN spans all the ADs in a region. Remote VCN peering can be used to connect VCNs securely and reliably across regions. VCNs are composed of subnets. Subnets and load balancers may be created at the AD or region level. Both subnet and load balancer HADR is improved when you use regional resources in a multi-AD region. Load balancers are commonly used for optimizing the utilization of backend resources as well as to provide scaling and high availability. A load balancer may be public or private and accepts incoming TCP or HTTP network traffic on a single IP address and distributes it to a backend set that comprises one or more compute instances in your VCN. In this context, the compute instances are known as backend servers. Each of these compute instances resides in either a public or private subnet.

When a private load balancer is created, you specify the VCN and private subnet to which it belongs. An active (primary) private load balancer obtains a private IP address from the CIDR range of a private subnet. A passive (standby) private load balancer is created automatically for failover purposes and also receives a private IP address from the same subnet. A floating private IP address serves as a highly available address of the load balancer. The active and passive private load balancers are highly available within a single AD. If the primary load balancer fails, the listener directs traffic to the standby load balancer and availability is maintained. A private load balancer is accessible from compute instances within the VCN where the subnet of the load balancer resides. You may improve the service availability across ADs by setting up multiple private load balancers and make use of private DNS servers to set up a round-robin DNS configuration with their IP addresses.

A public load balancer is allocated a floating public IP address that is routable from the Internet. When a public load balancer is created, two subnets are required, one for the active (primary) public load balancer and another for the passive load balancer. Incoming traffic from the public Internet on allowed ports and protocols is directed to the floating public IP address associated with the active load balancer. If the primary load balancer fails, the passive device is automatically made active. The public load balancer is a regional resource as opposed to a private load balancer, which is an AD-level resource. In regions with multiple ADs, it is mandatory to specify public subnets in different ADs for the active and passive load balancers.

Services are often accessed via DNS hostname resolution to an IP address of a load balancer or compute instance. Subnets provide primary private IP addresses to resident compute instances and private load balancers. Secondary private or reserved public IP addresses may be additionally allocated to compute instances. It is good HADR practice to bind services to DNS targets that resolve to secondary or floating IP addresses. In the event of a loss of a compute instance, the secondary IP address may be reassigned to a standby compute instance enabling a continuation of service. Secondary private IP addresses may only be assigned to standby compute instances resident in the same subnet as the primary instance. Reserved public IP addresses offer more flexibility and may be assigned to any standby compute instance and persist beyond the lifetime of the compute instance to which it is assigned.

Figure 8-2 depicts a potential website architecture. You may register your domain name in a public DNS registry that resolves to multiple public IP addresses that belong to public load balancer listeners located in different regions. The regional load balancer in region R1 forwards traffic to a backend set of instances that reside in separate ADs but share a common regional subnet. The public load balancer in region R2 routes traffic to a backend set of instances that despite residing in a single AD are guaranteed to run on separate hardware.

In this architecture, the website is protected from single server failure, entire AD failure, and even region failure, ensuring uninterrupted service and meeting stringent organizational HADR goals.

NOTE When a compute instance using floating IP addresses fails, it is often possible to automate the allocation of the floating IP address to a standby instance to minimize downtime.

To failover to a standby compute instance using a floating IP address still leaves you with the problem of data being out of sync between the primary and standby compute instances. There are several approaches to maintaining data availability and ensuring data integrity that involve using shared file systems or keeping file systems in sync. Databases are discussed later in this chapter.

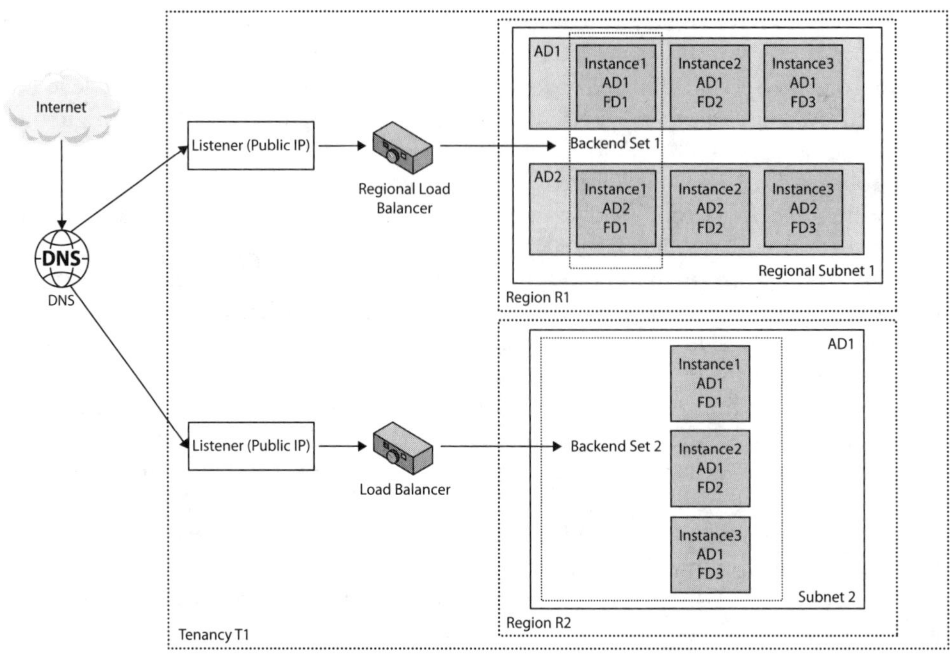

Figure 8-2 HADR architecture using regional network resources across multiple regions

VPN and FastConnect

Connecting a VCN to your on-premises network creates a new point of failure that must be mitigated. As discussed in Chapter 3, you may make use of IPSec VPN and FastConnect to connect discrete networks. You may set up a connection between your on-premises network's edge router (CPE or customer-premises equipment) and an OCI Dynamic Routing Gateway (DRG). High availability is provided for the network path between the CPE and DRG through a set of redundant IPSec VPN tunnels. When an IPSec VPN is set up, two tunnels are created for redundancy. These may be used in active-active mode or active-passive mode.

OCI provides FastConnect as a means to create a dedicated high-speed private connection between on-premises networks and OCI. FastConnect provides consistent, predictable, secure, and reliable performance. FastConnect supports the following uses:

- Private peering extends your on-premises network into a VCN and may be used to create a hybrid cloud. On-premises connections can be made to the private IP addresses of instances as if they were coming from instances in the VCN. Private peering can also occur between instances in VCNs in other regions.
- Public peering allows you to connect from resources outside the VCN, such as an on-premises network, to public OCI services such as object storage, over FastConnect without traversing the Internet.

FastConnect is actualized using several connectivity models:

- Colocation with Oracle allows direct physical cross-connects between your network and Oracle's FastConnect edge devices. HADR is achieved by ensuring that at least two cross-connects are set up, each connecting to a different router. New virtual circuits should be provisioned on both redundant links.
- Using an Oracle Network Provider or Exchange Partner, you can set up a FastConnect connection from your network to the provider or partner network that has a high bandwidth connection into Oracle's FastConnect edge devices. To mitigate loss of a FastConnect location, you can set up redundant circuits using a different FastConnect location provided by either the same provider or a different provider. This enables redundancy at both the circuit and data center levels.

Planned maintenance on routers involved in the FastConnect setup can impact availability. This may be mitigated by providing multiple paths and changing traffic patterns to use preferred paths by configuring Border Gateway Protocol (BGP) route preferences.

An alternative VPN HADR architecture involves using both IPSec VPN and FastConnect to provide redundancy in case one of these connection options fails, as shown in Figure 8-3. When both IPSec VPN and FastConnect virtual circuits connect to the same DRG, consider that IPSec VPN uses static routing while FastConnect uses BGP. You need to test your configuration to ensure that if BGP routes overlap with IPSec VPN routes, then BGP routes are preferred by OCI as long as they are available.

There has also been an increase in the availability of software-defined wide area networking (SD-WAN) solutions in the realm of cloud networking that are worth considering. SD-WAN appliances reside at your network edge locations—for example, in your VCN and on-premises networks—and evaluate the performance of multiple network routes using analytics and routing algorithms to dynamically route network traffic along the most efficient path.

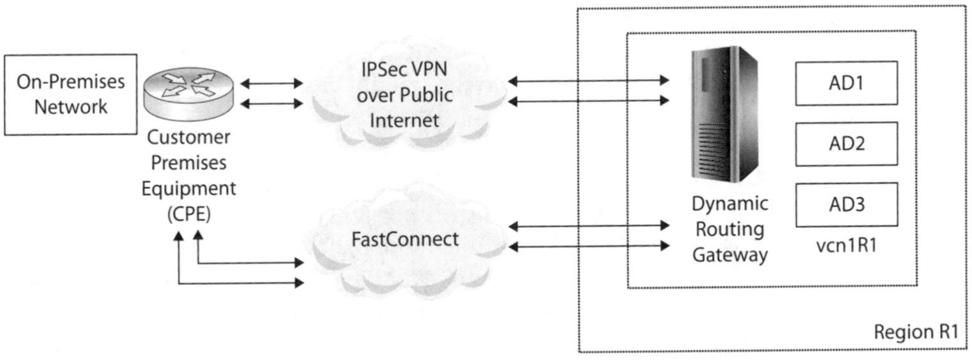

Figure 8-3 FastConnect and IPSec VPN HADR connecting VCN to an on-premises network

Storage and Compute Instances

File systems may be shared by compute instances in the same AD by using OCI file storage services, which provide an NFS-compliant shared network attached storage. If critical files are kept in a shared file storage location then loss of a compute instance may be tolerated with no service loss. An example of this may be a website where the static content or files with session state information are placed on shared file system. If multiple webserver compute instances reference the shared file storage, then a website may remain highly available even if an underlying webserver compute instance has failed.

NOTE The file storage service also provides a snapshot-based backup mechanism that supports the immediate restoration of files accidentally removed due to user error, which further supports RPO and RTO.

When primary and standby compute instances are in separate ADs, file systems may be synchronized to provide some measure of HADR. There are two basic approaches to synchronizing file systems:

- Synchronous replication refers to changes being shipped from the primary to the standby instance. Only once the changes are confirmed to have arrived at the standby are they committed on the primary site. Synchronous replication is dependent on network and block volume resources and can lead to queuing delays and waits, which could have a negative impact on performance. Instances in ADs in the same region benefit from the low-latency network backbone between the ADs and you may find that synchronous replication is a feasible approach that leads to synchronization between the two sites when no data loss can be tolerated.
- Asynchronous replication refers to changes to the primary instance being shipped to the standby with no need to wait for confirmation that the changes have been received and applied. There is no blocking or waiting with this approach and it is suitable for synchronizing data between instances in different regions. There is a risk of data loss, however, because a change may be written to a primary instance, which fails before the change is sent to the standby instance.

CAUTION DenseIO compute shapes include support for direct attached NVMe disks. This storage is not SAN-based and is presented as raw storage to the compute instance. There is no redundancy built in and it is your responsibility to set up appropriate redundancy. This could take the format of ASM redundancy if the NVMe volumes are used for Oracle databases or some sort of RAID configuration if they are used for generic file system storage. Configuring redundancy for locally attached NVMe storage provides redundancy and HADR in case of storage failure.

Object storage provides petabyte-scale storage that is resilient and has become a standard for general-purpose file storage in the cloud. The object storage system is Internet accessible, and you control the permissions and whether a bucket is publicly accessible or not. OCI object storage integrates with OCI's Identity and Access Management (IAM) to control permissions on object storage. Object storage is not suitable for high-speed computing storage requirements (such as those required to run databases) but provides flexible and scalable options for unstructured data storage and sharing as well as being great for big data and content repositories, backups and archives, log data, and other large datasets. Object storage is also not bound to an instance or an AD but is a region-level construct that provides a highly available file storage solution.

Performance-Based HADR

Service availability is sometimes impacted by poorly performing systems. Common causes of performance-related service outage include undersized compute infrastructure for the actual workload, distributed denial of service (DDoS) attacks, and software quality. Buggy or problematic software quality cannot be solved through HADR design but through a systematic quality assurance test and release cycle. Although this topic is beyond the scope of this book, it has happened too often that poorly tested code is released into the wild, exposing enterprises to avoidable critical security- and performance-related bugs. The undersized compute infrastructure problem is one that is dealt with quite easily.

The cloud computing paradigm revolves around sizing resources for average workloads to contain costs while planning for bursting or scaling during peak periods. Imagine a website hosted on a single compute instance running an HTTP server. You can create a custom image from this compute instance and use it as the basis for automatically provisioning additional preconfigured web server compute instances when your website is overloaded. Not all resource classes are capable of autoscaling but two key resources benefit from this automation: compute instances and autonomous databases, discussed later in the chapter. DBaaS instances benefit from explicit CPU scaling to increase CPU capacity.

Instance configuration and pools provide the basis for autoscaling, which is the dynamic addition or removal of instances from an instance pool based on an autoscaling policy. Instance configuration metadata forms the basis for pools of compute instances created using these regional templates. You can configure the automatic spawning and removal of compute instances based on a common instance configuration as the workload changes. Instance pools are a regional construct and may contain instances from multiple ADs. By attaching load balancers to instance pools, new auto-provisioned instances are added to the relevant backend sets. This is a useful feature to consider when designing for performance-based compute instance HADR.

Database HADR

Chapter 6 outlines the available database options in OCI. Oracle Database on OCI is a key driver to the adoption of OCI for many enterprises. Oracle databases usually support critical workloads and HADR is a primary consideration. Database backups are a key component of any HADR solution and are not discussed here. This section assumes you have read Chapter 6 or are familiar with these options for running Oracle databases on OCI.

Single-Instance Databases (SI)

You can manually configure and run a single-instance database on a compute instance or use DBaaS to have OCI provision a single-instance server. Automatically created single-instance DBaaS environments are preconfigured with Oracle Grid Infrastructure (GI). Because there are many points of failure similar to manually configured single-instance databases and similar approaches to mitigate these issues, these two methods of running single-instance databases are discussed together next. Manually configured instances offer both familiarity for on-premises DBAs as well as certain migration flexibility, but have limited HADR options. There are many points of failure, some of which are detailed next with suggestions to mitigate these issues.

- With a single-instance database manually configured on a compute instance, once you lose your compute instance, the database is no longer accessible. You could clone your boot image to create a custom image and use this to create a new standby instance that is available in the same AD as the source instance. A floating IP address could be attached to the source instance. In the event of an unrecoverable loss of the source instance, you could reallocate the floating IP address, detach the block volumes with the Oracle Home and Oracle database files from the source instance, and attach it to the standby instance.
- Access to the database is tied to the availability and accessibility of the database processes and listener process to database clients. If a listener fails, no new remote database connections are accepted. If a database process fails, so does the database. Oracle offers a technology (for single-instance databases) known as Oracle Restart, which is part of GI. GI should be installed for many reasons, especially for ASM. GI is installed with DBaaS instances. Oracle Restart periodically checks if key processes such as DB listeners, DB server processes, and ASM disk groups are available and restarts processes if a problem is detected. For Oracle RAC databases, similar functionality is managed by the Clusterware-related services.
- Sufficient disk storage must be allocated to allow for growth of database, audit, trace, and log files, as well as any redo logs. If the database is running in archivelog mode (as it should be in most cases), there must be sufficient space for growth of archived redo logs. Use Oracle Enterprise Manager (OEM) or Oracle Management Cloud (OMC) to monitor your server and alert you proactively to disk and other issues that could affect availability.
- Loss of key database files will also halt the database. If GI is installed, ASM disk groups may be configured with normal or high levels of redundancy, configuring either two or three copies of ASM extents respectively across the disks in the disk group. Placing key, or ideally all, database files in redundant disk groups ensures database availability.

Real Application Clusters (RAC)

RAC is an option that allows a set of database files to be mounted by multiple database instances concurrently. RAC relies on shared storage accessible by each instance participating in the cluster. RAC is included with all Exadata Cloud services, supporting up to eight nodes and is optional on VM-based DBaaS supporting a two-node format. RAC provides HADR for a database through two primary mechanisms:

- A RAC database is concurrently mounted by one or more database instances, each running on a separate compute node within an AD. RAC databases can tolerate the loss of a RAC node. As long as there is at least one RAC node available, the database remains accessible.
- Database listener services are provided by a special set of processes known as scan listeners that provide HADR for local database listeners. Three scan listeners are deployed on floating IP addresses and route network connection traffic to available local listeners on each RAC node based on their workload and availability. When a node is offline, the scan listeners relocate dynamically to available nodes to provide connection HADR to database clients.

RAC nodes or compute instances are created in separate fault domains within the same AD to protect the database from hardware failure. RAC additionally provides an HADR benefit during planned maintenance activities. Firmware on each RAC compute node may be updated, and even database software patches may be applied in a rolling manner to maximize database availability.

Data Guard

While RAC mitigates against node failure and ensures HA, Data Guard mitigates against node, shared storage, and even AD failure in multi-AD regions. Data Guard is a mature replication technology available with all Oracle Enterprise Edition versions. You may manually configure Data Guard between two manually configured databases (RAC or SI) or use the managed Data Guard DBaaS for OCI. The managed option is straightforward to set up and uses automation behind the scenes to ensure the standby is correctly configured. As of this writing, the managed Data Guard service is limited to inter-AD replication within a multi-AD region. You may choose to manually build a Data Guard standby for a manually configured database that is located in a different region or even on-premises. Keep in mind that network latency must be considered and may limit the replication mode, as discussed later in this section.

All Data Guard configurations consist of a primary database and at least one standby database. Each system is a fully operational Oracle server with nodes, instances, and independent sets of database files. The primary and standby systems are almost exclusively on separate infrastructure, in different fault domains, to provide business continuity in case there is a failure of the primary system. Two modes of Data Guard replication may be configured, physical and logical standby. An important differentiator is that with physical Data Guard, the entire database is replicated with no exception. With logical replication such as SQL Apply or even Oracle GoldenGate, only a subset of the database is replicated—user-specified schemas and objects.

Each database in a Data Guard architecture is designated a role. One database occupies the primary role while one or more databases occupy the standby role. Data Guard physical standby replication may be configured in one of three modes that determines how the redo stream of changes from the primary database is shipped and applied on the standby:

- **Maximum Performance** (optimized for performance) Replication is asynchronous and the primary database does not wait for confirmation that the captured redo stream has been successfully shipped or applied on the standby. Replication interruptions or issues do not impact the primary database.
- **Maximum Availability** (optimized for availability and protection) Under normal operation, changes are not committed on the primary database until all changes are written to the redo logs and confirmation that the captured redo stream has been successfully shipped or applied on the standby has been received. Issues with the replication cause the system to downgrade automatically to operate as if in maximum performance mode, and the availability of the primary database is not impacted.
- **Maximum Protection** (optimized for data protection and integrity of the standby) Zero data loss is possible. Replication is synchronous and the primary database waits for confirmation that the captured redo stream has been successfully shipped or applied on the standby. Replication interruptions or issues cause the primary database to shut down.

A role transition occurs when one of the standby databases assumes the primary role. The following are two types of role transitions:

- **Switchover** A planned role transition often to perform OS patching or hardware maintenance on the primary. No data loss is incurred during a switchover because there is a clean stop of changes in the primary, the standby is in sync, and the roles have transitioned. There is a small window (a few minutes at most, usually less than a minute) of unavailability during a switchover. The "old" standby database is now the primary (open read-write) while the "old" primary acts in a standby role. Managed recovery is paused, while maintenance is performed without interruption to the business. This provides HADR in a planned manner.
- **Failover** This is an unplanned role transition and, as the name suggests, a failure has occurred. One of the standby databases is designated as the new primary. Point-in-time recovery (PITR) occurs. Depending on the Data Guard configuration discussed earlier, minimal (max performance or max availability) or no data loss (max protection) may occur during failover. Max protection mode ensures that any last in-flight transactions are only committed on the primary if they are committed on the standby, so no data loss occurs.

Ideally, each database system resides in a separate availability domain in a multi-AD region, but at the very least, each system should reside in a separate fault domain.

In a two-system Data Guard configuration, one is designated the primary role while the other takes on the standby role. Applications and users connect to the primary database and as changes are made on the primary database, they are captured and shipped over the network to the standby database, where they are applied. This is a classical physical standby configuration.

Several important considerations for Data Guard systems include setting up a regional subnet in multi-AD regions. This simplifies networking configuration, and primary and standby database systems can be placed in different ADs. Data Guard also provides a monitoring agent known as an observer that ideally runs on different infrastructure from both the primary and secondary DB systems. The observer can be configured to determine when a failover is required and to automatically perform the failover. This provides a huge HADR advantage as no human involvement is required.

Data Guard may be enhanced by licensing the additional Active Data Guard (ADG) option. ADG is included with the Enterprise Edition—Extreme Performance on OCI. ADG allows standby databases to be opened in read-only mode, supporting the offloading of expensive queries and read-intensive activities such as exports and backups to the standby. ADG in 19c and later supports limited read-write operations on the standby database, which exposes some exciting HADR possibilities.

NOTE Consider the us-ashburn-1 region, which has at least three ADs. A best-practice HADR architecture may include a primary RAC database system in AD1 with each RAC node in a separate fault domain, with a standby RAC database system in AD2, again with both standby nodes in separate fault domains. Active Data Guard has been implemented for backup and query offloading. A Data Guard observer has been configured in AD3 to orchestrate a fast-start-fail-over (FSFO) if issues with the primary RAC database system are detected.

GoldenGate

Oracle GoldenGate provides logical replication between multiple databases using many different topologies. Each database may reside in separate ADs or even in separate regions if the network bandwidth is sufficient for the DB IOPS. These databases are kept in sync by transactional replication and potentially support updates from multiple master databases. The following GoldenGate topologies are supported on OCI:

- **Unidirectional** Source database transactions are sent to one target database. Typically used for offloading read-intensive operations such as Reporting, while providing a read-only synchronized standby database.
- **Broadcast** This is similar to Unidirectional but source database transactions are sent to multiple target databases, typically to distribute data to downstream systems.

- **Bi-directional** Source database transactions are sent to one target databases and vice versa, using predefined conflict resolution strategies to avoid data conflicts. This topology provides instant failover as both databases are active processing read and write transactions.
- **Peer-to-Peer** The same as Bi-directional with multiple master databases. So DB1 replicates to DB2, which replicates to DB3, and so on. This topology also provides excellent zero downtime HADR.
- **Consolidation** This is conceptually the opposite of Broadcast because transactions from many source databases are replicated to a single target database. It is typically used in a datamart or datawarehouse scenario.
- **Cascading** This conceptually consists of Unidirectional and Broadcast topologies.

Each topology has pros and cons and may be leveraged to design an appropriate HADR solution. Conflict-resolution strategies are usually designed when implementing GoldenGate. This solution can provide zero downtime for RPO/RPO requirements but comes at a financial and complexity cost.

Autonomous Databases

Oracle Autonomous Database (ADB) systems offer a hosted and managed option with an underlying Exadata service and the ability to dynamically scale up and scale down both the CPUs and storage allocated to your VM. This supports sizing your environment for average workload, scaling up during peak periods and scaling back down once the workload normalizes, thereby providing database-level performance-based HADR. Autonomous databases are opened by multiple nodes (RAC) when more than 16 OCPUs are enabled and are hosted on highly redundant Exadata infrastructure managed and monitored by Oracle.

NOTE Infrastructure-as-Code solutions, including Terraform and OCI Resource Manager, may also be leveraged in an HADR solution to rapidly provision infrastructure in a secondary region. Budgetary constraints and RPO/RTO requirements may determine if you set up a warm standby that is ready to go with minor CPU scaling adjustments or a cold standby that takes a longer time to provision.

Leverage OCI Security Features to Protect Your Cloud Infrastructure

Practically securing your OCI tenancy demands the consolidation of lessons on IAM, networking, compute instances, storage, and databases discussed in detail in previous chapters dedicated to each of these topics. The following is a set of high-level guidelines to consider when securing your tenancy.

IAM

OCI resources may be organized into compartments to logically separate applications and systems. IAM supports a flexible framework for granting the least-privilege required to secure access and govern OCI resources. IAM policies allow only authorized groups of IAM users and dynamic groups of principal instances to interact with OCI resources and are an effective mechanism for managing IAM.

Try to ensure that all resources are tagged with defined tags, enabling cost-tracking tags to implement a chargeback system. While your organization may not be ready for a chargeback system today, this approach also helps reduce unnecessary spend and allocates an owner to each resource. Each resource owner is the person or department that pays for a resource. This paradigm may encourage security-compliant behaviors that will contribute to the overall security of your tenancy and reduce the sprawl of resources commonly found in less well-governed environments.

There are many keys involved when accessing OCI resources. Consider rotating SSH keys periodically and allocating individual SSH or API keys to specific individuals who must have access to OCI resources. Corporate key stores should also be leveraged to hold master keys, TDE keys, and other key pairs to reduce resource access issues and to boost security posture. Authentication mechanisms granting users access to the OCI console, API access using API keys, and object storage access using Auth tokens must be formalized for IAM user management.

Recent collaboration with other cloud vendors, notably Azure, supports the federation of IAM systems across multi-cloud environments. While this is great for flexible multi-cloud architectures, you now have an additional level of IAM to carefully consider when designing your security posture. As discussed in Chapter 3, IAM federation is not limited to IDCS and can include AD, G Suite, and other SAML 2–compliant directory services. Federating identity providers from the start of your cloud journey is well advised.

Networking

When designing security for your VCN, many OCI networking components are available out of the box to support good practice, starting with private and public subnets. It is usually permissible to expose a public load balancer to the Internet for HTTP traffic to your public website or web applications. These points of entry need to be secured and protected. Sensitive databases should be located in private subnets. NAT gateways may be used for instances in private networks to gain one-way access to Internet resources and still be protected. Use the route table infrastructure to ensure that Dynamic Routing Gateways only route allowed traffic between your VCN and your on-premises network or other cloud networks.

Each subnet can have one route table comprising rules that route traffic to one or more targets. It is good practice for hosts that have similar routing requirements to use the same route tables across multiple ADs. It is also recommended that private subnets have individual route tables to control traffic flow. Traffic between all compute instances within a VCN is routable, but the VCN route table limits routing of traffic into and out of the VCN.

Each subnet may have multiple security lists, each of which supports multiple stateful and stateless ingress and egress rules. You must ensure that security lists behave like firewalls, managing traffic into and out of the VCN (known as North–South traffic) as well as managing internal VCN traffic between multiple subnets (known as East–West traffic).

If access to compute resources is required from the public Internet, it is good practice to create a Bastion host. A Bastion host, or server, is colloquially known as a jump-box designed and configured to withstand attacks.

Compute Instances

Security in OCI is a shared responsibility between you and Oracle. Using DBaaS and compute instances based on Oracle-supplied images is a safer bet than using custom images and manual software and database installations because the default images are already security hardened by the OCI security specialists at Oracle. It is highly recommended to start your customized compute and database system using a supplied image. Bare metal instances are available with no Oracle-managed software. These instances do not benefit from the security hardening and must be hardened by your internal security team.

Storage and Databases

Data is your biggest asset and must be protected. Place sensitive data in encrypted databases, which are encrypted at rest and in-transit. Set up auditing to track who accesses and updates data in both your file systems and databases. When backups are made, ensure these are encrypted, keeping encryption keys in corporate key vaults.

Formulate and formalize a data strategy for data stored in your tenancy that explicitly encourages the use of best practices when using local file systems on block volumes, object storage buckets, shared file storage, and databases to eliminate the risk of errant files with sensitive data being exposed.

Chapter Review

This chapter discussed high availability and disaster recovery architectural considerations as well as a consolidated high-level outlook on designing a future cloud security posture by embracing best practices and leveraging lessons from your own organizational security legacy.

There are many permutations of OCI resources that will address any HADR requirement. In reality, we are governed by three main considerations: budget, RPO, and RTO. Understanding that the HADR design exercise is constrained by these three considerations is likely to yield an optimal architecture. Not all systems require a zero downtime, zero data loss, sufficiently engineered solution. But some do.

Cloud is the future and cloud vendors continue to innovate and compete for your business. HADR and security are key areas to design correctly. But it is not over when you build it. These topics are highly visible, and it is highly recommended that you attend to the latest developments and innovations available to evolve your design to ensure a safe and highly available infrastructure that is resilient to disaster.

Questions

1. RTO is an important concept related to high availability and disaster recovery. What sentiment is associated with RTO?
   - A. RTO specifies the amount of data loss that is tolerable for a system without impacting the business too negatively.
   - B. RTO specifies the amount of time it takes to restore service for a system without impacting the business too negatively.
   - C. Oracle redo transactions are shipped to the Data Guard standby database.
   - D. Real-time Oracle is a logical replication solution that mirrors an existing system.
2. RPO is an important concept related to high availability and disaster recovery. What sentiment is associated with RPO?
   - A. RPO specifies the amount of data loss that is tolerable for a system without impacting the business too negatively.
   - B. RPO specifies the amount of time it takes to restore service for a system without impacting the business too negatively.
   - C. The Oracle redo process generates redo logs essential to instance recovery.
   - D. The Oracle replication process is a solution that clones an existing system.
3. Which type of IP address may be unassigned and reassigned between compute instances?
   - A. Public IP
   - B. Private IP
   - C. IPv6 IP
   - D. Floating IP
4. DenseIO compute shapes include support for direct attached NVMe disks. What steps, if any, are required to ensure redundancy for this type of storage?
   - A. This storage is mirrored at the SAN level. No further steps are required.
   - B. Object storage mirrors must be configured.
   - C. Direct attached NVMe disks are preconfigured as highly available storage.
   - D. Some RAID configuration must be implemented to support redundancy for generic file system storage.
5. Which of the following statements is true?
   - A. All OCI regions have three availability domains.
   - B. HADR is not possible in a region with only one AD.
   - C. Each AD has three fault domains.
   - D. All OCI regions have three fault domains.

6. What process coordinates a fast-start-fail-over event in a Data Guard setup that automates a primary database failover to its standby?
   - **A.** Observer
   - **B.** Watcher
   - **C.** Listener
   - **D.** Active Data Guard
7. Which of the following statements is true?
   - **A.** You can only interact with OCI resources using the CLI and Terraform.
   - **B.** You can only interact with OCI resources using the CLI, Terraform and SDKs.
   - **C.** You can only interact with OCI resources using the CLI, Terraform, SDKs, and the OCI console.
   - **D.** You can interact with OCI using any tool through the OCI API endpoints.
8. Which of the following statements is true? (Choose all that apply.)
   - **A.** A RAC database is concurrently mounted by one or more database instances, each running on a separate compute node.
   - **B.** RAC databases can tolerate the loss of a RAC node.
   - **C.** As long as there is at least one RAC node available, the database remains accessible.
   - **D.** Both primary and standby databases in a Data Guard configuration may be RAC databases.
9. Which of these options may provide zero data loss solutions for Oracle databases?
   - **A.** Oracle RAC
   - **B.** Oracle Data Guard in Maximum Performance mode
   - **C.** Oracle Data Guard in Maximum Protection mode
   - **D.** Oracle Data Guard in Maximum Availability mode
10. List two basic approaches to synchronizing general purpose file systems for HADR.
   - **A.** Private peering
   - **B.** Synchronous replication
   - **C.** File Storage Service snapshots
   - **D.** Asynchronous replication

Answers

1. **B.** RTO specifies the amount of time it takes to restore service for a system without impacting the business too negatively.
2. **A.** RPO specifies the amount of data loss that is tolerable for a system without impacting the business too negatively.

3. **D.** Floating IP addresses may be unassigned from one compute instance and reassigned to another. It is often possible to automate the allocation of a floating IP address to a standby instance to minimize downtime.
4. **D.** DenseIO compute shapes include support for direct attached NVMe disks. This storage is not SAN-based. There is no redundancy built in and it is your responsibility to set up appropriate redundancy using some sort of RAID configuration if they are used for generic file system storage.
5. **C.** Each AD has three fault domains providing physical server isolation for VMs created in separate FDs in the same AD.
6. **A.** A Data Guard observer is configured to orchestrate a fast-start-fail-over (FSFO) if issues with the primary database system are detected.
7. **D.** You can interact with OCI using any tool through the OCI API endpoints. You are not confined to using any specific tools.
8. **A, B, C, D.** RAC and Data Guard form a potent pair in providing HADR for Oracle databases.
9. **C.** Data Guard in Maximum Protection mode ensures synchronous replication achieving zero data loss at the cost of potential waits on the primary database for confirmation that the captured redo stream has been successfully shipped and applied on the standby.
10. **A, D.** Synchronous replication supports zero data loss but incurs waits while transported IOs are acknowledged and remote IOs are confirmed. Asynchronous replication risks data loss in the event of an outage, but changes to the primary site are shipped to the standby with no need to wait for confirmation that the changes have been received and applied. There is no blocking or waiting with this approach and it is suitable for synchronizing data between instances in different regions.

About the Online Content

This book comes complete with TotalTester Online customizable practice exam software with 140 practice exam questions.

System Requirements

The current and previous major versions of the following desktop browsers are recommended and supported: Chrome, Microsoft Edge, Firefox, and Safari. These browsers update frequently, and sometimes an update may cause compatibility issues with the TotalTester Online or other content hosted on the Training Hub. If you run into a problem using one of these browsers, please try using another until the problem is resolved.

Your Total Seminars Training Hub Account

To get access to the online content, you will need to create an account on the Total Seminars Training Hub. Registration is free, and you will be able to track all your online content using your account. You may also opt in if you wish to receive marketing information from McGraw-Hill Education or Total Seminars, but this is not required for you to gain access to the online content.

Privacy Notice

McGraw-Hill Education values your privacy. Please be sure to read the Privacy Notice available during registration to see how the information you have provided will be used. You may view our Corporate Customer Privacy Policy by visiting the McGraw-Hill Education Privacy Center. Visit the **mheducation.com** site and click **Privacy** at the bottom of the page.

Single User License Terms and Conditions

Online access to the digital content included with this book is governed by the McGraw-Hill Education License Agreement outlined next. By using this digital content you agree to the terms of that license.

Access To register and activate your Total Seminars Training Hub account, simply follow these easy steps.

1. Go to **hub.totalsem.com/mheclaim**
2. To register and create a new Training Hub account, enter your e-mail address, name, and password. No further personal information (such as credit card number) is required to create an account.

NOTE If you already have a Total Seminars Training Hub account, select **Log in** and enter your e-mail and password. Otherwise, follow the remaining steps.

3. Enter your Product Key: `22b3-3hh3-39fw`
4. Click to accept the user license terms.
5. Click **Register and Claim** to create your account. You will be taken to the Training Hub and have access to the content for this book.

Duration of License Access to your online content through the Total Seminars Training Hub will expire one year from the date the publisher declares the book out of print.

Your purchase of this McGraw-Hill Education product, including its access code, through a retail store is subject to the refund policy of that store.

Restrictions on Transfer The user is receiving only a limited right to use the Content for the user's own internal and personal use, dependent on purchase and continued ownership of this book. The user may not reproduce, forward, modify, create derivative works based upon, transmit, distribute, disseminate, sell, publish, or sublicense the Content or in any way commingle the Content with other third-party content without McGraw-Hill Education's consent.

Limited Warranty The McGraw-Hill Education Content is provided on an "as is" basis. Neither McGraw-Hill Education nor its licensors make any guarantees or warranties of any kind, either express or implied, including, but not limited to, implied warranties of merchantability or fitness for a particular purpose or use as to any McGraw-Hill Education Content or the information therein or any warranties as to the accuracy, completeness, correctness, or results to be obtained from, accessing or using the McGraw-Hill Education Content, or any material referenced in such Content or any information entered into licensee's product by users or other persons and/or any material available on or that can be accessed through the licensee's product (including via any hyperlink or otherwise) or as to non-infringement of third-party rights.

Any warranties of any kind, whether express or implied, are disclaimed. Any material or data obtained through use of the McGraw-Hill Education Content is at your own discretion and risk and user understands that it will be solely responsible for any resulting damage to its computer system or loss of data.

Neither McGraw-Hill Education nor its licensors shall be liable to any subscriber or to any user or anyone else for any inaccuracy, delay, interruption in service, error or omission, regardless of cause, or for any damage resulting therefrom.

In no event will McGraw-Hill Education or its licensors be liable for any indirect, special or consequential damages, including but not limited to, lost time, lost money, lost profits or good will, whether in contract, tort, strict liability or otherwise, and whether or not such damages are foreseen or unforeseen with respect to any use of the McGraw-Hill Education Content.

TotalTester Online

TotalTester Online provides you with a simulation of the Oracle Cloud Infrastructure Architect Associate (1Z0-1072) exam. Exams can be taken in Practice Mode or Exam Mode. Practice Mode provides an assistance window with hints, references to the book, explanations of the correct and incorrect answers, and the option to check your answer as you take the test. Exam Mode provides a simulation of the actual exam. The number of questions, the types of questions, and the time allowed are intended to be an accurate representation of the exam environment. The option to customize your quiz allows you to create custom exams from selected domains or chapters, and you can further customize the number of questions and time allowed.

To take a test, follow the instructions provided in the previous section to register and activate your Total Seminars Training Hub account. When you register you will be taken to the Total Seminars Training Hub. From the Training Hub Home page, select **Oracle Cloud Infrastructure Arch Assoc (1Z0-1072) TotalTester** from the Study drop-down menu at the top of the page, or from the list of Your Topics on the Home page. You can then select the option to customize your quiz and begin testing yourself in Practice Mode or Exam Mode. All exams provide an overall grade and a grade broken down by domain.

Technical Support

For questions regarding the TotalTester or operation of the Training Hub, visit **www.totalsem.com** or e-mail **support@totalsem.com**.

For questions regarding book content, e-mail **hep_customer-service@mheducation.com**. For customers outside the United States, e-mail **international_cs@mheducation.com**.

AD Availability domain. OCI represents a collection of resources, both virtualized and bare metal systems grouped in data centers known as availability domains (ADs).

ADB Autonomous database systems offer a hosted and managed option with an underlying Exadata service and the capability to dynamically scale up and scale down both the CPUs and storage allocated to your VM. ADB is a pluggable database and is available on a shared or dedicated Exadata infrastructure. ADW and ATP are two types of ADBs.

ADW, ADWC Autonomous data warehouse, or ADW cloud, is a type of ADB designed for analytic workloads, including data warehouses and marts, data lakes, and large machine learning databases with configuration parameters biased toward high-volume ordered data-scanning operations.

API Application programming interface. A defined method for interacting with Oracle Cloud Infrastructure resources using REST web services. In the context of interacting with Oracle databases, APIs are a defined method for manipulating data, typically implemented as a set of PL/SQL procedures in a package.

ASM Automatic Storage Management. An LVM provided with the Oracle database.

ATP Autonomous Transaction Processing is a type of ADB designed for OLTP databases, and configuration parameters are biased toward high-volume random data access typical of OLTP systems. ATP databases are also suitable for mixed workloads, including some batch processing reporting, IoT, and machine learning as well as transaction processing. ATP on dedicated infrastructure is known as ATP-D while serverless ATP is known as ATP-S.

auto scaling The auto scaling feature available for serverless autonomous databases enables dynamic CPU scaling as load demand fluctuates.

autoscaling Autoscaling refers to the dynamic addition or removal of instances from an instance pool based on an autoscaling policy that defines scaling limits and scaling rules that determine the conditions that trigger the scale-out or scale-in of instances in an instance pool.

backend set A backend set is a logical grouping of backend servers and a traffic distribution policy. Traffic from load balancers is sent to backend set instances.

block volumes Block volumes are provided to your compute instances by the OCI block volume service, which manages and carves out block storage volumes per your requirements. A block volume is initially equivalent to an unformatted disk with no partitioning or file system. Block volumes may be created, attached, connected, or detached from compute instances. There are two types of block storage volumes. A boot volume is used as the image source for a compute instance while a block volume allows dynamic expansion of storage capacity of an instance

BM Bare metal instances reside on physical equipment localized in a data center or AD. A BM instance executes on a dedicated x86 server providing strong isolation and highest performance.

BMCS Bare Metal Cloud Services. Oracle Cloud Infrastructure was previously known as BMCS.

boot volume A special type of block volume that contains a boot image.

bucket A logical container for objects that reside in a compartment and may exist at one of two tiers: standard tier and archive tier storage.

BYOH Bring Your Own Hypervisor. OCI provides support for installing several hypervisors on bare metal instances. Supported hypervisors include the following: kernel-based VM (KVM), Oracle VM (OVM), and Hyper-V.

BYOI Bring Your Own Image allows custom images to be imported into OCI in one of three modes: native, paravirtualized, and emulated mode.

BYOL Bring Your Own License. BYOL allows your pre-existing license to be reused on a DBCS system.

CIDR A Classless Inter-Domain Routing (often pronounced cider) block specifies a range of IP addresses that may be allocated to a VCN or subnet. CIDR notation is based on an IPv4 or IPv6 network or routing prefix separated by a slash from a number indicating the prefix length.

cluster A hardware environment where more than one computer shares access to storage.

compartments OCI resources are grouped into compartments. When an OCI account is provisioned, several compartments are automatically created, including the root compartment of the tenancy. An OCI resource can only belong to one compartment. Because compartments are logical structures, resources that make up or reside on the same VCN can belong to different compartments.

complete recovery Following a restore of damaged database files, a complete recovery applies all redo to bring the database up-to-date with no loss of data.

compute shape A predefined bundle of computing resources, primarily differentiated by OCPUs, memory, network interfaces, network bandwidth, and support for block and NVMe local storage.

connect identifier An Oracle Net service name.

connect string The database connection details needed to establish a session: the address of the listener and the service or instance name.

container database A database in a multitenant environment that hosts zero, one, or more pluggable databases (PDBs). It will always host the root container and the seed container.

CPE Customer Premises Equipment refers to the network edge router on your on-premises network. You may set up a connection between your CPE and a dynamic routing gateway in your VCN to connect these networks.

CPU Central processing unit. The chip that provides the processing capability of a computer, such as an Intel XEON 8260.

Data Guard Data Guard mitigates against node, storage, and even AD failure in multi-AD regions. Data Guard replication configuration consists of a primary database and at least one standby database. Each system is a fully operational Oracle server with nodes, instances, and independent sets of database files. The primary and standby systems are almost exclusively on separate infrastructure to provide business continuity in case there is a failure of the primary system.

Data Pump A facility for transferring large amounts of data at high speed into, out of, or between databases.

data residency Data residency refers to a data location policy usually associated with highly regulated and sensitive environments, which limits the consumption of data storage services to only resources within a particular locale.

data sovereignty Data sovereignty refers to a data management policy usually associated with highly regulated and sensitive environments, which limits the management of data to personnel located in a particular geographic region.

data transfer service Oracle offers an offline, secure data transfer service to upload data to your designated object storage bucket at no additional cost.

datafile The disk-based structure for storing data in the context of an Oracle database.

DBA Database administrator. The person responsible for creating and managing Oracle databases—this could be you.

DBaaS Database as a Service. *See* DBCS.

DBCS Database Cloud Service is a PaaS service that provides you with a fully functional and deployed Oracle database platform on a virtual machine (VM), bare metal (BM), or Exadata server.

DBMS Database management system. Often used interchangeably with RDBMS.

DHCP Dynamic Host Configuration Protocol services provide configuration information to compute instances at boot time. You can influence only a subset of the DHCP service offerings by setting DHCP options that apply to all compute instances created in the subnet or VCN.

DNS The Domain Name System is a directory that maps hostnames to IP addresses. The OCI DNS service is a regional service.

DRG A Dynamic Routing Gateway connects your VCN to other networks.

emulated mode A compute instance launched in emulated mode is fully virtualized and runs without modification on the OCI hypervisor.

ExaCS Exadata Cloud Service places the stable and mature Exadata engineered system within reach of any OCI tenancy. The Exadata platform is built with redundancy and high-performance components at its core and consists of preconfigured compute nodes, storage cells, and networking infrastructure. Exadata system software unlocks unique database software optimizations that include SmartScan, Storage Indexes, and Hybrid Columnar Compression.

fast incremental database backup An incremental backup that uses a block change tracking file to identify only changed blocks since the last backup.

FastConnect FastConnect is used to create a dedicated high-speed private connection between on-premises networks and OCI VCNs. FastConnect provides consistent, predictable, secure, and reliable performance.

fault domain Fault domains are sets of fault-tolerant isolated physical infrastructure within an AD. By choosing different fault domains for two VM instances, you ensure these are hosted on separate physical hardware, thus increasing your intra-availability domain resilience.

FSS The File Storage Service (FSS) provides network file systems (NFSv3) that provide shared storage to instances in the same region and offers exabyte scale storage.

FSS snapshots FSS snapshots are a read-only point-in-time backup of an FSS file system located in a hidden directory named .snapshot in the root directory of the FSS file system.

full database backup A backup containing all blocks of the files backed up, not only those blocks changed since the last backup.

GI Grid Infrastructure is specialized Oracle software used for supporting databases that use ASM for storage and provides cluster services used by RAC databases and the Oracle Restart feature, which improves database availability by automatically restarting various Oracle components.

GPU Graphical Processing Units. OCI compute instances based on GPU shapes are based on servers with NVIDIA GPUs.

HPC High Performance Computing. OCI compute instances based on HPC shapes offer supercomputer high-performance compute power.

HTTP Hypertext Transfer Protocol. The layered protocol, which runs over TCP/IP, enables the World Wide Web.

I/O Input/output. The activity of reading from or writing to disks—often the slowest point of a data processing operation.

IaaS Infrastructure as a Service. A collection of servers, storage, and network infrastructure onto which you deploy your platform and software. IaaS is an abstraction of these infrastructure components available in an online marketplace, enabling you to choose the most appropriate combination of these elements to meet your computing requirements. OCI and other IaaS vendors provide this fundamental service.

IaC Infrastructure as Code enables consistent, infrastructure architectures to be programmatically deployed using tools including the OCI CLI and Terraform.

image copy An RMAN copy of a file.

inconsistent backup A backup made while the database was open.

incremental database backup A backup containing only blocks that have been changed since the last backup was made.

instance configurations Instance configurations provide a system for creating configuration templates from existing compute instances.

instance pools Instance configurations form the basis for instance pools. These are pools of compute instances created using the instance configuration templates in a particular region.

instance recovery The automatic repair of damage caused by a disorderly shutdown of the database.

Internet gateway An Internet gateway is attached to any new VCN. It allows resources and services with public IP addresses to be reached over the Internet and for these instances to connect to the Internet.

IP Internet Protocol. Together with the Transmission Control Protocol, IP makes up the de facto standard communication protocol (TCP/IP) used for client-server communication over a network.

iSCSI Internet Small Computer Systems Interface. Block volumes can be connected to compute instances using the iSCSI protocol over a TCP/IP network connection. iSCSI is an established storage communications protocol and is supported on bare metal and VM instances.

JSON JavaScript Object Notation is an open-standard file format that describes data objects in terms of attribute-value pairs as well as supporting array data types. JSON format files may be used as an input or an output format for the OCI CLI.

level 0 incremental backup A full RMAN backup that can be used as the basis for an incremental backup strategy.

level 1 cumulative incremental backup An RMAN backup of all changed blocks since the last level 0 incremental backup.

level 1 differential incremental backup An RMAN backup of all changed blocks since the last level 0 or level 1 incremental backup.

listener, database The server-side process that listens for database connection requests from user processes, and launches server processes to establish sessions.

listener, load balancer Each listener in a load balancer defines a set of properties that include a unique combination of protocol (HTTP or TCP) and port number. Incoming network traffic to a load balancer is received by the listener and handed off to underlying backend set servers.

load balancer A load balancer is a network device that ultimately routes traffic to one or more reachable backend compute instances (called backend servers) that reside in any subnet in the VCN.

LPG A local peering gateway allows VCNs in the same region, regardless of tenancy, to act as peers and supports instances in one VCN connecting to instances in another VCN using private IP addresses.

LVM Logical Volume Manager. A layer of software that abstracts the physical storage within your computer from the logical storage visible to an application.

mounted database A situation where the instance has opened the database control file, but not the online redo logfiles or the datafiles. Traditional Data Guard physical standby databases operate in mount mode while Active Data Guard physical standby databases are in open mode.

MTTR Mean Time To Recover. The average time it takes to make the database available for normal use after a failure.

multiplexing To maintain multiple copies of files.

multitenant architecture An architecture that hosts many logical databases within one larger database instance to more efficiently use server resources such as memory, CPU, and I/O.

namespace A logical grouping of objects within which no two objects may have the same name.

NAT gateway A network address translation gateway allows instances with no public IP addresses to access the Internet while protecting the instance from incoming traffic from the Internet. When an instance makes a request for a network resource outside the VCN, the NAT gateway makes the request on behalf of the instance to the Internet and forwards the response back to the instance.

node A computer attached to a network.

non-CDB A standalone database that cannot automatically be plugged into a CDB and cannot host PDBs. A non-CDB can be at any database version, but to convert to a PDB directly, it must be at version 12.1.0.1 or newer. The non-CDB architecture was the only type of architecture available before release 12.

NVMe (Non-Volatile Memory express) The fastest, most expensive storage options available in OCI are NVMe SSD storage drives attached locally to a compute instance. This storage is typically used in high-performance computing where high IO speeds are required, such as an important transactional database, and provides terabyte-scale capacity.

OCI Oracle Cloud Infrastructure refers to a collection of IaaS and some PaaS offerings and forms part of the Oracle Public Cloud offering.

OCI CLI The OCI Command Line Interface or CLI is based on Python and makes use of JSON input and output formats. The Python code is a wrapper around OCI APIs. OCI CLI commands call these APIs that implement the required functionality supporting script–based OCI resource management.

OCI dynamic group Dynamic groups authorize member instances to interact with OCI resources at a tenancy level by using IAM policies.

OCI group OCI users are organized into groups. A user may belong to many groups.

OCI policy OCI policies are the glue that determines how groups of users interact with OCI resources that are grouped into compartments. Provides capabilities ("permissions").

OCI user An OCI user is an individual or system that has been granted access to OCI resources. There are three types of users: local users, federated users, and provisioned or synchronized users.

OCPU An Oracle Compute Unit is equivalent to a hyper-threaded CPU core in an x86 server. Each OCPU corresponds to two hardware execution threads, known as vCPUs.

offline backup A backup made while the database is closed.

OLAP Online Analytical Processing. Select, intensive work involving running queries against a (usually) large database. Oracle provides OLAP capabilities as an option, in addition to the standard query facilities.

OLTP Online Transaction Processing. A pattern of activity within a database typified by a large number of small, short transactions.

online backup A backup made while the database is open.

ORACLE_BASE The root directory into which Oracle products are installed.

ORACLE_HOME The root directory of any one Oracle product.

Oracle Net Oracle's proprietary communications protocol, layered on top of an industry-standard protocol.

OS Operating system. Typically, in the Oracle database environment this will be a version of Linux (perhaps Unix) or Microsoft Windows.

PaaS Platform as a Service. A collection of one or more preconfigured infrastructure instances usually provided with an operating system, database, or development platform onto which you can deploy your software.

parallelization Using multiple slave processes managed by a single coordinator process to perform queries or DML operations in parallel across multiple CPUs and I/O channels simultaneously. RMAN backups take advantage of parallelism by allocating multiple channels and improving backup performance by executing partitioned chunks of I/O in parallel.

paravirtualized mode Paravirtualized (PV) mode in OCI refers to a type of virtualization used when launching an imported custom image that provides drivers to directly access some of the underlying hardware interfaces instead of emulating these interfaces. An instance launched in PV mode will perform better than one in emulated mode. It is therefore preferable to migrate older systems to newer natively supported images.

PDB *See* pluggable database.

physical backup A copy of the files that constitute the database.

PL/SQL Procedural Language/Structured Query Language. Oracle's proprietary programming language, which combines procedural constructs, such as flow control, and user interface capabilities with the ability to call SQL statements.

pluggable database Also known as a PDB, or a pluggable container. A logical database that exists within a container database and shares the memory, process slots, and other resources with other logical databases within the CDB but is isolated from all other logical databases in the same container. Pluggable databases can be unplugged (removed) from the container database and plugged back in later to the same or different container.

preauthenticated requests A preauthenticated request enables object storage contents or buckets to be shared for a limited time.

private peering Private peering extends your on-premises network into a VCN and may be used to create a hybrid cloud. On-premises connections can be made to the private IP addresses of instances as if they were coming from instances in the VCN. Private peering can also occur between instances in VCNs in other regions.

public load balancer A public load balancer is allocated a public IP address that is routable from the Internet.

public peering Public peering allows you to connect from resources outside the VCN, such as an on-premises network to public OCI services including object storage, without traversing the Internet, over FastConnect.

RAC Real Application Clusters. Oracle database clustering technology, which allows several instances on different machines to open the same database for scalability, performance, and fault tolerance.

RAID Redundant Array of Inexpensive Disks. Techniques for enhancing performance and/or fault tolerance by using a volume manager to present a number of physical disks to the operating system as a single logical disk.

RAM Random access memory. The chips that make up the real memory in your computer hardware, as opposed to the virtual memory presented to software by the operating system.

RDBMS Relational database management system. Often used interchangeably with DBMS.

recovery window An RMAN parameter and time period that defines how far back in time the database can be recovered.

region A region consists of one or more availability domains within a specific geography.

resource consumer groups Groups of users or sessions that have similar resource needs.

restore point A database object containing either a system change number (SCN) or a time in the past used to recover the database to the SCN or timestamp.

retention policy The number of copies of all objects that RMAN will retain for recovery purposes.

RMAN Recovery Manager. Oracle's backup and recovery tool.

RPC A remote peering connection is created on the DRG in both regionally separated VCNs.

RPO Recovery Point Objective refers to how much data loss is tolerable for the organization in the event of a disaster.

route table Route tables contain rules that determine how network traffic coming in or leaving subnets in your VCN is routed.

RTO Recovery Time Objective refers to the duration of a service outage.

SaaS Software as a Service. Applications are deployed and maintained in a cloud and all you do is access them through your browser. SaaS applications range from webmail to complex ERP and BI Analytic systems.

security lists Security lists contain firewall rules for all the compute instances using the subnet. Ingress and egress rules specify whether certain types of traffic are permitted into and out of the VCN respectively. The traffic type is based on the protocol and port, and a rule can be either stateful or stateless. Stateful rules allow connection tracking and are the default, but stateless is recommended if you have high-traffic volumes.

service gateway Allows OCI instances to access OCI services using a private network path on OCI fabric without traffic needing to traverse the Internet.

service name A logical name registered by an instance with a database listener; can be specified by a user process when it issues a connect request.

session A user process and a server process, connected to the instance.

SGA System Global Area. The block of shared memory that contains the memory structures that make up an Oracle instance.

SID System identifier. The name of an instance, which must be unique on the computer the instance is running on. Alternatively, session identifier. The number used to identify uniquely a session logged on to an Oracle database instance.

SQL Structured Query Language. An international standard language for extracting data from and manipulating data in relational databases.

SSL Secure Sockets Layer. A standard for securing data transmission using encryption, checksumming, and digital certificates.

subnet A portion of your network or VCN that comprises a contiguous CIDR block that is a subset of the VCN CIDR block.

tag A tag is simply a key-value pair that you associate with a resource. There are two types of tagging: free-form and defined tags. Free-form tags are descriptive metadata about a resource, but they are not subject to any constraints. Defined or schema tagging is the recommended enterprise-grade mechanism for organizing, reporting, filtering, managing, and performing bulk actions on your OCI resources.

TCP Transmission Control Protocol. Together with the Internet Protocol, TCP makes up the de facto standard communication protocol (TCP/IP) used for client-server communication over a network.

TCPS TCP with SSL. The Secure Sockets version of TCP.

TDE Transparent Data Encryption is a feature of the Database Advanced Security Option that is included for database encryption across all editions using DBaaS on OCI.

Terraform Terraform is an industry standard declarative tool used to automate the full infrastructure lifecycle from the provision stage to updates and maintenance to the destroy stage. Terraform is developed by HashiCorp and is integrated into OCI through the Terraform provider for OCI.

TNS Transparent Network Substrate. The heart of Oracle Net, TNS is a proprietary layered protocol running on top of whatever underlying network transport protocol you choose to use—probably TCP/IP.

TSPITR Tablespace point-in-time recovery. A recovery method that is ideal for recovering a set of objects isolated to a single tablespace.

UI User interface. The layer of an application that communicates with end users—nowadays, frequently graphical: a GUI.

URL Uniform Resource Locator. A standard for specifying the location of an object on the Internet, consisting of a protocol, a hostname and domain, an IP port number, a path and filename, and a series of parameters.

user-managed recovery Using tools or commands outside of RMAN to recover a database or tablespace.

VCN A virtual cloud network, which works much like a traditional private, on-premises network. It is a regional resource that spans all ADs in a region and resides in a compartment. At least one VCN must be set up before compute instances may be provisioned.

VCN peering VCN peering refers to connecting your VCN to other networks.

vCPU A virtual CPU or vCPU is equivalent to a single CPU core hardware execution thread in an x86 server.

virtualization Virtualization of resources is the underlying philosophy behind IaaS. On premises, virtualization technologies like Oracle Virtual Machine (OVM) paved the way for consolidation and pooling of resources and sharing these between VMs to optimize hardware and infrastructure efficiency.

VM Virtual machines reside on physical equipment localized in a data center or AD. A VM is defined as an independent computing environment executing on physical hardware. Multiple VMs may share the same physical hardware.

vNIC A virtualized network interface card (NIC) resides in a subnet and is allocated to a compute instance, thus allowing the instance to connect to the subnet's VCN. Upon launch of a compute instance, a private, unremovable vNIC is assigned to the instance and allocated a private IP address.

volume groups Block volumes may be grouped with other block volumes to form a logical set known as a volume group. Volume groups may be backed up together to form a consistent point-in-time backup that is also useful for cloning.

whole-database backup A database backup that includes all datafiles plus the control file.

INDEX

A

A DNS record type, 122
AAAA DNS record type, 122
access control lists (ACLs), 297
accounts, creating, 4–8
ACFS (ASM File System), 242
ACTION commands in instance power management, 174
Active Data Guard (ADG) option, 293, 355
Active Directory in federated OCI, 64
AD attribute in block volumes, 189
ADB. *See* autonomous database (ADB) systems
Add SSH Key screen, 158
add-vnic command, 175
administration in autonomous database systems, 302–303
ADs. *See* availability domains (ADs)
ADW (Autonomous Data Warehouse) services, 239–240
  vs. ATP, 294
  resources, 53
ALIAS DNS record type, 122
Amazon Web Services (AWS), 11
AMD processors for compute shapes, 143
API keys
  OCI CLI, 327
  Terraform, 334
APIs
  federated OCI, 64–66
  IAM resources, 40
  OCIDs for, 47
  permissions, 36–38
apply command in HCL, 337–338
archive storage, 21–22
archive tier buckets, 215–217
ASM (Automatic Storage Management), 241–243
ASM File System (ACFS), 242
asynchronous replication, 350
ATP (Autonomous Transaction Processing) services, 239
  vs. ADW, 294
  description, 293
  resources, 53
Attach Dynamic Routing Gateway screen, 113
attaching block volumes, 192–195
authentication
  Auth tokens, 32
  autonomous database systems, 297
  database backups, 275
  federated OCI, 64–66
  IAM. *See* Identity and Access Management (IAM)
  OCI CLI, 325
automatic backups, 277, 279–281
Automatic Storage Management (ASM), 241–243
automation tools, 321
  OCI CLI, 321–333
  questions, 340–342
  review, 340
  Terraform, 333–339
Autonomous Data Warehouse (ADW) services, 239–240
  vs. ATP, 294
  resources, 53
autonomous database (ADB) systems
  backups and recovery, 300–301
  connecting, 297–300
  creating, 294–297
  HADR architecture, 356
  operating, 301–303
  variants, 293–294
Autonomous Transaction Processing (ATP) services, 239
  vs. ADW, 294
  description, 293
  resources, 53

autoscaling
- custom images, 147
- instance pools, 178–179

availability
- Data Guard, 354
- database migration, 308
- HADR architecture. *See* HADR architecture

availability domains (ADs)
- compute instances, 142
- description, 2–3
- HADR architecture, 345–346
- overview, 11–15
- resources, 43–47

AVAILABLE attribute in block volume lifecycle-state, 190

AWS (Amazon Web Services), 11

B

backend sets, 19, 130–132

backups
- autonomous database systems, 300–301
- block volumes, 189, 204–213
- console, 277–281
- copying, 212–213
- Database Cloud Services, 267–282
- dbcli utility, 267–273
- Exadata, 281–282
- full, 207
- manual, 205–206
- policies, 205
- RMAN, 273–277
- volume groups, 208–210

bandwidth of networks, 13

Bare Metal Cloud Services (BMCS), 240

bare-metal machines and database systems
- block volume connections, 192
- compute instances, 15, 20, 22, 142–143
- Database Cloud Services, 242–246
- Exadata, 247–248
- hypervisors, 142, 152
- IP address space and DNS requirements, 256
- network requirements, 250
- servers, 3
- virtual machines, 250, 257

Berkeley Internet Name Domain (BIND), 116

best practice architectures. *See* HADR architecture

BGP (Border Gateway Protocol), 90, 349

bi-directional topology in GoldenGate, 356

BIND (Berkeley Internet Name Domain), 116

blkid command, 200

block size in database migration, 307

block storage, 21
- attaching, 192–195
- backups, 204–213
- connecting, 195–198
- creating, 189–192
- deleting, 210
- file systems, 198–199
- formatting, 198–200
- groups, 207–210
- mounting, 199–200
- overview, 188–189
- presenting, 200–204
- recovery, 210–213

Block Volume service
- boot volumes, 150
- OCI CLI, 330

BMCS (Bare Metal Cloud Services), 240

boot volumes
- compute instances, 149–151
- description, 189

Border Gateway Protocol (BGP), 90, 349

Bring Your Own Hypervisor (BYOH), 151–152

bring your own license (BYOL), 23, 257–258, 286–287

broadcast addresses in CIDR, 76

broadcast topology in GoldenGate, 355

Bucket Resource-Type for permissions, 36–38

buckets
- archive tier, 215–217
- backups, 267–268, 270–271, 273–277
- credentials, 32
- multipart uploads, 219–220
- object storage, 21–22, 188, 213–215
- permissions, 36–38
- pre-authenticated requests, 220–221
- standard tier, 217–219

bulk loader in database migration, 310–311

business units in IAM, 31

bv backup command, 330
BYOH (Bring Your Own Hypervisor), 151–152
BYOL (bring your own license), 23, 257–258, 286–287

C

cascading topology in GoldenGate, 356
CDBs (container databases)
  Database Cloud Services, 250
  database migration, 307
certificate-based authentication, 297
Challenge Handshake Authentication Protocol (CHAP), 193, 195–198
character sets
  Database Cloud Services, 261
  database migration, 307
child compartments, 35
Choose Instance Type screen, 157
Classless Inter-Domain Routing (CIDR)
  OCI CLI, 332
  overview, 75–79
  VNC design, 18, 136
cloud computing models, 9–11
clusters. *See* Real Application Clusters (RACs)
CNAME DNS record type, 122
colocation model in FastConnect, 89
command-line interface. *See* OCI command line interface (CLI)
compartments
  block volumes, 189
  creating, 44–47
  IAM, 29–31
  policies, 35
  resources, 57–60
complexity in database migration, 307
compute instances, 20
  autoscaling, 178–179
  boot volumes, 149–151
  compute images, 144–152, 162–167
  compute service components, 142–152
  compute shapes, 142–144
  configurations, 176–179
  console connections, 179–182
  creating, 152–162
  dynamic groups, 67, 69
  HADR architecture, 346–348, 350–351, 358
  introduction, 141
  managing, 174–175
  metadata, 174
  multiple vNICs, 175
  pools, 176–178
  power management, 174
  questions, 183–185
  review, 182
  virtual cloud networks, 84
  Windows, 170–173
conditions in policies, 54–56
connections
  autonomous database systems, 297–300
  block volumes, 195–198
  compute instances, 179–182
  database migration, 304
console
  autonomous database systems, 294–297
  backups, 277–281
  compute instances connections, 179–182
  launching, 8
consolidation topology in GoldenGate, 356
container databases (CDBs)
  Database Cloud Services, 250
  database migration, 307
Copy Block Volume Backup screen, 212
copying backups, 212–213
cores in processor-based licensing, 284–285
costs
  database migration, 307
  IAM, 31
CPE (Customer Premises Equipment), 20
CPUs
  autonomous database systems, 301
  description, 2
Create Autonomous Database screen, 295
Create Backup screen, 278
create-backupconfig command, 271–272
Create Block Volume screen, 190–191
Create Compute Instance screen, 157, 164, 170–171
Create Custom Image screen, 163
Create Dynamic Routing Gateway screen, 112
Create File System screen, 226

Create Internet Gateway screen, 254
Create Load Balancer screen, 167–168
Create Local Peering Gateway screen, 107–108
Create Namespace Definition screen, 50–51, 58
Create NAT Gateway screen, 100–101
create-objectstoreswift command, 271
Create Pre-Authenticated Request screen, 220–221
Create Remote Peering Connection screen, 113
create-rmanbackupreport command, 281
Create Route Table screen, 101–102, 105
Create Service Gateway screen, 104, 253
Create Subnet screen, 97–98
Create Virtual Cloud Network screen, 96–97, 252
Create Volume Group screen, 208, 211
credentials for accounts, 32–33
cross-platform transportable tablespaces in abase migration, 313
CSI (Customer Support Identifier) numbers, 7
custom images
  compute instances, 146–149
  creating, 162–167
Custom Resolver, 118
Customer Premises Equipment (CPE), 20
Customer secret keys in federated OCI, 65
Customer Support Identifier (CSI) numbers, 7

D

data center failures, 288
DATA disk group
  bare metal database systems, 245
  database files, 243
  description, 241
  Exadata, 248–249
Data Guard
  database migration, 312
  HADR architecture, 343, 353–355
  high availability, 290–293
Data Pump, 309–310, 313–314
data residency regulations in GoldenGate, 28
Data Transfer Appliances, 305
data transfer service for base migration, 304–306, 308
Data Transfer Utility (DTU)
  database migration, 305
  resource locations, 39
Database as a Service (DBaaS)
  description, 9–10
  HADR architecture, 352
Database Cloud Services (DBCS), 239
  backups, 267–282
  bare metal database systems, 242–246
  Data Guard, 291–292
  dbcli utility, 265–267
  description, 22–23
  encryption, 287
  Exadata, 247–249
  licensing, 286–287
  network requirements, 250–267
  overview, 240–242
  patching, 282–283
  SQL Developer, 264–265
  SQL*Plus utility, 262–264
  VM, 250, 257–262
Database Connection screen, 299
database HADR, 351–356
database resource managers, 298
databases, 239–240
  autonomous database systems, 293–303
  bare-metal. *See* bare-metal machines and database systems
  Database Cloud Services, 283
  HADR architecture, 358
  high availability, 287–293
  licensing, 283–287
  migration. *See* migration of databases
  questions, 317–319
  review, 316–317
db version list command, 331
DBaaS (Database as a Service)
  description, 9–10
  HADR architecture, 352
dbcli utility
  backups, 267–273, 281
  Database Cloud Services, 265–267
  encryption, 287

DBCS. *See* Database Cloud Services (DBCS)
DBMS_CLOUD.CREATE_CREDENTIAL package, 300
DCS-10045 validation error in backups, 272
DDoS (distributed denial of service) attacks
  DNS protection for, 121
  HADR architecture, 351
defined tags, 50–52
deleting block volumes, 210
DenseIO compute, 350
describe-rmanbackupreport command, 281
destroy command in HCL, 337, 339
DHCP
  IP addresses, 84
  networks, 74–75
  options, 81, 98
  subnets, 117
  VCNs, 97, 118
Disaster Recovery (DR), 343
  autonomous database systems, 300–301
  availability domains, 13
  block volumes, 210–213
  HADR architecture. *See* HADR architecture
disk-based database backups, 268–270
distributed denial of service (DDoS) attacks
  DNS protection for, 121
  HADR architecture, 351
DNAME DNS record type, 122
dnsdomain command, 118
Domain Name System (DNS)
  concepts and features, 116–120
  Database Cloud Services requirements, 256
  description, 19
  HADR architecture, 347
  in OCI, 115–126
  records, 121–126
downloading objects, 216–218
DRGs. *See* Dynamic Routing Gateways (DRGs)
DTU (Data Transfer Utility)
  database migration, 305
  resource locations, 39
dynamic groups
  description, 38–39
  setting up, 66–69
Dynamic Routing Gateways (DRGs)
  Database Cloud Services, 250–251
  description, 20
  overview, 88–90
  RPCs, 94

E

East–West traffic, 137, 358
edge security in networking, 137
Edit Route Rules screen, 110, 115
Egress Rules screen, 256
egress security list rules, 282
emulated mode for custom images, 147–148
encryption
  block volumes, 189
  Database Cloud Services, 267, 287
  SSH key pairs, 154
  wallet backups, 270–271
end-to-end SSL, 129
ephemeral IP addresses, 85
equality operators for dynamic groups, 67
Establish Peering Connection screen, 109
/etc/fstab file, 198–199
/etc/hosts file, 119
/etc/nsswitch.conf file, 119
/etc/resolv.conf file, 119–120
Exadata
  backups, 281–282
  Database Cloud Services, 247–249
  servers, 239–240
Exadata Cloud at Customer (ExaCC), 309
Exadata on DBCS (ExaCS), 247
Exchange Partner for FastConnect, 349
export options and utilities
  database migration, 311–312
  FSS, 224

F

failover role transitions in Data Guard, 291, 354
family resource-types in policies, 52–54
Fast Application Notification (FAN) Event traffic, 251
Fast Recovery Area (FRA)
  backups, 273
  Database Cloud Services, 267
  Exadata backups, 282

fast-start-fail-over (FSFO) in Data Guard, 293
FastConnect
  autonomous database systems, 297
  database migration, 304
  description, 20
  Dynamic Routing Gateways, 89
  HADR architecture, 348–349
fault domains, 12
fault-tolerant data centers, 11
FAULTY attribute in block volume lifecycle-state, 190
fdisk command, 197–199
federated OCI, 64–66
file storage service (FSS), 187–188, 222
  concepts, 222–224
  creating, 225–232
  description, 22
  snapshots, 232–234
file systems, creating, 198–199
formatting block volumes, 198–200
FQDNs (fully qualified domain names), 116–118, 256
FRA (Fast Recovery Area)
  backups, 273
  Database Cloud Services, 267
  Exadata backups, 282
free-form tags, 49–50
FSFO (fast-start-fail-over) in Data Guard, 293
FSS. *See* file storage service (FSS)
full backups
  block volumes, 205
  creating, 207
  Exadata, 281–282
  managed, 277
  RMAN, 309
fully qualified domain names (FQDNs), 116–118, 256

G

gateways, 86
  BGP, 90, 349
  Database Cloud Services, 251–252
  database migration, 304
  DRGs, 20, 88–90, 94, 250–251
  dynamic routing, 88–90
  Internet, 87
  local peering, 93–94
  NAT, 87–88, 100–103
  remote peering connection, 93–95
  service, 90–93, 103–106
get command for Internet gateways, 87
global resources, 40–43
gold images, 146
GoldenGate topologies, 355–356
graph command in HCL, 337
Grid Infrastructure (GI)
  description, 241
  HADR architecture, 352
  patches, 283
  RAC, 288
groups
  block volumes, 207–210
  creating, 60–63
  dynamic, 38–39, 66–69
  IAM, 33–34
Guided Journey screen, 7–8

H

HADR architecture
  autonomous database systems, 356
  compute instances, 358
  Data Guard, 353–355
  database, 351–356
  designing, 344–356
  GoldenGate, 355–356
  IAM, 357
  networking, 357–358
  overview, 343
  performance-based, 351
  questions, 359–361
  RACs, 353
  regions and availability domains, 345–346
  review, 358
  security, 356–358
  single-instance databases, 352
  storage and compute instances, 350–351
  VCNs, load balancers, and compute instances, 346–348
  VPN and FastConnect, 348–349
hard disk drives (HDDs) in database migration, 305
hardware-based encryption, 287
HashiCorp Configuration Language (HCL), 333, 336–337

Health Checks for backend sets, 131–132
high availability (HA), 343
  Data Guard, 290–293
  HADR. *See* HADR architecture
  overview, 287–288
  RACs, 288–290
HIGH priority in autonomous database systems, 298
host address space in CIDR, 76–78
hostname command, 118
hostnames in load balancers, 129
Hybrid Columnar Compression, 247
Hyper-V hypervisors, 152
hyperthreading in processor-based licensing, 284–285
hypervisors, 151–152

I

IaaS (Infrastructure as a Service), 2, 9–11
IaC (Infrastructure-as-Code)
  automation tools, 321
  OCI CLI, 332
IAM. *See* Identity and Access Management (IAM)
iam region list command, 327
IANA (Internet Assigned Numbers Authority), 80, 116
ICANN (Internet Corporation for Assigned Names and Numbers), 116
IDCS (Identity Cloud Service)
  accounts, 6–7
  federated OCI, 64
Identity and Access Management (IAM)
  concepts, 27–28
  dynamic groups, 66–69
  federated OCI, 64–66
  FSS, 224
  groups, 33–34, 38–39
  HADR architecture, 351, 357
  introduction, 27
  overview, 16–18
  policies, 34–38, 52–56
  questions, 70–72
  resource creation, 56–63
  resource identifiers, 47–48
  resource locations, 39–47
  resource overview, 28–29
  review, 69
  tags, 49–52
  tenancy and compartments, 29–31
  users, 31–33
Identity Cloud Service (IDCS)
  accounts, 6–7
  federated OCI, 64
identity providers (IdPs) in federated OCI, 64–66
images, compute, 144–152, 162–167
import utilities in database migration, 311–312
incremental backups
  block volumes, 205
  console, 277, 279–281
indexing in autonomous database systems, 302
inequality operators for dynamic groups, 67
Infrastructure as a Service (IaaS), 2, 9–11
Infrastructure-as-Code (IaC)
  automation tools, 321
  OCI CLI, 332
Ingress Rules screen, 255
init command in HCL, 336
inspect verb for permissions, 36–38
installing
  OCI CLI, 322–325
  Terraform, 334–335
Internet and VCN Resolver, 118
Internet Assigned Numbers Authority (IANA), 80, 116
Internet Corporation for Assigned Names and Numbers (ICANN), 116
Internet gateways
  Database Cloud Services, 251
  database migration, 304
  overview, 87
Internet service providers (ISPs), 74
IP addresses
  CIDR, 76–77
  Database Cloud Services, 256
  DNS. *See* Domain Name System (DNS)
  gateways, 86–95
  load balancers, 347
  networks, 74–75
  private, 83–84

IP addresses (*cont.*)
public, 85–86
virtual cloud networks, 80, 83–86
IP hash policy for load balancers, 132
IPSec VPN
database migration, 304
Dynamic Routing Gateways, 89
iSCSI attachments, 192–198
iSCSI Commands & Information screen, 202
iscsiadm command, 197–198
isolation in availability domains, 13
ISPs (Internet service providers), 74

J

JSON files
free-form tags, 49
OCI CLI, 328, 330, 332–333
Terraform, 333, 336

K

Keep Policy Current option, 38
kernel-based VM (KVM), 152
key management system (KMS), 287
Key Vault for encryption, 287
keys
credentials, 32–33
federated OCI, 65
OCI CLI, 327–328
SSH, 154–156
tags, 50
Terraform, 334
KMS (key management system), 287
KVM (kernel-based VM), 152

L

labels in DNS, 116
large objects in multipart uploads, 219–220
latency in networks, 13
Launch DB System screen
bare metal systems, 244
DB systems on VMs, 257
high availability, 289
least connections policy for load balancers, 132
licensing databases, 283–287
list-backupconfigs command, 272
list-vnics command, 175
Listener Information screen, 133
listeners in load balancers, 19, 129–130
load balancers (LBs)
backend sets, 130–132
HADR architecture, 346–348
instance pools, 177
listeners, 129–130
networking, 19
in OCI, 126–135
private, 127
public, 127–129
routing traffic to web servers, 167–170
setting up, 132–135
terminology and concepts, 126–135
local peering gateways (LPGs), 93–94
local peering setup, 106–111
logical standby in Data Guard, 290–291
LOW priority in autonomous database systems, 298
LPGs (local peering gateways), 93–94

M

MAA (Maximum Availability Architecture) in database migration, 308, 310, 354
manage verb in policies, 34–38
managed recovery in Data Guard, 290
manual backups, 205–206
master images, 146
matching rules in dynamic groups, 67
Maximum Availability Architecture (MAA) in database migration, 308, 310, 354
Maximum Availability mode in Data Guard, 291, 354
Maximum Performance mode in Data Guard, 291, 354
Maximum Protection mode in Data Guard, 291
MEDIUM priority in autonomous database systems, 298
metadata in compute instances, 174
metrics
named user plus licensing, 286–287
processor-based licensing, 284–285
migration of databases, 303–304
approaches, 306–310
connectivity, 304

Data Guard, 312
Data Pump, 313–314
data transfer service, 304–306
export and import utilities, 311–312
multitenant approaches, 314–315
RMAN, 313
SQL Developer, 315–316
SQL*Loader, 310–311
monitoring autonomous database systems, 302–303
mount targets in FSS, 225–232
mounting block volumes, 199–200
multipart uploads for large objects, 219–220
multiple vNICs, 175
multitenancy
Database Cloud Services, 250
database migration, 307, 309, 314–315
MX DNS record type, 122

N

NAME component in DNS resource record, 122
named user plus (NUP) licensing, 283, 286–287
names
block volumes, 189
buckets, 214–215
DNS. *See* Domain Name System (DNS)
shapes, 20, 142
tags, 49–52
usernames, 32
native mode for custom images, 147–148
netmasks in CIDR, 77–78
network address translation (NAT) gateways
Database Cloud Services, 251
deploying, 100–103
overview, 87–88
network file system (NFS), 22, 222
network identifiers in CIDR, 76
Network Information screen, 133
network vcn command, 330, 332
network virtualization, off-box, 15–16
networks and networking, 2
CIDR, 75–79
concepts and terminology, 73–75
Database Cloud Services requirements, 250–267
DNS, 19, 115–126
Dynamic Routing Gateway, 20
edge security, 137
FastConnect, 20
HADR architecture, 357–358
introduction, 73
load balancers, 19, 126–135
performance, 13
questions, 138–140
review, 137–138
virtual cloud networks, 18–19
VNC design, 135–136
NFS (network file system), 22, 222
NFSv3 Unix security, 224
Nimbula Director, 4
node failures in high availability, 288
noisy neighbor situations, 15
non-volatile storage components, 1
North–South traffic, 137, 358
NS DNS record type, 122
nslookup command, 120
NUP (named user plus) licensing, 283, 286–287
NVIDIA processors for compute shapes, 142–143
NVMe disks in HADR architecture, 350

O

OAM (Oracle Access Manager), 64
object storage, 213
buckets, 213–219
Exadata backups, 282
multipart uploads, 219–220
overview, 21–22
pre-authenticated requests, 220–221
pseudo-hierarchies, 218–219
RMAN backups, 275–277
objectstoreswift resources for backups, 271
OCI command line interface (CLI)
buckets, 215
configuring, 325–328
installing, 322–325
overview, 321–322
resource locations, 39
supported database lists, 331–333
working with, 328–330

OCI console for buckets, 215
OCI users for Exadata backups, 282
OCIDs. *See* Oracle Cloud IDs (OCIDs)
OCPUs (Oracle Compute Processing Units), 3
 compute shapes, 142
 processor-based licensing, 284–285
OEM (Oracle Enterprise Manager), 241
off-box network virtualization, 15–16
olsnodes command, 282
OLTP-specific services, 298
on-premises networks, 73–74
one-off patches in database migration, 306
ONS (Oracle Notification Services), 251
OPC (Oracle Public Cloud), 4
optimizing autonomous database systems, 302
Oracle Access Manager (OAM), 64
Oracle Call Interface, 297
Oracle Cloud IDs (OCIDs), 35
 Dynamic Routing Gateways, 90
 FSS, 233
 images, 151
 policies, 35
 remote peering connection, 94
 resource identifiers, 47–48
 Terraform, 334
Oracle Cloud Infrastructure Classic, 1
Oracle Cloud Infrastructure (OCI) overview, 1
 accounts, 4–8
 cloud computing models, 9–11
 compute instances, 20
 Database Cloud Service, 22–23
 features and components overview, 11
 Identity and Access Management, 16–18
 introduction, 1–8
 load balancers, 126–135
 networking, 18–20
 off-box network virtualization, 15–16
 questions, 24–26
 regions and availability domains, 11–15
 review, 24
 storage, 20–22
Oracle Compute Processing Units (OCPUs), 3
 compute shapes, 142
 processor-based licensing, 284–285
Oracle Enterprise Manager (OEM), 241
ORACLE HOME location, 241
Oracle images, 145
Oracle Network Provider for FastConnect, 349
Oracle Notification Services (ONS), 251
Oracle Public Cloud (OPC), 4
Oracle Virtual Machine (OVM)
 description, 2
 hypervisors, 152

P

PaaS, 9–11
paravirtualized attachments in block volumes, 192
paravirtualized mode for custom images, 147–148
PARs (pre-authenticated requests) for object storage, 220–221
partitions for block volumes, 198–200
partner images, 145
passwords in federated OCI, 65
patching
 autonomous database systems, 302
 Database Cloud Services, 282–283
 database migration, 306
path route rules for load balancers, 129
Path Route Sets for load balancers, 19
PDBs (pluggable databases)
 Database Cloud Services, 250
 database migration, 307
peer-to-peer topology in GoldenGate, 356
PEM key pairs in Terraform, 334
performance
 Data Guard, 354
 networks, 13
performance-based HADR, 351
permissions
 overview, 35–38
 tags, 51
physical standby mode in Data Guard, 290
PITR (point-in-time recovery)
 backups, 280
 Data Guard, 291, 354
plan command in HCL, 337–338
platform images, 144–145
pluggable databases (PDBs)
 Database Cloud Services, 250
 database migration, 307

point-in-time recovery (PITR)
  backups, 280
  Data Guard, 291, 354
policies
  backups, 205
  conditions, 54–56
  creating, 60–63
  family resource-types, 52–54
  IAM, 34–38
  locations, 54–55
Policies Resource-Type for permissions, 37
pools in compute instances, 176–178
power management in compute instances, 174
pre-authenticated requests (PARs) for object storage, 220–221
presenting block volumes, 200–204
private IP addresses, 74, 83–84
private load balancers
  compartments, 127
  HADR architecture, 347
private peering in FastConnect, 89, 348
private subnets with dynamic routing gateways, 251
processor-based licensing, 283–285
protection
  Data Guard, 354
  HADR architecture, 356–358
providers in HCL, 336
PROVISIONING attribute in block volume lifecycle-state, 190
provisioning state in instance pools, 177
pseudo-hierarchies in object storage, 218–219
PTR DNS record type, 122
public IP addresses, 74, 85–86
public load balancers
  HADR architecture, 347
  overview, 127–129
public peering in FastConnect, 89, 348
public subnets with Internet gateways, 251–257
PuTTY Key Generator, 154–155

Q

QuickStart installation, 323–324

R

racks
  Exadata Cloud Service, 247
  failures, 288
RACs. *See* Real Application Clusters (RACs)
RCs (root compartments) in IAM, 30
RDATA component in DNS resource record, 122
RDLENGTH component in DNS resource record, 122
read verb for permissions, 36–38
Real Application Clusters (RACs)
  description, 240–242
  Exadata, 247
  HADR architecture, 353
  high availability, 288–290
RECO disk group
  bare metal database systems, 245
  description, 241
  Exadata, 248–249
  recovery-related files, 243
records, DNS, 121–126
recovery
  autonomous database systems, 300–301
  availability domains, 13
  block volumes, 210–213
  HADR architecture. *See* HADR architecture
Recovery Manager (RMAN)
  backup reports, 281
  database migration, 309–310, 313
  unmanaged database backups, 273–277
Recovery Point Objective (RPO), 344
Recovery Time Objective (RTO), 344
redundancy
  ASM, 242
  HADR architecture, 343
refresh command in HCL, 337
regions
  HADR architecture, 345–346
  overview, 11–15
  resources, 43–47
  subscribing to, 41–43
  volume backups, 212

reliability in database migration, 308
remote cloning in database migration, 309–310
remote peering connection (RPC), 93–95
remote VCN peering, 111–115
replication in HADR architecture, 350
reserved IP addresses, 85
RESET command in instance power management, 174
resolution, DNS, 117–118
resource identifiers, 47–48
resource locations, 39–40
  global resources, 40–43
  regional and availability domain–level resources, 43–47
resource records (RRs) in DNS, 116, 122–126
resources
  compartments, 57–60
  creating, 56–63
  family resource-types, 52–54
  HCL, 336
  IAM, 28–29
  regions and availability domains, 43–47
REST APIs for buckets, 215
restoring
  block volumes, 210–212
  objects, 216–218
RESTORING attribute in block volume lifecycle-state, 190
RMAN (Recovery Manager)
  backup reports, 281
  database migration, 309–310, 313
  unmanaged database backups, 273–277
roles in Data Guard, 291, 354
root compartments (RCs) in IAM, 30
Round Trip Time (RTT) in networks, 13
route tables
  creating, 101–103
  Database Cloud Services, 251
  description, 80
  routers, 75
routers in networks, 74–75
routing algorithms for load balancers, 19
routing traffic to web servers, 167–170
RPC (remote peering connection), 93–95
RPO (Recovery Point Objective), 344
RRs (resource records) in DNS, 116, 122–126
RSA key pairs in OCI CLI, 328
RTO (Recovery Time Objective), 344
RTT (Round Trip Time) in networks, 13
rules
  load balancers, 130
  routers, 75
running state in instance pools, 177

S

SaaS, 9–11
scaling
  autonomous database systems storage, 301
  custom images, 147
  instance pools, 178–179
schemas
  autonomous database systems, 302
  database migration, 314
  tags, 50–52
SCIM (System for Cross-domain Identity Management), 64
SD-WAN (software-defined wide area networking) solutions, 349
SDKs (Software Development Kits)
  buckets, 215
  resource locations, 39
secure shell (SSH)
  compute instances, 20, 180–182
  Database Cloud Services, 263
  key pairs, 154–156
Secure Sockets Layer (SSL)
  autonomous database systems, 297
  listeners, 129
security
  autonomous database systems, 302
  FSS, 224
  HADR architecture, 356–358
  networking, 137
security lists
  Database Cloud Services, 251
  edge security, 137
  Exadata backups, 282
  FSS, 224
  VCNs, 81
service gateways
  Database Cloud Services, 251
  deploying, 103–106

Exadata backups, 281
overview, 90–93
setup config command, 326
shapes, compute, 142–144
single-instance (SI) databases, 352
single sign-on (SSO), 64–66
size
boot volumes, 149
source databases in database migration, 307
SMTP credentials, 32
snapshots in FSS, 232–234
SOA DNS record type, 122
sockets in processor-based licensing, 284–285
SOFTRESET command in instance power management, 174
SOFTSTOP command in instance power management, 174
software-defined wide area networking (SD-WAN) solutions, 349
Software Development Kits (SDKs)
buckets, 215
resource locations, 39
source databases in database migration
platforms, 307
size, 307
version, 306
SPARSE disk group
description, 241
Exadata, 248–249
speed in database migration, 308
SQL Apply in Data Guard, 290
SQL Developer
autonomous database system connections, 298–300
Database Cloud Services, 264–265
database migration, 308–309, 315–316
SQL*Loader in database migration, 310–311
SQL*Plus utility, 262–264
ssh-keygen command, 155
SSH (secure shell)
compute instances, 20, 180–182
Database Cloud Services, 263
key pairs, 154–156
SSL (Secure Sockets Layer)
autonomous database systems, 297
listeners, 129
SSO (single sign-on), 64–66
standalone managed backups, 277–278
Standard Edition for databases, 241
standard tier for buckets, 214, 217–219
START command in instance power management, 174
starting state in instance pools, 177
static routes in Exadata backups, 282
STOP command in instance power management, 174
stopped state for instance pools, 178
stopping state for instance pools, 178
storage, 20–21, 187–188
archive, 21–22
block. *See* block storage
file service, 22
file storage service. *See* file storage service (FSS)
HADR architecture, 350–351, 358
object. *See* object storage
questions, 235–237
review, 234
scaling in autonomous database systems, 301
subnets
CIDR, 76
creating, 96–100
DNS, 117
edge security, 137
VCNs, 81–82
subscribing to regions, 41–43
switchover role transitions in Data Guard, 291, 354
synchronous replication, 350
System for Cross-domain Identity Management (SCIM), 64

T

tags
defined, 50–52
dynamic groups, 67
free-form, 49–50
taint command in HCL, 337
TCP/IP (Transmission Control Protocol/Internet Protocol), 74–75

TDE (Transparent Data Encryption)
  Database Cloud Services, 267, 287
  description, 242
  wallet backups, 270–271
tenancy
  Database Cloud Services, 250
  database migration, 307, 309, 314–315
  federated OCI, 66
  IAM, 29–31
TERMINATED attribute in block volume lifecycle-state, 190
terminated state in instance pools, 178
TERMINATING attribute in block volume lifecycle-state, 190
terminating state in instance pools, 178
termination of SSL traffic, 129
Terraform tool
  installing and configuring, 334–335
  overview, 333
  VCNs, 337–338
  working with, 336–337
threads in processor-based licensing, 284–285
tiers in buckets, 214–217
top-level domains (TLDs), 116
TP service in autonomous database systems, 298
TPURGENT service in autonomous database systems, 298
Transmission Control Protocol/ Internet Protocol (TCP/IP), 74–75
Transparent Data Encryption (TDE)
  Database Cloud Services, 267, 287
  description, 242
  wallet backups, 270–271
transportable tablespaces in database migration, 313–314
TTL component in DNS resource record, 122
tuning autonomous database systems, 302
tunneling SSL traffic, 129
TYPE component in DNS resource record, 122

U

unidirectional topology in GoldenGate, 355
unique identifiers (UUIDs) for partitions, 200
unmanaged database backups, 273–275
Unplug/Plug in database migration, 309–310, 314
untaint command in HCL, 337
update-database command, 272
update-tdekey command, 287
uploading
  large objects, 219–220
  objects, 216–218
use verb for permissions, 37–38
Use Version Date option, 38
users
  creating, 60–63
  credentials, 32–33
  IAM, 31–33
UUIDs (unique identifiers) for partitions, 200

V

variables
  HCL, 335–336
  policy conditions, 56
VCNs. *See* virtual cloud networks (VCNs)
vCPUs (virtual CPUs), 284–285
verbs for permissions, 35–38
virtual cloud networks (VCNs), 18–19
  creating, 44–47, 96–100
  design, 135–137
  DHCP options, 81
  gateways, 86–95
  HADR architecture, 346–348
  IAM, 28–29
  local peering, 106–111
  NAT gateways, 100–103
  networks, 74
  OCI CLI, 329, 332
  overview, 79–80
  peering, 80
  private IP addresses, 83–84
  public IP addresses, 85–86
  remote peering, 111–115
  route tables, 80
  security lists, 81
  service gateways, 103–106
  subnets, 81–82
  Terraform, 337–338
  virtual NICs, 83–84
virtual CPUs (vCPUs), 284–285
virtual hostnames for load balancers, 129
virtual machines (VMs)
  compute instances, 142–143
  Database Cloud Services, 250, 257–262

virtual network interface cards (vNICs)
multiple, 175
networks, 75
overview, 83–84
virtualization, off-box network, 15–16
VMs (virtual machines)
compute instances, 142–143
Database Cloud Services, 250, 257–262
VNC connections for compute instances, 180
vNICs (virtual network interface cards)
multiple, 175
networks, 75
overview, 83–84
volatile storage components, 2
VPNs in HADR architecture, 348–349

W

web servers
compute instances as, 156–162
routing traffic to, 167–170
weighted round robin policy for load balancers, 131
Windows
block volume instances, 200–204
compute instances, 170–173

Z

Zero Data Loss Recovery Appliance (ZDLRA) for database migration, 308, 310
Zero Downtime Migration (ZDM) for database migration, 308, 310
zones, DNS, 116, 121, 123–126